Recent Developments in Labor Economics
Volume III

The International Library of Critical Writings in Economics

Series Editor: Mark Blaug

Professor Emeritus, University of London, UK
Professor Emeritus, University of Buckingham, UK
Visiting Professor, University of Amsterdam, The Netherlands

This series is an essential reference source for students, researchers and lecturers in economics. It presents by theme a selection of the most important articles across the entire spectrum of economics. Each volume has been prepared by a leading specialist who has written an authoritative introduction to the literature included.

A full list of published and future titles in this series is printed at the end of this volume.

Wherever possible, the articles in these volumes have been reproduced as originally published using facsimile reproduction, inclusive of footnotes and pagination to facilitate ease of reference.

For a list of all Edward Elgar published titles visit our site on the World Wide Web at
www.e-elgar.com

Recent Developments in Labor Economics
Volume III

Edited by

John T. Addison

Hugh C. Lane Professor of Economic Theory
University of South Carolina, Columbia, USA
and Professor of Economics
Queen's University, Belfast, UK

THE INTERNATIONAL LIBRARY OF CRITICAL WRITINGS IN ECONOMICS

An Elgar Reference Collection
Cheltenham, UK • Northampton, MA, USA

Published by
Edward Elgar Publishing Limited
Glensanda House
Montpellier Parade
Cheltenham
Glos GL50 1UA
UK

Edward Elgar Publishing, Inc.
William Pratt House
9 Dewey Court
Northampton
Massachusetts 01060
USA

A catalogue record for this book is available from the British Library

Library of Congress Control Number: 2007921147

ISBN: 978 1 84064 925 3 (3 volume set)

Printed and bound in Great Britain by MPG Books Ltd, Bodmin, Cornwall

Contents

Acknowledgements

The editor and publishers wish to thank the authors and the following publishers who have kindly given permission for the use of copyright material.

American Economic Association for articles: Lawrence H. Summers (1989), 'Some Simple Economics of Mandated Benefits', *American Economic Review, Papers and Proceedings*, **79** (2), May, 177–83; Jonathan Gruber (1994), 'The Incidence of Mandated Maternity Benefits', *American Economic Review*, **84** (3), June, 622–41; Richard B. Freeman (1995), 'Are Your Wages Set in Beijing?', *Journal of Economic Perspectives*, **9** (3), Summer, 15–32; Stephen Nickell (1997), 'Unemployment and Labor Market Rigidities: Europe Versus North America', *Journal of Economic Perspectives*, **11** (3), Summer, 55–74; Olivier Blanchard and Pedro Portugal (2001), 'What Hides Behind an Unemployment Rate: Comparing Portuguese and U.S. Labor Markets', *American Economic Review*, **91** (1), March, 187–207.

Blackwell Publishing Ltd for articles: Thibaut Desjonqueres, Stephen Machin and John Van Reenen (1999), 'Another Nail in the Coffin? Or Can the Trade Based Explanation of Changing Skill Structures Be Resurrected?', *Scandinavian Journal of Economics*, **101** (4), December, 533–54; Olivier Blanchard and Justin Wolfers (2000), 'The Role of Shocks and Institutions in the Rise of European Unemployment: The Aggregate Evidence', *Economic Journal*, **110** (462), March, C1–C33.

Cornell University for articles: Alan B. Krueger (1991), 'The Evolution of Unjust-Dismissal Legislation in the United States', *Industrial and Labor Relations Review*, **44** (4), July, 644–60; David Card (2001), 'The Effect of Unions on Wage Inequality in the U.S. Labor Market', *Industrial and Labor Relations Review*, **54** (2), January, 296–315; John DiNardo and Kevin F. Hallock (2002), 'When Unions "Mattered": The Impact of Strikes on Financial Markets, 1925–1937', *Industrial and Labor Relations Review*, **55** (2), January, 219–33; Stephen Machin and Stephen Wood (2005), 'Human Resource Management as a Substitute for Trade Unions in British Workplaces', *Industrial and Labor Relations Review*, **58** (2), January, 201–18.

Elsevier for article: John T. Addison, Ralph W. Bailey and W. Stanley Siebert (2007), 'The Impact of Deunionisation on Earnings Dispersion Revisited', *Research in Labor Economics*, forthcoming.

MIT Press Journals for articles: Christopher J. Ruhm (1998), 'The Economic Consequences of Parental Leave Mandates: Lessons from Europe', *Quarterly Journal of Economics*, **CXIII** (1), February, 285–317; Stephen Machin and John Van Reenen (1998), 'Technology and Changes in Skill Structure: Evidence from Seven OECD Countries', *Quarterly Journal of Economics*, **CXIII** (4), November, 1215–44; Eli Berman, John Bound and Stephen Machin

(1998), 'Implications of Skill-Based Technological Change: International Evidence', *Quarterly Journal of Economics*, **CXIII** (4), November, 1245–79; Sandra E. Black and Lisa M. Lynch (2001), 'How to Compete: The Impact of Workplace Practices and Information Technology on Productivity', *Review of Economics and Statistics*, **83** (3), August, 434–45.

Southern Economic Association for articles: John T. Addison, Paulino Teixeira and Jean-Luc Grosso (2000), 'The Effect of Dismissals Protection on Employment: More on a Vexed Theme', *Southern Economic Journal*, **67** (1), July, 105–22; John T. Addison, John S. Heywood and Xiangdong Wei (2003), 'New Evidence on Unions and Plant Closings: Britain in the 1990s', *Southern Economic Journal*, **69** (4), April, 822–41.

Springer Science and Business Media for article: John T. Addison, Richard C. Barrett and W. Stanley Siebert (2006), 'Building Blocks in the Economics of Mandates', *Portuguese Economic Journal*, **5** (2), October, 69–87.

Transaction Publishers for articles: Barry T. Hirsch (2004), 'Reconsidering Union Wage Effects: Surveying New Evidence on an Old Topic', *Journal of Labor Research*, **XXV** (2), Spring, 233–66; Barry T. Hirsch (2004), 'What Do Unions Do for Economic Performance?', *Journal of Labor Research*, **XXV** (3), Summer, 415–55.

University of Chicago Press for articles: John T. Addison and John B. Chilton (1998), 'Self-Enforcing Union Contracts: Efficient Investment and Employment', *Journal of Business*, **71** (3), July, 349–69; Edward P. Lazear (1999), 'Personnel Economics: Past Lessons and Future Directions. Presidential Address to the Society of Labor Economists, San Francisco, May 1, 1998', *Journal of Labor Economics*, **17** (2), April, 199–236; David Card (2001), 'Immigrant Inflows, Native Outflows, and the Local Labor Market Impacts of Higher Immigration', *Journal of Labor Economics*, **19** (1), January, 22–64.

In addition the publishers wish to thank the Library of Indiana University at Bloomington, USA, for their assistance in obtaining these articles.

Part I
Technology, Trade, Immigration and Wages

[1]

TECHNOLOGY AND CHANGES IN SKILL STRUCTURE: EVIDENCE FROM SEVEN OECD COUNTRIES*

STEPHEN MACHIN AND JOHN VAN REENEN

This paper compares the changing skill structure of wage bills and employment in the United States with six other OECD countries (Denmark, France, Germany, Japan, Sweden, and the United Kingdom). We investigate whether a directly observed measure of technical change (R&D intensity) is closely linked to the growth in the importance of more highly skilled workers which has occurred in all countries. Evidence of a significant association between skill upgrading and R&D intensity is uncovered in all seven countries. These results provide evidence that skill-biased technical change is an international phenomenon that has had a clear effect of increasing the relative demand for skilled workers.

I. INTRODUCTION

The structure of wages and employment has dramatically shifted in many countries in recent years. There have been big increases in wage inequality in the United States and in the United Kingdom, while other countries (especially those in continental Europe) have had more stable wage structures. At the same time unemployment has risen sharply in several European countries, and almost all countries have seen shifts in employment structure that have adversely affected relatively unskilled workers.

Many commentators believe that much of the change in skill and wage structure in the United States stems from the impact of new technology. Indeed, it has been argued by a large body of economists (e.g., Bound and Johnson [1992]; Berman, Bound, and Griliches [1994], and Johnson [1997]) that certain skill-biased technological changes (SBTC) have favored the wage and employment prospects of relatively skilled workers, while simultaneously damaging the wages and employment of the less skilled. Furthermore, if one considers relative employment shifts in the

* We would like to thank Thibaut Desjonqueres and Annette Ryan for their exceptional research assistance on this paper (and its earlier versions). We have received a great deal of help with data from many people, notably Jean Bourdon, Richard Dickens, Par Hansson, Mary O'Mahony, Souichi Ohta, George Papaconstantinou, Marcus Rebick, and David Wilkinson. We would like to thank Olivier Blanchard, Lawrence Katz, and two referees for a number of helpful comments. In addition, Susanne Ackum-Agell, Eric Bartelsman, Eli Berman, Richard Blundell, Richard Dickens, Peter Gottschalk, Zvi Griliches, Daniel Hamermesh, Jonathan Haskel, Stephen Nickell, Andrew Oswald, John Schmitt, and participants in numerous seminars have offered useful suggestions. Financial assistance has come from the Leverhulme Trust and the Economic and Social Research Council.

The Quarterly Journal of Economics, November 1998

manufacturing sectors of a number of advanced countries, one sees a pattern similar to that observed in the United States, in that the share of relatively skilled workers in total wage costs and employment appears to have increased (see Berman, Bound, and Machin [1998]). Most of these shifts appear to have occurred within, rather than between industries, leading some commentators to come down in favor of SBTC as the key factor underpinning shifts in relative labor demand.

A difficulty with some of this work is that the effects of technology are inferred as indirect effects associated with particular correlation patterns, or linked to specific components from decompositions, rather than being based upon directly observed comparable measures of technical change across countries. In this paper we consider whether one directly observable indicator of technology, R&D intensity, is intrinsically associated with the degree of skill upgrading. We adopt an international perspective by looking at the relationship between changes in skill structure and R&D for comparable data in seven OECD countries: the United States, the United Kingdom (where wage inequality rose even faster in the 1980s than in the United States, albeit from a much lower level), two Continental European countries (France and Germany), two Scandinavian countries (Denmark and Sweden), and Japan. To do so, we construct an original industry-level panel data set from a wide variety of national and international sources.[1]

According to our analysis, there have been shifts in relative labor demand that have favored skilled workers in all seven countries. As in the United States, most of this shift has occurred within, rather than between, industries. Evidence of a significant complementarity of human capital with new technology is uncovered in all seven countries, and this is robust to alternative measures of skill and technology. We do not find that measures of trade, such as the share of imports originating from less developed countries, are important in explaining the change in within-industry skill structures. Our main findings are robust to alternative econometric specifications that allow for the possible endogeneity of technical change and spillover effects.

---

1. The focus on international comparisons using microeconomic data through time means that our work is closest in spirit to the recent comparison of wage and employment structures in the United States, Canada, and France by Card, Kramarz, and Lemieux [1996]. However, as will be seen below, we employ a somewhat different methodology.

Overall, our reading of these results is that they provide evidence that skill-biased technical change is an international phenomenon that has had a clear effect of increasing the relative demand for skilled workers. This should not be taken to mean that technology is the *only* factor in explaining the changing skill structures of the industrialized countries. We cannot deduce the full effect of technology on labor market structure without also closing the model by looking at supply side effects and the nonmanufacturing sector, which is beyond the scope of this paper. Our view is that the results presented here form a necessary, but not sufficient, part of the story that changes in the wage and employment distribution are closely tied to technical changes.

The plan of the paper is as follows. The next section describes the construction of the data set and offers some preliminary descriptive statistics. Section III outlines the econometric strategy, and gives a discussion of the basic regression results. Section IV goes on to test the robustness of the results by examining other technology measures, the effects of trade, the potential endogeneity of R&D, and international spillover effects. Some concluding remarks are made in Section V.

II. Data Description

A. Data Construction

We draw on a number of data sources to construct the industry-level panel data we use in our empirical analysis. The data on value added and investment come from an industry-level panel data set compiled by the OECD known as STAN (Standardized Analytical Database). This contains data which are internationally comparable having been compiled by OECD researchers working with the Central Statistical Offices of each country. The OECD also develops complementary databases to STAN. We use their Business Enterprise R&D (ANBERD) database for R&D data and the Bilateral Trade Database for international trade information.

STAN/ANBERD is the only data set we know of which contains information on industry-level R&D expenditures over time across industrialized countries. The industry R&D measure is comprised of the amount of R&D conducted by (but not necessarily financed by) the business sector, and this is the key technology measure we rely upon. Of course, we acknowledge from the outset that no single proxy for technology is perfect. However, when compared with other existing measures of innovation, R&D intensity has several advantages for the purposes of our study. First, it is measured in a broadly consistent way over time and across countries. Most industrialized nations use the Frascati Manual definition of R&D, and the OECD statisticians have made considerable efforts to make the measures consistent over time across the countries we consider.[2] Although a measure of investment in computers or information technology may have some advantages over R&D, these are generally only available for a subset of countries and even then only for a few recent years. Second, R&D is measured in "dollar terms" (or D-Marks, or pounds, etc). Most measures of innovation such as patents or innovation counts are qualitative in nature. The proportion of workers using a computer does not adjust for the differential amount of resources going into purchasing a computer, for example. Third, it is a direct measure of technology, unlike total factor productivity (TFP) which has the twin disadvantages of being highly endogenous and containing a variety of unknown influences unrelated to technology (such as unmeasured changes in the factor quality mix). Finally, more on the downside, R&D has the potential drawback that it is only an input (as are the physical investment flows we use to construct the fixed capital stock). Yet, even here, a long line of research has established that R&D expenditures do a reasonably good job at proxying the outputs of the innovative process.[3]

In terms of data on skills, STAN only has data on total employment by industry and does not disaggregate by skill category. To overcome this, we drew on the United Nations Industrial Statistics Database (UNISD) which includes data on the wage costs and numbers of production and nonproduction workers by industry. Merging the data sets together left us with country-specific time series data on relative wage costs, employment, and R&D for the same manufacturing industries (defined at about the two-digit level) in each country. From our data-matching procedures (see the Data Appendix) there are actually sixteen industries that make up the entire manufacturing sector

2. For a detailed discussion of the procedures used, see OECD [1997a].
3. For example, Griliches, Hall, and Pakes [1991] have investigated the informativeness of the patent count measure in a dynamic factor model of firm value, R&D, sales, and investment. They found that (with the exception of the pharmaceutical industry) patents provided little additional information on the economic variables above and beyond that contained in R&D spending.

in each country. However, when we need to consider the technology measures, we analyze data on fifteen industries, dropping the transport goods sector due to erratic R&D data. The sample of countries we use is dictated by the availability of data on skill structure and on R&D intensity. Full information on the matching and cleaning procedures and a listing of industries is given in the Data Appendix.

We have also generalized our empirical work in a number of directions. As one may have doubts about the use of the nonproduction/production worker distinction to proxy skill, we have also constructed education-based measures by aggregating individual-level cross-sectional data sources to industry-level in France, Germany, Japan, the United Kingdom, and the United States.[4] Despite problems of consistently defining education groups across countries, we have constructed education-based employment shares at exactly the same industry-level as the combined STAN/UNISD data through time. In this paper we look only at high education employment shares, which correspond to the proportion of workers in an industry with a college degree.

B. Descriptive Statistics

Some descriptive statistics on the key variables for the manufacturing sectors of the seven countries between 1973 and 1989 are reported in Table I. The first point to note is that the nonproduction worker share of the wage bill has risen in all countries and that, in absolute terms, the largest increase has been in the United Kingdom and the United States (with annualized increases of .6 and .5 percentage points per year) and the smallest in Sweden and Japan (both with annualized increases of about .25 percentage points per year). There is a similar pattern for employment shares, but one should notice that the United Kingdom and United States changes are less dramatic here and the size of the change is more in line with that of the other countries, due to the fact that wage differentials between nonproduction and production workers increased very rapidly in those two countries in the 1980s but remained relatively constant elsewhere. In the same way, more highly educated workers have

---

4. The data sources used are France—Enquete Emploi; Germany—Mikrozensus; Japan—Japanese Wage Census; the United Kingdom—Labour Force Survey; the United States—Current Population Survey. Note that for Germany and Japan the data on nonproduction shares also come from these sources and not from UNISD. More details are given in the Data Appendix.

TABLE I

NONPRODUCTION WAGE BILL AND EMPLOYMENT SHARES, RELATIVE WAGE
DIFFERENTIALS, HIGH EDUCATION EMPLOYMENT SHARES, AND R&D INTENSITY
IN MANUFACTURING

	1973	1977	1981	1985	1989
Nonproduction wage-bill shares					
Denmark	.336	.338	.359	.373	.402
Japan	.406 (1974)	.415	.428	.433	—
Sweden	.356	.385	.395	.395	.396
U. K.	.317	.333	.377	.392	.414
U. S.	.337	.351	.379	.406	.414
Nonproduction employment shares					
Denmark	.251	.270	.292	.293	.318
Germany	—	.292	.306	.318	.327
Japan	.339 (1974)	.350	.364	.369	—
Sweden	.271	.288	.299	.304	.303
U. K.	.260	.278	.311	.321	.325
U. S.	.246	.261	.285	.305	.303
Nonproduction/production wage differentials					
Denmark	1.511	1.382	1.359	1.434	1.437
Japan	1.331 (1974)	1.314	1.310	1.309	—
Sweden	1.487	1.549	1.532	1.493	1.509
U. K.	1.316	1.292	1.340	1.366	1.470
U. S.	1.553	1.531	1.532	1.559	1.623
High education employment shares					
France	—	.047	.057	.081	.093
Germany	—	.032	.044	.054	.066
Japan	—	.098	.111	.129	.135
U. K.	—	.039	.054	.065	.064
U. S.	—	.088	.126	.161	.167
R&D intensity (R&D/value added)					
Denmark	.021	.022	.027	.031	.039
France	.035	.037	.046	.056	.060
Germany	.032	.037	.043	.052	.055
Japan	.031	.036	.046	.060	.070
Sweden	.038	.050	.063	.080	.081
U. K.	.043	.046	.064	.062	.060
U. S.	.063	.062	.077	.097	.087

Nonproduction wage bills, employment, and wages are taken from UNISD or from country-specific micro-data (Germany—Mikrozensus; Japan—Wage Census); R&D intensity is drawn from ANBERD and STAN; high education shares from micro-data sources in each country (France—Enquete Emploi; Germany—Mikrozensus; Japan—Wage Census; U. K.—Labour Force Survey; U. S.—Current Population Survey). For more details see the Data Appendix. High education employment shares are also available for Sweden in two different years (1986 and 1993). Means are .090 in 1986 and .154 in 1993.

TECHNOLOGY AND CHANGES IN SKILL STRUCTURE 1221

increased their relative employment shares in the countries on
which we have data on education. The descriptive statistics in
Table I point to considerable shifts in skill structure that have
favored more-skilled workers.

The bottom panel of Table I also shows the pattern of R&D
spending across the countries. In 1989 R&D intensity (R&D
divided by value added) was highest in the United States and
lowest in Denmark. It is also interesting to note the time series
pattern. All countries have increased the proportion of value
added given over to R&D between 1973 and 1989, with the largest
increases occurring in Japan and Sweden. More detailed analysis
of the increasing R&D intensities reveals both an increasing
importance of high-tech industries and also a general increase in
manufacturing R&D across almost all industries [Van Reenen
1997].

As studied in much more detail in Berman, Bound, and
Machin [1998], the bulk of the change in skill proportions is going
on within, rather than between, industries. Our disaggregated
data on the sixteen industries within manufacturing also allows a
comparison of the within/between changes using education rather
than occupation as a definition of skill. Figure I reports the
familiar decomposition of aggregate changes in skilled wage-bill
and employment shares into within-industry and between-
industry components.[5] In all seven countries the vast majority of
skill upgrading is happening within industries, and this is true for
both the occupational and educational proxies for skill.[6]

Berman, Bound, and Machin [1998] also present empirical
evidence that faster skill upgrading is concentrated in similar
industries in different countries and argue that this is consistent
with the idea that SBTC has had a pervasive effect in shifting
relative labor demand in favor of skilled workers across countries.

5. The aggregate change in the skilled proportion over a given time period,
ΔP, can be decomposed (for industries $i = 1,2,\ldots,N$) as

$$\Delta P = \sum_i \Delta S_i \bar{P}_i + \sum_i \Delta P_i \bar{S}_i,$$

where $P_i = SK_i/L_i$ is the proportion of skilled workers in industry i and $S_i = L_i/L$ is
the share of total employment in industry i. A bar over a variable denotes a time
mean. The first term on the right-hand side of the equation is the change in the
aggregate proportion of skilled workers attributable to shifts *between* industries
with different proportions of skilled workers. The final term in the expression is
the change in the aggregate proportion of skilled workers attributable to changes
in the proportion of skilled workers *within* industries.
6. This pattern remains true in nonmanufacturing sectors and also for more
disaggregated industry definitions (see Machin and Van Reenen [1997]).

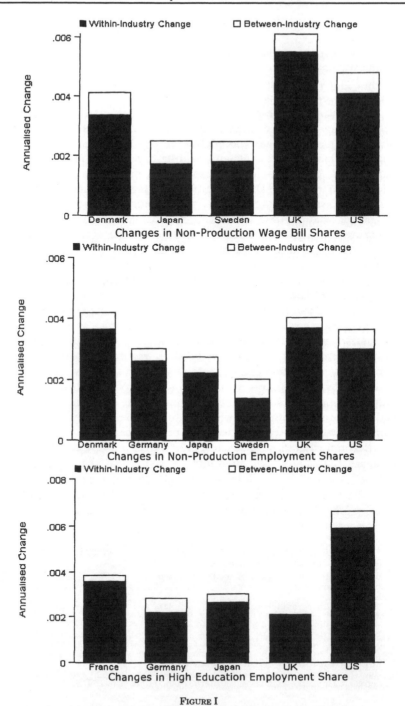

FIGURE I
Changes in Nonproduction Wage Bill and Employment Shares (1973–1989 except
Japan 1974–1985) and High Education Employment Shares
(1977–1989)—within/between Components of Annualized Changes

TECHNOLOGY AND CHANGES IN SKILL STRUCTURE   1223

In our data we are able to break down the overall change in the nonproduction or education shares into each of the manufacturing sectors and then rank the industries by their within-industry contribution to the overall change. It is clear by just eyeballing these rankings that, for the most part, the biggest changes are concentrated in the same industries across countries. The industries with the biggest individual contributions are computers and nonelectrical machinery, professional goods (i.e., instruments) and paper, printing, and publishing. The existence of cross-country correlations of industry skill upgrading is important and suggests that a key empirical strategy should be to isolate what factors are common to the industries in which faster skill upgrading is concentrated. Yet it remains difficult to be fully convinced that these kinds of cross-country industry correlations signify a SBTC shock in the absence of direct measures of technology.[7]

That technical change is clearly a candidate for explaining the observed shifts is indicated by the fact that the same industries tend to be R&D intensive across countries. This is shown in Table II which reports cross-country correlations in industrial R&D intensity (only fifteen industries are now considered because, as noted above, we drop the transport goods industry due to worries about the reliability of the R&D data). All pairwise correlations are positive, large in magnitude, and significantly different from zero.[8] This clearly mirrors the observation that faster skill upgrading is observed in similar industries in different countries, although the R&D correlations are clearly stronger than the skill upgrading correlations.[9] The latter suggests that other factors may also be at play. It is in the spirit of

---

7. Recent work by Haskel and Slaughter [1998] has also emphasized that technical change may have effects on the between-industry component as well as on within-industry shifts in relative employment.

8. Industries with consistently high R&D intensities were nonelectrical machinery (including computers), chemicals (including drugs) and electrical, radio, TV, and communications (mean R&D intensities across all seven countries for these three industries were .060, .102, and .134, respectively). On the other hand, consistently low (R&D/value added) was present in the textiles, apparel, and leather, and wood products and furniture industries (mean R&D intensities were .006 and .003).

9. The skill upgrading correlations in our data are in line with those in Berman, Bound, and Machin [1998] even though our data are more aggregated (they consider 28 industries, as compared with our 15). For example, for the ten possible pairwise comparisons of cross-country correlations in nonproduction wage-bill shares (for Denmark, Japan, Sweden, the United Kingdom, and the United States), all were positive, and five were statistically significant at the 5 percent level. For the 1980–1990 time period, and for a wider range of countries, Berman, Bound, and Machin [1998] report that 12 out of 36 cross-country correlations of changes in nonproduction wage-bill shares were significant.

TABLE II
CROSS-COUNTRY CORRELATIONS IN INDUSTRY R&D INTENSITY (FIFTEEN
MANUFACTURING INDUSTRIES, 1973–1989 AVERAGES, WEIGHTED BY CROSS-COUNTRY
MEAN INDUSTRY VALUE ADDED SHARES)

	Cross-country correlations of industry (R&D/Y)					
	Denmark	France	Germany	Japan	Sweden	U. K.
France	.68*					
	(.01)					
Germany	.79*	.97*				
	(.00)	(.00)				
Japan	.66*	.95*	.97*			
	(.01)	(.00)	(.00)			
Sweden	.73*	.97*	.97*	.96*		
	(.00)	(.00)	(.00)	(.00)		
U. K.	.73*	.98*	.95*	.92*	.98*	
	(.00)	(.00)	(.00)	(.00)	(.00)	
U. S.	.68*	.90*	.85*	.91*	.93*	.94*
	(.01)	(.00)	(.00)	(.00)	(.00)	(.00)

These are pairwise correlation coefficients based on fifteen manufacturing industries (except for correlations for Denmark which are based on fourteen industries due to missing data on the petroleum industry). They are weighted by the pairwise cross-country mean industry value added share in total value added. p-values testing the null of independence are in parentheses (an asterisk denotes significance at .05 level or better).

these data patterns that we next turn to regression models which essentially try to see whether it is in fact broadly the same industries that have simultaneously experienced skill upgrading and technical change.

III. EMPIRICAL MODELS OF CHANGES IN SKILL STRUCTURE AND TECHNOLOGY

A. Econometric Approach

Beginning from a simple restricted variable translog cost function for industry i in country j in year t, say $C[\log (W^{NP})_{ijt}, \log (W^{P})_{ijt}, \log (K_{ijt}), \log (Y_{ijt}), TECH_{ijt}]$, it is straightforward to derive a nonproduction wage-bill-share equation as

(1) $SHARE_{ijt} = \varphi_{ij} + \alpha_j \log (K_{ijt}) + \beta_j \log (Y_{ijt})$

$$+ \gamma_j \, TECH_{ijt} + \delta_j \log (W^{NP} / W^{P})_{ijt},$$

where *SHARE* is the nonproduction wage-bill share, K is the tangible capital stock (assumed to be a quasi-fixed factor), Y is value added, W^{NP} and W^P are the wage rates of nonproduction and production workers, and *TECH* is a measure of the stock of technology.[10] The j subscript attached to the coefficients allows them to vary across countries (although in practice we estimate separate equations for each country). We time difference equation (1) in order to sweep out the correlated industry-specific fixed effects φ_{ij}. The stochastic form of the estimating equation (with Δ being a difference operator and u a random error term) is therefore

$$(2) \quad \Delta SHARE_{ijt} = \alpha_j \Delta \log (K_{ijt}) + \beta_j \Delta \log (Y_{ijt})$$
$$+ \gamma_j (\text{R\&D/}Y)_{ijt} + \eta_{jt} D_{jt} + u_{ijt}.$$

Notice that the relative wage rates have been replaced by country-specific time dummies (D_{jt}) which will also capture common macroeconomic shocks. The differenced industry-specific relative wage terms could be entered separately in (2), but they are likely to be highly endogenous. In the absence of any convincing instruments, wages are assumed to move in tandem across the economy (levels are captured by the fixed effect). Some specification tests reported below relax this assumption and show the results to be robust to the inclusion or exclusion of the industry-specific relative wage.

More importantly in terms of specification issues, the main variable used to measure the change in the technology stock, $\Delta TECH$, is R&D/Y, the ratio of the flow of R&D expenditures to value added. As we have noted above, we think this is a good measure of technological progress and is the main variable we consider in our empirical work. Some results based on alternative technology measures are therefore also discussed below.

In terms of the specifications to be estimated, one should also note that, because industrial R&D intensity tends to be persistent over time, then in terms of timing, the way in which the variable is entered into equation (2) makes little difference to the nature of the results. For most of the analysis below we enter it as the average over the period used in differencing, but we also discuss results using lagged (R&D/Y) and the initial (1973) value.

Finally, because yearly variations in industrial R&D intensity tend to be small, one may believe that the estimation of

---

10. Notice that, in this framework, *SHARE* is the share of nonproduction worker wages in the overall wage bill, not total costs, as the only variable factors of production are the two labor types (since the capital and technology stocks are assumed quasi-fixed).

models based on annual industry data is not suitable. As such, the main results that we present specify equation (2) in longer frequency differences (four-year changes). Nevertheless, the results are robust to using shorter or longer changes, and we also report results from annual data. All reported results are based on annualizing the data to ensure comparability across models based on data of different frequencies.

B. Basic Regressions

Table III reports simple regressions of (annualized) four-year and one-year changes in skilled wage-bill and employment shares on R&D intensity (and year dummies). For the four-year models, where we have full data, these models cover four time periods (1973–1977, 1977–1981, 1981–1985, and 1985–1989), and exceptions to this are detailed in the notes to the table. Because the specifications cover the same industries in different time periods, we let the industry-specific errors be correlated over time (in other words, we allow for random effects in the differenced specifications). Each equation also incorporates a set of year dummies to control for country-specific common time effects.

In all cases, the estimated coefficients on the R&D variable are positive and are almost always statistically significant at the 5 percent level. Only in three cases out of seventeen in the four-year change models (Sweden, changes in nonproduction wage-bill shares; United Kingdom, changes in high education employment shares; United States, changes in high education employment shares) is the estimated coefficient on R&D intensity not significant at the 5 percent level, and even there the p-values testing the null hypothesis of no association are .15, .07, and .07, respectively. In the one-year change models fourteen of the sixteen of the estimated R&D coefficients are significantly different from zero (and the two that are not—high education employment shares in the United Kingdom and the United States—have p-values of .22 and .07, respectively).[11]

The regressions therefore paint a very clear picture about the relationship between skill upgrading and R&D intensity. It is clearly the more R&D-intensive industries that have seen faster

---

11. The same pattern of results is also preserved in longer differenced models. Exactly the same pattern also emerged if lagged (R&D/Y) was entered ($t - 1$ for the one-year changes, $t - 4$ for the four-year changes). Notice also that the one-year models use all the data we have compiled and in some countries this goes up to 1991. As such, the coefficients are not strictly comparable (but restricting to the same time period as the four-year models produced similar results).

TABLE III

BASIC REGRESSIONS OF CHANGES IN SKILL UPGRADING ON R&D
INTENSITY—FOUR-YEAR CHANGES (ANNUALIZED) AND ONE-YEAR CHANGES

			Changes in nonproduction wage-bill share	Changes in nonproduction employment share	Changes in high education employment share
Denmark	Four-year changes	Coefficient (standard error) on R&D/Y	.028 (.013)	.031 (.012)	
		Sample size	56	56	
	One-year changes	Coefficient (standard error) on R&D/Y	.024 (.011)	.021 (.009)	
		Sample size	173	173	
France	Four-year changes	Coefficient (standard error) on R&D/Y			.052 (.008)
		Sample size			42
	One-year changes	Coefficient (standard error) on R&D/Y			.047 (.003)
		Sample size			196
Germany	Four-year changes	Coefficient (standard error) on R&D/Y		.021 (.007)	.026 (.007)
		Sample size		45	39
	One-year changes	Coefficient (standard error) on R&D/Y		.024 (.007)	.022 (.007)
		Sample size		210	186
Japan	Four-year changes	Coefficient (standard error) on R&D/Y	.050 (.016)	.043 (.017)	.019 (.008)
		Sample size	45	45	45
	One-year changes	Coefficient (standard error) on R&D/Y	.037 (.015)	.034 (.014)	.020 (.008)
		Sample size	174	174	189
Sweden	Four-year changes	Coefficient (standard error) on R&D/Y	.013 (.009)	.020 (.008)	.032 (.007)
		Sample size	45	45	15
	One-year changes	Coefficient (standard error) on R&D/Y	.036 (.011)	.038 (.009)	
		Sample size	157	157	
U. K.	Four-year changes	Coefficient (standard error) on R&D/Y	.024 (.009)	.025 (.009)	.013 (.007)
		Sample size	60	60	45
	One-year changes	Coefficient (standard error) on R&D/Y	.026 (.009)	.026 (.009)	.011 (.009)
		Sample size	255	255	210
U. S.	Four-year changes	Coefficient (standard error) on R&D/Y	.024 (.007)	.020 (.007)	.025 (.014)
		Sample size	60	60	45
	One-year changes	Coefficient (standard error) on R&D/Y	.021 (.007)	.022 (.007)	.020 (.011)
		Sample size	270	270	210

Nonproduction shares: four-year changes are based on fifteen industry manufacturing panel data for four time periods (1973–1977, 1977–1981, 1981–1985, 1985–1989) for all countries except Germany (1977–1981, 1981–1985, 1985–1989), Japan (1974–1977, 1977–1981, 1981–1985), and Sweden (1973–1977, 1977–1981, 1981–1985). Full sample sizes are 60 but may be less due to data problems in some industries and years. Education shares: four-year changes are based on fifteen industry manufacturing panel data for three time periods (1977–1981, 1981–1985, 1985–1989) except for Sweden (1986–1993). One-year-change models use data on all available years. All four-year changes are annualized, and all regressions include a full set of time dummies. Regressions are weighted by industry size (wage-bill share or employment share). Estimation is by GLS/random effects where the industry errors are allowed to be correlated for industries over time. Heteroskedasticity-consistent standard errors are in parentheses.

increases in nonproduction wage-bill and employment shares and high education shares in the seven countries we study. We view the fact that a significant correlation is obtained for "skill" measures based on nonproduction and education-based shares as very reassuring for interpreting the observed changes as illustrating faster skill upgrading associated with higher industry R&D intensity in these countries.

C. Estimates of Extended Cost-Share Equations

The results of implementing the more detailed econometric models based on equation (2) are contained in Table IV. The table reports models analyzing changes in nonproduction wage-bill shares and reports four specifications for each country. The first two rows contain coefficient estimates from models based on four-year changes with the first row imposing constant returns to scale (CRS: $\alpha_j = -\beta_j$ in the context of equation (2)) and the second row relaxing this assumption. The third and fourth rows reports analogous models based on annual year-on-year changes.

Overall, the wage-bill share models in the upper panel of Table IV are very much in line with the skill-biased technological change hypothesis as there is evidence of a positive association between new technology and changes in skilled wage-bill shares in all five countries considered. The coefficient on R&D/Y is estimated to be positive across all specifications and is significantly different from zero in almost all cases.[12] We also find a positive correlation between the growth of capital intensity and the skill upgrading in every country except Japan. This is important as it is likely that some of the effect of technology on the labor market occurs through being "embodied" in more recent vintages of capital goods. What is more, the estimated coefficients are robust to specification of equations in four-year changes as compared with looking at annual year-on-year regressions.

---

12. In terms of equations (1) and (2) it is worth noting that we allow for industry fixed effects in the level of skill intensity but do not allow for fixed effects in the growth rates (i.e., we do not incorporate industry-specific trends in the levels equation). This is because allowing there to be permanent industry effects in the differenced equations is incoherent in the long run. Nevertheless, if we do include them in equation (2), the coefficients on (R&D/Y) are (unsurprisingly given the sample sizes) driven to insignificance. This is in line with well-known findings in the literature on productivity and R&D (e.g., Hall and Mairesse [1995]): most of the variance in R&D intensity is between rather than within units. Recovering the industry fixed effects and regressing them against R&D intensity reveals positive and significant correlations, illustrating that more R&D-intensive industries are those with faster skill upgrading.

TECHNOLOGY AND CHANGES IN SKILL STRUCTURE   1229

TABLE IV

CHANGE IN NONPRODUCTION WAGE-BILL SHARE EQUATIONS IN MANUFACTURING

		Changes in nonproduction wage-bill shares					
		(R&D/Y)	$\Delta \log (K/Y)$	$\Delta \log (K)$	$\Delta \log (Y)$	Sample size	Test of CRS (χ^2)
Denmark	Four-year changes CRS	.027 (.013)	.042 (.017)	.025 (.017)	−.079 (.019)	54	8.34 ($p = .00$)
	Relax CRS	.039 (.015)				54	
	One-year changes CRS	.022 (.014)	.082 (.014)	.035 (.014)	−.098 (.016)	173	17.25 ($p = .00$)
	Relax CRS	.037 (.011)				173	
Japan	Four-year changes CRS	.050 (.014)	−.035 (.011)	−.043 (.016)	.031 (.012)	45	.43 ($p = .51$)
	Relax CRS	.056 (.020)				45	
	One-year changes CRS	.038 (.015)	−.004 (.012)	−.017 (.022)	.001 (.015)	174	.31 ($p = .58$)
	Relax CRS	.046 (.020)				174	
Sweden	Four-year changes CRS	.039 (.014)	.037 (.017)	.083 (.024)	−.008 (.022)	39	9.04 ($p = .00$)
	Relax CRS	.020 (.014)				39	
	One-year changes CRS	.039 (.012)	.016 (.008)	.041 (.021)	−.013 (.008)	157	1.83 ($p = .18$)
	Relax CRS	.033 (.012)				157	
U. K.	Four-year changes CRS	.024 (.010)	.014 (.022)	.051 (.022)	.038 (.021)	60	9.99 ($p = .00$)
	Relax CRS	.013 (.008)				60	
	One-year changes CRS	.024 (.010)	.017 (.006)	.046 (.022)	−.011 (.005)	255	2.34 ($p = .13$)
	Relax CRS	.019 (.011)				255	
U. S.	Four-year changes CRS	.021 (.007)	.030 (.018)	.064 (.020)	−.014 (.015)	60	13.16 ($p = .00$)
	Relax CRS	.013 (.008)				60	
	One-year changes CRS	.018 (.007)	.042 (.011)	.070 (.019)	−.039 (.011)	270	3.59 ($p = .06$)
	Relax CRS	.013 (.008)				270	

Four-year changes are based on fifteen industry manufacturing panel data for four time periods (1973–1977, 1977–1981, 1981–1985, 1985–1989) for all countries except Germany (1977–1981, 1981–1985, 1985–1989), Japan (1974–1977, 1977–1981, 1981–1985), and Sweden (1973–1977, 1977–1981, 1981–1985). Full sample sizes are 60 but may be less due to data problems in some industries and years. One-year-change models use data on all available years. All four-year changes are annualized, and all regressions include a full set of time dummies. Regressions are weighted by industry size (wage-bill share). Estimation is by GLS/random effects where the industry errors are allowed to be correlated for industries over time. Heteroskedasticity-consistent standard errors are in parentheses.

We have also estimated employment share equations that reveal broadly supportive results, with R&D intensity being positively and significantly associated with faster growth of the proportion of skilled employees. These equations are reported in Appendix 1. One should note that the parameter estimates in the employment-share equations were robust to including relatively industry wage terms—defined as $\log(W^{NP}/W^P)_{ijt}$ —where the NP and P superscripts stand for nonproduction and production, respectively. However, this is where the only notable difference between the four-year and one-year growth models occurred. In the year-on-year regressions the coefficient on the relative wage is fairly precisely estimated and is significantly negative in all countries except Japan. Furthermore, they hint at a stronger (i.e., more negative) wage effect in the United States than elsewhere. This pattern is less clear in the longer differenced models where the wage effects are estimated with much less precision.

Finally, returning to the wage-bill-share equations, when the relative wage terms were included in the wage-bill-share specifications, their coefficients were estimated to be positive, but it should be noted that, since the dependent variable includes wage terms in its definition, the estimated coefficients on the relative wage terms are biased upward. Despite this, but most important for our focus, the coefficients on the R&D and physical capital terms were essentially unaffected by the inclusion of the industry-specific relative wage terms.[13]

D. Cross-Country Differences in the Size of the Technical Change Effect

To what extent is the effect of R&D similar across countries? Simply looking at the estimated coefficients in Table IV gives the impression that their magnitude differs, and given that skill upgrading has occurred to a different degree across countries, their ability to explain the observed changes varies across countries. The most pertinent observation here is that the R&D coefficients are smallest in the United Kingdom and the United

13. For the five countries considered (non-CRS specifications) they were as follows (standard errors are in brackets): four-year changes—Denmark .038 (.015); Japan .056 (.020); Sweden .022 (.008); the United Kingdom .015 (.011); the United States .012 (.008); one-year changes—Denmark .035 (.010); Japan .044 (.020); Sweden .032 (.007); the United Kingdom .021 (.012); the United States .013 (.008).

States, yet skilled wage-bill and employment shares rose fastest in those two countries.[14]

To probe the differences further, we pooled the data and tested restricting the R&D coefficients to be common across countries. One cannot reject moving from the most general specification (with all variables allowed to have different effects by country) to the restricted model where there is a common R&D coefficient. In the four-year change wage-bill and employment share models for the five countries with employment and wage data (Denmark, Japan, Sweden, the United Kingdom, and the United States), pooled data models with a common R&D effect produced coefficients (and associated standard errors) of .021 (.006) in the wage-bill-share equation and .021 (.007) in the employment-share equation. A $\chi^2(4)$ test of constancy of the estimated R&D effect across countries produced a test statistic of 6.96 for wage-bill shares and 7.11 for employment shares (5 percent critical value = 9.49).

A more detailed examination of these results, however, revealed that one can identify some country-specific variations around these average effects. In fact, for both wage bills and employment shares, a model that restricts the United Kingdom and the United States to have equal R&D effects, Denmark and Japan to have equal effects, and lets Sweden have its own R&D effect cannot be restricted to the common R&D coefficient model. In this model the R&D coefficients are smaller in the United Kingdom/United States case at .013 (.006) for wage-bill shares and .013 (.007) for employment shares (standard errors are in parentheses). In Sweden they are .022 (.013) and .025 (.007), respectively. And they are higher in Denmark/Japan at .048 (.012) and .046 (.012). The appropriate $\chi^2(2)$ test statistics of simplifying to a model with identical R&D effects in all countries can be rejected (with test statistics of 6.38 for wage bill shares and 6.26 for employment shares, 5 percent critical value = 5.99).

---

14. Our purpose in this paper is to focus on cross-country correlations between skill upgrading and R&D using data defined at the same level of disaggregation across countries. This insistence on cross-country consistency may well mean that we are making things more difficult in terms of identifying evidence of SBTC. That this may be true is borne out by the fact that our correlations for the United States seem, if anything, to be smaller than those based on much more disaggregated data as reported in Berman, Bound, and Griliches [1994] and Autor, Katz, and Krueger [1998]. However, a clear comparison is rather hard here for a number of reasons (e.g., those papers define R&D intensity as (R&D/sales), and we use (R&D/value added), and they cover different time periods).

The pattern that emerges is therefore an intriguing one. There is a significant association between skill upgrading and R&D intensity in all countries. Put more bluntly, technology matters everywhere. However, in the countries that have experienced bigger increases in wage inequality and faster skill upgrading, a unit increase in R&D intensity is associated with a significantly lower shift in skill structure. On the other hand, in countries where wage inequality has remained stable and smaller shifts in skill structure have occurred, our measure of technology can account for a larger fraction of the observed change.

IV. Further Considerations

There are many issues and extensions that follow from the nature of the specifications reported in the previous section. In this section we investigate some of these where we probe further the robustness of the key findings.

A. Computer Usage

A common alternative to R&D-based technology measures is some index of computer use across industries. For the United States and the United Kingdom, we calculated the proportion of workers in our industries who were using computers at work in the mid-1980s.[15] This is essentially the same variable used by Autor, Katz, and Krueger [1998] and has the advantage of being a direct measure of the diffusion of a new technology.[16] The correlation of computer use with R&D intensity was high (.78 in the United Kingdom and .83 in the United States), and the industry-based cross-country correlation is also high at .79. Rerunning the cost-share-based models in Table IV, replacing the R&D intensity variable with the computer usage variable gave similar results, uncovering an important complementarity between skill upgrading and this alternative measure of technology.[16]

---

15. Data come from the Current Population Survey in the United States and from the British Social Attitudes Survey in the United Kingdom.
16. The estimated coefficients (and associated standard errors) were as follows: United Kingdom—wage bill shares .010 (.004) [one year changes], .006 (.004) [four-year changes]; employment shares .011 (.003) [one year changes], .008 (.004) [four-year changes]; United States— wage-bill shares .011 (.005) [one-year changes], .011 (.005) [four year changes]; employment shares .011 (.004) [one-year changes], .010 (.004) [four-year changes].

B. Foreign Competition

The main alternative story to technology-driven changes is that increased foreign competition has damaged the position of less skilled workers [Freeman 1995; Wood 1994]. We have constructed two measures of changes in import competition for our industry panels (changes in the ratio of total imports to value added and in the ratio of imports from non-OECD countries to value added) and examined the extent to which one sees a cross-country correlation pattern by industry. At first glance, the cross-country patterns of increases in import competition look like they may be broadly supportive of the trade view. Like skill upgrading (and R&D intensity) bigger changes in import competition from 1973–1989 seem to be clustered in much the same industries over time. For the 21 pairwise comparisons of cross-country correlations that we can carry out with our data, all were positive for both import variables, 7 were significant (at the 5 percent level) for the total imports variable, and 17 were significant for the non-OECD imports variable. So it appears to be the case that faster increases in import competition, especially from non-OECD countries, were concentrated in similar industries over time (it is also true that higher levels of import intensity are concentrated in the same industries).

Taking the next step to see whether these import variables were correlated with the extent of skill upgrading, we then augmented our cost-share model with these extra variables. On some readings of the "trade hypothesis," one would expect the industries with faster rising import intensities to be reducing the proportion of their unskilled workers at a faster rate. Table V tests this hypothesis. To keep things clear, only non-CRS specifications in the four-year change models are reported (the same pattern of results is upheld in one-year models and if constant returns are imposed). Four specifications are reported for each country, the first two rows including the imports variables in levels, the final two incorporating the variable in changes. In no case was the coefficient on the imports variable correctly signed and significantly different from zero. In many cases the imports coefficient attracted a perverse negative sign. While rising import competition is concentrated in similar industries across countries over time, and the same is true of skill upgrading, they do not appear to be the same ones.

What is more, it is important to note that the R&D coefficient remains very robust to the inclusion of the trade varia-

TABLE V
WAGE-BILL SHARE EQUATIONS INCLUDING IMPORTS VARIABLES (FOUR-YEAR CHANGES)

Changes in nonproduction wage-bill shares (four-year change, annualized)

	Definition of I	I/Y	Δ(I/Y)	(R&D/Y)	Δ log (K)	Δ log (Y)	Sample size
Denmark	All imports	−.000 (.000)		.040 (.016)	.024 (.017)	−.079 (.020)	54
	Non-OECD imports	−.004 (.003)		.043 (.018)	.020 (.018)	−.079 (.021)	54
	All imports		−.002 (.009)	.039 (.015)	.025 (.017)	−.080 (.021)	54
	Non-OECD imports		.002 (.012)	.039 (.016)	.024 (.017)	−.079 (.019)	54
Japan	All imports	−.001 (.002)		.056 (.019)	−.044 (.016)	.031 (.012)	45
	Non-OECD imports	−.002 (.003)		.059 (.019)	−.049 (.017)	.032 (.012)	45
	All imports		.005 (.036)	.055 (.020)	−.043 (.016)	.032 (.015)	45
	Non-OECD imports		.007 (.034)	.055 (.020)	−.043 (.016)	.032 (.015)	45
Sweden	All imports	.001 (.001)		.013 (.019)	.088 (.025)	−.005 (.025)	39
	Non-OECD imports	−.002 (.002)		.027 (.010)	.082 (.025)	−.014 (.021)	39
	All imports		.001 (.007)	.020 (.015)	.083 (.023)	−.007 (.030)	39
	Non-OECD imports		.006 (.018)	.020 (.015)	.084 (.024)	−.006 (.027)	39
U. K.	All imports	.001 (.001)		.012 (.009)	.052 (.023)	.041 (.022)	60
	Non-OECD imports	.002 (.003)		.013 (.009)	.052 (.022)	.041 (.023)	60
	All imports		−.019 (.009)	.017 (.009)	.053 (.021)	.023 (.022)	60
	Non-OECD imports		−.014 (.015)	.013 (.009)	.052 (.023)	.036 (.021)	60
U. S.	All imports	−.003 (.002)		.017 (.008)	.059 (.018)	−.016 (.016)	60
	Non-OECD imports	−.004 (.003)		.016 (.008)	.058 (.020)	−.013 (.015)	60
	All imports		−.002 (.022)	.014 (.008)	.064 (.021)	−.015 (.018)	60
	Non-OECD imports		−.040 (.032)	.015 (.007)	.065 (.019)	−.019 (.016)	60

Imports data are taken from OECD STAN and Bilateral Trade databases. All equations include the same variables as the non-CRS specifications in Table IV. All four-year changes are annualized, and all regressions include a full set of time dummies. Regressions are weighted by industry size (wage-bill share). Estimation is by GLS/random effects where the industry errors are allowed to be correlated for industries over time. Heteroskedasticity-consistent standard errors are in parentheses.

bles.[17] Although this robustness is reassuring, a cautionary note must be added. Supporters of the trade-based explanation of changing skill structures emphasize that the effects of trade are a general equilibrium phenomenon. Thus, one may not necessarily expect there to be a positive correlation between within-industry shifts in import intensity and skill structure. In related work (Desjonqueres, Machin, and Van Reenen [1998]) we show that even if one examines disaggregated nontraded sectors it is possible to uncover evidence of skill upgrading—a fact which is hard to reconcile with a *pure* trade-based explanation.[18]

C. Potential Endogeneity of R&D

In common with most of the existing literature, we have so far taken technical change to be exogenous. This may be a problematic assumption. If firms expect skills to be growing at a particularly fast rate in their sector, it may be less costly for them to adopt new technologies and perform more R&D. Thus, the technology-skills correlation would be due to endogenous technological advance (as is suggested by some endogenous growth theories). To the extent that R&D only responds slowly to shocks to skills (e.g., because of high adjustment costs), this may be less of a severe problem (in econometric terms it is not strictly exogenous, but predetermined).[19]

It is notoriously hard to find convincing instruments for technology. Here we investigate the possibility of using government-funded business enterprise R&D. If government behavior

---

17. Work based on U. S. data (e.g., Autor, Katz, and Krueger [1998] and Feenstra and Hanson [1996]) has tended to find stronger effects of changes in export intensity or outsourcing (defined as imported inputs/total nonenergy material purchases). We have experimented with specifications that include changes in exports/value added but find little change in the nature of the results, in particular the estimated coefficient on industrial R&D intensity remains essentially unchanged (we do not have cross-country industry data on outsourcing to examine the Feenstra-Hanson hypothesis). It is also not obvious how one should read coefficients on changes in export intensity as the link between rising export propensities and the extent of competition is not clear.

18. This work also shows that (i) the "prize puzzle" of a weak correlation between industry skill intensity and price changes exists outside the United States; and (ii) patterns of skill change in developing countries are largely inconsistent with simple (Heckscher-Ohlin type) trade models. Of course, the existence of within-sector skill upgrading in nontraded sectors does not rule out the idea that trade could be a contributing factor, merely that it cannot be the only important source of increased labor demand for the more-skilled.

19. A second reason for instrumenting could be measurement error associated with the problem of "double counting." This is because few production workers are involved in R&D. However, since the number of R&D workers in an industry is small, this is likely to be a second-order problem.

can be taken as exogenous, then although government-funded R&D is likely to affect the amount of R&D conducted in the industry, it will be uncorrelated with the error term in the cost-share equation. Government-funded R&D varies across industries and over time, and we use this independent variation in constructing instrumental variable (IV) results. The first two columns of Table VI contain these results. The first row for each country reports the coefficient and standard error on the government R&D variable in the first-stage reduced-form "R&D equation." As can be seen, the instrument is highly significant in all cases. Next consider the second and third rows which present estimates of the IV R&D coefficient in the cost-share equations (with and without imposing constant returns). Compared with the models where R&D is assumed exogenous, the IV coefficient estimates, although estimated with less precision, are remarkably close. In some countries (such as Japan) the coefficient actually rises in magnitude, although the main pattern is no change or a small fall. In no case are the coefficients significantly different from the case where R&D is assumed exogenous, and the overall thrust of results remains very robust.

Issues to do with the timing of the R&D variable are also linked to endogeneity questions. We have also considered models where initial period (1973) R&D intensity is entered into the skill-upgrading equations. Specifications contained in the final column of Table VI show that the correlation between skill upgrading and R&D still holds when initial R&D intensity is used. In the same vein, when pooled wage-bill-share models were estimated exactly, the same story emerged: one can reject the null hypothesis of a common R&D coefficient across countries in favor of a model that groups the R&D coefficient for Denmark and Japan (coefficient = .055, standard error = .012), Sweden (.040, .014), and the United Kingdom and the United States (.012, .007), the appropriate $\chi^2(2)$ statistic being 10.59.

D. Spillovers

A further possible criticism of using own R&D as a measure of technology is that it ignores any international spillovers arising from the public good nature of knowledge. Constructing a spillover pool is by no means easy,[20] but one simple method is to calculate the amount of worldwide R&D for each industry using

---

20. See Coe and Helpman [1995] for a recent attempt to use trade flows to construct an international spillover measure.

TECHNOLOGY AND CHANGES IN SKILL STRUCTURE   1237

TABLE VI
POTENTIAL ENDOGENEITY OF (R&D/Y)

		Changes in nonproduction wage-bill shares (four-year changes, annualized)		
		Coefficient (se) on (R&D/Y), IV estimates	Coefficient (se) on (Government R&D/Y)	Coefficient (se) on initial period (R&D/Y)
Denmark	R&D equation		8.625 (1.271)	
	Wage-bill-share equation, CRS	.016 (.012)		.037 (.016)
	Wage-bill-share equation, relax CRS	.022 (.017)		.055 (.011)
Japan	R&D equation		30.193 (11.951)	
	Wage-bill-share equation, CRS	.059 (.029)		.052 (.012)
	Wage-bill-share equation, relax CRS	.070 (.030)		.055 (.018)
Sweden	R&D equation		11.263 (2.427)	
	Wage-bill-share equation, CRS	.031 (.028)		.063 (.018)
	Wage-bill-share equation, relax CRS	.030 (.024)		.037 (.015)
U. K.	R&D equation		2.218 (.217)	
	Wage-bill-share equation, CRS	.024 (.010)		.032 (.016)
	Wage-bill-share equation, relax CRS	.009 (.010)		.017 (.013)
U. S.	R&D equation		1.964 (.206)	
	Wage-bill-share equation, CRS	.021 (.010)		.019 (.007)
	Wage-bill-share equation, relax CRS	.013 (.009)		.009 (.008)

Government funded R&D is estimated from the OFBERD data set. Initial (R&D/Y) is dated 1973 (except for Japan which is 1974). R&D instrumentation equation and wage-bill-share equations include the same variables as the CRS and non-CRS specifications in Table IV. All four-year changes are annualized, and all regressions include a full set of time dummies. Regressions are weighted by industry size (wage bill share). Estimation is by (IV) GLS/random effects where the industry errors are allowed to be correlated for industries over time. Heteroskedasticity-consistent standard errors are in parentheses.

the entire STAN database (essentially all OECD R&D). After subtracting own R&D and normalizing on world value added in the industry (net of own value added), the spillover variable was entered alongside the own R&D variable. One should bear in mind that, as with the cross-country R&D correlations considered earlier (in Table II), own R&D and the spillover term are highly correlated so identification of separate effects is asking rather a lot. Nevertheless, the broad pattern that emerged is of some interest. In the United Kingdom and the United States the coefficient on the spillover variable was small and statistically insignificant. But in the other countries it was estimated to be positive and statistically significant, and the coefficient on own R&D was driven to insignificance.[21] Taken as a whole, the results suggest spillovers to be potentially more important in the smaller Scandinavian economies and Japan than in the United States and the United Kingdom.

V. CONCLUSIONS

This paper has reported evidence related to the question of whether the observed intertemporal shifts in the skill structure of international labor markets can be accounted for by skill-biased technological change. Using a newly constructed industry level database, we have contrasted the experience of seven industrialized nations: Denmark, France, Germany, Japan, Sweden, the United Kingdom, and the United States. Our countries provide an interesting comparison because, over the time period considered, there was skill upgrading in all cases, but there were also dramatic changes in the wage structure of the United Kingdom and the United States, with relative stability elsewhere. If a similar common technology shock hit the developed world, then the contrast between these countries should give some insight into the relative importance of different explanations for changes in the skill structure.

Our analysis leads to the conclusion that there exist important skill-technology complementarities across all countries. This finding was robust to experiments using different measures of

---

21. For the non-CRS case, in four-year change wage-bill share models, the following coefficients (standard errors) were obtained: Denmark, (R&D/Y) .001 (.006), spillover .040 (.006); Japan, (R&D/Y) .008 (.015), spillover .036 (.015); Sweden, (R&D/Y) −.066 (.050), spillover .097 (.050); the United Kingdom, (R&D/Y) .018 (.019), spillover −.006 (.021); the United States, (R&D/Y) .024 (.015), spillover −.015 (.024). The same pattern of results emerged in the CRS case (insignificant own R&D effects with positive significant spillovers in Denmark, Japan, and Sweden), except in the United Kingdom and, the United States where the positive own R&D effect was larger and more precisely determined (at .042 (.014) and .030 (.016), respectively). The coefficient on the spillover variable remained negative and insignificant in both these countries.-

TECHNOLOGY AND CHANGES IN SKILL STRUCTURE   1239

skill, introducing trade variables, and instrumenting R&D. Thus, it is likely that the move toward higher R&D intensities and increased computer usage (see also Autor, Katz, and Krueger [1998]) are factors that have contributed to reducing the relative demand for the unskilled.

To what extent can technical change account for changes in the structure of labor markets in industrialized nations? The results presented here can be interpreted as offering evidence that technology has been very important. It seems that R&D intensity pushes up the demand for skills and R&D intensity was higher in all countries in the 1980s than in the 1970s. There are several important caveats to be borne in mind, however. First, a full analysis needs to take into account the differential growth in the supply of skilled workers. Although this has been increasing across all countries, the rate of acceleration has been different, and equilibrium skill differentials will in part reflect these differences. Second, although R&D intensity is relatively high in the United Kingdom and the United States, the rate of growth has been slower, and the estimated coefficients on the R&D variable in skill upgrading equations appear to be somewhat lower in the United Kingdom and the United States than in other countries. Taken together with the fact that the skill structures were changing most rapidly in these two countries, it seems likely that there are other factors in addition to technology that have contributed to the declining labor market position of unskilled workers.

The additional factor that has received most attention to date is rising international trade, and it is natural that much current research focuses on this. However, we remain rather skeptical about the direct role of trade (i.e., through Heckscher-Ohlin type routes). A more fruitful path may well be to better integrate arguments to do with the declining role of labor market institutions into generating a fuller understanding of what lies behind the observed changes in skill structure. The ability of institutions to set wages, affect training, and reduce the power of firms to lay off unskilled workers is likely to impact on relative wages and employment. The cross-country pattern of results reported in this paper, coupled with the dramatic weakening of these institutions in the United Kingdom and the United States in the 1980s and their relative persistence in Europe, suggests that this could well be an important factor—in addition to technical change—in explaining the changing skill structure of the countries examined here.

DATA APPENDIX

The data used in this paper come from a variety of industry and individual level data sources. The main aim is to consider the relationship between skill upgrading and technology across countries in the same industries. This requires the matching of data from a number of sources and at different levels of industry disaggregation. We focus on the manufacturing sectors of seven countries (Denmark, France, Germany, Japan, Sweden, the United Kingdom, and the United States). From our matching of the relevant data sources described below, aggregate manufacturing can be broken down into sixteen industries at (broadly) the two-digit level. All the industry-based work in the paper that requires the use of R&D data focuses on fifteen industries only, dropping the transport goods sector because of problems with the R&D data for this sector (see below).

The fifteen sectors considered were chemicals (including drugs); electrical, radio, TV, and communications; food, beverages, and tobacco; iron and steel; metal products; nonelectrical machinery (including computers); nonferrous metals; nonmetallic mineral products; other manufacturing; paper products and printing; coal and petroleum products; professional goods; rubber and plastic goods; textiles, apparel, and leather; wood products and furniture.

The data sources used to set up the panel data for these industries over time were the following.

1. OECD STAN Database

STAN is a data set constructed in a long-term project by the OECD who work together with the Central Statistical Offices of OECD countries to compile consistent industry-level data over time from the early 1970s. All data are originally in unscaled national currencies. They can be converted to dollars using annual average values of the exchange rate. Industrial classifications are detailed in OECD [1997c]. There are three OECD databases which can be merged consistently in the STAN series.

(a) Business Enterprise R&D (ANBERD). This contains data on R&D conducted by industry regardless of funding source and is available from 1973 for the following countries: the United

Kingdom, France, Canada, Germany, Italy, Japan, the United States, Australia, Denmark, Finland, the Netherlands, and Sweden for 22 disaggregated industries (see OECD [1997b]). These figures have been adjusted to ensure comparability and so differ from the official figures for the individual countries. State-owned industries' R&D are included in all countries. As noted above, there appeared to be problems in constructing the R&D figure for the transport industries (this is related to the large amount of military/government expenditure, especially in the United Kingdom and the United States, erratic figures for the aerospace industries, and the fact that R&D data were missing for some subsectors of the transport industry). Consequently, this industry was dropped.

(b) OECD, DSTI(STAN/Industrial Database) contains data on investment, value added, and exchange rates. From the investment data capital stock measures were constructed using the perpetual inventory method and a depreciation rate of 8.4 percent (a weighted average of the depreciation rates for plant and machinery and buildings used in OECD [1991]). Initial year stocks assumed a presample growth rate of 5 percent. Data are National Accounts compatible where available, otherwise OECD estimates are made.

(c) Import and export data are from OECD's Compatible Trade and Production database (COMTAP). Figures are consistent across countries but may not be strictly comparable to trade flows published in other sources.

2. United Nations General Industrial Statistics Database (UNISD)

Data for wage bills and employment for production/nonproduction workers were obtained for Denmark, Sweden, the United Kingdom, and the United States from the Statistical Division of the United Nations from 1970 onward (up to 1991 in some countries). The key data are reported in terms of "employees" and "operatives," the latter of which are taken to be production workers, and nonproduction workers are the rest. More recent data are not available as the UN stopped collecting data disaggregated in this way after responsibility for the UNISD was moved from New York to Vienna. The UNISD database contains similar information (in particular on capital formation) to the STAN database, but differs from it in that the STAN database is derived from sample information which is then calibrated by national accounts numbers, whereas the UN figures report the survey results (e.g., from the United States Annual Survey of Manufactures or the United Kingdom Census of Production). After cleaning the data, consistently defined data on nonproduction shares were available for 1973–1989 (Denmark) and 1970–1985 (Sweden), 1970–1990 (United Kingdom), and 1970–1991 (United States).

3. OECD Bilateral Trade Database

Data on imports from non-OECD countries were matched in from the OECD Bilateral Trade Database.

4. OECD OFBERD

OFBERD ("Official" BERD) is an unpublished data set compatible with STAN/ANBERD which is compiled by the OECD. In OFBERD R&D performed by the business sector is broken down into sources of finance. Some data points were imputed using linear interpolation due to missing observations. We distinguish between R&D funded by government and by the private sector (domestic or foreign). Government-funded R&D is primarily direct grants and contracts.

5. Individual-Level Data Sources

Individual-level data sources were aggregated to industry level for the following.

(a) Nonproduction wage-bill and employment shares in Japan (*Source:* Japanese Wage Survey) and nonproduction employment shares in Germany (*Source:* Mikrozensus). As data were not available for all years, some values were imputed.

(b) High education employment shares (defined as the share of the workforce with a college degree) for France (1977–1991, *Source:* Enquete Emploi), Germany (1977–1991, *Source:* Mikrozensus), Japan (1977–1990, *Source:* Japanese Wage Survey), Sweden (1986 and 1993, provided by Par Hansson, data from ARSYS Regional Statistics Database, Statistics Sweden), the United Kingdom (1979–1991, *Source:* Labour Force Survey), and the United States (1977–1991, *Source:* Current Population Survey). In some cases data were not available annually so in these cases data were interpolated between years, and in Sweden only two years were available (1986 and 1993).

TECHNOLOGY AND CHANGES IN SKILL STRUCTURE 1243

APPENDIX 1: CHANGE IN NONPRODUCTION EMPLOYMENT SHARE EQUATIONS IN MANUFACTURING

Changes in nonproduction employment shares

			(R&D/Y)	$\Delta \log (K)$	$\Delta \log (Y)$	$\Delta \log (W^{NP}/W^{P})$	Sample size
Denmark	Four-year changes	Exclude relative wage	.040 (.015)	.019 (.020)	−.061 (.021)		54
		Include relative wage	.040 (.015)	.022 (.016)	−.068 (.017)	−.141 (.027)	54
	One-year changes	Include relative wage	.034 (.010)	.027 (.013)	−.074 (.012)	−.115 (.026)	173
Germany	Four-year changes	Exclude relative wage	.026 (.006)	−.021 (.013)	.000 (.007)		45
	One-year changes	Exclude relative wage	.029 (.007)	−.030 (.013)	−.002 (.003)		210
Japan	Four-year changes	Exclude relative wage	.046 (.015)	−.045 (.021)	.044 (.011)		45
		Include relative wage	.047 (.015)	−.045 (.021)	.044 (.013)	−.008 (.017)	45
	One-year changes	Include relative wage	.047 (.020)	−.026 (.026)	.002 (.015)	.017 (.014)	174
Sweden	Four-year changes	Exclude relative wage	.025 (.008)	.052 (.016)	−.001 (.013)		39
		Include relative wage	.024 (.007)	.056 (.012)	−.002 (.014)	−.034 (.078)	39
	One-year changes	Include relative wage	.034 (.006)	.035 (.016)	−.007 (.007)	−.074 (.020)	157
U. K.	Four-year changes	Exclude relative wage	.016 (.010)	.026 (.019)	.040 (.018)		60
		Include relative wage	.015 (.010)	.033 (.021)	.040 (.019)	−.063 (.079)	60
	One-year changes	Include relative wage	.021 (.011)	.028 (.018)	−.003 (.006)	−.088 (.031)	255
U. S.	Four-year changes	Exclude relative wage	.010 (.008)	.059 (.016)	−.011 (.011)		60
		Include relative wage	.012 (.008)	.061 (.017)	−.012 (.013)	−.124 (.088)	60
	One-year changes	Include relative wage	.013 (.008)	.073 (.020)	−.038 (.011)	−.203 (.021)	270

Four-year changes are based on fifteen industry manufacturing panel data for four time periods (1973–1977, 1977–1981, 1981–1985, 1985–1989) for all countries except Germany (1977–1981, 1981–1985, 1985–1989), Japan (1974–1977, 1977–1981, 1981–1985), and Sweden (1973–1977, 1977–1981, 1981–1985). Full sample sizes are 60 but may be less due to data problems in some industries and years. One-year-change models use data on all available years. All four-year changes are annualized, and all regressions include a full set of time dummies. Regressions are weighted by industry size (employment share). Estimation is by GLS/random effects where the industry errors are allowed to be correlated for industries over time. Heteroskedasticity-consistent standard errors are in parentheses.

1244   *QUARTERLY JOURNAL OF ECONOMICS*

DEPARTMENT OF ECONOMICS, UNIVERSITY COLLEGE LONDON AND CENTRE FOR ECONOMIC PERFORMANCE, LONDON SCHOOL OF ECONOMICS
DEPARTMENT OF ECONOMICS, UNIVERSITY COLLEGE LONDON, UNIVERSITY OF CALIFORNIA AT BERKELEY, AND INSTITUTE FOR FISCAL STUDIES

REFERENCES

Autor, David, Lawrence Katz, and Alan Krueger, "Computing Inequality: Have Computers Changed the Labor Market," *Quarterly Journal of Economics,* CXIII (1998), 1169–1213.
Berman, Eli, John Bound, and Zvi Griliches, "Changes in the Demand for Skilled Labor within U. S. Manufacturing Industries," *Quarterly Journal of Economics,* CIX (1994), 367–398.
Berman, Eli, John Bound, and Stephen Machin, "Implications of Skill-Biased Technological Change: International Evidence," *Quarterly Journal of Economics,* CXIII (1998), 1245–1279.
Bound, John, and George Johnson, "Changes in the Structure of Wages in the 1980s: An Evaluation of Alternative Explanations," *American Economic Review,* LXXXII (1992), 371–392.
Card, David, Francis Kramarz, and Thomas Lemieux, "Changes in the Relative Structure of Wages and Employment: A Comparison of the United States, Canada, and France," NBER Working Paper No. 5487, 1996.
Coe, David, and Elhanan Helpman, "International R&D Spillovers," *European Economic Review,* XLV (1995), 859–887.
Desjonqueres, Thibaut, Stephen Machin, and John Van Reenen, "Another Nail in the Coffin? Or Can the Trade-Based Explanation of Changing Skill Structure Be Resurrected?" Centre for Economic Performance, London School of Economics, mimeo, 1998.
Feenstra, Robert, and Gordon Hanson, "Globalization, Outsourcing and Wage Inequality," *American Economic Review Papers and Proceedings,* LXXXVI (1996), 240–245.
Freeman, Richard, "Are Your Wages Set in Beijing?" *Journal of Economic Perspectives,* IX (1995), 15–32.
Griliches, Zvi, Bronwyn Hall, and Ariel Pakes, "R&D, Patents and Market Value Revisited: Is There a Second (Technological Opportunity) Factor?" *Economics of Innovation and New Technology,* I (1991), 183–202.
Hall, Bronwyn, and Jacques Mairesse, "Exploring the Relationship between R&D and Productivity in French Manufacturing Firms," *Journal of Econometrics,* CXV (1995), 263–293.
Haskel, Jonathan, and Mathew Slaughter, "The Sector Bias of Skill-Biased Technological Change: Theory and International Evidence," Queen Mary and Westfield College, mimeo, 1998.
Johnson, George, "Changes in Earnings Inequality: The Role of Demand Shifts," *Journal of Economic Perspectives,* XI (1997), 41–54.
Machin, Stephen, and John Van Reenen "Technology and Changes in Skill Structure: Evidence from Seven Countries," Labour Market Consequences of Technical and Structural Change Discussion Paper No. 24, 1997.
OECD, "Taxing Profits in a Global Economy; Domestic and International Issues" (Paris: OECD, 1991).
OECD, "Research and Development Expenditure in Industry 1973–1995" (Paris: OECD, 1997a).
OECD, "ANBERD, Analytic Business Expenditure on R&D" (Paris: OECD, 1997b).
OECD, "STAN, Standardized Industrial Database" (Paris: OECD, 1997c).
Van Reenen, John, "Why Has Britain had Slower R&D Growth?" *Research Policy,* XXVI (1997), 493–502.
Wood, Adrian, *North-South Trade, Employment and Inequality* (Oxford: Clarendon Press, 1994).

[2]

IMPLICATIONS OF SKILL-BIASED TECHNOLOGICAL CHANGE: INTERNATIONAL EVIDENCE*

ELI BERMAN
JOHN BOUND
STEPHEN MACHIN

Demand for less-skilled workers plummeted in developed countries in the 1980s. In open economies, *pervasive* skill-biased technological change (SBTC) can explain this decline. SBTC tends to increase the domestic supply of unskill-intensive goods by releasing less-skilled labor. The more countries experiencing a SBTC, the greater its potential to decrease the relative wages of less-skilled labor by increasing the *world* supply of unskill-intensive goods. We find strong evidence for pervasive SBTC in developed countries. Most industries *increased* the proportion of skilled workers *despite* generally rising or stable relative wages. Moreover, the *same* manufacturing industries simultaneously increased demand for skills in *different* countries. Many developing countries also show increased skill premiums, a pattern consistent with SBTC.

I. INTRODUCTION

Less-skilled workers have suffered reduced relative wages, increased unemployment, and sometimes both in OECD economies over the 1980s. In the United States real wages of young men with twelve or fewer years of education *fell* by 26 percent between 1979 and 1993, and have not recovered since.[1] Between 1979 and 1992 the average unemployment rate in European OECD countries increased from 5.4 percent to 9.9 percent[2] and has remained high, with most of the unemployment concentrated among unskilled workers. In the same period relative wages of less-skilled workers declined slightly in several OECD countries and sharply in others. Several authors have documented the decline in the relative wages of less-skilled workers in the United States and the concurrent decline in their employment in manufacturing (e.g.,

* We appreciate the helpful comments and suggestions of Olivier Blanchard, Jonathan Eaton, Christine Greenhalgh, Lawrence Katz, Kevin Lang, John Martyn, Kenneth Troske, Daniel Tsiddon, two anonymous referees, and participants in numerous conferences and seminars. The Sloan Foundation supported plant visits. Berman acknowledges National Science Foundation support. We thank Thibaut Desjonqueres and Noah Greenhill for research assistance.
    1. Calculated for high school graduates with five years of labor market experience in Current Population Survey from Bound and Johnson [1995], table 1.
    2. Source: OECD [1992, 1993]. For specific countries the 1979–1992 increases in unemployment were 5.0 percent to 10.1 percent (United Kingdom); 3.2 percent to 7.7 percent (Germany), 7.6 percent to 10.7 percent (Italy), and 5.9 percent to 10.2 percent (France). All are considerably larger than the U. S. increase from 5.8 percent in 1979 to 7.4 percent in 1992.

The Quarterly Journal of Economics, November 1998

Murphy and Welch [1992, 1993]; Bound and Johnson [1992]; Katz and Murphy [1992]; and Blackburn, Bloom, and Freeman [1990]), and a number have documented similar trends in wages, employment, or unemployment in other OECD countries (e.g., Freeman [1988]; Freeman and Katz [1994]; Katz and Revenga [1989]; Katz, Loveman, and Blanchflower [1995]; Davis [1992]; Machin [1996a]; and Nickell and Bell [1995]). It is now well documented that labor market outcomes of less-skilled workers have worsened in the developed world in the past two decades, despite their increasing scarcity relative to the rapidly expanding supply of skilled labor.

The literature has proposed several reasons for this decline in the demand for unskilled labor, including both Stolper-Samuelson effects of increased exposure to trade from developing countries and skill-biased (or unskilled labor-saving) technological change (SBTC). While there is no consensus, labor economists generally believe that skill-biased technological change is the principal culprit. That belief is based on a combination of four findings: (1) employment shifts to skill-intensive sectors seem too small to be consistent with explanations based on product demand shifts, such as those induced by trade, or Hicks-neutral, sector-biased technological change [Bound and Johnson 1992; Katz and Murphy 1992; Berman, Bound, and Griliches 1994 (BBG); Freeman and Katz 1994]; (2) despite the increase in the relative cost of skilled labor, the majority of U. S. industries have increased their ratio of skilled to unskilled labor [Bound and Johnson 1992; Katz and Murphy 1992; Lawrence and Slaughter 1993; BBG], (3) there appear to be strong, within-sector correlations between indicators of technological change and increased demand for skills [Berndt, Morrison, and Rosenblum 1994; BBG; Autor, Katz, and Krueger 1998; Machin 1996b; Machin and Van Reenen 1998];[3] and (4) case studies conducted by the Bureau of Labor Statistics Office of Productivity and Technology that indicate the nature of innovations often mention innovations that lowered or are expected to lower production labor requirements [Mark 1987].

In this paper we claim that skill-biased technological change was pervasive over the past two decades, occurring simultaneously in most, if not all, developed countries. Thus, *it was not*

---

3. Plant-level studies using finer measures of technology adoption, such as use of computer-aided manufacturing, yield mixed results. Doms, Dunne, and Troske [1997] find that technology adoption is not correlated with changes in the proportion of nonproduction workers, although computer investment is. Siegel [1995] finds that technology adoption is correlated with increased proportions of high skill occupations.

SKILL-BIASED TECHNOLOGICAL CHANGE   1247

*only the major cause of decreased demand for less-skilled workers
in the United States, but also shifted demand from less-skilled to
skilled workers throughout the developed world.* Pervasiveness is
important for two reasons. First, at the current level of international communication and trade, it is hard to imagine major
productive technological changes occurring in one country without rapid adoption by the same industries in countries at the same
technological level. Thus, pervasive SBTC is an immediate implication of SBTC, which invites testing. If we did not observe
evidence of SBTC throughout the developed world, we would be
forced to doubt whether it occurred in any developed country, such
as the United States.

Second, the more pervasive the SBTC, the greater its potential to affect relative wages. To illustrate that point, we consider a
Heckscher-Ohlin (H-O) model with small open economies and two
factors of production. In that context the skill-bias of local
technological change is irrelevant to the wage structure in an H-O
model unless it is also sector-biased. On those grounds, Leamer
[1994] has objected to the notion that SBTC is the dominant factor
explaining the decline in the demand for skilled labor. This
critique is powerful, as the H-O model is widely considered to be a
relevant model for analyzing the long-run effect on wages of
increased exposure of developed economies to LDC manufacturing over the past few decades. (The long run is long enough for
factors to detach themselves from industries, allowing wages to be
set by perfectly elastic demand curves.)[4] However, as Krugman
[1995] has pointed out, *pervasive* skill-biased technological change
will affect relative wages, since an integrated world economy will
respond to such technological change as a closed economy would.
Under standard assumptions, including homothetic preferences,
skill-biased technological change releases less-skilled workers
from industries, depressing their relative wages by depressing the
world (relative) prices of goods intensive in less-skilled work.
Thus, pervasive skill-biased technological change in the developed world provides an explanation consistent with both increased wage premiums for skilled workers and within-industry

---

4. The H-O model has been criticized, as its property of perfectly elastic labor
demand curves is inconsistent with evidence that labor supply affects wages
[Freeman 1995]. One way to reconcile those two views is to recognize that the H-O
model applies only in the long run, so that the short- and long-run effects of a local
SBTC or of increased exposure to trade may differ. Since the trend increase in
relative demand for skilled labor seems to have persisted for decades, long-run
models deserve consideration.

substitution toward skilled workers, even in small open economy models.

Pervasive SBTC has two testable implications. 1. The within-sector shifts away from unskilled labor observed in the United States should occur throughout the developed world. 2. These shifts should be concentrated in the same industries in different countries. Using data on the employment of production and nonproduction workers in manufacturing from twelve developed countries in the 1980s, we find evidence consistent with both predictions. In all those countries we find large-scale within-industry substitution away from unskilled labor despite rising or stable relative wages in the 1980s. Moreover, the cross-country correlations of within-industry increases in employment of skilled workers are generally positive and often quite large.

The manufacturing industries that experience the greatest skill upgrading in our sample are those associated with the spread of microprocessor technology. Electrical machinery, machinery (including computers), and printing and publishing together account for 46 percent of the within-industry increase in relative demand for skills in our 1980s sample. Case studies reveal that these three industries underwent significant technological changes associated largely with the assimilation of microprocessors [United States Department of Labor 1982a, 1982b]. Casual empiricism suggests a pervasive spread of microprocessors within these and other manufacturing industries in the 1980s. This pattern strongly suggests a common technology linking similar patterns of skill upgrading across countries.

Evidence from the developing world is also consistent with the SBTC hypothesis. Several studies have found *increased* relative wages of skilled labor in LDCs undergoing trade liberalization in the 1980s, despite the opposite Stolper-Samuelson prediction [Feliciano 1995; Hanson and Harrison 1995; Robbins 1995]. We examine a larger sample of developing countries, finding that relative wages also increased in many developing countries during a decade of trade liberalization in the 1980s.

The paper proceeds as follows. In Section II we discuss skill-biased technological change in an H-O framework, contrasting the effects of local and pervasive SBTC on wages. In Section III we test one implication of SBTC, presenting evidence on within-industry changes in the employment of skills in OECD countries. We also examine alternative explanations for within-industry skill upgrading. Section IV presents further evidence of pervasive technological change, describing common technological changes across countries. In Section V we examine evidence that SBTC is pervasive in developing countries as well as in developed. Section VI concludes.

II. LOCAL VERSUS PERVASIVE TECHNOLOGICAL CHANGE IN OPEN ECONOMIES

How does skill-biased technological change affect the relative wages of skilled labor in open economies? In this section we argue that the pervasiveness of an SBTC is key to establishing its long-run influence on relative wages. In open economies the effect of *local* SBTC on relative wages is muted by the high price elasticity of product demand. In contrast, *pervasive* SBTC, occurring in many countries, will drive up the relative price of skill-intensive goods under fairly general conditions. That change in goods prices will induce an increase in the skill premium.

To illustrate the role of pervasiveness, we start with the extreme example of a small open economy, in which local SBTC has no effect on relative wages [Leamer 1994], but pervasive SBTC has a large effect [Krugman 1995]. While small economies provide a clear example, the mechanism is fairly general: the more pervasive the SBTC, the greater the effect on world prices and thus on wages. We discuss generalizations below.

Consider the two-factor, two-good small open economy version of Heckscher-Ohlin theory with local technological change [Helpman and Krugman 1985]: labor is either skilled or unskilled; two goods are produced by constant returns to scale, quasi-concave production functions; competition is perfect; all goods are produced in equilibrium; preferences are homothetic; world prices are parameters. These assumptions imply that goods are priced according to marginal cost as free entry of firms in any country and constant returns to scale dictate zero profits. The resulting zero profit condition is

$$(1) \qquad p_i = a_{Si}(w)w_S + a_{Ui}(w)w_U \qquad \text{for all } i,$$

where p_i is the world price of good i and a_{li} is the demand for factor l per unit of good i, which is a function of the wage vector, w. (For more detail see Berman, Bound, and Machin [1997].)

A. Stolper-Samuleson Effects and Sector-Biased Technological Change

The Lerner-Pierce diagram [Lerner 1952] in Figure I provides a clear illustration of the effects of trade and technological change on wages. Here the unit-value isoquants $C1$ and $C2$ trace out combinations of inputs that produce one dollar of goods 1 and 2, respectively. The line AB tangent to those curves describes zero profit combinations of inputs at equilibrium wages. Its slope is the wage ratio $-w_U/w_S$.

To illustrate the Stolper-Samuelson effect, consider a shift from autarky to trade for a skill-abundant country. The Heckscher-Ohlin-Vanek theorem implies an increase in the relative price of good 1, the skill-intensive good. In the diagram, that price change is reflected in the shift of $C1$ toward the origin, as fewer inputs are required to produce a dollar's worth of good 1. Preserving zero-profit, relative wages of skilled labor increase, a change reflected in the decrease in w_U/w_S as the line of tangencies shifts from AB to EF.

Now consider the effect on wages of technological change in the skill-intensive sector. Figure I can also be used to illustrate Hicks-neutral technological progress occurring only for good 1. Assuming that these goods are traded, their prices are exogenously fixed (under the small country assumption). Technological progress in good 1 production reduces factor requirements, shifting the unit value isoquant toward the origin from $C1$ to $C1'$. This shift is Hicks-neutral since at the old relative wage the ratio of inputs S/U is unchanged, a condition reflected in the diagram by CD being parallel to AB. Profit opportunities in good 1 production will bid up the relative wage of skill, as in the Stolper-Samuelson case, a change reflected, as before, in the decrease in w_U/w_S as the line of tangencies shifts from AB to EF. Note that within both sectors, rays from the origin to points of tangency reflect lower ratios of S/U. That is to say, whether the change in relative wages is driven by changes in sector-specific prices or productivity, there is within-sector substitution away from skilled labor due to its new, higher, relative wage.

B. Skill-Biased Technological Change

A skill-biased technological change is an exogenous change in the production function that increases the unit demand ratio a_{Si}/a_{Ui} at the current wage level. Figure II illustrates the effects of a skill-biased technological change on wages.

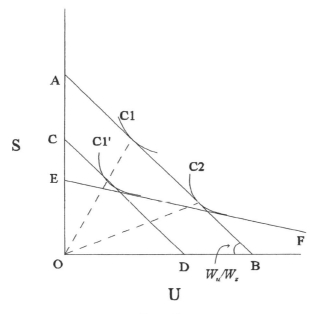

FIGURE I
The Stolper-Samuelson Effect or Sector-Biased Hicks-Neutral
Technological Change

Skill-biased technological change is reflected in the shift of unit cost curves C1 and C2 to C1' and C2'. This change is sector-neutral in the sense that both C1 and C2 shift to lower levels of inputs in a way that reduces costs by the same proportion in each sector. The line CD, tangent to C1' and C2' reflects the new zero-profit condition, and is parallel to AB, reflecting the same relative wage. These shifts are skill-biased as the new equilibrium ratios of skilled to unskilled workers are higher than the old. (Rays from the origin are steeper.) While a technological change that saves factors in the same proportion in each sector may seem artificial, it provides a useful contrast to the sector-biased technological change of Figure I. Note the testable implication: unlike Stolper-Samuelson effects, skill-biased technological change directly increases the proportion of skilled labor employed in each sector.

One feature of technological changes with fixed goods prices is that the skill bias of technological changes has no effect on

1252   *QUARTERLY JOURNAL OF ECONOMICS*

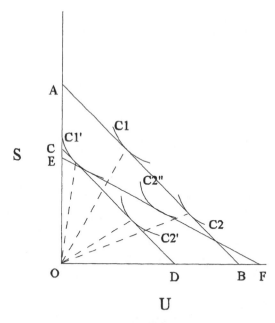

FIGURE II
Skill-Biased Technological Change

relative wages [Leamer 1994].[5] This appears particularly damning to the claim that skill-biased technological change increased the skill premium.

C. Pervasive Skill-Biased Technological Change

Now consider a *pervasive* skill-biased technological change occurring simultaneously in all economies in the production of some traded good. Imagine an integrated world economy consisting of many small open economies, each experiencing SBTC.[6] The response of prices and wages would be like that of a closed economy. SBTC would initially cause a disproportionate expan-

---

5. Imagine sliding the isovalue curve *C1'* along the unit-cost line so that the point of tangency is at a different ratio of skilled to unskilled workers. Any of those locations represent the same unit cost of production. Although the skill-biases of those locations (technologies) differ, they all share the same solution for relative wages.

6. The integrated world economy is discussed in Helpman and Krugman [1985]. It behaves like the closed economy in Jones [1965]. Baldwin [1994] provides a clear graphical presentation.

sion of production of the good intensive in unskilled labor (good 2) as each industry reduces its proportion of unskilled labor. Under homothetic preferences that disproportionate expansion would induce a decrease in the relative price of good 2 and in the relative wages of unskilled labor.[7] That decrease in the relative price of the good intensive in unskilled labor is illustrated as a shift of the unit cost curve from $C2'$ to $C2''$ as more inputs are required to provide the same value of output. That shift implies a decrease in the relative wages of unskilled labor, reflected in the slope of the line *EF*, which is shallower than that of *CD*. Thus, pervasive, sector-neutral, skill-biased technological change is a possible explanation for the increased skill premium even in the small open economy model. Note that unlike most alternative explanations of the increased skill premium, such as Stolper-Samuelson effects or factor-neutral sector-biased technological change, it implies within-industry increases in the proportion of skilled workers.

How general is the result that pervasive SBTC will affect relative wages more than local SBTC? It clearly generalizes to a number of models with product demand curves that are less than perfectly elastic, such as large open economies [Baldwin 1994], locally produced goods which are imperfect substitutes for traded goods [Johnson and Stafford, 1999] and models with barriers to trade, as long as perfectly elastic product demand is preserved.[8] In all these cases open economies behave more like the closed economies in the sense that SBTC can affect goods prices. While the contrast between the wage effects of a pervasive SBTC and those of a local SBTC is greatest in the small open economy model, it can also be large in more general models of trade, especially when product demand is elastic.

III. TESTING THE IMPLICATIONS OF ALTERNATIVE EXPLANATIONS

Section II established that pervasive SBTC can affect relative wages regardless of the degree of openness of the economy. It also showed that among candidate causes of increased relative wages SBTC has a unique prediction: within-industry skill upgrading. If

7. Homothetic preferences are sufficient but not necessary for the increased skill premium. Krugman [1995] points out that a limit on the cross-elasticity of demand will do.
8. With a little care, this result will also generalize to the $n > 2$ good case as in Ethier [1984]. Generalizations are much like those that allow the insensitivity of factor prices to changes in factor supplies [Leamer and Levinsohn 1995], which also relies critically on perfectly elastic product demand.

1254   *QUARTERLY JOURNAL OF ECONOMICS*

the dominant cause of increased skill premiums in the United States is indeed *pervasive* SBTC, then it must be evident in all developed countries. We begin this section by reporting evidence on plant-level skill upgrading despite increased relative wages in the United States and the United Kingdom. We then seek out the same pattern in a new, larger sample of OECD countries.

Table I reproduces evidence of skill upgrading in the presence of increasing relative wages in both U. S. and U. K. manufacturing, collecting estimates from several sources. The manufacturing sectors of both countries experienced large reductions in employ-

TABLE I
WITHIN-INDUSTRY SKILL UPGRADING: U. S. AND U. K. MANUFACTURING
IN THE 1980s

Period	United States		United Kingdom	
	1979–1987	1977–1987	1979–1990	1984–1990
Number of industries/ plants	450	360,000	100	402
Level of aggregation	4-digit SIC	plants	3-digit SIC	plants
Source	Annual Survey of Manufactures	Census of Manufactures	Census of Production	Workplace Industrial Relations Survey
Annual change in non-production employ- ment share (percent- age points)	.552	.483	.367	.41
Within-industry/plant component (percent)	.387 (70)	.341* (71)	.301 (82)	.34 (83)
Between-industry/plant component (percent)	.165 (30)	.077* (16)	.066 (18)	.07 (17)
Annual change in non-production wage bill share (percentage points)	.774	—	.668	—
Within-industry compo- nent (percent)	.468 (60)	—	.554 (83)	—
Between-industry com- ponent (percent)	.306 (40)	—	.114 (17)	—

Sources. U. S. industries—Berman, Bound, and Griliches [1994], Table IV, Using the Annual Survey of Manufactures [Bartelsman and Gray 1994]. U. S. plants—Dunne, Haltiwanger, and Troske [1997], Table 1, United Kingdom—Machin [1996b], Tables 7.2 and 7.3.
* This decomposition also includes a small negative cross-product term and a positive net entry term for the effect of entering and exiting plants. These terms are the sum of within and between components in 1977–1982 and 1982–1987 decompositions.

ment of less-skilled (production) workers in the 1980s and a trend increase in the share of skilled (nonproduction) workers in employment. In that work and in this paper nonproduction workers are treated as skilled and production workers as unskilled. That mapping is supported by comparisons of skill classifications of the same individuals in plant and household surveys reported in Berman, Bound, and Machin [1997], BBG, and Machin, Ryan, and Van Reenen [1996].[9] The table reports a decomposition of the increase in the aggregate employment share of nonproduction workers into between-industry and within-industry components using the following decomposition:

$$(2) \qquad \Delta Sn = \sum_i \Delta W_i \overline{Sn}_i + \sum_i \Delta Sn_i \overline{W}_i,$$

where

$$Sn \equiv \frac{S}{S + U}, \qquad W_i \equiv \frac{E_i}{\Sigma_i E_i}.$$

Here S are skilled workers, U are unskilled, E is employment, and an overstrike indicates a simple average over time. The weights are the industry employment shares in manufacturing employment. The first column reports that between 1979 and 1987 the aggregate proportion of nonproduction workers in U. S. manufacturing increased by 0.55 percentage points per year. Of that increase 70 percent occurred within the 450 four-digit industries. Dunne, Haltiwanger, and Troske [1997] replicate this result at the plant level using the entire Census of Manufactures, showing that 71 percent of the aggregate increase in Sn was due to within-plant shifts in demand. Machin [1996b] reports similar results from the United Kingdom. There as well, most of the sizable decrease in unskilled labor's share of manufacturing employment is due to

---

9. Berman, Bound, and Machin [1997] use the Worker Establishment Characteristics Database [Troske 1994], which matches the 1990 Census of Population to the Census of Manufactures. Standard occupational and educational measures correspond closely with the production/nonproduction classifications of skill in manufacturing plants. Seventy-five percent of nonproduction workers are in white-collar occupations; while 81 percent of production workers are in blue-collar occupations. Seventy-six percent of nonproduction workers have at least some college education, while 61 percent of production workers have a high school education or less. BBG also defend the production/nonproduction classification, showing that the proportion of nonproduction workers follows the same trend increase as the proportion of skilled workers in U. S. manufacturing. Machin, Ryan, and Van Reenen [1996] match manufacturing data and labor force surveys at the two-digit industry level, and find that the correlation of nonproduction/production categories with educational categories in the United Kingdom is similar to that in the United States.

within-industry (and apparently within-plant) decreases in demand for unskilled labor, despite its falling relative price.

If SBTC is pervasive, as in Section II, we should see the same pattern in all developed countries. The United Nations General Industrial Statistics Database [United Nations 1992] contains manufacturing employment and wage bill data for a large number of countries categorized into 28 consistently defined industries. We choose the most productive economies under the assumption that they are most likely to use the same production technologies as the United States. From the set of countries without serious data problems, we define our developed sample as the top twelve countries, ranked by GNP/capita in 1985. They range from the United States ($16,910) to Belgium ($8290). Appendix 1 reports the countries in order of rank. The Data Appendix describes these data and our selection criteria in more detail.

In most of these developed countries manufacturing employment declined substantially (Appendix 1). The decline of 9 percent in the United States was typical. That employment decline was particularly severe for the (less-skilled) production workers who lost employment share to nonproduction workers in all sampled countries.

Table II reports changes in nonproduction/production wage ratios (in column 6).[10] Relative wages of nonproduction workers rose by an average of 4 percent in these developed countries in the 1980s.[11] The U. S. increase of 7 percent was above average. Production workers lost employment share in all of these countries while suffering relative wage declines in seven of the ten. This pattern is roughly consistent with a common description of European labor markets in the 1980s: they share the same phenomenon of decreased demand for less-skilled workers but differ in how it is expressed. In the United States and United Kingdom where wages are more flexible, the relative wages of the

---

10. Variation in relative wage changes across countries need not be inconsistent with the framework of Section II. In the short run, local supply or institutional changes may affect relative wages even if small open economy assumptions apply in a longer run.

11. The wage ratio of nonproduction to production workers is a noisy measure of the preferable skill premium based on educational levels. In the 1980s the increased skill premiums in Table II are consistent with those reported in Davis [1992], Freeman and Katz [1994], and Gottschalk and Joyce [1998] for the United States, Australia, Japan, and the United Kingdom. The decreased skill premium we report for Sweden is inconsistent with those sources. In the 1970s the decreased skill premiums in Table II are consistent with those sources for the United States, Australia, and the United Kingdom, while the increased premiums are inconsistent for Sweden and Germany.

SKILL-BIASED TECHNOLOGICAL CHANGE   1257

TABLE II
PROPORTION OF INCREASED USE OF SKILLS "WITHIN" INDUSTRIES

Country	1970–1980			1980–1990			Note
	Change in % non-production (annualized)	% within	Change in wage ratio (%)	Change in % nonpro-duction (annualized)	% within	Change in wage ratio (%)	
U. S.	0.20	81	−2	0.30	73	7	
Norway	0.34	81	−3	−	−	−	1970,80,n/a
Luxembourg	0.57	90	6	0.30	144	12	
Sweden	0.26	70	3	0.12	60	−3	
Australia	0.40	89	−17	0.36	92	2	1970,80,87
Japan	−	−	−	0.06	123	3	n/a*,81,90
Denmark	0.44	86	−11	0.41	87	7	1973,80,89
Finland	0.42	83	−11	0.64	79	−2	
W. Germany	0.48	93	5	−	−	−	1970,79,n/a
Austria	0.46	89	7	0.16	68	7	1970,81,90
U. K.	0.41	91	−3	0.29	93	14	
Belgium	0.45	74	6	0.16	96	−5	1973,80,85
Average	0.40	84.3	−1.8	0.28	91.5	4.2	

a. The change in aggregate proportion of nonproduction workers can be decomposed into a component due to reallocation of employment *between* industries with different proportions of skilled workers and another due to changes in the proportion of skilled workers *within* industries. The percentage within is calculated by dividing the second term of equation (2) in the text by the sum of both terms.
b. *Source:* United Nations General Industrial Statistics Database.
c. There are 28 industries in this classification for all countries except Belgium (20), W. Germany (22), Japan (27), Luxembourg (9 in 1970–1980, 6 in 1980–1990), and Norway (26). For these countries aggregate changes and "within" calculations are based upon the reduced set of industries. Appendix 2 includes an industry list. See the Data Appendix for details.
* The sampling frame changed for Japanese data between 1970 and 1981.

less-skilled declined sharply, while in European countries with less flexible wages, reduced demand was expressed as unemployment [Freeman and Katz 1995; Krugman 1995].

A. Pervasive within-Industry Skill Upgrading

Table II reports the increased percentage of nonproduction workers in manufacturing employment and the percentage of that increase due to within-industry components in the 1970s and 1980s. Across countries with very diverse labor market institutions, two common features stand out. (1) The increased use of nonproduction workers in manufacturing is a universal phenomenon. The first and fourth column report that their proportion increased by an average of four percentage points in the 1970s and three percentage points in the 1980s. (2) In all these countries the vast majority of the aggregate substitution toward nonproduction workers was due to substitution toward nonproduction workers *within* industries in both decades.

The table shows strong evidence for pervasive skill-biased technological change in the 1980s. *In seven of the ten countries, positive "within" industry terms indicate that industries substituted nonproduction for production workers despite increasing relative wages.* Referring back to the discussion in Section II, increases in relative wages due (only) to Stolper-Samuelson effects imply negative "within" terms as firms substitute away from the input with an increasing relative wage. More generally, any increase in relative wages not due to a shift in the relative demand for skills at the industry level implies negative within terms. But a shift in relative demand for skills at the industry level (i.e., increased relative demand for skills, at fixed wages and prices) is by definition a skill-biased technological change.

Wage bill shares of nonproduction workers provide an additional way of looking at increased demand for skilled workers. If the elasticity of substitution between nonproduction and production workers is close to one, these shares provide a measure of demand robust to changes in relative wages. Table III reports increases in nonproduction wage bill shares in all countries in the 1970s and 1980s. Although the United States and United Kingdom show acceleration, the average rate of increase is constant. As in Table II, aggregate increases were mainly due to increases in within-industry skill upgrading.

It is not possible to tell from Tables II and III whether the rate of SBTC accelerated, remained constant, or decelerated during the 1980s [Bound and Johnson 1992; Katz and Murphy 1992; BBG]. In most of these countries within-industry skill upgrading occurred less in the 1980s than in the 1970s. However, the relative wage of nonproduction workers typically declined in the 1970s and increased in the 1980s, so that substitution effects alone could account for that decrease.[12] Without netting out those substitution effects, something that would be hard to do, it is impossible to tell whether the rate of SBTC accelerated, remained constant, or

___

12. These effects, in turn, are likely to be a symptom of decelerating skill supply, which can affect wages in the short run in small open economies or in an integrated equilibrium. All these countries show a trend increase in the proportion of college educated in the labor force in the 1970s, which decelerated in most of them in the 1980s [Organization for Economic Co-operation and Development (OECD) 1995; Barro and Lee 1997].

SKILL-BIASED TECHNOLOGICAL CHANGE 1259

TABLE III
PROPORTION OF INCREASED WAGE BILL SHARE OF SKILL "WITHIN" INDUSTRIES

Country	1970–1980			1980–1990			Note
	Change in % nonpro-duction (annualized)	% within	Change in wage ratio (%)	Change in % nonpro-duction (annualized)	% within	Change in wage ratio (%)	
U. S.	0.19	86	−2	0.51	76	7	
Norway	0.33	76	−3	—	—	—	1970,80,n/a
Luxembourg	0.90	95	6	0.73	123	12	
Sweden	0.38	81	3	0.07	25	−3	
Australia	0.07	51	−17	0.42	92	2	1970,80,87
Japan	—	—	—	0.14	84	3	n/a*,81,90
Denmark	0.12	42	−11	0.64	89	7	1973,80,89
Finland	0.27	82	−11	0.70	83	−2	
W. Germany	0.67	95	5	—	—	—	1970,79,n/a
Austria	0.69	93	7	0.36	76	7	1970,81,90
U. K.	0.39	91	−3	0.62	92	14	
Belgium	0.77	86	6	−0.06	92	−5	1973,80,85
Average	0.43	79.8	−1.8	0.41	83.2	4.2	

a. The change in aggregate wage bill share of nonproduction workers can be decomposed into a component due to reallocation of wage bill *between* industries with different shares of skilled workers and another due to changes in the shares of skilled workers *within* industries. The percentage within is calculated by dividing the second term of the following decomposition by the sum,

$$\Delta S_n^w = \sum_i \Delta W_i^w \overline{S_{n_i}^w} + \sum_i \Delta S_{ni}^w \overline{W_i^w},$$

where

$$S_n^w = \frac{w_S S}{w_S S + w_U U}, \qquad W_i^w = \frac{WB_i}{\Sigma_i WB_i},$$

and an overstrike indicates a simple average over time.

b. *Source:* United Nations General Industrial Statistics Database.

c. There are 28 industries in this classification for all countries except Belgium (20), W. Germany (22), Japan (27), Luxembourg (9 in 1970–1980, 6 in 1980–1990), and Norway (26). For these countries aggregate changes and "within" calculations are based upon the reduced set of industries. Appendix 2 includes an industry list. See the Data Appendix for details.

* The sampling frame changed for Japanese data between 1970 and 1981.

decelerated during the 1980s. Similarly, we are reluctant to interpret differences across countries in the rate of within-industry skill upgrading as evidence of cross-country patterns in the rate of technological change. Rather, these patterns could plausibly reflect cross-country differences in other factors that affect wage setting. Some of the cross-country variation in changes in the relative wages of nonproduction workers seems to be due to cross-country variation in the supply of college-educated workers (not shown),[13] a pattern consistent with the findings of Gottschalk and Joyce [1998] for several developed countries. Anticipating the discussion of an integrated equilibrium for developed countries below, the pattern of wages and employment in Table II is consistent with a trend increase in both supply and demand of skills, with either accelerated demand or decelerated supply in the 1980s increasing the skill premium on average, while local changes in supply affected relative wages as well.

In summary, in the developed countries for which we have manufacturing data in the 1970–1990 period, we find widespread within-industry substitution toward skilled labor, often despite increased relative wages. Applying the predictions of the analysis in the last section, that pattern indicates *skill-biased technological change in all of these countries.*

B. Alternative Explanations for within-Industry Skill Upgrading

To interpret positive within-industry upgrading despite increased relative wages as evidence for SBTC, one must assume homogeneous products within industries, which we did implicitly in Section II. Otherwise, an industry might reallocate employment from low-skill intensive products to high-skill intensive, perhaps in reaction to a change in product prices. That within-industry skill upgrading need not be due to SBTC. This problem of aggregation in measurement is more severe for the coarse 28-industry classification of Table II than for the finer plant-level data of Table I, allowing more room for composition effects to masquerade as within-unit effects. Yet, note that the "within" figures reported for the United States and the United Kingdom in Table II are not much higher than the comparable plant-level figures reported in Table I. Thus, a 28-industry decomposition seems to provide a good approximation of the plant-level substitution and composition effects that we report in Table I.

Within-plant skill upgrading could occur for a number of reasons besides SBTC. One possibility is capital investment combined with capital-skill complementarity. Previous work [BBG, Table VI] has found that capital accumulation in U. S. manufacturing was not large enough to generate the observed increase in relative wages using cross-sectional estimates of the elasticity of substitution.[14] Another possible explanation is intraplant demand

---

13. The OECD Employment Outlook provides figures [OECD 1993].
14. For a dissenting view see Krusell et al. [1997]. They find, using aggregate data, that if capital equipment, particularly computers, is evaluated using a

SKILL-BIASED TECHNOLOGICAL CHANGE 1261

shifts toward skill-intensive goods. Considering the size of inter-plant shifts, it seems unlikely that this effect can be large. Also, the increased relative price of skills should induce intraplant shifts in the opposite direction. Wood [1991] and Bernard and Jensen [1997] have argued that an increase in the relative price of skill-intensive goods, due to increased exposure to unskill-intensive developing countries, would induce intraplant substitution toward skill-intensive goods. BBG [Table IV] test that hypothesis, finding that only a tiny fraction of within-industry increase in the proportion of nonproduction workers can be explained by net imports using a fixed factor model, so that trade-induced within-plant composition effects are probably negligible. A third possibility is skill-biased product innovations, which can be thought of as SBTC for our purposes. A fourth possible explanation is intraplant skill upgrading induced by trade through an H-O effect whereby firms "outsource" low-skill parts of the production process abroad, replacing in-house production with imported materials [Feenstra and Hanson 1996a, 1996b, 1997].

While it is hard to measure outsourcing, let alone its effect on U. S. employment, two calculations suggest that outsourcing is responsible for at most a fraction of skill upgrading. First, BBG report that skill-upgrading occurred no more rapidly in import-intensive industries than in the rest of U. S. manufacturing in the 1980s [BBG, Table IV]. Second, the 1987 Census of Manufacturing reports that the total cost of imported material was 104 billion dollars, or 8 percent of materials purchased and 30 percent of imported manufactures. Imported materials substitute for domestically produced materials, but they only constitute outsourcing if they substitute for materials produced within the purchasing establishment. While we know of no reliable way to distinguish uses for imported materials, at most 7 percent of purchased materials (imported and domestic) come from an establishment's own industry.[15] This suggests that only a small fraction of imported materials represent outsourcing (as they do not replace domestic production in the same industry). Extending that calculation, assume that imported materials displace production but not nonproduction labor and that imported materials embody the

Gordon [1990] measure, its increase in value is fast enough to explain the increased demand for skills using a constant elasticity of substitution between capital and skill.

15. Materials files of the 1987 Census of Manufactures shows that 2 percent of materials purchased originate in the four-digit industry of the purchaser, and 7 percent originate in the same three-digit industry.

same amount of production labor as do domestically produced goods in the same industry (but no nonproduction labor). Thus, for each industry we calculate the number of production workers displaced by outsourcing as of 1987 as (imported materials/total shipments) × production employment. These calculations suggest that the employment of production workers would have been at most 2.8 percent higher in 1987 if there had been no outsourcing. This translates into a 0.76 percentage point increase in production workers' share in total employment. Within industry, production workers' share had dropped 4.22 percentage points between 1973 and 1987. Thus, this calculation indicates that outsourcing could directly account for at most 16 percent of the decline in the production worker share of employment over this time period, making the generous assumption of no outsourcing in 1973.[16]

While we expect that only a fraction of the materials that an establishment purchases from foreign sources represent outsourcing, the Census measure understates outsourcing in one respect. Census instructions state that "items partially fabricated abroad which reenter the country" should not be included as "foreign materials." Such items would normally enter the country under items 806 and 807, schedule 8 of the Tariff Schedule of the United States. In 1987 the value of such items totaled a not insignificant 68.6 billion dollars. However, the automobile industry, which accounted for only 3 percent of total skill upgrading accounted for roughly two-thirds of such imports. Eliminating both the auto industry and domestic content of such items reduces the 68.6 billion to 14.0 billion or roughly 0.5 percent of the value of

---

16. Feenstra and Hanson [1996b, 1997] use different methods to estimate the magnitude of foreign "outsourcing." First, they multiply materials purchased by the proportion of imports in their source industry. Their estimate is that, as of 1990, 11.6 percent of materials could represent outsourcing, rather than 8 percent. (Feenstra and Hanson emphasize that contract work could explain the difference between these estimates, since it is included in imports, but not in imported materials.) Nevertheless, both figures are likely to be substantial overestimates, as most imported materials probably do not replace in-house production. When Feenstra and Hanson redo their calculation restricting attention to purchases with an establishment's two-digit industry, their 11.6 percent estimate drops to 5.6 percent. Second, using regression techniques, Feenstra and Hanson [1997] estimate that outsourcing can account for as much as 15 percent of the within-industry shift away from production labor during the 1980s. Baru [1995] uses similar measures, but calculates outsourcing using only purchases within the same *three*-digit industry. She estimates a translog variable cost function using data on 51 three- and four-digit importing and exporting industries, and finds no association between changes in the price of imported materials and skill upgrading. Given the potential for measurement error in the variables and the apparent lack of robustness of the results, we put more stock in the back-of-the-envelope calculations, which are likely to exaggerate effects.

manufacturing shipments that year—too small a quantity to matter very much [United States International Trade Commission 1988].[17]

Our estimates are crude, but they err on the side of overestimating the effects of outsourcing on skill upgrading: not all foreign materials represent outsourcing. For those that do, some nonproduction labor is certainly embodied in domestic production replaced by outsourcing. Still, these calculations suggest that while outsourcing might be important for some industries, it cannot account for the bulk of the skill upgrading that occurred within manufacturing over the 1970s and 1980s. Calculations based on U. S. data also overstate the potential share of outsourcing in within-industry skill upgrading in the OECD as a whole, since the United States had a much greater increase in trade with the developing world than did the average developed country in the 1980s. We conclude that the majority of within-industry upgrading reported in Table II is due not to outsourcing, but to skill-biased technological change, implying pervasive SBTC among developed countries in the 1980s.

IV. Cross-Country Correlations: An Additional Test
of Pervasiveness

A. Cross-Country Correlations

The variation in rates of skill-upgrading across industries provides another testable implication of SBTC. We should find the same industries increasing their proportion of skilled workers at similar rates in different countries. Figure III displays a scatterplot of changes in the proportion of nonproduction workers (ΔSn) in U. S. manufacturing industries against changes in that proportion in their U. K. counterparts. Observations are weighted by industry employment shares in manufacturing employment (averaged over all countries in the developed sample), which is

---

17. Outsourcing may be important in some industries. For example, as of 1987, 806 and 807 imports represented 57 percent of imports in the auto industry and 44 percent of imports of semiconductors. A calculation similar to the one above suggests that these imports are sufficient to account for more than 100 percent of the shift away from production workers that occurred in the auto industry and one-third of the shift that occurred in semiconductors. (Figures on the overseas production of semiconductors are consistent with these calculations [United States International Trade Commission, 1982]. However, foreign outsourcing is concentrated enough in specific industries that it is hard to imagine it accounting for more than a small fraction of the total within-industry shift away from production labor.

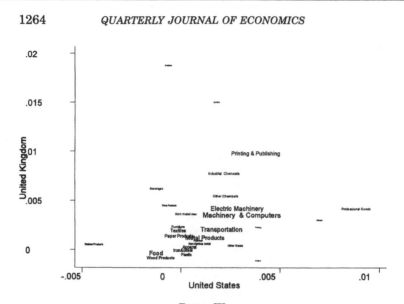

FIGURE III
Changes in Nonproduction Employment Shares:
United States and United Kingdom
Note: Each observation is a pair of "within"-industry increases in the proportion of nonproduction workers between 1980 and 1990. Text size is proportional to the industry share in manufacturing employment.
Source: United Nations General Industrial Statistics Database.

reflected in the size of the text. Among large industries there is certainly a positive correlation in rates of skill upgrading across countries. Printing and Publishing, Machinery and Electronics, Electrical Equipment, and Transportation all have high rates of skill upgrading in both countries, while Metal Products and Food industries have relatively low rates of skill upgrading in both. The weighted correlation coefficient corresponding to this scatterplot is 0.46.

Pervasive skill-biased technological change implies that (holding relative wages constant) within-industry changes in the use of skills will be positively correlated across all countries producing that good. So we test for pervasiveness by examining cross-country correlations of changes in the use of skills (ΔSn) for our entire developed sample.

Table IV presents a matrix of weighted correlations of ΔSn_{ci} with $\Delta Sn_{c'i}$, the cross-country, within-industry changes in the proportion of nonproduction workers for nine developed countries

SKILL-BIASED TECHNOLOGICAL CHANGE 1265

TABLE IV
CROSS-COUNTRY CORRELATIONS OF WITHIN-INDUSTRY CHANGES IN PROPORTION
NONPRODUCTION: 1980–1990

	U. S.	Sweden	Australia	Japan	Denmark	Finland	Austria	U. K.
Sweden	.55*							
	(.00)							
Australia	.25	.18						
	(.20)	(.35)						
Japan	.25	.19	−.09					
	(.21)	(.35)	(.65)					
Denmark	.43*	.17	.19	.25				
	(.02)	(.40)	(.33)	(.21)				
Finland	.45*	.41*	.11	.42*	.31			
	(.02)	(.03)	(.57)	(.03)	(.11)			
Austria	.09	−.21	.33	−.08	.24	.40*		
	(.65)	(.27)	(.09)	(.70)	(.23)	(.04)		
U. K.	.48*	.09	.20	.14	.31	.41*	.64*	
	(.01)	(.65)	(.30)	(.48)	(.11)	(.03)	(.00)	
Belgium	.48*	.58*	.14	.29	.16	.42	.13	.03
	(.03)	(.01)	(.57)	(.23)	(.50)	(.06)	(.60)	(.91)

a. These are cross-country correlations of ΔSn_{ci} and $\Delta Sn_{c'i}$ for countries c and c'. Observations are weighted by industry employment shares averaged over time and across all countries.

b. The number in brackets is the significance level of a two-tailed test that the correlation is zero. An asterisk denotes a significant correlation at the 5 percent level.

c. The sample was restricted to countries with GNP/capita of over $8000 US in 1985 and twenty or more consistently defined industries observed in 1980–1990.

d. The 28 industries in this classification are listed fully in Appendix 2.

e. All correlation coefficients are calculated using a full set of 28 industries, except those involving Japan (27), Belgium (20), and Japan and Belgium (19).

f. *Source*: United Nations General Industrial Statistics Database.

in the 1980s.[18] For example, the first column reports that skill upgrading (ΔSn) in U. S. industries is positively and highly correlated with skill upgrading in Sweden, Denmark, Finland, the United Kingdom, and Belgium and positively correlated with skill upgrading in the other three countries. Asterisks denote a significant correlation at the 5 percent level. Note that the correlations are nearly all positive (33 of 36) and some are quite high. Indeed, 11 of the 36 are significantly positive at the 5 percent level (which is much more than the expected 2.5 percent). These results are robust to changes in the choice of weights and to using wage bill

18. Luxembourg has been dropped, as it has only six observed industries in this period. Norway and Germany were dropped for lack of employment share figures in 1980–1990.

1266   *QUARTERLY JOURNAL OF ECONOMICS*

TABLE V

CROSS-COUNTRY CORRELATIONS OF WITHIN-INDUSTRY CHANGES IN PROPORTION
NONPRODUCTION: 1970–1980

	U.S.	Norway	Sweden	Australia	Denmark	Finland	W. Germany	Austria	U. K.
Norway	.59*								
	(.00)								
Sweden	.29	.53*							
	(.13)	(.01)							
Australia	−.09	−.26	.20						
	(.66)	(.20)	(.31)						
Denmark	.13	.44*	.46*	.07					
	(.51)	(.03)	(.01)	(.73)					
Finland	−.20	.14	−.07	−.07	.27				
	(.31)	(.48)	(.70)	(.72)	(.17)				
W. Germany	.34	.64*	.69*	−.08	.75*	.31			
	(.12)	(.00)	(.00)	(.72)	(.00)	(.15)			
Austria	.36	.60*	.45*	−.08	.37	.42*	.56*		
	(.06)	(.00)	(.02)	(.70)	(.05)	(.03)	(.01)		
U. K.	.46*	.46*	.52*	.01	.37	.19	.59*	.56*	
	(.01)	(.02)	(.00)	(.96)	(.05)	(.34)	(.00)	(.00)	
Belgium	−.12	−.11	.00	.10	.16	.23	.02	.22	.32
	(.61)	(.67)	(.99)	(.68)	(.50)	(.32)	(.93)	(.36)	(.16)

a. These are cross-country correlations of ΔSn_{ci} and $\Delta Sn_{c'i}$ for countries c and c'. Observations are weighted by industry employment shares averaged over time and across all countries.

b. The number in brackets is the significance level of a two-tailed test that the correlation is zero. An asterisk denotes a significant correlation at the 5 percent level.

c. The sample was restricted to countries with GNP/capita of over $8000 US in 1985 and over twenty consistently defined industries observed in 1980–1990.

d. The 28 industries in this classification are listed fully in Appendix 2.

e. All correlation coefficients are calculated using a full set of 28 industries, except those involving Belgium (20), W. Germany (22), and Norway (26). The cross-country correlations between these three countries are based on the following number of observations: Belgium and W. Germany (18), Belgium and Norway (18), and W. Germany and Norway (22).

f. *Source*: United Nations General Industrial Statistics Database.

rather than employment shares.[19] The high number of precisely estimated large positive correlations is remarkable considering the potential for measurement error. These data are collected from separate national institutions with heterogeneous methods and sampling techniques (see the Appendix). Moreover, the fairly aggregated industry classifications imply that the same (2.5-digit) industry may contain very different four-digit industries in different countries.

Table V replicates that result for a similar sample of ten developed countries the 1970s. It reports similarly high rates of

19. Correlations of wage bill shares show 12 of 36 to be significantly positive. All results are essentially unaffected by using employment weights averaged only over the two paired countries.

SKILL-BIASED TECHNOLOGICAL CHANGE   1267

correlated skill upgrading. In that earlier decade 36 of 45 correlation coefficients are positive, with 16 significantly so.

Is this convincing evidence of pervasive SBTC? An alternative interpretation of the positive correlations in Tables IV and V is that they reflect similarity within industries in their reaction to similar changes in relative wages.[20] Suppose that industries have elasticities of substitution between skilled and unskilled labor which are similar across countries. Industries faced with similar changes in relative wages in different countries would then respond with similar adjustments to their skill mix of employment, generating positive correlations in ΔSn.

To test that explanation, we compared correlations in country pairs with changes in relative wages in the same direction to correlations in country pairs with changes in wages in opposite directions. This alternative explanation implies that correlations only be positive for countries experiencing changes in relative wages with the same sign. Yet reexamination of Tables IV and V reveals that correlations of skill upgrading are just as high in pairs of countries with wage changes in opposite directions. In the 1980s, six of eighteen country pairs with wage changes in opposite directions have statistically significant positive correlations of ΔSn (at the 5 percent level). For comparison, five of the eighteen pairs with wage changes in the same direction have significantly positive correlations. In the 1970s the result is similar: 9 of 21 country pairs with wage changes in opposite directions have significantly correlated skill upgrading, while 7 of the other 24 have significant correlations. Not only are correlations not negative for country pairs with wage changes in opposite directions, they seem to be significantly positive. We conclude that correlated within-industry upgrading is not caused by changes in wages.

The cross-country correlations suggest that technological change in several of the countries is quite similar. A group of countries (Denmark, Finland, Sweden, the United Kingdom, and the United States) have very similar within-industry changes in the proportion of nonproduction employment. Consider the United States, on the one hand, and Sweden, Denmark, and Finland, on the other. These are economies with very different labor market institutions and very different trade and macroeconomic experiences in the 1980s. The similarity in the pattern of decreased use of production workers despite their different experiences is compel-

20. We thank the editors for this insight.

ling evidence for common technological changes as an underlying cause of decreased demand for unskilled labor.

B. Industries with Large Skill-Biased Technological Change

The industries that drive the correlations in Tables IV and V may indicate what the nature of these technological changes may be. Referring to Figure III, the United States-United Kingdom correlation in the 1980s is mainly due to the large common increases in the share of nonproduction employment in four industries: Machinery (and computers), Electrical Machinery, Printing and Publishing, and Transportation.

Rather than examine all 36 scatterplots, a more systematic way of looking for industries with large effects is to estimate industry effects in a country-industry panel. We estimate the following regression of "within"-industry terms on country and industry indicators:

$$(3) \qquad y_{ci} = \sum_{i=1}^{I} \alpha_i + \sum_{c=1}^{C} \beta_c + \epsilon_{ci},$$

where

$$y_{ci} \equiv \Delta Sn_{ci} \overline{W}_{ci},$$

$$Sn \equiv \frac{S}{E}, \; W_{ci} \equiv \frac{E_{ci}}{\Sigma_i E_{ci}}.$$

Here an overstrike indicates a simple average over time. The α_i are the average industry terms once country means have been removed. A precisely estimated industry effect reflects a "within" term common to many countries, while a large industry effect is evidence of a high average increase in Sn across countries.

Table VI reports the three largest of the statistically significant estimated industry effects. The third column reports that three industries: Electrical Machinery, Machinery (and computers), and Printing and Publishing, together account for 46 percent of the within-industry component (averaged across countries) in the 1980s. A full set of estimated industry effects is reported in Appendix 2. Case studies indicate that these industries introduced significant skill-biased technologies during this period, especially in the automation of control and monitoring of production lines [United States Department of Labor 1982a, 1982b]. For example, a principal source of SBTC in the printing and publishing industry was automated rather than manual typesetting.

TABLE VI
SELECTED INDUSTRY EFFECTS IN WITHIN-INDUSTRY TERMS: 1970–1980
AND 1980–1990

Industry	Industry effect/ within component		Average share of industry in employment	
	1970–1980	1980–1990	1970–1980	1980–1990
Printing & publishing	.078	.111	.056	.061
	(.021)	(.048)		
Machinery (incl. computers)	.128	.173	.114	.116
	(.025)	(.047)		
Electrical machinery	.131	.173	.090	.096
	(.029)	(.044)		
Sum (3 industries)	.337	.457	.260	.273
Number of observations	264	243		
Root MSE	.0392	.0676		

a. In a regression of "within"-industry terms on country and industry indicators,

$$y_{ci} = \Delta Sn_{ci}\, \overline{W}_{ci} = \sum_{i=1}^{I} \alpha_i + \sum_{c=1}^{C} \beta_c + \epsilon_{ci},$$

the table reports the three largest estimated industry effects α_i. y_{ci} is the change in the proportion of nonproduction workers in employment multiplied by the industry's weight in manufacturing employment.

b. A full set of industry effects is reported in Appendix 2.

c. Data are scaled so that the estimated coefficient represents the ratio of the industry effect to the cross-country average "within" component.

d. The root mean squared error of the left-hand side variable is .0670 for 1970–1980 and .0894 for 1980–1990.

e. Standard errors are calculated using the White heteroskedasticity robust formula.

f. *Source*: United Nations General Industrial Statistics Database.

These three industries had the highest rates of investment in computers in the United States in the 1980s, if we exclude defense and space-related investment [Berman, Bound, and Griliches 1993, Table 9]. Taken together, the evidence implicates microprocessors as a principal cause of SBTC throughout the developed world in the 1980s. That technological change may not have been unique to the 1980s. The same three industries account for only a slightly smaller share (34 percent) of within-industry upgrading in the 1970s.

V. GLOBAL SKILL-BIASED TECHNOLOGICAL CHANGE?

How pervasive is skill-biased technological change? So far, we have discussed SBTC in developed countries. Looking for evidence of SBTC in developing countries is interesting for two reasons. First, it provides another source of evidence. Second, the implications for income inequality may be greater in countries where less-skilled workers are already extremely poor.

In an H-O framework, for a country that is abundant in unskilled labor, the opening up to trade that occurred in the 1980s should have a negative Stolper-Samuelson effect on the relative wages of skilled workers. Thus, H-O and SBTC hypotheses have opposite predictions for relative wages in LDCs. The literature reports that relative wages of skilled labor have *risen* in some, though not all, LDCs undergoing trade liberalizations in the 1980s (e.g., Feliciano [1995], Hanson and Harrison [1995], Robbins [1996], and Feenstra and Hanson [1996a]. Figure IV reproduces that result using the United Nations data, showing that many low-income countries experienced an increase in the relative wages of nonproduction workers in manufacturing during the decade of trade liberalization between 1980 and 1990. The correlation of wage changes and per capita GNP across countries in the figure is (a precisely estimated) zero, a pattern inconsistent with the Stolper-Samuelson prediction but consistent with SBTC.

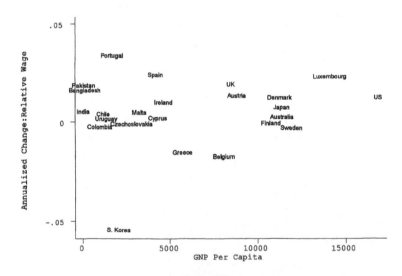

FIGURE IV

Change in Relative Wages in 1980s by GNP

The figure reports relative wages information for 24 countries judged to have reliable information over the 1980s. The annualized change in wage ratio of nonproduction to production workers is recorded between 1980 and 1990 where possible. Other endpoints are used when necessary.

Source: United Nations General Industrial Statistics Database.

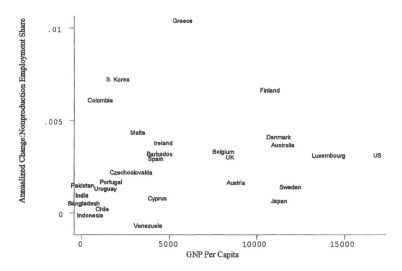

FIGURE V
Skill Accumulation in the 1980s by GNP
The figure reports changes in the proportion of nonproduction workers in manufacturing employment for 27 countries judged to have reliable information over the 1980s. The annualized change in the proportion of nonproduction workers is recorded between 1980 and 1990 where possible. Other endpoints are used when necessary.
Source: United Nations General Industrial Statistics Database.

Stable and rising relative wages are particularly interesting, considering that almost all of these developing countries experienced considerable increases in the proportion of skilled labor in manufacturing over the 1980s, as illustrated in Figure V.[21] For the developing world, that increase in the proportion of skilled labor was generally accompanied by rapid growth in manufacturing employment [Wood 1994]. While H-O logic suggests that increased exposure to trade should reduce relative demand for skilled workers in LDCs, their manufacturing sectors expanded rapidly and upgraded skills at the same time in the 1980s. Besides the effects of trade, some other effect must have more than compensated to keep wages of nonproduction workers stable especially as their proportion increased quickly in the 1980s. Skill-biased technological change is one possible explanation. Other causes could be increased investment and technology

21. Richardson's [1995] literature survey also reports widespread skill upgrading in the developing world.

transfer combined with capital-skill complementarity, or decreased protection of industries intensive in unskilled workers. Nevertheless, the combination of these findings and the evidence presented above that SBTC was pervasive in the developed world raise the intriguing possibility that SBTC is at work in the developing world as well.

VI. CONCLUDING REMARKS

In this paper we have presented strong evidence that the kind of skill-biased technological change which occurred in the United States in the 1980s was pervasive throughout the developed world. Our data show that (a) substitution toward skilled labor within industries occurred in all ten developed countries that we studied, despite generally constant or increasing relative wages of skilled labor; and (b) the same manufacturing industries that substituted toward skilled labor in the United States in the 1980s did so in the other developed countries as well. The three industries with the largest within-industry contributions to skill upgrading are machinery (and computers), electrical machinery, and printing and publishing. All three carried out significant microprocessor-based technological innovation, suggesting microprocessors as the technological link between common patterns of skill-upgrading across countries.

The debate in the literature over the effects of SBTC on relative wages has often turned on the relevance of the small, open economy assumptions [Freeman 1995; Leamer 1996]. Pervasiveness allows SBTC to reduce the relative wages of the unskilled even in a model that assumes small, open economies because its occurrence in a large number of countries allows analysis of the integrated equilibrium as if the OECD countries were a closed economy. In the context of that model, to calculate the size of the effect of different factors, we must gauge their relative effects on world goods prices. The relative price of skill-intensive (to low-skill-intensive) goods is in turn set by the factor content embodied in increased supplies of goods to the OECD countries. Using the U. S. experience as a guide, we see that *the factor content of SBTC in manufacturing alone implies a decrease in the proportion of less-skilled (production) workers about eight times that attributable to increased trade.* That calculation goes like this: referring back to Table I, in the 1979–1987 period, during which demand for less-skilled workers dropped sharply in the United States, the factor content of SBTC accounts for at least 70 percent of the displacement of unskilled workers (i.e., the increase in the proportion of skilled workers) in U. S. manufacturing. The factor content of trade accounts for about 9 percent [BBG, Table IV].[22] For the OECD countries as a whole, 70 percent is a typical figure for SBTC, but 9 percent is a generous estimate of the effects of trade as the United States experienced a much greater increase in trade with the developing world than did the other developed countries. Assuming that demand elasticities are approximately the same for imports and domestic production, that calculation implies that the effects of SBTC on relative wages are an order of magnitude larger than those of increased trade with the developing world.

Although the evidence we present is only from manufacturing, where measurement is easiest, the effects of SBTC on wages may be just as important in the service sectors. In retail and financial services, for example, microprocessor-based information processing technologies have dramatically changed accounting and secretarial work [Levy and Murnane 1996]. At a more aggregate level, Bound and Johnson [1992], Murphy and Welch [1992], and Katz and Murphy [1992] all present evidence of within-industry skill upgrading in other sectors, despite increased relative wages of skilled workers. Within-industry skill upgrading outside of manufacturing also occurred in the same industries in the United States as it did in the United Kingdom.[23] Skill-biased technological change outside of manufacturing may also have been pervasive and is an additional likely cause of decreased demand for less-skilled workers.

Even if pervasive SBTC is a principal explanation, there is no reason to believe that it is the sole explanation for increased relative demand for skills. Heckscher-Ohlin trade and sector-biased technical change[24] have presumably both played a role in shifting employment toward sectors of the economy that are intensive in skilled labor. Particular groups, such as very low-

22. For a justification of the use of factor content calculations in approximating the effects of trade flows on relative wages, see Krugman [1995] or Deardorff and Staiger [1988].
23. Calculations based on the U. S. Current Population Survey and the U. K. Labor Force Survey show a high cross-country correlation of increases in employment shares of people with postsecondary education in fifteen manufacturing industries in the 1980s. Much of the high correlation is driven by rapid skill upgrading in financial services.
24. Haskel and Slaughter [1998] and Jones [1965] analyze the possibility that technological change is both skill and sector biased.

1274   *QUARTERLY JOURNAL OF ECONOMICS*

skilled workers, may be disproportionately affected by increased imports. These effects may have increased in the 1990s with increased trade with LDCs. However, the observed between-industry employment shifts in the 1980s do not appear to be nearly large enough to explain the bulk of the shift in demand toward skilled labor.[25]

Pervasive skill-biased technological change suggests several avenues for interesting research. The source of SBTC, its rate of flow across borders, the identification of the technologies involved, and the likely implications for labor demand in the receiving country are all interesting and relevant. This is especially true for developing countries in which technological changes could exacerbate current high levels of income inequality.

DATA APPENDIX

The data are from the United Nations General Industrial Statistics Database. They cover 28 manufacturing industries at (broadly) the two- to three-digit level, consistently defined across countries and years. Data are collected by the United Nations directly from the appropriate statistical agencies in each country. The main purpose is to facilitate international comparisons relating to the manufacturing sector. Concepts and definitions are drawn from the International Recommendations for Industrial Statistics [Statistical Papers, Series M, No 48/Rev 1, United Nations Publication] and the classification by industry is taken from the International Standard Industrial Classification (ISIC) of All Economic Activities [Statistical Papers, Series M, No 4/Rev 2, United Nations].

For our analysis the key data included are the employment and wage bills of all employees and operatives. "Employees" is usually the average number of employees during the year (other than working proprietors, active business partners, and unpaid family workers). "Operatives" usually refers to employees directly engaged in production or related activities of the establishment, including clerks or working supervisors whose function is to record or expedite any step in the production process. Employees

---

25. Institutional factors such as the decline in the real value of the minimum wage and in unionization may have also played a role in explaining the rise in the relative wages of skilled workers in some countries. However, such factors have probably not contributed to within- and between-sectors shifts in employment, which have both favored skilled workers.

SKILL-BIASED TECHNOLOGICAL CHANGE   1275

of a similar type engaged in activities ancillary to the main activity of the establishment and those engaged in truck driving, repair and maintenance, and so on, are also considered to be operatives. Wages and salaries includes all payments in cash or in kind made to employees or operatives during the reference year (these include direct wages and salaries, remuneration for time not worked, bonuses and gratuities, housing allowances and family allowances paid directly by the employer and payments in kind).

The sample of countries selected was dictated by the availability of consistently defined data on employment and wage bills for all employees and operatives over time. The resulting developed country sample includes the twelve highest ranked countries (in 1985 GNP per capita) that meet our selection criteria. For the wider sample of countries used in Figures IV and V we required consistent data over the 1980–1990 period (or as close to those years as possible). This produced the 24 countries judged to have reliable wage data and the 27 judged to have reliable employment data used in the figures.

APPENDIX 1: NONPRODUCTION EMPLOYMENT, WAGE BILL SHARES, AND EMPLOYMENT GROWTH IN MANUFACTURING, 1970–1990

	Nonproduction employment shares			Nonproduction wage bill shares			Employment growth (%)		GNP per capita (US$)	
	1970	1980	1990	1970	1980	1990	1970–80	1980–90	1985	Notes
U. S.	.261	.281	.311	.355	.375	.425	5.5	−8.9	16910	
Norway	.222	.256	—	.291	.323	—	0.6	—	14560	1970,80,n/a
Luxembourg	.163	.209	.239	.253	.328	.394	−5.7	−5.4	14070	
Sweden	.269	.294	.307	.355	.393	.400	−6.0	−15.7	12040	
Australia	.217	.257	.282	.284	.290	.320	−10.8	−11.1	11760	1970,80,87
Japan	see note below						—	6.5	11430	n/a,81,90
Denmark	.251	.282	.318	.336	.344	.402	−10.7	2.5	11380	1973,80,89
Finland	.198	.240	.305	.296	.323	.393	14.9	−18.6	11000	
W. Germany	.247	.290	—	.327	.388	—	−12.9	—	10980	1970,79,n/a
Austria	.246	.296	.310	.335	.411	.443	2.3	−5.4	9100	1970,81,90
U. K.	.259	.300	.329	.320	.359	.421	−18.7	−25.9	8520	
Belgium	.211	.244	.260	.327	.383	.392	−20.3	−13.2	8290	1973,80,85

Sources: United Nations General Industrial Statistics Database (numbers for ISIC 3000, total manufacturing). GNP per capita data are from World Bank [1994], Table 1. Conversion to U. S. dollars is according to the World Bank *Atlas Method*, which averages exchange rates for that year and the preceding two years, and adjusts for differences in U. S. and domestic inflation rates.

The levels are not reliable for Japan as the number of operatives is only counted for a subsample of large firms, while employment is counted for all firms. The changes considered should be more reliable over the 1981–1990 period when the definition of large firms remained the same.

1276   *QUARTERLY JOURNAL OF ECONOMICS*

APPENDIX 2: INDUSTRY EFFECTS IN WITHIN-INDUSTRY TERMS

	1970–1980		1980–1990	
Code and industry	Coefficient (t-statistic)	Coefficient (t-statistic)	Coefficient (t-statistic)	Coefficient (t-statistic)
3110 Food	.039 (1.745)	.019 (.842)	−.004 (−.145)	−.008 (−.295)
3130 Beverages	.026 (2.602)	.005 (.513)	.035 (1.947)	.032 (1.580)
3140 Tobacco	.008 (1.960)	−.012 (−1.489)	.011 (2.149)	.004 (.339)
3210 Textiles	.037 (2.511)	.017 (1.169)	.047 (2.662)	.043 (2.363)
3220 Apparel	.022 (2.450)	.002 (.188)	.000 (0.017)	−.003 (−.174)
3230 Leather products	−.002 (−.300)	−.021 (−2.327)	.020 (1.310)	.017 (.871)
3240 Footwear	−.001 (−.367)	−.021 (−2.688)	.015 (2.030)	.011 (.991)
3310 Wood products	.054 (4.740)	.037 (2.680)	.041 (1.677)	.037 (1.775)
3320 Furniture	.028 (3.537)	.012 (1.351)	.019 (1.704)	.015 (1.088)
3410 Paper products	.044 (4.385)	.024 (1.835)	.034 (2.725)	.031 (2.606)
3420 Print & publishing	.099 (5.049)	.078 (3.771)	.114 (2.183)	.111 (2.291)
3510 Ind chemicals	.027 (2.233)	.011 (.760)	.053 (4.809)	.049 (4.219)
3520 Other chemicals	.035 (3.008)	.018 (1.569)	.051 (5.041)	.047 (3.651)
3530 Petr refineries	.000 (.143)	−.018 (−2.161)	.029 (1.429)	.026 (1.125)
3540 Petr & coal	.007 (2.166)	−.012 (−1.542)	−.009 (−.700)	−.012 (−.766)
3550 Rubber prod	.013 (3.061)	−.001 (−1.062)	.011 (1.288)	.008 (.594)
3560 Plastic prod	.027 (4.398)	.007 (.872)	−.000 (−.004)	−.003 (−.321)
3610 Pottery, china	−.004 (−1.458)	−.023 (−2.788)	.014 (2.041)	.010 (.833)
3620 Glass products	.014 (3.512)	−.006 (−.850)	−.005 (−.889)	−.009 (−.672)
3690 Nonmetal nec	.046 (3.794)	.027 (2.145)	.034 (3.364)	.030 (2.005)
3710 Iron & steel	.052 (4.479)	.033 (2.761)	.016 (1.070)	.012 (.842)
3720 Nonferrous metal	.009 (2.756)	−.010 (−1.399)	.007 (.943)	.003 (.198)
3810 Metal products	.074 (5.740)	.054 (4.296)	.050 (1.989)	.046 (2.192)
3820 Machinery, computers	.148 (5.747)	.128 (5.162)	.177 (3.265)	.173 (3.658)
3830 Electric machinery	.151 (4.887)	.131 (4.501)	.177 (3.914)	.173 (3.943)
3840 Transport equip	.061 (3.379)	.041 (2.240)	−.001 (−.013)	−.004 (−.089)
3850 Professional goods	.011 (1.129)	−.009 (−.722)	.072 (3.842)	.069 (2.876)
3900 Other goods	.014 (4.512)	−.006 (−.741)	.019 (2.404)	.015 (1.332)
Country effects	No	Yes	No	Yes
Observations	264	264	243	243
Root MSE	.0403	.0392	.0702	.0676

The estimating equation is equation (3) in the text. Coefficients are scaled so that the reported coefficient represents the ratio of the industry effect to the cross-country average "within" component. The root mean squared error of the left-hand side variable is .0670 for 1970–1980 and .0894 for 1980–1990. t-statistics are calculated using heteroskedasticity robust standard errors. Countries included are all those in Tables IV and V.

Source: United Nations General Industrial Statistics Database.

BOSTON UNIVERSITY AND NATIONAL BUREAU OF ECONOMIC RESEARCH
UNIVERSITY OF MICHIGAN AND NATIONAL BUREAU OF ECONOMIC RESEARCH
UNIVERSITY COLLEGE LONDON AND CENTRE FOR ECONOMIC PERFORMANCE, LONDON
SCHOOL OF ECONOMICS

REFERENCES

Autor, David, Lawrence F. Katz, and Alan Krueger, "Computing Inequality: Have Computers Changed the Labor Market?" *Quarterly Journal of Economics,* CXIII (1998), 1169–1213.

Baldwin, Robert E., "The Effects of Trade and Foreign Direct Investment on Employment and Relative Wages," *Organization for Economic Co-operation and Development Studies,* XXIII (1994), 7–54.

Bartelsman, Eric, and Wayne Gray, "National Bureau of Economic Research Manufacturing Productivity Database," National Bureau of Economic Research, mimeo, 1994.

Barro, Robert, and Jong-Wha Lee, "International Measures of Schooling Years and Schooling Quality," ftp://www.nber.org/pub/barro.lee, 1997.

Baru, Sundari, "Essays in Trade, Job Market Skills and Employment Changes," Ph.D. thesis, University of Michigan, 1995.

Berman, Eli, John Bound, and Zvi Griliches, "Changes in the Demand for Skilled Labor within U. S. Manufacturing Industries: Evidence from the Annual Survey of Manufacturing," NBER Working Paper No. 4255, 1993.

Berman, Eli, John Bound, and Zvi Griliches, "Changes in the Demand for Skilled Labor within U. S. Manufacturing Industries: Evidence from the Annual Survey of Manufacturing," *Quarterly Journal of Economics,* CIX (1994), 367–398.

Berman, Eli, John Bound, and Stephen Machin, "Implications of Skill-Biased Technological Change: International Evidence," NBER Working Paper No. 6166, 1997.

Bernard, Andrew B., and J. Bradford Jensen, "Exporters, Skill Upgrading and the Wage Gap," *Journal of International Economics,* XLII (1997), 3–31.

Berndt, Ernst, Catherine J. Morrison, and Larry S. Rosenblum, "High-Tech Capital Formation and Labor Composition in U. S. Manufacturing Industries: An Exploratory Analysis," *Journal of Econometrics, Annals of Econometrics,* LXV (1994), 9–43.

Blackburn, McKinley, David Bloom, and Richard Freeman, "The Declining Economic Position of Less-Skilled American Males," in *A Future of Lousy Jobs?* Gary Burtless, ed. (Washington, DC: Brookings, 1990).

Bound, John, and George Johnson, "Changes in the Structure of Wages during the 1980s: An Evaluation of Alternative Explanations," *American Economic Review,* LXXXII (1992), 371–392.

Bound, John, and George Johnson, "What Are the Causes of Rising Wage Inequality in the United States?" *Federal Reserve Bank of New York Economic Policy Review,* I (1995), 1–17.

Davis, Steven, "Cross-Country Patterns of Change in Relative Wages," *National Bureau of Economic Research Macroeconomics Annual 1992,* Olivier Jean Blanchard and Stanley Fischer, eds. (Cambridge, MA: MIT Press, 1992), pp. 239–292.

Deardorff, A., and R. Staiger, "An Interpretation of the Factor Content of Trade," *Journal of International Economics,* XXIV (1988), 93–107.

Doms, Mark, Timothy Dunne, and Kenneth R. Troske, "Workers, Wages, and Technology," *Quarterly Journal of Economics,* CXII (1997), 253–290.

Dunne, Timothy, John Haltiwanger, and Kenneth R. Troske, "Technology and Jobs: Secular Changes and Cyclical Dynamics," *Carnegie Rochester Conference Series on Public Policy,* XLVI (1997), 107–178.

Ethier, Wilfred J., "Higher Dimensional Issues in Trade Theory," *Handbook of International Economics,* Vol. 1, Ronald W. Jones and Peter Kenen, eds. (New York: North-Holland, 1984), pp 131–184.

Feliciano, Zadia, "Workers and Trade Liberalization: The Impact of Trade Reforms in Mexico on Wages and Employment," Queen's College, mimeo, May 1995.

Feenstra, Robert C., and Gordon Hanson, "Foreign Investment, Outsourcing, and Relative Wages," in *The Political Economy of Trade Policy: Papers in Honor of Jagdish Bhagwati,* Robert C. Feenstra, Gene M. Grossman, and Douglas A. Irwin, eds. (Cambridge, MA: MIT Press, 1996a), pp. 89–127.

Feenstra, Robert C., and Gordon Hanson, "Globalization, Outsourcing, and Wage Inequality" *American Economic Review Papers and Proceedings,* LXXXVI (1996b), 240–245.

Feenstra, Robert C., and Gordon Hanson, "Productivity Measurement and the Impact of Trade and Technology on Wages," NBER Working Paper No. 6052, 1997.

Freeman, Richard, "Evaluating the European View That the United States Has no Unemployment Problem," *American Economic Review Papers and Proceedings,* LXXVIII (1988), 294–299.

——, "Are Your Wages Set in Beijing?" *Journal of Economic Perspectives,* IX (1995), 15–32.

Freeman, Richard, and Lawrence Katz, "Rising Wage Inequality: The United States vs. Other Advanced Countries," in *Working Under Different Rules,* Richard Freeman, ed. (New York, NY: Russell Sage Foundation, 1994).

Gordon, Robert J., *The Measurement of Durable Goods Prices* (National Bureau of Economic Research Monograph Series, Chicago: University of Chicago Press, 1990).

Gottschalk, Peter, and Mary Joyce, "Cross-National Differences in the Rise of Earnings Inequality—Market and Institutional Factors," *Review of Economics and Statistics,* LXXX (November 1998).

Hanson, Gordon H., and Ann Harrison, "Trade, Technology and Wage Inequality," NBER Working Paper No. 5110, 1995.

Haskel, Jonathan E., and Matthew J. Slaughter, "Does the Sector-Bias of Skill-Biased Technological Change Explain Changing Wage Inequality?" Dartmouth College, mimeo, 1998.

Helpman, Elhanan, and Paul R. Krugman, *Market Structure and Foreign Trade* (Cambridge, MA: MIT Press, 1985).

Jones, Ronald W., "The Structure of Simple General Equilibrium Models," *Journal of Political Economy,* LXXIII (1965), 557–572.

Johnson, George, and Frank Stafford, "The Labor Market Implications of International Trade," in O. Ashenfelter and D. Card, eds., *Handbook of Labor Economics,* Vol. III (Amsterdam: North-Holland, 1999), forthcoming.

Katz, Lawrence F., Gary W. Loveman, and David G. Blanchflower, "A Comparison of Changes in the Structure of Wages in Four OECD Countries," in *Differences and Changes in Wage Structures,* Lawrence F. Katz and Richard Freeman, eds. (Chicago, IL: University of Chicago Press, 1995).

Katz, Lawrence F., and Kevin M. Murphy, "Changes in Relative Wages, 1963–1987: Supply and Demand Factors," *Quarterly Journal of Economics,* CVII (1992), 35–78.

Katz, Lawrence F., and Ana Revenga, "Changes in the Structure of Wages, The U. S. vs. Japan," *Journal of Japanese and International Economics,* III (1989), 552–553.

Krugman, Paul, "Technology, Trade and Factor Prices," NBER Working Paper No. 5355, November 1995.

Krusell, Per, Lee E. Ohanian, José-Victor Ríos-Rull, and Giovanni L. Violante, "Capital-Skill Complementarity and Inequality: A Macroeconomic Analysis," Federal Reserve Bank of Minneapolis Research Department Staff Report No. 239, 1997.

Lawrence, Robert, and Matthew Slaughter, "International Trade and U. S. Wages in the 1980s: Great Sucking Sound or Small Hiccup," *Brookings Papers on Economic Activity,* 2 (1993), 161–227.

Leamer, Edward, "Trade, Wages and Revolving Door Ideas," Working Paper No. 4716, 1994.

——, "What's the Use of Factor Contents?" NBER Working Paper No. 5448, 1996.

Leamer, Edward, and James Levinsohn, "International Trade Theory: The Evidence," in G. Grossman and K. Rogoff, eds. *Handbook of International Economics,* Vol. 3 (Amsterdam: North-Holland, 1995), pp. 1139–1194.

Lerner, A. P., "Factor Prices and International Trade," *Economica,* XIX (1952), 1–16.

Levy, Frank, and Richard J. Murnane, "With What Skills Are Computers a Complement?" *American Economic Review Papers and Proceedings,* LXXXVI (1996), 258–262.

Machin, Stephen, "Wage Inequality in the U. K." *Oxford Review of Economic Policy,* XII (1996a), 47–64.

——, "Changes in the Relative Demand for Skills in the U. K. Labor Market," in *Acquiring Skills: Market Failures, Their Symptoms and Policy Responses.* Alison Booth and Dennis Snower, eds. (Cambridge, MA: Cambridge University Press, 1996b).

Machin, Stephen, Annette Ryan, and John Van Reenen, "Technology and Changes in Skill Structure: Evidence from an International Panel of Industries," Center for Economic Performance Discussion Paper No. 297, 1996.

SKILL-BIASED TECHNOLOGICAL CHANGE 1279

Machin, Stephen, and John Van Reenen, "Technology and Changes in Skill Structure: Evidence from Seven OECD Countries," *Quarterly Journal of Economics*, CXIII (1998), 1215–1244.

Mark, Jerome S., "Technological Change and employment: Some Results from BLS Research," *Monthly Labor Review*, CX (1987), 26–29.

Murphy, Kevin M., and Finis Welch, "The Structure of Wages," *Quarterly Journal of Economics*, CVII (1992), 285–326.

Murphy, Kevin M., and Finis Welch, "Industrial Change and the Rising Importance of Skill," in *Uneven Tides: Rising Inequality in America*, Sheldon Danziger and Peter Gottschalk, eds. (New York, NY: Russell Sage Foundation, 1993).

Nickell, Stephen, and Brian Bell, "The Collapse in Demand for the Unskilled and Unemployment across the OECD Countries," *Oxford Review of Economic Policy*, XI (1995), 40–62.

Organisation for Economic Co-operation and Development, *Economic Outlook Historical Statistics 1960–1990*, (Paris: OECD Publications, 1992).

——, *Employment Outlook* (Paris: OECD Publications, 1993).

——, *OECD Education Statistics 1985–1992*. (Paris: OECD Publications, 1995).

Richardson, J. David, "Income Inequality and Trade: How to Think, What to Conclude," *Journal of Economic Perspectives*, IX (1995), 33–55.

Robbins, Donald J., "Trade, Trade Liberalization and Inequality in Latin America and East Asia—Synthesis of Seven Country Studies," Harvard University, mimeo, 1995.

Siegel, Donald, "The Impact of Technological Change on Employment: Evidence from a Firm-Level Survey of Long Island Manufacturers," Arizona State University, mimeo, 1995.

Troske, Kenneth R., "The Worker Establishment Characteristics Database," Center for Economic Studies, United States Census Bureau, mimeo, July 1994.

United Nations, Department of Economic and Social Affairs, Statistical Office, *Industrial Statistics Yearbook, Volume I: General Industrial Statistics* (New York, NY: 1992).

United States Department of Labor, BLS Bulletin 2104, "The Impact of Technology on Labor in Four Industries: Meat Packing/Foundries/Metalworking Machinery/Electrical and Electronic Equipment," written under the supervision of John J. Macut, Richard W. Riche, and Rose N. Zeisel; Authors: Robert V. Critchlow (electrical and electronic equipment), Gary E. Falwell (meat products), Richard W. Lyon (foundries), and A. Harvey Belitsky (metal working machinery) (Washington, DC: United States Government Printing Office, 1982a).

——, BLS Bulletin 2137, "The Impact of Technology on Labor in Five Industries: Printing and Publishing/Water Transportation/Copper Ore Mining/Fabricated Structural Metal/Intercity Trucking," written under the supervision of John J. Macut, Richard W. Riche, and Rose N. Zeisel; Authors: Robert V. Critchlow (printing/publishing, water transportation), Richard W. Lyon (copper), Charles L. Bell (fabricated structural metal), and A. Harvey Belitsky (trucking) (Washington, DC: United States Government Printing Office, 1982b).

United States International Trade Commission, *Summary of Trade and Tariff Information: Semiconductors*, Publication No. 841 (Washington, DC: United States Government Printing Office, 1982).

——, *Imports under Items 806.30 and 807.00 of the Tariff Schedules of the United States, 1984–1987*, Publication No. 2144 (Washington, DC: United States Government Printing Office, 1988).

Wood, Adrian, "How Much Does Trade with the South Affect Workers in the North?" *World Bank Research Observer*, VI (1991), 19–36.

——, *North-South Trade, Employment and Inequality, Changing Fortunes in a Skill-Driven World* (Oxford: Clarendon, 1994).

World Bank, *World Tables* (Washington, DC: Johns Hopkins University Press, 1994).

[3]

Journal of Economic Perspectives—Volume 9, Number 3—Summer 1995—Pages 15–32

Are Your Wages Set in Beijing?

Richard B. Freeman

In the 1980s and 1990s, the demand for less-skilled workers fell in advanced countries. In the United States, this showed up primarily in falling real wages for less-educated men, although hours worked by these men also declined. In OECD-Europe, it took the form of increased unemployment for the less skilled. Over the same period, manufacturing imports from third world countries to the United States and OECD-Europe increased greatly. In 1991, the bilateral U.S. merchandise trade deficit with China was second only to its deficit with Japan.[1]

The rough concordance of falling demand for less-skilled workers with increased imports of manufacturing goods from third world countries has created a lively debate about the economic consequences of trade between advanced and developing countries. This debate differs strikingly from the debate over the benefits and costs of trade in the last few decades. In the 1960s and 1970s, many in the third world feared that trade would impoverish them, or push them to the periphery of the world economy; virtually no one in advanced countries was concerned about competition from less-developed countries. In the 1980s and 1990s, by contrast, most of the third world has embraced the global economy; whereas many in the advanced world worry over the possible

---

[1] The 1992 merchandise trade net deficit was $18 billion for mainland China and $50 billion for Japan; for "Greater China" (including Taiwan and Hong Kong) the deficit was $28 billion; for the rest of the world it was $16 billion.

■ *Richard B. Freeman is Professor of Economics, Harvard University, and Research Associate, National Bureau of Economic Research, both in Cambridge, Massachusetts. This paper was written while he was a visitor at the Centre for Economic Performance, London School of Economics, London, Great Britain.*

adverse economic effects of trade. The new debate focuses on one issue: whether in a global economy the wages or employment of low-skill workers in advanced countries have been (or will be) determined by the global supply of less-skilled labor, rather than by domestic labor market conditions. Put crudely, to what extent has, or will, the pay of low-skilled Americans or French or Germans be set in Beijing, Delhi and Djakkarta rather than in New York, Paris or Frankfurt?

On one side of the new debate are those who believe in factor price equalization—that in a global economy the wages of workers in advanced countries cannot remain above those of comparable workers in less-developed countries. They fear that the wages or employment of the less skilled in advanced countries will be driven down due to competition from low-wage workers overseas. On the other side of the debate are those who reject the notion that the traded goods sector can determine labor outcomes in an entire economy or who stress that the deleterious effects of trade on demand for the less skilled are sufficiently modest to be offset readily through redistributive social policies funded by the gains from trade. They fear that neoprotectionists will use arguments about the effect of trade on labor demand to raise trade barriers and reduce global productivity.

The debate has created odd divisions and bedfellows among economists and within the broader society.

There is, first, an Atlantic Divide in the importance that is accorded trade (which is mirrored by the two papers that follow). American economists generally conclude that trade is not the primary cause of the economic problems of low-skilled workers in advanced countries. European economists, by contrast, generally champion the view that trade with the third world has caused joblessness in Europe and rising inequality in the United States. What is odd is that imports from developing countries are a greater share of GNP and increased more in the United States in the 1970s and 1980s than in the European Union. For example, U.S. imports from less-developed countries were 0.4 percent of GNP in 1970, before rising to 2.5 percent of GNP in 1990. Meanwhile, in the European Union, imports from less-developed countries increased from 0.5 percent in 1970 to 2.1 percent of GNP in 1990.[2]

Second, there is disagreement over the appropriate mode of analysis to assess the effects of trade on income distribution. Labor economists and some trade economists estimate the potential loss of low-skill employment in import-intensive industries by comparing employment in those sectors with what employment might be if imports were produced domestically. Some trade economists favor analyses that examine the effects of trade on the prices of goods produced by low-skill workers. What is unexpected is that the techniques are more complementary than opposite and give the same substantive answer: both

---

[2] These data are from the World Bank computer files.

find that, barring strong auxiliary assumptions, trade is not *the* cause of the labor market woes of less-skilled workers.

Third, there is a divide between professionals and populists. Most economists, including those who believe trade has caused immiseration of less-skilled workers, are opposed to renewed protectionism. They are opposed because such a policy would reduce national output, some of which could be redistributed to the less skilled. Most participants in the debate favor policies to upgrade skills, and many favor more direct redistributive schemes to deal with the immiseration of low-skill workers. Just as an environmental cure, glasses, resolves a largely genetic disease of myopia, so too can nontrade policies resolve the possible distributional costs of trade. By contrast, in the broader community, many in the disparate coalition of consumer advocates, union leaders, billionaires (Ross Perot in the United States; Sir James Goldsmith in Europe), and conservatives who believe that trade caused the job market problems of the less-skilled favor protectionism.

Fourth, there is a division between trade theorists and other economists about the possible relevance of the forces for factor price equalization to the real economy. Had you asked me a decade ago whom I would have expected to champion the idea that trade is important in income distribution, I would have said trade theorists, if only from self-interest. After all, what greater triumph for a fundamental proposition of trade theory than to explain the problem of rising inequality in earnings and employment in the late twentieth century? However, some trade experts have been in the forefront of those rejecting factor price equalization. By contrast, nontrade economists have taken factor price equalization more seriously.

This paper provides a viewer's guide to the debate. I review the two facts that motivate the debate: the immiseration of less-skilled workers in advanced countries and the increase in manufacturing imports from less-developed countries. Then I summarize the arguments and evidence brought to bear on them and give my scorecard on the debate. I conclude by examining the fear that, whatever trade with less-developed countries did in the past, it will impoverish less-skilled Americans and western Europeans in the future, as China, India, Indonesia and others make greater waves in the world economy.

The Immiseration of Low-Skill Workers in the United States and Europe

An economic disaster has befallen low-skilled Americans, especially young men. Researchers using several data sources—including household survey data from the Current Population Survey, other household surveys, and establishment surveys—have documented that wage inequality and skill differentials in earnings and employment increased sharply in the United States from the mid-1970s through the 1980s and into the 1990s. The drop in the relative position of the less skilled shows up in a number of ways: greater earnings differentials between those with more and less education; greater earnings differentials between older and younger workers; greater differentials between high-skilled and low-skilled occupations; in a wider earnings distribution overall and within demographic and skill groups (Mishel and Bernstein, 1994; U.S. Department of Labor, 1994); and in less time worked by low-skill and low-paid workers (Topel, 1993).

If the increase in earnings inequality had coincided with rapidly growing real earnings, so that the living standards of low-skill workers increased or fell a trifle, no one would ring alarm bells. But in the past decade or two, real earnings have grown sluggishly at best, and fallen for men on average.[3] The economic position of low-skill men has fallen by staggering amounts. For instance, the real hourly wages of males with 12 years of schooling dropped by some 20 percent from 1979 to 1993; for entry-level men with 12 years, the drop has been 30 percent! The real hourly earnings of all men in the bottom decile of the earnings distribution fell similarly since the early or mid-1970s, while that of men in the upper decile has risen modestly—producing a huge increase in inequality.[4]

Similar economic forces have led to somewhat different problems in Europe. For most of the period since World War II, OECD-Europe had lower unemployment rates than the United States. For example, in 1973, the rate of unemployment was 2.9 percent for OECD-Europe compared to 4.8 percent for the United States, and the ratio of employment to population was as high in Europe as in the United States. This changed in the 1980s. From 1983 to 1991 unemployment averaged 9.3 percent in OECD-Europe compared to 6.7 percent in the United States. Unemployment in OECD-Europe seems destined to remain above American levels throughout the '90s decade. The ratio of employment to the population of working age and the hours worked per employee has also fallen in Europe relative to the United States, adding to the U.S.-Europe gap in the utilization of labor. In addition, unemployment has been highly concentrated in Europe: in OECD-Europe, nearly half of unemployed workers are without jobs for over a year, compared to less than 10 percent of unemployed workers in the United States. The employment problem in Europe has generated numerous studies, culminating in the OECD Jobs Study (1994a).

If wage inequality had risen in Europe as much as in the United States, or was near U.S. levels, or if the real wages of low-skill Europeans had fallen, high joblessness would be a devastating indictment of European reliance on institutional forces to determine labor market outcomes. In effect, Europe would be

---

[3] The magnitude of change in real earnings depends on the years covered, the deflator used and treatment of fringe benefits.
[4] These figures are from Mishel and Bernstein (1994).

suffering unemployment with no gain in equality. But in general, Europe has avoided an American level of inequality or changes in inequality, and wages at the bottom of the distribution rose rather than fell (Freeman and Katz, 1994).[5] By the early 1990s, workers in the bottom tiers of the wage distribution in Europe had higher compensation than did workers in the bottom tiers in the United States (Freeman, 1994). Western Europe's problem was one of jobs, not of wages: the workers whose wages have fallen through the floor in the United States—the less skilled and (except in Germany) the young—were especially likely to be jobless in Europe.

The rise in joblessness in Europe is thus the flip side of the rise in earnings inequality in the U.S. The two outcomes reflect the same phenomenon—a relative decline in the demand against the less skilled that has overwhelmed the long-term trend decline in the relative supply of less-skilled workers. In the United States, where wages are highly flexible, the change in the supply-demand balance lowered the wages of the less skilled. In Europe, where institutions buttress the bottom parts of the wage distribution, the change produced unemployment. The question then is not simply why the United States and Europe experienced different labor market problems in the 1980s and 1990s, but what factors depressed the relative demand for low-skill labor in both economies?

Trade Between the United States and Europe with the Third World

One thing that distinguishes the 1980s and 1990s from earlier decades following World War II is the growth of the global economy, which in practical terms can be seen in reduced trade barriers, increased trade, highly mobile capital, and rapid transmission of technology across national lines. Multinationals, who locate plants and hire workers almost anywhere in the world, have replaced national companies as the cutting edge capitalist organization. The most commonly used indicator of globalization is the ratio of exports plus imports to gross domestic product. In the United States, this ratio rose from 0.12 in 1970 to 0.22 in 1990. Trade ratios rose substantially throughout the OECD (OECD Jobs Study, 1994, ch. 3). Although most trade is among advanced countries, trade with less-developed countries increased greatly. By 1990, 35 percent of U.S. imports were from less-developed countries, compared with 14 percent in 1970. In the European Community, 12 percent of imports were from less-developed countries, compared with 5 percent in 1970. (The less-developed country portion of European trade is lower largely because trade among U.S. states doesn't count as imports and exports, while trade among European countries does, thus inflating the overall total of intra-Europe trade.)

---

[5]The United Kingdom is a mixture. Inequality has risen as in the United States; unemployment has risen as in Europe. But real earnings, even for those in the bottom decile, have also risen.

In 1992, 58 percent of less-developed country exports to the western industrialized nations consisted of (light) manufacturing goods (OECD, 1994b), compared with 5 percent in 1955 (Wood, 1994).

The increase in manufacturing imports from less-developed countries presumably reflects the conjoint working of several forces. Reductions in trade barriers must have contributed: why else the huge international effort to cut tariff and nontariff barriers embodied in GATT, NAFTA, WTO and other agreements? The shift in development strategies of less-developed countries, from import substitution to export promotion, must also have played a part. Perhaps World Bank and IMF pressures on less-developed countries to export as a way of paying off their debts contributed as well. Advanced country investments in manufacturing in less-developed countries also presumably increased their ability to compete in the world market.

Changes in the labor markets of less-developed countries have also contributed to the increased role of those countries in world markets. The less-developed country share of the world workforce increased from 69 percent in 1965 to 75 percent in 1990; and the mean years of schooling in the less-developed country world rose from 2.4 years in 1960 to 5.3 years in 1986.[6] The less-developed country share of world manufacturing employment grew from 40 percent in 1960 to 53 percent in 1986. Finally, diffusion of technology through multinational firms has arguably put less-developed countries and advanced countries on roughly similar production frontiers. Skills, capital infrastructure, and political stability—rather than pure technology—have become the comparative advantage of advanced countries.

Given these two facts, it is natural to pose the question: to what extent might trade with less-developed countries be reducing demand for less-skilled labor in the advanced countries?

Economic Theory: Factor Price Equalization

At the conceptual heart of the debate over the effects of trade on the labor market is the strength of forces for factor price equalization. Consider a world where producers have the same technology; where trade flows are determined by factor endowments, so that advanced countries with many skilled workers compared to unskilled workers import commodities made by less-skilled workers in developing countries, while developing countries with more unskilled labor import commodities made by skilled labor in advanced countries; and where trade establishes a single world price for a good. Trade makes less-skilled labor in advanced countries and skilled labor in developing countries less scarce and can thus be expected to reduce their wages. By contrast, trade will increase the production of goods made by skilled labor in advanced countries and by

---

[6] My tabulations are based on World Bank data for individual countries given in the Bank's publicly available diskettes on Social Indicators.

less-skilled labor in developing countries and can thus be expected to raise their wages. In equilibrium, under specified conditions, the long-term outcome is that factor prices are equalized throughout the world: the less-skilled worker in the advanced country is paid the same as his or her competitor in a developing country; and similarly for the more-skilled workers.

But does factor price equalization (appropriately qualified to fit an n-factor/n-good world) capture economic reality? For years, many trade economists rejected factor price equalization as a description of the world. The wide, and in some cases increasing, variation in pay levels among countries seemed to make it a textbook proposition of little relevance.[7] Reflecting this view, in the recent debate Bhagwati and Dehejia (1994) have enumerated some of the "extraordinarily demanding" assumptions needed to establish factor price equalization. These include: identical technology and tastes; similar ranking of sectors by skilled to unskilled and capital to labor intensity at all prices; absence of scale effects; and perhaps most important, that countries are incompletely specialized—that is, they produce the full set of traded goods. Norman and Venables (1993) stress that in a Hecksher-Ohlin model where costs of trade are nonnegligible, goods trade alone does not equalize factor prices; flows of capital or labor would also be needed.[8] Other trade economists, however, treat factor price equalization as a core proposition of international economics (Leamer, 1984).

To labor economists, the observation that trade with less-developed countries places some economic pressures on low-skill westerners is a valuable reminder that one cannot treat national labor markets in isolation. If the West can import children's toys produced by low-paid Chinese workers at bargain basement prices, surely low-skilled westerners, who produce those toys at wages 10 times those of the Chinese, will face a difficult time in the job market. It isn't even necessary that the West import the toys. The threat to import them or to move plants to less-developed countries to produce the toys may suffice to force low-skilled westerners to take a cut in pay to maintain employment.[9] In this situation, the open economy can cause lower pay for low-skilled westerners even without trade; to save my job, I accept Chinese-level pay, and that prevents imports. The invisible hand would have done its job, with proper invisibility.

For the factor price equalization argument to carry weight, advanced countries should export commodities to less-developed countries made with relatively skilled labor and import commodities from less-developed countries produced by unskilled labor. U.S. trade operates in just this way. American

[7]For an exception to the prevailing view, see Krueger (1968).

[8]Wood (1994) argues that capital is so mobile that differences in capital should not be viewed as endowments. But the positive correlation between savings and investment rates found by Feldstein and Horioka (1980) implies that capital is not so mobile.

[9]As an example, in early 1995, the head of the Confederation of British Industry declared that western workers would have to lower wage expectations to compete in the global market with low-wage workers from developing countries (*Financial Times*, Jan. 13, 1995).

exports are skill intensive: our net exports are positive for such goods as scientific instruments, airplanes, and in intellectual property, including software. Imports make less intensive use of skilled labor: our net imports are positive for toys, footwear and clothing. Europe also imports low skill intensive goods from less-developed countries and exports high skill intensive goods. While factors other than labor skills affect trade—natural resource endowments, infrastructure capital, perhaps capital overall, technological changes that diffuse slowly—the flows of goods between advanced countries and less-developed countries seems to fit the Hecksher-Ohlin model well enough (Leamer, 1984) to raise the specter of factor price equalization for low-skilled westerners.

The argument for complete factor price equalization is, to be sure, an extreme one. It implies that in an economy fully integrated in the world trading system, domestic market developments have *no* effect on wages. Instead, there is a single global labor market that sets the factor prices for inputs, even if trade is only a small part of the economy. Whether 5 percent or 95 percent of less-skilled workers are employed in import-competing activities, their pay is determined in Beijing. Transportation costs, immediacy of delivery, and such factors are assumed to be irrelevant in differentiating the location of production. If unskilled labor can readily switch from traded goods to nontraded goods, it would be a single factor, so that the pay of even those working in nontraded goods or services would be set in the global market. Only when *all* less-skilled workers are employed in nontraded activities or if those in nontraded activities have sector-specific skills that make them "different" from workers in traded activities (for some period) will their pay depend on domestic market considerations.

These predictions run counter to a wide body of evidence that domestic developments do affect wages: for instance, that the baby boom affected the pay of young workers; that the relative number of college graduates altered the premium paid for education; that sectoral developments affect pay in certain industries; that your wages are likely to be higher if your firm does well than if it is doing poorly. In the United States, wage differences among states and localities have persisted for decades despite free trade, migration, and capital flows. Among countries, wage differences between workers with seemingly similar skills have also persisted for decades, albeit exaggerated by the divergence between purchasing power parities and exchange rates, and by differences in skills that are hard to measure.

Given these considerations, factor price equalization should not be viewed as the Holy Grail giving the answer of economic science as to why demand fell for low-skill western workers in the 1980s and 1990s. Instead, the theory is a flag alerting us to the possibility that increased linkages with less-developed countries *may have* contributed to the immiseration of the less skilled, and pointing to some routes through which such linkages *may have* worked. The gap between "may have" contributed and "has" contributed is large—bridgeable only by empirical analysis, with all of its compromises and difficulties.

Empirical Work

The effort to see whether or not trade has contributed to the growing immiseration of low-skill workers in developed economies has taken two forms. One set of studies exploits data on the "factor content" of import and export industries to estimate the implicit change in factor endowments in advanced countries due to trade. A second set of studies exploits price data to see if increased imports from less-developed countries have induced sizable drops in the prices of goods produced by low-skilled westerners, which would reduce demand for their labor and lower their pay or disemploy them. The debate has drawn attention to problems with both sets of calculations.

Factor Content Analysis: Can the Tail Wag the Dog?

In factor content studies, analysts estimate the impact of trade on the demand for labor at given wages or, alternatively, on the nation's "effective" factor endowments, that is, the domestic *and* foreign labor inputs used to produce society's consumption bundle. Since the U.S. imports goods that make heavy use of low-skilled labor, and exports goods that make heavy use of high-skilled labor, trade with developing countries reduces the relative demand for less-skilled labor in the United States, or, if you prefer, increases the relative supply of less-skilled labor.[10] Given estimates of the labor skills used in various sectors, one can estimate how changes in imports and exports altered the demand-supply balance for high- and low-skilled labor at given relative wages and prices. To see how the changed supply-demand balance for labor skills affected relative wages (the variable of interest in the United States), analysts transform the calculated shifts in quantities into changes in wages using estimates of the effect of changes in supply and demand on relative pay from other studies (for instance, studies of how the increase in the relative supply of college graduates on the domestic labor market affects their relative pay).

For example, if the United States imported 10 additional children's toys, which could be produced by five American workers, the effective supply of unskilled workers would increase by five (or alternatively, domestic demand for such workers would fall by five), compared with the alternative in which those 10 toys were produced domestically. This five-worker shift in the supply-demand balance would put pressure on unskilled wages to fall, causing those wages to fall in accord with the relevant elasticity. Any trade-balancing flow of exports would, contrarily, reduce the effective endowment of skilled workers (raise their demand) and thus increase their pay. In the context of a standard

---

[10] The *change* in endowments due to a *change* in trade is estimated as the multiplicand of a matrix of sectoral labor skill inputs (a_{ij}, where i = labor skill and j = industry) and a vector of changes in sectoral imports (M_j) minus exports (X_j). Since we are measuring a horizontal shift in "quantities," this is also the change in demand for skill i at existing wages due to actual trade flows.

trade model, Deardorff and Staiger (1988) show the conditions under which changes in the factor content of trade indicate how trade affects relative factor prices.

Several recent studies use factor content calculations to examine the possible effect of trade on the fall in relative pay of low-skilled workers during the 1980s and 1990s. Borjas, Freeman and Katz (1992) estimate what would happen to the relative employment of less-skilled Americans as a result of the change in trade in the 1980s and conclude that the reduction in employment was modest, due largely to the trade deficit. Sachs and Shatz (1994) analyzed trade flows with less-developed countries with a more extensive data set for the period 1978–1990 and also concluded that increased import penetration from less-developed countries reduced manufacturing employment modestly. Cooper (1994) estimated that the number of less-skilled workers displaced by imports in textiles, apparel and leather was small relative to employment in retail trade, which employs many such workers.

These studies find that changes in actual trade flows have not displaced all that many low-skill workers from manufacturing (taken as the major traded goods sector) for one basic reason: that only a moderate proportion of workers now work in manufacturing. In 1993, roughly 15 percent of American workers were employed in manufacturing. The vast majority of unskilled workers were in nontraded goods, such as retail trade and various services. In such a world it is hard to see how pressures on wages emanating from traded goods can determine wages economy-wide. To be sure, the strong version of factor price equalization argues that the wage of low-skilled labor is set in a global market, affecting workers in both traded goods and untraded services. But this seems implausible. Compare two situations: in the first, 50 percent of the nation's unskilled workers are in import-competing industries, and increased trade with less-developed countries displaces one in 10 of them; in the second, only 1 percent of unskilled workers are in import-competing industries, and trade displaces one in 10 of them. To argue that trade would have the same effect in both cases seems far-fetched, dependent on the simplifying assumptions of the trade model (notably that elasticities of supply are infinite, with no variation in products produced in developed and less-developed countries).

However, Adrian Wood's (1994) factor content study, which he discusses in his paper in this issue, reaches a different conclusion. Wood argues that standard factor content analyses understate the effect of trade on employment. Once the proper corrections are made, he argues, trade becomes the root cause of the fall in demand for less-skilled workers in advanced countries.

Wood (1994) begins by arguing that estimated changes in effective labor endowments, based on existing labor input coefficients in advanced countries, are biased against finding a big disemployment effect. The reason is that less-developed countries export different and noncompeting goods within sectors than the goods produced by advanced countries; for example, the United States might make high-tech toys, while the Chinese make low-tech toys. The typical factor content analysis would observe the import of low-tech Chinese toys and then multiply that by the quantity of labor, of various skills, used in the U.S. manufacture of high-tech toys. But if the low-tech toys were made in the United States, manufacturers would in fact use more less-skilled labor than in producing high-tech toys. To correct for this possible bias, Wood uses the labor input coefficients for developing countries, adjusted for labor demand responses to higher western wages, rather than those for the advanced countries. With this procedure, he estimates that labor demand due to imports of manufactures fell by "ten times the conventional ones" (Wood, 1994, p. 10).

The problem of differing mixes of products within industries is real. Ideally, one would like the change in labor input coefficients associated with the actual change in goods produced domestically as a result of imports. My guess is that the conventional factor content approach does underestimate the effect of trade on demand for low-skilled labor, but I also suspect that Wood's upward adjustment is probably excessive.[11]

Wood (1994) also asserts that trade with less-developed countries induced substantial labor-saving innovation in the traded goods sector. This further reduces demand for unskilled labor. Although there is no reason to expect innovation to respond to import competition any more or less than to any other form of competition, the problem of induced technical change is a real one, and Wood's adjustment is potentially in the right direction. But he may be claiming too much for this factor. For the 1980s, Sachs and Shatz (1994) find virtually no difference in the rate of change of total factor productivity in industrial sectors divided by skill intensity of labor, which runs against Wood's (1994) argument. They do, however, report that between 1960–1978 and 1978–1989 industrial sectors with lower skill intensity increased their rate of growth of total factor productivity more than sectors with high skill intensity, which could be a response to the greater low-wage competition from less-developed countries in the 1980s. But this is a weak reed. As the evidence stands, the claim that trade induces large labor-saving technological change in low-skill industries is not especially strong.

Standard factor content analysis studies indicate that trade can account for 10–20 percent of the overall fall in demand for unskilled labor needed to explain rising wage differentials in the United States or rising joblessness in Europe. If one accepts Wood's (1994) adjusted factor content analysis for traded goods and his estimate of induced technological change, then trade accounts for about half of the requisite fall in demand for labor. Where can we find the other half?

As a final step, Wood assumes that trade-induced labor-saving technological changes spill over to nontraded sectors, where most nonskilled workers are employed. This final assumption leads him to conclude that increased trade

[11] Factor content studies use base period labor input ratios by sector to measure skill usage. Thus, the input use in labor-intensive goods that presumably make up the increased imports are included in the sectoral labor usage ratio, but aggregated with the input use of other goods as well.

with less-developed countries accounts for all of the rise of inequality in the United States and all of the increase in unskilled unemployment in Europe.

If one is going to use a factor content approach to attribute immiseration of the less skilled in the West to globalization, Wood's clear and careful approach shows the way. But as he is fully aware, some of the steps along the way are arguable or problematic.

Criticisms of Factor Content Studies

Some trade economists criticize factor content studies because observed trade patterns "do not necessarily capture the effects of price pressures that operate through trade" (Lawrence, 1994, p. 16). Rather, "it is the absence of trade barriers, and not any measure of the volume or terms of trade, that affects factor prices" (Deardorff and Hakura, 1994, p. 78). These economists favor looking at prices rather than quantities to study how trade has affected demand for low-skilled workers. Putting aside the price approach until the next section, I discuss here the problems with the factor content studies that have been raised.

One problem is that factor content calculations treat changes in the production of goods as output shocks that affect employment at *existing* wages. But if wages in a sector adjusted rapidly as imports entered that market, this would reduce the competitive advantage of the foreign workers and limit import flows. In this scenario, the observed rise in imports understates trade pressures because it misses the feedback from domestic wages to imports. At the extreme, it is possible (as noted earlier) that the mere threat of imports may reduce wages absent any trade. If the forces for factor price equalization operate with little trade, or absent trade at all, factor content studies would understate the effects of trade on relative pay. Does this criticism devastate factor content studies? In the United States, the wages of less-skilled labor have fallen sharply, presumably limiting the entry of imports. In this setting, factor content studies may very well understate the contribution of trade to immiseration. If the pay of low-skilled Americans were, say, 20 percent higher, I would expect to see greater imports and accompanying loss of jobs, producing a greater estimated trade-induced disemployment. But the situation is different in western Europe, where labor market institutions maintain the wages of less-skilled labor. With roughly fixed relative wages, factor content studies should give a more accurate picture of trade effects in Europe than in the United States. If they showed much larger trade displacement effects than in the United States, we might reject standard factor content studies in the United States as seriously biased downward. I know of no evidence of larger trade displacement effects in Europe than in the United States.

A second problem is that the standard factor content studies ignore how demand for output may respond to changes in prices. Assume that less-developed countries did not produce low-price children's toys in the 1980s, so that the United States did not import any. The factor content calculations assume that without such imports, consumers would have bought the same amount of domestically produced low-tech goods, despite the fact that they would presumably be much higher priced than the imports. More likely, consumers would have bought fewer higher-priced low-tech toys and more high-tech toys or other commodities. By ignoring the likely consumer response to higher-priced domestic equivalents of imports, the factor content calculations overstate how much domestic production by low-skilled labor is displaced by imports. What is needed to assess the magnitude of this effect are elasticities and cross elasticities of product demand for various goods, which are not readily available. Wood makes some adjustments for the lower amount of goods that might be sold at a higher domestic price in his calculations, but they are not part of the standard analysis.

Some trade economists criticize standard factor content studies for failing to lay out adequately the counterfactual underlying the calculations. Deardorff and Hakura (1994, p. 78) stress that in the trade model, as in any comparative statics model of prices and quantities, "the volume of trade and the level of wages are simultaneously determined," so that the effect of trade on wages cannot be meaningfully explored without additional specification of what outside force caused trade to change. This directs attention to two related questions. Why did imports of manufactured goods from less-developed countries increase so much in the 1980s and 1990s? What would have happened to other elements of GDP had imports not risen?

Factor content calculations take the increase in imports as an exogenous event for the receiving country. Imports to the West could have risen for any and all of the reasons given earlier: reductions of trade barriers; increased skills of workers in third world countries; spread of technology that made less-developed country production more competitive. If the increase in trade is due to any of these factors, the assumption that the link is largely from trade to wages or employment is reasonable enough. But if increased imports are caused by increases in wages or technological change in the receiving country due to domestic labor market forces, or to macroeconomic expansion, the change in trade cannot be treated as an exogenous event in the spirit of factor content analysis. Analysts who use the factor content technique have implicitly (Borjas, Freeman and Katz) or explicitly (Wood) assumed that the increase in trade is due to reduced trade barriers, increased skills in developing countries, and the spread of technology, without testing this. One way to test this interpretation of causality is to estimate the effect of some outside factor on the volume of trade, and use the part of trade due to that factor as the independent variable explaining employment or wages (an instrumental variables approach). Ana Revanga (1992) has done this using changes in exchange rates as the factor causing trade flows and found that the effects of trade on employment or wages at an industry level in the United States are not markedly different than the effects estimated by assuming the volume of trade is exogenous to the American labor market.

This still leaves the problem of what might have happened to other parts of GDP absent increased imports. Since no one can say with confidence what would have happened had imports from less-developed countries remained constant or at the same proportion of GDP over time, perhaps the best response is for analysts to present a range of options, with separate estimated trade effects for each. Barring strong assumptions that reductions in imports would greatly reduce GDP growth, I doubt that such a range would alter the message of most factor content studies that trade has had at most a moderate effect on the demand for unskilled labor in advanced countries.

However, the criticisms and Wood's analysis tell us that while standard factor content studies offer a clue to how trade has affected relative wages, such studies are not the final word. We must look at other evidence as well.

Price Effects Studies and Other Evidence

Two additional bodies of evidence have been brought to bear on this debate: price data on the goods produced by low-skill labor; and data on changes in the employment of skilled and less-skilled workers in industries that produce traded and nontraded goods. In the trade model, price declines in import-competing sectors should lower the relative wages of unskilled labor, which those sectors use intensely, and ultimately the prices of all goods and services produced by those workers. The lower relative pay of the less skilled ought further to lead firms to substitute them for more expensive skilled labor throughout the economy.

Two studies have looked for evidence that the prices of sectors that extensively use unskilled labor have fallen greatly. Lawrence and Slaughter (1993) correlate changes in import prices with the share of production workers across industries and find that when prices are adjusted for changes in total factor productivity, the prices of less skill intensive goods fell only slightly.[12] Sachs and Shatz (1994) examine output prices for all of manufacturing, not just imports, which provides a larger sample of industries. After adjusting for productivity changes that should independently affect prices, they find a modest negative relation between the production worker share of employment and changes in industry prices.[13] They also find that prices fell faster in sectors that make more intensive use of low-skilled workers in the 1980s than in previous decades compared with sectors that use fewer low-skilled workers. They conclude that relative prices exerted some pressure on the pay of the less skilled, but not by enough to account for a significant widening of wage inequality.

The studies of prices have weaknesses. Price data is subject to serious measurement problems. Import prices exist for relatively few industries and cover only some goods in those industries. Output prices suffer from an aggregation problem, since the sectors with imports presumably include domestic goods that differ in important dimensions from the imports. Changes in the

---

[12] It is necessary to adjust the prices for technological progress (and other forces that might alter prices) to isolate the effect of the fall in the wages of less-skilled labor.

[13] They also include a dummy variable for computers, due to the likely inaccuracy of prices for this good.

quality of products not captured in the indices create measurement error, which may be correlated with the skill intensity of production. The use of the proportion of production workers in an industry as a measure of skill is exceedingly crude since it fails to recognize the difference between production workers across sectors and does not map readily into standard indicators of human capital, such as education or age. Moreover, since unskilled labor is only a modest proportion of cost in most industries (except in activities like untraded personal services, which these studies exclude), finding any link between changes in prices and the fraction of workers who are unskilled is fraught with difficulty.

Perhaps the biggest problem with these studies is that they ignore potential determinants of changes in sectoral prices and potential reasons for the proportion of unskilled workers in a sector to be correlated with changes in prices, save for trade. They do not, for example, examine possible shifts in consumer demand that might affect prices due, say, to increasing GDP per capita. They also ignore the possibility that prices in sectors that intensively use unskilled labor might fall for reasons independent of trade, such as the falling real value of the minimum wage. Consider an economy with no trade at all, but where the minimum wage affects the pay of low-skilled workers. Reduce the minimum and the prices in industries with many unskilled workers should fall, producing a correlation between skill intensity of production and relative prices that has (by assumption) nothing to do with trade. Finding relative price declines in sectors that intensively use less-skilled labor may be necessary to establish a trade effect that operates through prices, but it is not sufficient to establish a trade effect in a world where many forces influence relative prices.

Like the factor content studies, price studies provide a clue to how trade could affect relative wages—the greater the estimated import-induced reduction in the prices of goods produced by low-skill labor, the greater the likely trade effect on wages and employment—but they also are far from the final word.

Some additional evidence has been put forward on the possible connection between trade and wages. For example, as evidence that trade is not the prime cause of the decline in demand for the less skilled, Berman, Bound and Griliches (1992) point out that the ratio of unskilled workers fell in all sectors over this period. If trade was driving down wages of unskilled workers in traded sectors, then some of those workers should be displaced into the nontraded sectors. As a result, the ratio of unskilled workers should be rising or at least holding steady in some sectors. I find it hard to argue that trade is the full story of reduced demand for these workers in the face of the observed decline in the use of less-skilled workers in all sectors.

Those who argue for the importance of trade have also brought other evidence, not directly related to the trade models, to bear as well. Wood (1994) has pointed out that a composite indicator of changes in demand for skills based on changes in wage and unemployment differentials is strongly correlated with the share of imports from less-developed countries across a sample of 14 developed economies. Borjas and Ramey (1994) have found a strong correlation in time series data between the wage differentials between different levels of education and durable goods imports as a share of GDP. They argue that imports of durable goods account for most of the change in the wage differentials, by squeezing economic rents in relatively union-intensive sectors or in sectors that would have had great market power (and rents to share with workers) absent the imports.

Conclusion

The debate over whether increased trade with less-developed countries is the main cause of the immiseration of the less-skilled has raised numerous conceptual and empirical issues, as well as some hackles. Adherents of one side in the debate, or of one approach to the problem, have found it easy to criticize the other. Most criticisms have at least an element of truth, making scoring the debate a bit of a judgment call. Largely because neither the factor content nor the price analysis comes up with a smoking gun, and because demand for the less skilled has fallen even in nontraded goods sectors, my scorecard reads: trade matters, but it is neither all that matters nor the primary cause of observed changes.

That we lack compelling evidence that trade underlies the problems of the less skilled in the past does not, of course, rule out the possibility that trade will dominate labor market outcomes in the future. Indeed, it is commonplace in the trade-immiseration debate for those who reject trade as *the* explanation of the past decline in the demand for the less skilled to hedge their conclusion by noting that there is a good chance that in the future, pressures for factor price equalization will grow. Maybe your wages were not set in Beijing yesterday or today, but tomorrow they will be.

I have problems with this prognostication. Economists do not have a good record as soothsayers, and neither trade nor labor economists are exceptions. Trade economists once worried about the perpetual dollar shortage; believed that flexible exchange rates would be more stable than fixed exchange rates; and saw the Common Market as the cure-all to European problems. Labor economists declared unions were dead just before the formation of the CIO; worried about the falling return to skills and were as shocked as anyone else by the increased inequality of the 1980s; did not expect the Civil Rights Act to raise the demand for black workers; and so on. For what it is worth, I am not convinced that continued expansion of trade with less-developed countries spells doom for low-skill westerners. As more and more low-skilled western workers find employment in the nontraded goods service sector, the potential for imports from less-developed countries to reduce their employment or wages should lessen. In the standard trade model, a factor used exclusively in non-traded goods has its pay determined by the domestic economy. The closer western economies get to this situation, the smaller should be the trade-induced pressures on low-skilled workers. Wildly heralded trade agreements such as the U.S.-Canadian agreement, the Common Market, and NAFTA have not dominated our wages and employment in the ways their advocates or opponents forecast.

In the past, other factors have been more important than trade in the well-being of the less skilled: technological changes that occur independent of trade; unexpected political developments, such as German reunification and instability in various regions of the world; policies to educate and train workers; union activities; the compensation policies of firms; and welfare state and related social policies. In the future, I expect that these factors will continue to be more important. I could, of course, be utterly wrong. The best we can do is probe and poke at the evidence and arguments, and present our analyses and prognostications with appropriate humility.

References

Berman, Eli, John Bound, and Zvi Griliches, "Changes in the Demand for Skilled Labor Within U.S. Manufacturing Industries: Evidence from the Annual Survey of Manufacturing." NBER Working Paper, July 1992.

Bhagwati, Jagdish, and Vivek Dehejia, "Free Trade and Wages of the Unskilled: Is Marx Striking Again?" In Bhagwati, J., and Marvin Kosters, eds., *Trade and Wages.* Washington, D.C.: American Enterprise Institute, 1994, pp. 36–75.

Borjas, George, Richard Freeman, and Lawrence Katz, "On the Labor Market Effects of Immigration and Trade." In Borjas, G., and R. Freeman, eds., *Immigration and the Work Force.* Chicago: University of Chicago and NBER, 1992, pp. 213–44.

Borjas, George, and Valerie Ramey, "Time-Series Evidence on the Sources of Trends in Wage Inequality," *American Economic Review*, Papers and Proceedings, May 1994, *84*, 10–16.

Cooper, Richard, "Foreign Trade, Wages, and Unemployment." Paper delivered at Egon Sohmen Conference, Salzburg Austria, September 1994.

Deardorff, Alan, and Dalia Hakura, "Trade and Wages: What are the Questions?" In Bhagwati, J., and Marvin Kosters, eds., *Trade*

and Wages. Washington, D.C.: American Enterprise Institute, 1994, pp. 76–107.

Deardorff, Alan, and Robert Staiger, "An Interpretation of the Factor Content of Trade," *Journal of International Economics*, February 1988, *24*, 93–107.

Feldstein, Martin, and Charles Horioka, "Domestic Savings and International Capital Flows," *Economic Journal*, June 1980, *90*, 314–29.

Freeman, Richard, "How Labor Fares in Advanced Economies." In Freeman, R., ed., *Working Under Different Rules.* New York: Russell Sage Foundation, 1994, pp. 1–28.

Freeman, Richard, and Lawrence Katz, "Rising Wage Inequality: The United States vs. Other Advanced Countries." In Freeman, R., ed., *Working Under Different Rules.* New York: Russell Sage Foundation, 1994, pp. 29–62.

Krueger, Anne, "Factor Endowments and Per Capita Income Differences Among Countries," *Economic Journal*, September 1968, *78*, 641–57.

Lawrence, Robert, "The Impact of Trade on OECD Labor Markets." Group of Thirty, Occasional Paper 45, Washington, D.C., 1994.

Lawrence, Robert, and Matthew Slaughter, "Trade and U.S. Wages: Great Sucking Sound or Small Hiccup?" In *Brookings Papers on Economic Activity, Microeconomics*. Vol. 2. Washington, D.C.: Brookings Institution, 1993.

Leamer, Edward, *Sources of International Comparative Advantage*. Cambridge: MIT Press, 1984.

Mishel, Lawrence, and Aaron Bernstein, *The State of Working America, 1994–95*. New York: Economic Policy Institute, M.E. Sharpe, 1994.

Neary, J. P., and A. G. Schweinberger, "Factor Content Functions and the Theory of International Trade," *Review of Economic Studies*, July 1986, *53*, 421–32.

Norman, Victor, and Anthony Venables, "International Trade, Factor Mobility, and Trade Costs." CEPR Discussion Paper 766, February 1993.

OECD, *The OECD Jobs Study: Evidence and Explanation*. Paris: OECD, 1994a.

OECD, *Background Document for a Study on Economic and Other Linkages with Major Developing Economies*. Paris: OECD, August 1994b.

Revanga, Ana, "Exporting Jobs? The Impact of Import Competition on Employment and Wages in U.S. Manufacturing," *Quarterly Journal of Economics*, 1992, *107*:1, 255–84.

Sachs, Jeff, and Howard Shatz, "Trade and Jobs in U.S. Manufacturing," *Brookings Papers on Economic Activity*. Vol. 1. Washington, D.C.: Brookings Institution, 1994, pp. 1–84.

Topel, Robert, "What Have We Learned from Empirical Studies of Unemployment and Turnover?," *American Economic Review*, Papers and Proceedings, May 1993, *83*, 110–15.

United States Department of Labor, *Report on the American Work Force*. Washington, D.C.: U.S. Government Printing Office, 1994.

Wood, Adrian, *North-South Trade, Employment and Inequality*. Oxford: Clarendon Press, 1994.

[4]

Scand. J. of Economics 101(4), 533–554, 1999

Another Nail in the Coffin? Or Can the Trade Based Explanation of Changing Skill Structures Be Resurrected?*

Thibaut Desjonqueres

London School of Economics, London WC2A, England

Stephen Machin

University College, London WC1E 6BT and London School of Economics, London WC2A 2AE, England

John Van Reenen

University College, London WC1E 6BT and Institute for Fiscal Studies, London WC1E 7AE, England

Abstract

The skill structure of wages and employment has altered markedly in recent years. In some countries (most notably the UK and the US) wage inequality has risen sharply and in most countries relative demand has shifted unfavourably against the less skilled. In this paper we reassess the evidence that rising international competition from developing countries is the crucial factor underpinning these changes. Our results, based on newly constructed internationally comparable industry data, find little support for the predictions of the basic Heckscher-Ohlin (H-O) trade model.

Keywords: International trade; skill differentials; skilled employment shares

JEL classification: J31; F14

I. Introduction

The skill structure of wages and employment has altered markedly in recent years. In some countries (like the UK and the US) the wages of skilled workers have risen sharply *vis-à-vis* their less skilled counterparts, despite increases in their relative employment. As such the wage bill shares of more

*We would like to thank Lupin Rahman for excellent research assistance and many people for help with data (especially Naercio Menezes-Filho for Brazil). We have received helpful comments from Joe Altonji, David Card, Torbjørn Hægeland, Alan Manning, John Schmitt, Steve Nickell, Tony Venables, Adrian Wood, three anonymous referees and participants in seminars in Berkeley, Essex, Prague, LSE, Northwestern, the Royal Economic Society Conference at Warwick, University of San Paolo, UCLA and at the conference on 'Competition and Industrial Policies in Open Economies' in Bergen. Financial assistance has come from the Leverhulme Trust and the ESRC. The usual disclaimer applies.

534   *T. Desjonqueres, S. Machin and J. Van Reenen*

skilled workers have risen. In other countries, where wage inequality has remained relatively stable (like France, Germany or Japan), employment seems to have shifted in favour of the skilled. Even in some developing countries this pattern seems to be present, suggesting that skill upgrading has been widespread across the world.

Several explanations have been offered for these shifts, but the dominant one today is that skill biased technological shocks have favoured the wages and employment of skilled workers, but have been detrimental to the wages and employment of the less skilled. Probably the commonest example of this is the introduction of computers in the workplace[1].

Despite a feeling among many people that increased international competition from developing countries should be important in explaining the observed shifts in wage and employment structure, there is currently not much evidence in favour of this view. For example, a number of authors have shown that the effects of rising international competition on the relative demand for skills is surprisingly small; see, among others, Lawrence and Slaughter (1993), Krugman and Lawrence (1993) and Sachs and Shatz (1994). Wood (1991, 1995) argues that the effects are larger, but even here his more recent work argues that trade expansion has more to do with the 1980s *acceleration* in skill upgrading, rather than skill upgrading itself; see Wood and Anderson (1998). Our reading is that there is currently little evidence in support of the idea that, at least up to the start of the 1990s, increased trade was key to the deteriorating labour market position of the less skilled.[2]

Evidence that is more in line with the trade hypothesis is Krueger's (1995) analysis of what he refers to as the 'price puzzle', which attempts to link product price changes to the skill intensity of employment in US industries. Based on 4-digit industry data between 1989 and 1995, he presents some evidence that price changes rose by less in the low skill intensive US industries whose products compete with imports from low wage developing countries. The 1989–95 period showed relatively little change in skill differentials, however, so it is unclear whether these results can be generalised to earlier periods.

In this paper we reassess this evidence. We try to give the trade based explanation of changing skill structures as much scope as possible by examining several different empirical implications of rising international

---

[1]Berman, Bound and Griliches (1994), Berman, Bound and Machin (1998), Johnson (1997), Machin (1996), Machin and Van Reenen (1998), Krueger, (1993) and Autor, Katz and Krueger (1998).

[2]For an alternative perspective and a rather different reading of existing empirical work, see Wood (1998) who presents various arguments that globalisation may be more important, both more recently and in terms of indirect trade effects (e.g. induced innovation).

© The editors of the *Scandinavian Journal of Economics* 1999.

trade for relative wage and employment shifts. In Section II we outline the simple trade model on which we base our empirical tests. Internationally comparable industry data is then used in the rest of the paper to evaluate the trade hypothesis in a number of ways. We set the scene in Section III by presenting simple descriptive statistics on shifts in skill structure and international competition in the manufacturing and non-manufacturing sectors of a number of countries. In Section IV we report in some detail on what we view as a relatively strong test of a fundamental implication of the basic trade approach. This involves looking at what has happened to the skill structure of wages and employment in disaggregated non-manufacturing non-traded sectors. Section V then looks at international evidence on the 'price puzzle' discussed above. In Section VI we examine shifts in labour market structure in a sample of developing countries. The evidence presented in the earlier sections is evaluated and interpreted in Section VII. Although there is some *prima facie* evidence from the common cross-country patterns of changes in industry imports, these do not stand up to more rigorous empirical testing. Our reading is that the international evidence does not lend much support to the notion that rising international competition from developing countries is the key factor behind the deteriorating labour market position of less skilled workers.

II. Empirical Implications of the Basic Heckscher-Ohlin Model

In this paper the trade model from which we derive empirical implications is the simple Heckscher-Ohlin (H-O) model. The H-O assumptions are strong, but we derive empirically testable predictions and then discuss the effects of varying the underlying assumptions. We draw heavily on the excellent exposition in Johnson and Stafford (1999). There are two regions in the world: the "North" is abundant in skilled labour (S) and the "South" is abundant in unskilled labour (U). There are four industries. Two are internationally traded at prices P_1 and P_2, industry 1 is skill intensive and industry 2 is unskilled intensive. The other industries are non-tradeables (industry 3 is skill intensive and industry 4 is unskilled intensive). Supply is exogenous, labour markets are competitive and products are perfectly substitutable between countries for the same product.

The production function is

$$Q_i = A_i F^i(S_i, U_i)$$

where i = industry 1, 2, 3, 4 and Q = output. A_i is a technology parameter which is assumed (for now) to be the same across all countries. F^i is linear homogeneous and the shares of skilled and unskilled labour in each industry are β_i and $(1 - \beta_i)$, respectively ($\beta_1 > \beta_2$ and $\beta_3 > \beta_4$).

536   *T. Desjonqueres, S. Machin and J. Van Reenen*

The Stolper-Samuelson theorem concerns the relationship between wages and product market prices. Consider a small economy in the North. Following Jones (1965) we start from the zero profit conditions $P_i Q_i - W_S S_i - W_U U_i = 0$ where W_S and W_U are the wage rates of skilled and unskilled workers, respectively. Totally differentiating the zero profit conditions, we have two equations determining the proportional changes ($\wedge$) in the two wage rates:

$$\hat{P}_1 + \hat{A}_1 = \beta_1 \hat{W}_S + (1 - \beta_1) \hat{W}_U$$

$$\hat{P}_2 + \hat{A}_2 = \beta_2 \hat{W}_S + (1 - \beta_2) \hat{W}_U.$$

This implies that the skilled/unskilled relative wage depends on the relative prices of the two goods and the technology parameters:

$$(\hat{W}_S / \hat{W}_U) = \frac{1}{\beta_1 - \beta_2} \left(\frac{\widehat{P_1 A_1}}{P_2 A_2} \right).$$

The removal of trade barriers with the South increases the relative price of skill intensive industries. This means that the relative wages of skilled workers will rise in the North. The opposite will happen in the South, relative prices of the skill intensive industries fall and this will tend to compress wage differentials. Finally, note that the move from autarky to free trade will mean that the North specialises in the skill intensive industries where it has a comparative advantage. There will be a between industry shift to skilled workers. The fact that skilled workers are relatively more expensive means that within industries there is substitution towards more unskilled workers.

The three main predictions that we examine are:

    I. there should be a between sector movement towards skilled workers and a within sector movement away from skilled workers;
   II. relative prices should fall in the unskilled industries; and
  III. wage differentials should fall in developing countries.

Note that an increase in the domestic supply of skills does not affect the relative wage as it would in a closed economy (the factor price insensitivity theorem). This is because wages are set on the world market and each country is small compared to the world. A country which expands its human capital stock will specialise more in skill intensive sectors. The skill intensity within each sector will not change. Some generalisations of the model do imply a role for skill supply. Allowing foreign and domestic versions of the tradeable good to be imperfect substitutes, for example, means that the labour demand curve is no longer horizontal. It is still the case, however, that falls in the world price of unskilled goods will follow reductions in trade barriers (prediction II). This will increase wage differentials unless the growth in the supply of skills is sufficiently large. Thus, one would still expect increases in the within industry proportion of the less skilled (prediction I).

Second, the model as stated assumes that all countries produce the two tradeable goods. It is possible that competition from the South might make it unprofitable for the North to produce anything in industry 2 (unskilled intensive tradeables). In this case we are outside the 'cone of diversification' and although P_1 is determined internationally, other product prices are determined domestically. The labour market resembles that of a closed economy where domestic skill supply will affect relative wages. Note, however, that changes in the world price of the export good have no effect on relative wages, so there is no more role for trade to increase wage inequality in this model.

Third, consider the relaxation of the assumption of perfect competition in the labour market. There are many ways to incorporate the effects of institutions into the model. Let us assume that minimum wages or trade unions prevent unskilled wages from falling below a certain level in the North; see Davis (1998). Opening up trade will still mean that relative prices fall in unskill intensive industries (prediction II) and that differentials fall in the South (prediction III). Low skilled industries where the minimum wage covered more workers would shrink substantially (and their workers be unemployed). Unless relative wages are completely rigid we would still expect to see some within industry movements towards unskilled workers.[3]

Fourth, what if we allow differential technologies in the North and South? Such models are considered by, *inter alia*, Wood (1994) and Krugman (1979). Differential technologies, by themselves, leave the basic structure of the theory the same. What matters is if there is a different rate of technological progress in different regions; see Davis (1998). For example, let the North produce in tradeable industries 1 and 2 (skilled and less skilled as before). The South produces in industry 2 and a very unskilled industry 5 (the North finds it unprofitable to produce in this industry). All countries produce in the two non-tradable industries 3 and 4. The production function is now

$$Q_{ij} = A_{ij} F^i(S_{ij}, U_{ij})$$

---

[3]Borjas and Ramey (1995) consider a model where unions share in product market rents which are bid away by trade. Union rent sharing is unlikely to be a feature of non-traded sectors where we examine skill upgrading in detail.

538   *T. Desjonqueres, S. Machin and J. Van Reenen*

where $i = 1, 2, 3, 4, 5$; $j = n$ (north) and s (south) and $A_{is} < A_{in}$. The assumptions about skill intensity imply $\beta_1 > \beta_2 > \beta_5$. An experiment we may wish to perform is to allow the South to have faster technological progress than the North – say allowing A_{2s} to rise towards A_{2n} due, say, to multinational investment in the South. This means that relative wages in the South will be given by[4]

$$(\widehat{W_{Ss}/W_{Us}}) = \frac{1}{\beta_{2s} - \beta_{5s}}(\hat{P}_2 + \hat{A}_2).$$

Falls in the price of the unskilled good P_2 following an opening up of trade have the usual effect of decreasing the wage differential in the South. The technological change also has the indirect effect of reducing prices, but this will be swamped by the direct effect of A_2 which increases wage relativities. So the upshot is that faster technological progress in the South could swamp prediction III above.

Finally, consider global technical change. Let us assume that we can parametrise the production function as

$$Q_i = A_i (b_i S_i)^{\beta i} U_i^{1-\beta i}.$$

where A_i is the skill neutral technical parameter, b_i is the quantity of efficiency units of skilled labour realised per unit of S_i (*intensive* skill biased technical change) and β_i increases when skilled workers get better at both skilled and unskilled tasks (*extensive* skill biased technical change). In the open economy case, we can take the logarithmic derivatives of the zero profit conditions allowing all three types of technology to vary. Holding relative prices constant we obtain

$$(\widehat{W_S/W_U}) = (\beta_1 - \beta_2)^{-1}$$

$$\times \left[(\hat{A}_1 - \hat{A}_2) + (\beta_1 \hat{b}_1 - \beta_2 \hat{b}_2) + \left(\ln\left(\frac{b_1 S_1}{U_1}\right) d\beta_1 - \ln\left(\frac{b_2 S_2}{U_2}\right) d\beta_2 \right) \right].$$

The qualitative effect of changes in A or β will depend on the sector bias of technical change as argued by Leamer (1994) and Haskel and Slaughter (1998). It is still the case, however, that intensive technical change (δ) in both tradeable sectors will increase wage inequality. One implication of this is that we should try to hold technical change constant when we look at whether prices have fallen in the less skilled industries (prediction II). A

---

[4]We are assuming Cobb Douglas preferences here.

second implication is that technical change may also be the reason why we observe within industry shifts (prediction I) and these overwhelm the trade effects.

These last two points emphasise what we can and cannot test. Both trade and technology can imply mandated higher wage inequality. Sufficiently large amounts of technical change could neutralise the predictions from the H-O model (I and III in particular). But this would suggest that technology rather than trade was the dominant force in shifting labour demand. It may be, as recently argued by Wood (1998), that trade has *accelerated* the demand for skilled workers since the 1980s. Testable implications of this view rest partially on whether prices have fallen particularly rapidly in the unskilled industries in the 1980s relative to previous periods (prediction II).

III. Descriptions of Changing Trade Patterns and Shifts in Skill Structure

Changing Trade Patterns and Shifts in Relative Employment in Manufacturing

Table 1 shows the changing pattern of trade with non-OECD countries in 1970 and 1990 in the manufacturing sectors of nine OECD countries.[5] Although the size of the flows remains relatively small, there are some large changes over time: for example, the imports/value of production ratio in the US more than quadrupled, going from 1.2 percent in 1970 to 5.4 percent by 1990.[6] At the same time, exports to non-OECD countries did not increase as rapidly.

A second observation reflects the tendency for the same industries across the OECD to have experienced the fastest increases in imports from developing countries. This can be seen by examining the upper panel of Table 2 which reports correlation coefficients for cross-country changes in non-OECD import intensity for the same 16 manufacturing industries[7]

---

[5]These numbers are computed from the OECD Bilateral Trade database. We stop in 1990 as our data on skill structure of wages and employment from the United Nations database that we use later also stop there. However, import shares have continued to rise post-1990. The 1994 import shares for the countries in the table are: Australia .084; Denmark .073; Finland .055; Germany .053; Japan .029; Sweden .051; UK .051; US .074.

[6]The only notable exception is Finland where it is probably the collapse of trade with Eastern Europe that distorts the non OECD import figure in 1990.

[7]The 16 sectors are the ones used in our earlier work as follows: Transport Goods; Chemicals, Electricity & Radio, TV & Communications; Food, Beverages & Tobacco; Iron & Steel; Metal Products; Non-Electrical Machinery; Non-ferrous Metals; Non-metallic Mineral Products; Other Manufacturing; Paper Products & Printing; Petroleum Refineries & Products; Professional Goods; Rubber & Plastic Goods; Textiles, Apparel & Leather; Wood Products and Furniture; see Machin and Van Reenen (1998).

540   *T. Desjonqueres, S. Machin and J. Van Reenen*

Table 1. *Trade patterns with non-OECD countries (manufacturing, 1970–1990)*

Country	Imports with non-OECD countries/ Value of production in manufacturing		Exports with non-OECD countries/Value of production in manufacturing	
	1970	1990	1970	1990
Australia (AU)	0.016	0.057	0.034	0.048
Denmark (DE)	0.037	0.060	0.054	0.071
Finland (FI)	0.049	0.037	0.068	0.078
France (FR)	0.018	0.037	0.044	0.059
Germany (GE)	0.018	0.038	0.036	0.051
Japan (JA)	0.012	0.027	0.040	0.049
Sweden (SW)	0.031	0.035	0.016	0.053
UK	0.026	0.044	0.049	0.049
US	0.012	0.054	0.018	0.040

Source: OECD Bilateral Trade Database and Standardised Analytical Database.

Table 2. *Cross-country correlations of industrial changes in trade patterns with non-OECD countries, 1970–1990*

Change in imports with non-OECD countries/Value of production (1970–1990)

	US	UK	GE	JA	SW	DE	AU
UK	0.91*						
GE	0.86*	0.93*					
JA	0.46	0.54*	0.63*				
SW	0.69*	0.74*	0.74*	0.16			
DE	0.64*	0.69*	0.67*	0.31	0.64*		
AU	0.70*	0.44	0.52*	0.16	0.65*	0.33	
FI	0.62*	0.55*	0.58*	−0.06	0.92*	0.62*	0.64*

Change in exports with non-OECD countries/Value of production (1970–1990)

	US	UK	GE	JA	SW	DE	AU
UK	0.02						
GE	0.25	0.61*					
JA	0.53*	0.22	−0.10				
SW	0.30	0.16	0.67*	−0.38			
DE	0.27	−0.14	0.03	−0.15	0.24		
AU	0.39	0.44	0.48	0.17	0.48	0.21	
FI	0.41	0.55*	0.58*	0.32	0.32	0.35	0.50*

Notes: Correlation coefficients are weighted by industry shares of total production (mean shares for each pairwise comparison). * denotes significant correlations at the 5 percent level.

between 1970 and 1990. Of the 28 pairwise comparisons, 27 have positive correlation coefficients and 21 of these are statistically significant at the 5 percent level or better.[8] However, the concentration of intertemporal changes in the same industries is not true of export intensity, where the cross-country industry correlations reported in the lower panel of the table show a much more mixed pattern (only six of the pairwise correlations are positive and statistically significant).

Since it is also the case that the proportion of skilled workers has generally risen in the same type of industries across different countries, as reported by e.g. Berman, Bound and Machin (1998), the fact that rising import intensities are concentrated in similar industries across countries might be viewed as *prima facie* evidence in favour of the trade hypothesis. This conclusion is not warranted, however. Deeper investigation reveals that the industries that have reduced their shares of unskilled workers most rapidly *are not the same ones* that have had the largest increases in imports from developing countries.

For our 16 manufacturing industries we have compiled data on changes in employment shares based on two measures of skill, the first based on the non-production/production classification, the second based on comparisons of high and low education workers.[9] The data used come from a variety of sources, with the non-production/production comparisons based on data from the United Nations Industrial Statistics Database (UNISD) and the education comparisons on micro-data sources in the relevant countries (e.g. in the UK they are based on Labour Force Survey data and in the US on Current Population Survey data). Table 3 reports simple regressions showing that, in almost all cases, there is actually a perversely signed negative (although typically statistically insignificant) association between the growth of skilled workers and the rise in imports from LDCs. If outsourcing were an important factor in explaining within industry skill upgrading we would expect a stronger positive association between import penetration and skills, see Feenstra and Hanson (1996).

This lack of correlation may not contradict the basic H-O approach. In general equilibrium there is a single economy-wide wage differential which moves in favour of the skilled when the economy opens up to trade. Within each industry there is a move away from unskilled workers. We therefore

---

[8]Similar patterns emerge if one looks at data from the United Nations Industrial Demand-Supply Database, although one cannot carry out identical computations as the definition of developing countries differs across the two datasets. In the UN database fewer countries are covered and the data only begin at the start of the 1980s.

[9]The precise definition of high/low education differs across countries according to the nature of the educational system. More details are given in the Data Appendix to Dejonqueres, Machin and Van Reenen (1998).

542   *T. Desjonqueres, S. Machin and J. Van Reenen*

Table 3. *Descriptive regions of changes in within-industry employment shares on changes in imports/value of production across industrialised countries*

	Dependent variable: within-industry component of change in white-collar employment share		Dependent variable: within-industry component of change in non-production employment share		Dependent variable: within-industry component of change in high education employment share	
	Coefficient (standard error) on change in imports with non-OECD countries/value of production					
	(1)	(2)	(3)	(4)	(5)	(6)
Australia	0.001 (0.002)		−0.008 (0.008)	−0.012 (0.008)		
Denmark	0.003 (0.002)					
Finland	−0.004 (0.003)	−0.004 (0.003)				
Germany	−0.009 (0.007)	−0.009 (0.007)			−0.001 (0.005)	−0.002 (0.005)
Japan			−0.000 (0.002)	0.000 (0.002)		
Sweden			−0.008 (0.008)	−0.012 (0.008)		
UK	−0.009 (0.005)	−0.010 (0.004)	−0.006 (0.003)*	−0.007 (0.003)*	−0.002 (0.003)	−0.003 (0.003)
US	−0.001 (0.001)	−0.001 (0.001)	−0.005 (0.003)*	−0.005 (0.002)*	−0.007 (0.005)	−0.007 (0.005)

Notes: Regressions (2), (4) and (6) include the change in log(value of production) as an independent variable. Standard errors are in parentheses. * denotes significant at the 5% level.

prefer to look at other ways of testing the H-O approach more rigorously in
the next section.

IV. Within-Industry Skill Shifts

Changes in Within-Industry Employment Shares

In some countries wage differentials tended to widen in the 1980s compared
to the 1970s. The 1980s rate of increase was far greater in the UK and the
US than elsewhere; see Machin (1996). However, in other countries (especially in continental Europe) wage differentials remained largely unchanged.
As noted above, a direct implication of wage differentials rising as a
response to an increase in international trade should be falls in within-
industry skilled employment shares.

The decomposition used to consider within and between changes in wage
and employment structure is by now standard; see Berman, Bound and
Griliches (1994). If S_j is the share of skill j workers in aggregate employment, the overall change in the skilled share can be decomposed into two
components, one due to the reallocation of employment *between* industries
with different proportions of skilled workers, the other due to changes in the
proportion of skilled workers *within* industries:

$$\Delta S_j = \sum_i \Delta E_i \overline{S}_{ji} + \sum_i \Delta S_{ji} \overline{E}_i \qquad (1)$$

where E_i denotes the (total) employment share of industry i in aggregate
employment and a bar indicates a simple average over time.

Figures 1 to 4 report the results of carrying out this decomposition for

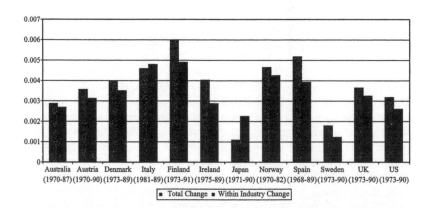

Fig. 1. Changes in a non-production/production employment shares in manufacturing

544   *T. Desjonqueres, S. Machin and J. Van Reenen*

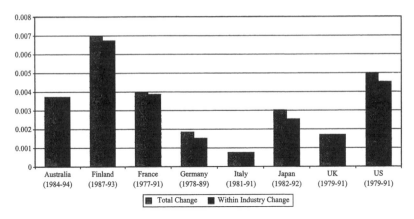

Fig.2 . Changes in high education employment shares in manufacturing

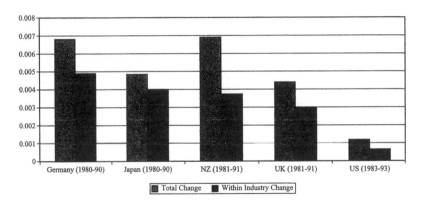

Fig. 3. Changes in non-production/production employment shares in non-manufacturing

different skill measures and for both manufacturing and non-manufacturing. The pattern is very clear. We observe evidence of important shifts toward an increased use of more skilled workers in the manufacturing sectors of all countries considered, regardless of their respective changes in wage differentials. This is true of comparisons based on non-production/production (Figure 1) or education based definitions of skill (Figure 2). Figures 3 and 4 repeat the analysis for non-manufacturing showing a similar pattern. If one takes the trade model presented earlier above at value, then the model predicts falls in within-industry skilled employment shares. This prediction is clearly not supported by the data.

© The editors of the *Scandinavian Journal of Economics* 1999.

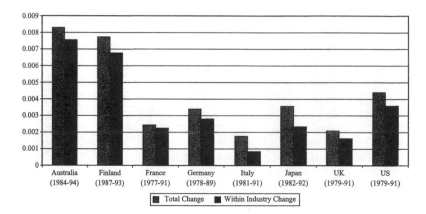

Fig. 4. Changes in high education employment shares in non-manufacturing

An obvious criticism of this is that each sector we use contains a mixture of heterogeneous industries. Some of these sectors are skill intensive and expanding, others are unskill intensive and contracting. By aggregating over the two we may mask the real within-industry fall in skill intensity within the more disaggregated industries. Although moving to a much more disaggregated level does not change the predominance of within effects,[10] some argue that even this level is too aggregated. To counter this view we next turn to what has happened in disaggregated non-traded sectors.

Changes in Within-Industry Employment Shares in Non-Traded Sectors

Rather than get involved in what is likely to be a difficult and probably irresolvable discussion about the appropriate level of (dis)aggregation, we prefer to take another route and examine the extent of shifts in skill structure in non-traded sectors. Taking the trade model in Section II seriously would imply that, in the absence of any other offsetting factors, there should be strong within-industry shifts in skill structure in non-traded industries towards the less skilled who, after an opening up to trade, are (relatively) much cheaper to employ. Yet it is striking, and very hard to rationalise in terms of the basic trade approach, that when looking at changes in within-

---

[10]We carried out decompositions of changes in high education employment shares for 299 UK industries and 227 US industries in the 1980s: the bulk of the increase in skill upgrading is within, rather than between, industries in both cases (68 percent in the UK, 91 percent in the US). Establishment level work also finds that the bulk of upgrading is within plant, see Haskel and Heden (1999) and Dunne, Haltiwanger and Troske (1996).

546   *T. Desjonqueres, S. Machin and J. Van Reenen*

industry skilled employment shares in non-traded sectors, one does observe skill upgrading.

Table 4 reports changes in education based employment shares and relative wages in a number of non-manufacturing industries that we characterise as non-traded for five countries (Brazil, Japan, Germany the UK and the US). These are the only countries for which we could get consistently defined industry data on employment and (in some cases) wages by skill within sectors over time.[11] Table 4 shows a pattern of relative increases in the employment shares of skilled workers in all of the industries we consider. This pattern of skill upgrading in non-traded sectors is very hard to reconcile with the pure trade based model.

Is this seemingly perverse pattern due to the fact that the general wage trends favourable to skilled workers are not present in these industries? It could be, for example, that skilled workers are unable to find employment in 'good jobs' and are therefore forced to take lower paid jobs in these nontraded sectors. The relative wage trends in Table 4 show that this cannot be the full story. Skilled wage differentials have generally risen in the non-traded industries at the same time as skilled employment shares. Shifts in relative demand in favour of the skilled have also occurred in disaggregated non-traded sectors. Trade alone seemingly cannot explain the extent of skill upgrading that has occurred over time.[12]

V. Investigating the 'Price Puzzle'

A necessary condition for the trade based explanation to hold is that import prices have fallen faster in the less skilled industries than in the more skilled industries over time. Existing evidence for this proposition is, at best, rather weak. Lawrence and Slaughter (1993) claimed to refute it, although Sachs and Schatz (1994), Krueger (1997) and Schmitt and Mishel (1996) have recently put forward more supportive evidence. All of this is based only on the US, however; recent exceptions are Fitzenberger (1996) and Neven and Wyplosz (1998). Table 5 reports evidence from a wider range of countries.

The basic regression price growth model we estimate is of the form:

$$\Delta \log(price_{it}) = \alpha + \beta SKILL_{i,t-1} + \varepsilon_{it} \qquad (2)$$

---

[11] Data no doubt exist for other countries but, at the time of writing, we did not have access to detailed micro-data on employment and wages at the disaggregated level over time for other countries.

[12] Of course, within-sector skill upgrading in non-traded sectors does not rule out trade as a contributing factor, merely that it cannot be the only important source of relative demand shifts in favour of the more skilled and that rather large offsetting effects from another factor are required if trade is important.

Table 4. *Changes in relative employment shares and wage differentials in disaggregated non-traded sectors*

Country	Industry	Time period	High education employment share		High/low education relative wage	
			Last period level	Change	Last period level	Change
Brazil	Personal & Household Services	1981–89	0.016	0.010	3.55	0.50
	Hotels & Restaurants	1981–89	0.044	0.019	3.79	1.31
	Wholesale Trade	1981–89	0.084	0.032	3.23	0.83
Germany	Personal & Household Services	1982–89	0.017	0.002	–	–
	Hotels & Restaurants	1982–89	0.031	0.010	–	–
	Wholesale Trade	1982–89	0.048	0.011	–	–
Japan	Hotels & Restaurants	1981–90	0.074	0.055	1.52	0.12
	Wholesale Trade	1981–90	0.114	0.043	1.26	0.01
UK	Personal & Household Services	1981–90	0.021	0.006	–	–
	Hotels & Restaurants	1981–90	0.021	0.005	–	–
	Wholesale Trade	1981–90	0.057	0.006	–	–
US	Personal & Household Services	1980–90	0.055	0.013	1.54	0.13
	Beauty Parlours & Hairdressers	1983–90	0.029	0.003	1.65	0.07
	Hotels & Restaurants	1983–90	0.085	0.024	2.22	−0.04
	Eating & Drinking Places	1983–90	0.066	0.005	2.08	0.16
	Wholesale Trade	1983–90	0.22	0.08	1.87	0.11

Notes: Calculated from country-specific sources – Brazil, National Survey of Households (Pesquisa Nacional Amostra de Domicilios); Germany, Mikrozensus; Japan, Japanese Wage Survey; UK, Labour Force Survey; US, Current Population Survey. The high education classification denotes workers with a degree or higher.

548   T. Desjonqueres, S. Machin and J. Van Reenen

Table 5. Regressons of industry price changes on initial skilled employment shares

	Coefficient on proportion of non-production workers in initial year						Coefficient on proportion of highly educated workers in initial year					
	No computer dummy			Computer dummy			No computer dummy			Computer dummy		
	74–89 (1)	74–80 (2)	80–89 (3)	74–89 (4)	74–80 (5)	80–89 (6)	74–89 (7)	74–80 (8)	80–89 (9)	74–89 (10)	74–80 (11)	80–89 (12)
PANEL A: Dependent variable: Product prices												
UK	-0.0001 (0.0006)	0.0012 (0.001)	-0.0009 (0.0005)	-0.0006 (0.0005)	0.0003 (0.0010)	-0.0011 (0.0006)			-0.0032* (0.0015)			-0.0035* (0.0016)
GE	-0.0007 (0.0008)	-0.0029 (0.0014)	0.0001 (0.0008)	-0.0002 (0.0008)	-0.0016 (0.0013)	0.0003 (0.0009)			-0.0035 (0.0020)			-0.0036 (0.0020)
JA	0.0000 (0.0022)	0.0018 (0.0031)	-0.0013 (0.0008)	0.0001 (0.0023)	0.0022 (0.0032)	-0.0014 (0.0009)			-0.0025 (0.0016)			-0.0026 (0.0017)
US	0.0009* (0.0004)	0.0016* (0.0007)	0.0001 (0.0007)	0.0011* (0.0002)	0.0014* (0.0007)	0.0006 (0.0005)			-0.0004 (0.0012)			0.0001 (0.0008)
DE	0.0007 (0.0006)	0.0003 (0.0011)	0.0007 (0.0004)	0.0006 (0.0006)	0.0003 (0.0011)	0.0006 (0.0005)						
SW	-0.0002 (0.0008)	0.0002 (0.0009)	-0.0006 (0.0007)	-0.0002 (0.0009)	-0.0001 (0.0009)	-0.0006 (0.0008)						

(continued over)

PANEL B: Dependent variable: Effective prices

UK	0.0000	0.0014	-0.0010	-0.0006	0.0002	-0.0013	-0.0033	-0.0037
	(0.0007)	(0.0020)	(0.0008)	(0.0007)	(0.0019)	(0.0009)	(0.0026)	(0.0028)
GE	0.0001	-0.0036*	0.0012	0.0005	-0.0025	0.0015	-0.0008	-0.0009
	(0.0009)	(0.0015)	(0.0009)	(0.0009)	(0.0015)	(0.0010)	(0.0028)	(0.0030)
JA	0.0022	0.0046	-0.0013	0.0023	0.0048	-0.0013	-0.0028	-0.0027
	(0.0027)	(0.0034)	(0.0014)	(0.0029)	(0.0036)	(0.0015)	(0.0027)	(0.0029)
US	0.0014*	0.0019	0.0006	0.0016*	0.0018	0.0013*	0.0005	0.0013
	(0.0005)	(0.0010)	(0.0010)	(0.0003)	(0.0010)	(0.0006)	(0.0016)	(0.0011))
DE	0.0007	0.0003	0.0007	0.0006	0.0002	0.0008		
	(0.0006)	(0.0013)	(0.0006)	(0.0006)	(0.0013)	(0.0006)		
SW	0.0001	0.0007	-0.0008	0.0000	0.0001	-0.0007		
	(0.0010)	(0.0014)	(0.0010)	(0.0011)	(0.0015)	(0.0011)		

PANEL C: Dependent variable: TFP growth

UK	0.0001	0.0001	0.0000	-0.0002	-0.0001		0.0003	0.0002
	(0.0003)	(0.010)	(0.0006)	(0.0003)	(0.0011)	(0.0007)	(0.0018)	(0.0020)
GE	0.0007	-0.0007	0.0012	0.0007	-0.0008	0.0011	0.0030	0.0031
	(0.0005)	(0.0006)	(0.0007)	(0.0006)	(0.0007)	(0.0008)	(0.0017)	(0.0016)
JA	0.0018*	0.0028*	0.0001	0.0018*	0.0026*	0.0002	-0.0001	0.0001
	(0.0006)	(0.0010)	(0.0006)	(0.0007)	(0.0010)	(0.0006)	(0.0012)	(0.0013)
US	0.0005	0.0004	0.0005	0.0005	0.0004	0.0006	0.0009	0.0011
	(0.0003)	(0.0004)	(0.0003)	(0.0003)	(0.0004)	(0.0004)	(0.0007)	(0.0006)
DE	0.0002	0.0004	0.0001	0.0002	0.0004	0.0001		
	(0.0002)	(0.0006)	(0.0003)	(0.0002)	(0.0006)	(0.0003)		
SW	0.0002	0.0005	0.0000	0.0002	0.0002	0.0000		
	(0.0004)	(0.0007)	(0.0005)	(0.0004)	(0.0007)	(0.0005)		

Notes: * Denotes significant at the 5% level. All equations are weighted by employment shares; Germany (1977 to 1989) and Japan (1974 to 1987).

where $price_{it}$ is prices in industry i in period t, $SKILL_{i,t-1}$ is the proportion of skilled workers in the initial year $(t-1)$ and ε_{it} is an error term.

In Table 5 we report estimates of β from a wide range of simple regressions using the specification in equation (2). These estimated equations measure skill in terms of the employment share of both non-production workers and highly educated workers for a number of time periods. In panel A the dependent variable is the average annual change in industry prices. Because of the very different evolution of prices in the computer industry, a dummy variable equal to 1 for that industry and 0 elsewhere is included in the regressions in columns (4) through (6) and column (12). The results in panel A show that, for all countries except the US, the coefficient on the skills variable is statistically insignificant (and in some cases the estimated coefficient on the initial skill level variable is actually negative). Only in the US can we pin down any positive, statistically significant relationship between price increases and industry initial skill intensity. This analysis may, be misleading, however, if low price increases in some high skilled industries are due to the fact that high skilled industries experienced a faster rate of technological progress and therefore had faster falls in price. These falls in price are probably not due to trade (although Wood (1994) argues that trade induced innovation may be important) and may disguise a 'true' positive relationship between skills and relative prices. Indeed, in the lowest panel, (C), we see that there is indeed a positive correlation between the skill level of the industry and its rate of technological progress as proxied by total factor productivity (TFP).

Panel B follows Leamer (1994) and others in constructing an index of effective prices (actual prices + an estimate of TFP).[13] The average change in this index is then used instead of actual product prices. This change does cause the estimated coefficient on initial skills to become positive as the trade model predicts. Nevertheless, the coefficient is statistically insignificant for all countries except the US. Furthermore, even in the US, falls in producer prices do not appear to be faster in the 1980s than the 1970s.

VI. Evidence from non-OECD Countries

The key premise of the Heckscher-Ohlin/Stolper-Samuelson approach is that high skill and low skill intensive countries should specialise in producing goods and services using the type of labour with which they are most endowed. So, labour market responses to trade should work in opposite

---

[13]Although theoretically more appropriate, TFP is notoriously difficult to measure. As is standard, we assumed that labour's share in value added was 0.7, capital's 0.3 and used these for the weights across all observations. The qualitative nature of the results was preserved in experiments with other methods (e.g. using the actual industry-country specific weights).

directions in high and low skill intensive countries. We now extend this logic to present some descriptive statistics on shifts in relative wage differentials and employment structure in the manufacturing sectors of developing countries. In what follows we find little systematic evidence of shifts in wage and employment structure in developing countries that move in the opposite direction to the industrialized nations.

Table 6 reports changes in skilled wage differentials in (a small number of) developing countries: Brazil, Chile, Colombia, India and Pakistan. There is a rather mixed pattern of changes. Non-production/production worker wage differentials rise in Chile and (in the 1980s) in Pakistan, they fall in Colombia and are more-or-less constant in Brazil and India.

On the other hand, Table 7 shows that the employment shares of non-production workers rise in five of the six countries and, like the developed countries considered earlier, the bulk of the shifts is occurring within industries.[14] The same is true for the only country on which we have education data (Brazil). Consistent with the trade hypothesis there is a negative between-industry contribution (and positive within effects) in three of the countries (Brazil, Chile and Pakistan). Three others contradict the basic trade perspective and there is a positive between-industry contribution.

Table 6. *Changes in wage differentials in developing countries (manufacturing)*

Changes in non-production/production wage differentials

	1970	1975	1980	1985	1990
Brazil	–	–	2.01 (1981)	1.96	1.98
Chile	2.16 (1973)	2.39	3.07	3.38	3.43 (1986)
Columbia	2.33 (1973)	2.27	1.93	1.77	1.89
India	–	–	2.04	2.02	2.07 (1987)
Pakistan	–	1.37 (1978)	1.22	1.32	1.52 (1988)

Changes in high education/low education wage differentials

	1970	1975	1980	1985	1900
Brazil	–	–	3.75 (1981)	3.68	3.61 (1989)

Sources: Non-production/production wage differentials for Chile, Columbia, Ecuador, India and Pakistan: United Nations Industrial Statistics Database; Brazil: Brazilian Annual Household Survey (PNAD) – employees in the formal sector only are included.

---

[14]The within-industry comparisons are based on the same 16 manufacturing sectors as used in the earlier analysis and described in footnote 7.

552   *T. Desjonqueres, S. Machin and J. Van Reenen*

Table 7. *Changes in relative employment shares in developing countries (manufacturing)*

Changes in non-production/production employment shares

	Time period	Shares in last year	Total change	Within industry	Percent within
Brazil	1981–89	0.286	0.0047	0.0067	143.5
Chile	1973–86	0.264	0.0371	0.0410	112.9
Columbia	1973–90	0.327	0.1055	0.0845	80.2
Ecuador	1970–90	0.286	0.940	0.0852	90.7
India	1980–87	0.210	0.0060	0.0039	38.4
Pakistan	1978–88	0.215	−0.0346	−0.0422	122.1

Changes in high education employment shares

	Time period	Shares in last year	Total change	Within industry	Percent within
Brazil	1981–89	0.104	0.0172	0.0174	101.0

Sources: Non-production employment shares for Chile, Colombia, Ecuador, India and Pakistan: United Nations Industrial Statistics Datablase; Brazil: Brazilian Annual Household Survey (PNAD) – employees in the formal sector only are included.

VII. Conclusions

It is commonplace to hear the statement that globalisation is leading to the demise of unskilled workers. Although empirical work by labour economists has generally not found much evidence for the importance of direct trade effects, some of their methods have recently come under criticism. In this paper we have tried to tackle some of the issues directly by examining several pieces of evidence in an attempt to support a trade based explanation for the declining labour market fortunes of the less skilled. For this purpose we have gathered a large amount of industry data from a number of different countries rather than relying on the experience of just one nation.

On the whole our conclusion must be that the trends in the data are rather unfavourable to the pure trade explanation. Even within narrowly defined non-traded sectors there is a shift towards the use of more skilled workers despite their increased relative wages. Furthermore, the trends in developing countries do not appear to go in the expected direction. The most we could find in favour of the trade story was related to some US results showing that imports from non-OECD countries and movements in product prices are consistent with increasing competition from less developed countries reducing relative prices in low skilled industries. Even here, however, we cannot find such a mechanism operating outside the US.

The next stage of research in this area requires acknowledging more fully the interactions between competing explanations.[15] This would involve the development of econometric models incorporating technology, trade and institutional effects in an interactive manner (i.e., rather than looking for effects from each as a single factor). It may be that better measurements of quality-adjusted prices or trade-induced technological progress will help shore up the globalisation thesis. The current state of knowledge does suggest, however, that at least up to the start of the 1990s, increased trade with developing countries, unless augmented by one or more of the other relevant competing hypotheses, has only had a minor influence on the growth of earnings and employment inequality in the OECD.

References

Aghion, P., Howitt, P. and Violante, G. (1999), Technology, Knowledge and Inequality, mimeo, University College London.

Autor, D., Katz, L. F. and Krueger, A. (1998), Computing Inequality: Have Computers Changed the Labor market?, *Quarterly Journal of Economics 113*, 1169–1215.

Berman, E., Bound, J. and Griliches, Z. (1994), Changes in the Demand for Skilled Labor within US Manufacturing Industries: Evidence from the Annual Survey of Manufacturing, *Quarterly Journal of Economics 109*, 367–98.

Berman, E., Bound, J. and Machin, S. (1998), Implications of Skill Biased Technological Change: International Evidence, *Quarterly Journal of Economics 113*, 1245–80.

Borjas, G. and Ramey, V. (1995), Foreign Competition, Market Power and Wage Inequality, *Quarterly Journal of Economics 110*(4), 246–61.

Davis, D. (1998a), Does European Unemployment Prop up American Wages? National Labour Markets and Global Trade, *American Economic Review 88*(3), 748–494.

Davis, D. (1998b), Technology, Unemployment and Relative Wages in Global Economy, *European Economic Review 42*(9), 1613–1633.

Desjonqueres, T., Machin, S. and Van Reenen, J. (1998), Another Nail in the coffin? The Labour Market Consequences of Technical and Structural Change, Discussion Paper Series no. 34, Oxford Institute of Economics and Statistics.

Dewatripont, M., Sapir, A. and Sekkat, K. (1998), *Trade and Jobs in Europe: Much Ado about Nothing?*, Clarendon Press, Oxford.

Dunne, T., Haltiwanger, J. and Troske, K. (1996), Technology and Jobs: Secular Changes and Cyclical Dynamics, NBER Working Paper no. 5656.

Feenstra, R. and Hanson, G. (1996), Globalization, Outsourcing and Wage Inequality, *American Economic Review Papers and Proceedings 86*, 240–45.

Fitzenberger, B. (1996), Wages, Prices and International Trade: Trends across Industries for an Export Champion, Discussion Paper II-323, University of Konstanz.

Freeman, R. (1995), Are Your Wages Set in Beijing?, *Journal of Economic Perspectives 9* (Summer), 15–32.

Freeman, R. and Revenga, A. (1998), How Much has LDC Trade Affected Western Job Markets?, in M. Dewatripont, A. Sapir and K. Sekket (eds.), *Trade and Jobs in Europe: Much Ado about Nothing*, Clarendon Press, Oxford.

---

[15]Theory has made some advances in this direction; see Aghion, Howitt and Violante (1999) and Davis (1998a,b).

554   *T. Desjonqueres, S. Machin and J. Van Reenen*

Haskel, J. and Heden, Y. (1999) Computers and the Demand for Skilled Labour: Industry and Establishment Level Panel Evidence for the UK, *Economic Journal* 109, C68–C79.

Haskel, J. and Slaughter, L. (1998), Does the Sector Bias of Skill Biased Technological Change Explain Changing Wage Inequality?, mimeo, Dartmouth College.

Johnson, G. (1997), Changes in Earnings Inequality: The Role of Demand Shifts, *Journal of Economic Perspectives* 11 (Spring), 41–54.

Johnson, G. and Stafford, F. (1998), The Labour Market Implications of International Trade, forthcoming in O. Ashenfelter and D. Card (eds.), *Handbook of Labor Economics*, North Holland, Amsterdam.

Krueger, A. (1993), How Computers have Changed the Wage Structure, *Quarterly Journal of Economics* 108, 33–60.

Krueger, A. (1995), Labour Market Shifts and the Price Puzzle Revisited, mimeo, Princeton University.

Lawrence, R. and Slaughter, M. (1993), International Trade and US Wages in the 1980s: Great Sucking Sound or Small Hiccup, *Brookings Papers on Economic Activity*, 161–227.

Leamer, E. (1994), Trade, Wages and Revolving Door Ideas, NBER Working Paper no. 4716.

Machin, S. (1996), Changes in the Relative Demand for Skills in the UK Labour Market, in A. Booth and D. Snower (eds.), *The Skills Gap and Economic Activity*, Cambridge University Press, Cambridge.

Machin, S. and Van Reenen, J. (1998), Technology and Changes in Skill Structure: Evidence from Seven OECD Countries, *Quarterly Journal of Economics* 113, 1215–44.

Minford, P., Riley, J. and Nowell, E. (1995), Trade, Technology and Development in the World Economy, *Journal of Development Studies 34*, 2, 1–34.

Nickell, S. and Bell, B. (1995), The Collapse in Demand for the Unskilled and Unemployment across the OECD, *Oxford Review of Economic Policy 11*, 40–62.

Neven, D. and Wyplosz, C. (1998), Relative Prices, Trade and Restructuring in European Industry in M. Dewatripont, A. Sapir and K. Sekket (eds), *Trade and Jobs in Europe: Much Ado about Nothing*, Clarendon Press, Oxford.

Sachs, J. and Shatz, H. (1994), Trade and Jobs in US Manufacturing, *Brookings Papers on Economic Activity*, 1–84.

Schmitt, J. and Mishel, L. (1996), Did International Trade Lower Less-skilled Wages during the 1980s? Standard Trade Theory and Evidence, mimeo, Economic Policy Institute, Washington, DC.

Wood, A. (1991), How Much does Trade with the South Affect Workers in the North?, *World Bank Research Observer 6*, 19–36.

Wood, A. (1994), *North-South Trade, Employment and Inequality, Changing Fortunes in a Skill-Driven World*, Clarendon Press, Oxford.

Wood, A. (1998), Globalization and the Rise in Labour Market Inequalities, *Economic Journal 108*, 1463–1482.

Wood, A. and Anderson, E. (1998), Does Heckscher-Ohlin Theory Explain why the Demand for Unskilled Labour in the North First Accelerated then Decelerated? mimeo, Institute for Development Studies, University of Sussex.

[5]

Immigrant Inflows, Native Outflows, and the Local Labor Market Impacts of Higher Immigration

David Card, *University of California, Berkeley*

This article uses 1990 census data to study the effects of immigrant inflows on occupation-specific labor market outcomes. I find that intercity mobility rates of natives and earlier immigrants are insensitive to immigrant inflows. However, occupation-specific wages and employment rates are systematically lower in cities with higher relative supplies of workers in a given occupation. The results imply that immigrant inflows over the 1980s reduced wages and employment rates of low-skilled natives in traditional gateway cities like Miami and Los Angeles by 1–3 percentage points.

Over the past 3 decades, immigration rates into the United States have risen while the real wages of younger and less-educated workers have fallen (Levy and Murnane 1992). Despite the coincidental timing, a growing body of research finds only modest evidence that immigrant competition has hurt the labor market opportunities of low-wage natives. A series of studies has correlated the fraction of immigrants in different

The first draft of this article was written while I was a fellow at the Center for Advanced Study in the Behavioral Sciences in Stanford, California (CASBS). I am grateful to the National Science Foundation, for fellowship support at the CASBS, and to the Industrial Relations Section of Princeton University and the Center for Labor Economics at Berkeley, for research support. Thanks to seminar participants at Berkeley, University of California at Los Angeles, and the Public Policy Institute of California, for helpful comments, and to Michael Greenstone, Gena Estes, and Ethan Lewis, for outstanding research assistance.

[*Journal of Labor Economics*, 2001, vol. 19, no. 1]

cities with native wages, employment rates, and unemployment rates.[1] Typically, a 10-percentage-point increase in the fraction of immigrants (roughly the difference between Detroit and Houston) is estimated to reduce native wages by no more than 1 percentage point. This evidence seems to confirm the rather surprising experiences of Miami in the aftermath of the 1980 Mariel boatlift. Although the boatlift instantaneously raised the fraction of low-skilled workers in the Miami labor force, there was no discernable effect on wages or unemployment rates of less-skilled natives in the city (Card 1990).

Nevertheless, the entire strategy of estimating the impact of immigration by comparing labor market outcomes across cities has come under attack, most notably by Borjas, Freeman, and Katz (1992, 1996) and Borjas (1994). There are three key conceptual problems in the cross-market approach: (1) an increase in the fraction of immigrants in a city does not necessarily raise the supply of low-skilled labor, since natives may move out in response to immigrant inflows; (2) the cross-sectional correlation between immigrant inflows and native wages may be upward-biased by local demand shocks that raise wages and attract in-migrants; (3) in the long run, an immigration-induced increase in the supply of labor to a particular city can be diffused across the economy by intercity trade. In light of these problems, Borjas et al. (1992, 1996) and Borjas (1994) downplay findings from the cross-market studies, and they rely instead on a priori theoretical models to deduce the effects of immigration on native opportunities.[2]

In this article I attempt to reassess the effect of immigration on the local labor market opportunities of native workers while addressing some of the limitations of earlier cross-market studies. My starting point is a recognition of the enormous heterogeneity in the population of U.S. immigrants. As noted by Butcher and DiNardo (1998), an average immigrant worker is only slightly less skilled than an average native worker. In many cities, immigrants actually earn higher wages than natives. For example, in 66 of the 175 major cities analyzed below, the mean log hourly wage of immigrant men (based on data from the 1990 census) is higher than the mean log hourly wage of native-born men.[3] Given this heterogeneity, the overall fraction of immi-

---

[1] For recent surveys of this literature, see Borjas (1994) and Friedberg and Hunt (1995). Grossman (1982) is one of the earliest studies of immigrant impacts on local labor markets. Subsequent research includes Borjas (1987); Altonji and Card (1991); and Schoeni (1996). LaLonde and Topel (1991) use a somewhat different strategy that is closer in spirit to the analysis here.

[2] A similar approach is followed by Jaeger (1995) who simulates the effects of immigration on the relative wages of different education groups under various assumptions about technology.

[3] Cities where immigrant men earn more than native men include Baltimore, Buffalo, Cincinnati, Cleveland, Louisville, Memphis, St. Louis, and Wilmington.

grants in a city is simply too crude an index of immigrant competition for any particular subgroup of natives.

To proceed, I make the simplifying assumption that local labor markets are stratified along occupation lines. Assuming a constant elasticity of substitution (CES) technology, the fraction of a city's population who would normally be expected to work in a given occupation provides a summary measure of relative local labor market competition facing that group. Within this framework, immigrant inflows affect the structure of wages by raising or lowering the relative population shares of different occupation groups. An inflow of immigrants that raises the fraction of the population in a particular group would be expected to put downward pressure on wages and employment rates for workers in the group. On the other hand, a balanced inflow of immigrants that leaves the relative population shares unchanged would not be expected to affect the relative wage structure.

This framework also clarifies the role of mobility in offsetting the effects of immigrant inflows. In the absence of offsetting mobility flows, each newly arriving immigrant in a particular occupation group adds one person to the local population of that group. To the extent that immigrant inflows lead to outflows of natives or earlier immigrants in the same skill group, however, each newly arriving immigrant contributes less than one person to the net population of his or her skill group.

To operationalize the notion of occupation-specific labor markets, while recognizing that individuals have some flexibility in choosing occupations, I assign nationally based probabilities for working in different occupations to each person. These probabilities are estimated for a standardized national labor market, using observed characteristics such as education, age, ethnicity, and country of origin. The local supply of workers in a given occupation is defined as the sum of the probabilities for working in that occupation across all individuals in the local labor market. Conceptually, this is an estimate of the number of people who would be expected to work in the occupation in the absence of any distortions caused by local demand or supply pressures. Similarly, city-specific wages and employment rates for the occupation group are defined as weighted averages across all individuals in the local labor market, using the occupation-specific probabilities as weights.[4]

A second novel feature of the analysis in this article is a focus on recent immigrants—individuals who have moved to the United States within the past 5 years. This focus is motivated by two considerations. First, as will be shown below, recent immigrants are concentrated in the same occu-

---

[4] This procedure is a generalization of the more standard procedure of assigning each individual to a specific skill group with a probability of one.

Impacts of Immigration   25

pations as low-skilled native workers. Much of the policy concern over
higher immigration is, therefore, naturally directed toward the labor
market impacts of newly arrived immigrants. Second, because many
newly arriving immigrants settle in enclaves established by earlier immigrants from the same source countries, it is possible to develop a measure
of the supply-push component of recent immigrant inflows to a particular
city that is arguably exogenous to local demand conditions. Such a
measure is needed to identify the causal effect of immigrant inflows in the
presence of unobserved city- and skill-group-specific demand shocks.

I. Theoretical Framework

A useful benchmark model for analyzing the effect of relative supplies
of different skill groups on the structure of wages is one with a single
output good in each city. Assume that output in city c (Y_c) is produced
by a competitive industry with a production function

$$Y_c = F(K_c, L_c),$$

where K_c is a vector of nonlabor inputs (capital, etc.) and L_c is a CES-type
aggregate of the quantities of labor N_{jc} in various skill categories or
occupations $j = 1, \ldots J$:

$$L_c = [\Sigma_j (e_{jc} N_{jc})^{(\sigma-1)/\sigma}]^{\sigma/(\sigma-1)}.$$

For the moment, assume that individuals are assigned to unique occupations and ignore any variation in hours per worker, so N_{jc} is just a count
of the number of individuals in occupation group j employed in city c.
The variables e_{jc} represent city- and occupation-specific productivity
shocks, while the parameter σ is the elasticity of substitution between
different occupations. If w_{jc} represents the wage rate of occupation group
j in city c and q_c is the selling price of output from city c, then the
first-order condition that equates the marginal product of an occupation
group with its real product wage can be written as

$$\log N_{jc} = \theta_c + (\sigma - 1) \log e_{jc} - \sigma \log w_{jc}, \qquad (1)$$

where $\theta_c = \sigma \log [q_c F_L(K_c, L_c) L_c^{1/\sigma}]$ represents a common city-specific
component shared by all groups. Although equation (1) is not a proper
labor demand function, it nonetheless captures the effect of the local wage
structure on the relative demands for different occupations, holding
constant citywide factors.

Let P_{jc} represent the population of individuals in occupation j in city c,

26   Card

and assume that the labor supply function (or participation function) for
the group is log-linear:

$$\log (N_{jc}/P_{jc}) = \varepsilon \log w_{jo} \qquad (2)$$

where $\varepsilon > 0$. Equations (1) and (2) lead to the following expressions for
the wage rate and employment-population rate of occupation j in city c:

$$\log w_{jc} = 1/(\varepsilon + \sigma)\{(\theta_c - \log P_c)$$
$$+ (\sigma - 1) \log e_{jc} - \log (P_{jc}/P_c)\}, \qquad (3)$$

$$\log (N_{jc}/P_{jc}) = \varepsilon/(\varepsilon + \sigma)\{(\theta_c - \log P_c)$$
$$+ (\sigma - 1) \log e_{jc} - \log (P_{jc}/P_c)\}, \qquad (4)$$

where P_c is the total population in city c. These equations show that
wages and employment rates are determined by three factors: a common
city-specific component, an occupation and city-specific productivity
component, and the relative population shares of the groups. The CES
functional form implies that each group's relative wage depends only on
its population share and on the group-specific productivity component.

Equations (3) and (4) are used as the basis for the empirical work in this
article. I assume that the productivity component can be decomposed as

$$\log e_{jc} = e_j + e_c + e_{jc}',$$

where e_j represents a common occupation effect, e_c is a city-effect, and
e_{jc}' represents an occupation and city-specific productivity term. Let f_{jc}
$= P_{jc}/P_c$ denote the fraction of the population of city c in occupation
group j. Then equations (3) and (4) lead to simple regression models of
the form

$$\log w_{jc} = u_j + u_c + d_1 \log f_{jc} + u_{jc} \qquad (3')$$

and

$$\log (N_{jc}/P_{jc}) = v_j + v_c + d_2 \log f_{jc} + v_{jc}, \qquad (4')$$

where u_j, v_j, u_c, and v_c are occupation- and city-fixed effects, u_{jc} and v_{jc}
are unobserved error components that depend on e_{jc}' (and other factors,
such as sampling errors), and the coefficients d_1 and d_2 are functions of
the elasticities of substitution and supply: $d_1 = -1/(\varepsilon + \sigma)$; $d_2 = -\varepsilon/(\varepsilon + \sigma)$. City fixed effects absorb any citywide variables that might otherwise influence the levels of wages or employment in the local labor

market.[5] Any occupation-specific local productivity shocks, however, remain in the error terms. To the extent that local productivity shocks raise wages and lead to an increase in the population of a particular occupation group, the error components in equations (3′) and (4′) will be positively correlated with the population shares, leading to positive biases in the estimates of d_1 and d_2. This bias can be reduced or eliminated if there is an instrumental variable that is correlated with f_{jc} but uncorrelated with the city- and occupation-specific productivity shock. As discussed in more detail below, the supply-push component of the immigrant inflows to a particular city, which is based on historical settlement patterns and the total number of newly arriving immigrants from different source countries, is a potential candidate for such an instrumental variable.

The assumption that all individuals in a given occupation supply the same units of labor and earn the same wage is obviously quite restrictive, and this is unlikely to hold when men and women are pooled in the same occupations (as they are below). In an earlier version of this article (Card 1997), I showed how this assumption can be relaxed by assuming that different demographic subgroups within each occupation are perfect substitutes in production but supply different efficiency units of labor (e.g., by working more hours per period) or have different intercepts in their labor supply functions. This assumption leads to versions of equations (3) and (4) that depend on an adjusted count of the relative populations of different occupation groups, where the adjustment factors vary by demographic subgroup within occupations, reflecting differences in the relative efficiency and relative tastes of different subgroups. It is important to note that if the subgroup composition of different occupations is roughly constant across cities, then the adjustment factors will be constant, and equations (3′) and (4′) will continue to hold with a reinterpretation of the occupation-specific fixed effects. Otherwise, it is necessary to estimate the relative adjustment factors using data on per capita earnings for each subgroup in a given occupation.

Limitations of the Model

Before proceeding to the data analysis, it is useful to underscore the limitations of the theoretical framework underlying equations (3) and (4). Perhaps the most important limitation is the assumption of one output good. More generally, the demand for labor in a city is generated by many

[5] Many previous studies (e.g., Altonji and Card 1991; Schoeni 1996) focus on a single skill group in each city and therefore rely on longitudinal data to eliminate permanent city effects. Lalonde and Topel (1991) compare the relative wages of different cohorts of immigrants within cities: their approach is, therefore, quite similar to the one in this article.

different industries, some of which produce goods or services that can be exported to other cities. In this situation, the impact of an increase in the relative fraction of the population in a given skill group can be mitigated by the expansion of export industries that use the relatively abundant skill-group more intensively.[6] Such an endogenous shift in industry structure is observationally equivalent to occupation-specific local demand shocks that are positively correlated with the relative supplies of different occupation groups. However, since the market signal that triggers an endogenous change in local industry structure is a shift in relative wages, one would expect an exogenous rise in the local population share of a given occupation group to exert at least a short-run impact on wages.

In particular, consider the responses of different local labor markets to inflows of new immigrants over the 1980s. Given the unprecedented magnitude of these flows, it seems unlikely that employers could have adjusted their product mixes and capital stocks to fully accommodate the shifts in relative labor supplies. Nevertheless, employers in some immigrant gateway cities could have anticipated some fraction of the relative supply shifts that actually occurred, leading to some specialization and a lessening of impacts on the relative wage structure. Ordinary least squares estimates of the effects of relative population shares derived from equations (3') and (4') are, therefore, likely to be smaller in magnitude than the effects that would arise with a fixed industry structure, but they are likely to be larger than the effects that would emerge in the very long run if the industry structure could fully adjust. Instrumental variable estimates based on exogenous short-run supply shifts (such as the supply-push component of immigrant inflows to each city) should be larger in magnitude and closer to the parameter values that would arise with a fixed industry structure.

A second limitation of the model is the assumption (arising from the CES functional form) that the relative wage of a particular skill group depends only on the relative population share of that group. This assump-

---

[6] Standard trade theory results imply that if each industry has the same production function in all cities, there are enough different tradeable goods with sufficiently diverse production technologies, and relative supplies of different skill groups are not too unbalanced, then in the long run one would expect the same wages in all cities regardless of the skill proportions in particular labor markets. See Johnson and Stafford (1999) and Leamer (1995) for rigorous statements. There is surprisingly little evidence on the extent of product-mix specialization at the city level. Altonji and Card (1991) show that low-wage manufacturing industries increased their relative employment shares between 1970 and 1980 in high-immigrant cities relative to low-immigrant cities. The actual changes in the levels of employment in these industries, however, are small (and in some cases even negative), suggesting that low-wage manufacturing industries could not have absorbed large inflows of immigrants.

tion is widely used in the wage inequality literature (e.g., Bound and Johnson 1992), and it provides a natural starting point for analyzing the effect of relative supply shifts.[7] As a specification test, I conduct some analysis using only a subset of occupations. As long as two or more groups are included per city, equations (3′) and (4′) are estimable, and under the CES assumption, the parameter estimates should be invariant to the choice of which occupation groups are included. On the other hand, if some subset of occupations are closer substitutes to one another, one would expect the magnitude of the estimated elasticity of substitution to rise when only those groups are included in the analysis.[8]

II. Data Description and Implementation Issues

The empirical analysis in this article is based on 1990 census data pertaining to labor market outcomes in 1989. Throughout the article, I restrict attention to men and women between the ages of 16 and 68 with at least 1 year of potential labor market experience in 1989. (The latter restriction is meant to eliminate students.) I use total annual earnings (including self-employment and wage and salary earnings) along with data on weeks worked and hours per week over the year to construct an hourly wage measure and a simple indicator for employment status. The appendix provides more detailed information on the sample extracts. I use 100% of all foreign-born individuals in the 5% public use micro sample of the 1990 census (roughly 840 thousand observations) and a 25% random sample of all U.S.-born individuals (roughly 1.8 million observations).

A. Defining Local Labor Markets

An immediate issue that arises in any study of local labor markets is the definition of individual markets. Large urban agglomerations such as the New York metro area pose a particular problem: at one extreme, the entire area can be considered as a single labor market; at the other, individual cities within the metro area can be treated separately. In this article, I consider each metropolitan statistical area (MSA) as an indepen-

---

[7] Katz and Murphy (1992) consider a more general technology in their analysis of the role of demand shifts in wage inequality, although they reach substantially the same conclusions as Bound and Johnson (1992). Moreover, they do not simultaneously consider supply and demand shocks.

[8] For example, suppose that labor input in each city can be decomposed as $G(L_{Ac}, L_{Bc})$, where L_{Ac} is a CES subaggregate of low-skill labor (with substitution with parameter σ_A) and L_{Bc} is a CES subaggregate of high-skill labor (with substitution with parameter σ_B). Then, estimation of eqq. (3′) and (4′) on the subset of low-skill occupations will recover σ_A and a corresponding labor supply elasticity for these groups.

dent labor market. I also consider individually identified cities within larger agglomeration of cities as separate local labor markets.[9] A total of 324 individual MSAs and subcities within consolidated metropolitan statistical areas (CMSA) are identified on the 1990 census public-use files.[10] Since the sample sizes for many of the smaller cities are limited, I restricted attention to the 175 largest cities, ranked by the number of native-born adults in the city. Using this criterion, the smallest city included in the sample is Ann Arbor, Michigan, while the largest city excluded from the sample is Naples, Florida. A list of included cities is available on request.

Table 1 presents some descriptive information on the characteristics of U.S. adults who lived in the largest 175 cities and elsewhere, along with comparisons between natives and immigrants in the larger cities. About 65% of the adult population resided in larger cities in 1990.[11] Residents of larger cities are more likely to be black, Hispanic, and foreign-born, and they are slightly better-educated than other adults. The employment-population rate and average hours of work of big-city residents and other adults are very similar, although hourly wages are about 25% higher in larger cities.

In 1990, 14% of the adult population of the 175 largest U.S. cities were born abroad. Of these, about one-fifth arrived in the United States between 1985 and 1990. The three right-hand columns of table 1 illustrate some of the similarities and differences between natives, recent immigrants, and immigrants who arrived before 1985. Immigrants differ from natives in several dimensions: for example, immigrants are 10 times more likely to be of Hispanic ethnicity, and they have 1–2 years less education on average. Recent immigrants tend to be younger than the other two groups. The labor market outcomes of natives and pre-1985 immigrants are surprisingly similar, whereas recent immigrants have significantly

[9] For example, New York City, Nassau and Suffolk Counties, and Newark are each considered as separate cities, although all three belong to the New York Consolidated Metropolitan Statistical Area (CMSA). The classification of large urban areas into separate entities is somewhat arbitrary. Areas with over a million people may be subdivided if population and commuting criteria are met and if there is local political support for creating separate entities (U.S. Bureau of the Census 1994).

[10] Some individuals who live in geographic areas that straddle an MSA boundary (or boundaries) are not assigned an MSA in the public use micro data samples. As explained in the appendix, in cases where more than one-half of the population of such an area live in one MSA, I assigned all the individuals in the geographic area to that MSA.

[11] The rest of the population consists of individuals who do not live in MSAs or CMSAs (25% of the population) and individuals who live in smaller MSAs (10% of the adult population).

Impacts of Immigration   31

Table 1
Characteristics of Natives and Immigrants

	All United States	In 175 Largest Cities	Outside of Largest Cities	In 175 Largest Cities		
				Natives	Pre-1985 Immigrants	Recent Immigrants
Weighted count (millions)	160.0	102.0	58.0	87.9	11.1	3.0
Immigrants (%)	10.2	13.9	3.7	.0	100.0	100.0
Immigrated, 1985–90 (%)	2.1	3.0	.7	.0	.0	100.0
Black (%)	9.9	11.5	7.0	12.3	6.8	6.8
Hispanic (%)	8.0	10.1	4.3	4.7	42.3	48.4
Average education (years)	12.6	12.9	12.2	13.1	11.6	11.1
Average age	39.9	39.6	40.3	39.7	40.7	31.9
Labor market outcomes:						
Worked in 1989 (%)	77.9	78.7	76.6	79.6	76.0	63.5
Average hours worked in 1989	1,403	1,427	1,360	1,445	1,390	1,025
Average hourly wage in 1989	11.92	12.82	10.25	12.99	12.30	9.20
Distribution of workers:						
By hourly wage (%):						
<$6.00	25.6	21.8	32.8	20.8	24.6	44.3
$6.00–$9.99	28.4	27.4	30.4	27.1	29.2	29.3
$10.00–$15.00	22.0	23.1	19.8	23.6	21.4	13.1
>$15.00	24.0	27.7	17.0	28.5	24.8	13.2
By location (%):						
Living in Los Angeles, New York, or Chicago	8.4	13.1	.0	10.0	31.6	35.1
Major city residents who lived elsewhere in 1985[a]	...	20.5	...	19.6	27.6	...

NOTE.—Figures are based on tabulations of the 1990 Census sample. Samples include men and women ages 16–68 with 1 or more years of potential experience in 1989.
[a] Percent of current residents of larger cities who did not live in the same city 5 years ago. Post-1985 immigrants were excluded from the calculation.

lower wages and employment rates. For example, 21% of natives and 25% of pre-1985 immigrants earned less than $6 per hour in 1989, as compared with 44% of recent immigrants. Similarly, 29% of natives and 25% of pre-1985 immigrants earned over $15 per hour, as compared with only 13% of recent immigrants.

Another difference between native workers and immigrants is geographic location. In 1990, about 28% of all immigrants lived in the three largest cities (Los Angeles, New York, Chicago), as compared with only 6% of natives. Immigrants and natives also differ in their intercity mobility rates. As shown in the bottom row of table 1, about 20% of the adult population of larger cities reported living in a different city in 1990 than did so in 1985.[12] Even though natives are better-educated and slightly younger than pre-1985 immigrants (both factors that normally increase migration rates), a smaller fraction of natives left their 1985 city of residence by 1990. The mobility patterns of both groups are discussed in more detail below.

B. Defining Occupation Groups

A second issue that arises in estimating the impact of immigration is the question of "who competes with whom?" Specifically, which groups of workers are perfect substitutes for each other, and how many independent types of labor are present in any local labor market? Most existing studies treat immigrant workers as one factor of production and various subgroups of natives as separate factors (a notable exception is Jaeger 1995). As noted in the introduction, however, the immigrant workforce is remarkably diverse, and it varies widely across cities. An alternative to treating immigrants and natives as separate skill groups is to define skill categories within which immigrants and natives are perfect substitutes and to classify individual immigrants and natives into these groups. This approach allows a more precise characterization of the degree of competition between natives and immigrants in different cities, but it does so at the cost of some arbitrariness in the definition of skill groups.

One potentially appealing assumption is that labor markets are stratified along occupation lines and that individuals who work in the same occupation are perfect substitutes with each other regardless of their gender or national origin.[13] A problem with this assumption is that individuals can move between occupations, and they would be expected to do so if there is a relative oversupply of workers in a particular occupation. Another difficulty is that occupations are only observed for those who work: thus, it may be difficult to measure the population of individuals in a given city who could potentially work in an occupation. Both of these problems can be solved by considering an individual's occupation as a probabilistic outcome that depends on underlying characteristics such as age, education, race, gender, national origin, and length of time in the country. Suppose that occupations are partitioned into a set $j = 1, \ldots, J$ and that a given individual, i, has probabilities $\pi_{i1}, \pi_{i2}, \ldots,$

---

[12] The census form asks each individual where they lived 5 years ago, and the public-use micro data samples report Public Use Micro data Area (PUMA) identifiers for 1985 place of residence. I assigned these to MSAs using the mapping between PUMAs and MSA for 1990 place of residence.

[13] This assumption is built in to U.S. immigration law, which requires employers who sponsor applicants for permanent residence status to certify that the applicant is not undercutting wages of workers in the same occupation in his or her local labor market.

π_{ij} of working in the different occupations in some reference labor market (e.g., a nationally representative city). Then, the number of people who would be expected to work in occupation j in any particular local labor market is just the sum of the π_{ij}'s across the local population.[14] (Of course, the number who actually work in the occupation could depend on conditions in the local market, such as the wage for the occupation.) Moreover, estimates of the employment rate and mean wages for individuals who would be expected to work in occupation j can be obtained by forming weighted averages of employment and wages across the population of the city, using the π_{ij}'s as weights.

To implement this idea, I estimated a set of multinomial logit models (by gender and immigrant status) for the probabilities of working in six different broad occupation groups, using a sample of individuals from the 175 largest cities. The models for native men and women included identical flexible functions of age and education, race, marital status, and disability status in each branch of the logit model. To abstract from any distortions in the occupation distribution in high-immigrant cities, the models also include dummies for the 30 largest cities and dummies for living in California, Texas, Florida, New York, or other northeastern states. The models for immigrants included the same basic covariates, plus dummy variables for 17 different origin countries (or groups of countries), a polynomial in the number of years in the United States, and interactions of four broad origin groups with education.[15] The estimated coefficients from these four models were then used to assign probabilities of working in different occupations assuming that an individual lives in an average smaller city outside the four major immigrant-receiving states and the northeast.

Table 2 summarizes the characteristics of individuals in each of the six predicted occupation groups. The groups are laborers and low-skilled service workers; operatives and craft workers; clerical workers; sales workers; managers; and professional and technical workers. The six groups each represent 10%–20% of the national labor force, and they are ordered by the mean level of education in the group. The first group, laborers and less-skilled service workers, has the lowest average education and the lowest average hourly wages; this group also has the highest representation of blacks, Hispanics, and immigrants. At the other end of

[14] A similar assumption is widely used in the wage inequality literature to measure the supply of high-school-equivalent and college-equivalent labor—see, e.g., Katz and Murphy (1992).

[15] The origin groups are explained below. See the appendix for a fuller description of these models. In principle, the models could be estimated on weighted samples, where the weight for each individual represents his or her relative probability of working (since occupations are only observed for workers).

Table 2
Characteristics of Predicted Occupation Groups

	Occupation Group					
	I	II	III	IV	V	VI
Percentage female	53.9	23.8	81.8	55.9	45.8	53.8
Mean education	11.1	11.4	12.8	13.0	14.4	15.6
Percentage black	19.4	12.3	11.3	7.3	6.2	8.2
Percentage Hispanic	16.9	16.6	12.1	10.5	7.2	6.2
Percentage immigrant	19.1	16.9	11.9	11.5	9.4	10.6
Percentage recent immigrant	5.4	3.7	2.0	2.4	1.3	1.8
Percentage Mexican immigrant	4.7	5.5	2.3	1.8	.2	.1
Mean years in the United States						
among immigrants	14.4	15.5	18.3	17.4	20.5	18.7
Mean log wage	2.10	2.29	2.18	2.30	2.52	2.56
Percentage of workers	17.4	23.2	16.2	11.3	12.0	19.8
Percentage of population	19.5	22.8	17.2	11.4	11.0	18.1

NOTE.—Occupation groups are I, laborers, farm workers, and low-skilled service workers; II, operatives and craft workers; III, clerical workers; IV, sales workers; V, managers; and VI, professional and technical workers. Characteristics for each occupation group are formed as weighted averages over the entire adult population, where the weights are the predicted probabilities of working in the occupations. See text for further details.

the spectrum, professional and technical workers have the highest average education and the highest average wage, and they have the lowest fraction of Hispanics and Mexican immigrants. As shown in the bottom two rows of the table, the fractions of the overall adult population and of the employed adult population assigned to the six occupation groups are somewhat different, and there is a greater relative representation of nonworkers in the the lowest occupation group.[16]

The occupational composition of the local population varies widely across cities. Table A1 in the appendix shows the predicted fractions of the population in each occupation group for the 30 largest cities, normalized relative to the corresponding averages for all cities. Compared with the all-city average, Miami has 30% more of its local population in the lowest occupation group. Los Angeles and New York also both have relatively high fractions in the lowest occupation group (roughly 18% above the national average in each case). By comparison, Seattle and Denver have relatively low fractions in this group. At the other end of the skill distribution, the populations of Washington, DC, and San Francisco are overrepresented in the highest occupational category (roughly 40% above the national average), whereas Riverside and Miami have relatively low fractions in this group. Across all 175 major cities, St. Louis has a

---

[16] While not shown in the table, the characteristics of workers in each predicted occupation group match very closely with the characteristics of actual workers in each occupation.

Table 3
Predicted Occupation Distributions of Natives, Older Immigrants, and
Recent Immigrants

	Predicted Percentage of Occupation						Index of Competition
	I	II	III	IV	V	VI	
Natives:							
All	18.3	21.9	17.6	11.8	11.6	18.8	.98
Dropouts	37.5	36.5	12.7	9.1	2.6	1.6	1.31
High school	22.6	28.4	22.0	12.2	7.9	6.9	1.08
Some college	14.8	19.6	21.2	13.9	13.4	17.2	.93
College or more	3.3	5.2	9.7	10.2	21.1	50.5	.67
Pre-1985 immigrants:							
All	24.5	27.5	15.6	9.5	8.3	14.6	1.09
Dropouts	38.5	41.8	10.5	6.8	1.6	.8	1.35
High school	25.7	28.4	20.4	11.7	7.4	6.4	1.12
Some college	18.5	21.9	20.9	12.1	11.7	15.0	.99
College or more	6.9	9.0	11.7	8.0	16.4	48.0	.74
Recent immigrants (all)	35.1	28.3	11.8	9.2	4.8	10.8	1.22

NOTE.—Predictions are based on a multinomial logit model fitted to workers but applied to the entire population of individuals ages 16–68 with 1 or more years of labor market experience in 1989 who lived in one of the 175 largest cities in 1990. Occupations groups are I, laborers, farm workers and low skilled service workers; II, operatives and craft workers; III, clerical workers; IV, sales workers; V, managers; and VI, professional and technical workers. Index of competition measures the relative impact of an increase in the supply of recent immigrants on the particular group of natives or earlier immigrants. See text for details.

predicted occupation distribution closest to the national average. Other cities that are very similar to the national average include Columbus (Ohio), Indianapolis, Louisville, and Fort Worth. Looking across cities, the predicted fraction of the population in the lowest education group is highly correlated with the fraction of immigrants and with the fraction of recent immigrants (the population-weighted correlations are 0.46 and 0.42, respectively). It is interesting to note that mean log wages are also positively correlated with the fractions of immigrants or recent immigrants in the city (the weighted correlations are 0.41 and 0.42, respectively).

C. The Degree of Competition between Natives and Immigrants

The hypothesis that labor markets are stratified by occupation suggests a simple metric for assessing the degree of competition between subgroups of immigrants or natives. Intuitively, two groups with very similar predicted occupation distributions are in direct competition, whereas two groups with very different distributions are not. Table 3 shows the mean predicted occupation distributions for natives, pre-1985 immigrants, and recent immigrants, as well as for various subgroups of natives and pre-1985 immigrants. An examination of these distributions shows that natives and older immigrants are fairly similar, although the latter are slightly more likely to work in the two lowest occupations. By comparison, the predicted occupation distribution of recent immigrants is heavily skewed toward blue-collar occupations (laborers, operatives, and crafts). Indeed, the occupation distribution of recent immigrants is quite similar to that of natives who did not finish high school.

More formally, the degree of competition between groups can be summarized by an index (I) that measures the effective increase in labor supply experienced by one group as the population of another group rises (Altonji and Card 1991). Let f_j^1 and f_j^2 denote the fractions of groups 1 and 2 (e.g., natives and recent immigrants) employed in occupation j, and let f_j denote the fraction of the overall workforce employed in this occupation. Now consider an increase in the population of group 1 that generates a 1-percentage-point increase in the total workforce. Assuming that the new members of group 1 adopt the same occupation distribution as the existing members of the group, the percentage increase in the workforce of occupation j is f_j^1/f_j. For members of group 2, the weighted average increase in the supply of labor to their occupation-specific labor markets is $I_{1,2} = \Sigma_j f_j^2 f_j^1/f_j$. Note that if $f_j^2 = f_j$ or $f_j^1 = f_j$, (i.e., if either group 1 or group 2 has the same occupational distribution as the overall workforce), then the index takes a value of one. On the other hand, if groups 1 and 2 work in completely different occupations, then the index is zero. Finally, $I_{1,2}$ can be bigger than one if groups 1 and 2 have similar occupation distributions and if both groups are concentrated in a subset of occupations.

The right-hand column of table 3 presents estimates of the index of competition between recent immigrants and the various subgroups of natives and pre-1985 immigrants. Note, first, that the own-index of labor market competition between recent immigrants and themselves is greater than one (1.22). This reflects the fact that recent immigrants are disproportionately crowded into occupations I–IV. It is interesting that the cross-indexes of competition between recent immigrants and the least-educated subgroups of natives and older immigrants are even higher. Thus, the supply pressure exerted by an inflow of new immigrants is even bigger for poorly educated natives than for new immigrants themselves. This arises because a sizeable fraction of recent immigrants are predicted to work in the two highest occupations, whereas poorly educated natives are largely confined to the four lowest occupation groups, which experience disproportionate increases in supply when there is an inflow of new immigrants. Both informal comparisons of predicted occupation distributions and the more formal index of competition therefore confirm that inflows of new immigrants put substantial supply pressure on labor markets for less-educated natives.

III. Immigrant Inflows and Intercity Mobility Patterns

One of the most important unresolved questions about U.S. immigration is whether immigrant inflows to particular cities lead to offsetting mobility flows by natives and earlier immigrants (see, e.g., Filer 1992; Frey 1995*a*, 1995*b;* White and Hunter 1993; and Wright, Ellis, and Reibel 1997). To the extent that existing residents of a city respond to inflows of new immigrants by moving to other cities or that potential in-movers from other cities alter their migration plans and move elsewhere, the effect of new immigration is quickly diffused across the national labor market. In the absence of such flows, however, new immigrant inflows directly shift the skill distribution of local labor markets, and they can be used as instrumental variables for the shares of the local population in different occupation groups, potentially overcoming endogeneity issues arising from the presence of skill-group specific local demand shocks.

This section analyzes the effect of immigrant inflows on the migration behavior of natives and earlier immigrants and on net population growth. Unlike most of the previous literature, I focus on skill-group specific migration flows, in order to assess the effect of immigrant inflows on the composition (rather than the total population) of local labor markets. The analysis uses information collected in the 1990 census on each individual's current location and place of residence in 1985. To fix ideas, let N^{90} represent the 1990 population of a given city in a certain occupation group, and let N^{85} represent the 1985 population of the same skill group. Note that N^{85} represents the number of people who lived in the city in 1985 and would be assigned to the occupation group as of 1990. Next, let N^t_1, N^t_2, and N^t_3 represent the numbers of city residents in the occupation in period t ($t = 85$ or 90) from three mutually exclusive groups: natives (N^t_1), immigrants who arrived in the U.S. before 1985 (N^t_2), and immigrants who arrived in the United States after 1985 (N^t_3). By definition, $N^{85}_3 = 0$. For natives and older immigrants,

$$N^{90}_1 = N^{85}_1 + N^J_1 - N^L_1 \qquad (5)$$

and

$$N^{90}_2 = N^{85}_2 + N^J_2 - N^L_2, \qquad (6)$$

where the superscript *J* denotes joiners—people who moved into the city between 1985 and 1990—and the superscript *L* denotes leavers—people who left the city between 1985 and 1990. Finally, let s_1 denote the fraction of natives in the occupation group in 1985. Then, the overall growth rate of the local population of the occupation group between 1985 and 1990 can be written as

$$N^{90}/N^{85} = 1 + s_1(J_1 - L_1) + (1 - s_1)(J_2 - L_2) + R, \qquad (7)$$

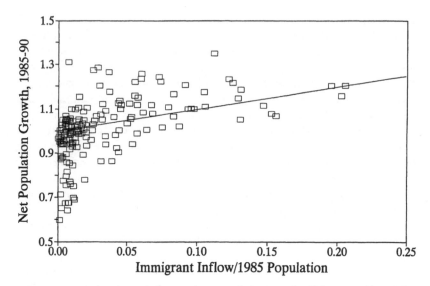

FIG. 1.—Recent immigrant inflows and net population growth of laborers and less-skilled service workers. Line shows population growth assuming no offsetting mobility.

where $J_g = N_g^J/N_g^{85}$ is the inflow rate of group g ($g = 1$ for natives and 2 for pre-1985 immigrants), expressed as a fraction of its 1985 population, $L_g = N_g^L/N_g^{85}$ is the outflow rate of group g, and $R = N_3^{90}/N^{85}$ is the inflow rate of new immigrants in the occupation group.

Equation (7) is a simple accounting identity that expresses the growth rate of the population of a specific occupation group as a weighted average of the net population growth rates of natives and older immigrants in the group, plus the inflow rate of new immigrants. If immigrant inflows have no effect on the location decisions of natives or older immigrants in the same skill group, this equation shows that the occupation-specific growth rate will vary one-for-one with inflows of new immigrants in the group. In terms of a graph, this means that observations on city-specific growth rates for a given occupation group will lie on a line with an intercept of 1 and a slope of 1 when plotted against the recent immigrant inflow rate. On the other hand, if previous residents of a city respond to inflows of new immigrants by moving away or if natives and older immigrants who might otherwise move to the city choose other places to go, then immigrant inflows will generate less-than-proportionate increases in the size of the occupation group, which will lead to a scatter of points below the line with intercept of 1 and slope of 1.

Figure 1 graphs the 1985–90 growth rates of the population of occupation group I (laborers and low-skilled service workers) for the 175 largest U.S. cities against the immigrant inflow rates of new immigrants in this occupation, along with a reference line that represents the benchmark

Impacts of Immigration   39

case of no offsetting migration by natives or earlier immigrants. Across cities, the 5-year immigrant inflow rate for the lowest occupation group ranges from 0 to over 20%.[17] Even at these very high rates of new immigration, however, there is little indication of offsetting migration flows. In fact, a population-weighted OLS regression fit to the data in figure 1 yields a coefficient of 1.26 between immigrant inflows and population growth (with a standard error of 0.13).

A problem with this regression is that favorable demand conditions in a city may stimulate inflows of both immigrants and natives, leading to an upward bias in the partial correlation between N^{90}/N^{85} and R. This can be overcome by pooling the data for all six occupation groups and including city-specific fixed effects that capture any unobserved characteristics of a particular city that lead to greater population inflows (or lower outflows) for both immigrants and natives. More generally, each of the components of occupation-specific local population growth can be modeled as a function of observable city- and occupation-specific factors, a general citywide effect, and the occupation-specific new-immigrant inflow rate:

$$y_{jc} = Z_{jc}\beta + \gamma R_{jc} + d_j + \theta_c + e_{jc}, \tag{8}$$

where y_{jc} represents a particular component of population growth for occupation group j in city c (e.g., the out-migration rate of natives), Z_{jc} represents a vector of observable factors that affect this growth rate (e.g., the characteristics of the group measured in 1985), R_{jc} is the inflow rate of recent immigrants in skill group j to city c, d_j is a skill-group fixed effect, θ_c is a city fixed effect, and e_{jc} is a error term. In light of equation (7), the estimate of γ for total population growth will be a weighted average of the γ's for the individual components, plus 1.

Table 4 reports a series of estimates of the coefficient γ for seven different population growth components: native outflow rates, native inflow rates, net native population growth, pre-1985 immigrant outflow rates, pre-1985 immigrant inflow rates, net population growth of pre-1985 immigrants, and, finally, total population growth (i.e., N^{90}/N^{85}). The covariates in these models include the means of age, age-squared, education, and the fraction of blacks among the particular group in the city in 1985, as well as the fraction of immigrants in 1985.[18] Row A

---

[17] The maximum immigrant inflow rates for occupation group I are 0.21 for Anaheim-Santa Ana, CA, and 0.20 for Los Angeles, CA, and Miami, FL. Other cities with high inflow rates are San Francisco, CA (0.16), Jersey City, NJ (0.15), San Jose, CA (0.15), Salinas, CA (0.13), and New York, NY (0.13).

[18] The covariates in the models for overall population growth include all the mean characteristics for both natives and pre-1985 immigrants in the city in 1985.

Table 4
Effects of Recent Immigrant Inflows on Migration Rates of Natives and Earlier Immigrants in the Same-Skill Group

	Native Out- and Inflows				Earlier Immigrant Out- and Inflows				Total Population Gain per New Immigrant
	Outflow Rate		Inflow Rate	Net Population Growth	Outflow Rate		Inflow Rate	Net Population Growth	
	Raw	Adjusted			Raw	Adjusted			
Ordinary least squares estimation:									
A. 175 cities weighted	.02 (.02)	.02 (.02)	.13 (.02)	.11 (.03)	.13 (.04)	.08 (.04)	.09 (.06)	-.04 (.07)	1.25 (.04)
B. 175 cities unweighted	.05 (.03)	.05 (.03)	.08 (.05)	.02 (.06)	.13 (.07)	.06 (.07)	-.16 (.10)	-.29 (.12)	1.19 (.06)
C. Top 50 cities weighted	.00 (.03)	.01 (.03)	.18 (.03)	.17 (.04)	.08 (.05)	.05 (.04)	.14 (.08)	.07 (.09)	1.30 (.05)
D. 158 cities outside California weighted	-.11 (.04)	-.08 (.04)	.11 (.05)	.22 (.06)	.16 (.07)	.04 (.07)	.19 (.10)	.03 (.12)	1.36 (.07)
Instrumental variables estimation (instrument is predicted immigrant inflow):									
E. 175 cities weighted	.02 (.02)	.03 (.02)	.13 (.03)	.11 (.03)	.14 (.04)	.10 (.04)	.14 (.06)	.00 (.07)	1.25 (.05)
F. Top 50 cities weighted	.00 (.03)	.01 (.03)	.16 (.03)	.16 (.04)	.10 (.05)	.07 (.04)	.24 (.09)	.13 (.09)	1.28 (.05)
G. Three least-educated occupations only	-.06 (.02)	-.03 (.03)	.11 (.03)	.15 (.03)	.08 (.05)	.00 (.05)	.26 (.07)	.19 (.08)	1.25 (.04)
H. Laborers/low-skill services and professional/technical only	-.12 (.05)	-.08 (.05)	.15 (.05)	.27 (.07)	.16 (.08)	.06 (.07)	.14 (.11)	-.02 (.13)	1.43 (.08)

NOTE.—Entries are estimated regression coefficients of recent immigrant inflow rate in models for dependent variable listed in column heading. Sample includes six occupation groups in 175 cities (1,050 observations) except as noted in rows G and H. All models include occupation group dummies, mean age, mean age-squared, mean education, and percentage black; and (for immigrants only) mean years in the United States for the skill group in the particular city in 1985. Adjusted outflow rates are obtained from a set of linear probability models fitted by occupation group to the event of leaving one's city of residence in 1985. Standard errors are in parentheses.

reports weighted OLS estimates of equation (8) for each of the dependent variables, using the 1985 city population as a weight for the observations from occupation group j in city c.[19] Row B reports corresponding un-weighted estimates, while row C reports estimates based on only the 50 largest cities. As a further check on the sensitivity of the results, row D reports results based on a subsample that excludes any California cities.

The addition of average population characteristics to the right-hand side of equation (8) is meant to adjust for differences in the observable characteristics of the populations of different cities that might be corre-lated with mobility rates and immigrant inflow rates. In the case of the outflow rates, a finer adjustment is potentially useful. As motivation for this procedure, suppose that the out-migration probability for individual i in occupation group j who lived in city c in 1985 is

$$P_{ijc} = X_{ijc}b_j + Z_{jc}\beta + \gamma R_{jc} + d_j + \theta_c + \zeta_{jc},$$

where X_{ijc} is a vector of characteristics of individual i, b_j is a set of skill-group-specific coefficients, Z_{jc} is a set of other group-level characteristics that affect the mobility rate of group j in city c (such as the fraction of immigrants or nonwhites in 1985), d_j and θ_c are skill-group and city dummies, R_{jc} is the inflow rate of new immigrants in occupation j to city c, and ζ_{jc} is a residual component. The coefficient γ can be estimated in two steps by first estimating a micro-level linear probability model for the event of leaving one's city of residence in 1985 that includes unrestricted city and occupation-group effects:

$$P_{ijc} = X_{ijc}b_j + \mu_{jc}, \tag{9}$$

and then regressing the estimated μ_{jc}'s on city dummies, occupation dummies, the other group-level controls Z_{jc}, and the inflow rate of new immigrants:

$$\mu_{jc} = Z_{jc}\beta + \gamma R_{jc} + d_j + \theta_c + \zeta_{jc}.$$

The adjusted outflow rates used in the models in table 4 are simply the

---

[19] The motivation for the weighted estimates is the fact that the number of observations in the sample ranges from over 100,000 for Los Angeles to around 2,000 for some of the smaller cities. If the variances of the estimated flow rates are proportional to the sample sizes for each city-occupation group cell, then weighted estimates are more efficient. To reduce the risk of a correlation between the weight for each city/occupation-group cell and the dependent variables, I use the 1985 city population for all occupation groups as a weight for each occupation group in the city.

first-stage estimates of the μ_{jc}'s, derived from linear probability models fit to samples of natives and pre-1985 immigrants.[20] These models include a much richer set of covariates than the limited number included at the aggregate level, allowing for very detailed adjustments to the raw outflow rates.[21] In principle, it is possible to derive an analogous set of adjusted inflow rates for each skill group and city. In practice, however, the population at risk to move into a given city between 1985 and 1990 (i.e., the population who lived somewhere else in 1985) is very similar for all cities. Thus, there is no real advantage in attempting to construct adjusted inflow rates.

The estimated effects of recent immigrant inflows on the raw or adjusted outflow rates of natives in rows A–C of table 4 are very modest in size and fairly similar across specifications. When California cities are excluded, the effects become slightly negative, suggesting that occupation-specific outmigration responses to immigrant inflows may be different for California cities. Nevertheless, the coefficients are still small in magnitude, implying that any native out-migration response is modest. The effects of new immigrant inflows on the outflow rates of earlier immigrants are also positive, but they are modest in magnitude and (in the case of the adjusted outflows) uniformly insignificant. With respect to inflow rates, the estimated effects of new immigrant inflows are generally positive for both natives and pre-1985 immigrants. For natives, the positive effect on inflows is larger than the positive effect on outflows, so that the estimated impact of recent immigration on net native population growth is positive. For pre-1985 immigrants, there is more variability across specifications, but, apart from the unweighted OLS estimates, the coefficients are not significantly different from zero. Finally, the estimated coefficients in the extreme right-hand column of the table for the overall population growth rate are uniformly above one, suggesting that the net mobility responses of natives and older immigrants do little to dampen the impacts of new immigrants and that they may actually complement recent immigrant inflows, even when citywide demand factors are taken into account by including city-fixed effects.[22]

Even after accounting for unobserved city-specific factors, the estimates in rows A–D of table 4 suggest that the net mobility flows of

---

[20] For occupation j, the models are fitted over the entire population of the city but use as weights the probabilities that each individual works in occupation j.

[21] See the appendix for a description of the first-stage models.

[22] The estimate of γ for total population growth when city-fixed effects are excluded is larger than any of the estimates in table 4 (1.59, with a standard error of 0.10). Thus, it appears that unobserved city factors are positively correlated with new immigrant inflows and complementary mobility flows of natives and earlier immigrants.

natives and earlier immigrants may be positively related to new immigrant inflows—the opposite of what would be expected if new immigrants depress wages and force other people to move out. One explanation for this finding is that there are unobserved city- and occupation-specific factors (like the productivity shocks introduced in the theoretical model of Sec. I) that attract recent immigrants of a particular skill group and at the same time slow down the outflow of natives. In the presence of such occupation-specific demand-pull factors, an instrumental variable for occupation-specific immigrant inflows is needed to identify the true causal effect of inflows.

The tendency of newly arriving immigrants to move to enclaves established by earlier immigrants from the same source country (Bartel 1989) suggests one such instrument. In particular, suppose that the total number of immigrants from a given source country who enter the United States is independent of occupation-specific demand conditions in any particular city. The actual inflow of immigrants from a given source country moving to a city can then be decomposed into an exogenous supply-push component, based on total inflows from the country and the fraction of earlier immigrants from that country who live in the city, and a residual component reflecting any departures from the historical pattern. Multiplying the total inflow from a given source country by a factor reflecting the national fraction of immigrants from that country who fall into a certain occupation group gives an estimate of the supply-push component of recent immigrant inflows of a given skill group that can be used as an instrumental variable in the estimation of equation (8).

Formally, let M_g represent the number of immigrants from source country g who entered the United States between 1985 and 1990, and let λ_{gc} represent the fraction of immigrants from an earlier cohort of immigrants from country g who are observed living in city c in 1985. Finally, let τ_{gj} represent the fraction of all 1985–90 immigrants from source country g who fall into occupation group j. In the absence of demand-pull factors, the number of immigrants from country g in skill group j who would be expected to move into city c between 1985 and 1990 is $\tau_{gj}\lambda_{gc}M_g$. If τ_{gj}, M_g, and λ_{gc} are independent of occupation-specific demand conditions in city c over the 1985–90 period, then this estimate is independent of any demand-pull conditions in the city.[23] Summing across

[23] If city- and occupation-group specific productivity shocks are highly persistent and immigrant inflows from different source countries are persistently concentrated in specific occupation groups, then the fraction of earlier immigrants from a given source country who settled in a given city may be correlated with the current city- and skill-group specific productivity shock for the predominant skill group(s) from that country. In this case the proposed measures of supply-push immigration are not strictly exogenous. One could potentially overcome this

source countries, an estimate of the supply-push component of recent
immigrant inflows in occupation group j and city c is

$$SP_{jc} = \Sigma_g \tau_{gj} \lambda_{gc} M_g. \tag{10}$$

To construct this measure, I used a set of 17 source country groups,
identified in table 5.[24] The first column of the table gives the fraction of
all 1985–90 immigrants from each source (i.e., M_g/M, where M is the total
inflow of new immigrants), while the second column shows the mean
education of recent immigrants from each source country group. Mexico
is the largest single source country, accounting for 26% of the approximately 3.4 million adult immigrants who entered the United States between 1985 and 1990. The Philippines is the second largest individual
source country, accounting for about 5% of all recent immigrants. Other
source-country groups account for 1%–8% of recent immigrants.

The right-hand columns of table 5 show the predicted fractions of
recent immigrants from each source country group in the six occupation
groups. There are notable differences in the skill distributions of immigrants from different source countries. For example, 81% of Mexican
immigrants and 71% of Central American immigrants are predicted to
work in the two lowest occupation groups, versus only 40% of immigrants from Canada, England, Australia and New Zealand, or from Korea
and Japan. Cities that receive most of their new immigrants from Mexico
or Central America, therefore, tend to have relatively low-skilled inflows,
whereas cities that receive a larger fraction of Canadian or European
immigrants have more highly skilled inflows.

The final set of unknowns in equation (10) are the city distribution
shares for each source country—the λ_{gc}'s. I use the 1985 geographic
distribution of immigrants who entered the United States between 1975
and 1984 (reported retrospectively in the 1990 census) to estimate these
shares. A table of the resulting estimates (available on request) shows
many interesting patterns. For example, Los Angeles attracted the largest
share of 1975–84 immigrants (18%), with 41% of Central American
immigrants and 28% of Mexican immigrants living there in 1985. New
York City accounted for the next largest share (10%), with 43% of
Caribbean immigrants and 22% of immigrants from the former Commu-
nist countries of Europe, but a very small share of Mexicans (0.7%). Even

---

problem by finding a set of instruments that explain the location choices of earlier
immigrants from different sources countries and using predicted settlement patterns of the earlier cohort to construct the supply push indexes.

[24] The groupings were selected on the basis of geography and ethnic similarity
and are reported in order of population size.

Table 5
Countries of Origin and Predicted Occupation Distributions of Recent
Immigrants

	Percent of Total	Mean Education (Years)	Predicted Fraction in Occupation Groups					
			I	II	III	IV	V	VI
All source countries	100.0	11.0	35.0	28.4	11.6	9.3	4.8	11.0
Mexico	26.2	8.0	39.3	41.9	10.3	7.5	.6	.4
Caribbean countries	8.4	11.1	37.6	26.0	17.7	8.3	4.4	6.0
Central America	8.2	9.0	39.9	31.3	13.2	8.3	3.4	4.0
China, Hong Kong, and Singapore	6.2	13.0	32.3	16.9	9.3	9.7	8.3	23.4
South America	6.0	12.2	32.0	26.0	18.1	8.7	6.2	8.9
Indonesia, Malaysia, and Brunei	6.0	11.3	42.5	23.7	9.8	8.4	4.3	11.1
Korea and Japan	5.9	13.6	29.9	18.0	8.5	17.0	9.0	17.6
Philippines	5.1	13.4	33.6	18.3	15.0	7.3	5.4	20.4
Burma, Loas, Thailand, and Vietnam	4.6	9.3	36.7	38.8	7.2	6.8	2.4	8.1
Australia, New Zealand, Canada, and United Kingdom	4.4	14.0	24.8	16.6	12.0	11.1	10.8	24.6
India, Pakistan, and Central Asia	4.1	14.0	21.9	17.1	12.2	12.8	8.0	28.0
Russia, Central Europe	4.0	13.0	33.3	28.3	7.1	7.2	5.7	18.3
Turkey, North Africa, and the Middle East	3.4	13.1	28.2	17.5	9.2	17.3	8.8	19.1
Northwestern Europe and Israel	2.9	14.3	27.5	15.9	11.3	11.7	9.6	23.9
Southwestern Europe	2.0	12.1	36.4	25.1	6.8	9.4	6.7	15.6
Africa (excluding North Africa)	1.7	13.3	29.9	24.0	18.7	7.0	6.8	13.7
Cuba	1.0	10.5	39.2	32.2	8.9	7.3	4.1	8.3

NOTE.—Figures are based on immigrants who entered the United States between 1985 and 1990, were ages 16–68 in 1990, and had more than 1 year of potential experience. The sample size is 171,230, representing a population of 3.43 million. See table 3 for descriptions of the occupation groups and the occupation prediction method.

cities that currently receive relatively few immigrants show long-established enclave patterns. For example, Detroit accounted for only 0.6% of total immigrants but for 5% of immigrants from the Middle East and North Africa.

How do the observed immigrant inflows over the period from 1985–90 compare with the supply-push flows predicted by equation (10)? Figure 2 plots the actual immigrant inflow rate for laborers and low-skilled service workers in each city against the corresponding supply-push flows. For reference, I have superimposed a 45-degree line on the figure. The correlation between the actual and supply-push inflows is strong, although there are many cities with bigger or smaller inflows than would have been predicted on the basis of earlier immigrant settlement patterns and national immigration inflows over the 1985–90 period. The set of Texas cities is a case in point. The nine Texas cities in the sample are plotted with a different symbol in figure 2 and uniformly lie below the 45-degree line. The shortfall presumably reflects the relatively unfavorable labor market in Texas following the collapse of oil prices in the mid-1980s.

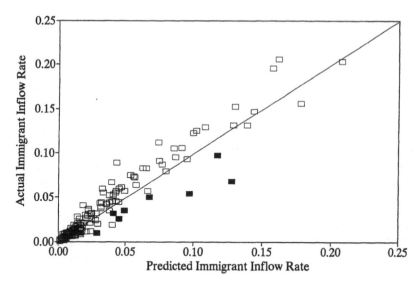

FIG. 2.—Actual and supply-driven immigrant inflows of laborers and less-skilled service workers. Texas cities shown with filled squares.

The lower panel of table 4 presents instrumental variables (IV) estimates of the effect of immigrant inflows on mobility rates of natives and earlier immigrants, using the supply-push component of immigrant inflows as an exogenous determinant of the recent immigrant inflow rate. Row E reports estimates for the 175 largest cities, while row F reports estimates based on only the largest 50 cities. The point estimates of the coefficient γ are very similar to the corresponding OLS estimates (from rows A and C, respectively) providing no evidence of endogeneity bias attributable to occupation-specific local demand shocks that draw new immigrants and other migrants in specific skill groups to certain cities.

Another specification test is provided by the IV estimates in row G, which are based on mobility patterns for only the three lowest occupation groups. (The OLS estimates for these specifications are very similar to the IV estimates.) Based on the similarity of these estimates with the estimates in rows E and F, there is little indication that less-educated occupation groups have systematically different responses to new immigrant inflows than do other groups. Although not shown in the table, IV estimates for the subset of cities outside of California are very similar to the OLS estimates, which again suggests that the main results are quite robust.

A final set of models were estimated to assess the effect of immigrant inflows on the population shares of different occupation groups. This analysis is directly relevant to the theoretical model in Section I, since in that model wages and employment rates of different occupation groups vary with the log population shares of the groups. An analysis of the

Impacts of Immigration   47

effects of new immigrant inflows on population shares also provides a useful check on the implicit assumption underlying the models in table 4 that the mobility flows of an occupation group depend only on the immigrant inflows of people in that group. Specifically, if the population growth rate of a given occupation group varies one-for-one with the immigrant inflow rate of the group, then the log of the population share of the group will also vary one-for-one with group-specific immigrant inflows. More generally, however, inflows of one group could affect the mobility decisions of other groups, leading to a bigger or smaller effect of immigrant inflows on the log population share.[25] Ordinary least squares regression models similar to those in table 4 reveal that the elasticity of population share with respect to new immigrant inflows is close to one, with most estimates clustering somewhat above one. The IV estimates, using the supply-push component of immigrant inflows, are generally as big or only slightly smaller. These findings are consistent with the results in table 4, which suggests that mobility flows of natives and earlier immigrants are, if anything, slightly complementary to recent immigrant inflows.

Taken as a whole, the results in table 4 confirm that mobility flows of natives and older immigrants are not very sensitive to inflows of new immigrants. This conclusion is consistent with some previous studies of city-level population growth rates over the 1980s (Butcher and Card 1991; White and Liang 1994), but not with others. Most notably, Frey (1995*a*, 1995*b*) has argued that out-migration rates of low-skilled natives were higher from cities that received larger immigrant inflow rates over the 1985–90 period—particularly California cities.[26] In an effort to verify the results in table 4, I performed a variety of checks. First, as shown in figure 3, I plotted the outflow rates of natives in the lowest skill group for each city against the corresponding immigrant inflow rate. As the figure makes clear, the leaving rates of low-skilled natives from the 17 California

[25] I also fitted some models that included inflows of immigrants in the laborer and low-skilled service occupations as an additional explanatory variable for mobility flows of other occupation groups. The effects of the low occupation inflows were generally small and statistically insignificant.

[26] Studies by Filer (1992) and White and Hunter (1993) of migration patterns in the 1970s also point to a negative correlation between immigrant inflows and native outmigration. A recent paper by Wright, Ellis, and Reibel (1997) reexamines the connection between net internal migration and immigration inflows, using both 1975–80 and 1985–90 data. After comparing various specifications, these authors surmise that differences in findings across previous studies result from a failure to separate city size effects from immigrant flow effects. They conclude that "the net loss of native workers from large metropolitan areas in the United States in the late 1970s and late 1980s occurs for reasons other than mass immigration to these places" (Wright et al. 1997, p. 250).

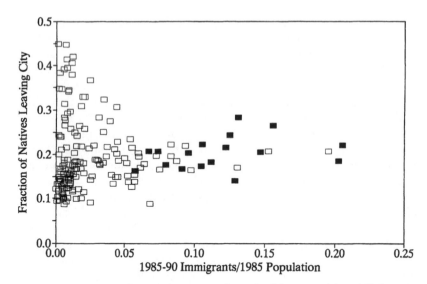

FIG. 3.—Immigrant inflows and native outflows for laborers and less-skilled service workers. California cities shown with filled squares.

cities in the sample are similar to the rates for other cities. Consistent with the estimates from the more complex models in table 4, the raw data in figure 3 suggest that out-migration rates of low-skilled natives are not systematically higher in high-immigrant cities. Second, I estimated the migration response models using only data from the 17 California cities in the sample. These estimates showed that even within California, occupation-specific mobility flows are relatively insensitive to immigrant inflows.[27]

One caveat to the conclusion that native migration patterns are insensitive to immigrant inflows is the time frame implicit in table 4. At least one-fifth of the recent immigrants measured in the empirical analysis entered the United States in 1989 or early 1990, leaving relatively little time for previous residents of a city to respond. More generally, the correlation of 5-year mobility flows of natives and earlier immigrants with 5-year immigrant inflow rates cannot capture long lags in any behavioral responses. Nevertheless, the evidence in table 4 suggests that immigrant inflows exert a powerful short-run effect on the relative supplies of different types of labor in different cities.[28]

[27] For example, the coefficient of immigrant inflows on native outmigration is 0.05 (standard error 0.05); and the coefficient on total occupation-specific population growth is 1.15 (0.13).

[28] A similar conclusion is reached by Wright et al. (1997), although they do not

IV. Effects of Local Population Shares on Employment and Wages of Natives and Older Immigrants

This section turns to an analysis of the effects of changes in the skill composition of the local labor force on the labor market outcomes of different occupation groups. The investigation is conducted within the framework of the theoretical model in Section I, which specifies that the relative wages and employment rates of each group depend on the population shares of the groups. Although the population shares are computed using the entire adult population of each city, I fitted separate models for the outcomes of native men, native women, immigrant men, and immigrant women. Under the assumption that local labor markets are defined by occupation (rather than by nativity or gender), a shift in the share of the local population in a specific occupation should have the same effect on the employment and wages of all four gender-nativity subgroups. Thus, a comparison of the effects of shifting local population shares on the labor market outcomes of the four subgroups provides a test of the assumption of occupationally based labor markets.[29] As noted in Section I, a key concern in interpreting the effect of relative supplies on the structure of city-specific wages is that occupation-specific local demand shocks may be correlated with the relative supplies of labor in a city. Following the approach in the previous section, I use the supply-push component of recent immigrant inflows to each city as an instrumental variable for the population shares of the various occupation groups.

Table 6 presents estimates of the effect of occupation-specific local population shares on the employment rates of individuals who would be expected to work in that occupation in the absence of unusual local labor market competition. The format of the table is similar to that of table 4: thus each column presents results for a different demographic subgroup, and each row pertains to a different estimation method or sample. In addition to the log population share of the occupation group, the models include city and occupation dummies and a set of controls for the characteristics of the local population (e.g., the mean age and education of

---

distinguish among skill groups within cities. I conducted an analysis along the lines of table 4 using total adult city populations to see if total population growth is depressed by immigrant inflows (regardless of the skill composition of the inflows). The results (available on request) confirm the findings of Wright et al. (1997): total population growth of a city responds positively to new immigrant inflows.

[29] A similar test is suggested by Jaeger (1995), using changes for 50 large cities between 1980 and 1990. He concludes that immigrants and natives are nearly perfect substitutes within broad occupation groups.

Table 6
Effects of Skill Group Population Shares on Employment-Population Rates
of Natives and Earlier Immigrants

	Natives		Pre-1985 Immigrants	
	Men	Women	Men	Women
Ordinary least squares estimation:				
A. 175 cities weighted	−.028	−.045	−.019	−.023
	(.004)	(.005)	(.005)	(.007)
B. 175 cities unweighted	−.035	−.047	−.032	−.020
	(.005)	(.005)	(.006)	(.008)
C. Top 50 cities weighted	−.022	−.046	−.007	−.035
	(.008)	(.009)	(.006)	(.009)
Instrumental variables estimation (instrument is predicted immigrant inflow):				
D. 175 cities weighted	−.202	−.081	−.096	−.146
	(.042)	(.018)	(.040)	(.036)
E. Top 50 cities weighted	−.185	−.070	−.041	−.072
	(.056)	(.020)	(.027)	(.032)
F. Three least-educated occupations only	−.068	−.032	−.020	−.045
	(.019)	(.014)	(.020)	(.036)
G. Laborers/low-skill services and professional/ technical only	−.040	−.060	−.022	−.038
	(.010)	(.010)	(.011)	(.013)

NOTE.—Entries are estimated regression coefficients of the log population share of a specific occupation group in a model for the employment rate of individuals in the occupation group. Models are fitted separately by gender and nativity: each model is estimated on a sample of six occupation groups in 175 cities, except as noted in rows F and G. All models include occupation group dummies, city dummies, mean age, mean education, percentage black, and percentage married; and (for immigrants only) mean years in the United States and fractions of immigrants from Western Europe, Asia, and Mexico for the gender/origin/skill group in the particular city in 1990. The employment rates for each city and occupation group are adjusted for the characteristics of individuals in the particular city and occupation using a first-stage regression model, as described in the text. Standard errors are in parentheses.

individuals in the specific occupation and demographic subgroup). The upper panel reports OLS estimates, while the lower panel reports IV estimates that use the predicted inflow rate of new immigrants as an instrument for the log population shares.

The city-specific employment rates for each demographic group are obtained from a 2-step procedure similar to the one used to derive the adjusted outflow rates used in table 4. Specifically, the dependent variables are estimated city dummies taken from a series of 24 weighted linear probability models for employment status, fitted by occupation and demographic subgroup to national samples of individuals and using as weights the predicted probabilities of working in the occupation in a standardized labor market.[30] These first-stage models include a rich set of

[30] Although eq. (4) specifies the log of the employment rate as the dependent variable, I use the employment rate itself, since this simplifies the procedure for obtaining adjusted employment rates. The coefficients can be translated into

individual-specific characteristics (see the appendix) that control for any observable differences in the characteristics of each subgroup in each city that might happen to be correlated with average employment rates and the relative population shares.

Rows A–C of table 6 report weighted and unweighted OLS estimates for the 175 major cities and for the subset of 50 largest cities. Consistent with the theoretical model, the estimated effects of an increase in population share are uniformly negative and are similar in magnitude across the four subgroups. The estimates are also similar across specifications. Although not reported in the table, estimates using actual employment rates, rather than regression-adjusted employment rates, are very close to the ones in table 6.

I also fitted a set of parallel models that used an augmented population share measure, based on formulas presented in Card (1997). Specifically, the observed occupation shares were adjusted for intercity differences in the population shares of six subgroups: native men, native women, pre-1985 immigrant men, pre-1985 immigrant women, post-1985 immigrant men, and post-1985 immigrant women. The adjusted shares were derived by weighting the counts of individuals in each demographic subgroup by their relative annual earnings (estimated nationally by occupation). Empirically, however, there is very limited intercity variation in the adjustment factors. Estimates from these specifications are, therefore, quite close to those shown in the table.

Rows D–F of table 6 present IV estimates that use the supply-push component of recent immigrant inflows as an instrument for the population shares. Although not shown in the table, the first-stage equations for the IV models show large and highly significant effects of predicted immigrant inflows on the log of the population share, with t-ratios over 5. The IV estimates are uniformly more negative than the corresponding OLS estimates (compare rows D and E to rows A and C, respectively), which suggests the presence of skill-group-specific local demand shocks that are correlated with local population shares. They are also a little more variable across the four demographic subgroups, but they are generally significantly different from zero.

The existence of a strong reduced-form correlation between the supply-push component of immigrant inflows and the employment-population rate of individuals in the same occupation group is illustrated in figure 4, using data for native men in the laborers and low-skilled services occupation group. Although there is substantial variability in average employment rates across cities, a negative relationship between employ-

---

effects on the log employment rate by multiplying by the inverse of the average employment rate (0.85 for men, 0.70 for women).

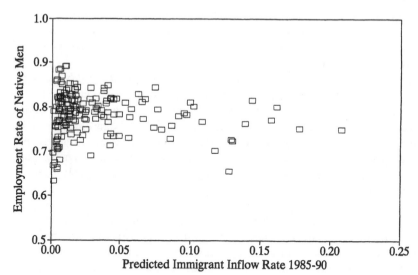

FIG. 4.—Predicted immigrant inflows and employment rate of native men in laborer and less-skilled service occupations.

ment and the supply-push component of immigrant inflows is clearly discernable.[31] Thus, both simple evidence, such as the scatter in figure 4, and estimates from the structural models in table 6 point to an impact of immigrant inflows on employment outcomes.

The assumption of a CES technology implies that the relative employment rate of each occupation group depends only on its own population share. One way to test this assumption is to reestimate the model on a subset of occupations. For example, the IV estimates in row F are based on outcomes for the three least-educated occupation groups. The point estimates of the population share coefficient are somewhat smaller than in the corresponding estimates that pool all six occupation groups, potentially indicating a higher elasticity of substitution within these three groups than across all groups. (Recall that the coefficient of the log population share in eq. [4'] is $d_2 = -\varepsilon/(\varepsilon + \sigma)$, which will be smaller in absolute value, the larger the elasticity of substitution, σ.) It is interesting, however, that estimates from a specification that pools only the lowest and the highest occupation groups (shown in row G) are also smaller in absolute value than the estimates that pool all six occupation groups.

Taken as a whole, the estimates in table 6 point to a modest effect of

[31] A simple weighted regression of the adjusted native male employment rate on the predicted immigrant inflow rate has a coefficient of −0.29, with a standard error of 0.10.

relative population shares on local employment rates. In terms of the theoretical model, the OLS estimates in row A imply that the coefficient d_2 from equation 4' is in the range of -0.03 to -0.06, whereas the IV estimates in row F point to a larger estimate: one in the range of -0.1 to -0.2.[32] The IV estimates suggest that a rise in the local population share of the lowest occupation group from 20% to 24% (equivalent to the difference between St. Louis and New York) would be expected to reduce the employment-population rate for individuals in this occupation by 0.02 to 0.04. Translated into an impact of new immigrant inflows, a 0.10 inflow rate of new immigrants in the lowest occupation group (comparable to the rate for Oakland, California, or Bergen County, New Jersey, between 1985 and 1990) would be expected to increase the log population share of the group by 0.10 and to depress the employment rate of natives and earlier immigrants in the occupation group by about 0.01–0.02. A massive 0.20 immigrant inflow rate—comparable with the impact of the Mariel boatlift—would be expected to have about twice as big an effect.[33]

Table 7 presents a parallel analysis for the effect of skill group population shares on mean log wages of the four demographic subgroups. An important difference between the analyses of employment and wages is the fact that wages are only observed for workers. Thus, there is a potential selectivity bias in the measured effect of population shares on wages. In particular, if higher-wage individuals in a given occupation are more likely to remain employed in the face of declining demand conditions, the coefficient estimates in table 7 will be biased toward zero. I return to this issue below.

The OLS estimates in rows A–C of table 7 show systematically negative effects of higher local population shares on the relative wages of different occupation groups. The estimates are roughly comparable in magnitude with the corresponding estimates in table 6, which suggests that the elasticity of labor supply (or, more precisely, employment participation) is around one. In comparison with the relatively stable OLS estimates, the IV estimates in rows D–G are more variable across specifications and between the four demographic groups. If unobserved occupation-specific local demand shocks are positively correlated with local population shares, one would expect the IV estimates in row D or row E to be systematically more negative than the corresponding OLS estimates

---

[32] Recall that the theoretical model is written in terms of the log employment rate, so the coefficients in table 6 have to be divided by the average employment rate to calculate the implied estimate of d_2.

[33] In my 1990 paper, I estimated that the boatlift increased the Miami labor force by 7%. Assuming that three-quarters of the Marielitos were in laborer and less-skilled service occupations, the boatlift would have increased the relative population share of these occupations by about 25%.

Table 7
Effects of Skill Group Population Share on Mean Log Wages of Natives and
Earlier Immigrants

	Natives		Pre-1985 Immigrants	
	Men	Women	Men	Women
Ordinary least squares estimation:				
A. 175 cities weighted	−.025	−.058	−.051	−.041
	(.005)	(.005)	(.010)	(.010)
B. 175 cities unweighted	−.010	−.051	−.037	−.022
	(.006)	(.004)	(.013)	(.012)
C. Top 50 cities weighted	−.054	−.058	−.059	−.064
	(.009)	(.007)	(.013)	(.012)
Instrumental variables estimation (instrument is predicted immigrant inflow):				
D. 175 cities weighted	−.099	.063	.037	−.251
	(.033)	(.020)	(.073)	(.055)
E. Top 50 cities weighted	−.039	.050	−.022	−.116
	(.038)	(.023)	(.055)	(.042)
F. Three least-educated occupations only	−.041	.020	−.018	−.213
	(.020)	(.012)	(.036)	(.054)
G. Laborers/low-skill services and professional/ technical only	−.031	−.056	−.057	−.048
	(.012)	(.008)	(.022)	(.019)

NOTE.—Entries are estimated regression coefficients of the log population share of a specific occupation group in a model for the hourly wage of individuals in the occupation group. Models are fitted separately by gender and nativity: each model is estimated on a sample of six occupation groups in 175 cities, except as noted in rows F and G. All models include occupation group dummies, city dummies, mean age, mean education, percentage black, and percentage married; and (for immigrants only) mean years in the United States and fractions of immigrants from Western Europe, Asia, and Mexico for the gender/origin/skill group in the particular city in 1990. The mean wages for each city and occupation group are adjusted for the characteristics of individuals in the particular city and occupation using a first-stage regression model, as described in the text. Standard errors are in parentheses.

in row A or row 3. This pattern is true for native men and immigrant women, but not for the other two subgroups. The IV estimates for the subset of the three least-educated occupations (row F) are a little more stable across demographic groups, while those based on wages for the lowest and highest occupation groups (row G) are quite similar across subgroups.

An issue in the interpretation of the estimates in table 7 is selectivity bias. One way to assess the potential magnitude of any such bias is to posit a specific model for the employment outcomes of individuals within each occupation group. Following Gronau (1974), suppose that individual wages (i.e., the wages that individuals could receive if they worked) are distributed within occupation/city cells according to

$$\log w_{ijc} = \log w_{jc} + \xi_{ijc},$$

where w_{jc} is the mean wage for individuals in occupation j and city c, and

ξ_{ijc} is normally distributed with mean 0 and standard deviation $\sigma(\xi)$. Suppose that individual i's employment outcome is determined by the sign of a latent index, $H_{ijc} = d_{jc} + \alpha\xi_{ijc} + v_{ijc}$, where v_{ijc} is another normally distributed error. In this case, the mean of observed wages for workers in city c and occupation j is related to the unconditional mean by

$$E(\log w_{ijc}|H_{ijc} \geq 0) = \log w_{jc} + E(\xi_{ijc}|H_{ijc} \geq 0) = \log w_{jc} + \rho\sigma(\xi)\lambda(\pi_{jc}),$$

where ρ is the correlation coefficient between ξ_{ijc} and the composite error $\alpha\xi_{ijc} + v_{ijc}$, π_{jc} is the employment rate of group j in city c, and $\lambda(\pi)$ $= \phi(\Phi^{-1}(\pi))/\pi$ is the inverse Mill's ratio function. The selectivity bias component in the mean of observed wages is $\rho\sigma(\xi)\lambda(\pi_{jc})$, which is positive and decreasing in π if $\rho > 0$. Since the function $\lambda(\pi)$ is approximately linear over most of its range, the assumption of joint normality of the error components implies that the selectivity bias component is approximately a linear function of the employment rate of the group. Indeed, for $0.4 < \pi < 0.9$, $\lambda(\pi) \approx 1.5 - 1.5\pi$. Assuming that $\sigma(\xi)$ is approximately equal to 0.5, the selectivity bias in the mean observed wages of occupation j in city c is

$$\text{Bias}_{jc} \approx 0.75\rho - 0.75\rho\pi_{jc}.$$

To illustrate the implications of this formula, note that the estimates in table 6 suggest that the employment rate of a skill group is negatively related to the log population share of the group with a coefficient of (roughly) -0.15. Using this estimate, the implied selectivity bias in a regression of observed mean log wages on log population shares is approximately 0.11ρ. Since ρ cannot exceed one, an upper bound on the selectivity bias is 0.11, and a more reasonable bound might be 0.05 (assuming $\rho < 0.5$).

Given that most of the estimates in table 7 range from -0.10 to 0, a reasonable lower bound on the coefficient d_1, taking account of potential selectivity biases, is -0.15, with a somewhat larger bound for immigrant women. This range of estimates can be combined with evidence on the range for the coefficient d_2 from table 6 to construct estimates of the theoretical parameters underlying equations (3') and (4')—the participation elasticity ε and the substitution elasticity σ. Assuming that $-0.15 \leq d_1 \leq -0.05$ and $-0.20 \leq d_2 \leq -0.10$, the data point to an estimate of $\varepsilon = d_2/d_1$ that is on the order of one. This is somewhat above estimates based on comparisons of the aggregate changes in wage and employment rates of different demographic groups over the 1980s (e.g., Juhn 1992; Card, Kramarz, and Lemieux 1999), but given the range of uncertainty in the estimates of d_1, it is hard to draw strong inferences. The implied estimate of the substitution elasticity, $\sigma = -(1 + d_2)/d_1$, is large—at least 5, and probably more like 10, using the midpoint of the estimates. This magnitude is consistent with the observation that relative wages are not much different in cities that have substantially different relative population shares of different occupation groups.[34] In terms of implications for immigrant inflows, an estimate of $d_1 = -0.15$ implies that an inflow rate of 10% for one occupation group (which raises the log population share of the group by about 0.1) would reduce relative wages for the occupation by 1.5%. An inflow of 20% — equivalent to the highest rates seen in the data between 1985 and 1990 —would be expected to lower relative wages by 3%.

It is worth noting that the findings in tables 6 and 7 are qualitatively and quantitatively similar to findings in an earlier version of this article (Card 1997) that used a different skill group classification system, based on 10 intervals of predicted wages rather than six predicted occupations. The use of the smaller number of occupation-based skill groups leads to somewhat stronger evidence that the relative wages of different groups are affected by their relative population shares, while the estimated impacts on relative employment are very similar under the two classification systems. In light of the uncertainty over how to define skill groups and how many skill groups to define, this comparability is reassuring.

V. Summary and Conclusions

The findings in this article point to three substantive conclusions. First, inflows of new immigrants to individual cities over the 1985–90 period did not generate large offsetting mobility flows by natives or earlier immigrants in the same skill groups. As a result, cities that received large inflows of new immigrants generally experienced large increases in the relative size of their less-skilled populations. Second, shifts in the population shares of different skill groups are associated with systematic changes in relative employment. Ordinary least squares estimates of the effect of an increase in the relative population share of an occupation group suggest that a 10% increase in population share is associated with up to a 0.5-percentage-point reduction in the employment rate of the group. Instrumental variables estimates using the supply-push component of recent immigrant inflows are two to three times bigger. The larger IV estimates are consistent with the existence of skill-group specific local demand shocks that are positively correlated with relative population shares of different groups. Such demand shocks may be attributable to exogenous factors, or they could potentially represent an endogenous

---

[34] Jaeger (1995) also obtains relatively large elasticities of substitution.

adaptation of local industry structure to the local supplies of different skill groups, as predicted by multisector trade models. Taken together, these first two findings imply that, in the short run at least, inflows of new immigrants in the 1985–90 period reduced the relative employment rates of natives and earlier immigrants in laborer and low-skilled service occupations by up to 1 percentage point, and by up to 3 percentage points in very high-immigrant cities like Los Angeles or Miami.

A third and more tentative finding is that shifts in relative population shares are associated with changes in relative wages. On balance, the estimates suggest that the elasticity of relative wages with respect to relative population shares is comparable with, or slightly smaller than, the elasticity of relative employment. While OLS estimates of the relative wage effects are fairly stable, the IV estimates vary across demographic subgroups, and they are also somewhat sensitive to specification choices. Moreover, the measured wage effects are potentially biased by selective labor force participation behavior. Despite these sources of uncertainty, it seems likely that immigrant inflows over the late 1980s reduced the relative wages of laborers and less-skilled service workers in high immigrant cities by no more than 3%. The effects in other cities, and for other occupation groups that were less affected by new immigrant arrivals, were probably much smaller.

In the context of the simple theoretical model developed in this article, the estimation results suggest that the elasticity of substitution between different skill categories is relatively high. Given this high degree of substitutability, shifts in the relative supply of different occupations do not affect the relative wage structure very much. This is true even in the short run in response to supply-push immigrant inflows over the preceding 5 years. Shifts in the relative supply of the different skill groups may, of course, affect the overall level of wages in a city, but a complete examination of this possibility is beyond the scope of this article.[35]

In comparing the findings of this article with the results in the existing literature, it is worth noting that most earlier studies make no distinction among different subgroups of immigrants: rather, native wage and employment outcomes are correlated with levels or changes in the overall fraction of immigrants in different local labor markets. The analysis here, on the other hand, assumes that local labor markets are occupation-specific, and it focuses on the effect of immigrant inflows on the relative supplies of different occupation groups in different cities. Even with these distinctions, the measured effects of immigrant inflows on the native wage

---

[35] It should be noted that in the cross-section of major cities studied here, average wages are significantly higher in cities with high overall immigrant inflow rates (see table A1). This is consistent with the existing literature, e.g., with Schoeni (1996).

structure are small. The results in this article are, therefore, consistent with most of the existing literature on immigration and native wages. They are also consistent with the results of Lalonde and Topel (1991), who find relatively modest effects of immigrant inflows on immigrant relative wages.

The conclusion that immigrant inflows affect native employment rates is new. However, the implied effects for natives as a whole are very small. Even for workers in the bottom of the skill distribution, I find relatively modest employment effects of recent immigrant inflows in all but a few high-immigrant cities. Between 1985 and 1990, however, a handful of U.S. cities experienced immigrant inflows that expanded their unskilled labor forces by as much or more than the Mariel boatlift affected the Miami labor market. The results in this article suggest that these massive expansions may have significantly reduced employment rates for younger and less-educated natives in these cities.

Appendix
Data Appendix
A. Basic Sample Criteria

I begin with a 25% random sample of all native-born individuals ages 16–68 in the 5% public use samples of the 1990 census, and 100% of all foreign-born individuals in the same age range. The resulting sample sizes are 965,132 native women; 921,034 native men; 428,789 foreign-born women; and 418,258 foreign-born men. I further restrict the sample to individuals whose potential labor market experience (age minus years of education minus five) is greater than one in 1990. Years of education are assigned to the education codes used in the 1990 census following Park (1996). The minimum age restriction eliminates about 4.5% of natives and 4% of immigrants from the sample.

Labor market outcomes are based on earnings and hours of work in 1989. Individuals are coded as employed if they reported positive earnings, including wage and salary and self-employment earnings, and positive weeks of work and positive usual hours per week in 1989. An hourly wage was assigned by dividing total earnings by the product of weeks worked and usual hours per week. I did not exclude allocated responses for earnings or hours. Wage rates less than $2 per hour or greater than $90 per hour were set to missing.

B. Assigning MSA Codes

The finest level of geographic information on the 1990 public use samples is the PUMA (public-use micro sample area). Most individuals who live in a metropolitan area are also assigned a metropolitan area identifier (i.e., an MSA or CMSA code). However, some PUMAs straddle the boundary of one or more MSAs, and in these mixed PUMAs, an MSA code is not assigned. I used the Geographic Equivalency file to identify the MSA that contributed the largest fraction of the population to any such mixed PUMAs. If over 50% of the PUMA population was attributable to a single MSA, I then assigned all individuals in that PUMA to the majority MSA. The computer code for this assignment, which affects 213 PUMAs, is available on request.

C. Assigning 1985 MSA Codes

The public use samples also include information on place of residence in 1985, coded to the PUMA level. I used the Geographic Equivalency files to map 1985 PUMA codes into MSAs. The computer code for this assignment is available on request. A small fraction of immigrants who are coded as having arrived in the United States between 1985 and 1990 report data on their place of residence in 1985. For simplicity, however, I assume these individuals lived outside of the United States in 1985, and I ignore them in constructing 1985 population counts for individual MSAs.

D. Models Used to Determine Occupation Groups

Separate multinominal logit models were fitted for native-born and immigrant men and women, using the samples of individuals living in the largest 175 cities with valid wages in 1990, as described above. The native models included a linear education term; a quartic in potential experience; indicators for black, Asian, or Aboriginal race; indicators for marital status, disability status, and veteran status; interactions of education with the race indicators and linear and quadratic experience; interactions of the race indicators with marital status and veteran status; and indicators for the 30 largest cities and cities in California, Texas, Florida, or the northeast region. In addition, the model for native women included indicators for the presence of own children less than 6 years of age and between 6 and 17 years of age.

The immigrant models included a linear education term; a quartic in potential experience; a quadratic function of years in the United States fully interacted with education; a dummy for having moved to the United States before age 6; 17 origin dummies; and interactions of years of education with indicators for three main origin groups (immigrants from Mexico, Canada/Australia/Europe; and Asia); dummies for black and Asian race, being married, and reporting a disability; and indicators for the 30 largest cities and cities in California, Texas, Florida, or the northeast region. Finally, the model for immigrant women included indicators for the presence of own children less than 6 years of age and between 6 and 17 years of age.

Predicted probabilities of working in each occupation were formed for each individual, using the estimated coefficients from the appropriate model and assuming residence outside the 30 largest cities, or California, Texas, Florida, or the northeast region.

E. Models Used to Construct Adjusted Outmigration Rates

The adjusted outflow rates used in table 4 are city dummies estimated from a set of linear probability models for the event of moving out of the 1985 city of residence by 1990. A total of 12 models are fitted for the six different occupation groups by nativity. The models for each occupation are fitted by weighted least squares, using as weights the predicted probabilities of working in the occupation. For each occupation-nativity group, I fitted a linear probability model with unrestricted dummies for the particular city of residence in 1985. For natives, the other covariates included in the models were a gender dummy; age, age-squared, and a dummy for age under 30; interactions of the three age variables with the gender dummy; years of education; interactions of education with indicators for gender, age under 30; and the interaction of gender and age under 30; a dummy for black race; and interactions of education with indicators for black men and black women. For immigrants, the covariates included age, age-squared, and a dummy for age under 30; a gender dummy; years of education; interactions of education with indicators for gender, age under 30, and gender × age under 30; 16 dummies for country of origin; interactions of the country-of-origin dummies with years since arrival in the United States, and with years since arrival squared.

F. Models Used to Construct Adjusted Employment and Wage Rates

The employment rates and wage rates used as dependent variables in tables 6 and 7 are city dummies estimated from separate sets of models fit by occupation group and gender-nativity to samples of individuals who lived in one of the 175 largest cities in 1990. The models used to construct the employment rates are linear probability models for the event of reporting positive earnings and hours in 1989, while the models used to construct the average wages are models for the log of average hourly wages in 1989. The models for each occupation are fitted by weighted least squares, using as weights the probabilities of working in that occupation. For native men and women, the other covariates included in the models were years of education and an indicator for holding a college degree; a cubic function of experience; an indicator for being married; and interactions of race indicator with education, experience, and the marital status indicator. For immigrant men and women, the other covariates included years of education and an indicator for holding a college degree; a cubic function of experience; an indicator for marital status; 16 dummies for country of origin; interactions of the country-of-origin dummies with years since arrival in the United States, and with years since arrival squared; and interactions of education with years in the United States and indicators for three main origin groups (immigrants from Mexico, Canada/Australia/Europe, and Asia).

Table A1

Population, Immigrant Fraction, and Occupational Distributions in 30 Largest Cities

	Adult Population	Percentage of Immigrants		Relative Population Shares of Six Major Occupation Groups						Relative Level and Dispersion of Wages	
		All	Recent	I	II	III	IV	V	VI	Level	SD
All major cities	102,108	13.9	3.0	1.00	1.00	1.00	1.00	1.00	1.00	1.00	1.00
Los Angeles, CA	5,638	41.1	10.6	1.17	1.12	.92	.93	.84	.88	1.05	1.04
New York, NY	4,425	38.1	8.1	1.18	.96	.97	.90	.91	1.00	1.16	1.02
Chicago, IL	3,309	17.5	3.4	1.03	.97	.97	.96	1.00	1.06	1.08	.98
Philadelphia, PA	2,606	7.3	1.2	.98	.97	1.01	1.01	1.02	1.03	1.09	.96
Washington, DC	2,559	16.0	4.4	.92	.80	.92	.91	1.13	1.40	1.19	.97
Detroit, MI	2,247	6.4	.8	1.04	1.01	1.03	1.02	.98	.92	1.06	1.01
Houston, TX	1,886	17.3	3.3	1.06	1.05	.96	.95	.95	.98	.97	1.05
Nassau-Suffolk, NY	1,784	13.8	2.0	.83	.87	1.01	1.06	1.17	1.20	1.26	1.02
Boston, MA	1,746	14.8	3.9	.84	.82	.95	1.02	1.16	1.34	1.18	.95
Atlanta, GA	1,704	5.6	1.4	1.01	.97	.99	.95	1.01	1.07	1.01	.97
Anaheim, CA	1,668	29.6	8.5	.94	.99	.95	1.02	1.05	1.08	1.15	1.03
Dallas, TX	1,659	11.6	2.6	.96	.98	.98	.99	1.04	1.07	.99	1.01
San Diego, CA	1,578	22.0	5.2	.96	1.00	.99	1.00	1.00	1.04	.98	1.02
Baltimore, MD	1,501	5.2	.8	1.04	.99	.98	.96	.99	1.03	1.06	.95
Riverside, CA	1,439	19.4	4.5	1.05	1.14	1.03	1.01	.90	.80	1.02	.99
Oakland, CA	1,365	21.1	4.6	.93	.88	.96	.98	1.10	1.22	1.19	.98
Tampa, FL	1,322	9.5	1.5	.97	1.02	1.07	1.05	1.01	.90	.86	.96
Newark, NJ	1,305	18.5	3.6	1.00	.92	.98	.97	1.05	1.11	1.20	.99
St Louis, MO	1,302	2.7	.5	.99	.99	1.02	1.01	1.02	1.00	.98	.98
Phoenix, AZ	1,291	9.5	2.2	.90	.98	1.02	1.06	1.08	1.03	.94	.99
Pittsburgh, PA	1,235	2.4	.4	.94	1.02	1.07	1.06	1.01	.93	.92	1.01
Seattle, WA	1,217	10.1	2.1	.81	.86	1.00	1.07	1.20	1.22	1.07	.95
Minneapolis, MN	1,211	3.9	.9	.84	.93	1.03	1.08	1.14	1.10	1.03	.95
Miami, FL	1,201	57.6	11.1	1.30	1.10	.96	.83	.80	.82	.87	1.01
Cleveland, OH	1,075	6.3	.8	1.02	.99	1.03	1.00	.99	.97	.98	.96
San Jose, CA	1,041	28.7	7.1	.91	.92	.93	1.00	1.09	1.22	1.21	.99
San Francisco, CA	1,025	32.1	7.2	.90	.82	.89	.96	1.16	1.37	1.20	1.01
Denver, CO	1,007	6.7	1.2	.82	.89	1.01	1.05	1.18	1.18	.99	.98
Sacramento, CA	927	12.6	2.5	.89	.94	1.02	1.04	1.10	1.10	1.04	.95
Fort Worth, TX	902	8.2	1.6	.96	1.04	1.01	1.02	1.02	.96	.93	1.00
Correlation with:											
Fraction immigrant	···	1.00	.98	.46	.07	−.66	−.62	−.32	.04	.41	.48
Fraction recent immigrant	···	.98	1.00	.42	.06	−.70	−.60	−.30	.07	.42	.49

NOTE.—Adult population is thousands of people ages 16–68 with 2 or more years of potential experience. Relative population shares of the six occupation groups are the fraction of adults in the city in each of six occupation groups, divided by the national average fractions of adults in the same occupation. Occupation groups are I, laborers, farm workers, and low-skilled service workers; II, operatives and craft workers; III, clerical workers; IV, sales workers; V, managers; and VI, professional and technical workers. Relative level of wages is 1 plus the difference in mean log wages between the city and the national mean. Relative standard deviation of wages is the ratio of the standard deviation of log wages in the city to the standard deviation nationally. Correlations in the bottom two rows are weighted correlations over all 175 major cities between immigrant fractions and the variables represented by the column headings.

References

Altonji, Joseph G., and Card, David. "The Effects of Immigration on the Labor Market Outcomes of Less-Skilled Natives." In *Immigration, Trade and Labor,* edited by John M. Abowd and Richard B. Freeman. Chicago: University of Chicago Press, 1991.

Bartel, Anne P. "Where Do the New U.S. Immigrants Live?" *Journal of Labor Economics* 7 (October 1989): 371–91.

Borjas, George J. "Immigrants, Minorities, and Labor Market Competition." *Industrial and Labor Relations Review* 40 (April 1987): 382–92.

———. "The Economics of Immigration." *Journal of Economic Literature* 32 (December 1994): 1667–1717.

Borjas, George J.; Freeman, Richard B.; and Katz, Lawrence F. "On the Labor Market Effects of Immigration and Trade." In *Immigration and the Work Force: Economic Consequences for the United States and Source Areas,* edited by George J. Borjas and Richard B. Freeman. Chicago: University of Chicago Press, 1992.

———. "Searching for the Effect of Immigration on the Labor Market." Working Paper no. 5454. Cambridge, MA: National Bureau of Economic Research, 1996.

Bound, John, and Johnson, George. "Changes in the Structure of Wages in the 1980s: An Evaluation of Alternative Explanations." *American Economic Review* 82 (June 1992): 371–92.

Butcher, Kristin F., and Card, David. "Immigration and Wages: Evidence from the 1980s." *American Economic Review* 81 (May 1991): 292–96.

Butcher, Kristin F., and DiNardo, John E. "The Immigrant and Native-Born Wage Distributions: Evidence from the United States Censuses." Working Paper no. 6630. Cambridge, MA: National Bureau of Economic Research, 1998.

Card, David. "The Impact of the Mariel Boatlift on the Miami Labor Market." *Industrial and Labor Relations Review* 43 (January 1990): 245–57.

———. "Immigrant Inflows, Native Outflows, and the Local Labor Market Impacts of Higher Immigration." Working Paper no. 5927. Cambridge, MA: National Bureau of Economic Research, 1997.

Card, David; Kramarz, Francis; and Lemieux, Thomas. "Changes in the Relative Structure of Wages and Employment: A Comparison of the United States, Canada, and France." *Canadian Journal of Economics* 32 (August 1999): 843–77.

Filer, Randall K. "The Impact of Immigrant Arrivals on Migratory Patterns of Native Workers." In *Immigration and the Work Force: Economic Consequences for the United States and Source Areas,* edited by George J. Borjas and Richard B. Freeman. Chicago: University of Chicago Press, 1992.

Frey, William H. "Immigration and Internal Migration 'Flight': A California Case Study." *Population and Environment* 16 (1995): 353–75. (*a*)

———. "Immigration Impacts on Internal Migration of the Poor: 1990 Census Evidence for U.S. States." *International Journal of Population Geography* 1 (1995): 51–67. (*b*)

Friedberg, Rachel M., and Hunt, Jennifer. "The Impact of Immigrants on Host Country Wages, Employment, and Growth." *Journal of Economic Perspectives* 9 (Winter 1995): 23–44.

Gronau, Reuben. "Wage Comparisons: A Selectivity Bias." *Journal of Political Economy* 82 (November/December 1974): 1119–43.

Grossman, Jean B. "The Substitutability of Natives and Immigrants in Production." *Review of Economics and Statistics* 64 (November 1982): 596–603.

Jaeger, David A. "Skill Differences and the Effects of Immigrants on the Wages of Natives." Working Paper no. 273. Washington, DC: U.S. Bureau of Labor Statistics, 1995.

Johnson, George, and Stafford, Frank. "The Labor Market Implications of International Trade." In *Handbook of Labor Economics*, vol. 3, edited by Orley Ashenfelter and David Card. Amsterdam and New York: Elsevier, 1999.

Juhn, Chinhui. "Decline of Male Labor Market Participation: The Role of Declining Market Opportunities." *Quarterly Journal of Economics* 107 (February 1992): 79–122.

Katz, Lawrence F., and Murphy, Kevin M. "Changes in Relative Wages, 1963–1987: Supply and Demand Factors." *Quarterly Journal of Economics* 107 (February 1992): 35–78.

LaLonde, Robert J., and Topel, Robert H. "Labor Market Adjustments to Increased Immigration." In *Immigration, Trade and Labor*, edited by John M. Abowd and Richard B. Freeman. Chicago: University of Chicago Press, 1991.

Leamer, Edward E. *The Heckscher-Ohlin Model in Theory and Practice.* Princeton Studies in International Finance, vol. 77. Princeton, NJ: Princeton University, Department of Economics, International Finance Section, 1995.

Levy, Frank, and Murnane, Richard J. "U.S. Earnings Levels and Earnings Inequality: A Review of Recent Trends and Propose Explanations." *Journal of Economic Literature* 30 (September 1992): 1333–81.

Park, Jin Heum. "A Comparison of Old and New Measures of Education from the Current Population Survey." *Economics Letters* 50 (March 1999): 425–28.

Schoeni, Robert F. "The Effect of Immigrants on the Employment and Wages of Native Workers: Evidence from the 1970s and 1980s." Unpublished manuscript. Santa Monica, CA: Rand, 1996.

United States Department of Commerce Bureau of the Census. "Statistical Brief: Metropolitan Areas." SB/94-9. Washington, DC: U.S. Government Printing Office, 1994.

White, Michael J., and Hunter, Lori. "The Migratory Response of Native Born Workers to the Presence of Immigrants in the Labor Market."

Population Studies and Training Center Working Paper no. 93-08.
Providence, RI: Brown University, 1993.

White, Michael J., and Liang, Zai. "The Effect of Immigration on the
Internal Migration of the Native Born Population, 1981–90." Unpublished manuscript. Providence, RI: Brown University, 1994.

Wright, Richard A.; Ellis, Mark; and Reibel, Michael. "The Linkage
between Immigration and Internal Migration in Large Metropolitan
Areas in the United States." *Economic Geography* 73 (June 1997):
234–54.

Part II
Institutions and Labor Market Outcomes

[6]

THE EVOLUTION OF UNJUST-DISMISSAL LEGISLATION IN THE UNITED STATES

ALAN B. KRUEGER*

In the past decade, many state courts have ruled in favor of employees alleging they were improperly dismissed. The author of this paper advances an evolutionary theory of unjust-dismissal legislation in which employer groups, responding to the threat of large and variable damage awards imposed by the judicial system, eventually support unjust-dismissal legislation in order to clearly define property rights, reduce uncertainty, and limit employer liability. Based on evidence from a case study of legislation enacted in Montana and an empirical analysis of the determinants of proposed unjust-dismissal legislation in a panel of states, the author concludes that proposals of unjust-dismissal legislation are a response to court rulings that weaken and obfuscate the employer's right to dismiss employees at will.

For the past 100 years, job security in the United States has been governed by the common law "employment-at-will" doctrine. Under this doctrine, an employer can legally dismiss an employee for a good reason, a bad reason, or no reason at all, so long as the dismissal does not violate the provisions of a specific statute such as the National Labor Relations Act or the Civil Rights Act of 1964. The employer's unmitigated right to dismiss at-will employees, however, has been weakened by autonomous state court rulings in several jurisdictions in the 1980s. In addition, legislation to broadly

require some form of "just cause" to dismiss at-will employees has been introduced in ten state legislatures. And in 1987, Montana passed landmark legislation requiring firms to have a "just reason" to fire a worker. Epstein (1984), Lazear (1987), Posner (1988), and others have argued that judicial and legislative departures from the employment-at-will doctrine should be resisted because they have deleterious economic effects.

This paper focuses on the *positive* issue of the origin of unjust-dismissal legislation instead of the *normative* issue of whether such legislation is desirable. I advance the hypothesis that independent judiciary decisions lead a state's legislative branch to propose an unjust-dismissal law to clarify employment rights and limit employer liability. Under the strict employment-at-will doctrine, the property rights to jobs—meaning the set of actions that either party to an employment relationship could take to terminate the relationship—are clearly defined and enforced.

* The author is Assistant Professor of Economics and Public Affairs at Princeton University. He thanks Angela Chang, Timothy Kastelle, and Philip Levine for research assistance. In addition, he is grateful to Robert Gibbons, Lawrence Katz, Morris Kleiner, Lisa Krueger, Jonathan Leonard, Jack Stieber, and seminar participants at the University of Minnesota, the University of Chicago, and the NBER for helpful comments.

The data and computer programs used in this study are available on request to the author.

Industrial and Labor Relations Review, Vol. 44, No. 4 (July 1991). © by Cornell University.
0019-7939/91/4404 $01.00

Once state courts modify the common law, however, the property rights to jobs become uncertain and incomplete. Moreover, unjust-dismissal suits impose large legal costs on all parties concerned, and carry the prospect of unpredictable, highly variable, and occasionally excessive awards. I hypothesize that when the judicial costs of firing workers are perceived to be high, unjust-dismissal legislation is more likely to occur.

Two types of evidence are used to test this hypothesis. First, a case study of the forces leading to the passage of the nation's first unjust-dismissal law in Montana is presented. Second, pooled time-series/cross-sectional data on states from 1981 to 1988 are used to empirically examine whether unjust dismissal legislation is more likely to be proposed in states that have experienced a judicial break from the employment-at-will doctrine. The results suggest that employers are willing to accept a just cause firing standard in exchange for limited liability in states where they have lost their traditional common law right to fire workers at will. This conclusion is inconsistent with the conventional political economy view of unjust-dismissal legislation.

At-Will Employment and the Coase Principle

As a benchmark, it is useful to consider the conditions under which departures from the employment-at-will doctrine will affect economic efficiency.[1] As is well known, the Coase principle holds that if property rights are clearly defined and tradeable with zero transactions costs, then economic efficiency is *independent* of the original distribution of property rights.[2]

---

[1] Ehrenberg (1985) provides a useful survey of theoretical implications of the employment-at-will doctrine. Hamermesh (1990) provides some time-series evidence on the impact of the erosion of the employment-at-will doctrine on employment adjustment in the United States.

[2] See Coase (1960). This conclusion is only a partial equilibrium one because income effects may alter the equilibrium. In addition, the Coase theorem

Under these assumptions, the allocation of property rights will have distributional consequences for the parties involved, but will not affect the allocation of resources or the Pareto optimality of a market economy. This result has important implications for the legal controversy over employment-at-will.

In particular, if the rights to jobs (for example, the restrictions and review procedures that govern firings) are clearly defined and tradeable, and if transaction costs are insignificant, then a direct application of the Coase principle would imply that economic efficiency is independent of whether the right to terminate an employment relationship at will is originally assigned to the employer or to the employee. To illustrate this point, consider the equivalence of the following two examples.

In the first example, employers have the legal right to arbitrarily fire employees at will. Suppose that employees value protection from arbitrary dismissal such as that accorded by grievance procedures at $100 per year, and employers value the option to fire employees arbitrarily (for example, to avoid having grievance procedures to review disputed discharges) at $50 per year. The efficient allocation of resources in this situation would dictate that grievance procedures be provided. Because the employee in this example would be willing to forgo up to $100 per year in wages to "purchase" grievance procedures, and the employer would be willing to provide grievance procedures for $50 or more, the parties will privately contract to introduce grievance procedures. Voluntary exchange would lead to the efficient outcome.

In the second example, the employee is initially assigned the right to a grievance hearing if he or she should desire to challenge a dismissal. In this situation, the employer would be willing to pay up to $50 to have the employee waive this right, but the employee would decline the employer's offer because the provision of grievance procedures is valued at $100. Again, the efficient allocation of resources

---

rests on the assumption of complete information (see Farrell 1987).

results. The only substantive difference between the two examples is that the employee does not have to forgo $50 in wage payments when he or she is initially assigned the property right to protection from unjust dismissal.

Under the "Coasian" assumptions, opposition to wrongful-discharge legislation must rest on distributional arguments rather than efficiency arguments, because economic efficiency is not affected by the presence or absence of such legislation. On the other hand, if the assumptions of the Coase principle are violated, a move from the employment-at-will doctrine to an unjust-dismissal standard will affect economic efficiency.

An obvious assumption to question is whether property rights could be traded at zero transaction costs under a court-enforced just cause firing standard. In the first example discussed above, economic efficiency would clearly be reduced if the parties were forbidden from trading the opportunity to have grievance procedures. If explicit trades over job security were forbidden, however, it would still be possible for trades to take place along other margins. For example, even if it were nominally illegal to pay a worker a wage premium to relinquish the property right to protection from arbitrary dismissal, an employer could overcome this prohibition by offering a severance payment to a dismissed employee conditional on the employee not challenging the dismissal.[3] Although there is potential for trades along other dimensions of jobs, there are different transactions costs associated with alterations in the employment-at-will doctrine. If transactions costs inhibit trades, the efficient allocation would be to assign the right to termination review to the party that values it most highly.[4]

A related issue is whether job termination rights can be clearly defined under alternative legal schemes. As discussed in the next section, the current common law system generates considerable uncertainty over the ownership of job property rights and over the penalties for violations of those rights. Even for cases with similar circumstances, awards in unjust-dismissal suits vary depending on the particular judge and jury. This uncertainty can be characterized by an award distribution that is positively skewed, ranging from zero (which includes situations in which an employee does not bring a suit) to a large award. *Ex ante* uncertainty will inhibit efficient transactions because parties do not know their endowments. Moreover, if the parties are risk-averse, the introduction of a fixed award in unjust-dismissal judgments—or a limited liability rule that truncates the award distribution—can be Pareto improving.[5]

Institutional Analysis

In 1987, Montana became the first state in the United States to pass a broad law to protect at-will employees from unjust dismissal.[6] Curiously, Montana has historically been a leader in labor law: it passed the nation's second compulsory workers' compensation law in 1909, and was among the first states to pass a mandatory maternity leave law and sexual harassment prevention law. A case study of the forces that led to the proposal and enactment of unjust-dismissal legislation in Montana is instructive.

In the early 1980s, state courts in Montana issued several decisions that weakened the prevailing employment-

---

[3] Evidence suggests that this strategy is actually used: a Bureau of National Affairs (BNA) survey conducted in 1985 found that 23% of employers reported the "use of severance agreements with terminated employees for release of any claims against the organization" (BNA 1985:1).

[4] In addition, it may be efficient to shift the right to job security over time. For instance, given the

uncertainty of job matches, employers may value the right to dismiss at will more highly for newly hired workers than for long-service employees—as suggested by the existence of probationary periods during which new employees can be more easily dismissed.

[5] Although it is typical to treat employers as risk-neutral, in this instance employers may reasonably be thought of as risk-averse, since it is difficult to diversify risks associated with dismissals.

[6] This law was held constitutional by the Montana Supreme Court in *Meech v. Hillhaven West, Inc.* (Mont. 46 P.2d 88-410) in June 1989.

at-will doctrine. These decisions resulted in large judgments against employers in several unjust-dismissal cases shortly before the introduction and passage of the "Wrongful Discharge from Employment Act" (Mont. Code Ann. 39-2-901) by the state legislature in January 1987.

For example, in one well-publicized case (*Mildred Flanigan v. Prudential Federal Savings,* 720 P.2d 257, Mont. 1986) a 62-year-old employee was judged to have been wrongfully discharged from her job as an assistant loan counselor and was awarded $1.3 million for punitive damages, $100,000 for emotional distress, and $93,000 for economic losses by a Montana jury. The circumstances of this case were as follows. Flanigan, after 34 years of service at Prudential Federal, was given four months' notice that she would be terminated because of economic conditions. She was advised subsequently, however, to attend a week-long training program in Salt Lake City, Utah, to prepare for a new job as a bank teller. Despite having attended the training course, Flanigan was discharged without notice or hearing less than one month after assuming a position as a teller. She was given six months' pay as a severance benefit. She was also later offered an opportunity to return as a part-time teller, but refused. The court reasoned that Flanigan's discharge violated the covenant of good faith and fair dealing implicit in employment relationships. Moreover, the *Flanigan* verdict and award were both affirmed on appeal by the Montana Supreme Court in June 1986.

In another influential case (*Farrens v. Meridian Oil,* CV 85-229-BLG), Michael Farrens was discharged for allegedly using one mud supplier exclusively, for purchasing drilling mud from the supplier at inflated prices, for taking bribes from the mud supplier, and for being a member of the mud supplier's board of directors. A Billings jury found these charges to be factually incorrect, and awarded the 34-year-old mechanical engineer $2.5 million for economic losses. After appeal, the Ninth Circuit Court of Appeals upheld the liability claim but ruled that the

evidence supported a $1.7 million award for economic damages. At the time he was dismissed, Farrens was earning $85,500 per year: $63,000 in salary, $11,000 in bonus, and $11,500 in fringes.

Although the *Flanigan* and *Farrens* cases are extreme examples, they reflect the potential losses that employers faced if they were challenged in an unjust-dismissal case.

Employer groups protested the large magnitude of some of the awards in unjust-dismissal cases, and objected to the uncertainty and expense created by the evolving common law.[7] As a consequence, many employer groups vigorously supported unjust-dismissal legislation. Consider, for example, the testimony of Kay Foster before the Montana State legislature:

I am a business owner and Deputy Mayor of Billings, appearing on behalf of the Billings Area Chamber of Commerce. The Billings Chamber supports HB241 [the Wrongful Discharge from Employment Act] and the positive impact it will have, particularly on the business community in our area. Wrongful discharge has become the favored tort claim in the Billings District and Federal Courts with the number of cases swelling from 2 in 1981 to 89 in 1985. The rising number of claims allowed under present Montana statutes has become a major disincentive to local business development and expansion of employment. (Quoted from Kay Foster's written testimony on HB241, Submission by the Montana Association of Defense Counsel, Exhibit E, January 28, 1987)

The unjust-dismissal legislation that was proposed and enacted in Montana was appealing to employers because, although it requires a standard of "just cause" for dismissal (and for other personnel actions, such as demotions), it limits an employee's ability to recover punitive damages to cases in which it is established that the employer acted with "actual fraud or

---

[7] In addition to direct legal fees, other transactions costs incurred in unjust-dismissal claims are likely to include a loss of management time during preparation of the case, damages to employee relations, deterioration of the firm's public image, and the release of confidential and proprietary information that may be exploited by competitors.

actual malice."[8] When actual fraud or actual malice cannot be established—as, in the vast majority of cases, it cannot—the maximum award an employee can recover is limited to four years of wages and fringes from the date of discharge, with interim earnings deducted. In addition, parties are encouraged to resolve their disputes via binding arbitration, which generally confers smaller awards than jury trials. The law has the effect of assigning employees the property right to a job (after a probationary period) as long as they adequately perform their work and are not laid off because of fluctuations in demand, but limits the potential damages that employers can be assessed if they violate this property right.

Unions and other employee representatives in Montana were either indifferent to or, like employer groups, supportive of the bill requiring just cause and limiting employers' liability in unlawful-dismissal suits. Some employee groups appeared to welcome the Wrongful Discharge from Employment Act because it codified a just cause firing requirement into law. Although some economists have argued that limits on employment-at-will have been detrimental to union organizing efforts (for example, Neumann and Rissman 1984), labor unions in Montana did not testify in opposition to legislation that extended unjust-dismissal protection to nonunion workers.

Nationwide Developments

Exceptions to the employment-at-will doctrine recognized by state courts in recent years may be categorized into three main classes.[9] First, and most common,

the judiciary in most states will not allow a cause of action alleging that an employee was fired for performing an act that was in the interest of public policy, such as serving jury duty, filing a workers' compensation claim, or refusing to commit perjury (the "public policy exception"). Second, many state courts have held that an implicit contract exists between an employer and his or her employees that binds the employer to statements made in personnel handbooks, company manuals, or oral promises (the "implied contract exception"). For example, some jurisdictions will hold an employer liable for damages if he or she fires an employee who is absent from work five times if a personnel handbook states that six absences are required for a dismissal.

Third, a minority of states have ruled in favor of employees in unjust-dismissal cases under the legal theory that an implied covenant of good faith and fair dealing exists between an employee and employer (the "good faith exception").[10] In essence, the good faith exception requires an employer to treat employees in a fair and reasonable manner, which is the essence of a just cause firing clause in a union contract. An example of such a precedent would be a court ruling against a firm that fired a worker for no other reason but to avoid paying the worker a Christmas bonus. The good faith exception is probably the most radical departure from the traditional employment-at-will doctrine, because it holds employers to a standard of behavior that is not prescribed by public policy and not set forth in an oral or written statement.

Table 1 reports the year in which a judicial precedent under each of these

---

[8] The act defines a dismissal as wrongful if it is not "for good cause," or if it is "in retaliation for the employee's refusal to violate public policy," or if it violates an express provision of the employer's personnel policy. Layoffs because of insufficient demand or other "business-related" reasons are not proscribed by the act. See Table 3.

[9] See Jacoby (1982) for an historical overview of employment at will. St. Antoine (1985:563) has claimed that "the most significant development in the whole field of labor law during the past decade was

the growing willingness of the courts to modify the traditional doctrine of employment-at-will." In addition to the three legal exceptions to the employment-at-will doctrine considered here, less common causes of action have been fraud and intentional or negligent infliction of emotional distress (see Shepard et al. 1989:127–47).

[10] It should be noted that requirements similar to the good faith and fair dealing exception and the implied contract exception are embodied in the existing law that applies to commercial contracts.

UNJUST-DISMISSAL LEGISLATION   649

Table 1. Chronology of Exceptions to the Employment-At-Will Doctrine in Each of the Fifty States.

	Year Exception Recognized				Year Exception Recognized		
State	*Public Policy Exception*	*Implied Contract Exception*	*Good Faith Exception*	*State*	*Public Policy Exception*	*Implied Contract Exception*	*Good Faith Exception*
Alabama		1984		Montana	1980	1983	1983
Alaska		1983	1981	Nebraska			
Arizona	1985	1984		Nevada	1984	1986	1987
Arkansas	1982	1985		New Hampshire	1974		
California	1980	1976	1980	New Jersey	1980	1985	
Colorado		1983		New Mexico		1980	
Connecticut	1980	1986	1984	New York		1982	
Delaware				North Carolina	1985		
Florida				North Dakota	1987		
Georgia				Ohio		1984	
Hawaii	1982			Oklahoma		1976	
Idaho	1977	1977		Oregon	1975	1979	
Illinois	1981	1986		Pennsylvania	1978		
Indiana	1980			Rhode Island			
Iowa			1984	South Carolina	1985		
Kansas	1981	1984		South Dakota		1983	
Kentucky	1982			Tennessee	1985		
Louisiana				Texas	1985		
Maine		1977		Utah			
Maryland	1981	1987		Vermont	1986	1985	
Massachusetts	1982		1977	Virginia	1985		
Michigan	1976	1980		Washington	1984	1978	
Minnesota	1987	1983		West Virginia	1978	1986	
Mississippi				Wisconsin	1980	1985	
Missouri	1979			Wyoming			

Sources: Derived from Bureau of National Affairs (1982, 1988) and Shepard, Heylman, and Duston (1989).

three legal theories was first established by either the state supreme court or by another court in each state.[11] The exemptions to the employment-at-will doctrine, as well as the years in which these exemptions were first recognized, vary considerably among the states. In addition, there may be conflicting decisions within a state—an exception may be recognized by some courts in the state but not by others. There is no obvious chronological order to the exceptions recognized by state courts. In 25 states the public policy exception was the first allowable cause of action, whereas in 14 states the implied contract exception preceded the public policy exception.

It should be stressed that the entries in

Table 1 represent state court rulings that break from the traditional common law; they are not based on legislation approved by the state legislature. The selection process and length of service of state court justices vary across states. These judges are typically appointed by the governor and serve terms ranging from two years to life.[12] As a result, the process by which state court precedents are generated differs from that by which bills are proposed and adopted by the state legislature. Because these state court precedents reflect the extent of erosion of the common law employment-at-will doctrine, they form the key explanatory variables in the empirical analysis below.

Although precise information on the number of unjust-dismissal suits brought to state courts or settled out of court is

[11] For the present analysis, whether a precedent is set by a state supreme court or by a lower court is of little consequence, because both erode the employment-at-will doctrine, create uncertainty, and reallocate property rights.

[12] See Klein (1977) for an overview of the state court system.

unavailable, one estimate is that there were more than 20,000 suits alleging termination without cause pending in state courts in 1987 (Westin and Feliu 1988). Furthermore, a recent survey of 255 employers by the Administrative Management Society indicated that 27% of respondents had been sued for wrongful discharge (Bureau of National Affairs 1990).

State-by-state information on the average or variance of the awards in unjust-dismissal suits (or in cases settled out of court) is not available. In some well-publicized cases, however, awards granted to unjust-dismissal claimants have exceeded the prize for winning the state lottery! In contrast, awards granted in unjust-dismissal cases in countries that require just cause firing by statute typically limit the maximum amount an employee can recover to one or two years of back wages.[13]

Recent surveys by the Rand Institute (Dertouzos et al. 1988) and by the Bureau of National Affairs (Shepard et al. 1989) provide an indication of the average award granted in unjust-dismissal cases, and of the considerable legal costs of an unjust-dismissal suit.[14] The Rand survey examined 120 unjust-dismissal cases that were decided by a jury trial between 1980 and 1986 in California. In the 82 cases decided in favor of the plaintiff (employee), the average initial award was $646,000, but the median was $177,000. Moreover, post-trial activities such as appeals and settlements reduced the initial jury award by about 55%, on average. Similarly, the BNA nationwide survey of 260 wrongful-termination cases between January 1986 and October 1988 found that in the 166 cases won by employees, the average award was $602,302, and the median award was $158,800.[15] Both of

these surveys indicate that the award distribution is positively skewed.

Another finding of the Rand survey is that the average cost of litigation incurred by an employer in defending an unjust-dismissal suit is $80,073, and the median is $65,000. In addition, litigation costs for employees are typically based on a contingency of 40% of the award. Thus, with combined legal fees exceeding $150,000 on average, the cost of litigation is nearly as great as the average total monetary amount awarded to successful employees in unjust-dismissal cases.

Proposed State Legislation

The ten states in which a bill to require just cause firing has been introduced in the state legislature are listed in Table 2. The laws that have been proposed in these states are similar in many respects to the Montana law. Moreover, these laws were often proposed following well-publicized and costly rulings against employers. In California, for example, a $20 million verdict preceded a legislative proposal.

Table 3 summarizes the salient characteristics of several of the laws. The proposed unjust-dismissal laws typically limit employer liability by requiring arbitration rather than jury trials, or by denying damage awards, or by pursuing both approaches. In addition, the laws tend to cover a wide range of personnel actions, including forced resignations and

Table 2. States Where Just Cause Firing Legislation Has Been Introduced into the State Legislature.

State	Year(s)
California	1984, 1985, 1986, 1988
Colorado	1981
Connecticut	1975
Michigan	1982
Montana	1987
New Jersey	1980, 1984
Pennsylvania	1981, 1985
Vermont	1988
Washington	1987
Wisconsin	1982

Sources: Bureau of National Affairs (1982); Bakaly and Isaacson (1983:12–13); Hill (1988); and personal telephone calls to each state by Timothy Kastelle.

[13] See Dickens, Hart, Jones, and Weekes (1984) for evidence on Great Britain.
[14] An important limitation of both of these surveys is that they exclude cases that were settled prior to trial, as well as those that were decided in a bench trial.
[15] The BNA survey did not report the typical reduction in awards due to post-trial activities.

Table 3. Characteristics of Proposed Unjust-Dismissal Laws.

State, Year, and Bill No.	Coverage	Standard for Just Dismissal	Dispute Procedures	Remedies
California, 1986[a] [SB 2800]	Private sector workers with 5 years or more of tenure who worked 1,000 hours or more per year. Employees whose total annual remuneration exceeds $100,000 are excluded. Employees covered by a collective bargaining agreement or bilateral contract are excluded.	A discharge is wrongful if there is not "good cause" or a legitimate business reason for the discharge. Employee has burden of proof.	Parties may voluntarily agree to final and binding arbitration; otherwise, parties may bring the case to court.	There shall be no damages for pain and suffering or emotional distress and no compensatory damages or punitive damages. Awards are limited to reinstatement and back pay. An employer who violates the act must pay a civil penalty to the state of $500 to $2,000 per violation.
California, 1988[b] [SB 1827]	Private sector workers earning less than $100,000 per year with more than 6 months of tenure. Employees covered by a union contract providing arbitration of unjust dismissal claims are excluded; employers with fewer than 5 employees are excluded.	"Just cause" is required for dismissal. Immediate discharge is legal if continued employment would endanger the health of others, or if the employee engaged in sabotage or willful misconduct.	Employer must notify employee of intent to discharge. Employee may file for a state-appointed mediator to mediate dispute. Failing a settlement, the state will assign an arbitrator who will issue a final and binding award. Financed by a .25% payroll tax on employees.	The arbitrator may award, among other things, reinstatement, back pay, and attorney fees.
Colorado, 1981 [HB 1495]	Private sector workers not represented by a union.	"Unjust dismissal prohibited."	Employee has a cause of action in contract if unjustly dismissed.	Court may award lost wages during spell of unemployment, relocation expenses, reasonable attorney fees, and other appropriate relief. Punitive damages allowed if dismissal is for refusal to perform an act that violates public policy.
Michigan, 1982 [HB 5892]	Private sector workers not covered by a collective bargaining agreement or contract. Public sector workers not protected by civil service. Coverage begins after a 6-month probationary period.	"An employer shall not discharge an employee except for just cause."	15 days of advance notice of reasons for discharge required; then mediation, followed by binding and final arbitration.	The arbitrator may award reinstatement with or without back pay, or severance pay.

Table 3. (Continued)

State, Year, and Bill No.	Coverage	Standard for Just Dismissal	Dispute Procedures	Remedies
Montana, 1987 [HB 241]	Public and private sector workers who have successfully completed the probationary period.	A discharge is wrongful if it is not for "good cause," or if it is in retaliation for employee's refusal to violate public policy, or if it violates written personnel policy. "Business-related" layoffs are lawful.	Before filing a complaint, employees must exhaust all internal grievance procedures. Employers have up to 90 days to reach a decision on internal grievances. Failing voluntary resolution, parties may choose to bring the case to arbitration or state court.	Compensatory damages are limited to four years of back wages and fringe benefits. Employee must establish by clear and convincing evidence that employer engaged in actual fraud or actual malice to recover damages for pain, suffering, and emotional distress, or punitive damages.
Pennsylvania, 1981 [HB 1742]	All employees excluding those protected by a collective bargaining agreement, civil service, or a fixed-length contract.	"An employer may not discharge an employee except for just cause."	15 days advance notice of reasons for discharge required; then mediation, followed by binding and final arbitration.	The arbitrator may reinstate the employee with no, partial, or full back pay, or award a severance payment with no reinstatement.
Vermont, 1988 [SB 299]	All public and private sector employees employed by firms with 5 or more employees in Vermont.	An employee may be discharged only for "just cause." An employee fired for refusal to perform what he in good faith believes to be illegal is not a just dismissal. Layoffs and plant relocations are just cause.	Employer must notify employee of reasons for discharge in writing within 15 days after discharge. Employee may bring suit to state court. Employer has burden of proving that discharge was for just cause.	Employee may be awarded an injunctive order, and may recover from the employer damages, court costs, and attorney fees.
Washington, 1987 [HB 1133]	Public and private sector workers with three or more years of service in a firm with 8 or more employees. Individuals covered by a collective or individual contract are exempt.	"Just cause" is required for dismissal. Just cause means there is a sufficient reason, judged by a "standard of reasonableness," for the discharge. Employer has burden of proving by preponderance of evidence "just cause" for dismissal.	Employee must file an appeal within 60 days of discharge to the county superior court. The court assigns an arbitrator, whose decision is final and binding.	Arbitration award may include compensation for all economic loss, reinstatement, and up to 3 years of future lost wages. No punitive damages provided.
Wisconsin, 1981	All private sector workers.	Any dismissal that employee believes to be "improper" can be challenged.	Employee must file a complaint to the Dept. of Industry, Labor and Human Relations within 20 days of discharge. An informal conference will be held between the employee and employer.	None. Bill only calls for a conference between the parties and voluntary settlement.

Source: Compiled from original laws by the author.

a California Bill No. SB 2800 is identical to California Bill No. AB 1400, which was introduced in 1985.
b California Bill No. SB 1827 is identical to California Bill No. 1348, which was introduced in 1985.

UNJUST-DISMISSAL LEGISLATION   653

demotions, but to *exclude* layoffs due to slack demand and employee-initiated turnover. The reliance on arbitration and a uniform definition of just cause are intended to reduce legal fees. Finally, although reinstatement of fired workers is a remedy that is typically unavailable under the common law, the proposed laws frequently allow reinstatement in wrongful termination cases.

Business groups have often supported the proposed unjust-dismissal laws in the states where they have been proposed. For example, a 1985 report of the California Manufacturers' Association encouraged employers to support a state unjust-dismissal law (SB 2800) because it would "provide a more expedient means by which an employee may be compensated for a truly wrongful discharge—such as through the opportunity to arbitrate—and remove an employer's exposure to punitive damages." On the other hand, the same California Manufacturers' Association opposed an alternative unjust-dismissal bill (SB 1348) proposed in the same year because it would not have shielded employers from large damage suits.

Hypothesis

A logical hypothesis to explain why employer and employee groups often jointly support just cause dismissal laws is that such laws are an acceptable compromise between limited employer liability and assumption of fault.[16] This compromise is reminiscent of the "great industrial bargain" that is said to have occurred in the development of workers' compensation insurance, whereby employers surrendered the common law defenses available in work-related injury cases in exchange for limited liability regardless of fault. After initial opposition, the AFL supported workmen's compensation legis-

lation in 1909, and President Gompers was a leader in the workmen's compensation movement. In the same year, a survey of the membership of the National Association of Manufacturers found a majority of businesses in favor of workmen's compensation legislation (see Somers and Somers 1954:31).

In the case of job security, many employers are willing to support unjust-dismissal legislation and accept a "just cause" firing requirement in exchange for the implementation of a strict standard for employees to recover punitive damages and a consistent, well-defined legal definition of unjust dismissals. An additional benefit of legislation is that it would likely reduce the uncertainty and expense inherent in common law unjust-dismissal suits. Legislation becomes an attractive alternative for employers when state courts break from the traditional common law employment-at-will doctrine.

A testable implication of this hypothesis is that unjust-dismissal legislation is more likely to be proposed and ultimately enacted into law in states where the courts have recognized exceptions to the traditional employment-at-will doctrine than in states where they have not. Although only one state has actually enacted an unjust-dismissal law to date, bills containing just cause firing requirements have been introduced in several state legislatures in the 1980s. Moreover, it is not unusual for legislation to be proposed several times before it is finally enacted into law. The empirical analysis is an attempt to explain the occurrence of these proposed laws.[17]

Statistical Framework

To structure the analysis, I assume that employer resistance to, or support for, an unjust-dismissal statute in a state is based

---

[16] This hypothesis contrasts with the conventional political economy view of unjust-dismissal legislation implicit in Blades (1967), Stieber (1979), and elsewhere, which predicts that such protective labor legislation will be supported by employees and opposed by employers.

[17] Examples of other empirical analyses of the economic factors leading to the passage of laws include Leffler's (1978) and Bloch's (1975) analyses of support for the minimum wage, Farber's (1988) analysis of the determinants of state public sector bargaining laws, and Feenberg and Rosen's (1987) examination of states' decisions to index tax laws.

on a comparison between the expected operating costs under a statute and under the common law. Specifically, employer support for legislation is summarized by a latent variable, y^*, determined by $y^* = C_N - C_L + \varepsilon$, where C_N is the expected costs in the absence of legislation, C_L is the expected costs under legislation, and ε is a random disturbance. Greater values of y^* indicate increasing employer support for unjust-dismissal legislation to limit liability and clarify property rights.

To focus on employer incentives, it will be assumed that employees are never opposed to unjust-dismissal legislation. This assumption may be justified either because a transfer of property rights to employees will increase their wealth or because risk-averse employees prefer legislation that would result in less uncertainty than is present under the current common law.[18] With this stipulation, the probability that a bill will be endorsed by employer groups and eventually gain enough support to be proposed and enacted by the state legislature is given by prob $[y^*] > 0$, or, equivalently, by prob $[C_L - C_N] > \varepsilon$.

In the empirical implementation of this model, it will be assumed that ε has a logistic cumulative distribution function. The proposal of a bill in the state legislature will be used as an indicator of the latent variable y^*. In particular, the variable y_t is set equal to one if a law is proposed in year t and to zero in all other years.[19]

Dummy variables for the three main types of exceptions to the employment-at-will doctrine recognized by the court system in each state will proxy for employers' expected costs in the absence of legislation. Specifically, suppose exception i is first recognized in year t^*; then the dummy variable $E_{i,t}$ is defined to equal one if $t \geq t^*$ and zero if $t < t^*$.[20] These dummy variables are a plausible proxy for the cost under the common law because they reflect the incompleteness of property rights, the magnitude and variability of awards, and the legal transaction costs involved in unjust-dismissal suits.

Exceptions to the common law doctrine are likely to have a delayed effect on the proposal of legislation. Some state legislatures, for example, only meet every other year. Consequently, the basic equation estimated is

$$(1) \quad y_t = F(E_{1,t-1}, E_{2,t-1}, E_{3,t-1}, X_t),$$

where X_t is a vector of state-level explanatory variables and $F(\ )$ is the logistic cumulative distribution function (CDF). In addition, estimates that are presented below (in the section headed "Causality") allow for different assumptions about the timing of the relationship between the common law exceptions and the proposal of wrongful-termination laws.

The Determinants of Proposed Unjust-Dismissal Laws

To examine the possible effect of exceptions to the employment-at-will doctrine, I have assembled data on proposed unjust-dismissal statutes and court rulings by state for each year from 1981 to 1988.

---

[18] If awards granted employees become large enough (with a constant variance), employees will prefer the common law to an unjust-dismissal statute. The assumption that employees uniformly support legislation, however, is necessary for identification in this model because we only observe the occurrence of proposed legislation. Moreover, the assumption that employees do not oppose unjust-dismissal legislation seems consistent with casual empirical observation. The AFL-CIO Executive Council, for example, endorsed just cause firing legislation in February 1987.

[19] An alternative approach, which was suggested by a referee, is to let y_t equal one every year after a law has been first proposed in a state. Estimation with this dependent variable leads to more significant coefficients on the legal exceptions in Table 4. For

example, the coefficient and standard error on the exceptions in the specification in column 6 of Table 4 are 1.13 and 0.22 when this alternative dependent variable is used. The definition of y_t given in the text is used in the empirical analysis, however, because it gives a precise indication of current support for legislation.

[20] Because none of the exceptions was unambiguously reversed during the period under study, the exceptions are assumed to hold in every year after they were first recognized.

UNJUST-DISMISSAL LEGISLATION   655

The Appendix contains descriptive statistics for the data set. Table 4 presents maximum likelihood logit estimates of the occurrence of proposed unjust-dismissal laws for the pooled sample of states.

The first column presents estimates of the effect of the three exceptions to the common law without controlling for covariates. The results show that if a state court system allows one of the exceptions to the employment-at-will doctrine in a given year, the probability that an unjust-dismissal bill will be introduced in the state legislature the following year is increased. The likelihood ratio test of the joint significance of the three exceptions reported in the last row of the table indicates that together the exceptions are highly statistically significant. Furthermore, in spite of the high correlation among the three dummy variables, the good faith

exception and the public policy exception are individually statistically significant.

Several covariates are included in columns 2 and 3 to control for political and economic factors that might influence the introduction of an unjust-dismissal law. The good faith and public policy exceptions to the employment-at-will doctrine are individually statistically significant when these additional variables are included in the equation, and the exceptions continue to be jointly highly statistically significant. The point estimates in column 3 imply that, on average, the probability that a state legislature proposes an unjust-dismissal law is increased by 6.7 percentage points if its court system has recognized the good faith exception, by 8.5 percentage points if the public policy exception has been recognized, and by 2.0 percentage points if the implied contract

Table 4. Logit Estimates of Unjust-Dismissal Laws Proposed in State Legislatures, 1981–1988.

Variable	Coefficient (Std. Error)					
	(1)	(2)	(3)	(4)	(5)	(6)
Intercept	−5.947***	−6.112***	−6.664***	−5.419***	−5.898***	−6.590***
	(1.051)	(1.781)	(1.987)	(0.694)	(1.620)	(1.873)
Good Faith	1.616***	1.825***	1.994***	—	—	—
Exception	(.612)	(.649)	(.703)			
Public Policy	2.561**	2.537**	2.508**	—	—	—
Exception	(1.052)	(1.057)	(1.099)			
Implied Contract	0.856	0.645	0.604	—	—	—
Exception	(0.606)	(0.627)	(0.665)			
Total Number of	—	—	—	1.505***	1.474***	1.534***
Exceptions Allowed				(0.333)	(0.350)	(0.367)
Proportion of Employees in State	—	7.912	6.314	—	7.184	6.129
Who Are Union Members		(5.121)	(5.603)		(4.728)	(5.230)
Proportion of Democrats	—	−2.463	−2.580	—	−1.655	−1.730
in State Legislature		(2.233)	(2.245)		(2.199)	(2.193)
Proportion of Employees in State	—	—	1.641	—	—	3.341
Who Are in Manufacturing			(4.725)			(4.467)
Unemployment Rate	—	—	8.177	—	—	2.812
			(13.163)			(12.592)
Log Likelihood	−47.68	−46.01	−45.75	−48.83	−47.47	−47.15
χ² for Exceptions[a]	26.01	23.36	23.72	20.43	17.74	17.47
[Prob. Value]	[0.0000]	[0.0000]	[0.0000]	[0.0000]	[0.0000]	[0.0000]

Source: See Appendix table.

Notes: The sample size is 400. The three exceptions to the common law pertain to year $t-1$. The mean of the dependent variable is .035.

[a] The likelihood ratio tests of the joint contribution of the three exceptions to employment-at-will in columns 1–3 have three degrees of freedom. The critical value for such a test at the .005 level is 12.8. In columns 4–6, the χ² test is for the variable measuring the total number of exceptions allowed.

*Significantly different from 0 at the .10 level; ** significantly different from 0 at the .05 level; *** significantly different from 0 at the .01 level (2-tail tests).

656   INDUSTRIAL AND LABOR RELATIONS REVIEW

exception has been recognized.[21] Put another way, the probability that a law is proposed is more than quadrupled if these causes of action have been allowed in a state.

A positive but statistically insignificant relationship is found between the union membership rate and the likelihood that an unjust-dismissal law is proposed in a state.[22] A positive coefficient on the union rate is probably to be expected, as protective labor legislation is likely to receive greater support from legislators in states that have a higher union rate. In addition, an unjust-dismissal law appears less likely to be proposed in states with legislatures having a greater proportion of Democratic members, but this effect is statistically insignificant. The variables measuring the proportion of employment that is in the manufacturing sector and the unemployment rate both have coefficients that are much smaller than their standard errors.

Because of strong multicollinearity between the three common law dummy variables, columns 4–6 report specifications that use the total number of exceptions recognized in a state each year $(E_{1,t-1} + E_{2,t-1} + E_{3,t-1})$ instead of the three common law dummies.[23] Estimation of the new specification yields results that are similar to those of the unrestricted specification in columns 1–3. The total number of exceptions to the employment-at-will doctrine in a state has a positive and statistically significant effect on the probability that unjust-dismissal legislation will be proposed by the legislature in the following year. According to the point estimate in column 4, each additional

exception allowed by the courts increases the probability that legislation is proposed by 5.2 percentage points. Moreover, likelihood ratio tests of the restricted specifications that sum the exceptions (columns 4–6) compared to the specifications that enter the exceptions as separate dummy variables (columns 1–3) do not reject the restrictions imposed in columns 4–6.[24]

Causality

The results presented so far have documented that a relationship exists between the erosion of the employment-at-will doctrine and the proposal of unjust-dismissal legislation. A much more difficult question to answer is whether this relationship is a causal one or is due to omitted factors that are correlated with the erosion of the common law and with the proposal of legislation in a state. Although causality is difficult to establish even when a randomized experiment has been conducted, the issue of causality should be addressed here because it is central to the explanation of the evolution of unjust-dismissal legislation given in this paper.

The timing of the recognition of exceptions to employment at will provides some leverage to determine causality. If the erosion of the traditional common law causes support for legislation, then one would expect the erosion of the common law to precede, rather than succeed, the proposal of unjust-dismissal legislation. The first five columns of Table 5 contain estimates of the determinants of proposed legislation using varying lags and leads of the common law variables to explore the relationship between the timing of exceptions and the proposal of laws. These equations use the total number of common law exceptions as an indicator of the

---

[21] These derivatives were calculated as $100 \times \bar{y}$ $(1-\bar{y})\beta_i$, where $\bar{y} = .035$ is the proportion of state/year cells to have proposed legislation, and β_i is a logit coefficient estimate.

[22] Because state-level union rates are no longer available from the Bureau of Labor Statistics, a series was estimated by the author from the May and March Current Population Survey (CPS) from 1981 to 1987. The 1982 state union rates were interpolated because the CPS did not collect union data in that year.

[23] Although other methods of aggregating the dummies are possible, this approach is simple and is not rejected by the data.

[24] Two times the absolute difference in the value of the log likelihood function asymptotically follows a chi-square with two degrees of freedom. For example, the chi-square statistic for a test of the hypothesis that columns 3 and 6 perform equally well is 1.40, and the critical value for such a test at the .10 level is 4.61.

Table 5. Examination of Casuality: Logit Estimates of the Proposal of Unjust-Dismissal Laws, 1981–1985.

Variable[a]	Coefficient (Std. Error)					
	(1)	(2)	(3)	(4)	(5)	(6)
Intercept	−4.979***	−4.826***	−4.787**	−4.894**	−4.710**	−4.745**
	(1.915)	(1.869)	(1.862)	(1.918)	(1.865)	(1.879)
Total No. of Exceptions $(t-2)$	1.277***	−	−	−	−	−
	(.428)					
Total No. of Exceptions $(t-1)$	−	1.026**	−	−	1.370	.995**
		(.428)			(1.044)	(.431)
Total No. of Exceptions $(t+1)$	−	−	.798*	−	−.400	−
			(.444)		(1.074)	
Total No. of Exceptions $(t+2)$	−	−	−	.758*	−	−
				(.446)		
Law Proposed $(t-1)$	−	−	−	−	−	.789
						(1.217)
Proportion of Workers in State Who Are Union Members (+)	10.719*	10.105	9.972*	10.014*	10.171*	9.649
	(6.520)	(6.195)	(5.934)	(5.929)	(6.153)	(6.232)
Proportion of Democrats in State Legislature (+)	−3.604	−3.328	−3.179	−3.079	−3.316	−3.322
	(2.960)	(2.864)	(2.795)	(2.805)	(2.826)	(2.899)
Log Likelihood	−27.87	−29.50	−30.67	−30.80	−29.42	−29.32

Notes: The sample size is 250. The mean of the dependent variable is .032.
[a] The dependent variable indicates whether an unjust-dismissal law was proposed in year t. The year that the independent variables pertain to is listed in parentheses next to the variable name.
* Significantly different from 0 at the .10 level; ** significantly different from 0 at the .05 level; *** significantly different from 0 at the .01 level (2-tail tests).

erosion of the common law because this variable is a simpler summary than separate dummy variables for each exception, and because the exceptions are highly multicollinear.[25]

The results in columns 1–4 indicate that past recognition of exceptions to the common law have a greater impact on the occurrence of proposed legislation than do future exceptions to the common law. Both the future and past court rulings, however, are found to have a statistically significant effect at the .10 level, which may be due to the high degree of serial correlation in the common law decisions within the states. Indeed, the first-order serial correlation in the exceptions is .90. Once an exception is recognized, a precedent is established that is infrequently reversed, inducing serial correlation.

The high level of serial correlation in

the exceptions to the common law makes it infeasible to include adjacent lags of the exceptions in the same equation. Nevertheless, column 5 includes the number of exceptions to the common law in the preceding year and the following year. Although both variables are statistically insignificant at the .10 level, the results suggest that recognizing more exceptions to the traditional common law in the past increases the likelihood that legislation is proposed, whereas exceptions recognized in the future have a small, negative effect on the proposal of current legislation.

Unfortunately, because the exceptions are so highly serially correlated, only a limited Granger-Sims causality test can be estimated. Column 6 presents an estimate of a logit equation that includes a one-year lag of the dependent variable (whether a law was proposed) and a one-year lag of the number of exceptions to the common law.[26] These results indicate that the

[25] Also note that observations for states after 1985 were dropped from the sample so that the equations would be estimated for a consistent set of observations. This step was necessary because future values of the exceptions are unknown for years after 1985.

[26] Unfortunately, when the equations were estimated including both one- and two-period lags of the

INDUSTRIAL AND LABOR RELATIONS REVIEW

number of exceptions to the common law recognized as of the previous year has a positive and statistically significant effect on the probability that legislation is introduced. On the other hand, the proposal of legislation in the past year has a statistically insignificant, though positive, effect on the chance of legislation being proposed in the current year. Although far from unambiguous, the results in Table 5 provide some support for the view that changes in the common law precipitate the proposal of unjust-dismissal legislation.

Finally, two additional pieces of evidence are also consistent with the interpretation that the erosion of the common law has caused the state legislature in many jurisdictions to consider unjust-dismissal legislation. First, available evidence suggests that the pattern of recognition of exceptions to the employment-at-will doctrine by state courts is haphazard, unrelated to the wage level, unemployment rate, region, or demographic characteristics of states (see Dertouzos et al. 1988). This finding suggests that the common law exceptions are uncorrelated with omitted variables because they occur more or less randomly. Second, the political and economic variables that are included in the equations in Table 4 have little explanatory power and do not reduce the effect of the common law exceptions. Notably, if omitted political factors were responsible for both the erosion of the common law and the proposal of unjust-dismissal legislation, it is likely that the proportion of Democrats in the state legislature and the extent of unionization in the state would have a greater effect on the occurrence of proposed legislation.

Conclusion

In many states the common law employ-

ment-at-will doctrine has been eroded over the past decade by state court rulings. I have argued that the new *employment-sometimes-at-will* common law doctrine has produced uncertain and incomplete property rights to jobs, often leaving employers and employees unsure of the legality of personnel actions. Moreover, when disputes arise over improper dismissals, the current judicial system imposes large transactions costs and highly variable awards on the parties.

I have presented evidence showing that unjust-dismissal legislation is more likely to be proposed in states where the departure from the traditional employment-at-will doctrine by the courts has been most extreme. When proposed, this legislation is typically designed to limit employer liability, expedite dispute settlements, reduce legal costs, and clarify property rights. There is a possibility, of course, that unjust-dismissal legislation could, at least initially, increase uncertainty and disputes over property rights.

As a practical matter, unjust-dismissal legislation may be Pareto superior to the withered employment-at-will doctrine.[27] The anecdotal evidence that employer groups in some states actually support and sponsor unjust-dismissal legislation to limit liability suggests that such "no-fault-firing" legislation is a viable political and economic alternative to the *ad hoc* court system. If state courts continue to dilute the employment-at-will doctrine, the analysis presented in this paper would predict that many states will follow Montana by proposing and enacting legislation to limit employer liability, clearly redefine property rights, and reduce legal costs.

A natural question to raise is, why has only one state been successful so far in passing wrongful-termination legislation? Two answers suggest themselves. First, the

dependent variable and of the legal exceptions, the variables were too highly correlated to estimate the logit. Also, I was unable to estimate an equation in which the number of legal exceptions recognized as of period *t* was the dependent variable if such an equation included a lagged dependent variable.

[27] An alternative response by employers, which was suggested by a referee, would be to lobby for legislation to place an across-the-board ceiling on all damage awards. This strategy, however, seems unlikely to be pursued in response to the erosion of the employment-at-will doctrine because, unlike wrongful-termination legislation, it is not a viable political compromise.

threat to employers under the common law is not great enough in most states to provoke sufficient support for legislation. Second, a nontrivial waiting period is often required before legislation can be successfully steered through the legislature. For example, more than a decade passed before Alabama became the first state to enact a right-to-work law after such laws were sanctioned by the Taft-Hartley Amendments of 1947.[28] Similarly, there were long and variable lags in the adoption of public sector bargaining laws in many states (Farber 1988).

The results in this paper suggest that in the long run, the prospects for the passage of unjust-dismissal legislation are linked to the erosion of the common law employment-at-will doctrine. Although it is difficult to predict the future course of the common law, Donald Horowitz (1977:12) has noted that "doctrinal erosion in particular is not easily stopped" because precedents make it difficult for courts to reverse

themselves, and because judges typically serve long terms. On the other hand, a recent decision by the California Supreme Court (*Foley v. Interactive Data Corp.*, CA Sup. Ct., 3 IER 1729), which, among other things, limits damage awards in cases over a breach of the covenant of good faith and fair dealing, and recent rulings in Michigan (for example, *Bankey v. Storer Broadcasting Co.*, Mich. Sup. Ct., No. 78200) suggest that the dramatic transformation of the employment-at-will doctrine may be abating in some jurisdictions.

Finally, the explanation for proposed unjust-dismissal legislation developed in this paper may also be relevant in a variety of other contexts. As noted, the legislative history of state workers' compensation laws—which were enacted with the support of both the American Federation of Labor and the National Association of Manufacturers at the beginning of the twentieth century—closely parallels the recent developments in unjust-dismissal laws. The idea that no-fault, limited liability legislation is a response to *ad hoc* changes in the common law may have broad applications.

---

[28] Six states, however, passed right-to-work laws of dubious legal status prior to the Taft-Hartley Amendments.

Appendix
Means and Standard Deviations

Variable	Law Proposed	No Law Proposed	All States
Good Faith Exception ($t-1$)	.429 (.514)	.080 (.272)	.093 (.290)
Public Policy Exception ($t-1$)	.929 (.267)	.430 (.496)	.448 (.498)
Implied Contract Exception ($t-1$)	.643 (.497)	.319 (.467)	.330 (.471)
Total Number of Exceptions Allowed ($t-1$)	2.000 (1.038)	.829 (.791)	.870 (.828)
Union Membership Rate	.213 (.053)	.171 (.072)	.172 (.072)
Democratic Legislature	.538 (.064)	.598 (.194)	.596 (.191)
Proportion Manufacturing	.191 (.063)	.186 (.074)	.186 (.074)
Unemployment Rate	.079 (.027)	.075 (.024)	.075 (.024)

Notes. The sources used to derive the common law variables are listed in Table 1. The union rate was calculated by the author based on the CPS. The unemployment rate and proportion of the work force in manufacturing are from *Geographic Profile of Employment and Unemployment* (Washington, D.C.: U.S. Bureau of Labor Statistics, 1987). The fraction of the legislature that belongs to the Democratic party is derived from various issues of *Statistical Abstract of the United States* (Washington, D.C.: Department of Commerce, Bureau of the Census).

REFERENCES

Bakaly, Charles, Jr., and William Isaacson. 1983. *Employment-at-Will and Unjust Dismissal: The Labor Issues of the '80s.* New York: Law and Business, Inc.

Blades, Lawrence E. 1967. "Employment at Will vs. Individual Freedom: On Limiting the Abusive Exercise of Employer Power." *Columbia Law Review,* Vol. 67, No. 8 (December), pp. 1404–36.

Bloch, Farrell. 1975. "Political Support for Minimum Wage Regulations." Princeton University, Industrial Relations Section, Working Paper No. 71.

Bureau of National Affairs. 1982. *The Employment-at-Will Issue.* Washington, D.C.

———. 1985. *Employee Discipline and Discharge.* PPF Survey No. 139, January.

———. 1988. *Individual Employment Rights Manual.*

———. 1990. *Daily Labor Report,* No. 25 (Feb. 6), pp. A8–A9.

Coase, Ronald. 1960. "The Problem of Social Cost." *Journal of Law and Economics,* Vol. 3, No. 1, pp. 1–44.

Dertouzos, James, Ellaine Holland, and Patricia Ebener. 1988. "The Legal and Economic Consequences of Wrongful Termination." The RAND Institute for Civil Justice, R-3602-ICJ.

Dickens, Linda, Moira Hart, Michael Jones, and Brian Weekes. 1984. "The British Experience Under a Statute Prohibiting Unfair Dismissal." *Industrial and Labor Relations Review,* Vol. 37, No. 4 (July), pp. 497–514.

Ehrenberg, Ronald G. 1985. "Workers' Rights: Rethinking Protective Labor Legislation." NBER Working Paper No. 1754, November.

Epstein, Richard A. 1984. "In Defense of the Contract at Will." *University of Chicago Law Review,* Vol. 51, No. 4, pp. 947–82.

Farber, Henry. 1988. "The Evolution of Public Sector Bargaining Laws." In R. Freeman and C. Ichniowski, eds., *When Public Sector Workers Unionize.* Chicago: University of Chicago Press.

Farrell, Joseph. 1987. "Information and the Coase Theorem." *Journal of Economic Perspectives,* Vol. 1, No. 2, pp. 113–29.

Feenberg, Daniel, and Harvey Rosen. 1987. "Promises, Promises: The States' Experience with Income Tax Indexing." Mimeo, Princeton University, January.

Hamermesh, Daniel. 1990. "Employment Protection: Theoretical Implications and Some U.S. Evidence." Unpublished paper, Michigan State University, March.

Hill, Andrew. 1988. *"Wrongful Discharge" and the Derogation of the At-Will Employment Doctrine.* Philadelphia: Wharton Industrial Research Unit, University of Pennsylvania.

Horowitz, Donald. 1977. *The Courts and Social Policy.* Washington, D.C.: Brookings Institution.

Jacoby, Sanford. 1982. "The Duration of Indefinite Employment Contracts in the United States and England: An Historical Analysis." *Comparative Labor Law,* Vol. 5, No. 1 (Winter), pp. 85–128.

Klein, Fannie. 1977. *Federal and State Court Systems: A Guide.* Cambridge, Mass.: Ballinger.

Lazear, Edward. 1987. "Employment at Will, Job Security, and Work Incentives." In *Proceedings of the Conference on Employment, Unemployment and Hours of Work.* London: Allen & Unwin.

Leffler, Keith. 1978. "Minimum Wages, Welfare, and Wealth Transfers to the Poor." *Journal of Law and Economics,* Vol. 21 (October), pp. 345–58.

Neumann, George, and Ellen Rissman. 1984. "Where Have All the Union Members Gone?" *Journal of Labor Economics,* Vol. 2, No. 2 (April), pp. 175–92.

Posner, Richard. 1988. "Hegel and Employment at Will: A Comment." Mimeo, University of Chicago Law School.

Shepard, Ira, Paul Heylman, and Robert Duston. 1989. *Without Just Cause: An Employer's Practical and Legal Guide on Wrongful Discharge.* Washington, D.C.: Bureau of National Affairs.

Somers, Herman, and Anne Somers. 1954. *Workmen's Compensation.* New York: John Wiley & Sons.

St. Antoine, Theodore. 1985. "The Revision of Employment-at-Will Enters a New Phase." *Labor Law Journal,* Vol. 36, pp. 563–67.

Stieber, Jack. 1979. "The Case for Protection of Unorganized Employees Against Unjust Discharge." In *Proceedings of the Industrial Relations Research Association* (December), pp. 155–63.

Westin, Alan, and Alfred Feliu. 1988. *Resolving Employment Disputes Without Litigation.* Washington, D.C.: Bureau of National Affairs.

[7]

Southern Economic Journal 2000, 67(1), 105–122

The Effect of Dismissals Protection on Employment: More on a Vexed Theme

John T. Addison,* Paulino Teixeira,† and Jean-Luc Grosso‡

This paper presents new results on the relationship between severance pay and labor market performance for a sample of 21 OECD countries, 1956–1984. Specifically, it evaluates Lazear's empirical argument that severance pay reduces employment and elevates joblessness. His findings are shown not to survive correction for errors in the data and the application of correct estimation procedures. Furthermore, adverse labor market consequences of severance pay are not detected in a dynamic characterization of the Lazear model. Limitations of the approach followed here are also addressed and contextualized.

1. Introduction

Concern over the adverse employment consequences of employment protection legislation is a recurring theme in labor market analysis. Recent, and conflicting, applied treatments include Scarpetta (1996) and Nickell (1997). The unfolding empirical analysis of the effects of employment protection shares certain similarities with investigation of the covariation of collective bargaining structures and macroeconomic outcomes (see, e.g., Calmfors and Driffill 1988; OECD 1997). In both cases, the models are typically reduced form and the empirical evidence rather mixed.

The present paper offers a replication and critique of Lazear's (1990) famous empirical model of employment protection, which is the sole extant empirical treatment to allow for changes in a measure of employment protection over an extended time interval. Our concern is not so much with theoretical issues as with the sensitivity of Lazear's results to data problems. Suffice it to say here that the theoretical analysis of the long-run effects of employment protection produces ambiguous results (e.g., Bentolila and Bertola 1990; Bertola 1991; Hopenhayn and Rogerson 1993; Bentolila and Saint-Paul 1994; Saint-Paul 1995). Accordingly, there is a premium on empirical analysis.[1]

It should perhaps come as no surprise to learn that Lazear (1990) did not deny that employment protection could be benign—in perfectly functioning markets, the parties would ef-

* Department of Economics, Darla Moore School of Business, University of South Carolina, Columbia, SC 29208, USA, and Department of Commerce, University of Birmingham, Birmingham B15 2TT, UK; E-mail ecceaddi@darla. badm.sc.edu; corresponding author.

† Faculdade de Economia, Universidade de Coimbra, Av. Dias da Silva, 165, 3000 Coimbra, Portugal; E-mail paulinot@sonata.fe.uc.pt.

‡ Department of Business Administration and Economics, University of South Carolina–Sumter, Sumter, SC 29150, USA; E-mail jlgrosso@uscsumter.edu.

We thank, without implicating, two anonymous referees and coeditor Kathy Hayes for their helpful comments on earlier drafts of this paper.

Received July 1998; accepted November 1999.

[1] That said, there is no substitute for carefully parameterized models of individual employment protection mandates. For one such attempt, see Addison and Chilton (1997).

106   *Addison, Teixeira, and Grosso*

ficiently negotiate around a severance pay mandate via appropriate side payments from worker to firm—or argue that outcomes were independent of the stage of the cycle (see Hamermesh 1993) or, for that matter, assert that negative effects would be observed across all outcome indicators (adverse effects being more clear-cut for employment than for unemployment, where discouragement could even generate a reduction in unemployment). Rather, his position was that, in the presence of constraints on efficient contracts, employment protection rules might be expected to bind in regular (and especially European) markets. His tests were designed accordingly.

Our criticism of Lazear is that, quite apart from errors in his data, he did not adequately investigate the statistical problems stemming from his use of pooled cross-sectional and time-series data, even if recognition of the problems emphasized in the present treatment is apparent in his narrative. We refer in particular to the problems of country heterogeneity and autocorrelation. We shall report that almost all of the statistical significance attaching to Lazear's key employment protection measure evaporates once the appropriate econometric procedures are employed. This is not the end of the story, however, because of the limitations of the employment protection variable and the parsimonious nature of the estimating equations used here. Both issues will be addressed in the context of the developing employment protection research literature.

2. Data and Methodology

The data and variables used in this inquiry in principle follow those of Lazear (1990), to whom we are indebted for supplying us with a diskette containing the raw data (and programs) used in his study. The data have been corrected for the errors of omission and commission identified by Addison and Grosso (1996). Appendix A illustrates the main issues. We note that the data errors do not overturn Lazear's principal findings, taken at face value, even if they do serve substantially to alter the point estimates.

In estimating the employment effects of statutory job protection, Lazear initially uses data on 20 OECD countries for the sample period 1956–1984. His data are not complete for all variables and years. Lazear actually collected data on 22 countries but subsequently dropped two nations (Canada and Hong Kong). Our sample of countries and time frame are the same as Lazear's, with the exceptions noted in Appendix A. Suffice it to say that sample differences were not material to any of the results reported below.

Lazear examines the determinants of four outcome indicators: the employment–population ratio (EMPPOP), the unemployment rate (UNRATE), the labor force particiaption rate (LFPR), and the average hours worked by production workers (HOURS). Values of each of the first three dependent variables differ slightly from those used by Lazear because we were able to obtain updated estimates of the size of the population, civilian labor force, and employment used in their construction. Rather more important changes were introduced into the HOURS variable, chiefly because of the need to provide a consistent time series and also to substitute a correct measure of weekly hours for Italy to replace the erroneous daily hours measure inadvertently used by Lazear (1990, table I, column 3).

Turning to the independent variables, the crucial employment protection measure is severance pay (SEV). This is defined as the statutory entitlement in months of pay due to a blue-collar worker with 10 years of service on termination for reasons unconnected with his/her behavior. The measure thus pertains to no-fault individual dismissals for economic reasons. Comment on the efficacy of this measure is provided below.

The remaining covariates are a quadratic time trend, represented by YEAR and YEAR^2; a demographic control for the population of working age (WRKAGE);[2] and the growth in per capita gross domestic product (GROWTH), which accommodates the notion that a growing economy vitiates at least in part the probabilistic costs of a severance pay mandate (see Gavin 1986). Unusually, in his fitted regressions, Lazear only enters the latter variable in interaction with severance pay. As is more conventional, we include both GROWTH and its interaction with severance pay (GROWTH.SEV).

The majority of Lazear's estimates are from outcome equations that include just the time trend variables YEAR and YEAR^2 and the key dismissals protection indicator. This has perhaps served to amplify the principal criticisms of the model, namely, that it abstracts from many variables that may be expected to affect structural unemployment and employment rates, while its key independent variable, severance pay, is at best a partial indicator of the legal regulations applying in a particular country. (There is also the neglected issue of other constraints operating through the collective bargaining system.) But we note parenthetically that Lazear (1990) does at least use his expanded set of variables to explain changes in unemployment rates in a spec- ification that combines cross-section and time-series variation. He concludes that, in some coun- tries, more generous severance pay "can go a long way in explaining the changes in employment over time" (Lazear 1990, p. 720). Singled out as cases in point are France, Portugal, Italy, and Israel.

Although our interest is primarily in reassessing Lazear's model *per se,* both criticisms have to be addressed at this point. Consider first the dismissals protection variable. Recent work in the employment protection area has sought to widen the definition of dismissals protection. Perhaps the best known measure has been constructed by Grubb and Wells (1993), who identify three elements of a system of employment protection: restrictions on dismissals, restrictions on temporary forms of employment contract (so-called atypical work), and restrictions on working hours.

The first element covers not only severance pay, as in Lazear, but also procedural delays and unfair dismissal provisions. (Note, however, that there is no recognition of regulations concerning collective dismissals.)[3] The second element encompasses restrictions on the use of fixed-term contracts and temporary agency work, such as the permissible grounds for their use, the maximum number of successive contracts, and their maximum cumulated duration. Finally, hours restrictions cover such things as the length of the normal working week, annual overtime limits, minimum rest periods, and restrictions on night work.

Using simple unweighted averages of rankings, Grubb and Wells (1993) provide summary indexes for each component together with a grand ranking for the overall strictness of the regulatory climate that is reproduced in column 3 of Table 1. An analogous procedure is em- ployed by the OECD (1994) to (average) rank countries by the severity of their legal restrictions on regular and atypical work, the results of which are reported in column 4 of Table 1. In each case, the ranking is from least to most regulated, and the data describe the situation in the late

---

[2] On the important contribution of growth in the working age population to employment development, see Krueger and Pischke (1997).

[3] The OECD (1999, table 2.4) has recently incorporated information on collective dismissal regulations in a revised measure of the overall strictness of employment protection legislation (OECD 1999, table 2.5).

Table 1. Severance Pay and Alternative Indicators of the Stringency of Employment Protection

Country	(1) Severance Pay Entitlement (Months)ª	(2) Bertola Ranking	(3) Grubb–Wells Ranking	(4) OECD Index	(5) IOE Employer Survey Index, 1985	(6) EC Employer Survey Index, 1985	(7) WCR Flexibility Index, 1984–1990
Belgium	0	9	5	10.50	2.5	113	41.83
Denmark	0	2	2	3.25	1.0		61.76
France	1	8	6	9.50	2.5	134	42.33
Germany	0	6	7	12.0	2.5	83	41.49
Greece	1		10	11.0		130	30.28
Ireland	1.5		3	2.75	1.5	111	47.57
Italy	8.8	10	8	14.25	3.0	151	39.87
The Netherlands	0	3	4	7.25	2.5	73	46.70
Portugal	10		11	12.50	2.0		33.12
Spain	6.6		9	11.25	3.0		29.81
United Kingdom	2.5	4	1	2.25	0.5	39	58.08
Austria	4			9.0	1.5		41.29
Finland	0			10.50	1.0		50.11
Norway	0			9.75	1.5		40.89
Sweden	0	7		8.50	2.0		40.77
Switzerland	0			1.75			61.69
United States	0	1		0.36			72.66
Japan	0	5		3.71			55.43
Australia	0			3.26			38.45
New Zealand	5.5			0.72		—	40.95
Spearman rank correlation coefficientᵇ		0.654ᶜ	0.361	0.389	0.097		0.434

Sources: Bertola (1990), European Commission (1986), Di Tella and MacCulloch (1999), Grubb and Wells (1993), IOE (1985), OECD (1994).

ª The entries in column (1) are taken from the present study and pertain to 1984. All other index/ranking values are for the late 1980s unless otherwise indicated. The construction of the various indexes/rankings is discussed in the text.

ᵇ The rank correlation exercise is for the first 11 countries in the table, where missing values are based on OECD (1994, table 6.7, panel B) interpolations.

ᶜ Statistically significant at the 0.05 level.

1980s. We note that the OECD ranking in column 4 has commonly been used in most of the recent employment protection studies (see below).[4]

Given that legislative rules may be only part of the story, other researchers have exploited less ambitious but potentially more encompassing reputation indexes based on surveys of employers. One such index is provided in column 5 of Table 1. It uses data from a survey conducted by the International Organization of Employers (IOE) (1985) as distributed to European and non-European employer federations. The survey seeks to identify the importance of obstacles to the termination of regular employment and the deployment of atypical workers. The entries in column 5 are taken from the OECD (1994) and measure the reported levels of difficulty on an ascending scale of 0–3 (regulatory constraints were classified as insignificant, minor, serious, or fundamental) averaged over regular and fixed-term contracts.

Two other employment protection indexes derived from employer surveys have also been used in the literature. Column 6 of Table 1 provides results from an *ad hoc* survey of some 8000 industrial firms conducted by the European Commission (1986) at the end of 1985. The survey inquires of the management respondents which of a number of reasons explained their not employing more people at the time of the survey and asks them to indicate whether each one was "very important," "important," or "not important." One such reason is "insufficient flexibility in shedding labor." The entries in column 6 of Table 1 are obtained by assigning a value of 2 (1) to the percentages of firms responding that this reason was "very important" ("important"). Clearly, other weighting procedures can be used (see, e.g., OECD 1994).

A broader based survey of employers, the *World Competitiveness Report* (WCR), has recently been used to provide another measure of the stringency of cross-country employment regulations.[5] Di Tella and MacCulloch (1999) exploit one question in the WCR survey to obtain an indicator of labor market flexibility. The survey question asks respondents to rate the "flexibility of enterprises to adjust job security and compensation standards to economic realities" on a scale of 0 to 100, where 0 indicates "none at all" and 100 "a great deal." Column 7 of Table 1 provides values of this flexibility index averaged over 1984–1990. (Di Tella and MacCulloch 1999, table A).

Yet other researchers have offered more impressionistic indexes of the severity of the regulatory regime. One such index, used by Bertola (1990) and based on an (unstated) mix of employer perceptions and legal rules, is given for completeness in column 2 of Table 1. Finally, severance pay entitlements as of 1984 for our own sample of 21 countries are given in the first column of Table 1. If these are then ranked in ascending order of generosity, we can compare the relation between our index (i.e., the Lazear measure) and that of the other studies, at least for the 11 countries common to each, using OECD (1994) interpolations for the odd missing values. The rankings evidently display some diversity, our measure of the stringency of employment protection correlating most closely with that of Bertola (1990).

This diversity is inevitable. As Grubb and Wells (1993, p. 33) caution, "there is no simple and objective way of defining" an overall index of the severity of the regulatory climate. Their own index fails to consider nonlegal constraints (e.g., union restrictions) or, indeed, issues of legal interpretation. Moreover, there is the inevitable problem of additional subjectivity introduced by any weighting scheme—implicit in their case. In these circumstances, might not

---

[4] A useful survey of these studies is provided by the OECD (1999, table 2.C.1).

[5] The survey covers 21 countries. The number of returned questionnaires varies by year, averaging 1531 between 1984 and 1990. There was no survey in 1987. The flexibility question was changed in 1990 and was subsequently dropped.

rankings derived from employer surveys better capture "the many dimensions that such institutional arrangements associated with employment protection laws encompass" (Di Tella and MacCulloch 1999, p. 8)? The fact that some employer surveys are available in a time-series form might appear an added bonus in this regard. Unfortunately, apart from the issue of their representativeness (the firm heterogeneity point), there is the problem of precision of response. Employers may have difficulty in interpreting questions as to the flexibility or otherwise of the regulatory climate. As a case in point, Addison and Siebert (1999) have noted that there is little correspondence in ranking between two subsequent *ad hoc* employers conducted by the European Commission in 1989 and 1994. Major changes in ranking do not seem to correspond to observed changes in national employment protection laws or their application. In addition, employer responses are likely to be mediated by the cycle, and it is not clear that this relationship has been convincingly sterilized in extant treatments (e.g., Morgan 1998). Consistency problems may thus severely reduce the usefulness of employer surveys as a partial solution to the moment-in-time limitation of more comprehensive OECD-type indexes of employment protection.

This brings us to post-Lazear studies that not only use a more comprehensive measure of employment protection than severance pay but also a richer array of controls. The best known treatments are by Nickell (1997) and Scarpetta (1996), who use moment-in-time estimates of employment protection taken from the OECD (1994) Jobs Study. The studies cover almost identical time periods—1983–1994 and 1983–1993, respectively—and each employs a comprehensive set of rather similar independent variables. The latter include unemployment benefits, expenditures on active labor market policies, measures of the tax wedge, union density, and the degree of coordination of collective bargaining. The sample of countries is 20 for Nickell and 17 for Scarpetta.

Nickell's dependent variables are short- and long-term unemployment and the employment–population ratio. Estimation is via generalized least squares (GLS) random effects using averaged data for two subperiods, 1983–1988 and 1989–1994. He reports that the effects on employment protection are largely statistically insignificant. Scarpetta focuses on unemployment: overall unemployment, youth unemployment, long-term unemployment, and nonemployment. Unlike Nickell, he uses time-series variation in his key variables, other than the employment protection argument. That said, much of this variation is obtained by extending single data point observations. He concludes to the contrary that employment protection causes unemployment, particularly among youths. A harsh reading of both studies would be that the use of a more extensive set of controls is achieved at the cost of no small imprecision of the explanatory variables. Although the lack of variation in the employment protection variable may be less of a problem given the short time frame of the studies, the different conclusions reached regarding its impact are disturbing.

Disquiet over this conflicting evidence has generated a wave of new studies. Of these, perhaps the most interesting is by Di Tella and MacCulloch (1999), who combine a Lazear-type treatment with a new time series on employment protection derived from the WCR, discussed earlier. The dependent variables follow Lazear, the main difference being the inclusion of a variable proxying the generosity of national unemployment benefits, using the OECD (1994) summary measure of the unemployment insurance system. Using data on 20 countries for 1984–1990, Di Tella and MacCulloch report robust, positive associations between flexibility and employment and the labor force participation rate. Less clear-cut, however, is the role of labor market flexibility in reducing unemployment.[6]

---

[6] At issue is whether the short time series of this study is really sufficient to capture actual changes in the regulatory

Supportive evidence regarding the costs of employment protection has also been reported by Garibaldi and Mauro (1999). Following the Nickell procedure of averaging several years of data over the interval 1980–1998, the authors examine the association between the growth in total civilian employment and employment protection legislation (using the OECD index) for a 21-country sample. Their controls include the unemployment insurance net replacement ratio, union density, the extent of bargaining coordination, overall taxes, payroll taxes, population growth, and the average change in inflation (to proxy the business cycle and the macro policy regime). They report strongly negative associations between the degree of employment protection and employment growth in cross section. That said, the coefficient estimates of the employment protection variable are imprecisely estimated in panel regressions, which they attribute to the time-invariant nature of the variable.

Further support for the Lazear argument is provided by Elmeskov, Martin, and Scarpetta (1998) in what is largely an extension of Scarpetta's (1996) analysis. Apart from including more countries and covering a modestly longer time interval, the principal innovation of this follow-up study resides in its use of a second data point for the OECD employment protection index (see below). The dependent variable is structural unemployment as measured by the predicted nonaccelerating wage inflation rate of unemployment. Broadly speaking, the results reported by the authors suggest that structural unemployment is elevated in more generous employment protection regimes. That said, they also argue that the effects of employment protection are mediated by the collective bargaining environment. Specifically, its adverse consequences are reduced in countries characterized by either centralized and coordinated or decentralized collective bargaining compared with nations where sectoral wage bargaining predominates with limited coordination.[7]

Finally, a new study by the OECD (1999), which provides updated and revised information on its comprehensive index of job protection, has created considerable controversy precisely because of its finding of insignificant associations between that index and either unemployment or employment (Taylor 1999). These results are obtained using two-period panel regressions in the manner of Nickell (1997) that employ the now familiar battery of controls. And they hold for disaggregations of the employment protection measure and for the main demographic components of the two outcome measures.

Against this backdrop, the Lazear approach has advantages and disadvantages. The advantage is the use of a long time series on dismissals protection that is consistent across time and requires relatively few judgment calls on the part of the investigator. The disadvantages are twofold. First, that indicator can offer only a partial view of the regulatory apparatus. Second, there is the separate issue of an omitted variables problem. Given our 1956–1984 sample period, we were unable to construct a long enough time series on variables such as union density and aspects of the unemployment insurance system emphasized in more recent studies. To this extent, our point estimates of the effect of dismissals protection could well be biased, although we have indicated that we are not reassured by extant treatments that have deployed a richer mix of covariates. In evaluating the Lazear model, however, the prime initial consideration must be one of replication, using appropriate econometric techniques. Nevertheless, despite the prob-

---

environment, which are infrequent. The limited time span may also mean that it is difficult to identify patterns of adjustment implicit in the model's use of lagged variables.

[7] A worrying feature of the study is its heavy reliance on collective bargaining systems. Classifying countries by the coordination or otherwise of collective bargaining and the degree of centralization and cooperation is a nontrivial task. It shares certain commonalities with the construction of an employment protection index in this regard.

112   *Addison, Teixeira, and Grosso*

lems of assembling the relevant time series, future work using more contemporary data must seek to include a wider array of independent variables than considered here. Yet we have also indicated that the construction of a time series on employment protection, the essential contribution of Lazear, remains central. Absent this, discussion over the disemployment effects of employment protection will continue to be mired in controversy.

3. Econometric Issues

The use of a panel of data to study the effects of employment protection on labor market performance seems to be a useful approach because it combines cross-section and within-country variation. Although a simple cross-section data set is able to provide enough variation in both the dependent and independent variables of the model, it necessarily fails to capture the dynamic effects of severance pay entitlements on labor market outcomes. For its part, a single-country time series would probably not produce statistically significant coefficient estimates for the key dismissals protection argument because changes in employment protection are fairly sporadic even over more than two decades.

However, if panel estimation has the strength (and richness) of combining cross-section and time-series information, it can also reflect the problems specific to each. Nations have their own characteristics—in particular, labor market institutions differ widely across countries—so that no single model can be expected to explain the behavior of a given set of outcome variables. In this case, the pooled ordinary least squares (OLS) regression (ultimately favored by Lazear) should be avoided because it will produce biased estimates. The appropriate procedure would be to deploy a model with fixed or random effects. Both approaches assume a common slope and different intercepts, intercepts that in the random effects specification shift around an estimated mean in accordance with an individual error component specific to each cross-section unit and an error component that is associated with time rather than being assumed to be fixed for each unit.

A second problem stems from the time-series nature of the data. We refer to the likely presence of serially correlated errors. If present, the latter have implications for the efficiency of the estimation and may lead to erroneous statistical inference. In these circumstances, transformation of the data is necessary to satisfy the standard assumptions of zero covariance between residuals through time.

To anticipate our findings, we do indeed detect the presence of highly correlated residuals in each of the cross-section units in both the fixed effects and random effects models run on the untransformed data. The individual autocorrelation coefficients are highly significant and large in absolute magnitude, a result that may, of course, flag poor specification. Abstracting from the latter issue, we address the autocorrelation problem by (a) running a fixed effects model on the pooled data, (b) computing the autocorrelation coefficient $\hat{\rho}$, and (c) re-estimating the model (fixed or random effects) on the transformed data, where the transformed variables are given by $y_{it}^* = y_{it} - \hat{\rho} y_{it-1}$ and $x_{it}^* = x_{it} - \hat{\rho} x_{it-1}$. This is the asymptotic efficient estimator noted by Hsiao (1986), who recommends finding a consistent estimate of ρ from a first-stage fixed effects model and then applying the covariance method to the transformed data. A standard Lagrange multiplier (LM) test was duly performed on the estimated residuals to check whether autocorrelation was removed.

In addition, we employ a feasible GLS procedure that, in a first stage—to control for serial

Table 2. Pooled Estimations, No Country Dummies[a]

Independent Variable	Dependent Variable[b]			
	EMPPOP	UNRATE	LFPR	HOURS
Intercept	−0.254***	0.103***	−0.228***	48.336***
	(0.048)	(0.028)	(0.045)	(3.659)
SEV	−0.0045***	0.0021***	−0.0038***	0.095
	(0.0008)	(0.0005)	(0.0008)	(0.064)
GROWTH	−0.066	0.029	−0.054	11.274**
	(0.073)	(0.042)	(0.068)	(5.535)
GROWTH.SEV	−0.002	0.004	0.0004	−0.753
	(0.017)	(0.010)	(0.0162)	(1.294)
WRKAGE	1.044***	−0.097**	1.032***	−5.333
	(0.074)	(0.043)	(0.069)	(5.633)
R^2	0.38	0.41	0.41	0.29
$\hat{\sigma}$	0.041	0.024	0.038	3.060
n	536	536	536	513

[a] Regressions include YEAR and YEAR^2, $\hat{\sigma}$ is the standard error of the estimated regression. Standard errors of the coefficient estimates are given in parentheses.
[b] ***, **, * denote statistical significance at the 0.01, 0.05, and 0.10 levels respectively.

correlation, transforms the data using the estimated $\hat{\rho}$ obtained from OLS (or fixed effects) on the untransformed data and then applies the GLS estimator, assuming that the residuals are both cross-sectionally correlated and heteroskedastic (Kmenta 1997, chap. 12). This estimation applies a seemingly unrelated regressions technique (Parks estimator) and is implemented using the software EViews.

Two remaining issues are tackled prior to a final substantive exercise that evaluates the properties of the Lazear model in the specific context of dynamic panel estimation (Arellano and Bond 1991). First, we informally address the potential contribution of influential observations to our central and essentially negative results. Second, given the infrequent nature of changes in the key severance pay argument, which may not therefore have immediate effects on labor markets, we investigate the sensitivity of our results to the use of a smoothed severance pay variable obtained through a Hodrick–Prescott filter.

4. Findings

Table 2 contains results of fitting the Lazear model to the pooled cross-section time-series data without country-specific effects. The regressions are the exact counterpart of those in Lazear (1990, table VII). As in Lazear, the severance pay argument is statistically significant in the first three regressions. The odd man out is the hours worked equation, where the coefficient estimate of SEV is positive and insignificant at conventional levels. We believe the latter result has more to do with the inaccuracy of Lazear's hours data than anything else.

The positive association between severance pay and unemployment and the negative relationship between severance pay and employment and labor force participation seem to illustrate the adverse labor market consequences of more generous severance pay regimes. Also consonant with Lazear, the GROWTH.SEV (and GROWTH) covariate is statistically insignificant and the population control, WRKAGE, is strongly significant. It seems therefore that,

114   *Addison, Teixeira, and Grosso*

Table 3. Fixed Effects Regressions[a]

Independent Variable	Dependent Variable[b]			
	EMPPOP	UNRATE	LFPR	HOURS
SEV	0.00076	0.0013***	0.0012**	0.053
	(0.00050)	(0.0004)	(0.0005)	(0.045)
GROWTH	0.024	0.016	0.033	12.231***
	(0.033)	(0.029)	(0.032)	(3.029)
GROWTH.SEV	−0.0087	0.0084	−0.0049	−0.461
	(0.0074)	(0.0063)	(0.0074)	(0.670)
WRKAGE	0.548***	0.350***	0.710***	2.650
	(0.062)	(0.056)	(0.061)	(5.681)
R^2	0.90	0.77	0.89	0.83
$\hat{\sigma}$	0.017	0.015	0.017	1.510
LM	22.92	17.14	7.34	17.13
n	536	536	536	513

[a] Regressions include YEAR and YEAR^2, $\hat{\sigma}$ is the estimated standard error of the regression. Standard errors of the coefficient estimates are given in parentheses. LM is the first-order autocorrelation test statistic. The estimated autocorrelation coefficients $\hat{\rho}$ resulting from applying a Marquardt nonlinear least squares algorithm that simultaneously estimates the coefficients β and ρ are 0.94 (0.02), 0.83 (0.03), 0.94 (0.05), and 0.84 (0.02), respectively.
[b] ***, **, * denote statistical significance at the 0.01, 0.05, and 0.10 levels, respectively.

although our data differ in many respects from those of Lazear, there is broad confirmation of his preferred specification.

When country dummies are included in the regressions and again abstracting from the hours result, there is again reasonable correspondence with Lazear. The findings in Table 3 are for a fuller specification than in Lazear, who provides fixed effects results for specifications containing only severance pay and the year variables (see Lazear 1990, table V). The most important (common) result is the positive and statistically significant coefficient of SEV in the unemployment equation (Lazear reports that SEV is negative and insignificant in the employment equation and positive and insignificant in the labor force participation equation.)

As we have argued, however, the real issue is whether or not these results can be used to make predictions about the role of severance pay in generating, say, unemployment (see Lazear 1990, table VIII). The pooled OLS results evidently produce biased estimates, while the fixed effects specification, although controlling for country heterogeneity, may yield misleading statistical inference if there is serial correlation in the error structure. From the LM test statistics in Table 3, it can be seen that the null of no autocorrelation can be rejected. We note parenthetically that implementation of a nonlinear procedure that simultaneously estimates the parameters of the model and the autocorrelation coefficient confirmed that the latter coefficient was indeed highly significant.

There can be no question that Lazear (1990) is aware of the issues, but in our view, he does not adequately tackle the data problems. Rather, he elects to tackle one problem at a time; that is, he compares (a) the pooled OLS with the fixed effects results and then (b) the OLS and the random effects model (REM) specifications before (c) finally addressing the autocorrelation issue.

The point is that, in (b), the error component associated with time is not present in his error components specification, only the cross-country effect, while in (c), country fixed effects are ignored. In any event, we note that the REM specification assumes that the autocorrelation of the residuals remains constant irrespective of the time distance between them, while the commonly assumed first-order autocorrelation implies that autocorrelation declines over time.

Table 4. Fixed Effects Regressions with Correction for Autocorrelation[a]

Independent Variable	Dependent Variable[b]			
	EMPPOP	UNRATE	LFPR	HOURS
SEV	−0.00047	0.00052	−0.00028	−0.0076
	(0.00034)	(0.00050)	(0.00031)	(0.0434)
GROWTH	0.0022	−0.0218*	−0.0071	3.988***
	(0.0091)	(0.0150)	(0.0087)	(1.310)
GROWTH.SEV	0.0032	0.0037	0.0049***	0.113
	(0.0021)	(0.0032)	(0.0018)	(0.276)
WRKAGE	0.337***	0.398**	0.477***	−15.095
	(0.106)	(0.132)	(0.095)	(12.260)
R^2	0.35	0.41	0.39	0.34
$\hat{\sigma}$	0.006	0.009	0.006	0.780
LM	39.76	18.37	6.22	18.77
n	536	536	536	513

[a] Regressions include YEAR and YEAR², $\hat{\sigma}$ is the estimated standard error of the regression. Standard errors of the coefficient estimates are given in parentheses. LM is the first-order autocorrelation test statistic.
[b] ***, **, * denote statistical significance at the 0.01, 0.05, and 0.10 levels, respectively.

And, according to our tests, application of random effects to the untransformed data did not remove autocorrelation.

Given the clear autoregressive pattern of the residuals, the data have to be differenced according to the estimated autocorrelation coefficients. After this transformation, we obtain the fixed effects results given in Table 4. (Results for the alternative random effects specification are similar and are provided in Appendix B.) The consequences of controlling for the autocorrelation present in the time series are quite dramatic: The effects of SEV are now statistically insignificant throughout. At this stage, then, there is no statistical corroboration of the claim that tougher dismissals protection leads to more unfavorable labor market outcomes.

It is worth pointing out that, once we difference the data and rerun the model, the problems of autocorrelation do appear to be solved if we use a REM rather than a fixed effects specification. The results are provided in Appendix B, where it can be seen that the LM tests on the residuals strongly reject the presence of first-order autoregressive errors, with the possible exception of the employment equation. This is because the random effects model additionally corrects for the remaining posttransformation nonzero covariance between residuals over time.

Inspection of the variance of the residuals on each pooled unit in Table 4 (and Appendix B) fails to indicate the presence of heteroskedasticity. As an additional check on the homoskedasticity of the residuals, we applied a weighted least squares regression procedure in which the data were transformed according to the residual variance for each country (see Kmenta 1997, chap. 12). The results, which are available from the authors on request, do suggest that, after controlling for autocorrelation and introducing country-specific effects, it is indeed correct to assume an homoskedastic error structure.

Another concern is the possible presence of cross-sectional correlation. Here the issue is whether or not the economic interdependence between the countries in the sample influences our results. After controlling for autoregressive errors and cross-section heterogeneity, we applied the SUR weighted least squares option available in EViews. (The results are given in Appendix C.) Compared with the REM estimation, for example, the parameters generally maintained their signs and magnitudes, and we observe a slight increase in the statistical significance

116   *Addison, Teixeira, and Grosso*

Table 5. Fixed Effects Regressions with Correction for Autocorrelation (Hodrick–Prescott Smoothed Series)[a]

Independent Variable	Dependent Variable			
	EMPPOP	UNRATE	LFPR	HOURS
SEV	0.00174	0.00097	0.0015	0.119
	(0.00108)	(0.00113)	(0.0014)	(0.073)
GROWTH	0.010	−0.029**	−0.004	3.471***
	(0.006)	(0.013)	(0.009)	(0.765)
GROWTH.SEV	0.0004	0.007	0.0038	−0.142
	(0.0042)	(0.012)	(0.0048)	(0.312)
WRKAGE	0.309***	0.413***	0.462***	−1.089
	(0.067)	(0.155)	(0.095)	(9.514)
R^2	0.41	0.44	0.43	0.37
$\hat{\sigma}$	0.006	0.009	0.005	0.788
LM	18.53	24.51	18.13	13.92
n	536	536	536	513

[a] Regressions include YEAR and YEAR², $\hat{\sigma}$ is the estimated standard error of the regression. Standard errors of the coefficient estimates are given in parentheses. LM is the first-order autocorrelation test statistic.
[b] ***, ** denote statistical significance at the 0.01 and 0.05 levels, respectively.

of the GROWTH and GROWTH.SEV point estimates. Again, this conformity is to be expected because the REM model assumes a nonzero correlation coefficient between the residuals of different cross-section units at a given point in time.

It is also worth observing that our results do not appear to be driven by outliers. The unemployment regression is the most susceptible in this regard since cross-country differences in unemployment are quite large and because unemployment development varies across countries. Visual inspection of our data indicates that Spain and Israel are the most likely outlier candidates. Unemployment in Spain increased from 5.2% in 1979 (the first observation for this country) to 20.3% in 1984. For its part, Israel shows some sharp movements in unemployment in 1967 and again in 1975. Deleting the two countries from the sample produced virtually no change in the statistical significance of the covariates reported earlier. This is a rather informal statement of the issue. We did not attempt a formal sensitivity analysis for reasons of tractability. First, it is a nontrivial exercise to interpret potential outliers in a very long panel of data of this type. Second, and more important, the conventional methods used to detect leverage points and influential data are derived assuming a standard linear model (e.g., Belsley, Khu, and Welsch 1980). There is no guarantee that the usual diagnostic checking procedures can easily be applied under the very different estimation methods used here.

Because regulations on employment protection change only from time to time, a further issue is whether it is appropriate to impose an immediate reaction of employment and unemployment to changes in severance pay. To investigate this issue, we applied a Hodrick–Prescott filter to the severance pay data. As can be seen from Table 5, smoothing the employment protection variable produced only a slight increase in the precision of the point estimates of SEV, none of which achieved statistical significance at conventional levels.

The strong residual autocorrelation detected in the untransformed data points to persistence in the outcome indicators. As a final exercise, therefore, it seems sensible to look in detail at the dynamic properties of the model. Our approach uses the generalized method of moments (GMM) estimator developed by Arellano and Bond (1991), a methodology that extends the first

Table 6. Dynamic Specification of the Lazear Model: GMM Estimates[a]

Independent Variable	Dependent Variable Y_{it}[b]							
	EMPPOP		UNRATE		LFPR		HOURS	
	OLS[c]	GMM[d]	OLS	GMM	OLS	GMM	OLS	GMM
$Y_i(t-1)$	0.930***	0.763***	0.942***	0.722***	0.929***	0.799***	0.886***	0.498**
	(0.024)	(0.134)	(0.065)	(0.147)	(0.032)	(0.113)	(0.020)	(0.224)
SEV	0.00007	-0.0010	0.00028	0.000064	0.00021	-0.0010**	-0.024	0.058***
	(0.00012)	(0.0008)	(0.00024)	(0.000903)	(0.00017)	(0.0005)	(0.016)	(0.025)
GROWTH	0.070***	0.054*	-0.134***	-0.094***	0.0119	0.010	7.264***	5.901**
	(0.021)	(0.029)	(0.031)	(0.030)	(0.0919)	(0.019)	(1.713)	(2.602)
GROWTH.SEV	-0.00099	0.0059	0.0081*	0.0033	0.0031	0.0092***	0.558	0.251
	(0.00272)	(0.0036)	(0.0045)	(0.0037)	(0.0021)	(0.0022)	(0.449)	(0.474)
WRKAGE	0.052	0.120	0.085	0.488	0.095**	0.282***	-1.912	10.895
	(0.034)	(0.081)	(0.058)	(0.318)	(0.040)	(0.097)	(3.120)	(11.858)
m_2[e]		-2.11		-1.60		0.22		1.02
Wald[f]		100.8 [5]		299.0 [5]		348.3 [5]		16.6 [5]
R^2	0.88		0.85		0.91		0.88	
n	536	536	535	514	536	515	505	484

[a] The equations were estimated using the DPD software developed by Arellano and Bond (1991). The version used in this study was made available by Dr. Jurgen Doornik of the Oxford University Institute of Economics and Statistics. Standard errors of the coefficient estimates are given in parentheses.

[b] ***, **, * denote statistical significance at the 0.01, 0.05, and 0.10 levels, respectively.

[c] OLS is the within-group (i.e., fixed effects) estimation in levels of the variables.

[d] The GMM method estimates the model in first differences. The variables SEV, GROWTH, GROWTH.SEV, and WRKAGE are assumed exogenous and are used as instruments.

[e] The m_2 is a test for lack of second-order serial correlation in the first difference residuals; the Wald statistic is a test of the joint significance of the independent variables (degrees of freedom for χ^2 are in brackets). The m_2 and Wald tests are both asymptotically robust to general heteroskedasticity.

118   *Addison, Teixeira, and Grosso*

difference instrumental variables method suggested by Anderson and Hsiao (1981) to dynamic fixed effects models. (Fixed effects estimation of an autoregressive model produces biased estimates.) This technique yields asymptotic standard errors that are robust to general cross-section and time-series heteroskedasticity under the null hypothesis of no serial correlation in the errors. To test this hypothesis, Arellano and Bond developed a first- and second-order serial correlation test statistic based on the GMM residuals.

Results of fitting this dynamic version of the Lazear model are given in Table 6. (The estimation was implemented using the Dynamic Panel Data [DPD] software made available by Dr. Jurgen Doornik of the Oxford University Institute of Economics and Statistics.)[8] The most important result is the failure to observe statistically significant effects of SEV on the key outcome indicators EMPPOP and UNRATE. That said, there is some indication that severance pay has an impact on the remaining outcome indicators, even if the LFPR effect is perverse from a conventional (and Lazear) perspective. In all cases, the coefficient estimates of the autoregressive terms are highly significant. The use of OLS methods can be seen to produce upwardly biased coefficient estimates and understated standard errors. The GROWTH variable also seems to become more important in explaining labor market outcomes than was previously the case, while the WRKAGE covariate evidently loses some of its explanatory power. All the regression statistics perform as expected. Thus, the Wald statistic is very large and the hypothesis that there is no second-order serial correlation in the first difference residuals, given by the m_2 statistic, cannot be rejected. In sum, our dynamic representation of the Lazear model casts further doubt on the argument that severance pay has adverse consequences for employment and unemployment development.

5. Concluding Remarks

This paper has re-estimated Lazear's influential empirical model of the effects of dismissals protection on employment and unemployment using corrected data for all variables and taking account of econometric problems associated with cross-country heterogeneity and serial correlation in the time series for each country. The upshot was that the adverse labor market consequences of more generous severance pay detected by Lazear were not confirmed in either static or dynamic representations of his model.

These results do not, of course, imply that the effects of dismissals laws, or employment protection legislation more generally, are benign. They pertain solely to the effects of severance pay in the framework of Lazear's parsimonious estimating equation. The use of severance pay to characterize the entire regulatory apparatus of dismissals protection is clearly an oversimplification and possibly a poor proxy for the stringency of dismissals protection. Clearly, any two countries with the same recorded severance pay entitlements may be expected to differ in other aspects of dismissals protection. Similarly, the sparse formal representation of employment/unemployment determination in the model raises a potentially severe omitted variables problem.

To be sure, recent studies that include a more encompassing measure of dismissals protection and a wider array of control variables have yielded some support for Lazear's empirical

---

[8] This procedure assumes a homogeneous lagged response, an assumption that is probably violated in the population. Given that the time series is relatively short for analyzing an autoregressive error structure, however, this assumption is unlikely to cause major problems and was necessary to gather sufficient information for parameter estimation.

conjectures, if not his methodology. More stringent employment protection has thus been linked to elevated unemployment, lower employment/labor force participation, and reduced employment growth. Absence of a suitable time series on variables used in such post-Lazear studies, however, precluded our testing the adequacy of the severance pay argument or assessing the importance of the omitted variables problem. We have also noted the problems attaching to alternative employment protection measures and the dubious pedigree of some explanatory variables popular in the new literature. Moreover, the evidence on adverse labor market consequences of employment protection is not overwhelming. For example, studies using updated measures of the OECD index that provide two data points for this comprehensive measure of employment protection either fail to detect adverse effects on the employment and unemployment aggregates in two-period panel regressions (and first differences) or seem to downplay negative effects, where these are observed, by emphasizing interactions between employment protection and the collective bargaining and tax regimes.

Just as with our own findings, we would not conclude from the latter studies that employment protection is benign after all. A more balanced view would be that the research focus has been too oblique. That is to say, the impact of employment protection on unemployment and employment aggregates is somewhat indirect and difficult to isolate from other causal factors. One alternative research strategy would be to focus on the point at which dismissals protection can be expected more directly to affect behavior. An obvious example is the speed of employment adjustment to demand shocks. Here the immediate goal would be to discover whether observed differences in the employment adjustment process are linked in a systematic way to extant representations of the stringency of national employment protection rules (see Addison and Teixeira 1999). Another example would be to analyze job flow data (see Blanchard and Portugal 1998; Garibaldi 1998). In both cases, the ultimate goal would be to trace the implications of changes in employment adjustment and flows to average levels and durations of employment and unemployment.[9]

Despite the conflicting results reported here, it is assuredly of importance to get a better grip on the effects of employment protection. This is perhaps nowhere more important than in Europe at a time when the European Union is seeking to implement a wide range of job protection and analogous mandates at a European level (Addison and Siebert 1999). It would be particularly unfortunate were the results of our own cross-country inquiry, and the mixed evidence of the wider literature, to encourage the perception that supranational legislation is benign.

Appendix A: Data

This paper uses data from Lazear (1990) that have been corrected for errors of omission and commission. Full details are supplied by Addison and Grosso (1996). The sample period is identical to Lazear, while the (initial) sample of countries has been expanded by one nation, namely, Finland. Lazear collected data on Finland but treated them as nonapplicable, presumably because there is no requirement in Finnish law for employers to pay severance pay (over and above pay for notice periods). But it became possible for employees to be dismissed for economic reasons in 1979, and so Finland enters our data set from that date and severance pay is duly coded as 0 month.

Unlike Addison and Grosso (1996), we follow Lazear in including Portugal within the sample. Indeed, the Portuguese data cover the entire sample period, 1956–1984, rather than 1970–1984 as in Lazear. The reasons for this extension have to do with the legal definition of collective dismissals in Portugal. The employment threshold is so low that we

---

[9] Another option of course would be to temporarily abandon cross-country analyses in favor of national studies, in which framework individual mandates can more easily be parameterized and any tradeoffs rendered more transparent.

120   Addison, Teixeira, and Grosso

treat the law on collective dismissals as applicable to individual dismissals. (For an elaboration of this argument, as well as the problems with Lazear's own measure of Portuguese severance pay, see Addison and Teixeira 1997).

The countries listed in Table 1 plus Israel make up our 21-nation sample. Israel is not included in the table because of the nature of the comparisons being effected there. By contrast, Lazear's final sample is just 18 countries.

Most of the differences between ourselves and Lazear pertain to the severance pay variable, although many of the same sources are used in its construction (see Addison and Grosso 1996, fn. 5). The more important differences in this regard include the following. First, there are no statutory severance pay entitlements in Denmark, as claimed by Lazear; such obligations are instead fixed under collective bargaining. Denmark is thus coded here as 0 month throughout and not as 0 for 1956–1970 and 1 for 1971–1984. Second, for four countries (France, Italy, Norway, and Spain), severance pay fails to reach the levels indicated by Lazear. Third, Germany has no statutory severance pay—although service-related compensation for "socially unwarranted" dismissals is set down under 1969 legislation—and is here coded 0 throughout rather than as 1 as in Lazear. Fourth, legislation covering severance pay has long applied in the United Kingdom but is unaccountably neglected by Lazear. Relatedly, Lazear adopts the convention of discarding all data for a particular country/year if data for any one of the four dependent variables are missing. This procedure serves to further truncate the overall sample size, largely because of missing data on hours. As a practical matter, however, constraining the number of observations to be equal across all four outcome measure regressions did not materially affect any of the results reported here.

Appendix B Random Effects Regressions with Correction for Autocorrelation[a]

Independent Variable	Dependent Variable[b]			
	EMPPOP	UNRATE	LFPR	HOURS
SEV	−0.00054	0.00069	−0.00035	−0.0070
	(0.00034)	(0.00049)	(0.00030)	(0.0424)
GROWTH	0.0022	−0.0207	0.0070	4.016***
	(0.0098)	(0.0148)	(0.0087)	(1.303)
GROWTH.SEV	0.0031	0.0039	0.0049***	0.108
	(0.0021)	(0.0031)	(0.0018)	(0.274)
WRKAGE	0.364***	0.283**	0.501***	−13.620
	(0.103)	(0.121)	(0.092)	(11.261)
R^2	0.32	0.38	0.36	0.31
$\hat{\sigma}$	0.006	0.009	0.005	0.775
LM	9.05	0.82	1.07	1.86
n	536	536	536	513

[a] Regressions include YEAR and YEAR², $\hat{\sigma}$ is the estimated standard error of the regression. Standard errors of the coefficient estimates are given in parentheses. LM is the first-order autocorrelation test statistic.
[b] ***, ** denote statistical significance at the 0.01 and 0.05 levels, respectively.

Appendix C Feasible GLS Estimation for Cross-Sectionally Correlated Residuals[a]

Independent Variable	Dependent Variable[b]			
	EMPPOP	UNRATE	LFPR	HOURS
SEV	−0.00020	0.00065	−0.00017	0.00006
	(0.00016)	(0.00046)	(0.00014)	(0.01631)
GROWTH	0.0018	−0.0073	−0.0066**	4.417***
	(0.0042)	(0.0071)	(0.0030)	(0.531)
GROWTH.SEV	0.0033***	0.0035	0.0048***	−0.216
	(0.0012)	(0.0071)	(0.0015)	(0.178)
WRKAGE	0.304***	0.336***	0.483***	−12.417**
	(0.042)	(0.054)	(0.026)	(5.693)
R^2	0.35	0.40	0.38	0.34
$\hat{\sigma}$	0.006	0.009	0.006	0.781
LM	2.00	1.86	2.12	1.96
n	515	465	515	489

[a] Regressions include YEAR and YEAR², $\hat{\sigma}$ is the estimated standard error of the regression. Standard errors of the coefficient estimates are given in parentheses. LM is the first-order autocorrelation test statistic.
[b] ***, ** denote statistical significance at the 0.01 and 0.05 levels, respectively.

References

Addison, John T., and John B. Chilton. 1997. Nondisclosure as a contractual remedy: Explaining the advance notice puzzle. *Journal of Labor Economics* 15:143–64.

Addison, John T., and Jean-Luc Grosso. 1996. Job security provisions and employment: Revised estimates. *Industrial Relations* 35:585–603.

Addison, John T., and W. Stanley Siebert. 1999. Labor market regulation in the European Union: More costs than benefits? Hobart Paper 138. London: Institute of Economic Affairs.

Addison, John T., and Paulino Teixeira. 1997. Dismissals protection and employment: Does the Lazear model work for Portugal? Unpublished paper, Universidade de Coimbra.

Addison, John T., and Paulino Teixeira. 1999. Is Portugal really so arteriosclerotic? Results from a cross-country analysis of labor adjustment. Discussion Paper No. 99-30, Zentrum für Europäische Wirtschaftsforschung.

Anderson, T. W., and Cheng Hsiao. 1981. Formulation and estimation of dynamic models with error components. *Journal of the American Statistical Association* 76:598–606.

Arellano, Manuel, and Stephen Bond. 1991. Some tests of specification for panel data: Monte Carlo evidence and an application to employment equations. *Review of Economic Studies* 58:277–97.

Belsley, David, Edwin Khu, and Roy Welsch. 1980. *Regression diagnostics: Identifying influential data and sources of collinearity.* New York: Wiley.

Bentolila, Samuel, and Giuseppe Bertola. 1990. Firing costs and labor demand: How bad is Eurosclerosis? *Review of Economic Studies* 57:81–102.

Bentolila, Samuel, and Gilles Saint-Paul. 1994. A model of labor demand with linear adjustment costs. *Labour Economics* 12:303–26.

Bertola, Giuseppe. 1990. Job security, employment and wages. *European Economic Review* 34:851–86.

Bertola, Giuseppe. 1991. Labor turnover costs and average labor demand. Discussion Paper No. 601, Center for Economic Performance, London School of Economics.

Blanchard, Olivier, and Pedro Portugal. 1998. What hides behind an unemployment rate: Comparing Portuguese and U.S. unemployment. NBER Working Paper No. 6636.

Calmfors, Lars, and John Driffill. 1988. Bargaining structure, corporatism and macroeconomic performance. *Economic Policy* 6:13–61.

Di Tella, Rafael, and Robert MacCulloch. 1999. The consequences of labor market flexibility: Panel evidence based on survey data. Unpublished paper, Harvard Business School.

Elmeskov, Jørgen, John P. Martin, and Stefano Scarpetta. 1998. Key lessons for labor market reforms: Evidence from OECD countries' experiences. *Swedish Economic Policy Review* 5:205–52.

European Commission. 1986. Employment problems: Views of businessmen and the workforce. *European Economy* 27: 5–110.

Garibaldi, Pietro. 1998. Job flow dynamics and firing restrictions. *European Economic Review* 42:245–76.

Garibaldi, Pietro, and Paulo Mauro. 1999. Deconstructing job creation. Unpublished Paper, Research Department, International Monetary Fund.

Gavin, Michael K. 1986. Labor market rigidities and unemployment: The case of severance pay costs. International Finance Discussion Paper No. 248, Board of Governors of the Federal Reserve System.

Grubb, David, and William Wells. 1993. Employment regulations and patterns of work in EC countries. *OECD Economic Studies* 21:7–58.

Hamermesh, Daniel S. 1993. Employment protection: Theoretical implications and some U.S. evidence. In *Employment security and labor market behavior—Interdisciplinary approaches and international evidence,* edited by Christoph F. Buechtemann. Ithaca, NY: ILR Press, pp. 126–43.

Hopenhayn, Hugo, and Richard Rogerson. 1993. Job turnover and policy evaluation: A general equilibrium analysis. *Journal of Political Economy* 101:915–38.

Hsiao, Cheng. 1986. *Analysis of panel data.* Cambridge, UK: Cambridge University Press.

IOE. 1985. *Adapting the labor market.* Geneva: International Organization of Employers.

Kmenta, Jan. 1997. *Elements of econometrics.* New York: Macmillan.

Krueger, Alan B., and Jörn-Steffen Pischke. 1997. Observations and conjectures on the U.S. employment miracle. NBER Working Paper No. 6146.

Lazear, Edward P. 1990. Job security provisions and employment. *Quarterly Journal of Economics* 105:699–726.

Morgan, Julian. 1998. Employment security and the demand for labor in Europe. Unpublished paper, National Institute of Economic and Social Research.

Nickell, Stephen. 1997. Unemployment and labor market rigidities: Europe versus North America. *Journal of Economic Perspectives* 11:55–74.

OECD. 1994. *The OECD jobs study, evidence and explanations, Part II: The adjustment potential of the labor market.* Paris: OECD.

122   *Addison, Teixeira, and Grosso*

OECD. 1997. Economic performance and the structure of collective bargaining. *Employment Outlook* (July):63–92.

OECD. 1999. Employment protection and labor market performance. *Employment Outlook* (June):49–132.

Saint-Paul, Gilles. 1995. The high unemployment trap. *Quarterly Journal of Economics* 110:527–50.

Scarpetta, Stefano. 1996. Assessing the role of labor market policies and institutional settings on unemployment: A cross-country analysis. *OECD Economic Studies* 26:43–98.

Taylor, Robert. 1999. OECD backs down as finding on jobless is attacked. *The Financial Times*, 9 July, p. 1.

Journal of Economic Perspectives—Volume 11, Number 3—Summer 1997—Pages 55–74

Unemployment and Labor Market Rigidities: Europe versus North America

Stephen Nickell

ere is the received wisdom. The European job market is rigid and inflexible. Result: high unemployment. The North American job market is dynamic and flexible. Result: low unemployment. So Europeans had better do something about their labor markets unless they want permanent double digit unemployment.

In fact, this is not *totally* wrong. There are features of the labor markets in some European countries that help sustain high levels of unemployment. Some of these features can be thought of as rigidities. However, there are many other so-called rigidities that do not cause high unemployment and, indeed, may serve a useful purpose. So it is important to know which features of the labor market cause high unemployment and which do not. This is the subject of what follows.

Labor Market Outcomes in Europe and North America

While it is sometimes convenient to lump all the countries of western Europe together in order to provide a suitable contrast to North America, most of the time it is a rather silly thing to do. Different European countries are effectively different labor markets with the intercountry movement of labor being very small, mainly because of language and cultural barriers. Partly as a consequence of these differences, labor markets in Europe exhibit enormous diversity; in fact, differences within Europe are much greater than are the difference between the European average and North America. This section looks at some of these differences, first

■ *Stephen Nickell is Professor of Economics, Institute of Economics and Statistics, University of Oxford, Oxford, United Kingdom.*

56   Journal of Economic Perspectives

Table 1
Unemployment Rates in the OECD

	1983–96	1983–88			1989–94		
	Total	Total	Short-term	Long-term	Total	Short-term	Long-term
Austria	3.8	3.6	na	na	3.7	na	na
Belgium	9.7	11.3	3.3	8.0	8.1	2.9	5.1
Denmark	9.9	9.0	6.0	3.0	10.8	7.9	3.0
Finland	9.1	5.1	4.0	1.0	10.5	8.9	1.7
France	10.4	9.8	5.4	4.4	10.4	6.5	3.9
Germany (W)	6.2	6.8	3.7	3.1	5.4	3.2	2.2
Ireland	15.1	16.1	6.9	9.2	14.8	5.4	9.4
Italy	7.6	6.9	3.1	3.8	8.2	2.9	5.3
Netherlands	8.4	10.5	5.0	5.5	7.0	3.5	3.5
Norway	4.2	2.7	2.5	0.2	5.5	4.3	1.2
Portugal	6.4	7.6	3.5	4.2	5.0	3.0	2.0
Spain	19.7	19.6	8.3	11.3	18.9	9.1	9.7
Sweden	4.3	2.6	2.3	0.3	4.4	4.0	0.4
Switzerland	1.8	0.8	0.7	0.1	2.3	1.8	0.5
U.K.	9.7	10.9	5.8	5.1	8.9	5.5	3.4
Canada	9.8	9.9	9.0	0.9	9.8	8.9	0.9
U.S.	6.5	7.1	6.4	0.7	6.2	5.6	0.6
Japan	2.6	2.7	2.2	0.5	2.3	1.9	0.4
Australia	8.7	8.4	5.9	2.4	9.0	6.2	2.7
New Zealand	6.8	4.9	4.3	0.6	8.9	6.6	2.3

Source: OECD Employment Outlook, U.K. Employment Trends, U.S. Bureau of Labor Statistics.

with regard to unemployment and then with regard to other labor market outcomes, notably job and worker mobility, and wage flexibility.

Table 1 sets out some information on unemployment[1] where we focus on the recent past, namely the period following the major recession of the early 1980s. The first column provides an up-to-date summary picture; the other columns present averages over two subperiods, which will be used for more detailed analysis. The immediate point that stands out is the enormous variation in European rates. Taking the period 1983–1996, these stretch from 1.8 percent in Switzerland to 19.7 percent in Spain. This variation means that around 30 percent of the popu-

[1] Table 1 uses OECD standardized rates, with the exception of Austria, Denmark and Italy. For Austria and Denmark, the table presents national registered rates. For Italy, the table presents the unemployment rate as calculated by the U.S. Bureau of Labor Statistics "on U.S. concepts." Aside from Italy, the OECD rates and BLS rates are very similar. For Italy, the OECD rates appear to include the large number of Italians who are registered as unemployed but have performed no active job search in the previous four weeks. Finally, the unemployment rate here is for *West* Germany, both to maintain comparability across time and because including a "transition economy" in the data would weaken comparability across countries.

lation of OECD Europe lives in countries and operates in labor markets with average unemployment rates lower than that of the United States.

A closer look at Table 1 raises two additional points. First, the European countries with the lowest unemployment rates (Austria, West Germany, Norway, Portugal, Sweden and Switzerland) are not noted for the flexibility of their labor markets. Britain, on the other hand, has always had the most flexible labor market in Europe on standard measures and yet has an average unemployment rate higher than half of its European neighbors.

Second, it is worth remarking on the fact that the variation in short-term unemployment is substantially smaller than that in long-term unemployment, where long-term is defined as a duration of more than a year. Thus, while countries require some short-term unemployment, long-term unemployment appears to be an optional extra. The reason is that long-term unemployment, in contrast to the short-term variety, contributes very little to holding down wage pressure and hence inflation (OECD, 1993, p. 94). The long-term unemployed are far enough away from the active labor market that their presence has little influence on wages. So if some suitable microeconomic policy can eliminate long-term unemployment, this will have few adverse macroeconomic implications. That is, it will not require much of a rise in short-term unemployment to maintain stable inflation.

Instead of concentrating on unemployment rates, some commentators prefer to focus on total employment, noting, for example, that North American employment has risen much faster in recent years than has European employment. Such a contrast is not helpful, however, because there is no control for different rates of growth in the population of working age. Controlling for this by normalizing on the size of the labor force takes one back to unemployment. A more reasonable alternative is to focus on employment/population ratios, although these tend to be strongly influenced by all the social and cultural factors that affect the labor market participation of married women. Table 2 presents evidence on alternative labor supply measures, like the employment/population ratio.

The first two columns of Table 2 show the ratio of employed persons to the total working-age population and the ratio for males ages 25–54. The cross-country variation in overall employment/population ratios is due to a variety of factors. Particularly important are variations in the participation rates of married women (which are very low in southern Europe), variations in the retirement rates of those over the age of 55 (OECD, 1996, p. 188) and variations in the employment rates of prime-age men, shown in the second column of the table. The third column of the table shows annual hours worked by the average worker in these different economies. Differences in this column are dominated by the extent of part-time working and by variations in weekly hours and annual holiday entitlements. Many countries in continental Europe have low annual hours actually worked even excluding part-time workers, because of their low weekly hours and long annual holidays compared to those of the United States and Japan. This does not imply that European workers would like to work more paid hours per year. Indeed, across the EC, more people would like to work *fewer* paid hours than would like to work more paid hours at

Table 2
Alternative Labor Supply Measures

	Employment/Population Ratio (%) (whole working age population)	Employment/Population Ratio (%) (males age 25–54)	Annual Hours Worked per Worker	Overall Labor Supply (%)
Austria	67.3	86.6	1600	51.6
Belgium	56.1	87.4	1580	42.6
Denmark	75.0	86.6	1510	54.5
Finland	67.1	82.4	1770	57.1
France	59.8	87.9	1650	47.4
Germany (W)	65.2	87.0	1600	50.0
Ireland	53.2	80.3	1750	44.8
Italy	54.0	84.3	1730	44.9
Netherlands	62.2	86.5	1510	45.2
Norway	73.3	87.4	1430	50.4
Portugal	69.3	90.6	2000	66.6
Spain	47.5	81.5	1820	41.6
Sweden	75.6	88.2	1510	52.0
Switzerland	78.6	94.7	1640	62.0
UK	69.6	86.7	1750	58.6
Canada	70.6	84.7	1740	59.0
U.S.	73.1	88.2	1940	68.2
Japan	73.4	95.9	1960	69.2
Australia	68.2	86.5	1870	61.3
New Zealand	68.0	86.6	1830	59.8

Source: OECD Employment Outlook (1996), Tables A, B and C.

given hourly rates (European Economy, 1995, Table 25a). The final column, "over-all labor supply," combines the annual hours worked and employment/population ratios. Take the annual hours worked as a percentage of 2080 hours, which represents a full-time year of working 40 hours a week for 52 weeks. Multiply this by the employment/population ratio. The result can be thought of as the proportion of total "potential" hours worked in the economy. Total labor supply varies enormously across countries, with Japan, Portugal and the United States all supplying about two-thirds of potential hours, while Spain and Belgium supply barely 40 percent of potential.[2]

Another way of putting the unemployment/rigidity story into a broader perspective is to look at job and worker mobility. Job turnover is defined as the sum of the gross job creation and job destruction rates across companies; that is, the total of all new jobs generated plus all old jobs destroyed. Worker mobility includes

[2] Of course, these numbers exclude unmeasured labor input into, for example, the "black economy." However, these total labor supply numbers are worth bearing in mind when comparing GDP per capita across countries.

all job turnover, but also includes the numerous occasions where workers enter or leave a job in a company when the overall number of jobs remains fixed, because of quits, retirements and so on. Of course, there are problems of comparability with cross-national data such as these (Contini et al., 1995), but there is no evidence that jobs are created and destroyed at a more rapid rate in North America than they are in Europe. However, workers do appear to circulate faster through the existing jobs in North America (OECD, 1996, Tables 5.1, 5.2). This is also consistent with the finding that the United States has relatively high levels of regional mobility: about 3 percent of U.S. households change their region of residence in a year, compared to closer to 1 percent in the United Kingdom, Germany and France, and even lower in Italy and Spain. However, regional mobility rates in Norway and Sweden are similar to those in the United States (OECD, 1990, Table 3.3). Since the encouragement of regional mobility has always been a feature of Norwegian and Swedish labor market policy, this outcome is no surprise.[3]

A final perspective on the aggregate labor market is to look at the evidence on wage flexibility. Table 3 presents some measures of the responsiveness of overall wages to unemployment, derived from both aggregate time series and individual survey data. Of course, this is only one feature of wage flexibility; for example, it is not informative about the flexibility of relative wages across different groups. However, for this particular aspect of wage flexibility, there is no dramatic contrast between Europe and North America. If anything, Canada and the United States veer toward the inflexible end of the spectrum.

To summarize, the contrast between Europe and North America is more complex than is commonly realized. Unemployment is higher in the majority of European countries than in the United States, but there is considerable variation across Europe. Rates of job turnover are no higher in North America than in Europe and neither are overall wages any more flexible, but it does seem that U.S. workers are more mobile than are many Europeans both geographically and between jobs. The next step is to focus on a large number of separate features of the labor market and to try to isolate those that have some responsibility for the high levels of unemployment in many European countries.

What Features of the Labor Market Generate High Unemployment?

Our aim in this section is to pinpoint precisely which features of the labor market generate unemployment and which do not. Then we can discuss how these facts relate to the view that high unemployment in Europe is due to rigid and inflexible labor markets.

The first step is to look at labor market characteristics in different countries. Table 4 presents direct measures of labor market rigidities and summary statistics

---

[3] The "regions" in all these countries are comparable in size, so these comparisons have some meaning.

Table 3
**Wage Flexibility: The Percentage Increase in Wages in Response to a One
Percentage Point Fall in the Unemployment Rate**

	Aggregate Time Series Measure		Microeconometric Measure
	Short-run	Long-run	
Austria	1.43	3.11	2.43
Belgium	0.65	4.06	
Denmark	0.66	1.74	
Finland	0.48	1.55	
France	2.22	4.35	
Germany (W)	0.55	1.01	2.06
Ireland	0.80	1.82	2.35
Italy	2.07	12.94	1.32
Netherlands	0.66	2.28	1.98
Norway	1.96	10.59	1.95
Spain	0.17	1.21	
Sweden	2.31	12.16	
Switzerland	1.32	7.33	7.06
U.K.	0.98	0.98	0.82
Canada	0.50	2.38	0.92
U.S.	0.32	0.94	1.52

Source: Aggregate time series measures; Layard et al. (1991), chapter 9, Table 2. Microeconomic measures;
Blanchflower and Oswald (1994), Table 9.1. These later numbers are derived by dividing the Blanch-
flower/Oswald numbers by the average unemployment rate, because they only report the elasticity of
wages with respect to unemployment.

on the treatment of the unemployed. The employment protection index in the first
column was drawn up by the OECD and is based on the strength of the legal
framework governing hiring and firing. The countries are ranked from 1–20, with
20 being the most strictly regulated. The countries of southern Europe have the
toughest regulations and, roughly speaking, these regulations get weaker as one
moves further north. Switzerland, Denmark and the United Kingdom have the
weakest laws in Europe, and these laws are comparable to those in place outside
Europe.

The labor standards index in the second column was also drawn up by the
OECD and refers to the strength of the legislation governing a number of aspects
of the labor market. The index ranges from 0 to 10, with each country being scored
from 0 (lax or no legislation) to 2 (strict legislation) on each of the five dimensions:
working time, fixed-term contracts, employment protection, minimum wages and
employees' representation rights (on works councils, company boards and the like).
The scores are then added up. The picture is similar to the employment protection
column. The United Kingdom and the United States have very weak legislation in
this area, whereas Spain and Italy have many strict rules and regulations. So it is
undoubtedly true that if we are to think of inflexibility as referring to legal restric-

Table 4

Features of OECD Labor Markets I, 1989–1994

	Direct Rigidities		Treatment of the Unemployed		
	1 *Employment* *Protection*	*2* *Labor* *Standards*	*3* *Benefit Replacement* *Rate (%)*	*4* *Benefit Duration* *(years)*	*5* *Active Labor* *Market* *Policies*
Austria	16	5	50	2	8.3
Belgium	17	4	60	4	14.6
Denmark	5	2	90	2.5	10.3
Finland	10	5	63	2	16.4
France	14	6	57	3	8.8
Germany (W)	15	6	63	4	25.7
Ireland	12	4	37	4	9.1
Italy	20	7	20	0.5	10.3
Netherlands	9	5	70	2	6.9
Norway	11	5	65	1.5	14.7
Portugal	18	4	65	0.8	18.8
Spain	19	7	70	3.5	4.7
Sweden	13	7	80	1.2	59.3
Switzerland	6	3	70	1	8.2
U.K.	7	0	38	4	6.4
Canada	3	2	59	1	5.9
U.S.	1	0	50	0.5	3.0
Japan	8	1	60	0.5	4.3
Australia	4	3	36	4	3.2
New Zealand	2	3	30	4	6.8

Source: OECD *Jobs Study* (1994), Part II, Table 6.7, column 5. OECD *Employment Outlook* (1994), Table 4.8, column 6 (extended by author). U.S. Department of Health and Social Services, *Social Security Programmes Throughout the World* (1993). OECD Employment Outlook (1995), Table T.

tions on the operation of the labor market, southern and continental Europe are the most inflexible. As an offset to this, however, it is worth remarking that southern Europe also has the highest rate of self-employment in the OECD (OECD, 1994, Table 6.8). The self-employed are, presumably, among the most flexible of all workers.

Benefit systems vary quite dramatically. The "replacement rate," which shows what share of income is replaced by unemployment benefits, and the duration of these benefits (four years means indefinite duration) are typically fairly generous by U.S. standards (50 percent replacement rate for six months). Italy, however, barely had an unemployment benefit system at all for most of the postwar period.[4]

---

[4] Until recently, the unemployed in Italy were entitled to 800 lira per day (around 50 cents). A small proportion of the "unemployed" would be covered by the CIG scheme for industrial workers who are in danger of being laid off. These typically do not amount to more than 1 percentage point of unemployment.

Some of the countries with the most generous benefit levels have strictly time-limited systems, notably in Scandinavia, like Sweden's 80 percent replacement rate, which is limited to 1.2 years. The next column, "active labor market policies," refers to expenditures on activities for the unemployed that are geared to help them back into work and are popular in many, although not all, European countries. These include labor market training, assistance with job search, subsidized employment and special measures for the disabled. The numbers in this column are derived by taking active labor market spending per unemployed person as a percentage of GDP per member of the labor force. Thus, Sweden's figure of close to 60 shows that expenditure on active policies per unemployed person is nearly 60 percent of national output per potential worker, which is extraordinarily high. Spain, on the other hand, is notable for its combination of a generous benefit system and a low level of expenditure on active labor market policies.

The first few columns of Table 5 present variables that summarize the structure of wage determination systems. In most European countries, with the exception of the United Kingdom and Switzerland, trade unions play a very significant role in wage determination. The union density column shows the proportion of trade union members as a percentage of all wage and salary earners. However, this does not tell the whole story. In many nations, union wage negotiations determine the wages of workers who are not explicitly part of the union. In Spain and France, for example, only about 10 percent of workers are union members, but the wages of over 70 percent of all workers are covered by union bargaining. Thus, the "union coverage index" presents a summary of the share of workers actually covered by union bargaining, where 3 means over 70 percent covered, 2 means from 25–70 percent, and 1 is under 25 percent.

The next column of the table shows the extent of coordination in wage bargaining, on the part of both unions and employers. In each country, the degree of union and then employer coordination is ranked from a low of 1 to a high of 3. In some of these countries, both unions and, more significantly, employers coordinate their wage bargaining activities, particularly in central Europe and Scandinavia. In those countries where unions play a lesser role, although still an important one like the United Kingdom, Switzerland, and all non-European countries except the United States—there is very little coordination over wage bargaining, with the notable exceptions of Switzerland and Japan, where employer coordination is very important.

The final two columns of the table give information on the tax burden on labor. First we have the payroll tax rate, defined as the ratio of labor costs to wages (less unity) and then we show the total tax rate, which is the sum of the average payroll, income and consumption tax rates. The latter are based on aggregate tax and income data. The payroll tax rate varies dramatically across countries, with Denmark levying no payroll taxes and France and Italy with a rate close to 40 percent. The total tax rate is less variable and represents a crude measure of the tax wedge between real labor costs and real take-home pay. This is arguably the correct measure of the tax burden on labor.

Unemployment and Labor Market Rigidities: Europe versus North America   63

Table 5

Features of OECD Labor Markets II, 1989–1994

	1 *Union Density* *(%)*	*2* *Union Coverage* *Index*	*3* *Co-ordination* *Union*	*Employer*	*4* *Payroll Tax* *Rate (%)*	*5* *Total Tax* *Rate (%)*
Austria	46.2	3	3	3	22.6	53.7
Belgium	51.2	3	2	2	21.5	49.8
Denmark	71.4	3	3	3	0.6	46.3
Finland	72.0	3	2	3	25.5	65.9
France	9.8	3	2	2	38.8	63.8
Germany (W)	32.9	3	2	3	23.0	53.0
Ireland	49.7	3	1	1	7.1	34.3
Italy	38.8	3	2	2	40.2	62.9
Netherlands	25.5	3	2	2	27.5	56.5
Norway	56.0	3	3	3	17.5	48.6
Portugal	31.8	3	2	2	14.5	37.6
Spain	11.0	3	2	1	33.2	54.2
Sweden	82.5	3	3	3	37.8	70.7
Switzerland	26.6	2	1	3	14.5	38.6
U.K.	39.1	2	1	1	13.8	40.8
Canada	35.8	2	1	1	13.0	42.7
U.S.	15.6	1	1	1	20.9	43.8
Japan	25.4	2	2	2	16.5	36.3
Australia	40.4	3	2	1	2.5	28.7
New Zealand	44.8	2	1	1	—	34.8

Source: Layard et al. (1991), Annex 1.4, and *OECD Employment Outlook* (1994), p. 175–85. Centre for Economic Performance (LSE), OECD data set.

Overall, therefore, there are quite substantial differences between European and North American labor markets as well as important differences within Europe. The consequences of these differences for unemployment and labor supply form our next topic.

The Labor Market and Unemployment

Our purpose in what follows is to investigate the relations between unemployment and other measures of labor supply, and labor market institutions. Table 6 presents three regressions relating to unemployment. Each regression is based on two cross-sections dated 1983–88 and 1989–1994. The dependent variables are the unemployment rates reported in Table 1, and the values of the independent variables for the time period 1989–1994 are from Tables 4 and 5. The corresponding values of the independent variables for 1983–88 are not presented here but are available from the author. Some variables take the same values for both periods,

Table 6

Regressions to Explain Log Unemployment Rate Percentage

(20 OECD countries, 1983–88 and 1989–1994)

	1 Total Unemployment	2 Long-term Unemployment	3 Short-term Unemployment
Employment Protection (1–20)	−0.0032 (0.03)	0.051 (0.034)	−0.046 (0.024)
Replacement Rate (%)	0.011 (0.0050)	0.011 (0.0080)	0.011 (0.0060)
Benefit Duration (years)	0.088 (0.055)	0.25 (0.089)	0.043 (0.062)
Active Labor Market Policies [a]	−0.024 (0.0087)	−0.039 (0.013)	−0.012 (0.0098)
Union Density (%)	0.012 (0.0063)	0.010 (0.0096)	0.0082 (0.0071)
Union Coverage Index (1–3)	0.45 (0.22)	0.83 (0.35)	0.39 (0.24)
Co-ordination (Union + Employer) (2–6)	−0.46 (0.087)	−0.54 (0.15)	−0.37 (0.11)
Total Tax Rate (%)	0.026 (0.0087)	0.023 (0.013)	0.025 (0.010)
Change in Inflation (% pts. p.a.)	−0.17 (0.11)	−0.30 (0.17)	−0.18 (0.10)
Dummy for 1989–94	0.20 (0.095)	0.30 (0.16)	0.17 (0.089)
R^2	0.76	0.84	0.60
N (countries, time)	40 (20, 2)	38 (19, 2)	38 (19, 2)

Notes: Estimation is by GLS random effects using two time periods (1983–88 and 1989–1994). Standard errors are in parentheses.

[a] The variable is instrumented. Because the active labor market policies variable refers to percentage of GDP normalized on *current* unemployment, this variable is highly endogenous. So we renormalized the current percentage of GDP spent on active labor market measures on the average unemployment rate in 1977–79 to create the instrument. Insofar as measurement errors in unemployment are serially uncorrelated, this will help with the endogeneity problem.

but many are different. We chose to use six-year averages in order to smooth out both the cycle and year-on-year noise. On the other hand, we felt there was enough useful information here to warrant the use of two cross-sections rather than one 12-year average. The regression coefficients are estimated using the standard random effects generalized least squares procedure, which is essentially ordinary least squares corrected for the fact that the two successive observations for each country cannot be treated as independent random draws. Finally, note that the dependent variables are the logs[5] of the unemployment rate (column 1), the long-term rate (column 2) and the short-term rate (column 3). Thus, if the right-hand side of the equation increases by 0.1, log unemployment goes up by 0.1, so unemployment rises by just over 10 percent. From a baseline unemployment rate of 5 percent, this would represent an increase of half a percentage point to 5.5 percent.

In Table 7 we report similar regressions explaining other aspects of labor supply, notably the employment/population ratios and overall labor supply reported

---

[5] The use of the log of the unemployment rate follows from the fact that many investigations of wage determination find that the use of log u in a wage equation is preferable to the use of u. See Blanchflower and Oswald (1994), for example.

Table 7

Regressions to Explain Labor Supply Measures

(20 OECD countries, 1983 and 1989–1994)

	Employment/Population Ratio (%)		
	1 Whole Working Age Population	*2* Males Aged 25–54	*3* Overall Labor Supply
Employment Protection (1–20)	−0.94 (0.30)	0.040 (0.18)	−0.70 (0.39)
Replacement Rate (%)	−0.026 (0.072)	−0.052 (0.043)	−0.037 (0.091)
Benefit Duration (years)	−1.26 (0.63)	−0.61 (0.43)	−0.32 (0.73)
[a] Active Labour Market Policies	0.16 (0.11)	0.081 (0.073)	−0.028 (0.14)
Union Density (%)	−0.082 (0.086)	−0.11 (0.053)	−0.18 (0.11)
Union Coverage Index (1–3)	−0.96 (2.54)	−1.36 (1.74)	−2.24 (2.84)
Coordination (Union + Employer) (2–6)	5.03 (1.23)	2.71 (0.74)	4.20 (1.58)
Total Tax Rate (%)	−0.24 (0.12)	−0.16 (0.075)	−0.26 (0.16)
Change in Inflation (% pts. p.a.)	−2.12 (0.93)	−0.97 (0.72)	−2.02 (0.97)
Dummy for 1989–94	1.87 (0.79)	−2.09 (0.63)	0.041 (0.83)
R^2	0.81	0.63	0.51
N (countries, time)	(20, 2)	(20, 2)	(20, 2)

Notes: Estimation is by GLS random effects using two time periods (1983, 1989–1994). Standard errors are in parentheses.

[a] Active labor market prices are instrumented as in Table 6.

in Table 2. Again we use two cross-sections with the same independent variables. In this case, the dependent variables are not in logs.

Before we go on to discuss particular rigidities, it is worth commenting briefly on the status of these results. First, we see them as a helpful overview of the correlations in the data and nothing more. Like all simple cross-section correlations, care must be taken with their interpretation because of issues of reverse causality and the like. Second, despite the use of six-year averages, there may still be significant long-term variations across countries in the stance of macroeconomic policy. We control for the average change in inflation as one attempt to deal with this problem. Third, there may be factors that explain cross-country differences in unemployment that are not associated with the labor market. For example, it can be argued that higher levels of product market competition tend to reduce unemployment (Layard, Nickell and Jackman, 1991, chapters 7 and 9, for example). Unfortunately, it has not proved possible to obtain measures of product market competition that are consistent across enough countries to include in the regressions.

Finally, and most importantly, why focus only on the 1980s and 1990s? Underlying this question is the reasonable argument that in the 1960s, the unemployment rankings across countries were completely different but, roughly speaking, the labor market institutions were the same. So how can the labor market institutions have anything to do with unemployment? Part of the answer has to be that the institutions had a big impact on the way in which each of the economies of the different countries responded to the major adverse shocks of the 1970s *and* the way in which some of these responses, notably unemployment, persisted through the 1980s and 1990s. In part, this effect is what our regressions are picking up. There remain a number of unanswered questions concerning the evolution of labor markets since the 1960s. Here, our main concern is much more limited, namely the question of which institutions, for whatever reason, appear to be important in understanding recent unemployment levels across the OECD. So let us consider various institutions in turn.

Direct Rigidities

Labor market legislation is typically put in place to protect employees from arbitrary, unfair or discriminatory actions on the part of employers. In so doing, it may raise the effective cost to firms of employing workers and/or raise the effective cost of adjusting levels of employment. The impact of the former on unemployment depends crucially on the extent to which the extra costs are shifted onto employees by a suitable adjustment of the wage. The general evidence on payroll taxes (as we shall see) is that the major part of the burden of such costs is typically shifted onto workers in the long run, thereby nullifying their impact on unemployment. While this obviously cannot be the case for minimum wages, there is no evidence in our data that high labor standards overall have any impact on unemployment whatever. For example, if we add our labor standards variable (Table 4, column 1) to our unemployment regression (Table 6, column 1), it has a negligible and completely insignificant coefficient.[6]

Laws that raise the cost of employment adjustment, notably those relating to employment protection, will tend to reduce the inflow into unemployment and, because they make firms more cautious about hiring, will also reduce the flow out of unemployment into work. This will almost certainly reduce short-term unemployment (via the reduced inflow) and raise long-term unemployment (via the reduced outflow). The overall impact on unemployment is likely to be rather small, as these effects would tend to cancel out. The results in the first row of Table 6 are entirely consistent with this discussion and confirm the analysis of Bentolila and Bertola (1990).

However, as the coefficients in the first row of Table 7, columns 1 and 3, indicate, there is some evidence of a negative correlation between employment protection and measures of labor supply that go beyond unemployment (see also Lazear, 1990). Much of this correlation arises, in fact, because participation rates among married women in southern Europe are very low and employment protection laws in these countries are very tough (OECD, 1994, Table 6.9). Thus, as the first row of Table 7 also indicates, if we focus on prime-age men (column 2), there

---

[6] The coefficient is 0.019 with a standard error of 0.063.

is no effect. A speculative hypothesis might be that low female participation and tough employment protection laws in southern Europe are both consequences of a culture that places a great deal of weight on the position of the (male) head of household, which is not to be undermined either by the presence of a high-earning wife or by the loss of a job.

The Treatment of the Unemployed

There are two aspects of the treatment of unemployed individuals, which might be termed passive and active. The passive is exemplified by the payment, as of right, of unemployment benefit for a given period. Active policies, on the other hand, consist of measures that attempt to ensure that the unemployed individual is able and willing to take up work.

On the passive side, generous benefit systems influence unemployment via two mechanisms. First, they reduce the fear of unemployment and hence directly increase upward pressure on wages from employees (via unions, for example). Second, they reduce the "effectiveness" of unemployed individuals as potential fillers of vacancies, by allowing them to be more choosy. The impact of a high benefit replacement ratio on unemployment is well documented (Layard, Nickell and Jackman, 1991; OECD, 1994, chapter 8) and is confirmed by the significant coefficient on the replacement rate in Table 6. The other important feature of the benefit system is the duration of entitlement. Long-term benefits generate long-term unemployment (Table 6, row 3; OECD, 1991, Chart 7.1B). Of course, it can be argued that countries might introduce more generous benefit systems when unemployment is a serious problem, so that in cross-country correlations, the causality runs from unemployment to benefits rather than the other way round. However, the microeconometric evidence on the positive impact of benefit levels and entitlement durations on the duration of individual unemployment spells (Narendranathan, Nickell and Stern, 1985; Meyer, 1990) suggests that at least part of the observed cross-country correlation can be taken at face value.

The impact of a relatively generous benefit system might be offset by suitable active measures to push the unemployed back to work. Such policies seem to work particularly well when allied to a relatively short duration of benefit entitlement, reducing long-term unemployment while alleviating the social distress that might be caused by simply discontinuing benefits without offering active assistance toward a job. Their effects are well summarized in OECD (1993, ch. 2), and their significant impact in reducing long-term unemployment is illustrated in the fourth row of Table 6.

While benefits affect unemployment, our evidence suggests that the benefit system seems to have little impact on overall labor supply as shown in Table 7. There is a suggestion here that while high benefits lead to high unemployment, they also lead to high participation because they make participation in the labor market more attractive, because participation is necessary to be eligible for the high benefits. This is consistent with a weak impact of benefits on employment/population ratios, because the higher unemployment effect and the higher labor market participation effect tend to cancel out.

Wage Determination and Unions

The key features of wage determination systems are the extent to which wages are determined collectively, via union bargaining (union coverage), and the degree to which employers and unions coordinate their wage bargaining activities given that wages are determined collectively. Of course, if wages are not generally determined collectively, as in the United States, the extent of coordination simply does not apply.

Unions tend to raise pay, and thus one would expect the extent of union activity in an economy to influence unemployment. This is confirmed by the results in rows 5 and 6 of Table 6, where greater union density and especially union coverage tend to raise unemployment. However, Table 6, row 7, also shows that this is offset if unions and employers can coordinate their bargaining activities. For example, leapfrogging is a common feature of decentralized, uncoordinated, union-dominated systems; that is, each union tends to take an earlier pay settlement in a related sector as a baseline to be exceeded in its own negotiations. This generates an additional source of inflationary pressure that requires more unemployment to quash it. If unions and employers can coordinate their wage bargaining activities, such leapfrogging may be eliminated.

It is important to note that coordination does not mean centralization, which typically implies government involvement in wage bargaining. Both Japan and Germany have a high degree of coordination in wage bargaining, particularly across employers, but neither system is centralized. And as OECD (1994, Table 5.16) makes clear, coordination appears to have a significant negative impact on wages, whereas the centralization of wage bargaining does not. To summarize, therefore, unions are bad for jobs, but these bad effects can be nullified if both the unions and the employers can coordinate their wage bargaining activities.

Labor Taxes

Lowering payroll taxes is a very popular recommendation by those concerned with reducing unemployment (OECD, 1994; Phelps, 1994). It is easy to understand this advice if a payroll tax is viewed as a tax on jobs. Things are not, however, quite as they seem. The first point to recognize is that, broadly speaking, the key tax rate for the labor market is the sum of the payroll tax rate, the personal income tax rate and the consumption tax rate. Switching between these taxes will not have an important impact, so payroll taxes, per se, are of little consequence. This result has nothing to do with the incidence of these taxes, which we shall address later. It derives from the logic of supply and demand.

Consider a simple example. Suppose we have a labor market where total labor costs per employee are $100, payroll taxes paid by the employer are $10 (so pretax wages are $90), income taxes paid by the employee are $10, and post-tax wages are $80. Suppose this labor market is in equilibrium. Thus, firms are just willing to employ at $100 all the workers who are willing to work at $80. Now suppose that income taxes are reduced to $5 and payroll taxes are raised to $15 to maintain revenue. Further, suppose that as a result of this change, firms pay pretax wages of $85. Then labor costs per employee are $100; post-tax wages are $80. This remains an equilibrium because firms are still willing to employ at $100 all the workers who want to work at $80. Nothing substantive has changed except that pretax wages have fallen from $90 to $85. But this is irrelevant; the only prices that interest the agents in this economy are labor costs per employee and post-tax wages.

But what about consumption taxes? Employees are interested in what their wages can buy. So if their income taxes are cut by 10 percent and the cost of consumption is raised by 10 percent, post-tax real wages are unchanged and so is labor market behavior. So, broadly speaking, what really counts is the sum of payroll taxes, income taxes and consumption taxes; the total tax burden on labor. Of course, this is not exactly correct for a variety of reasons. For example, income tax is charged on nonlabor income whereas payroll tax is not, so that a cut in payroll tax and a rise in income tax will reduce nonlabor income, raise labor supply and reduce unemployment. But, in practice, this is not important because individuals who are likely to become unemployed have little or no nonlabor income.[7] Our conclusion is that payroll taxes, *per se*, can be expected to have little impact on unemployment but the total tax burden might.

The fundamental question, therefore, is whether or not this total tax burden is entirely shifted onto labor. That is, does real labor cost per worker remain unaffected by variations in the total tax burden, at least in the long run?

If capital is internationally mobile and labor is not, then we should expect to see labor bearing all of the tax burden. In this case, employment and unemployment will, in the long run, remain unaffected by changes in the overall tax rate on labor. There is, however, one situation where it is impossible to shift payroll taxes onto workers. That is where there is a rise in the payroll tax and an employee is already receiving the minimum wage. The burden of the extra tax must then fall on the employer because the wage cannot adjust.

What happens in practice? The balance of the evidence suggests that lowering payroll taxes and raising consumption taxes will have no long-run impact on unemployment (OECD, 1990, Annex 6A; OECD, 1994, Table 9.5).[8] This result is confirmed by the fact that if we include the payroll tax rate in any of the regressions in Table 6 or 7, its coefficient is always negligible.[9] It also helps to explain why Denmark, which uniquely has no payroll taxes, has unemployment on a par with

---

[7] For example, in Britain in 1987–88, only 7 percent of the unemployed had savings in excess of 3,000 pounds, enough to produce an annual interest income of around 10 percent of unemployment benefit (Layard, Nickell and Jackman, 1991, Table A6).

[8] There are some individual country time series results that appear to give a role to payroll taxes in individual countries—see OECD (1994, Chapter 9, p. 247) for a summary. However, in relatively short time series, it is often very difficult to distinguish between long-lasting short-run effects and long-run effects.

[9] For example, in columns of Table 6 its coefficient is -0.014, with a standard error of 0.06.

the European average and appears to derive no special employment benefit from its lack of these taxes.

The evidence on the total tax burden is less clear. One careful cross-country study has ruled out any long-run impact of the total tax burden on employment (OECD, 1990, Annex 6A). However, the results in Tables 6 and 7, row 8, which are in agreement with the findings of Bean, Layard and Nickell (1986), suggest that the overall tax burden may raise unemployment and reduce labor supply. A 10 percentage point fall in the total tax burden reduces unemployment by around 25 percent and raises labor supply by around 2 percentage points on every measure. Of course, a 10 percentage point fall in the total tax burden is enormous. Most countries find permanently reducing expenditure by 1 percent of GDP an extremely difficult task. To generate a 10 percentage point shift would mean, for example, transferring the whole of the UK health service to the private sector.[10]

Minimum Wages

While it is impossible to produce a single cross-country variable that captures the impact of minimum wage laws or related legislation (like extending union pay bargains to the nonunion sector), it is still worth discussing the potential impact of minimum wages on unemployment. A reading of Card and Krueger (1995) and its various reviews in the July 1995 issue of the *Industrial and Labor Relations Review* reveals that there is no consensus on the impact of minimum wages on unemployment. However, the following conclusions do seem to be consistent with the evidence. First, where the minimum wage applies, it is low enough not to have an important effect on the unemployment rates of adult men. Second, minimum wages do have a significant though small adverse impact on youth unemployment rates, particularly in countries like France and Spain where payroll taxes are high and there is little in the way of an age adjustment to the minimum wage (Dolado et al., 1996; Abowd et al., 1996).

Labor Supply Measures

Two much-canvassed solutions to unemployment are reduced hours of work and early retirement. Advocates of these measures often seem to imagine that there is some exogenously given level of work to be done. In fact, all historical evidence shows that, for a given institutional structure, the amount of work to be done tends to adjust in line with the available supply of labor, leaving equilibrium unemployment unaffected. So we can expect that an *imposed* cut in hours or reduction in the labor force will raise wage pressure in a way that can only be offset by an equivalent cut in jobs. Indeed if, in a standard wage equation, we allow wages to depend

---

[10] Even if there were some macroeconomic benefits to this, there could easily be substantial costs; for example, total health expenditure in the United Kingdom is 4–5 percentage points of GDP less than health expenditure in the United States, without there being notable differences in the overall health of the two populations. Moving health care to the private sector might impair efforts to hold down costs, or result in greater inefficiency.

separately on (the logs of) labor force and employment instead of on unemployment, we typically obtain equal and opposite coefficients. This indicates that a fall in the labor force relative to employment raises wage pressure just as much as a rise in employment relative to the labor force (Layard, Nickell and Jackman, 1991, p. 504; Jackman, Layard and Nickell, 1996, p. 28). Similarly, if one adds measures of labor supply like hours worked per worker to the unemployment regressions in Table 6, no significant effect is found.

Shifts in the Demand for Skills and Unemployment

It has become commonplace to argue: "The rise in joblessness in Europe is thus the flip side of the rise in earnings inequality in the U.S." (Freeman, 1995, p. 19). This view is based on the notion that first, in all countries, there has been an increase in the relative demand for skilled workers (as against unskilled workers) that has been greater than the increase in their relative supply. Then the argument goes that in Europe, the inflexibility of the labor market has turned this shift into higher unemployment whereas in the United States, labor market flexibility has translated this shift into increased inequality. Finally, this shift explains the majority of the rise in European unemployment relative to that in the United States.

Despite this being a commonly held view, a variety of facts cast doubt on it (Card, Kramarz and Lemieux, 1995; Nickell and Bell, 1995, 1996; Nickell, 1996; Jackman et al., 1996). First, it appears to be the case that in Britain and the United States the demand for skill outran the supply by more than in the rest of Europe. Second, for a variety of European countries including Britain, the evidence suggests that skill shifts account for between 0 and 20 percent of the rise in unemployment from the 1970s. There is no evidence that this number is lower in "flexible" Britain than it is anywhere else in Europe. In any event, the vast majority of the rise in European unemployment is due to other factors. Third, there has been a substantial rise in unskilled unemployment in the United States since the early 1970s (over 100 percent) despite (because of?) the fall in unskilled real wages. Fourth, the adverse impact of the fall in the relative demand for unskilled workers on the wages and unemployment of this group is strongly attenuated in those countries whose education and training systems are particularly effective at raising the human capital of those at the lower end of the ability range (notably middle Europe[11] and Scandinavia).

Overall, therefore, there is no evidence that these skill shifts have made a substantial contribution to the rise in European unemployment nor that labor market inflexibility per se is associated in any simple way with such effects as have been observed.

Special Cases and the Demand Side

Our aim has been to understand what generates high average levels of unemployment over long periods. Business cycle effects and autonomous demand shocks of

---

[11] That is, Switzerland, Austria, Germany and Holland.

various kinds should wash out if we take a long enough period—and our focus has been on 1983–1996, a 14-year stretch. Despite the length of this period, it is possible to argue that because of exceptional problems, policy mismanagement, very high levels of hysteresis and the like, the average unemployment figures give a distorted picture of the underlying equilibrium rate. If we were just considering the 1990s, this argument might be applied to a number of countries, such as Sweden. But over the longer period, there is only one country where truly exceptional problems have distorted the long period average dramatically, namely Finland. In the three years from 1990 to 1993, Finnish unemployment rose from 3.4 to 17.7 percent. This increase was generated first by the collapse of an enormous domestic credit boom, which was, in its turn, brought about by a mismanaged deregulation of the financial sector. Real house prices fell by over 50 percent between 1990 and 1993. This disaster was reinforced by the more or less complete elimination of Soviet trade over the same period, which had previously been responsible for about one-third of Finnish exports. Without these exceptional events, there is no question that average unemployment would have been substantially lower over the relevant period and this lower number would more accurately reflect the equilibrium rate in Finland.

Conclusions

High unemployment is associated with the following labor market features: 1) generous unemployment benefits that are allowed to run on indefinitely, combined with little or no pressure on the unemployed to obtain work and low levels of active intervention to increase the ability and willingness of the unemployed to work; 2) high unionization with wages bargained collectively and no coordination between either unions or employers in wage bargaining; 3) high overall taxes impinging on labor or a combination of high minimum wages for young people associated with high payroll taxes; and 4) poor educational standards at the bottom end of the labor market.

Labor market rigidities that do not appear to have serious implications for average levels of unemployment include the following: 1) strict employment protection legislation and general legislation on labor market standards; 2) generous levels of unemployment benefit, so long as these are accompanied by pressure on the unemployed to take jobs by, for example, fixing the duration of benefit and providing resources to raise the ability/willingness of the unemployed to take jobs; and 3) high levels of unionization and union coverage, so long as they are offset by high levels of coordination in wage bargaining, particularly among employers.

Suppose we define high unemployment as above 120 percent of the U.S. rate over the 1983–1996 period (7.8 percent). Then, looking at Table 1, we see there are eight European countries in this category out of 15, as well as Canada. These eight include three major countries (France, Spain and United Kingdom) of which the last has far and away the most flexible labor market in Europe, as normally measured. The remaining countries with high unemployment are Belgium, Denmark, Finland, Ireland and the Netherlands.

Unemployment is high in these countries (excluding Finland, for reasons already explained) partly because, on average, they have reasonably generous benefits with very long periods of entitlement and little in the way of active policies to push the unemployed into work. Wages are typically bargained collectively, so unions apply pressure on wages, but coordination is not high, particularly among employers. Education levels at the lower end of the ability range are generally weak. Of course, not all of these apply to every country, and the country to which they apply least, the Netherlands, is now moving out of the high-unemployment group. Most importantly for the topic of this paper, many features of the labor market that are popularly viewed as serious rigidities apply no more to this high-unemployment group than they do to the low-unemployment group. These include high payroll taxes, high overall taxes, strict employment protection legislation, high labor market standards (legally enforced), high unionization and high benefit replacement rates.

It is clear that the broad-brush analysis that says that European unemployment is high because European labor markets are "rigid" is too vague and probably misleading. Many labor market institutions that conventionally come under the heading of rigidities have no observable impact on unemployment.

■ *I am most grateful to Tracy Jones and the Leverhulme Trust (Programme on Unemployment and Technical and Structural Change) for their help in the preparation of this paper. My thanks are also due to Alan Krueger, Bradford De Long and Timothy Taylor for their very useful comments on an earlier draft.*

References

Abowd, J., F. Kramarz, T. Lemieux, and D. Margolis, "Minimum Wages and Youth Employment in France and the United States," mimeo, Cornell University, 1996.

Bean, C., R. Layard, and S. J. Nickell, "The Rise in Unemployment: A Multi-Country Study," *Economica*, Supplement 1986, *53*, S1–S22.

Bentolila, S., and G. Bertola, "Firing Costs and Labour Demand: How Bad is Eurosclerosis," *Review of Economic Studies*, 1990, *57:3*, 381–402.

Blanchflower, D., and A. Oswald, *The Wage Curve*. Cambridge: Massachusetts Institute of Technology Press, 1994.

Card, D., and A. Krueger, *Myth and Measurement: The New Economics of the Minimum Wage*. Princeton, N.J.: Princeton University Press, 1995.

Card, D., F. Kramarz, and T. Lemieux, "Changes in the Relative Structure of Wages and Employment: A Comparison of the United States, Canada, and France." Industrial Relations Section, Working Paper No. 355, Princeton University, December 1995.

Contini, B., L. Pacelli, M. Filippi, G. Lioni, and R. Revelli, "A Study of Job Creation and Job Destruction in Europe," study for the European Commission, D.G.V., Turin, R. & P., 1995.

Dolado, J., F. Kramarz, S. Machin, A. Manning, B. Margolis, and C. Teulings, "The Economic Impact of Minimum Wages in Europe," *Economic Policy*, October 1996, *23*, 319–72.

European Economy, "Performance of the EU Labour Market: Results of an *ad hoc* Labour Market Survey." Reports and Studies, No. 3, European Commission, Directorate-General for Economic and Financial Affairs, B–1049, Brussels, 1995.

Freeman, R. B., "Are Your Wages Set in Beijing?," *Journal of Economic Perspectives*, Summer 1995, *9:3*, 15–32.

Jackman, R., R. Layard, and S. Nickell, "Combatting Unemployment: Is Flexibility Enough?" Centre for Economic Performance, DP No. 293, London School of Economics, 1996.

Jackman, R., R. Layard, M. Manacorda, and B. Petrangolo, "Skills Mismatch: The Race Between Demand and Supply," mimeo, Centre for Economic Performance, London School of Economics, 1996.

Layard, R., S. Nickell, and R. Jackman, *Unemployment: Macroeconomic Performance and the Labour Market.* Oxford: Oxford University Press, 1991.

Lazear, E. P., "Job Security Provisions and Employment," *Quarterly Journal of Economics,* 1990, *105*:3, 699–726.

Meyer, B. D., "Unemployment Insurance and Unemployment Spells," *Econometrica,* 1990, *58*:4, 757–82.

Narendranathan, W., S. Nickell, and J. Stern, "Unemployment Benefits Revisited," *Economic Journal,* June 1985, *95*, 307–29.

Nickell, S. J., "Unemployment and Wages in Europe and North America." Leverhulme Trust Programme on the Labour Market Consequences of Technical and Structural Change, Discussion Paper No. 6, University of Oxford, 1996.

Nickell, S. J., and B. Bell, "The Collapse in Demand for the Unskilled and Unemployment across the OECD," *Oxford Review of Economic Policy,* Spring 1995, *11*:1, 40–62.

Nickell, S. J., and B. Bell, "Changes in the Distribution of Wages and Unemployment in OECD Countries," *American Economic Review,* May 1996, *86*, Papers and Proceedings, 302–8.

OECD, *Employment Outlook.* Paris: OECD, 1990.

OECD, *Employment Outlook.* Paris: OECD, 1991.

OECD, *Employment Outlook.* Paris: OECD, 1993.

OECD, *Jobs Study: Evidence and Explanations.* Paris: OECD, 1994.

OECD, *Employment Outlook.* Paris: OECD, 1996.

Phelps, E. S., "A Program of Low Wage Employment Tax Credits." Russell Sage Foundation Working Paper No. 55, 1994.

[9]

The Economic Journal, 110 (*March*), C1–C33. © Royal Economic Society 2000. Published by Blackwell Publishers, 108 Cowley Road, Oxford OX4 1JF, UK and 350 Main Street, Malden, MA 02148, USA.

THE ROLE OF SHOCKS AND INSTITUTIONS IN THE RISE OF EUROPEAN UNEMPLOYMENT: THE AGGREGATE EVIDENCE*

Olivier Blanchard and Justin Wolfers

Two key facts about European unemployment must be explained: the rise in unemployment since the 1960s, and the heterogeneity of individual country experiences. While adverse shocks can potentially explain much of the rise in unemployment, there is insufficient heterogeneity in these shocks to explain cross-country differences. Alternatively, while explanations focusing on labour market institutions explain current heterogeneity well, many of these institutions pre-date the rise in unemployment. Based on a panel of institutions and shocks for 20 OECD nations since 1960 we find that the interaction between shocks and institutions is crucial to explaining both stylised facts.

Fig. 1 shows the evolution of unemployment in Europe since 1960. The figure plots average unemployment rates over 5-year intervals, starting in 1960, both for the OECD-Europe as a whole (the line) and for 15 individual OECD-Europe countries.[1] It shows the increase in the overall unemployment rate, from 1.7% in the early 1960s to 11.0% in the mid 1990s, together with the large dispersion in unemployment rates across countries, from 4.0% in Switzerland to more than 20% in Spain in the mid 1990s.

Explanations for these evolutions fall into three classes:

- Explanations that focus on the role of adverse economic shocks. Adverse shocks can indeed increase the unemployment rate, at least for some time. And there are many plausible candidates for such adverse shocks over the last 30 years. As unemployment started rising in the 1970s, the focus was on oil price increases and the TFP growth slowdown. Since then, the evolution of the real interest rate, and other shifts in labour demand have been added to the list. Explanations based solely on shocks run, however, into a major empirical problem. Shocks can potentially explain the general increase in unemploy-

---

* Harry Johnson Lecture. We thank Steve Nickell, Ed Lazear, John Addison and Paula Adam at the OECD for providing us with some of the data. We also thank Daron Acemoglu, Alberto Alesina, Tito Boeri, Bill Brainard, David Blanchflower, Peter Diamond, Ben Friedman, Jenny Hunt, Larry Katz, Steve Nickell, Andrew Oswald, Steve Pischke, Chris Pissarides, Chris Sims, Betsey Stevenson, and Robert Solow for useful suggestions and comments. An appendix containing the data, the programs, and describing the construction of the data, is available at http://web.mit.edu/blanchar/www/articles.html

[1] The 8 time periods are 1960–4 to 1990–4, and 1995+ (typically 1995–6.) The 15 countries included in OECD-Europe are Austria (AUT), Belgium (BEL), Denmark (DNK), Finland (FIN), France (FRA), Germany (DEU), Ireland (IRE), Italy (ITA), the Netherlands (NLD), Norway (NOR), Portugal (PRT), Spain (ESP), Sweden (SWE), Switzerland (CHE) and the United Kingdom (GBR). Left out are Greece, Iceland and Luxembourg, for which we could not construct time series for all the explanatory variables used later in the article. The unemployment rates are the rates according to national definitions, rather than standardised rates—which typically do not exist back to 1960. (For the period when both unemployment rates exist, using one or the other makes little difference.) Also, while the figures only show what has happened in Europe, the regressions we run later look at all available OECD countries; they include, in addition to Europe, the United States (USA), Canada (CAN), Australia (AUS), New Zealand (NZL) and Japan (JPN).

Note: line links average unemployment rate for the E15.
Mnemonics are listed in footnote 1.

Fig. 1. *Unemployment Rate*, E15

ment over time. But, as we shall see, they do not differ enough across countries
to explain the cross-country variation so evident in Fig. 1.

• Explanations that focus on the role of adverse labour market institutions.
Labour market institutions affect the nature of unemployment, and some can
indeed potentially generate a high unemployment rate. With the persistence
of high unemployment for now more than two decades, explanations based on
adverse institutions ('labour market rigidities') have become steadily more
popular. Explanations based solely on institutions also run however into a
major empirical problem: many of these institutions were already present
when unemployment was low (and similar across countries), and, while many
became less employment-friendly in the 1970s, the movement since then has
been mostly in the opposite direction. Thus, while labour market institutions
can potentially explain cross country differences today, they do not appear
able to explain the general evolution of unemployment over time.

• Explanations that focus on the interaction of adverse shocks with adverse
market institutions. Some institutions may affect the impact of shocks on
unemployment. For example, better coordination in bargaining may lead to a
faster adjustment of real wages to a slowdown in productivity growth. Some
institutions may affect the persistence of unemployment in response to shocks.
For example, if labour market institutions lead to a labour market with long
unemployment duration, adverse shocks are more likely to lead some of the
unemployed to become disenfranchised, reducing the pressure of unemployment on wages, thereby slowing, and possibly even halting the return to lower

unemployment. It is easy to see what makes this third class of explanations attractive. It has the potential to explain not only the increase in unemployment over time (through adverse shocks), but also the heterogeneity of unemployment evolutions (through the interaction of the shocks with different labour market institutions).

In a companion paper (Blanchard, 1999), we took stock of the underlying alternative theories. We looked at whether and how different shocks and different institutions may affect the unemployment rate. We looked at the channels through which shocks and institutions might interact. This led us to argue in favour of the third class of explanations. In this article, we look at the aggregate empirical evidence more formally, at the role of shocks, institutions, and interactions, in accounting for the evolution of European unemployment.

To do so, we look at the data through two panel data specifications. In the first, we assume unobservable but common shocks across countries. In the second, we construct and use country-specific time series for a number of shocks. In both specifications, we allow for an interaction between shocks and institutions: The effect of a given shock on unemployment is allowed to depend on the set of labour market institutions of the country.

We see the results as surprisingly (at least given our priors) good: Specifications that allow for shocks, institutions, and interactions can account both for much of the rise and much of the heterogeneity in the evolution of unemployment in Europe. The magnitudes of the effects of the shocks on unemployment are plausible. The magnitudes of the effects of institutions are equally so. And their interactions explain much of the difference across countries.

These results notwithstanding, three caveats are in order. First, the results are preliminary. In many cases, we do not have time series for institutions, and the series we have may not be very good. Second, the results are typically weaker when we allow for time-varying rather than time-invariant measures for institutions. This gives some reasons to worry. Last, the fact that the specifications fit the data does not prove that the underlying theories are right; just that they are not obviously inconsistent with the aggregate data.

We believe we are the first to analyse the panel data evidence looking simultaneously at shocks, institutions and interactions. But we build on a large number of previous studies. Bruno and Sachs (1985) were among the first to emphasise both shocks and institutions in the initial rise in unemployment. An empirical attempt to explain UK unemployment as a result of shocks, institutions, and interactions was presented by Layard *et al.* (1991) in their book on unemployment. Two recent influential studies are by Phelps (1994) and by Nickell (1997). We differ mostly from Phelps by allowing for institutions, and for interactions. We differ mostly from Nickell by allowing for observable shocks, and by having a panel data dimension going back to the 1960s. Our results are partly consistent with those of Phelps with respect to shocks, and largely consistent with those of Nickell with respect to institutions.

Our article is organised as follows: Section 1 looks at shocks, both across countries and over time. Section 2 does the same for institutions. Section 3 discusses potential interactions between shocks and institutions. Section 4 reports the results of estimation under the assumption of unobservable but common shocks across countries. Section 5 reports the results of estimation using country-specific time series for shocks. Section 6 concludes.[2]

1. Shocks

Three shocks appear to have played an important role in the increase in European unemployment. (This short declarative sentence conveys more certainty than is justified. Caveats follow.)

1.1. *The Decline in TFP Growth*

Starting in the early 1970s, Europe suffered a large decrease in the underlying rate of total factor productivity (TFP) growth. This is shown in Fig. 2.[3] The two lines in Fig. 2*a* give the evolution of the average rate of TFP growth for the 15 countries of OECD-Europe (E15 in what follows) and for the 5 largest European countries, France, Germany, Italy, Spain, and the United Kingdom (E5). To give a sense of the heterogeneity across countries, Fig. 2*b* gives the evolution of TFP growth in each of the E5 countries. (Showing all 15 countries would clutter the figure but yield similar conclusions). TFP growth which had been close to 5% in the 1960s decreased to 3% in the first half of the 1970s, and to 2% in the second half of the 1970s. It has remained around 2% since then. The decline has affected countries in roughly similar fashion.[4]

The decrease in TFP growth was initially partially hidden by the large increase in the relative price of oil and other raw materials. Thus, much of the focus of the initial research (for example Bruno and Sachs (1985)) was on this increase in relative prices rather than on the slowdown in TFP growth. In retrospect, the slowdown in TFP growth from its unusually high level in the first 30 years after World War II was surely the more important shock of the period.[5]

There is no question that a slowdown in TFP growth can lead to a higher equilibrium unemployment rate for some time (we prefer to use 'equilibrium rate' rather than 'natural rate', but the meaning is the same.) All that is needed is that it takes some time for workers and firms to adjust expectations to the new lower underlying rate, leading to wage growth in excess of pro-

[2] We shall use the existence of the companion paper as an excuse for keeping our discussion of theoretical issues, and of relevant references, to a minimum.

[3] We first construct the rate of TFP growth for each year and each country. We do so by computing the Solow residual for the business sector, and then dividing it by the labour share in the sector. Under the assumption of Harrod neutral technological progress—the assumption that allows for steady state growth—this is the right measure of technological progress, and gives the rate at which real wages can grow along the balanced growth path. We then take averages for each 5-year period, for each country. E5 and E15 are constructed as simple (unweighted) averages of TFP growth over countries.

[4] Note that, in contrast to the other observations which are based on five yearly observations, the observation for 1995 is typically based on only one year (1995) or two years (1995 and 1996). Thus, one year can make a lot of difference. This is the case for Italy in this figure.

[5] An early article on that theme is Grubb *et al.* (1982).

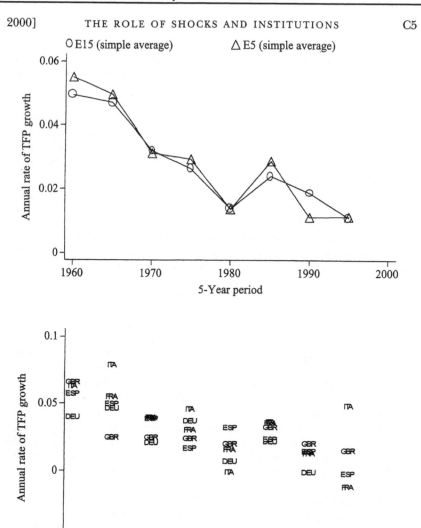

Fig. 2. *TFP Growth* (*a*) E15 and E5 (*b*) E5

ductivity growth for some time. Can the effects of such a slowdown on unemployment be permanent? Theory suggests that the answer, to a first approximation, is no. Once expectations have adjusted, the effect on unemployment should mostly go away. There lies the first puzzle of European unemployment. The initial shock is clearly identified. But, after more than twenty years, it is hard to believe that its effects are not largely gone. So, what accounts for today's high unemployment? There is much less agreement here, but two other shocks appear relevant.

1.2. *The Real Interest Rate*

Fig. 3*a* gives the evolution of the average real interest rate for both the E15 and the E5. Fig. 3*b* gives the real interest rate for each of the E5 countries.[6]

Fig. 3 shows that, both for the E15 and E5 countries, the real rate turned from positive in the 1960s to sharply negative in the second half of the 1970s, and then to large and positive in the 1980s and the 1990s. For some countries, the decline in the 1970s was nearly as dramatic as the ensuing increase. Fig. 3*b* shows how the real rate in Spain went down from 2% in the 1960s to −5% in the mid 1970s, back to 5% in the 1980s and the 1990s. For others, such as Germany, the real rate has remained much more stable.

Why might such changes in the real interest rate affect the equilibrium unemployment rate?[7] Because they are likely to affect capital accumulation, and so, at a given wage (and thus a given ratio of employment to capital), to shift labour demand. Are the effects on unemployment likely to be permanent? Theory is largely agnostic here. Again, a plausible answer is that long run effects, if present, are likely to be small.

It is clear from Fig. 3 that the pattern of interest rates may help explain why unemployment kept increasing in the 1980s, even as the effects of lower TFP growth on unemployment were—presumably—declining. This suggests that, had real interest rates been stable, unemployment would have been higher in the 1970s, and lower in the 1980s. Put another way, the low real interest rates of the 1970s delayed some of the increase in unemployment by a decade or so. The higher real interest rates since the early 1980s may help explain why unemployment has remained high in the 1980s and the 1990s.

1.3. *Shifts in Labour Demand*

Fig. 4 gives the evolution of the log of the labour share for both the E15 and the E5 (normalised to equal zero in 1960). For both groups of countries, the evolution of the share is quite striking. After increasing in the 1970s, the labour share started decreasing in 1980s and the decline has continued since then. For the E5, the labour share is now 10% lower than it was in 1960; for the E15, it is 8% lower.

Why look at the evolution of the labour share? Suppose that technology were

---

[6] We first compute the real interest rate for each year and each country, as the nominal long rate on government bonds minus a five-year average of lagged inflation. We then take averages for each 5-year period.

[7] The focus here is on the effects on the equilibrium unemployment rate. Changes in the real interest rate also affect the deviation of actual unemployment from the equilibrium rate. We focus on that effect below.

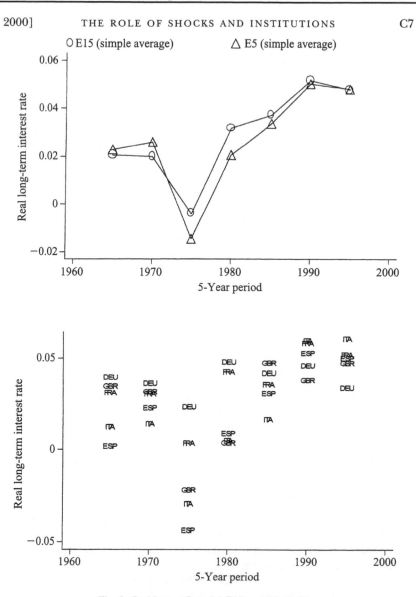

Fig. 3. *Real Interest Rate.* (*a*) E15 and E5 (*b*) E5

characterised by a Cobb-Douglas production function, both in the short and
the long run. The decrease in the share since the 1980s would then reflect
either technological bias away from labour—a decrease in the coefficient on
labour in the production function—or a decrease in the wage relative to the
marginal product of labour. In either case, the implication would be an

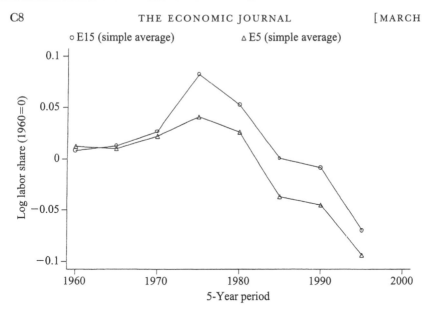

Fig. 4. *Log Labour Share, E15 and E5*

adverse shift in labour demand and thus a potential source of unemployment in the 1980s and 1990s.[8]

The elasticity of substitution may be equal to one in the long run, but is surely less than one in the short run. In that case, movements in the share will also reflect the dynamic response of factor proportions to factor prices. Indeed, much of the increase in the labour share in the 1970s surely reflects the effects of the increase in the real wage relative to TFP growth together with a low short-run elasticity of substitution, and some of the decrease since then reflects the adjustment of proportions over time. In Blanchard (1997), we argued however that more has been at work than the adjustment of factor proportions to factor prices, and that the large decline in the share reflects a genuine adverse shift in labour demand.

We shall use the measure of the shift in labour demand constructed in that earlier article. This measure can be thought of as the log of the labour share purged of the effects of factor prices on the share in the presence of a low elasticity of substitution in the short run. Fig. 5a plots the evolution of this measure of the labour demand shift for both the E5 and the E15. Fig. 5b plots the evolution of the measure for each of the E5 countries. Both figures show how the adjustment eliminates much of the increase and subsequent unwind-

---

[8] Let $Y = N^a K^{1-a}$. Let the ratio of the wage to the marginal product of labour $w/Y_n \equiv \mu$. μ is equal to 1 under perfect competition in both goods and labour markets, but may differ from 1 otherwise. Then the share of labour $\alpha = a\mu$. A decrease in α reflects a decrease in a or a decrease in μ. Also labour demand can be written as $\log N = \log Y - \log w + \log \alpha$. A decrease in $\log \alpha$ leads to an equal decrease in $\log N$ given output and the wage. This is why we look at the log share.

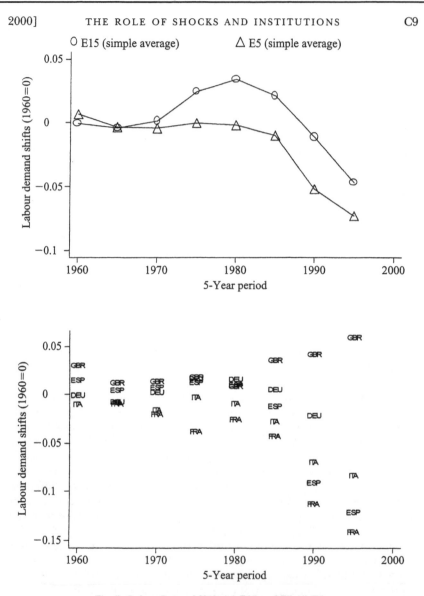

Fig. 5. *Labour Demand Shifts* (*a*) E15 and E5 (*b*) E5

ing in the share in the 1970s (visible in Fig. 4). Fig. 5*a* shows little movement in the measure until the mid 1980s, with a strong decrease thereafter. Fig. 5*b* shows the sharp difference between the United Kingdom where, if anything the shift has been positive (the underlying labour share has remained roughly constant) and countries such as Spain or France (where the adverse shift has exceeded 10%).[9]

Such an adverse shift in labour demand can clearly lead to higher equilibrium unemployment for some time. Its dynamic effects however are quite different from those of the two shocks we looked at earlier. Think for example of the shift as coming from a reduction in labour hoarding by firms—one of the interpretations suggested in Blanchard (1997). As firms get rid of redundant workers, the result will be a decrease in employment, and so an increase in unemployment. Thus, such a shift has the potential to explain why unemployment has remained high in many countries in the 1990s. But the decrease in labour hoarding also leads to higher profit, which in turn should lead, over time, to capital accumulation and higher employment. This is a relevant point to keep in mind when one thinks about the future. If it is the case that such a shift is indeed responsible for some of the unemployment of the 1990s, then this suggests a brighter future, as the favourable effects start dominating and lead to an increase in employment over time.

1.4. *Equilibrium Versus Actual Unemployment*

We have focused so far on factors that affect equilibrium unemployment. There is no question however that part of the evolution of unemployment in Europe comes from the deviation of actual unemployment from equilibrium unemployment.

In environments of low to medium inflation, the change in inflation is likely to be a good signal of where equilibrium unemployment is relative to actual unemployment. Decreasing inflation is likely to reflect an unemployment rate above the equilibrium rate; increasing inflation reflects the reverse. Fig. 6*a* shows the evolution of the change in inflation for the E5 and the E15. Fig. 6*b* shows the evolution of the change in inflation for each of the E5.[10] The change in inflation was positive in the 1970s, suggesting an actual unemployment rate below the equilibrium rate. The change in inflation has been negative since then, suggesting the equilibrium rate has been lower than the actual rate. In other words, macroeconomic policy probably delayed some of the increase in unemployment from the 1970s to the 1980s. And, as inflation is still slowly declining, actual unemployment probably exceeds equilibrium unemployment at this point. By how much is difficult to say: the relation between the change in inflation and the deviation of unemployment from its equilibrium may well be different at very low inflation.

Two caveats as we end this section. First, what we have taken as 'shocks' are

---

[9] This distinction between Anglo-Saxon and Continental countries is discussed in Blanchard (1997). The differences in evolutions reflects divergence rather than convergence of the shares in levels: For the last period (1995+), the labour share in the business sector was 62% for France and Spain, versus 70% for the United Kingdom and 67% for the United States. (The caveat about the dangers of comparing share levels across countries applies.)

[10] We first construct the change in inflation (using the business sector GDP deflator) for each year and each country. We then take the average for each 5-year period.

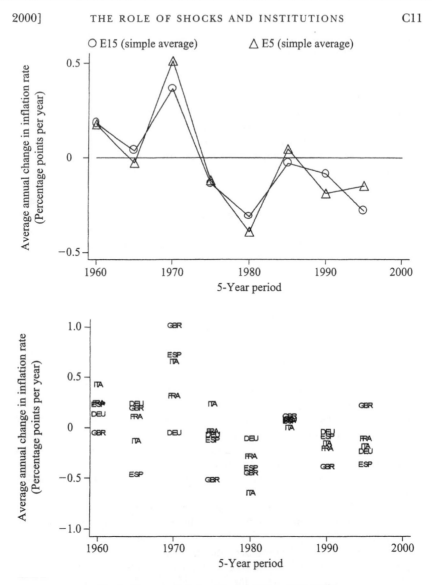

Fig. 6. *Change in Inflation Rate* (*a*) E15 and E5 (*b*) E5

at best proximate causes, and should be traced to deeper causes. This is particularly clear for real interest rates and labour demand shifts. Second, there may well have been other shocks, from increased turbulence (although the quantitative evidence on this is not very supportive), to shifts in the relative demand for skilled and unskilled workers (although, on this point as well, the evidence for Europe is mixed. See for example Nickell and Bell (1994).) We have not explored their role here.

To conclude: This section suggests the following story. Europe was hit with major adverse shocks in the 1970s, oil price increases, but also, and more importantly, a large and sustained decrease in TFP growth. Unemployment increased, but the adverse impact was initially softened both by lower real interest rates and an expansionary macroeconomic policy leading to less of an increase in actual than in equilibrium unemployment. As the effect of the adverse shocks of the 1970s receded, higher interest rates and tight macro-economic policy contributed to higher equilibrium and actual unemployment in the 1980s. Finally, adverse labour demand shifts can potentially account for why unemployment has remained high in the 1990s. Thus, shocks appear to have the potential to explain the broad evolution of European unemployment. But, at least to the naked eye, differences in the evolution of unemployment across countries seem difficult to trace back to differences in shocks.

2. Institutions

While in the 1970s the discussion of the rise of unemployment focused primarily on shocks, the persistence of high unemployment for another two decades has led to a shift in focus from shocks to labour market institutions. Indeed, many discussions of European unemployment ignore shocks alto-gether, and focus exclusively on 'labour market rigidities'. What typically follows is a long list of so-called 'rigidities', from strong unions, to high payroll taxes, to minimum wages, to generous unemployment insurance, to high employment protection, and so on.

We have learned however from theory that things are more complicated. Some of the so-called rigidities may represent rough institutional corrections for other distortions in the labour market. Some institutions may be bad for productivity, for output, and for welfare, but may not lead to an increase in unemployment. A short summary of the large literature—a literature largely triggered by the rise in European unemployment—goes as follows:[11]

- Some labour market institutions increase the equilibrium unemployment rate. First among them is the unemployment insurance system. More generous insurance increases unemployment through two separate channels: The first, and the focus of most microeconomic empirical work, is lower search intensity. The second is the effect on the bargained wage at a given rate of unemploy-ment. Both combine to increase equilibrium unemployment duration, and, by implication, the equilibrium unemployment rate.[12]
- Some labour market institutions change the nature of unemployment,

---

[11] A longer discussion is given in our companion paper. A nice theoretical discussion is given by Mortensen and Pissarides (1998). A wider ranging presentation of both theory and facts is given by Nickell and Layard (1998).

[12] The steady state unemployment rate is equal to unemployment duration times the flow into unemployment as a ratio to the labour force. Unemployment benefits increase duration, and leave the flow roughly unchanged, increasing the unemployment rate.

but have an ambiguous effect on the equilibrium unemployment rate. This is the case for employment protection. Employment protection both decreases the flows of workers through the labour market, and increases the duration of unemployment. This makes for a more stagnant labour market, with a higher proportion of long-term unemployed. But the effect of lower flows and higher duration on the equilibrium rate itself is ambiguous.

- Some labour market institutions may not have much effect either on the rate or on the nature of unemployment. Their incidence may be mainly on the wage, not on unemployment. This is the case for many of the components of the so called 'tax wedge'. Some of these components are really not taxes, but rather payments for health benefits, or retirement: the effect of these components on unemployment should be small. As to the tax component, what matters is how taxes affect the ratio of after-tax unemployment benefits to after-tax wages. Taxes which by their nature apply equally on the unemployed and the employed, such as consumption or income taxes, are likely to be roughly neutral. And if the unemployment insurance system tries to achieve a stable relation of unemployment benefits to after-tax wages—a reasonable assumption—even payroll taxes may not matter very much.

Turning to the evidence, the two relevant questions are: How much do labour market institutions vary across countries? And how have they evolved over time?

Thanks to work by the OECD and by a large number of researchers, we have fairly good answers to the first question. The state of knowledge has recently been summarised by Nickell (1997) and Nickell and Layard (1998).[13] In much of what we do later, we shall use the data for institutions put together by Nickell and described in those two articles. For the moment, suffice it to say that, based on the measures which have been constructed for various labour market institutions, and the cross section evidence: (1) there is substantial heterogeneity across European countries and (2) this heterogeneity appears to have the potential to explain differences in unemployment rates across countries *today*: countries with high unemployment rates typically have less employment-friendly institutions.

This raises the second question, the evolution of institutions over time. The basic question is a simple one. Have European labour market institutions become steadily worse since the early 1970s (in which case explanations based solely on institutions can potentially explain the evolution of unemployment)? Or do they in fact date back much further, to a time when unemployment was still low (in which case explanations based solely on institutions face a major puzzle)? The question is simple, but the answer is not.

Time series for at least part of the period and a subset of countries have been put together for some institutions—replacement rates, unionisation, the tax wedge—by the OECD and other researchers. But, in general, our know-

---

[13] In addition to the references in these two articles: For a recent comparison of various measures of unemployment insurance, see Salomaki and Munzi (1999). For a recent comparison of measures of employment protection, see OECD (1999), Chapter 2.

ledge of the evolution of institutions is rather limited. We shall look here at two institutions only, unemployment insurance, and employment protection.

• The OECD has constructed a measure of the replacement rate for each country, every two years, going back to 1961. The measure is an average of the replacement rates for different categories of workers, different family situations, and different durations of unemployment. Each replacement rate is constructed as the ratio of pre-tax social insurance and social assistance benefits to the pre-tax wage. Fig. 7*a* gives the evolution of this measure of the replacement rate, for each 5-year period, for each of the E5 countries. The figure clearly shows the different evolutions across countries. In Germany, France, and the United Kingdom, the replacement rate was relatively high to start; it has increased a bit in France, decreased a bit in Germany, decreased a bit more in the United Kingdom. In Spain and Italy, the replacement rate was very low at the start. It increased in the 1960s in Spain, and only more recently in Italy. Both are now at levels comparable to other countries. In short, there is no simple common trend.

The OECD measure is a summary measure of the replacement rate, and in some ways, not a very attractive one. It gives equal weight to the replacement rate in year 1 of an unemployment spell, to the average replacement rate in years 2 and 3, and to the average replacement rate for years 4 and 5; but given the exit rate from unemployment, the generosity of benefits in years 4 and 5 for example is clearly less important for the determination of unemployment than the generosity of unemployment in year 1. Fig. 7*b* provides a different angle by showing the *maximum* replacement rate over all categories and all durations of unemployment for each country and each subperiod. What clearly comes out is how this rate increased until the late 1970s, and how (except for Italy, which has converged from a low maximum replacement rate to the European average) it has decreased since then. In other words, the worst excesses have been largely eliminated. This may be more important than changes in the average replacement rate.

• Putting together series on employment protection is difficult. We have taken a first step by constructing series based on recent work by the OECD (see OECD (1999)), as well as on earlier work by Lazear (1990)). Details of construction are given in the appendix. There are a number of reasons why these series are at best rough approximations to the evolution of employment protection. In particular, the OECD data, which we use to construct the measures from 1985 on, are based on a much broader set of dimensions of employment protection than the Lazear series (notice period and severance pay for a blue collar worker with ten years seniority) which we use to construct the series before 1985.

This caveat notwithstanding, Fig. 8 shows the evolution of the employment protection index for the E5 countries since 1960. (The figure for the E15 would be harder to read, but yield similar conclusions). Note again the diversity of evolutions, and the lack of a simple answer.

Spain and Italy appear to have had high employment protection

Recent Developments in Labor Economics III

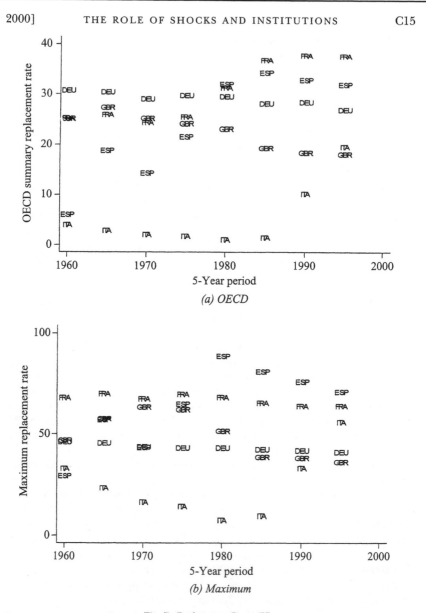

Fig. 7. *Replacement Rates, E5*

throughout. Employment protection in Spain was high even under Franco, before unemployment increased. In both countries, employment protection has decreased since the mid 1980s—in Spain, largely because of the development of fixed term contracts rather than the weakening of protection for workers on indefinite contracts. In France and Germany, employment protec-

C16   THE ECONOMIC JOURNAL   [MARCH

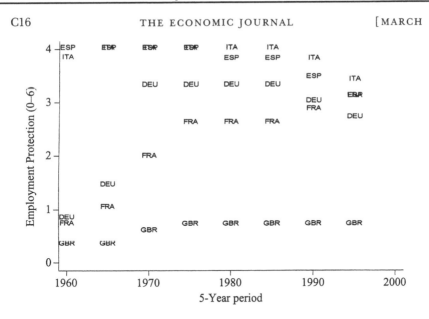

Fig. 8. *Constructed Employment Protection Index, E5*

tion was low to start with, then increased in the late 1960s and early 1970s, and has been roughly stable since then.[14]

To conclude: There is enough heterogeneity in labour market institutions within Europe to explain potentially differences in unemployment rates today. As to the evolution of institutions over time, it is clear that neither the view that labour market institutions have been stable through time, nor the view that labour market rigidities are a recent development are right. Some countries have had these institutions for a long time, others have acquired them more recently. There clearly was an increase in employment-unfriendly institutions in the late 1960s and early 1970s. Since then, there appears to have been a small but steady decline.

3. Interactions

Our review of facts makes clear why it is tempting to look for explanations of the rise of European unemployment based on the interaction of shocks and institutions: Adverse shocks can potentially explain the general increase in unemployment. Differences in institutions can potentially explain differences in outcomes across countries. This is indeed the direction that has been

[14] Informal evidence suggests that employment protection was high in France even in the 1960s. Again, this is not reflected in the Lazear measure, and by implication, not reflected in our measure either. This may be an issue for other countries as well.

explored in much of the recent research on unemployment. This section gives a brief assessment of the current state of knowledge.[15]

One can think of labour market institutions as shaping the effects of shocks on unemployment in two ways. First, they can affect the impact of shocks on unemployment. Second, they can affect the persistence of unemployment in response to shocks.

Most of the initial research explored the first direction, focusing on how the nature and the details of collective bargaining might determine the response of unemployment to various shocks.[16] It pointed for example to the importance of indexation clauses in labour contracts. It also pointed to the potential importance of the level and the structure of collective bargaining: it might be easier for example to achieve a slowdown in wage growth in response to a slowdown in productivity growth if bargaining takes place at the national rather than the firm or sectoral level—where aggregate trends may be less well perceived and understood, and coordination of the slowdown may be more difficult to achieve.

As unemployment remained high, the research shifted to how labour market institutions might also explain the persistence of unemployment in response to shocks.[17] The general idea is as follows. Take an adverse shock which leads to higher unemployment. The normal adjustment mechanism is then for unemployment to put downward pressure on wages until unemployment has returned to normal. To the extent that some labour market institutions reduce the effect of unemployment on wages, they will increase the persistence of unemployment in response to shocks. Research has identified a number of such channels. Here is a non-exhaustive list:

- A rise in unemployment typically comes with higher unemployment duration (rather than higher flows in and out of unemployment). If some of the unemployed remain unemployed for a long time, they may either stop searching or lose skills. Indeed, the two factors reinforce each other: if firms perceive the long term unemployed as more risky, they may be reluctant to hire them, decreasing the incentives of the long term unemployed to search for a job. But if they are not actively searching or employable, these unemployed workers become irrelevant to wage formation. Firms do not consider them. Employed workers do not see them as competition. The pressure of unemployment on wages decreases, and unemployment becomes more persistent. Layard and Nickell (1987) were the first to point to the potential macroeconomic relevance of such duration dependence.

  Why should institutions matter in this context? Because of their effect on the average duration of unemployment. A well documented fact about European labour markets is that, probably because of institutions such as more

---

[15] Again, see our companion paper for references, and discussion.

[16] This was indeed one of the main themes of Bruno and Sachs (1985).

[17] This was the motivation behind the admittedly crude 'hysteresis model' of unemployment in Blanchard and Summers (1986). Research since then has shown that while full hysteresis (permanent effects of shocks) is unlikely, institutions can lead to high persistence.

generous benefits and employment protection, a given unemployment rate is associated with much longer duration than in the United States.[18] And the longer the average duration of unemployment to begin with, the more likely the effects above are to play an important role. If an increase in the unemployment rate from 5 to 10% is associated with an increase in unemployment duration from 3 to 6 months, few of the unemployed will become long-term unemployed. If instead, the same increase in the unemployment rate implies an increase in duration from 1 to 2 years, then disenfranchising effects are much more likely to be important.

- Higher unemployment falls unevenly on different groups in the labour market. In most countries, higher unemployment tends to fall disproportionally on the youngest workers and the less educated.

Labour market institutions affect the compostion of the unemployed, thus affecting the effects of unemployment back on wages. For example, a high minimum wage can both increase the effect of adverse shocks on the unemployment rate of the less educated workers, and—because the minimum wage is fixed—reduce the effect of unemployment on wages. Collective bargaining, to the extent that it reflects primarily the preferences and the labour market prospects of prime-age workers, may also lead to little response of wages to youth unemployment, and thus lead to more persistence in unemployment.

- Higher unemployment may lead to a change in norms—an argument developed in particular by Wilson (1987) in the context of urban poverty in the United States, and by Lindbeck in the context of European unemployment (for example Lindbeck (1995)). As long as unemployment is low, workers may be largely ignorant of the rules governing unemployment insurance, or there may be a stigma attached to being unemployed. After a period of high unemployment, ignorance is likely to disappear; attitudes vis-a-vis unemployment are likely to change. Thus, countries with a more generous welfare system may end up with higher unemployment, even when the shocks are gone.

Other channels have been explored as well: Sargent and Ljundqvist (1995) have explored the effect of unemployment insurance rules on the relation between 'turbulence' shocks and equilibrium unemployment. Mortensen and Pissarides (1999) have explored the effect of unemployment insurance and employment protection on the relation between relative demand shifts and equilibrium unemployment. Our understanding of the specific channels and their empirical relevance remains rather primitive. This is still very much work in progress, and there is a need for substantially more theoretical and empirical work. Nevertheless, the general thrust is sufficiently clear for us to explore the potential role of interactions in explaining the evolution of unemployment. This is what we do in the rest of the article.

---

[18] See for example the comparison of the labour markets in Portugal and the United States in Blanchard and Portugal (1999).

4. Common Unobservable Shocks and Interactions

In looking more formally at the data, we proceed in two steps. In this section, we treat shocks as unobservable but common across countries—in effect we treat them as time effects. In the next, we treat shocks as observable and country specific.

Our first specification in this section relies on the set of time invariant measures of institutions used by Nickell (1997).[19] The specification we use is the following:

$$u_{it} = c_i + d_t \left(1 + \sum_j b_j X_{ij} \right) + e_{it} \tag{1}$$

where i is a country index, t a (5-year) period index, and j an institution index. The dependent variable, u_{it}, is the unemployment rate in country i in period t. c_i is the country effect for country i. d_t is the time effect for period t. X_{ij} is the value of institution j in country i (in this first specification, we do not allow for time variation in institutions, so there is no index t.) The specification allows for the effects of the common time effects on unemployment to depend on the specific set of labour market institutions of a country. This dependence is captured by the parameters b_j.

The specification of (1) is clearly more a description of the data than the outcome of a tightly specified theory of interactions. It does not distinguish in particular between the effects of institutions on the impact or on the persistence of shocks on unemployment. But it captures the basic hypothesis that, given the same shocks, countries with worse institutions will experience higher unemployment.

We estimate this equation using data from 20 countries—the E15 countries listed and examined earlier, plus the United States, Canada, New Zealand, Australia and Japan. (These countries are clearly important controls for any story about European unemployment.) There seems to be little point in looking at year-to-year movements in institutions or in shocks unless one wants to learn more about dynamic effects, and this would take us too far. So, as in earlier figures, we divide time into 8 five-year periods, from 1960–4 to 1995+.

Following Nickell, we use measures for eight 'labour market institutions' (the reader is referred to Nickell (1997) for more details):

• Three are measures of different dimensions of the unemployment insurance system: the replacement rate (*RR*), the number of years over which unemployment benefits are paid (*Ben*), and a measure of active labour market policies (*ALMP*).
• One is a measure of employment protection (*EP*).
• One is a measure of the tax wedge (*Tax*).
• The last three measure aspects of collective bargaining: union contract coverage (*Cov*), union density (*Den*), and (union and employer) coordination of bargaining (*Coor*).

[19] Nickell gives values for these institutions for both 1983–8, and 1989–94. We use the average of the two.

The results of estimation of (1) (by non-linear least squares) are presented in Table 1. All the measures of labour market institutions are defined so that an increase in the measure is expected to increase the effect of an adverse shock on unemployment: the expected sign of each b_j is positive.[20] Also, all measures of institutions are constructed as deviations from the cross-country mean; this way the time effects gives the evolution of unemployment for a country with mean values for all 8 institutions.

The results of Table 1 are surprisingly strong (relative to our priors). The estimated equation gives the following description of the data:

• Estimated time effects account for an increase in the unemployment rate equal to 7.3%. That is, the equation implies that, if a country had had mean values for all eight institutions, its unemployment rate would have grown by 7.3% over the period.

• Coefficients on all 8 institutions have the predicted sign: Higher replacement rates, longer duration of unemployment benefits, higher employment protection, a higher tax wedge, higher union contract coverage and density, lead to a larger effect of shocks on unemployment. Active labour market policies and coordination lead to a smaller effect (remember our sign convention in defining each institution).

All coefficients, except for the union coverage variable, are statistically significant.[21]

Table 1
Time Effects Interacted with Fixed Institutions

	(1) Coefficients	(2) Range of independent variable		(3) Implied range of effect of shock (mean = 1)	
Time effects*	7.3%				
Replacement rate	0.017 (5.1)	−46.3	32.6	0.21	1.55
Benefit length	0.206 (4.9)	−2.0	1.6	0.60	1.33
Active labour policy	0.017 (3.0)	−47.2	9.5	0.20	1.16
Employment protection	-0.045 (3.1)	−9.5	9.5	0.58	1.42
Tax wedge	0.018 (3.2)	−17.8	22.2	0.68	1.40
Union coverage	0.098 (0.6)	−1.7	0.3	0.83	1.03
Union density	0.009 (2.1)	−30.4	39.6	0.73	1.36
Coordination	0.304 (5.1)	−2.0	2.0	0.40	1.60
Country effects	yes				
$\bar{R}^2$	0.863				

* Time effects: Estimated time effect for 1995+ minus estimated time effect for 1960–64. Column (1): regression results, t-statistics in parentheses. Number of observations: 159.

[20] Thus, we multiply the original Nickell measures of active labour market policies and of coordination by −1. We take the expected effect of employment protection to be that more employment protection leads to a larger effect of adverse shocks on unemployment, and the expected effect of coordination that more coordination reduces the effects of adverse shocks on unemployment.

[21] The t-statistics are computed under the assumption of iid residuals. The residuals show however both spatial and serial correlation, and adjusted t-statistics would probably be lower.

To give a sense of magnitudes, column (2) gives the range for each institutional measure (recall that these are deviations from the cross country mean). Column (3) then shows the effect of a given shock for the lowest and highest value of the corresponding institution. The way to read the column is as follows. Take three countries, each with mean values for all institutions except one—say, employment protection (line 5). Take an adverse shock which would raise unemployment by 1 percentage point in the country with the mean value of employment protection. Then the same shock will have an effect of only 0.58 percentage point in the country with the lowest employment protection, but an effect of 1.42 percentage point in the country with the highest employment protection. The conclusion one should draw from column (3) is, given the existing variation in labour market institutions, the range of the effects of institutions on the impact of a given shock on unemployment is roughly similar across institutions.

- Not only are the coefficients on institutions plausible, but the model does a good job of explaining the differential evolution of unemployment rates across countries. Fig. 9 plots the change in the actual and the fitted unemployment rates from 1965–9 to 1995+. The fit is quite good. Interactions between common shocks and different institutions can account for much of the actual difference in the evolution of unemployment rates across countries (Recall that a pure time effect model with no interactions would predict no variation in predicted unemployment rates across countries: all the points would lie on a horizontal line.)

- Another way of thinking about these results is as follows. Consider a

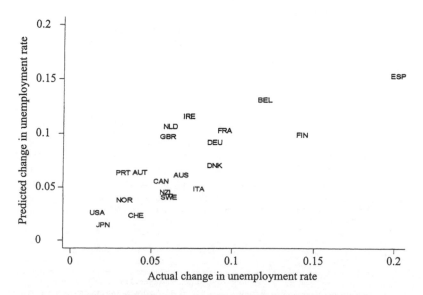

Fig. 9. *Actual and Predicted Change in u, 1995+ over 1965–9*

model with unobservable shocks and unobservable institutions—equivalently a
model with time, country, and interacted time and country effects:

$$u_{it} = c_i + d_t(1 + b_i) + e_{it}. \qquad (1')$$

Equation (1) can then be thought of as imposing the restriction that b_i
be a linear function of country i's institutions: $b_i = \sum X_{ij} b_j$. This raises the
question of how much better we would do if we did not impose this restriction
and estimated $(1')$ instead. One way to answer the question is to look at two
$\overline{R}^2$s. The $\overline{R}^2$ from estimation of $(1')$ is 0.903, compared to 0.863 in Table 1.
The $\overline{R}^2$ from a second state regression of the estimated $\hat{b}_i$ on labour market
institutions X_{ij}'s is 0.57. We read these results as saying that (1) the statistical
description of the evolution of unemployment as the result between shocks
and institutions has the potential to give a good description of the data (as
reflected in the first stage $\overline{R}^2$), and that (2) labour market institutions do a
good job of explaining country interaction effects (as reflected in the second
stage $\overline{R}^2$).

In short, (1) gives a good description of the heterogeneity of unemployment
evolutions as the result of interactions between shocks and institutions. These
results are indeed consistent with the two cross sections estimated by Nickell,
and show that his results are robust both to the use of a longer time period
and the introduction of country effects.[22]

One must worry however that these results are in part the result of research
Darwinism. The measures used by Nickell have all been constructed *ex-post
facto*, by researchers who were not unaware of unemployment developments.
When constructing a measure of employment protection for Spain, it is hard
to forget that unemployment in Spain is very high... Also, given the complexity in measuring institutions, measures which do well in explaining unemployment have survived better than those that did not. Thus, in the rest of this
section, we look at robustness.

4.1. *Dropping Institutions, Countries, or Country Fixed Effects*

To give a sense of robustness with respect to the set of institutions, column (1)
in Table 2 reports the results of 8 separate regressions, each regression
allowing interactions with only one of the 8 measures for institutions. When
introduced on their own, three measures are highly significant: the length of
benefits, the degree of employment protection, and the degree of union
coverage (which is insignificant in the multivariate specification). In contrast,
the replacement rate, which is highly significant in the multivariate specification, is insignificant when introduced alone. Another strategy is to see what
happens when we drop one institution at a time. The results (not reported)
indicate that the coefficients reported in Table 1 are robust to such a variation.

---

[22] There are however some differences between estimated coefficients. In particular: employment
protection is significant here, not in Nickell. Union contract coverage is not significant here, but is
significant in Nickell.

Table 2
Time Effects Interacted with Fixed Institutions. Alternative Specifications

	(1) Institutions entered individually		(2) No country effects
Time effects			7.1%
RR	0.004	(1.0)	0.017 (4.1)
Ben	0.268	(6.6)	0.213 (4.1)
ALMP	0.007	(1.4)	0.017 (2.4)
EP	0.043	(4.0)	0.049 (2.8)
Tax	0.012	(2.2)	0.017 (2.4)
Cov	0.532	(4.9)	0.049 (0.2)
Dens	−0.002	(−0.5)	0.009 (1.8)
Coor	0.048	(1.1)	0.301 (4.3)
CE		yes	no
$\overline{R}^2$			0.797

Column (1): each coefficient is estimated using a different regression, allowing interactions between the time effects and the specific institution variable. Column (2): Levels of institutional measures entered, but coefficients not reported. Number of observations: 159.

Second, we look at robustness with respect to the set of countries. In general, dropping one country at a time makes little difference to the results (not reported here). The only exception is the importance of Spain in determining the coefficient on employment protection. When dropping Spain, the coefficient on employment protection goes from 0.045 in Table 1 to 0.015.

Third, we look at robustness with respect to the treatment of country effects. Column (2) in Table 2 reports the results of estimation of (1), replacing country effects by the set of (time invariant) measures of labour market institutions for each country. That is, it imposes the constraint that all differences in unemployment rates be explained by differences in institutions; such a constraint is surely too strong, but it is worth seeing how it affects the results. Only the coefficients on interactions are reported in column (2). They are roughly the same as in Table 1. The coefficients on the levels of the labour market institutions (not reported) are typically insignificant. The fit is significantly worse than in Table 1.

4.2. *Looking at Alternative Measures of Institutions*

Table 3 looks at the implications of using alternative measures for some of the institutions. This is the work-in-progress part of our article. Our goal is eventually to construct time series for all 8 institutions. So far, we have done so only for replacement rates and for employment protection. Columns (1) and

Table 3

Time Effects Interacted with Institutions. Alternative Measures

	(1) Alternative replacement rates	(2) Time varying replacement rates	(3) Alternative employment protection	(4) Time varying employment protection
Time effects	7.3%	6.2%	7.3%	7.1%
(N) *RR*			0.017 (5.2)	0.017 (4.7)
(N) *Ben*			0.238 (5.6)	0.205 (4.4)
(Alt) *RR*1	0.009 (2.6)	0.007 (2.0)		
(Alt) *RR*25	0.009 (1.4)	0.019 (2.7)		
(N) *ALMP*	0.014 (1.6)	0.005 (0.5)	0.019 (3.2)	0.017 (2.6)
(N) *EP*	0.024 (1.4)	0.032 (1.7)		
(Alt) *EP*			0.294 (4.3)	0.167 (2.2)
(N) *Tax*	0.016 (2.4)	0.015 (2.1)	0.019 (3.5)	0.021 (3.7)
(N) *Cov*	0.413 (2.1)	0.395 (1.9)	0.085 (0.5)	0.287 (1.8)
(N) *Dens*	0.004 (0.8)	0.000 (0.0)	0.010 (2.5)	0.008 (1.7)
(N) *Coor*	0.272 (4.9)	0.325 (4.5)	0.392 (6.5)	0.361 (5.3)
CE	yes	yes	yes	yes
$\overline{R}^2$	0.824	0.831	0.872	0.857

(N) means Nickell measure. Column (1): estimation using time-invariant values of *RR*1 and *RR*25, equal to their average values for 1985–9. Column (2): estimation using the time series for *RR*1 and *RR*25. Column (3): estimation using the value of *EP* for the late 1980s. Column (4): estimation using the time series for *EP*. Number of observations: 159.

(2) report our results using alternative measures for replacement rates. Columns (3) and (4) report our results using alternative measures for employment protection.

Using the OECD database on replacement rates for each country since 1961, we construct an alternative set of measures for the generosity of unemployment insurance. The first measure, *RR*1, is the replacement rate during the first year of an unemployment spell, averaged over all categories. The second, *RR*25, is the average replacement rate during years 2 to 5 of an unemployment spell, averaged over all categories.

Column (1) shows the results of estimation using time invariant values for *RR*1 and *RR*25. For comparisons with the results using Nickell's measures which apply to the late 1980s and early 1990s, we use the mean value of the two replacement rates for the period 1985–9. Measures for the other 6 institutions are the same as in Table 1. The fit is a bit worse than in Table 1. The two replacement rates are both individually significant, and jointly highly significant. Coefficients on the other labour market institutions are often less significant than in Table 1. In particular, the coefficient on employment protection is smaller, and less significant.

Column (2) shows the results of estimation using time-varying measures for *RR*1 and *RR*25. Relative to column (1), the fit, measured by $\overline{R}^2$, is marginally improved (but is still worse than in Table 1). The part of the increase in unemployment due to time effects decreases from 7.3% to 6.2%. Coefficients on labour market institutions are largely the same as in column (1).

Columns (3) and (4) use the index of employment protection discussed in Section 2. In contrast to the Nickell index, which is a ranking of countries and thus ranges from 1 to 20, this index is a cardinal index, ranging theoretically from 0 to 6, empirically from 0 to about 4. Thus, in comparing coefficients to those obtained using the Nickell specification, keep in mind that the coefficients should be about 5 times larger to generate the same effect on unemployment.

Column (3) shows the results of estimation using time-invariant values of the index, equal to its value for 1985–9. The results are very similar to Table 1. $\bar{R}^2$ is a little higher. The effect of employment protection is similar in magnitude to that in Table 1 (i.e. the coefficient is about 5 times larger), and highly significant.

Column (4) shows the results of estimation using the time varying values of the employment protection index. Allowing for time variation does not improve the results: $\bar{R}^2$ is slightly lower. The coefficient on the employment protection index decreases by nearly half and becomes less significant. These results can be read in three ways. First, the effects of employment protection are indeed less strong than suggested by previous regressions using time-invariant measures. Two, the time series we have constructed for employment protection are not very reliable; as we discussed in Section 2, we are worried about the evolution of the index in the early part of the sample. Three, our earlier and apparently stronger results come in fact from reverse causality. Under this intepretation, the rise in unemployment has led over time to more employment protection, which is why there is a close relation between employment protection at the end of the sample and unemployment. But employment protection has little effect on unemployment, which is why the relation is weaker when using time series. Given the lack of strong evidence about the presence of a strong and reliable feedback from unemployment to institutions, we are sceptical; but we cannot exclude this interpretation.

To conclude: a model with common unobservable shocks and interactions with institutions provides a good description of the evolution of unemployment rates across time and countries. The description appears reasonably robust—although less so with respect to time variation in institutions. This conclusion leaves open the issue of what these shocks might have been, and whether they have indeed been similar across countries. For this reason, we now turn to a specification based on observable shocks.

5. Country Specific Observable Shocks, and Interactions

The benchmark specification we use in this section is the following:

$$u_{it} = c_i + \left(\sum_k Y_{kit} a_k \right) \left(1 + \sum_j X_{ij} b_j \right) + e_{it} \tag{2}$$

where the notation is the same as before, but the unobservable common shocks of Section 3 are now replaced by a set of country specific shocks; Y_{kit} denotes shock k for country i in period t.[23] Again our benchmark relies on time invariant measures of institutions, thus the lack of an index t for X. Later on, we look at results allowing for time variation for institutions.

Following the discussion in Section 2, we consider three sources of shocks and construct three variables for each country and each period. They are the rate of TFP growth, the real rate of interest, and the labour demand shift measure, respectively. We enter them as levels, but, given the presence of country dummies in the regression, they can be thought of as deviations from country averages—or from their 1960 values. To make it easy to read the tables, each variable is measured so an increase is expected to increase unemployment initially; therefore the original measure of TFP growth is multiplied by -1. Due to some missing data for some countries, the panel is (slightly) unbalanced. Also, one observation requires special treatment. As discussed in Blanchard (1997), the Portuguese revolution was associated with a large permanent increase in the measured labour share (20% of GDP)—without a corresponding increase in unemployment. While this evolution is interesting in its own right, we have decided to ignore it by allowing for a dummy for Portugal, from 1960 to 1974.[24]

The natural first question is: Ignoring differences in institutions across countries, how much of the evolutions of unemployment across time and countries can be explained by our three shocks? The answer is given in Table 4 and in Fig. 10.

Column 1 in Table 4 presents regressions of the unemployment rate on the three shocks, leaving institutions out. Two of the three shocks (TFP growth, and the real interest rate) are significant. A decrease in TFP growth of 3 percentage points, as has happened in many countries, translates into an increase in the unemployment rate of about 1.5%. An increase in the real

Table 4

Shocks only

Dependent var	(1) u	(2) u^* sacrifice ratio $= 0.2$	(3) u^* sacrifice ratio $= 4.0$
TFP growth	0.47 (3.1)	0.36 (2.6)	0.25 (1.7)
Real rate	0.67 (5.6)	0.63 (6.1)	0.63 (6.1)
LD shift	0.07 (1.1)	0.08 (1.5)	0.09 (1.7)
CE	yes	yes	yes
$\overline{R}^2$	0.566	0.590	0.584

Number of observations: 131.

[23] Most theories predict that the interaction of institutions and shocks may be different for different shocks. But allowing for different interactions between each shock and each institution struck us as asking too much from our limited data set (131 data points for the regressions in this section).

[24] The difference between macro and labour panel data regressions is that, in macro, each data point is intimately known by the researcher ...

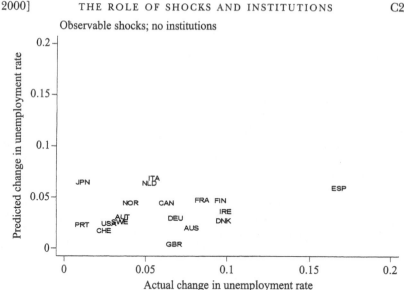

Fig. 10. *Actual and Predicted Change in u, 1965–9 to 1990-4*

interest rate of 5 percentage points leads to an increase in the unemployment rate of 3%. A decrease in the adjusted labour share of 10 percentage points, such as happened in France and Spain since the mid 1980s, leads to an increase in the unemployment rate of about 1%. So, these shocks appear indeed to explain part of the evolution of the unemployment rate across time and countries.

Do differences in the magnitude of shocks explain the cross country heterogeneity in unemployment increases? The answer, as shown in Fig. 10, is no. The figure plots the change in fitted unemployment against the change in actual unemployment from 1965–9 to 1990–4 (this is the longest time span for which data are available for all countries.). The relation is positive, but poor. The Netherlands and Spain have the same predicted increase in unemployment, yet very different outcomes. In short, the heterogeneity of shocks cannot account for much of the heterogeneity of unemployment evolutions.

Columns (2) and (3) in Table 4 present a rough attempt to adjust unemployment for deviations of actual from equilibrium unemployment. We start from the assumption that the following 'Phillips curve' relation holds between the change in inflation, the actual and the equilibrium rate of unemployment:

$$\Delta \pi_{it} = -a(u_{it} - u_{it}^*).$$

We then contruct 'equilibrium unemployment' as $u_{it}^* = u_{it} + (1/a)\Delta\pi_{it}$; $1/a$ is often called the sacrifice ratio. Estimates of a for Europe for annual data typically range from 0.25 to 0.50.[25] Column (2) constructs u^* using a sacrifice ratio of 2.0; column (3) does the same using a ratio of 4.0.[26] The fit in columns (2) and (3) is better than in column (1)—the dependent variable is not the same however. The effects of each of the three shock variables are roughly similar.

Table 5 presents the results of the specification that allows for both shocks and interactions with institutions. Column (1) presents the results from estimating the benchmark specification (2).

All three variables measuring shocks are now very significant. The effects of TFP growth and the labour demand shift are larger than in Table 4, the effects of the real interest rate slightly smaller. A decrease in TFP growth of 3 percentage points translates into an increase in the unemployment rate of about 2%. An increase in the real interest rate of 5 percentage points leads to an increase in the unemployment rate of 2.5%. A decrease in the adjusted labour share of 10 percentage points leads to an increase in the unemployment rate of about 2%.

Coefficients on 7 of 8 institutions have the expected sign. Only union coverage is negative, but insignificant. The most significant coefficients are on the replacement rate, the length of benefits, union density and coordination. Except for union coverage, the pattern of coefficients is the same as in Table 1

Table 5

Shocks Interacted with Fixed Institutions

	(1) Benchmark equation		(2) Institutions entered individually		(3) u^* sacrifice ratio = 2.0	
TFP growth	0.71	(5.0)			0.58	(4.5)
Real rate	0.47	(5.1)			0.49	(5.7)
LD shift	0.19	(2.7)			0.15	(2.4)
RR	0.025	(3.7)	0.013	(2.4)	0.025	(3.7)
Ben	0.267	(3.0)	0.203	(2.3)	0.313	(3.3)
ALMP	0.028	(1.4)	−0.009	(−0.7)	0.033	(1.6)
EP	0.095	(2.7)	0.047	(2.7)	0.090	(2.6)
Tax	0.033	(2.4)	0.026	(2.6)	0.037	(2.6)
Cov	−0.501	(−1.1)	0.639	(3.0)	−0.466	(−1.0)
Dens	0.033	(3.2)	−0.002	(−0.3)	0.033	(2.8)
Coor	0.414	(2.9)	−0.039	(−0.4)	0.439	(2.9)
CE	yes		yes		yes	
$\overline{R}^2$	0.674				0.702	

Number of observations: 131.

[25] If our approach to measuring the equilibrium unemployment rate is right however, then most existing estimates of a, which rely on a much rougher measure of equilibrium unemployment, are not right. We did not take up the task of estimating a in this article.
[26] In doing so, we are implicitly assuming that the sacrifice ratio is not related to institutions. This is probably incorrect.

(estimated with unobservable shocks), up to a factor of proportionality greater than 1. That is, they are in general 1.5 to 2 times larger than in Table 1. The mechanical explanation is that the observable shocks explain less of the general increase in unemployment, and the interactions must therefore explain more. The $\bar{R}^2$ is much lower than in Table 1: despite the fact that they can differ across countries, the 3 observable shocks do not do as good a job as the set of 8 time effects in Table 1.

The specification does a good job of explaining differences in unemployment evolutions across countries. This is shown in Fig. 11, which plots the change in fitted unemployment against the change in actual unemployment, from 1965–9 to 1990–4. The fit is quite good; clearly much better than in Fig. 10, if not quite as good as in Fig. 9. Fig. 12 gives another way of looking at fit, by plotting the actual and fitted unemployment rate for each of the 20 countries over time. The visual impression is one of a good fit in nearly all cases. (To facilitate comparison of unemployment rates across countries, the vertical scale is the same for all countries. The drawback is that it is harder to assess the fit for each country.)

Column (2) looks at the effects of entering institutions one at a time. The conclusions are largely similar to those in the previous section. In particular, union coverage is very significant on its own, but not in combination with other institutions. Column (3) replaces actual by equilibrium unemployment, assuming as sacrifice ratio of 2.0. The fit is better, but the results are otherwise very similar.

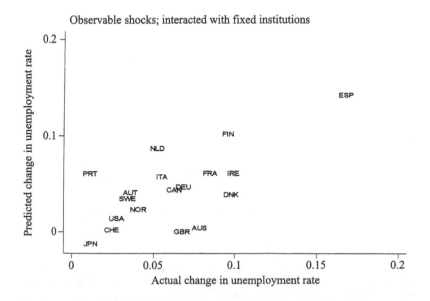

Fig. 11. *Actual and Predicted Change in u, 1965–9 to 1990–4*

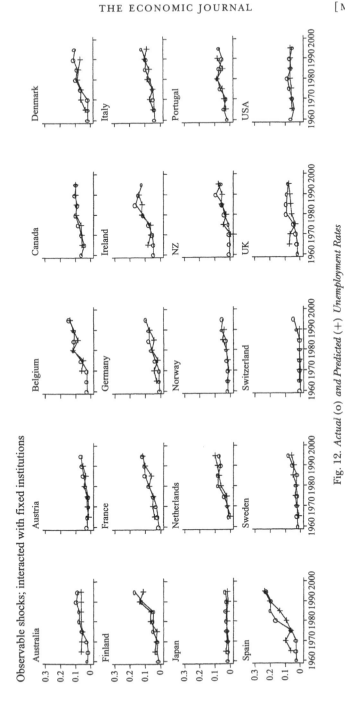

Fig. 12. *Actual* (o) *and Predicted* (+) *Unemployment Rates*

Table 6 looks at alternative measures of institutions. Its structure is the same as that of Table 3. Columns (1) and (2) look at the effects of using the two alternative measures of replacement rates using OECD data. Column (1) uses a time invariant value equal to the average for 1985–9; column (2) uses the time series. Columns (3) and (4) do the same for employment protection. The table suggests two conclusions, both worrisome: replacing the Nickell measures by alternative, but time invariant measures, substantially decreases the $\bar{R}^2$. Going from the time invariant to the time varying measures further decreases the fit. The coefficients on institutions remain consistently positive, but are typically smaller than in Table 5, and less significant. These results lead to the same discussion as in Section 3: Luck, or data mining, when the standard set of measures is used? Poor time series for institutions, interacting here with the fact that we are looking at their product with time varying and also imperfectly measured shocks? Or reverse causality (although the fact that the deterioration of fit happens when replacing one time invariant measure by another is not supportive of this hypothesis).

To conclude: one can indeed give a good account of the evolution of unemployment across countries and times by relying on observable shocks and interactions with labour market institutions. The fact that the results are weaker when using time varying institutions is worrying. But, again, the results strike us as surprisingly good overall.

Table 6

Shocks Interacted with Institutions. Alternative Measures of Institutions

	(1) Alternative replacement rates	(2) Time varying replacement rates	(3) Alternative employment protection	(4) Time varying employment protection
TFP growth	0.57 (3.7)	0.54 (3.6)	0.61 (4.2)	0.65 (4.3)
Real rate	0.50 (4.6)	0.51 (4.8)	0.49 (4.9)	0.51 (5.2)
LD shift	0.18 (2.1)	0.17 (2.2)	0.17 (2.3)	0.17 (2.2)
(N) *RR*			0.022 (2.9)	0.020 (3.0)
(N) *Ben*			0.199 (2.1)	0.157 (2.0)
(Alt) *RR1*	0.014 (1.8)	0.008 (1.1)		
(Alt) *RR25*	0.006 (0.4)	0.013 (0.9)		
(N) *ALMP*	0.014 (0.6)	0.001 (0.0)	0.017 (0.8)	0.008 (0.4)
(N) *EP*	0.051 (1.1)	0.049 (1.1)		
(Alt) *EP*			0.224 (1.3)	0.083 (1.1)
(N) *Tax*	0.023 (1.5)	0.018 (1.1)	0.037 (2.4)	0.032 (2.3)
(N) *Cov*	0.087 (0.2)	0.213 (0.5)	0.186 (0.6)	0.394 (1.5)
(N) *Dens*	0.020 (1.7)	0.013 (1.1)	0.026 (2.1)	0.020 (2.0)
(N) *Coor*	0.341 (2.3)	0.285 (1.9)	0.524 (2.8)	0.458 (2.9)
CE	yes	yes	yes	yes
$\bar{R}^2$	0.624	0.618	0.656	0.654

6. Conclusions

We see our results as preliminary. We see our dynamic specification of the effects of shocks as much too crude. We still need to construct and introduce time series for some labour market institutions. We worry about the endogeneity of labour market institutions. Nevertheless, we believe that the results so far suggest that an account of the evolution of unemployment based on the interaction of shocks and institutions can do a good job of fitting the evolution of European unemployment, both over time and across countries.

If our account is correct, one can be mildly optimistic about the future of European unemployment. The effects of some of the adverse shocks should go away. The real interest rate is likely to be lower in the future than in the recent past. The dynamic effects of what we have identified as adverse labour demand shifts should eventually prove favourable to employment. Institutions are also slowly becoming employment-friendly. Our results suggest that the more favourable macroeconomic environment and the improvement in institutions should lead to a substantial decline in unemployment.

MIT and NBER

Harvard University

References

Blanchard, O. (1997). 'The medium run', *Brookings Papers on Economic Activity*, no. 2, pp. 89–158.
Blanchard, O. (1999). 'European unemployment: the role of shocks and institutions', Baffi Lecture, Rome, (forthcoming, 1999).
Blanchard, O. and Portugal, P. (1998). 'What hides behind an unemployment rate. Comparing Portuguese and U.S. unemployment', NBER Working Paper 6636.
Blanchard, O. and Summers, L. (1986). 'Hysteresis and the European unemployment problem', *NBER Macroeconomics Annual* no. 1, pp. 15–78 (S. Fischer, ed), MIT Press.
Bruno, M. and Sachs, J. (1985). *The Economics of Worldwide Stagflation*, Oxford: Basil Blackwell.
Grubb, O., Jackman, R. and Layard, R. (1982). 'Causes of the current stagflation', *Review of Economic Studies*, vol. 49(5), pp. 707–30.
Layard, R. and Nickell, S. (1987). 'The labour market', In (R. Dornbusch and R. Layard, eds) *The Performance of the British Economy*, Oxford: Clarendon Press.
Layard, R., Nickell, S. and Jackman, R. (1991). *Unemployment; Macroeconomic Performance and the Labour Market*, Oxford: Oxford University Press.
Lazear, E. (1990). 'Job security provisions and employment', *Quarterly Journal of Economics*, vol. 105-3, pp. 699–725.
Lindbeck, A. (1995). 'Hazardous welfare-state dynamics', *American Economic Review*, vol. 85(2), pp. 9–15.
Mortensen, D. and Pissarides, C. (1998). 'Job reallocation, employment fluctuations, and unemployment differences, mimeo (forthcoming, *Handbook of Macroeconomics*).
Mortensen, D. and Pissarides, C. (1999). 'Unemployment responses to "skill biased" shocks: the role of labour market policy', ECONOMIC JOURNAL, vol. 109, pp. 1–24.
Nickell, S. (1997). 'Unemployment and labour market rigidities: Europe versus North America', *Journal of Economic Perspectives*, vol. 11(3), pp. 55–74.
Nickell, S. and Bell, B. (1994). 'Would cutting payroll taxes on the unskilled have a significant effect on unemployment?', Presented at CEPR conference on Unemployment Policy, Vigo, Spain, September.
Nickell, S. and Layard, R. (1998). 'Labour market institutions and economic performance', CEP Discussion Paper 407 (forthcoming, *Handbook of Labor Economics*).
OECD (1999). *OECD Employment Outlook*, OECD, Paris.
Phelps, E. (1994). *Structural Slumps. The modern equilibrium theory of unemployment, interest and assets*, Cambridge MA: Harvard University Press.
Salomaki, A. and Munzi, T. (1999). 'Net replacement rates of the unemployed. Comparisons of various

approaches', Economic Paper 133, European Commission, Directorate General for Economic and Financial Affairs.

Sargent, T. and Ljundqvist, L. (1995). 'The European unemployment dilemma', WP 95-17, Federal Reserve Bank of Chicago.

Wilson, W. J. (1987). *The Truly Disadvantaged*, Chicago: University of Chicago Press.

[10]

What Hides Behind an Unemployment Rate: Comparing Portuguese and U.S. Labor Markets

By OLIVIER BLANCHARD AND PEDRO PORTUGAL*

Behind similar unemployment rates in the United States and Portugal hide two very different labor markets. Unemployment duration is three times longer in Portugal than in the United States. Symmetrically, flows of workers into unemployment are three times lower in Portugal. These lower flows come in roughly equal proportions from lower job creation and destruction, and from lower worker flows given job creation and destruction. A plausible explanation is high employment protection in Portugal. High employment protection makes economies more sclerotic; but because it affects unemployment duration and worker flows in opposite directions, the effect on unemployment is ambiguous. (JEL E2, J3, J6)

At first glance, Portugal would appear to have avoided the European unemployment disease. Indeed, the right comparison would seem to be to the United States. Over the past 15 years, Portugal and the United States have had the same average unemployment rate, about 6.3 percent. And in the last quarter of 1999, the Portuguese unemployment rate stood at 4.1 percent, the same as the U.S. rate.

A closer look reveals, however, two very different labor markets. Mean unemployment duration in Portugal is more than three times that of the United States. Symmetrically, flows of workers into unemployment in Portugal are, in proportion to the labor force, less than a third of what they are in the United States. More informally, if the image of U.S. unemployment is one of a way station between jobs, the image of Portuguese unemployment is that of a stag-

nant pool, with low flows in and out, and long unemployment duration.

The purpose of our paper is to further characterize the differences, and offer a tentative explanation, namely the importance of employment protection in Portugal. It is organized in four sections.

Sections I and II are empirical and primarily descriptive. As a matter of logic, low flows of workers in and out of unemployment can come from a combination of three factors:

- Low flows of job creation and job destruction.
- Low flows of workers given job flows.
- Low flows of workers through unemployment relative to worker flows directly from employment to employment, or through nonparticipation.

Using evidence from Portuguese micro-data sets together with U.S. evidence collected by others, we compare job flows and the structure of worker flows across the two countries. Such international comparisons are always difficult because of differences in available data sets and methodology. We pay particular attention to these difficulties. Section I looks at job flows, Section II at worker flows. We conclude that the low flows in and out of unemployment in Portugal reflect in roughly equal part low job flows, and low worker flows given job flows. The third potential factor, low worker flows through

* Blanchard: Department of Economics, Massachusetts Institute of Technology, 50 Memorial Drive, Cambridge, MA 02139, and National Bureau of Economic Research; Portugal: Departamento de Estudos Económicos do Banco de Portugal, Avenida Almirante Reis, 71, 1150 Lisboa, Portugal, and Universidade Nova de Lisboa. We thank Lucena Vieira for computational assistance. We thank Hoyt Bleakley, Tito Boeri, Peter Diamond, Andrew Figura, Chris Foote, Victor Gaspar, John Haltiwanger, Larry Katz, José Mata, Bruce Meyer, and Andrei Shleifer for comments and help. We thank three anonymous referees for their suggestions. We thank the Fundação para a Ciência e Tecnologia and the National Science Foundation for financial assistance.

Recent Developments in Labor Economics III

unemployment relative to total worker flows, does not appear to play an important role.

We then argue in Section III that these facts, together with the high duration of unemployment, point to the importance of high employment protection in Portugal. To do so, we develop a simple model aimed at capturing the effects of employment protection on the labor market. We show how employment protection decreases job flows, decreases worker flows even more, and increases unemployment duration, thus fitting the basic facts of the Portuguese labor market. We show that, while the effect on output and welfare is (in our model) unambiguous, the effect on unemployment is ambiguous, and depends on the shape of the distribution functions for the shocks affecting the economy.

Assessing whether and how our conclusions extend to other Organization for Economic Cooperation and Development (OECD) countries would require doing the same type of data analysis for each country as we do here for Portugal. We have not done so. But we provide in Section IV what we find to be tantalizing evidence of the role of employment protection in explaining differences in the nature of unemployment across countries. We construct for each OECD country the average flow into unemployment—as a proportion of the labor force—and average unemployment duration, for the period 1985–1994. We then regress each one on the index of employment protection constructed by the OECD for the late 1980's. We find a strong negative relation between the flow into unemployment and employment protection, and a similarly strong positive relation between unemployment duration and employment protection. Employment protection appears to have strong effects on reallocation and the nature of unemployment. But the effect on the unemployment rate, the product of flow times duration, turns out to be both theoretically and empirically ambiguous.

Our paper is related to the growing literature on the nature of flows in the labor market, the role of employment protection, and differences between U.S. and European labor markets:

• It confirms the empirical validity of the conclusions of the recent theoretical research on the effects of employment protection. Em-

ployment protection profoundly affects the nature of the labor market, decreasing reallocation, and increasing the duration of unemployment. These effects may well decrease output and welfare. But they need not show up as higher unemployment.

• It sheds light on a puzzle in the recent empirical research on job creation and job destruction flows across countries. The prior belief was that employment protection led to lower rates of creation and destruction in Europe relative to the United States. But the constructed measures—typically annual rates of job creation and destruction—have turned out to be surprisingly similar across countries. Our examination of Portugal and the United States provides a potential explanation. *Annual rates* of job creation and destruction are indeed roughly similar in Portugal and in the United States; but *quarterly rates* are much lower in Portugal than in the United States, suggesting that the effect of employment protection is primarily to reduce transitory employment variations, much less permanent ones.

I. Job Flows

Following the work of the Organization for Economic Cooperation and Development (OECD, 1987) and of Steven J. Davis et al. (1996) for the United States, empirical research on job reallocation has focused on "job flows"—changes in employment at the establishment level over time. We follow the same strategy, and start by looking at job flows in Portugal and the United States.

In the case of Portugal, we rely on two data sets. The first is an annual data set, *Quadros de Pessoal,* collected by the Ministry of Employment, that gives point-in-time employment levels, for all Portuguese establishments, yearly. This allows us to construct annual measures of job creation and job destruction, for each year from 1983 to 1995. The second is a quarterly data set, the *Employment Survey,* that gives point-in-time employment levels for a sample of Portuguese establishments, quarterly. From that survey, we construct a probability-weighted sample, from which we construct series for job creation and job destruction for each quarter

TABLE 1—ANNUAL JOB CREATION AND DESTRUCTION IN MANUFACTURING, PORTUGAL AND THE UNITED STATES

	Job creation			Job destruction			Sum
	Entry	Expansion	Sum	Exit	Contraction	Sum	
Portugal							
1. All	5.3	6.1	11.4	5.5	6.3	11.8	23.2
2. ≥5 employees	4.9	5.7	10.6	5.3	6.3	11.6	22.2
3. Size adjusted	(3.0)	(4.5)	(7.5)	(4.2)	(5.9)	(10.1)	(17.6)
United States							
4. ≥5 employees	1.5	7.4	8.9	2.5	7.7	10.2	19.2
5. Ratio P/U.S.			1.19			1.13	1.16

Notes: All numbers: Percentage of employment. Averages over the relevant period.
Line 1. From the *Quadros de Pessoal,* 1983–1995. Includes all establishments.
Line 2. Same source. Excludes establishments with less than five workers.
Line 3. Same source. Uses U.S. establishment employment-size shares instead of Portugal shares to construct size-adjusted job creation and destruction.
Line 4. From Davis et al. (1997) for 1973–1993.
Line 5. Ratio of line 2 to line 4.

from 1991:1 to 1995:4.[1] In the case of the United States, we rely on series constructed by others, as indicated below.

A. *Manufacturing: Annual Measures*

Given that the Longitudinal Research Database (LRD), the main data set available to compute job flows for the United States, covers only manufacturing, we start by looking at job creation and destruction in manufacturing. We construct the series for Portugal using the same methodology and definitions as Davis et al. (1996). The average values of the two series and their components (job creation due to entries or to expansions in continuing establishments, job destruction due to exits or to contractions in continuing establishments) are given in line 1 of Table 1.

The series reported in line 1 include all manufacturing establishments. The U.S. series constructed by Davis et al. (1996) exclude firms with less than five workers. Thus, for comparison, we give, in line 2, the numbers for job creation and destruction in Portugal excluding establishments with less than five workers

[1] The Appendix at the end of the article gives a short description of the three Portuguese data sets we use in this study. A longer Appendix, giving a more detailed description of the data sets, the construction of the series, and the construction of the tables, is available at http://econ-wp.mit.edu/RePEc/2000/blanchar/portugal_data.pdf.

(these firms account for 3.4 percent of manufacturing employment in Portugal). Small establishments tend to have more volatile employment; excluding them leads to slightly lower numbers for creation and destruction.

Given that job creation and destruction typically decrease with establishment size, and that Portugal has a larger proportion of small firms than the United States (for example, establishments with less than 50 employees account for 32 percent of manufacturing employment in Portugal, compared to 14 percent in the United States), we then carry out the following exercise. We divide establishments in class sizes (following the grid size in Davis et al., 1996 Table 4-1), compute job creation and destruction for each class size, and then compute overall job creation and destruction, using *U.S.* rather than Portuguese shares of employment in each class. In short, this computation gives "firm size-adjusted" job creation and destruction for Portugal. The results are shown in line 3.

Finally, line 4 gives the U.S. numbers, from the updated data base constructed by Davis et al. (1997) from the LRD for the period 1973–1993.

The comparison of Portuguese and U.S. numbers yields three sharp conclusions. (The average values correspond to different time spans across the two countries. Comparing mean values for the period over which both sets of observations are available, 1983–1993, yields identical conclusions):

TABLE 2—QUARTERLY JOB CREATION AND DESTRUCTION IN MANUFACTURING, PORTUGAL AND THE UNITED STATES

	Job creation			Job destruction			Sum
	Entry	Expansion	Sum	Exit	Contraction	Sum	
Portugal							
1.	1.2	2.0	3.2	1.0	2.9	3.9	7.1
2. Memo: annual 1	(4.8)	(4.7)	(9.5)	(6.8)	(7.1)	(13.9)	(23.4)
3. Memo: annual 2		(4.0)			(7.5)		
United States							
4.	0.6	4.6	5.2	0.8	4.8	5.6	10.8
5. Memo: annual	(1.5)	(7.4)	(8.9)	(2.5)	(7.7)	(10.2)	(19.2)
6. Ratio P/U.S.			0.61			0.69	0.66
7. Memo: annual			(1.05)			(1.34)	(1.21)

Notes: All numbers: Percentage of employment. Averages over the period.

Line 1. Quarterly changes. Expansions and contractions, from quarterly *Employment Survey,* 1991:1 to 1995:4. Entries and exits computed from annual data as in Table 1, line 2, but for 1991:1 to 1995:4, divided by 4. Exits further adjusted as described in the Appendix.

Line 2. Annual changes, constructed as in Table 1, but for 1991:1 to 1995:4.

Line 3. Annual changes (expansions and contractions only), constructed from the *Employment Survey.*

Line 4. Quarterly changes. Davis et al. (1997) for 1972:2 to 1993:4.

Line 5. Annual changes, from line 4 in Table 1.

Line 6. Ratio of line 1 to line 4.

Line 7. Ratio of line 2 to line 5.

- First, annual job creation and destruction are actually *higher* in Portugal than in the United States. Comparing line 2 and line 4, job creation in Portugal is equal to 119 percent of the U.S. value, job destruction to 113 percent of the U.S. value. This observation is in line with the findings of other studies, which have found that annual job creation and destruction appears to be often as large or larger in Europe as in the United States.[2]

- Second, the high rates in Portugal reflect in part smaller firm size, and associated higher job turnover. Comparing line 3 and line 4, "size-adjusted" job creation in Portugal is equal to 84 percent of the U.S. value, job destruction to 99 percent of the U.S. value.

- Third, the composition of both creation and destruction is quite different across the two countries. The proportion of job creation due to entries and the proportion of job destruction due to exits are both about twice as large in Portugal as in the United States.

This difference could be due to measurement issues, with firms either failing to report on time, or misreporting their identification numbers, or actually going through the process of closing and reopening in order to avoid various legal obligations. As described in the detailed data Appendix, we have explored a number of checks on the series, and concluded that most of the entries and exits are indeed genuine. If so, one hypothesis is that employment protection—the role of which we shall explore at more length below—may lead to less employment adjustment in continuing firms, but at the cost of more closings of existing firms.

B. *Manufacturing: Quarterly Measures*

We turn next to the quarterly evidence, still for manufacturing. For Portugal, using the *Employment Survey,* we can construct series for quarterly job creation due to expansions, and job destruction due to contractions, for the period 1991:1 to 1995:4. The mean values of the flows are given in line 1 of Table 2. While the data set does not allow us to construct series for job creation due to entry, and job destruction due to exit, we construct estimates of mean entry and exit rates from annual numbers. For entries, we simply use the annual rate divided by four. For exits, matters are more complex. As firms which

---

[2] See, for example, Giuseppe Bertola and Richard Rogerson (1997), or OECD (1994 Ch. 6).

exit typically have decreases in employment in the quarters preceding their exit, some of the "job flows due to exits" in annual data show up as "job flows due to contractions" in quarterly data. As described in the detailed data Appendix, we use an adjustment factor to scale down the annual exit rate appropriately.

For comparison with the annual numbers, we report in line 2 the numbers for annual job creation and destruction from the annual data set, computed in the same way as line 1 of Table 1, but over the same period as for the quarterly rates. For purposes of assessing comparability between the annual and the quarterly data sets, we also compute annual numbers for both expansions and contractions from the quarterly data set. The results are reported in line 3. A comparison of lines 2 and 3 suggests that the two data sets are roughly consistent.

Lines 4 and 5 give the corresponding numbers for the United States. Line 4 gives the numbers constructed from the LRD by Davis et al. (1997) for the period 1972:2 to 1993:4. Corresponding annual numbers are given in line 5.

One issue we could not resolve in comparing the two sets of numbers is that the quarterly LRD results are for production workers only (about 70 percent of all workers for the period at hand), while the Portuguese numbers are for all workers; we do not have the information needed to create series just for production workers for Portugal. Based on various pieces of evidence, we believe it is not a major issue.[3] Another issue is the fact that the time periods for the two countries are quite different. The Portuguese data start in 1991, the U.S. data end in 1993. But the mean values of the flows for the United States appear stable over time; results are nearly identical when using, say, only the 1980's.

Comparison of the two sets of numbers, and of these numbers with those in Table 1, yields an important conclusion:

In contrast to the results using annual numbers, quarterly job creation and job destruction in manufacturing are substantially lower in Portugal than in the United States. Quarterly job creation in Portugal is equal to 61 percent of the U.S. value, job destruction to 69 percent of the U.S. value.

The interpretation of the difference between quarterly and annual results is a simple one: Movements in job destruction and job creation in the United States have a larger transitory component than in Portugal. This is indeed confirmed by constructing persistence rates (defined as in Davis et al., 1996) for Portugal and comparing them to U.S. numbers.[4] Persistence rates are higher in Portugal than in the United States, especially for job destruction: When a Portuguese establishment decreases employment, it is much less likely to increase it later on than is its U.S. counterpart.[5] We see this finding as suggestive of a role of employment protection in Portugal. Think of firms' desired employment as having both a transitory and a permanent (unit-root) component. The higher the cost of adjusting employment, the more firms will smooth the transitory component; but they will have little choice other than to adjust to the permanent one. The lower the frequency at which we look at employment changes, the more important will be the permanent component relative to the transitory component, and thus the smaller will be the effect of employment protection on employment movements.

We do not know whether a similar result holds for other European countries. To the extent that it does, this may give a key to the puzzle of the similar annual job creation/destruction measures on both sides of the Atlantic mentioned earlier. Employment protection may lead firms to smooth quarter-to-quarter movements, but the effect may be smaller when looking at year-to-year movements.

---

[3] Production workers account for between 72 and 75 percent of employment in manufacturing in Portugal. While we cannot compute separate quarterly flows for production and nonproduction workers, we can compute annual flows. Average job destruction and creation numbers are roughly similar for production and nonproduction workers. This does not quite settle the issue: It could be that while annual flows are similar, quarterly flows are different. This we cannot tell.

[4] Comparison of persistence rates across countries raises a number of issues of comparability, which are discussed in the detailed Appendix. Our best estimates of the quarterly persistence rates for job destruction for continuing establishments in manufacturing are 0.85 for Portugal, versus 0.68 for the United States.

[5] Yet another piece of evidence comes from looking at the seasonality: U.S. job destruction has a large seasonal component, which is nearly absent in Portugal.

TABLE 3—ANNUAL AND QUARTERLY JOB CREATION AND DESTRUCTION IN ALL SECTORS, PORTUGAL
AND THE UNITED STATES

	Job creation			Job destruction			Sum
	Entry	Expansion	Sum	Exit	Contraction	Sum	
			Annual				
Portugal							
1. All	7.8	7.1	14.9	6.4	7.3	13.7	28.6
2. ≥5 employees	6.5	6.3	12.9	5.8	7.6	13.4	26.3
3. Size-sector adjusted	(5.7)	(5.2)	(10.9)	(4.3)	(4.7)	(9.0)	(19.9)
United States							
4.	2.0	9.6	11.6	3.3	10.0	13.3	25.0
5. Ratio P/U.S.			1.11			1.01	1.05
			Quarterly				
Portugal							
6.	1.8	2.2	4.0	1.1	2.8	3.9	7.9
United States							
7.	0.8	6.0	6.8	1.0	6.3	7.3	14.0
8. Ratio P/U.S.			0.59			0.53	0.56

Notes: All numbers: Percentage of employment. Averages over the period.
Line 1. From the *Quadros de Pessoal,* 1983–1995. Includes all establishments.
Line 2. Same source. Excludes establishments with less than five workers.
Line 3. Same source, but uses U.S. employment size and sectoral shares to construct size-sector adjusted job creation and destruction.
Line 4. Estimates of U.S. job creation and destruction constructed using annual numbers from Davis et al. (1997) for 1973–1993, from Table 1, multiplied by 1.3.
Line 5. Ratio of line 2 to line 4.
Line 6. Quarterly changes. Expansions and contractions, from quarterly *Employment Survey,* 1991:1 to 1995:4. Entries and exits computed from annual data as in Table 3, line 2, but for 1991:1 to 1995:4, divided by 4. Exits further adjusted as described in the Appendix.
Line 7. Quarterly manufacturing numbers from Davis et al. (1997) for 1972:2 to 1993:4, from Table 2, line 4, multiplied by 1.3.
Line 8. Ratio of line 6 to line 7.

C. All Sectors

As the Portuguese data sets cover all sectors, we can carry the same exercises for the Portuguese economy as a whole. The problem is the lack of an appropriate counterpart data set for the United States. But, one can still get a sense of the relative magnitudes. The basic conclusion is that the main results obtained for manufacturing apply to the overall economy.

For Portugal, we construct annual data for job creation and destruction in the same way as we did for manufacturing. The numbers are given in line 1 of Table 3. Corresponding numbers, but excluding firms with less than five workers, are given in line 2.

Not only does Portugal have a higher proportion of smaller firms than the United States, but the sectoral composition of employment is different. Agriculture, a sector with higher job

creation and destruction than the others, is for example larger in Portugal than in the United States. Thus, following the logic followed in Table 1, we construct firm-size *and* sector-adjusted job creation and destruction numbers, using U.S. size/sector shares for employment. The results are reported in line 3.

For the United States, the only available source of information for firms outside of manufacturing is from the states' unemployment-insurance (UI) systems. This information has been examined by a number of researchers, Jonathan S. Leonard (1987) for Wisconsin from 1978 to 1982, Patricia Anderson and Bruce Meyer (1994) for eight states from 1978 to 1984, and more recently, Christopher Foote (1998) for Michigan from 1978 to 1988. Because of differences between firm-based data and unemployment-insurance-based data, the results from these studies cannot be directly compared to the Portuguese numbers.[6] But they can be used to get a sense of the ratio of job creation/destruction for the economy as a whole relative to that in manufacturing, and to adjust the LRD manufacturing numbers accordingly. This is what we do here. We read these studies as suggesting a ratio of job turnover for the economy as a whole relative to manufacturing around 1.3 (see detailed data Appendix). We therefore construct the numbers for the United States by multiplying the manufacturing numbers by 1.3. The resulting numbers are given in line 4.

The comparison of line 2 to line 4 yields one main conclusion: Annual job creation appears slightly higher in Portugal than in the United States. Annual job destruction is similar in both countries. Composition plays an important role: When adjusted for firm size and sector composition, the Portuguese number for job reallocation (job creation plus job destruction) is 20 percent lower than that for the United States.

The next two lines give the quarterly rates of job creation and destruction for the economy as whole. Line 6 gives the numbers for Portugal, constructed in the same way as for manufacturing earlier. Line 7 gives the corresponding U.S. numbers, obtained by multiplying the numbers in Table 2 by an adjustment factor of 1.3.

Line 8 gives the ratio of Portuguese to U.S. flows. It suggests that, for the economy as a whole, quarterly job creation and job destruction are substantially lower in Portugal than in the United States. Quarterly job creation in Portugal is equal to 59 percent of the U.S. value, job destruction to 53 percent of the U.S. value.

II. Worker Flows

In a well-functioning economy, many separations are not due to desired changes in the level of employment of the firm, but rather to match-specific problems: A firm no longer likes a particular worker, or a worker no longer likes his job. Thus, worker flows typically exceed job flows. We focus in this section on these worker flows and their relation to job flows, in both Portugal and the United States.

Two data sets are available for Portugal. One is the *Inquérito ao Emprego* household survey conducted by the Instituto Nacional de Estatística (INE). Its relative strength, for our purposes, is that it is comparable in design to the U.S. *Current Population Survey* (CPS) (but available quarterly instead of monthly) and thus allows for comparisons between Portuguese and U.S. numbers on worker flows. The other is the *Employment Survey* described and used earlier. Its relative strength, for our purposes, is that, because firms are asked not only about quarterly net changes in employment, but also about gross changes, the data set can be used to construct internally consistent job and worker flows, at least for continuing firms.

We start with a comparison of numbers based on the two household surveys. Quarterly worker flows for Portugal can be constructed for the period 1993:2 to 1996:4 by matching adjacent INE surveys. By using observations on workers in adjacent quarters, we can construct flows from employment to unemployment, to nonparticipation, and to other employment. (One of the strengths of the survey is that it allows one to compute employment-to-employment flows; see the detailed data Appendix.) The resulting mean values of quarterly worker flows from employment are given in column 1 of Table 4. Line 1 gives the value of worker outflows for all workers.[7] To look at a universe of workers consistent with that in the firms' surveys, line 2 gives the value of worker outflows for all workers except public employees (a large proportion of total employment in Portugal, with lower turnover than in the private sector), the self-employed, and private household employees.

Quarterly worker flows from employment for the United States are constructed by multiplying the monthly numbers from Blanchard and Peter Diamond (1990) by 3. Those numbers were in turn constructed as the sum of flows from employment to unemployment and nonparticipation, constructed from the CPS for the period 1968:1 to 1986:5 and adjusted by Abowd and Zellner, plus estimated employment-to-employment flows. Two remarks are needed here. First, during that

---

[6] For a discussion of the differences between LRD and UI-based numbers, see, for example, Foote (1998).

[7] To lighten the presentation, we present results only for worker outflows (and job destruction). The results are very similar for worker inflows (and job creation).

TABLE 4—QUARTERLY WORKER OUTFLOWS AND JOB
DESTRUCTION, PORTUGAL AND THE UNITED STATES

	Worker outflows	Job destruction	Ratio worker to job
(Data from household surveys)			
Portugal			
1. All workers	3.1		
2. Excluding public			
employees	4.1	(3.9)	(1.1)
United States			
3.	11.1–14.1	(7.3)	(1.5–1.9)
4. Ratio P/U.S.	0.21–0.28	0.53	
(Data from establishment surveys)			
Portugal			
5. All sectors	4.3	3.0	1.4
6. Manufacturing	4.0	2.9	1.4
United States			
7. All sectors	17.8–23.0	7.9	2.3–3.9

Notes: All numbers: Percentage of employment, unless otherwise indicated. Averages over the relevant period.
Lines 1 to 4. Workers outflows from household surveys, job destruction from firm surveys.
Line 1. Worker outflows, from INE household survey, 1993:2 to 1996:4. All workers.
Line 2. Same as line 1, but excludes public employees, the self-employed, and private household employees. Job destruction, constructed as in line 6 of Table 3, but for 1993:2 to 1995:4.
Line 3. Worker outflows, from CPS, 1968:1 to 1986:5, adjusted in Blanchard and Diamond (1990). The range reflects upper and lower bounds on the estimates. Job destruction, constructed as in line 7 of Table 3.
Line 5. Worker outflows and job destruction from *Employment Survey*, 1991:1 to 1995:4 (the numbers do not include worker outflows and job destruction due to exit of firms).
Line 6. Same as line 5, for manufacturing only.
Line 7. Worker outflows and job destruction, as constructed by Anderson and Meyer (1994) (see text).

period, employment-to-employment movements were not recorded in the CPS, so that the estimates of employment-to-employment flows are estimates based on retrospective information from workers; the range of values reported in line 3 for worker flows from employment in the United States reflects the range of estimates in Blanchard and Diamond.[8] The other is whether, for the pur-

[8] Since 1994, a new question in the CPS allows computation of employment-to-employment movements. The series of employment-to-employment movements from 1994:1 to 1996:12 has been constructed by Hoyt Bleakley, in unpublished work at the Federal Reserve Bank of Boston.

poses of comparison between the two countries, we should compare (the raw) Portuguese numbers to the raw U.S. flows or to the U.S. flows adjusted by Abowd and Zellner for spurious transitions. To the extent that many spurious transitions in monthly estimates are likely to be reversed in the following month, we believe that the problem of spurious transitions is likely to be more serious with cumulated monthly transitions than with quarterly transitions, and thus that it is better to add the Abowd-Zellner adjusted than the raw series.

The numbers for job destruction reported in column 2 are constructed in the same way as in Table 3, but for the period closest to that used to measure worker flows (for Portugal, 1993:2 to 1995:4). The last column gives the ratio of worker outflows to job destruction in each case.

Lines 1 to 4 yield one main conclusion: *Worker flows (as a proportion of employment) stand in Portugal at 21 to 28 percent of U.S. levels.*

A comparison of worker flows with job destruction shows that this comes from low job flows (which we documented in the previous section) and from low worker flows given job flows: Worker outflows in Portugal barely exceed job destruction. The ratio of worker outflows to quarterly job destruction is only 1.1. In contrast, the ratio of worker outflows to quarterly job destruction in the United States ranges from 1.5 to 1.9.

One problem, however, with the comparison of worker flows and job destruction in lines 1 to 3 is that the numbers for worker and job flows come from different sources. A more reliable set of estimates for *worker flows relative to job flows* in Portugal can be obtained by relying on a common source, namely the *Employment Survey*. Quarterly worker outflows from employment, as well as job destruction series, can be constructed for the period 1991:1 to 1995:4 (recall, however, that these numbers do not include job destruction and worker outflows due

The raw series, i.e., not corrected for potential measurement error bias, implies a ratio of monthly employment-to-employment flows to initial employment of about 2.5 percent for the period, higher than the mean upper bound of the range estimated by Blanchard and Diamond for the earlier period 1968–1986, namely 1.6 percent. We have not tried to reconcile these numbers here.

TABLE 5—QUARTERLY WORKER OUTFLOWS BY DESTINATION, PORTUGAL AND THE UNITED STATES

	Flows from employment to:			Sum	Ratio
	Unemployment	Inactivity	Employment		
Portugal					
1. All workers	1.0	1.0	1.0	3.0	0.33
2. Excluding public employees	1.6	1.1	1.3	4.0	0.40
United States					
3.	3.9	4.8	2.4–5.4	11.1–14.1	0.28–0.35

Notes: All numbers: Percentage of employment. Averages over the period.
  Column 4. Sum: sum of flows from employment to unemployment, inactivity, employment.
  Column 5. Ratio: ratio of flows from employment to unemployment to total flows.
  Line 1. Portugal. From INE household survey, 1993:2 to 1996:4.
  Line 2. Same, excluding public employees, the self-employed, and private household employees.
  Line 3. From CPS, 1968:1 to 1986:5, as adjusted in Blanchard and Diamond (1990), monthly numbers multiplied by 3.

to exit of firms). The mean values of the series for all sectors, and for manufacturing firms only, are given in lines 5 and 6.

No comparable data set exists for the United States. In line 7, we give—with some trepidation—the results of the Anderson-Meyer (1994) study of worker flows and job flows based on unemployment-insurance records. The trepidation comes from the numerous differences in the nature of the data sets in the Portuguese and the U.S. studies, and from the fact that the Anderson-Meyer estimates of worker flows are high compared to other estimates for the United States. Line 7 gives two numbers for worker flows. The second number in each case is the original Anderson-Meyer estimate; the first number gives the estimate subtracting the largest estimated bias according to Anderson and Meyer, namely 5.2 percent.

Lines 5 to 7 yield one main conclusion. The ratio of worker flows to job flows in Portugal is a bit higher in lines 5 or 6 than in line 2, around 1.4 rather than 1.1. But it is much lower than the range of 2.3 to 2.9 implied by the Anderson-Meyer results for the U.S. ratio.

One interpretation of these facts—which will be useful below—is in terms of layoffs and quits. Job destruction is not necessarily associated with layoffs: Firms may rely partly on quits to decrease employment. Worker outflows in excess of job destruction are not necessarily associated with quits: Firms may lay off a worker for cause, and replace him with another worker. Yet, thinking of job destruction primarily as layoffs, and worker outflows in excess of job destruction as quits, is probably not mis-

leading. In these terms, our conclusions so far are that not only layoffs are lower in Portugal, but so are quits.

The third potential factor behind the differences in flows between Portugal and the United States listed in the introduction was low flows through unemployment relative to total worker outflows. From line 4, the ratio of worker flows out of employment in Portugal relative to the United States (both normalized by employment) is between 0.2 and 0.3. This ratio is roughly equal to the ratio of flows into unemployment (both normalized by employment) between the two countries. Thus, it does not look as if this third factor plays an important role. But we can get some direct evidence on this as well. Using the household surveys, we can construct, for each country, movements from employment to employment, to unemployment, or to nonparticipation, and look at the proportion of outflows from employment that goes through unemployment.

The available evidence on implied quarterly flows from employment is presented in Table 5. The numbers for Portugal are from the INE survey, for the period 1993:2 to 1996:4. Line 1 gives the flows for all workers. Line 2 excludes public employees, the self-employed, and private household employees. Line 3 gives the numbers for the United States from Blanchard and Diamond, for the period 1968:1 to 1986:1.

The numbers in the table confirm our earlier conclusions. Flows from employment to unemployment account for 33 percent of total flows from employment in Portugal, 40 percent when excluding public employees. The corresponding numbers for the United States range from 28 to 35 percent. The proportions of flows from employment going through unemployment thus appear similar across the two countries.[9]

III. An Interpretation Based on Employment Protection

Our empirical findings are easy to summarize: Both layoffs and quits are much lower in Portugal than in the United States, leading to lower flows in general, and lower flows in and out of unemployment in particular. But, because mean unemployment duration is much longer in Portugal than in the United States, both countries have roughly similar unemployment rates.

While there are surely many factors at work, a natural explanation for these differences is the high degree of employment protection in Portugal relative to the United States:

- Employment protection, which is actually enshrined in Article 53 of the Portuguese Constitution, is very high in Portugal. The rules and costs of employment protection are described in Olympia Bover et al. (2000). In short, the legislation on collective dismissals imposes a long, complex, and costly process on employers. The OECD has consistently ranked Portugal as the country with the highest degree of employment protection among OECD countries.[10] Other rankings (for example, Bertola [1990]) also put Portugal at or close to the top. The United States, when included, is always at the bottom.[11]
- Differences in employment protection naturally deliver the observed differences between the two countries. Higher employment protection directly leads to lower layoffs. Be-

cause it increases the costs of firms while, at the same time, strengthening the bargaining power of workers, higher employment protection also naturally generates longer unemployment duration: Longer duration, and therefore more painful unemployment, is the mechanism through which the demands of workers are reconciled with the realities of lower feasible wages. And because quits depend on the state of the labor market, longer unemployment duration lowers quits.

The purpose of the model we present in this section is to formalize this last argument; to show the different effects at work; to explore, through a rough calibration, whether differences in employment protection can explain the differences between the two labor markets; and finally, to use the calibrated model to look at the potential output and welfare effects of employment protection.[12]

A. Assumptions

The economy is composed of workers and jobs. The labor force—the number of workers—is equal to 1. Workers are either employed or unemployed. The number of unemployed—equivalently the unemployment rate—is equal to u. The number of jobs is determined endogenously by a zero profit condition. Firms can create jobs at cost k.

The Churning Process.—To produce a positive level of output, a job must be matched with a worker. The match then produces output level $y \geq 0$, and delivers utility of work $z \leq 0$. Churning comes from shocks to y and shocks to z:

- All matches start with output level $\bar{y}$. The level of output then changes according to a Poisson process with arrival rate λ. Each time

---

[9] To the extent that they extend to other countries, these results shed doubt on the conjecture by Tito Boeri (1999) that the low flows through unemployment in Europe hide high job-to-job movements.

[10] See the *OECD Jobs Study* (1994) for the 1980's, and the *OECD Employment Outlook* (1999) for the 1980's and the 1990's.

[11] Other labor-market institutions look more similar across the two countries. For example, unemployment benefits used to be very low in Portugal; while they have increased, they are still modest by European standards. For more on Portuguese labor-market institutions, see Bover et al. (2000).

[12] The model is in the tradition of flow models with endogenous destruction, following Dale T. Mortensen and Christopher A. Pissarides (1994). It builds directly on Blanchard (1997) (which did not include endogenous quits). It is also a close cousin to one of the extensions sketched in Mortensen and Pissarides (1999); but that paper does not offer a full characterization of the equilibrium or of the effects of employment protection.

output changes, the new level of output y is drawn from a distribution $F(y)$.

- All matches start with utility level $\bar{z}$. The level of utility then changes according to a Poisson process with arrival rate μ. Each time utility changes, the new level of utility z is drawn from a distribution $G(z)$.[13]

- The matching process has "workers waiting at the gate": Firms can hire a new worker instantaneously. Workers have to wait. They are hired with instantaneous probability x, where $x = h/u$, with h being the flow of hires, and u the number of unemployed.

Firing Costs and Bargaining.—As explained earlier, we want to capture three effects of firing costs on the equilibrium. First, that, by making layoffs more expensive, firing costs decrease the flow of layoffs. Second, that, by forcing firms to pay firing costs, or keep less productive workers, they increase the cost of production for firms. Third, that they strengthen the hand of workers in bargaining, leading to an increase in equilibrium unemployment duration. To do so, we make the following assumptions:

- Firms can terminate a match and lay off a worker at (firing) cost c; c is waste rather than a transfer to the worker.[14] This assumption naturally delivers the first two effects, the decrease in the flow of layoffs, and the increase in cost for firms.

- Workers can terminate a match and quit a job at no cost. This assumption implies that any effect of firing costs on quits is indirect, i.e., come from the equilibrium effects of firing costs on the labor-market prospects of workers, were they to quit their current job.

- Wages are determined by Nash bargaining between workers and firms. Bargaining takes

place once, at the instant after the firm has hired the worker.

The assumption that the firm has to pay cost c if it does not want to keep the worker it just hired, implies that firing costs increase the bargaining power of workers, one of the effects we want to capture.

The assumption that the wage is set for the duration of the match and is not contingent on the realizations of either y or z yields a clear distinction between quits (separations initiated by a worker, and for which the firm does not have to pay the firing cost) and layoffs (separations initiated by a firm, and for which the firm has to pay the firing cost).

Given the earlier assumption that all matches look the same *ex ante*, this assumption also implies that all matches have the same wage, w, simplifying the analytics below.

In short, these assumptions imply that there are two sources of flows in the economy, shocks to productivity, which lead to layoffs, and shocks to utility of work, which lead to quits. Firms that lay off a worker face a financial cost, but can hire a new worker right away. By contrast, workers who quit face no direct cost, but have to wait to be hired by another firm. This is the asymmetry between workers and firms (quits and layoffs) in the model.

The structure of the model implies that the (steady-state) equilibrium in this economy is characterized by:

- A critical level of output y^* below which firms lay off a worker, and hire another one. This determines the flow of layoffs, $\lambda F(y^*)$.
- A critical level of utility z^* below which workers quit a job, and look for another one. This determines the flow of quits, $\mu G(z^*)$.
- A wage w such that firms make zero expected pure profit when creating a job (call it the feasible wage).
- An exit rate from unemployment, x (inversely, an expected unemployment duration $1/x$) such that the wage set in bargaining is equal to the feasible wage.

B. *Value Equations*

To characterize the equilibrium, one must first derive the relevant value equations for firms and workers.

---

[13] These two independently and identically distributed (i.i.d.) assumptions lead to a simple characterization of the equilibrium. They prevent us, however, from capturing the difference between relative annual and relative quarterly flows between Portugal and the United States discussed earlier. To do so would require having shocks with both permanent and transitory components.

[14] The equilibrium implications of thinking about firing costs as transfers to workers or as waste have been explored by others. See, for example, Edward Lazear (1990). What is important for our purposes is that at least some proportion of firing costs is waste.

198   THE AMERICAN ECONOMIC REVIEW   MARCH 2001

Let $V(y)$ be the value for a firm of a match with current output equal to y. $V(y)$ satisfies:

$$rV(y) = (y - w)$$

$$+ \lambda F(y^*)(V(\bar{y}) - V(y) - c)$$

$$+ \lambda \int_{y^*}^{\infty} (V(y') - V(y)) \, dF(y')$$

$$+ \mu G(z^*)(V(\bar{y}) - V(y)).$$

The term on the right on the first line is current profit. The term on the second line captures what happens if a sufficiently bad output shock takes place and the worker is laid off. The term on the third line captures what happens if an output shock takes place but the firm keeps the worker. The term on the fourth line captures what happens if a sufficiently bad utility shock takes place and the worker quits. (Note that if the worker is hit with a utility shock which does not trigger a quit, nothing changes from the point of view of the firm.)

Let $V_e(z)$ and V_u be the values for a worker of being employed with level of utility z, and being unemployed, respectively. $V_e(z)$ satisfies:

$$rV_e(z) = (w + z) + \lambda F(y^*)(V_u - V_e(z))$$

$$+ \mu G(z^*)(V_u - V_e(z))$$

$$+ \mu \int_{z^*}^{0} (V_e(z') - V_e(z)) \, dG(z').$$

The first term on the right captures current net income (the wage plus the current utility of work—which is nonpositive). The second term captures what happens if a sufficiently bad output shock takes place and the worker is laid off. The third term captures what happens if a sufficiently bad utility shock takes place and the worker quits. The fourth term captures what happens if a utility shock takes place but the worker decides not to quit.
V_u is given by:

$$rV_u = x(V_e(\bar{z}) - V_u).$$

For notational simplicity, there is no utility of leisure and no unemployment benefit. Current net income when unemployed is thus equal to zero. The instantaneous probability of being hired when unemployed is equal to x. All new matches start with value $V_e(\bar{z})$.

C. *The Equilibrium*

We can now derive the four relations between y^*, z^*, w, and x that characterize the equilibrium.

(i) *The critical level of output y^* below which firms lay off the worker and hire another worker must satisfy:*

$$V(y^*) = V(\bar{y}) - c.$$

Using the equation for $V(y)$ and solving gives:

$$(1) \qquad y^* = \bar{y} - c(r + \lambda + \mu G(z^*)).$$

If c is positive, the critical level of output is lower than $\bar{y}$, the level associated with a new match. The higher the firing cost, the lower the critical level of output at which firms lay off a worker, the lower the layoff rate.[15]

(ii) *The critical level of utility z^* below which a worker decides to quit and become unemployed must satisfy:*

$$V_e(z^*) = V_u.$$

Using the relations for $V_e(\cdot)$ and V_u gives an implicit characterization of z^*:

$$(2) \qquad w + z^* + \frac{\mu}{r + \lambda F(y^*) + \mu}$$

$$\times \int_{z^*}^{0} (z' - z^*) \, dG(z')$$

$$= x \, \frac{\bar{z} - z^*}{r + \lambda F(y^*) + \mu}.$$

---

[15] There is an interesting interaction between z^* and y^*: A higher value of z^*, which implies a higher quit rate $\mu G(z^*)$ leads to a lower value of y^*. Equivalently, a higher quit rate leads to a lower layoff rate: If the worker is likely to quit, the firm may decide to take the chance that he will leave on his own, in which case the firm will avoid paying the firing cost. This effect is quantitatively small in the calibration below. It would be larger in a model in which firms were collections of jobs, and workers could be reallocated to other jobs within the firm.

The left side of the equation gives the annuity value of being in a match with level of utility z^*, $rV_e(z^*)$. The right side gives the annuity value of quitting and becoming unemployed, rV_u. By the definition of z^*, the two sides must be equal.

To get a better sense of what determines z^*, focus on the effect of labor-market conditions, captured by x, on z^*.

Suppose first that workers can get a new job right away if they become unemployed, that $x = \infty$. Then, to maintain equality, the fraction on the right side must be equal to zero. This in turn implies $z^* = \bar{z}$: Workers will not stay unless they get what they could get in a new match, i.e., $\bar{z}$.

As x decreases from infinity, z^* decreases: Workers are willing to stay even if the utility from the current job is lower than the utility in a new match, and so the quit rate falls. The worse the labor-market conditions, the lower the critical level of utility z^*, the smaller the quit rate.

If $x = 0$, so workers have no chance of getting another job when unemployed, the right side of the equation is equal to zero. Workers stay in a job if the annuity value of disutility is less than the wage. If, in addition, $\mu = 0$, then workers stay if and only if $w + z \geq 0$, if current net income is nonnegative. If $\mu > 0$, $w + z^* < 0$: Workers may stay even if current net income is negative, because of the option value associated with a better utility draw in the future.

(iii) *The feasible wage*, the wage that satisfies the zero pure-profit condition is given by:

$$V(\bar{y}) = k$$

Using the equation for $V(\cdot)$ and solving gives the feasible wage:

(3)

$$w = (\bar{y} - rk)$$

$$+ \frac{\lambda}{r + \lambda + \mu G(z^*)} \int_{y^*}^{\infty} (y' - \bar{y}) \, dF(y')$$

$$- \lambda F(y^*)c.$$

The first two terms on the right give the annuity value of output associated with a new job. The first term is the initial level of output, net of the capital cost. The second term is the expected present value of future output. The third term reflects the direct effect of the firing cost on cost (there are also indirect effects, which work through the effect of c on y^* and on z^*).

(iv) *The bargained wage.* Symmetric Nash bargaining implies:

$$V_e(\bar{z}) - V_u = V(\bar{y}) - (V(\bar{y}) - c).$$

The left side gives the surplus to a worker of being in a new match, the difference between the value of being employed in a match with current utility level $\bar{z}$, and the value of being unemployed. The right side gives the surplus to the firm of being a new match, with current output level $\bar{y}$. The first term gives the value of keeping the current worker. The second term gives the value associated with hiring a new worker (at the same level of output $\bar{y}$), minus the cost of laying off the current worker c. This equation simplifies to:

$$V_e(\bar{z}) - V_u = c.$$

From the equations for $V_e(\cdot)$ and V_u, the surplus to the worker of being in a match with current output $\bar{y}$, $(V_e(\bar{z}) - V_u)$ satisfies:

$$r(V_e(\bar{z}) - V_u)$$

$$= (w + \bar{z}) + \lambda F(y^*)(V_u - V_e(\bar{z}))$$

$$+ \mu G(z^*)(V_u - V_e(\bar{z}))$$

$$+ \frac{\mu}{(r + \lambda F(y^*) + \mu)}$$

$$\times \int_{z^*}^{0} (z' - \bar{z}) \, dG(z')$$

$$- x(V_e(\bar{z}) - V_u).$$

The first term on the right gives the current flow surplus from a match with utility $\bar{z}$. The second term captures the fact that a bad output draw leads to a layoff. The third term captures the fact that a bad utility draw leads to a quit. The fourth captures what happens if the utility draw does not lead to a quit. The fifth term reflects the probability of finding a new job if unemployed.

Solving for $(V_e(\bar{z}) - V_u)$ and replacing in the Nash bargaining condition gives the bargained wage:

$$(4) \quad w + \bar{z} + \frac{\mu}{(r + \lambda F(y^*) + \mu)}$$

$$\times \int_{z^*}^{0} (z' - \bar{z}) \, dG(z')$$

$$= c(r + \lambda F(y^*) + \mu G(z^*) + x).$$

The important aspect of this relation for our purposes is the direct effect of c on w. For given y^*, z^*, and exit rate x, an increase in c leads to an increase in w: A higher value of the firing cost increases the bargaining power of workers.

In equilibrium, the wage set in bargaining [equation (4)] must be equal to the feasible wage [equation (3)]. This implicitly defines the equilibrium exit rate, x, or its inverse, unemployment duration $(1/x)$.

The system of equations (1) to (4) characterize the equilibrium values of y^*, z^*, w, and x. Layoffs and quits are then given by $\lambda F(y^*)$ and $\mu G(z^*)$, respectively. Duration is given by $(1/x)$. The unemployment rate is given by flows times duration, i.e., $(\lambda F(y^*) + \mu G(z^*))/x$.

Further analytical characterization is cumbersome except in the case where there are no quits—in that case, the system is recursive. We start with that case, and then turn to the general case using calibration.

D. Equilibrium with no Quits

Assume that μ is equal to zero, so the disutility of work is constant and there are no quits. The system is then recursive:

- From equation (1), the critical level of output y^* is given by:

$$(1') \quad y^* = \bar{y} - c(r + \lambda).$$

The higher the firing cost, the lower the critical level of output. The layoff rate is equal to $\lambda F(y^*)$. So, from equation (1'), the effect of the firing cost on the layoff rate is given by:

$$(1'') \quad d \text{ layoff rate} = -\lambda(r + \lambda) f(y^*) \, dc.$$

The higher the firing cost, the lower the layoff rate.

- From equation (3), the feasible wage w depends on c and y^*:

$$(3') \quad w = (\bar{y} - rk)$$

$$+ \frac{\lambda}{r + \lambda} \int_{y^*}^{\infty} (y' - \bar{y}) \, dF(y')$$

$$- \lambda F(y^*)c.$$

Differentiating with respect to c, taking into account the effect of c on y^*, gives:

$$(3'') \quad dw = -\lambda F(y^*) \, dc.$$

The feasible wage is a decreasing function of the firing cost. A higher firing cost decreases average productivity and increases the cost of labor through the payment of firing costs; both effects decrease the feasible wage.

- From equation (4), the bargained wage depends on c, y^*, and x:

$$(4') \quad w + \bar{z} = (r + x + \lambda F(y^*))c.$$

From equation (3'), a higher firing cost decreases the feasible wage. From equation (4') for given labor-market conditions, a higher firing cost increases the bargained wage.[16] Thus, to reconcile the bargained wage with what firms

---

[16] This requires that $\lambda F(y^*)$ not decrease too much when c increases, or more precisely, that the following condition holds: $(r + x + \lambda F(y^*)) - c\lambda(r + \lambda) f(y^*) > 0$. For plausible choices of the parameters, x, the exit rate from unemployment, is much larger than the other terms in the expression, and the condition holds.

can afford to pay, labor-market conditions must worsen: The exit rate from unemployment, x, must be lower. Equivalently, its inverse, unemployment duration, must increase.

In steady state, the unemployment rate is equal to the flow of layoffs times unemployment duration. As we have just seen, firing costs decrease layoffs but increase duration. Which of the two effects dominate is ambiguous.

Starting from a zero firing cost, we know that unemployment—which, in our model, is equal to zero absent firing costs—will increase. But, starting from a positive firing cost, the effect becomes ambiguous. Equations $(1')$ and $(3')$ show that what matters for the effect on layoffs is the *density function* of output shocks at the critical level of output, but what matters for the effect on the feasible wage, and by implication for the effect on unemployment duration, depends on the *cumulative distribution* of output shocks up to the critical level.

Depending on the shape of the distribution function, it is easy to construct cases where unemployment goes one way or the other. Take for example the case where adverse output shocks decrease output to zero. In this case, over some range, the firing cost will have no effect on layoffs, but will still both decrease the feasible wage and increase the bargained wage for given labor-market conditions, leading to an increase in equilibrium unemployment duration. Unemployment will then unambiguously increase. If, instead, the density function is very large at the initial critical level of output, a small increase in the firing cost will lead to a large decline in layoffs, leading to a decrease in unemployment.

E. *Equilibrium with Quits*

In the presence of endogenous quits, the system characterizing equilibrium is no longer recursive. A rough calibration, however, gives a sense of the effects at work, and of their potential magnitude.

The model is too crude in too many ways to allow convincing calibration. To mention the most obvious problems: Many flows from employment, especially in the United States, are either directly to employment or to nonparticipation; in our model, all flows are to unemploy-

ment. This means that we cannot match at the same time data on outflows from employment, on unemployment duration, and on the unemployment rate. (In our model, the unemployment rate is the product of the first two; in reality, it is the product of the flows to unemployment times duration, and is smaller.) Our model has only match-specific, i.i.d. shocks to both output and utility. The reality is one of partly match-specific, partly job-specific shocks, and of likely serial correlation in both. So we proceed as follows.

First, we summarize the evidence from our empirical work by a set of stylized numbers for layoffs, quits, and unemployment duration, for both the United States and Portugal. We interpret job flows as layoffs, worker flows minus job flows as quits. We take the unemployment rate to be the product of unemployment duration times total flows from employment, leading to constructed unemployment rates larger than the official unemployment rates. These stylized numbers are summarized in the first two columns of Table 6:

- Total monthly outflows from employment for the United States are equal to 3 percent, average unemployment duration to three months, leading to an unemployment rate of 9 percent.
- Total monthly outflows for Portugal are equal to 1 percent, average unemployment duration to nine months, also leading to an unemployment rate of 9 percent.

Second, we choose parameters and distributions to roughly fit these stylized facts, imposing that, except for the firing cost c, parameters and distributions be the same across the two countries. The specific assumptions, very much obtained by a process of trial and error (searching in particular over the mean and standard deviations for the two distributions), are as follows.

- The interest rate, r, is 1 percent monthly. Capital, k, is equal to annual output $\bar{y}$, so 12 times monthly output.
- Initial output $\bar{y}$ is equal to 1. This is simply a normalization. The monthly probability of an output shock is 5 percent. As for most parameter values the critical level of

202 THE AMERICAN ECONOMIC REVIEW MARCH 2001

TABLE 6—STYLIZED NUMBERS FOR U.S. AND PORTUGAL, AND SIMULATION RESULTS, FOR LOW AND HIGH FIRING COSTS

	Stylized		Simulation	
	United States	Portugal	United States $(c = \bar{y})$	Portugal $(c = 5\bar{y})$
Layoff rate	2.0	1.0	2.3	0.8
Quit rate	1.0	0.0	1.6	0.2
Exit rate	0.33	0.11	0.5	0.08
Duration	3.0	9.0	2.0	13.0
Unemployment rate	9.0	9.0	8.0	9.2
Total output			1.12	0.97
Total net output			0.74	0.56

Notes: All flows are in percent per month. In the two simulation columns, layoffs are $\lambda F(y^*)$, quits are $\mu G(z^*)$, the exit rate is x, unemployment duration is $1/x$, the unemployment rate is $(\lambda F(y^*) + \mu G(z^*))/x$, total output is $E(y|y > y^*)(1 - u)$, total net output is $(E(y|y > y^*) - E(z|z > z^*))(1 - u)$.

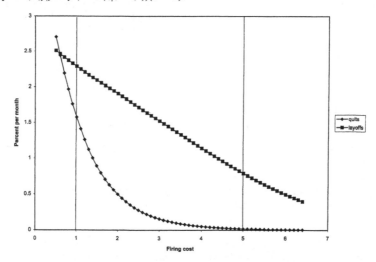

FIGURE 1. QUITS AND LAYOFFS VERSUS FIRING COSTS

output, y^*, is below the median; this implies a layoff rate below 2.5 percent per month. The distribution $F(y)$ is lognormal, with mean equal to $\bar{y} = 1$, and standard deviation equal to 30 percent.

- Initial utility $\bar{z}$ is equal to -0.45. The monthly probability of a utility shock is 10 percent. As for most parameter values, the critical level of utility is far below the median; this implies a quit rate far below 5 percent. The distribution of $-z$, $G(-z)$ is lognormal, with mean equal to $-\bar{z}$ = 0.45, and standard deviation equal to 30 percent.

We then characterize the equilibrium for values of c ranging from 1—one month of (initial)

output—to 6—six months of (initial) output. We think of the United States as being at the low end of this range, say around 1, and Portugal being at the high end of the range, say around 5.

The main results are shown in Figures 1 to 3. The values of the main variables for $c = 1$ and $c = 5$ are given in columns 3 and 4 of Table 6.

Figure 1 plots the layoff rate and the quit rate against the firing cost. Over the range of firing costs we consider, layoffs decrease roughly linearly with the firing cost, from 2.3 percent of the labor force per month for $c = 1$, to 0.8 percent for $c = 5$, reflecting the steady decrease of y^* as c increases. Quits decrease very rapidly. The reason is that they

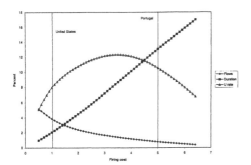

FIGURE 2. FLOWS, DURATION, AND UNEMPLOYMENT RATE

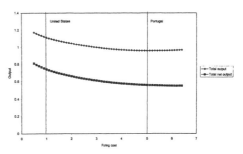

FIGURE 3. TOTAL OUTPUT AND TOTAL NET OUTPUT

depend primarily on unemployment duration, which (as shown in Figure 2) increases rapidly with the firing cost. Quits, which are equal to 1.6 percent for $c = 1$, are equal to only 0.2 percent for $c = 5$. Despite the fact that quits are not subject to firing costs, labor-market conditions are sufficiently bad that workers stay even in jobs they very much dislike.

Figure 2 plots flows, unemployment duration, and the unemployment rate against the firing cost. The behavior of flows follows from Figure 1: The sum of layoffs plus quits decreases from 3.9 percent for $c = 1$ to 0.8 percent for $c = 5$. Duration increases nearly linearly with the firing cost, going from two months when $c = 1$ to 13 months for $c = 5$. The evolution of flows and duration imply a hump-shaped evolution of the unemployment rate as a function of the firing cost. The unemployment rate increases from 8 percent for $c = 1$, to 12 percent for $c = 3.5$, and then decreases, reaching 9 percent for $c = 5$, and 8 percent for $c = 6$.[17]

The model formalizes the idea that two labor markets may have the same unemployment rate, yet be very different: The market with a high firing cost is sclerotic, with lower average productivity, and lower average utility. Indeed, the calibrated model allows us to get a sense of the loss in output and welfare which might come from firing costs. Figure 3 plots the behavior of

total output, i.e., average output per worker times one minus the unemployment rate, and total net output, i.e., average output minus the average disutility of work, times one minus the unemployment rate. Total output decreases from 1.12 for $c = 1$ to 0.97 for $c = 5$, a decrease of about 14 percent. Total net output decreases from 0.74 for $c = 1$ to 0.56 for $c = 5$, a decrease of about 27 percent. These numbers, rather than the unemployment rate, show the economic costs of firing costs. They suggest that the low Portuguese unemployment rate may hide large output and welfare costs.

IV. A Glimpse at Other Countries

The way to strengthen our argument that employment protection explains much of the difference between the Portuguese and the U.S. labor markets would be to compute job and worker flows for a larger group of countries. This would, however, require doing for each country the type of empirical work we have done for Portugal, and this will have to wait.

A simple exercise can however be carried out—that of looking, across countries, at the relation between, on the one hand, flows through unemployment, unemployment duration, and the unemployment rate and, on the other hand, the degree of employment protection. The results of this exercise are presented in Figure 4, which can be thought as plotting the empirical cross-country counterparts to the three curves in Figure 2.

Monthly flows into unemployment are constructed as the average number of workers unemployed for less than one month, for the period 1985–1994, divided by the average labor

[17] The unimodal shape of unemployment is not a general result, and depends in particular on the class of distribution functions used to generate shocks.

204   THE AMERICAN ECONOMIC REVIEW   MARCH 2001

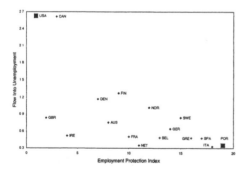

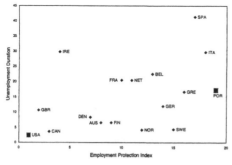

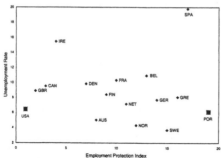

FIGURE 4. UNEMPLOYMENT AND EMPLOYMENT PROTECTION

period 1985–1994 to the flow into unemployment constructed above.

The employment protection index (EPL) is the overall index constructed by the OECD for the late 1980's (*Employment Outlook*, 1999 Tables 2–5); this index is a rank index for 19 countries, going from low to high protection. (The index is based solely on institutional aspects of employment protection, not on labor-market outcomes.) The value of the index goes from 1 for the United States to 19 for Portugal (17 for Spain, 18 for Italy).

The top part of the figure shows a clear negative relation between the flow into unemployment (as a ratio to the labor force) and employment protection.[19] (The points corresponding to Portugal and the United States are the foremost right and foremost left points, respectively.) The middle figure shows a clear positive relation between unemployment duration and employment protection. The bottom figure shows roughly no relation between the unemployment rate and employment protection.

Regressions of the log flow, log duration, and the log unemployment rate on the employment protection index give:[20]

$$\log \text{flow} = 0.49 - 0.076 \text{ EPL}$$
$$\bar{R}^2 = 0.46 \quad (\text{sd} = 0.020)$$

$$\log \text{duration} = 1.64 + 0.073 \text{ EPL}$$
$$\bar{R}^2 = 0.21 \quad (\text{sd} = 0.033)$$

$$\log u \text{ rate} = 2.14 - 0.003 \text{ EPL}$$
$$\bar{R}^2 = -0.06 \quad (\text{sd} = 0.015).$$

Thus, an increase in employment protection leads to a decrease in flows, and a decrease in duration. But the two effects cancel each other when looking at unemployment.

force during the same period, for each OECD country. The source for these data is the OECD duration database.[18]

Unemployment duration is constructed as the ratio of the average unemployment rate for the

---

[18] The numbers for Finland in this database are for the number of workers unemployed two months or less. We simply divide this number by 2.

[19] This negative correlation is also shown in Table 1 in Boeri (1999).

[20] The results using levels are very similar. We report regressions using logs because the log of the unemployment rate is the sum of log flow and log duration, making it easy to decompose the two effects of employment protection on the unemployment rate.

V. Conclusions

Looking at the Portuguese and U.S. labor markets, we have shown how a similar unemployment rate can hide profoundly different labor markets.

We have shown how unemployment in Portugal reflects much lower flows and much higher duration than in the United States. We have shown how these flows, in turn, reflect much lower job flows, and much lower worker flows given job flows in Portugal than in the United States.

We have argued theoretically that these differences may come from much higher employment protection in Portugal than in the United States. We have shown how, looking across countries, higher employment protection appears to be associated with lower flows through unemployment and higher unemployment duration.

Our conclusions raise in turn a number of issues. There are at least two we want to explore further.

The first is the output and welfare costs of employment protection in Portugal. One overly strong way of stating our results is that employment protection eliminates three out of every four desirable separations in Portugal.[21] One would expect, and our calibration suggests, that such reduction might have large efficiency effects on output and welfare. At the same time, one of our empirical results is that employment protection appears to have much less effect on year-to-year than on quarter-to-quarter movements in firm-level employment. If this is the case, can the smoothing of intra-year variations have a very large effect on efficiency?

The second is the "Spain versus Portugal" puzzle [see Blanchard and Juan F. Jimeno (1995)]. Given that both Spain and Portugal have high employment protection (although the large increase in the proportion of workers under fixed-term contracts in Spain, now up to 35 percent compared to 10 to 15 percent in Portugal, is rapidly changing the nature of that labor

market), why are the unemployment rate outcomes so different? (In Figure 4, Spain is the country with the highest unemployment duration, and the third highest EPL value.) Our model suggests that any outcome is possible depending on the distribution of shocks; but this is not a very appealing answer. Differences in both union power and in unemployment insurance may hold some of the keys. The evidence points to lower wage dispersion, and larger returns to tenure in Spain than in Portugal, typically two telltale signs of union power; representation rules appear more favorable to insiders in Spain than in Portugal. Evidence from Sonsoles Castillo et al. (1997) suggests that the relative consumption level of the unemployed is lower in Portugal than in Spain. This could explain the higher unemployment duration in Spain. Another tentative explanation is that high employment protection may affect not only the level and the nature of the equilibrium rate of unemployment, but also its dynamics. If this is the case, higher unemployment in Spain than in Portugal may reflect in part the effects of a different set of shocks over the last 20 years. This, however, remains to be shown, both theoretically and empirically.[22]

Appendix

This Appendix gives a brief description of the three Portuguese data sources used in our study.

A. *The Quadros de Pessoal Survey*

The first data set, *Quadros de Pessoal,* is based on an annual survey conducted by the Portuguese Ministry of Employment; it covers all establishments with wage earners. Answering this survey is mandatory, and the survey collects detailed information on both the wages and the characteristics of each individual employee (regular wages, subsidies, hours worked, date of admission, age, gender, schooling, qualification level, part-time status, occupation, type of collective agreement, promotions, etc.) as well as basic information about the establishment and the firm (size, ownership, shipments,

---

[21] There are at least three ways in which this statement is overly strong. It assumes that the reduction in flows is fully due to employment protection. It takes the United States as the natural benchmark. And it assumes that all these separations would be efficient.

[22] For a start along these lines, see Stephen Nickell (1997) and Blanchard and Justin Wolfers (2000).

SIC codes, location, etc.). Each year the survey collects information on around 140,000 establishments and 2 million individuals.

By law, this information is made available to every worker in a public space of the establishment. This requirement facilitates the work of the services of the Ministry of Employment that monitor compliance of firms with the law (e.g., illegal work). The administrative nature of the data and its public availability imply a high degree of coverage and reliability.

The Ministry of Employment has been conducting this survey since 1982 and the employment and wage data refer to the month of March for the period 1982–1993 and the month of October since 1994. In our analysis we use information for the period 1982 until 1995. The raw data that we use is organized in three data sets corresponding to the level of aggregation of the information: individual level, establishment level, and firm level.

B. *Inquérito ao Emprego Estruturado (Employment Survey)*

The second data set, *Inquérito ao Emprego Estruturado* (*Employment Survey*), is a quarterly survey of establishments also run by the Portuguese Ministry of Employment, for the purpose of collecting information about job and worker turnover. It also contains detailed information on the composition of the establishment workforce: employment by age, gender, type of contract (open-ended, fixed-term, or temporary contracts), and part-time status.

The sample is designed to include all establishments with 100 or more employees, and establishments with 1–99 employees with probabilities that increase with the size of the establishment (according to five size groups). We use these probabilities to properly weigh each plant in order to obtain a representative sample. Each year the sample is obtained from the *Quadros de Pessoal* survey and it covers all firms with wage earners in all sectors of the economy with the exception of agriculture and fishery. Since it is a survey of firms, it does not include the public administration. On average, for the period 1991–1995, the *Employment Survey* surveyed approximately 6,000 establishments each quarter.

A strength of this data set is the fact that establishments are asked about gross worker flows. That is, the survey contains information on the number of workers that either exited or joined the establishment over the course of the previous quarter. In addition, such flows can be decomposed according to a number of reasons: job creation, job substitution, return from a temporary exit, job destruction, voluntary exits, and temporary exits. (Temporary exits are not temporary layoffs. There are no temporary layoffs in Portugal, despite legislation introduced in the early 1980's with the purpose of making them available to firms.)

C. *Inquérito ao Emprego (INE Household Survey)*

The third data set is a CPS-type household survey conducted by the Instituto Nacional de Estatística (INE). Every quarter the INE surveys around 40,000 individuals to obtain information about the labor market. The basic structure of the survey follows the instructions of Eurostat, making the definitions of the basic labor-market indicators identical to those in other European countries (e.g., employment, unemployment, inactivity). We had access to the raw data from the INE survey for the 1992–1996 period.

Each quarter, $\frac{1}{6}$ of the sample is rotated out. Thus, each quarter, we can compute the labor status of a worker in quarter $t - 1$ and t for $\frac{5}{6}$ of the workers in the current sample. To make sure that we were tracking the same individual, we used a number of filters beyond the ID number: the order number, age, and gender. Preliminary work on the relevance of labor status measurement error (of the type documented by Abowd and Zellner for the United States) has led us to believe that this is not a serious issue in this survey. We find negligible evidence of inconsistencies in the observed labor-market transitions. One reason is a high—18 percent—reinterview rate. Another is the lack, relative to the United States, of high frequency movements in and out of unemployment.

REFERENCES

Anderson, Patricia and Meyer, Bruce. "The Extent and Consequences of Job Turnover." *Brookings Papers on Economic Activity, Microeconomics*, 1994, pp. 177–236.

Bertola, Giuseppe. "Job Security, Employment and Wages." *European Economic Review,* June 1990, *34*(4), pp. 851–79.

Bertola, Giuseppe and Rogerson, Richard. "Institutions and Labor Reallocation." *European Economic Review,* June 1997, *41*(6), pp. 1147–71.

Blanchard, Olivier Jean. "Comments on 'Labor-Market Flexibility and Aggregate Employment Volatility,' by Hugo Hopenhayn and Antonio Cabrales." *Carnegie-Rochester Conference,* June 1997, *46,* pp. 189–228.

Blanchard, Olivier and Diamond, Peter. "The Cyclical Behavior of the Gross Flows of U.S. Workers." *Brookings Papers on Economic Activity,* 1990, (2), pp. 85–143.

Blanchard, Olivier and Jimeno, Juan, F. "Structural Unemployment: Spain versus Portugal." *American Economic Review,* May 1995 (*Papers and Proceedings*), *85*(2), pp. 212–18.

Blanchard, Olivier and Wolfers, Justin. "Shocks and Institutions in the Rise of European Unemployment: The Aggregate Evidence." *Economic Journal,* March 2000, *110*(1), pp. 1–33.

Boeri, Tito. "Enforcement of Employment Security Regulations, On-the-Job Search, and Unemployment Duration." *European Economic Review,* January 1999, *43*(1), pp. 65–89.

Bover, Olympia; Garcia-Perea, Pilar and Portugal, Pedro. "Labour Market Outliers: Lessons from Portugal and Spain." *Economic Policy,* October 2000, *31,* pp. 379–428.

Castillo, Sonsoles; Dolado, Juan and Jimeno, Juan. "The Fall in Consumption from Being Unemployed in Portugal and Spain." Mimeo, FEDEA, 1997.

Davis, Steven J.; Haltiwanger, John C. and Schuh,

Scott. *Job creation and destruction,* Cambridge, MA: MIT Press, 1996.

_____. *Data set, update to 1993.* 1997.

Foote, Christopher L. "Trend Employment Growth and the Bunching of Job Creation and Destruction." *Quarterly Journal of Economics,* August 1998, *113*(3), pp. 809–34.

Lazear, Edward. "Job Security Provisions and Employment." *Quarterly Journal of Economics,* August 1990, *105*(3), pp. 699–726.

Leonard, Jonathan S. "In the Wrong Place at the Wrong Time: The Extent of Frictional and Structural Unemployment," in Kevin Lang and Jonathan S. Leonard, eds., *Unemployment and the structure of labor markets.* New York: Blackwell, 1987, pp. 141–63.

Mortensen, Dale T. and Pissarides, Christopher A. "Job Creation and Job Destruction in the Theory of Unemployment." *Review of Economic Studies,* July 1994, *61*(3), pp. 397–415.

_____. "Job Reallocation, Employment Fluctuations, and Unemployment Differences," in John Taylor and Michael Woodford, eds, *Handbook of macroeconomics.* New York: Elsevier Science, 1999, pp. 1171–228.

Nickell, Stephen. "Unemployment and Labor Market Rigidities: Europe versus North America." *Journal of Economic Perspectives,* Summer 1997, *11*(3), pp. 55–74.

Organization for Economic Cooperation and Development (OECD). *OECD employment outlook.* Paris: OECD, 1987.

_____. *OECD jobs study.* Paris: OECD, 1994.

_____. *OECD employment outlook.* Paris: OECD, 1999.

Part III
Regulation Selected Mandates

[11]

WHAT CAN ECONOMICS CONTRIBUTE TO SOCIAL POLICY?[†]

Some Simple Economics of Mandated Benefits

By Lawrence H. Summers*

When it has been decided that universal access to a good is to be provided, governments in some cases provide it directly, as with public education and old-age benefits almost everywhere and health benefits in many countries. In other cases, governments mandate that employers provide benefits to workers or that persons obtain benefits directly themselves. Requirements that employers keep workplaces safe and provide Workman's Compensation Insurance represent a clear example. Unemployment insurance provides an interesting middle ground. While in most European countries it is financed from general revenues, in the United States, employers are required to pay for the benefits their workers receive, because unemployment insurance taxes are experience rated, albeit imperfectly.

As a general proposition, liberals rank alternative strategies in the order of public provision, mandated benefits, then no action for addressing social concerns. Conservatives have exactly the opposite preferences, ranking the alternatives no action, mandated benefits, and then public provision. With these preference patterns, it is little wonder that governments frequently turn to mandated benefits as a tool of social policy. Mandated benefits raise a host of questions, however: What determines the choices governments make? Are there differences in the real effects of mandated benefits and tax-financed programs? Are there efficiency arguments for the use of mandated benefits?

These questions played a prominent role in the recent presidential campaign, with its debates over mandated health insurance, parental leave, and plant closing notification. More generally, there has been a great deal of recent interest in mandated benefits as a tool of social policy. As Frank McArdle notes: "[There is] an intense interest in mandated benefits issues.... Most of the current inspiration consists of extending to the non-covered population valuable, extensive, and socially desirable benefits policies that many companies provide on their own or through collective bargaining" (1987, pp. *xxxiv–xxxv*). Economists have generally devoted little attention to mandated benefits— regarding them as simply disguised tax and expenditure measures. Uwe Reinhardt's reaction is probably typical: "[Just because] the fiscal flows triggered by mandate would not flow directly through the public budgets does not detract from the measure's status of a *bona fide* tax" (1987, p. 124).

This paper tries to sort out some basic analytic points that need to be kept straight in considering the economics of mandated benefit proposals. Judgments about specific policy proposals must depend on the particulars, but I find that there are important differences in the efficiency and distributional consequences of standard public provision and mandated benefit programs. Essentially, mandated benefits are like public programs financed by benefit taxes. This makes them more efficient but less equitable than standard public programs. Section I lays out some efficiency arguments favoring government intervention in private employment contracts. Section II disputes the assertion that mandated benefits are really just disguised taxes, and contrasts the effects of government-mandated benefits with taxes and public provision. Section III discusses

[†]*Discussants*: Martin S. Feldstein, Harvard University; Robert M. Solow, MIT; James Tobin, Yale University.

*Harvard University, Cambridge, MA 02138. I am grateful to Jim Hines, Larry Katz, Alan Krueger, and especially David Cutler for useful discussions.

178   *AEA PAPERS AND PROCEEDINGS*   *MAY 1989*

some problems with the use of mandated benefits.

I. Efficiency Arguments for Mandating Employee Benefits

Analysis of competitive equilibrium militates against mandating employer benefits, just as it militates against other government interventions. Imagine that employers can compensate their workers in different ways: with cash, by providing them with insurance, or by giving them consumption goods directly. If employers and employees can negotiate freely over the terms of the compensation package, they will reach a mutually efficient outcome. If a health benefit that would cost an employer $20 to provide is worth $30 to prospective employees, employers could provide the benefit and reduce the employee's salary by between $20 and $30, leaving both better off. Reasoning of this sort demonstrates that benefits will be provided up to the point where an extra $1 spent by employers on benefits is valued by employees at $1.

When is there ever a case for mandating benefits or publicly providing goods that employers could provide their workers? Most obviously, there is the paternalism, or "merit goods," argument that individuals value certain services too little. They may irrationally underestimate the probability of catastrophic health expenses, or of a child's illness that would require a sustained leave. In the pension context, this argument may be especially persuasive since individuals are likely to be especially inept at making intertemporal decisions. A closely related argument involves the idea that society cares more about equal consumption of some merit good commodities than about others.

There are at least two further rationales for mandating benefits that do not assume individual irrationality. First, there may be positive externalities associated with the good—externalities that cannot be captured by either the provider or the recipient. The most obvious example is health insurance. Society cares about preventing the spread of contagious diseases more than any individual does or would take account of. Further,

people prefer for their friends and relatives to remain healthy, yet they cannot individually subsidize health insurance for all other consumers.

Much more important is the externality that arises from society's unwillingness or inability to deny care completely to those in desperate need, even if they cannot pay. The Congressional Budget Office estimates that there are 23 million American employees without health insurance. Health insurance for this group would cost about $25 billion. Currently, these uninsured employees incur $15 billion in health care costs for which they do not pay. The costs are borne in part by physicians and other providers of health care, but most of the cost is passed on to other consumers in the form of higher insurance and medical costs.

The externality here is quite large. About 60 percent of the benefit of employer-provided health insurance accrues ultimately to neither employer nor employee. Even with the current tax subsidy to employer-provided health insurance, there might be a further case for government action.

There is an interesting relationship between the paternalism arguments and the "protect others from paying" argument for mandating benefits. Folklore has it that universities mandated pension contributions for professors because they did not want to incur the costs of dealing with imprudent and impecunious retired professors and their spouses. By mandating contributions and forcing professors to save for themselves, universities avoided the problem. Where those who do without are institutionally able to foist themselves on someone other than their employer, there is a similar efficiency argument for government action.

Externality arguments can be used to justify other mandated benefits. Since unemployment insurance is only partially experience rated, layoffs at one firm raise taxes at others, creating an efficiency case for policies that would interfere with the private layoff decision. Mandatory plant closing notification is one such policy. There is an externality case for it also insofar as layoffs have adverse consequences for communities. The externality case for parental leave is more difficult to make, though even here there is the question of whether the benefits to the child of parental leave provide some justification for public policy intervention.

There is a second, perhaps stronger, argument for government intervention in the market for fringe benefits based on adverse selection considerations, as discussed for example in Michael Rothschild and Joseph Stiglitz (1976). If employees have more information about whether they will need parental leave or face high medical bills than their employers do, then employers that provide these benefits will receive disproportionately more applications from employees who require benefits and so will lose money. The market thus discourages provision of any fringe benefits.

Suppose, for example, that for the 10 percent of the population that knows it has health problems, health insurance is worth $300 and costs $270 to provide, and for the 90 percent of the population without preexisting conditions, health insurance is worth $100 and costs $90 to provide. Assume that individuals know whether they have problems or not, but employers cannot tell healthy from unhealthy individuals. Now consider what happens if employers do not offer health insurance. Any employer offering health insurance and a salary reduction of less than $100 would attract both classes of workers and would lose money, since the average cost of insurance would be $.9·90 + .1·270 = $108. Firms could offer insurance and reduce wages by between $270 and $300. This would attract only unhealthy individuals. Even leaving aside the consideration that for productivity reasons, firms might not prefer a personnel policy that was most likely to attract unhealthy workers, it is clear that the market solution will not provide universal insurance even though all individuals are willing to pay more than it costs to insure themselves.[1]

The same argument holds in the case of other employee benefits. Workers know much

better than their employers whether they are likely to go on parental leave or become disabled. They probably also know something about whether they are likely to become enmeshed in employment disputes. This suggests that there are efficiency arguments for limiting employers ability to fire workers at will.

These two considerations suggest that it may be optimal for the government to intervene in the provision of goods that some employers provide their workers.[2] In the next section, I take up the question of the form of government provision.

II. Mandated Benefits or Public Provision

It is often asserted that mandated benefits are just hidden taxes with the same efficiency and incidence implications as taxes, so that the choice between public provision and mandated benefits should depend only on the relative efficiency with which employers and the government can provide a service. I challenge the equivalence of these methods of provision below. But even granting the equivalence, there should be at least some presumption in favor of mandated benefits. Mandated benefits preserve employers' ability to tailor arrangements to their workers and to offer more than minimum packages. This avoids what might be called the "government provision trap" discussed in the context of higher education by Sam Peltzman (1973). Suppose that the government provides universal free health care of modest quality. This will be more attractive to many than paying the costs of high-quality care themselves, even though if they had

---

[1] The point is made more vivid by considering a strategy of attracting workers by offering a superior AIDS insurance policy.

[2] An alternative argument towards the same conclusion is that in a noncompetitive labor market such as one with either efficiency wages or monopsony power, there is no assurance that efficient compensation packages will be attained. In the Shapiro-Stiglitz (1984) model, for example, where firms will seek to structure employment arrangements to maximize workers' costs of job loss rather than to maximize their utility given their costs, there is no reason to expect the provision of efficient fringe benefits. I do not stress this argument because its predictions about the details of compensation are not very clear.

to pay for all their care they would have selected high- rather than low-quality care.[3]

Another argument in favor of mandated benefits rather than public provision is that mandated provision avoids the deadweight loss of tax-financed provision. Estimates of the marginal deadweight loss from a $1 increase in taxes range from the $1.07 suggested by Charles Stuart (1984) to the $1.21 suggested by Edgar Browning (1987) to the $1.33, as in Charles Ballard et al. (1985). These figures are probably underestimates since they recognize only a few of the many distortions caused by the tax system. This suggests that there are substantial efficiency gains to accomplishing social objectives in ways other than government taxation and provision. There is also the consideration that at the present time in the United States, the nature of budgetary bargaining makes it difficult to find funds even for programs that are very widely regarded as having substantial benefit-cost ratios.

Mandated benefits do not give rise to deadweight losses as large as those that arise from government tax collections. Suppose that the government required that all employers provide a certain benefit, say a leave policy, that cost employers $.10 per employee hour to provide. What would happen? Consider first employers whose employees previously valued the benefit at more than $.10 per hour and so had a leave package greater than $.10 per hour. They would not be affected at all by the government mandate, since they were previously in compliance with the law. For employees who valued the benefit at less than $.10 an hour, they would then receive the plan, at the cost of $.10.

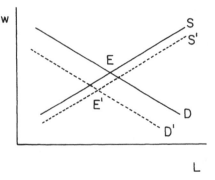

FIGURE 1. THE EFFECTS OF MANDATED BENEFITS

What would happen to the wages of those receiving the benefit? Figure 1 illustrates the answer. Requiring employers to pay for employee leaves shifts their demand curve downwards by $.10. Guaranteeing the benefit to employees shifts their supply curve downward by an amount equal to the value of the benefit. A new equilibrium level of employment and wages is reached, with lower wages and employment, but in general employment will be reduced by less than it would be with a $.10 tax.

Two special cases are instructive. First, suppose that the mandated benefit is worthless to employees. In this very special case, the change in employment and wages corresponds exactly to what would be expected from a $.10 tax on employers. Since the mandated benefit is worthless to employees, it is just like a tax from the point of view of both employers and employees. Second, consider the case where employees valuation of the policy is arbitrarily close to $.10. In this case, the mandated benefit does not affect the level of employment, the employer's total employee costs, or the employee's utility.

The general point should be clear from this example. In terms of their allocational effects on employment, mandated benefits represent a tax at a rate equal to the *difference* between the employers cost of providing the benefit and the employee's valuation

---

[3] This difficulty could in principle be avoided by public programs that partially compensated those seeking high-quality private sector care. In practice, it is hard to imagine the government contributing substantially to medical costs for veterans who do not use the VA hospital system, providing the cost of a public school education to parents who send their children to private schools, or giving rebates to the poor who choose not to take advantage of low-income housing programs.

VOL. 79 NO. 2 *WHAT CAN ECONOMICS CONTRIBUTE TO SOCIAL POLICY?* *181*

of it, *not* at a rate equal to the cost to the employer of providing the benefit.

With this in mind, contrast the effects of mandating benefits with the effects of taxing all employers and using the proceeds to finance a public parental leave program. In the latter case, employers would abandon their plans, and the government would end up paying for all parental leave. This would mean far more tax distortions than in the mandated benefits case for two reasons. First, employers and employees who were unaffected by the mandated benefit program would be taxed for the parental leave program. This creates a larger deadweight loss. Second, for those employers and employees who are affected, the tax levied is equal to the full cost of parental leave, not the difference between the employers cost and the workers' benefit.

Where is the efficiency difference between the two approaches coming from? To see the answer, suppose that the public parental leave program was exactly tied to the number of hours an employee worked in the past and to his or her wage. In this case, with rational employees, the program would not be distortionary because the extra parental leave one would get by working more hours would offset the extra tax payments. Mandated benefits have effects paralleling benefit tax-financed public programs. Without close links between taxes and benefits, that tend to be lacking in public programs, large distortions can result.

Exactly the same analysis could be carried out with respect to health insurance, but one extra complication must be recognized. Workers do not get more health insurance if they work more hours. Hence, mandating employer health insurance should not affect employees' decisions about working a marginal hour. A public program could achieve the same effect if it was financed by a lump sum tax on employees rather than on payroll or income, but such taxes are not normally contemplated. In the case of health insurance, a lump sum tax is the appropriate benefit tax, since benefits do not rise with income. If labor force participation is very inelastic, but hours of work are quite elastic,

then a mandated benefit program will involve less distortion than a tax-financed benefit program given the government's normal tax instruments.

This analysis suggests at least two possible advantages of mandated benefits over public provision of benefits. First, mandated benefits are likely to afford workers more choice. Second, they are likely to involve fewer distortions of economic activity. Why then should not all social objectives be sought through mandated benefits? I take this question up in the next section.

III. Some Potential Problems with Mandated Benefits

The most obvious problem with mandated benefits is that they only help those with jobs. Beyond the 25 million employed Americans without health insurance, another 13 million nonemployed Americans do not have health insurance. Mandated benefit programs obviously do not reach these people. There is certainly a case for public provision in situations where there is no employer who can be required to provide benefits.

A more fundamental problem comes when there are wage rigidities. Suppose, for example, that there is a binding minimum wage. In this case, wages cannot fall to offset employers' cost of providing a mandated benefit, so it is likely to create unemployment. This is a common objection to proposals for mandated health insurance, given that a large fraction of employees who are without health insurance are paid low wages. It is not clear whether this should be regarded as a problem with mandated benefits or minimum wages. Note that a payroll tax on employers directed at financing health insurance benefits publicly would have exactly the same employment displacement effects as a mandated health insurance program.

A different type of wage rigidity involves a requirement that firms pay different workers the same wage even though the cost of providing benefits differs. For example, the cost of health insurance is greater for older than for younger workers and the expected cost of parental leave is greater for women than

182 *AEA PAPERS AND PROCEEDINGS* *MAY 1989*

men. If wages could freely adjust, these differences in expected benefit costs would be offset by differences in wages. If such differences are precluded, however, there will be efficiency consequences as employers seek to hire workers with lower benefit costs. It is thus possible that mandated benefit programs can work against the interests of those who most require the benefit being offered. Publicly provided benefits do not drive a wedge between the marginal costs of hiring different workers and so do not give rise to a distortion of this kind.

Another objection to mandated benefits is that they reduce the scope for government redistribution. Consider the example of old-age benefits. Many of the arguments I have discussed could be used to support a proposal to privatize Social Security. The principal problem with this proposal is that it would make the redistribution of lifetime income that is inherent in the operation of the current Social Security system impossible. Assuming perfectly flexible markets, wages for each type of worker would fall by the amount of benefits they could expect to receive from a mandated pension; there would be no transfer from poor to rich. If the government sought to prevent redistribution by preventing wage adjustments, unemployment among those most in need would result. The nonredistributive character of mandated benefit programs is a direct consequence of the fact that, as with benefit taxes, workers pay directly for the benefits they receive.

A different sort of objection to mandated benefits as a tool of social policy follows along the lines of the traditional conservative position that "the only good tax is a bad tax." If policymakers fail to recognize the costs of mandated benefits because they do not appear in the government budget, then mandated benefit programs could lead to excessive spending on social programs. There is no sense in which benefits become "free" just because the government mandates that employers offer them to workers. As with value-added taxes, it can plausibly be argued that mandated benefits fuel the growth of government because their costs are relatively

invisible and their distortionary effects are relatively minor.

IV. Conclusions

The thrust of this analysis is that mandated benefits are like public programs financed through benefit taxes, thus saving many of the inefficiencies of government provision of public goods. There is an additional difference, however, in that mandated benefits typically allow more choice to employers and employees than public provision. From this perspective it is not surprising that conservatives tend to prefer mandated benefits to public provision, as evidenced, for example, in proposals to privatize Social Security or in proposals in the 1970s to mandate employer health insurance as the "conservative" alternative to national health insurance. Nor is it surprising that liberals tend to prefer mandated benefits to no public action, but have some preference for public provision over mandated benefits.

There is no question that debates about mandated benefits will continue for some time. Despite their potential importance, the role of mandated benefits as a tool for providing social insurance has received relatively little attention from students of public finance. In future work, it will be desirable to examine more formally the conjectures put forth here. It would also be valuable to begin the task of assessing empirically the effect of various programs on wage and employment decisions.

REFERENCES

Ballard, Charles L., Shoven, John B. and Whalley, John, "General Equilibrium Computations of the Marginal Welfare Costs of Taxes in the United States," *American Economic Review*, March 1985, *75*, 128–38.

Browning, Edgar, "On the Marginal Welfare Cost of Taxation," *American Economic Review*, March 1987, *77*, 11–23.

McArdle, Frank B., "The Pressure for New Legislated Mandates," in *Government Mandating of Employee Benefits*, Washington: Employee Benefit Research Institute (EBRI), 1987.

Peltzman, Sam, "The Effect of Subsidies-in-Kind on Private Expenditures: The Case of Higher Education," *Journal of Political Economy*, January/February 1973, *81*, 1–27.

Reinhardt, Uwe, "Should All Employers be Required by Law To Provide Basic Health Insurance Coverage for Their Employees and Dependents?," in *Government Mandating of Employee Benefits*, Washington: EBRI, 1987.

Rothschild, Michael and Stiglitz, Joseph E., "Equilibrium in Competitive Insurance Markets: An Essay on the Economics of Imperfect Information," *Quarterly Journal of Economics*, November 1976, *90*, 629–50.

Shapiro, Carl and Stiglitz, Joseph E. "Equilibrium Unemployment as a Worker Disciplining Device," *American Economic Review*, June 1984, *74*, 433–44.

Stuart, Charles, "Welfare Costs per Dollar of Additional Tax Revenue in the United States," *American Economic Review*, June 1984, *74*, 352–62.

[12]

PEJ (2006) 5:69–87
DOI 10.1007/s10258-006-0009-2

ORIGINAL PAPER

Building blocks in the economics of mandates

John T. Addison · Richard C. Barrett ·
W. Stanley Siebert

Received: 15 March 2006 / Accepted: 8 July 2006 /
Published online: 28 September 2006
© Springer-Verlag 2006

Abstract The paper constructs an asymmetric information model to investigate the efficiency and equity cases for government mandated benefits. A mandate can improve workers' insurance, and may also redistribute in favour of more 'deserving' workers. The risk is that it may also reduce output. The more diverse are free market contracts—separating the various worker types—the more likely it is that such output effects will on balance serve to reduce welfare. It is shown that adverse effects can be reduced by restricting mandates to larger firms. An alternative to a mandate is direct government provision. We demonstrate that direct government provision has the advantage over mandates of preserving separations.

Keywords Asymmetric information · Labour mandates · Compensation packages

JEL Classification D82 · J33

1 Introduction

In recent years, the case for government regulation of labour markets has been supplemented by a new literature that exploits asymmetric information. Thus,

J. T. Addison (✉)
Department of Economics, Moore School of Business, University of South Carolina,
1705 College Street, Columbia, SC 29208, USA
e-mail: ecceaddi@moore.sc.edu

J. T. Addison
GEMF Universidade de Coimbra, Coimbra, Portugal

J. T. Addison · W. S. Siebert
IZA, Bonn, Germany

R. C. Barrett · W. S. Siebert
University of Birmingham, Birmingham, UK

🍃 Springer

Summers (1989, p. 179) has argued that government mandates requiring firms to provide benefits can bring about an improvement in welfare in circumstances in which company schemes would be overwhelmed by adverse selection stemming from workers' or firms' private information.

Summers sees adverse selection as relevant specifically to the fringe benefits of health insurance, parental leave, and dismissals protection. In each of these cases, the worker may suffer some unforeseen contingency and the employer then provide a 'wage,' or 'benefit,' not matched by work done. This may be an insurance payout (health insurance); or an insurance payout and a guarantee of the job on return to work (parental leave); or the job and a wage when the employer's ability to fire at will is restricted (dismissals protection). And in each case, adverse selection due to asymmetric information may discourage firms from providing the fringe benefit. In the ensuing labour literature, Levine (1991) on dismissals protection, Ruhm (1998) on parental leave, and Encinosa (1999) on health insurance develop the point. Krueger (2000, p. 119) also points to the importance of adverse selection problems as a rationale for government mandates. Aghion and Hermalin (1990) is another progenitor of the basic idea.

The labour market literature is closely related to a more general and more developed literature on adverse selection in insurance markets, for which the seminal work is by Rothschild and Stiglitz (1976) and Wilson (1977). This general insurance market literature finds that the problem of adverse selection is reduced if insurance companies can offer loss-making contracts subsidised by profit-making contracts (Cave 1984; Stewart 1994); or again if in a multiperiod framework insurance companies can use loss experience to reclassify policy holders (Dionne and Lasserre 1987; Cooper and Hayes 1987). However, we have not thought it appropriate to incorporate these refinements. They imply that a firm routinely offers its workers a rich and varied menu of contracts. Such menus would embrace differing levels of health insurance, parental leave, dismissals protection, and so on, and they are not observed in practice. Indeed, as well as their complexity, adopting a variety of standards for a fringe benefit would typically conflict with 'norms of fairness' (Levine 1991, p. 296), and also confront legal constraints.

The discussion of labour market mandates has mostly proceeded informally. However, Summers (1989, p. 182) has called for more formal analysis, the provision of which is a principal task of our paper. The model we build for this purpose is in direct line of descent from Wilson (1977). We follow Hellwig's (1987) game theoretic development of Wilson, translating the model to a labour market context that is richer than the original in view of its technological complexity. We also make central the issue of the role of government.

The question at issue is this: can government by mandating labour market benefits increase welfare? In our simple model, where firms are distinguished only by product, in both the separating and pooling cases, a mandate can achieve efficient allocation of income across states (i.e. secure 'full insurance'), accompanied by a redistribution of income among workers. In some instances, this redistribution appears equitable—it favours 'deserving' workers. In this way, both the Summers' (1989) case and the redistributive case for mandates is formalised. However, in our general model, with firms differentiated in more important ways, the mandate is shown to reduce output in the separating case. This is because, whereas the free market exploits separation to match worker types efficiently to firms, a mandate imposes pooling and substitutes a random allocation of workers to firms. Whenever a sorting mechanism based on separation exists, it is necessarily eliminated by the imposition of a mandate. In our model, then, a mandate imposing dismissals protection, for example, does not simply affect the economy's pattern of adjustment to shocks, but may reduce productivity directly by causing worker misallocation.[1] In the separating case, a mandate could thus cause a loss of productive efficiency, making it less likely that the mandate is desirable.

One may be able to get round such misallocation when, for example, heterogeneity derives from a distinction between 'small' and 'large' firms, and where the government is able to target large firms. We show that, in a likely scenario, such a 'restricted' mandate can short-circuit adverse effects on labour allocation, thereby providing a case for restricting mandates to large firms. It is clear though that the general problem of firm heterogeneity remains.

Summers (1989) also discusses the advantages of the mandate over direct government provision of the benefit in terms of its not distorting prices. We can, however, point to an advantage of direct government provision. Direct government provision of the benefit can help to preserve separation, and so avoid the mandate's adverse effects on labour allocation.

The outline of the paper is as follows. "The model" develops the asymmetric information model and analyses the case of (essentially) homogeneous firms. The scope for achieving welfare improvements within this framework is examined in "Gains in welfare". The effects of introducing firm heterogeneity are discussed in "Heterogeneous firms". "Government provision" tackles the issue of government provision as an alternative to mandates. The last section presents the "Conclusion".

2 The model

There are two types of firm, each type producing a different good, and two types of worker (as defined below). Many firms of each type and many workers of each type play a three-stage game. In stage 1, each firm offers a contract; in stage 2, each worker accepts one of the contracts on offer; and in stage 3, a firm may if it wishes withdraw the contract offered in stage 1. (Allowing firms to withdraw contracts is consistent with the notion of long-run competitive behaviour. It also ensures that the game has a solution: see Hellwig 1987.) There are two states of nature for each worker. After completion of the game's three stages, the state of nature is in each case realised and firms and workers receive their payoffs.

The two states of nature correspond to 'success' or 'failure' on the part of the worker, where for example a worker may fail because of ill health, maternity leave, or an inability to cope with the job. The effect is that a worker's product is less in the 'bad' state (failure) than the 'good' state (success).

---

[1] A similar fall in labour productivity, although not on this occasion arising from the asymmetric information mechanism, obtains in the model of Hopenhayn and Rogerson (1993).

A worker has a continuously differentiable Neumann–Morgenstern utility function, $U(.)$ (the same for all workers), that is separable in income and prices. Thus, fixing the general level of prices (defined appropriately), the worker's utility depends, ex ante, only on the probability of failure and the income received in the different states. Suppose that if a worker accepts a contract (b,w), $U=U_F(b)$ if the bad state occurs and $U=U_S(w)$ in the good state. That is, ex post, utility is state-dependent. Further, suppose that workers are risk averse and worker types distinguished by the probability of failure, P_L for 'low-risk' types and P_H for 'high-risk' types ($P_L<P_H$).

Labour is the only factor of production and each good is produced under constant returns. For concreteness, call the two firm types 'large' firms and 'small' firms, even though strictly within the terms of the model, for simplicity, the size of firms is indeterminate. A worker's product is one unit in the good state, e units in the bad state if employed by a large firm ($e<1$), and e_m units in the bad state if employed by a small firm ($e_m<1$). Intuitively, the dependence on type of firm is because the failure of a worker may cause greater difficulties for some types than others. For example, we would argue that absence through illness is more disruptive in small firms than in large firms, where it is easier to arrange cover for absence.[2]

Firms are competitive and risk neutral: competition in the markets for goods and labour drives their expected profits—revenue minus wages—to zero. Let S and S_m be the prices of the goods produced by large and small firms, respectively. Then, for large firms revenue per worker is S in the good state and $F=eS<S$ in the bad state; for small firms it is S_m in the good state and $F_m=e_mS_m<S_m$ in the bad state.

Assume to start with that $e=e_m$, so that $S_m=S$ and $F_m=F$. (If, say, $S>S_m$ and so $F>F_m$, then workers would do better moving from small to large firms.) Thus we deal first with the case of (essentially) homogeneous firms—the same contracts on offer in the two sectors, workers indifferent between sectors, and supply adjusting to equate prices.

Consider any firm. According to the terms of a contract, the firm pays wages b in the bad state and w in the good state. Thus a contract is a pair of values, (b,w), where b may include a 'benefit.' Define this benefit as $b-F$—a benefit is paid if the wage in the bad state is greater than the worker's revenue product. Assuming the benefit cannot be negative, we have $b\geq F$. In addition, however, a higher minimum level for b—fixed either in absolute terms or as a proportion of w—can be mandated by the government. (The government could also provide the benefit directly; this issue is taken up in "Government provision".)

Recall that the probability of failure is P_L for a 'low-risk' type and P_H for a 'high-risk' type. The corresponding odds ratios are $Q_L=P_L/(1-P_L)$ and $Q_H=P_H/(1-P_H)$. Thus, the slope of an indifference curve is, for a low-risk type,

$$dw/db = -Q_L U_F'/U_S' \qquad (1)$$

---

[2] The OECD (1995, p. 190) surveys parental leave in 19 countries, and states that the absence of a key worker for a long period created difficulties for small firms. This explains the exemption, for example, of firms employing less than 50 workers from the provisions of the 1993 US Family and Medical Leave Act.

and, for a high-risk type,

$$dw/db = -Q_H U_F'/U_S'. \tag{2}$$

As $Q_L < Q_H$, at any point in (b,w) space the low-risk worker's indifference curve is flatter than that of the high-risk worker—the 'single crossing property' holds. In Fig. 1, $U_L = U_L^*$ and $U_H = U_H^*$ (on which more below) are indifference curves of low-risk and high-risk workers, respectively.

Three zero profit lines are also shown in Fig. 1. Contracts for which the firm breaks even (on average) when employing a low-risk worker are described by

$$R_L = P_L(F - b) + (1 - P_L)(S - w) = 0. \tag{3}$$

The corresponding zero profit line for a high-risk worker is

$$R_H = P_H(F - b) + (1 - P_H)(S - w) = 0. \tag{4}$$

The 'pooling line' is

$$R = P(F - b) + (1 - P)(S - w) = 0, \tag{5}$$

where $P = \theta P_L + (1-\theta)P_H$ and θ is the proportion of low-risk workers. Thus the pooling line describes break-even contracts for randomly selected workers. Let the odds ratio corresponding to P be $Q = P/(1-P)$.

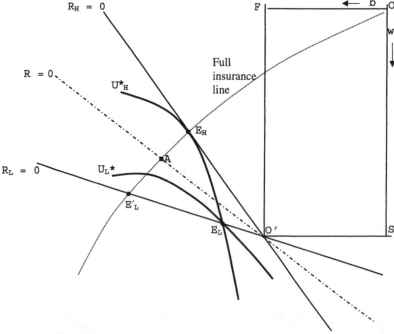

Fig. 1 Separating equilibrium

The respective slopes of the three zero profit lines are $-Q_L$, $-Q_H$ and $-Q$, where $Q=P/(1-P)$ and $Q_L<Q<Q_H$. This means the pooling line has a slope which is steeper than $R_L=0$ and flatter than $R_H=0$. Since P approaches P_1 as $\theta\rightarrow 1$, we have also the results that Q approaches Q_L and $R=0$ approaches $R_L=0$, as $\theta\rightarrow 1$.

The model is one of asymmetric information. Workers know their own type, but since this is private information firms cannot distinguish among workers. There are two possible solutions to this informed worker/ignorant firm model—a separating equilibrium and a pooling equilibrium. In describing these, it is helpful to define four special contracts, which we denote by E_H, E'_L, E_L and E.

First, contract E_H is the contract that maximises the high-risk type's utility,

$$U_H = P_H U_F(b) + (1 - P_H)U_S(w),\qquad(6)$$

subject to $R_H=0$ (Eq. 4). E_H is the best the high-risk worker can do, given that the firm knows the worker's type and breaks even. Let $E_H=(b_H,w_H)$. E_H is characterised by[3]

$$U'_F(b_H) = U'_S(w_H)\qquad(7a)$$

$$w_H = S - Q_H(b_H - F).\qquad(7b)$$

We denote by U^*_H the level of utility attained by the high-risk type at E_H.

Second, and analogously, contract E'_L maximises the low-risk type's utility

$$U_L = P_L U_F(b) + (1 - P_L)U_S(w),\qquad(8)$$

subject to $R_L=0$ (Eq. 3). Let $E'_L=(b'_L,w'_L)$. Accordingly, E'_L is characterised by

$$U'_F\left(b'_L\right) = U'_S\left(w'_L\right)\qquad(9a)$$

$$w'_L = S - Q_L\left(b'_L - F\right).\qquad(9b)$$

E_H and E'_L are the points where $R_H=0$ and $R_L=0$, respectively, intersect the 'full insurance' line. Shown as the dashed line in Fig. 1, the full insurance line is defined by $U'_F(b)=U'_S(w)$, and its slope is

$$dw/db = U''_F\Big/U''_S.\qquad(10)$$

---

[3] The Lagrangean is

$$P_H U_F(b) + (1 - P_H)U_S(w) + \lambda[P_H(F - b) + (1 - P_H)(S - w)].$$

Differentiating with respect to b and w and equating to zero,

$$P_H U'_F(b) = \lambda P_H$$

$$(1 - P_H)U'_S(w) = \lambda(1 - P_H).$$

Equation 7a follows from these two equations. The constraint gives Eq. 7b.

 Springer

Note that, in the case of state-independent utility, we have $U_F(.)=U_S(.)$ and the full insurance line becomes a 45-degree line through the worker origin O.

Because workers are assumed to be risk averse, both U_F'' and U_S'' are negative and the full insurance line has a positive slope. To the left of the line, $U_F'(.)<U_S'(.)$; and to the right, $U_F'(.)>U_S'(.)$. We assume $U_F'(F)>U_S'(S)$, that is, workers are underinsured at the firm origin O' where they are paid according to their productivity in the two states.

Given $Q_L<Q_H$ (flatter zero profit line associated with the low-risk worker), the full insurance line's positive slope implies $b_L'>b_H'$ and $w_L'>w_H'$. Thus, wages are higher at E_L' than at E_H in both good and bad states, and at E_L' we have $U_H>U_H^*$ (the high risk-type's utility at E_H).

Third, consider the contract, E_L, which comes into play when the firm does not know the worker's type. E_L maximises the low-risk type's utility, U_L, subject to $R_L=0$ and $U_H\leq U_H^*$, the incentive compatibility condition. When the latter condition holds, high-risk types have no incentive to switch from contract E_H to E_L, and since $U>U_H^*$ at E_L' the condition is binding. It follows that E_L is determined by the intersection of the indifference curve, $U_H=U_H^*$, and the zero profit line, $R_L=0$, and lies between E_L' and the firm origin, O'.[4] Let $E_L=(b_L,w_L)$. By Eqs. 3 and 6, E_L is characterised by

$$U_H^* = P_H U_F(b_L) + (1 - P_H)U_S(w_L) \tag{11a}$$

$$w_L = S - Q_L(b_L - F). \tag{11b}$$

We denote by U_L^* the level of utility attained by the low-risk type at E_L.

Finally, E is the contract that maximises the low-risk type's utility, U_L, subject to $R=0$, namely, the pooling line given by Eq. 5. Let $E=(b_P,w_P)$. Using Eq. 8, and proceeding as in footnote 2, E is characterised by

$$Q_L U_F'(b_P) = Q U_S'(w_P) \tag{12a}$$

$$w_P = S - Q(b_P - F). \tag{12b}$$

Since $Q_L<Q$, Eq. 12a implies that $U_F'>U_S'$ at E, and E lies on the pooling line to the right of the full insurance line. We will denote by U_L^{**} and U_H^{**}, respectively, the levels of utility attained by low-risk and high-risk types at E.

We now describe the two possible solutions. First of all, a separating equilibrium occurs when $U_L^*>U_L^{**}$, as depicted in Fig. 1. In this equilibrium, firms offer workers the pair of contracts (E_L, E_H), with all low-risk types accepting E_L and all high-risk

---

[4] We can show that U_L declines to the right of E_L' on the line $R_L=0$ (Fig. 1). From Eq. 8, since $R_L=0$ has slope$-Q_L = -P_L/(1-P_L)$,

$$dU_L/db = P_L U_F' + (1 - P_L)U_S'(dw/db) = P_L\left(U_F' - U_S'\right).$$

As E_L' lies on the full insurance line, we know that, to the right of E_L', $U_F'>U_S'$. Thus, from the above equation, to the right of E_L', $dU_L/db>0$, and U_L declines as benefits are reduced. U_H likewise declines to the right of E_L' on the line $R_L=0$, and declines also to the right of E_H on the line $R_H=0$ (the proofs are similar).

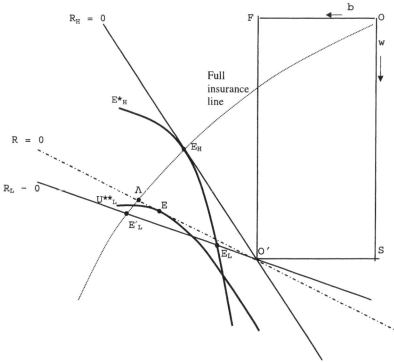

Fig. 2 Pooling equilibrium

types accepting E_H. Competition ensures that (E_L, E_H) is the pair of contracts offered. Because firms are risk neutral, in equilibrium they bear all the risk in relation to high-risk types, who are fully insured at the point E_H. Because of asymmetric information, firms cannot similarly offer low-risk types the contract E'_L. Firms need instead to identify low-risk types by offering E_L, a contract with a high wage in the good state and a low benefit in the bad state. E_L and E_H both lie on the indifference curve $U_H = U_H^*$, so that high-risk types have no incentive to "mimic" the behaviour of low-risk types.[5] A pooling equilibrium does not result in Fig. 1 because $U_L = U_L^*$, the low-risk type's indifference curve through E_L, does not intersect the pooling line. In other words, there is no contract on the pooling line that the low-risk types prefer to E_L.

Second of all, a pooling equilibrium occurs when $U_L^* < U_L^{**}$. In this equilibrium, as depicted in Fig. 2, only one contract is offered: contact E. The difference between Figs. 1 and 2 is that $U_L = U_L^*$ now intersects the pooling line. This means that, in comparison with the separating contracts (E_L, E_H), both types now do better at E. Firms can 'deviate' profitably from (E_L, E_H), and so (E_L, E_H) is not the equilibrium.

---

[5] An assumption here is that the high-risk type cannot obtain insurance outside the firm (cannot 'top up' with insurance), on terms that, starting from E_L, allow the high-risk type to attain levels of utility higher than U_H^*.

🌱 Springer

Low-risk types do better at E than at E_L, although mimicked at E by the high-risk types, and accordingly a pooling equilibrium results.

In determining whether pooling rather than separation obtains, the magnitude of θ is critical. The larger θ, the more likely is pooling. If θ is close to one, so that the pooling line is close to $R_L=0$, low-risk types suffer little from being pooled with their high-risk counterparts (who are relatively few in number), and low-risk types find separation is not worth its cost in the form of low insurance against the bad state.

In sum, there are two possible solutions to the model. In the case of a separating equilibrium (Fig. 1), low-risk types are identified by their choice of contract, namely, a high-wage/low-benefit contract. This is an example of 'screening' which benefits low-risk types even if they face a cost in that they cannot be fully insured. In the case of a pooling equilibrium (Fig. 2), high-risk types mimic the behaviour of their low-risk counterparts and gain in comparison with their full information contract, E_H. High-risk types gain by pooling. We now proceed to examine the justification for a government mandate in these two situations.

3 Gains in welfare

It is clear in our model that, since a firm is free to offer any contract it wishes, no government-mandated floor can engineer a Pareto improvement. Rather, competition will ensure that opportunities to make workers better off while firms still break even are not neglected. The mandate can only restrict the set of contracts on offer, transforming a separating equilibrium into a pooling equilibrium (Fig. 1), or a pooling equilibrium into a pooling equilibrium with a higher level of benefit (Fig. 2). In either case, low-risk workers are made worse off. In Fig. 1 they are better off at E_L than at any point on the pooling line; and in Fig. 2 better off at E than at any different point on the pooling line.

Summers (1989), however, makes the point that unregulated labour markets with asymmetric information fail to achieve efficiency across states (which requires workers to be fully insured). A mandate can achieve this outcome by imposing as a minimum the benefit corresponding to A in Figs. 1 and 2, where A is the point where the pooling and full insurance lines intersect. Such a mandate may be desirable even though it also has a redistributive effect that needs to be taken into account.

To formalise the discussion, we adopt a generalisation of Harsanyi's (1977) social welfare function due to Blackorby et al. (1997), namely,

$$W = \theta f(U_L) + (1 - \theta) f(U_H).^6 \qquad (13)$$

---

[6] An alternative approach that might be considered relies on the concept of a "potential" Pareto improvement. (A potential Pareto improvement occurs when 'winners' can compensate 'losers' and still come out ahead.) However, when applying this concept in our context, intransitivities arise. A in Fig. 1 is a potential Pareto improvement on (E_H, E_L), since redistribution is possible from A to (E_H, E_L') which itself is a Pareto improvement on (E_H, E_L). Thus A is 'better' than (E_H, E_L). On the other hand, redistribution is possible also from (E_H, E_L) back to A, so that (E_H, E_L) is no worse than A. A second problem with the concept of a potential Pareto improvement, in our context, is that winners compensating losers would in practice be impossible. When for example A is mandated, forcing pooling, low-risk types cannot be compensated by high-risk types, since the latter are not identifiable. Though a popular tool in many contexts, the concept of a potential Pareto improvement is not useful here.

🅰 Springer

Such a social welfare function may be thought to overstate utilitarian principles at the expense of individual rights, which figure so much in recent social choice literature (see for example Pattanaik 1994). But it has the advantage of simplicity and will provide us with insights. Varying our previous notation, let (b_L, w_L) denote the contract accepted by low-risk types and (b_H, w_H) that accepted by high-risk types. Maximising social welfare subject to the population, risk, and productivity conditions, the Lagrangean is

$$
\begin{aligned}
&\theta[P_L U_F(b_L) + (1 - P_L)U_S(w_L)] + (1 - \theta)[P_H U_F(b_H) + (1 - P_H)U_S(w_H)] \\
&+ \lambda\{\theta[P_L F + (1 - P_L)S] + (1 - \theta)[P_H F + (1 - P_H)S] \\
&- \theta[P_L b_L + (1 - P_L)w_L] - (1 - \theta)[P_H b_H + (1 - P_H)w_H]\}.
\end{aligned}
\tag{14}
$$

The first order conditions then give, together with the zero profit condition,

$$
U_F'(b_L) = U_S'(w_L) = U_F'(b_H) = U_S'(w_H).
\tag{15}
$$

From Eq. 15, the 'first-best' outcome assigns contract A to each worker. (Recall that $U_F'(b) = U_S'(w)$ defines the full insurance line.)

Thus, given our social welfare function, the government can achieve the first-best outcome by mandating full insurance. Mandating A is optimal for two reasons. First, A is on the full insurance line and so we have efficiency across states. Second, A is common to all workers and so we also have efficiency across workers. The redistribution (neglected by Summers) which accompanies the mandate, from low-risk to high-risk workers, is optimal because it equalises the marginal utility of income across workers.

It is worthwhile analysing the change which a mandate brings about. Starting from (E_L, E_H) in Fig. 1 or from E in Fig. 2, we may think of movement to A as taking place in two steps. There is an initial shift for each type along corresponding 'actuarially fair' isoprofit lines, which takes them to the full insurance line. This is a Pareto improvement. Then there is a second shift for each type, which unites them at A. Define 'redistribution' as the latter movement.

Under Eq. 13, redistribution is good because high-risk types are relatively deprived and therefore also good 'utility generators' (that is, they have a high marginal utility of income). An illustration is Summers' example of mandated company health insurance. Here it seems right for the unhealthy to benefit at a minor cost to the healthy. Note, however, that were one to introduce moral hazard into the discussion, high-risk types would no longer automatically emerge as "deserving." Society might prefer to reward a worker for his or her achievement of low risk.

It remains that, with homogeneous firms, mandates can improve efficiency across worker states, and will have redistributive effects that in many cases are seen as desirable. The policy implications are indeed quite striking. Yet, as we shall see, the picture can alter quite dramatically once we relax the assumption of identical firms.

 Springer

4 Heterogeneous firms

The problem in a nutshell is that enforced pooling may lead to the misallocation of workers in a world of heterogeneous firms. As noted earlier, employing high-risk workers creates greater difficulties for small than for large firms. To demonstrate that misallocation may occur, we replace our assumption, $e_m=e$, by $e_m<e$. A worker's product in the bad state is now less in the small-firm sector than in the large-firm sector. This implies $F_m<F$ and $S_m>S$. (Note that $S_m \leq S$ implies $F_m<F$, and $F_m \geq F$ implies $S_m>S$, so alternative revenue structures satisfying $e_m<e$ are not consistent with equilibrium. In "Gains in welfare", given $e_m=e$, a similar argument justified $F_m=F$ and $S_m=S$.) Assume there is a separating equilibrium (Fig. 3). Intuition suggests that efficiency now requires differences in contracts between small and large firms so as to bring about an appropriate matching of workers to firms. We explore this.

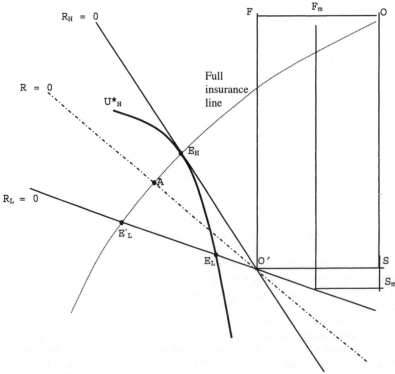

Fig. 3 Separation with two boxes

As before, let the separating contracts be (E_L, E_H), where $E_L = (b_L, w_L)$ and $E_H = (b_H, w_H)$. Firms are competitive and cannot make positive profits employing either worker type. Thus,

$$P_L b_L + (1 - P_L)w_L \geqslant P_L F_m + (1 - P_L)S_m \qquad (16a)$$

$$P_H b_H + (1 - P_H)w_H \geqslant P_H F + (1 - P_H)S \qquad (16b)$$

$$P_L b_L + (1 - P_L)w_L \geqslant P_L F + (1 - P_L)S \qquad (16c)$$

$$P_H b_H + (1 - P_H)w_H \geqslant P_H F_m + (1 - P_H)S_m. \qquad (16d)$$

Suppose, hypothetically, that low-risk types work for large firms and high-risk types for small firms. We can replace weak inequality in Eqs. 16c and 16d by equality. Substituting Eq. 16c into Eq. 16a and Eq. 16d into Eq. 16b, and re-arranging, gives

$$S_m - S \leqslant Q_L(F - F_m) \qquad (17a)$$

$$S_m - S \geqslant Q_H(F - F_m). \qquad (17b)$$

Since $S_m > S$, $F_m < F$ and $Q_H > Q_L$, this is a contradiction. Low-risk types working for large firms and high-risk types working for small firms does not occur.

We are left with just three possibilities:

(A) only high-risk types work for large firms and only low-risk types for small firms;
(B) a mix of low- and high-risk types works for large firms, but only low-risk types for small firms; and,
(C) a mix of low- and high-risk types works for small firms, but only high-risk types for large firms.

Case (B), which seems the most likely, is illustrated in Fig. 3. Since both types of firm employ low-risk workers, the zero profit line, $R_L = 0$, is common to the two types of firm and touches the corner of each box. Large firms offer both E_L and E_H, separating the low-risk from the high-risk types. Small firms offer only E_L.

We now investigate what happens when pooling replaces separation. In general, prices alter, so let the new prices be S' and S'_m. After pooling, for large firms revenue per worker is S' in the good state and $F' = eS'$ in the bad state; for small firms it is S'_m in the good state and $F'_m = e_m S'_m$ in the bad state. New revenues per worker will have the same structure as old revenues per worker, that is, $F'_m < F'$ and $S'_m > S'$.

A common feature of (A), (B) and (C) is low-risk types work for small firms and high-risk types work for large firms, and it follows that weak inequality can be replaced by equality in Eqs. 16a and 16b. Substituting Eq. 16a into Eq. 16c, and Eq. 16b into Eq. 16d, gives

$$S_m - S \geqslant Q_L(F - F_m) \qquad (18a)$$

$$S_m - S \leqslant Q_H(F - F_m). \qquad (18b)$$

The break-even relations under pooling are, from Eq. 6,

$$Pb_P + (1 - P)w_P = PF'_m + (1 - P)S'_m \qquad (19a)$$

$$Pb_P + (1 - P)w_P = PF' + (1 - P)S'. \qquad (19b)$$

Equating the two right hand sides of Eqs. 19a and 19b gives, for pooling,

$$S'_m - S' = Q\left(F' - F'_m\right). \qquad (20)$$

Recall that the general level of prices is fixed, so when pooling replaces separation prices S and S_m vary in opposite directions. We consider the three cases in turn.

Case A Weak inequality can be replaced by strict inequality in Eqs. 16c and 16d, and so too in Eqs. 18a and 18b. Clearly, prices in the large-firm sector may either rise or fall, with opposite variation in the small-firm sector.

Case B Weak inequality can be replaced by equality in Eq. 16c, and so too in Eq. 18a. Since $Q > Q_L$, it follows from Eqs. 18a and 20 that prices rise in the large-firm sector and fall in the small-firm sector. Intuitively, the effect pooling has on small firms is to worsen the mix of workers.

Case C Weak inequality can be replaced by equality in Eq. 16d, and so too in Eq. 18b. Since $Q < Q_H$, it follows from Eqs. 18b and 20 that prices fall in the large-firm sector and rise in the small-firm sector. Intuitively, the effect pooling has on large firms is that costs rise, due to workers are no longer being identifiable as high-risk.

Diagrammatically in case (B), the (F, S) box contracts and the (F_m, S_m) box expands to the point where the pooling line touches the corners of each. The large-firm sector expands and the small-firm sector contracts. Under pooling, competition requires the two types of firm to have a common pooling line (Fig. 3).

We now come to an important result we wish to prove, which is that in any of the three cases the switch in regime from separation to pooling causes a decline in average income. Rigorously, we can show this decline in each of the three cases. First note that, since both sectors break even, average income under pooling is $PF' + (1-P)S' = PF'_m + (1-P)S'_m$.

🖄 Springer

Case A From Eqs. 16a and 16d, average income under separation is greater than $PF_m+(1-P)S_m$ and, from Eqs. 16b and 16c, also greater than $PF+(1-P)S$. Whether $S'<S$ (and so $F'<F$), or $S'>S$ (and so $F'>F$), average income falls.

Case B From Eqs. 16b and 16c, average income under separation equals $PF+(1-P)S$. Since average income under pooling is $PF'+(1-P)S'$, and we also know $S'<S$ (and so $F'<F$), average income falls.

Case C From Eqs. 16a and 16d, average income under separation equals $PF_m+(1-P)S_m$. Since average income under pooling is $PF'_m+(1-P)S'_m$, and we also know $S'_m<S_m$ (and so $F'_m<F_m$), average income falls.

   The situation is different where market forces have already resulted in pooling. If workers are randomly allocated to begin with, designers of mandates do not have this type of misallocation to worry about.
   Our discussion suggests that it may be desirable to restrict the coverage of mandates. We focus on case (B), which as we have said seems the most likely of the three cases. Suppose full insurance is mandated in case (B), but with the mandate restricted to large firms. Small firms are free to screen out high-risk types. A curious situation results, which is they do so by offering the same contract as large firms.

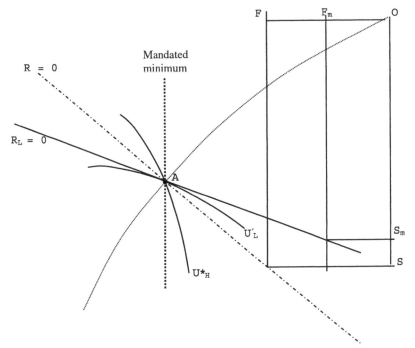

Fig. 4 Restricted mandate

To demonstrate this, let E_L be the contract which small firms offer. The contract which large firms offer is A, located (as before) where the large-firm pooling line intersects the full insurance line (see Fig. 4). Recall that the low-risk type's indifference curve through A is flatter than the high-risk type's indifference curve through A (an instance of the single crossing property). Denote these two indifference curves by U_L' and U_H'. The argument is simple. Firstly, since low-risk workers work in both sectors, they are indifferent between E_L and A, so E_L lies on U_L'; secondly, by the incentive compatibility condition, high-risk workers too are indifferent between E_L and A, so E_L lies on U_H'. Thus, $E_L=A$.

Although $E_L=A$, small firms are able to screen out high-risk types. Intuitively, this is because they are free to offer a high-wage/low-benefit contract that is attractive to low-risk types, but not to high-risk types. Large firms cannot follow suit. The restricted mandate benefits small firms, since low-risk types, pooled with high-risk types in large firms, are cheaper. There is also no loss of output, since exempted small firms continue to employ only low-risk types. Thus, in spite of firm heterogeneity, the restricted mandate avoids misallocation of workers.

The caveat in all of this is that there may be additional forms of heterogeneity, other than the small firm/large firm distinction. Mandates may need to be restricted in further and more complex ways if misallocation is to be avoided.

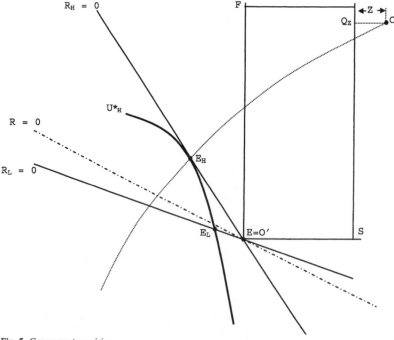

Fig. 5 Government provision

 Springer

5 Government provision

As an alternative to mandates, governments may themselves provide the fringe benefit directly. For expositional convenience, we will analyse such provision in the framework of the simpler one-box $(e_m = e)$ model. Prices are equal $(S = S_m)$, and worker revenue is S in the good state and $F(=F_m)$ in the bad state.

Suppose the government pays a worker a benefit z in the bad state, so that the worker's utility becomes $U_F(b+z)$. This provision is financed by a break-even tax of Qz on the worker in the good state, so that in the good state the worker's utility is $U_S(w - Qz)$. (Recall that $Q = P/(1-P)$.) Diagrammatically, an increase in government provision shifts the worker origin, O, rightward and downward in relation to the revenue box (see Fig. 5).

We investigate first the effect of varying government provision on E, the low-risk worker's preferred contract on the pooling line. Recall that $b \geq F$—the benefit paid by a firm cannot be negative. Thus E can be either an interior solution to the left of the firm origin, O', or the corner solution, $E = O'$. As an interior solution, E is characterised by[7]

$$Q_L U'_F(b_P + z) = Q U'_S(w_P - Qz) \tag{21a}$$

$$w_P - Qz = S - Q(b_P + z - F). \tag{21b}$$

Equations 21a and 21b determine $b_P + z$ and $w_P - Qz$ uniquely. Thus, when E is an interior solution, any variation in government provision of the benefit is exactly offset by a compensating variation in firm provision. An increase in z neither affects the total benefit, $b_P + z$, nor the net wage, $w_P - Qz$, while worker utilities at E, U_L^{**} and U_H^{**}, are likewise unaffected. Intuitively, the explanation for this result is that E is governed by the low-risk type's preferences, and the terms on which the low-risk type obtains additional benefits are the same irrespective of whether these are provided by firms or by government. In either case, cost is based on *average* risk. Consequently, as z increases, b_P is reduced until eventually $b_P = F$. Diagrammatically, E moves toward the revenue box until it coincides with the firm origin O' (Fig. 5). Ultimately, if not initially, we arrive at the corner solution, $E = O'$, where the firm provides no benefit.

We can also investigate the effect of varying government provision on the pair of separating contracts for high-risk and low-risk workers, E_H and E_L (as defined in "The model"), and on worker utilities associated with these contracts. Omitting proofs (which are available from the authors on request), the results are twofold.

(A) At E_H, the utility of high-risk types increases with government provision z, and total benefit, $b_H + z$, also increases. The intuitive explanation for this increased

---

[7] Adapting Eqs. 5 and 8, the Lagrangean for the determination of E is

$$P_L U_F(b+z) + (1 - P_L) U_S(w - Qz) + \lambda[P(F - b) + (1 - P)(S - w)].$$

Differentiating with respect to b and w, and equating to zero, $P_L U'_F = \lambda P$ and $(1 - P_L) U'_S = \lambda(1 - P)$. Dividing gives Eq. 21a. The constraint gives Eq. 21b.

 Springer

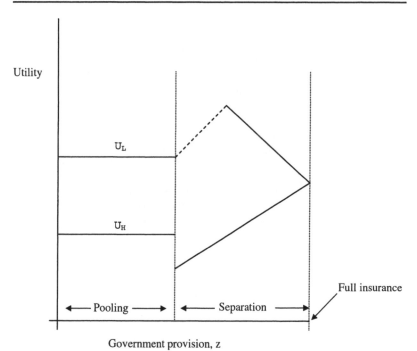

Fig. 6 Welfare effects of government provision—state independent utility

utility of high-risk types is that they obtain additional benefits on good terms. Although they experience greater than average risk of failure, they are taxed at just average risk.

(B) At E_L, the utility of low-risk types may or may not increase with government provision z, though total benefit, $b_L + z$, will again increase. The redistributive effect in this case operates against low-risk types—experiencing lower than average risk of failure, they are taxed at average risk. However, there is a further effect. As z increases, low-risk types can receive a higher level of benefit without being mimicked by high-risk types and, paradoxically, this beneficial effect can more than offset the pure redistributive effect.[8]

We now draw some conclusions about the effects of direct government provision on labour markets. Absent government provision, there can be either pooling or separation, but for the sake of argument let us suppose pooling. Figure 6 illustrates.

Equations 21a and 21b show that, as z increases from zero, there is at first no net effect on workers' benefits, wages, or welfare. But this situation does not persist. At

---

[8] This Pareto improvement result is also derived heuristically by Wilson (1977, p. 200), although he errs in claiming that Pareto improvements can always be achieved. A similar effect occurs when a firm, which is able to offer more than one contract, uses a profit-making contract aimed at low-risk types to balance a loss-making contract designed for high-risk types. The advantage gained is that the subsidised high-risk types are less inclined to mimic the low-risk types (see Cave 1984, in the insurance market context).

some point, as z increases, there occurs a switch in regime from pooling to separation. There has to be separation when E reaches $E=O'$, as low- and high-risk types are both better off with the separating contracts, (E_L, E_H), than with pooling at O'. Each type gains from obtaining insurance at a cost that is actuarially fair. Interestingly, as depicted in Fig. 6, there may be a range within which increases in z achieve Pareto improvements (see (A) and (B) above). Beyond this, an increase in z, by subsidising high-risk types at the expense of their low-risk counterparts, continues to make high-risk types better off, but now penalises low-risk types.

We see that government provision has the advantage over a mandate that it is able to retain separation, and also convert pooling into separation. Losses, arising under mandates due to the misallocation of labour (documented in "Heterogeneous firms"), are avoidable with government provision. Another advantage is that the taxes which fund government provision can be progressive. Taxes are, however, distortionary. These distortions, which are crucial to the argument of Summers (1989), fail to appear in our model because of the full employment assumption and also by reason of the focused nature of the taxes concerned. Relaxation of these assumptions means that distortions would surface. That said, we have demonstrated that government provision has certain advantages over mandates ignored in the extant literature.

6 Conclusion

This paper has provided the infrastructure for asymmetric information arguments favouring government labour market mandates. We have shown that mandates may improve welfare both by redistributing and by overcoming adverse selection. They can bring about an efficient allocation of income across worker states, and the accompanying redistribution of income across workers will in some instances accord with notions of equity. Mandates may, however, also reduce output. Specifically, where worker types are separated in a world of heterogeneous firms, mandates may lower productive efficiency, substituting a random allocation of labour for the purposive sorting mechanism that in regular markets exploits separation. We have reported that targeting may be able in some measure to side step these inefficiencies.

A further concern of the paper has been the issue of direct provision of the benefit by government. It is conventional to argue that mandates dominate government provision because of the greater tax distortions associated with the latter. Yet, we were able to show that direct provision can have the advantage of avoiding any misallocation attendant upon pooling and the consequent randomisation of labour allocation. Direct provision may thus be a more efficient redistributive tool, less costly in its implied output losses.

To conclude, our framework has been broad. An important task for the future is to identify and parameterise those mandates that fit the mould of adverse selection. We will then be able to assess the practical importance of adverse selection, and the redistributive (and possible disincentive) effects of mandates. Other issues that may need to be accommodated within the existing insurance framework include the availability of external insurance (allowing workers to top-up their firm benefits), and cross-subsidisation (even though ruled out here on grounds of complexity and institutional barriers).

 Springer

Acknowledgments We would like to thank seminar participants at the University of Birmingham, the EIIW-Potsdam, the ZEW-Mannheim, and the EMRU workshop at Lancaster University. We retain responsibility for any errors.

References

Aghion P, Hermalin B (1990) Legal restrictions on private contracts can enhance efficiency. J Law Econ Organ 6(2):381–409

Blackorby C, Donaldson D, Weymark JA (1997) Aggregation and the expected utility hypothesis. Mimeograph, University of British Columbia

Cave J (1984) Equilibrium in insurance markets with asymmetric information and adverse selection. RAND Report R-3015-HHS

Cooper R, Hayes B (1987) Multi-period insurance contracts. Int J Ind Organ 5(2):211–231

Dionne G, Lasserre P (1987) Adverse selection and finite horizon insurance contracts. Eur Econ Rev 31 (4):843–861

Encinosa W (1999) Regulating the HMO Market. Mimeograph, Agency for Health Care Policy and Research, US Department of Health and Human Services

Harsanyi J (1977) Rational behaviour and bargaining equilibrium in games and social situations. Cambridge University Press, Cambridge, UK

Hellwig M (1987) Some recent developments in the theory of competition in markets with adverse selection. Eur Econ Rev 31(1–2):319–325

Hopenhayn H, Rogerson R (1993) Job turnover and policy evaluation: a general equilibrium analysis. Eur Econ Rev 101(5):915–938

Krueger AB (2000) From Bismarck to Maastricht: the march to the European Union and the labor compact. Labour Eco 7(2):117–134

Levine DI (1991) Just-cause employment policy in the presence of worker adverse selection. J Labor Econ 9(3):294–305

OECD (1995) Long term leave for parents in OECD countries, Employment Outlook 1995, pp. 171–202

Pattanaik PK (1994) Some non-welfaristic issues in welfare economics. In: Dutta, B (ed) Welfare Economics, Oxford University Press, London, UK, pp. 196–248

Rothschild M, Stiglitz JE (1976) Equilibrium in competitive insurance markets: an essay on the economics of imperfect information. Q J Econ 90(4):629–650

Ruhm CJ (1998) The economic consequences of parental leave mandates: lessons from Europe. Q J Econ 113(1):285–317

Stewart J (1994) The welfare implications of moral hazard and adverse selection in competitive insurance markets. Econ Inq 32(2):193–208

Summers LH (1989) Some simple economics of mandated benefits. Am Econ Rev 79(2):177–183

Wilson C (1977) A model of insurance markets with incomplete information. J Econ Theory 16 (2):167–207

[13]

The Incidence of Mandated Maternity Benefits

By JONATHAN GRUBER*

I consider the labor-market effects of mandates which raise the costs of employing a demographically identifiable group. The efficiency of these policies will be largely dependent on the extent to which their costs are shifted to group-specific wages. I study several state and federal mandates which stipulated that childbirth be covered comprehensively in health insurance plans, raising the relative cost of insuring women of childbearing age. I find substantial shifting of the costs of these mandates to the wages of the targeted group. Correspondingly, I find little effect on total labor input for that group. (JEL I18, J32, H51)

In an era of tight fiscal budget constraints, mandating employer provision of workplace benefits to employees is an attractive means for a government to finance its policy agenda. Consequently, in recent years there has been a growth of interest in mandated benefits as a tool of social policy. For example, the centerpiece of President Bill Clinton's health-care proposal is mandated employer provision of health insurance, and more than 20 states have mandated some form of maternity leave since 1987.

Aside from their political attraction, there may be an efficiency argument for mandates, relative to public expenditure, as a means of financing benefit expansions. As highlighted by Lawrence H. Summers (1989), publicly financed benefits require an increase in government revenue-raising, with the resulting deadweight loss from taxation.

Mandates, however, are financed by a benefits tax; if employees value the benefit that they are receiving, then the deadweight loss from financing that benefit will be lower than from tax financing. In the limit, with full valuation of the benefit by employees, wages will fall to offset the cost of the benefit to the employer, and there will be no efficiency cost. In fact, recent research has suggested that the increased costs of one workplace mandate, workers compensation, were largely shifted to wages with little effect on employment (Jonathan Gruber and Alan B. Krueger, 1991).

This efficiency argument, however, may not apply to a popular type of policy, the "group-specific mandate," which mandates the expansion of benefits for a demographically identifiable group within the workplace.[1] In the case of mandates such as maternity leave, there is likely to be less scope for the free adjustment of wages to

*Department of Economics, Massachusetts Institute of Technology, Cambridge, MA 02139. I am grateful to Gary Chamberlain, David Cutler, Richard Freeman, Rachel Friedberg, Jerry Hausman, Olivia Mitchell, Rodrigo Vergara, seminar participants at Harvard, MIT, and the NBER, and two anonymous referees for helpful comments; to Josh Angrist, Larry Katz, Jim Poterba, and Larry Summers for both valuable suggestions and guidance; and to the Sloan Foundation and the Harvard Chiles Fellowship for financial support.

[1]Given the prevalence of experience rating in insurance markets, any social insurance mandate may be group-specific, since different individuals may cost the employer different amounts. In this paper, I define group-specific mandates as those which affect a demographically identifiable group only. It is unclear whether the results can be extended to cases in which workers are distinguished along more subtle dimensions.

VOL. 84 NO. 3   GRUBER: INCIDENCE OF MANDATED MATERNITY BENEFITS   623

reflect the valuation of the benefit by the targeted group, since there are barriers to *relative* wage adjustment within the workplace (such as antidiscrimination rules or workplace relative-pay norms) which do not affect the adjustment of overall workplace wage levels. Without the ability of relative wages to adjust, there may be substantial deadweight loss from these mandates even if the benefit is valued by that group. Thus, in considering the efficacy of these mandates, a central consideration is whether the cost of the mandate is shifted to the wages of the group that benefits.

This paper uses a set of "natural experiments" to estimate the response of the labor market to a group-specific mandate: state and federal laws that mandated comprehensive coverage for childbirth in health insurance policies. A commonly accepted feature of health insurance benefits before the mid-1970's was limited coverage for childbirth. Maternity coverage was sometimes excluded from basic health benefits; if included, it was often subject to flat-rate cash amount limits regardless of the cost of delivery. This differential coverage was widely perceived as discriminatory (Geraldine Leshin, 1981; Alan Guttmacher Institute, 1987). Many states responded to this perception in the 1975–1978 period by passing laws which prohibited treating pregnancy differently from "comparable illnesses" in health insurance benefits. Then, in October 1978, the Federal Government passed the Pregnancy Discrimination Act (PDA), which prohibited any differential treatment of pregnancy in the employment relationship.

This set of laws offers two advantages for studying the labor-market impact of a group-specific mandate. First, they affected a readily identifiable group, women of child-bearing age and their husbands (under whose insurance these women may have been covered), so that I am able to study their impact based on observable characteristics. Second, they were fairly costly for these individuals, due both to the widespread existence of differential maternity benefits before 1978 and the large fraction

of health insurance costs for women of childbearing age which are accounted for by maternity benefits.

I use the Current Population Survey (CPS) to study the extent to which the cost of these group-specific mandates was shifted to the targeted group's wages and the effect on net labor input. I begin by examining changes in wages, hours worked, and employment for married women of child-bearing age in states which passed these "maternity mandates," relative to a set of control individuals within the state and relative to similar states which did not pass this legislation. I then assign each worker an individual-specific cost of the mandate, which is a function of the age-specific cost of maternity coverage, the probability that the worker receives insurance on the job, and the predicted type of insurance coverage that she receives. This allows me to use individual variation in identifying the impact of the mandate and to estimate more precisely the extent of shifting. Finally, I note that, with the passage of the 1978 federal law, the existing state laws provide a natural set of controls; I exploit this "reverse experiment" to confirm my earlier findings. The findings consistently suggest shifting of the costs of the mandates on the order of 100 percent, with little effect on net labor input.

The paper proceeds as follows. Section I presents some background on health insurance benefits for maternity in the 1970's and discusses the economics of a group-specific mandated benefit. After describing the data and my estimation strategy in Section II, I estimate the impact of the state mandates on the labor-market outcomes of women of childbearing age (and their husbands) in Section III. In Section IV, I study the federal mandate. Section V concludes by discussing the welfare implications of these findings and suggesting directions for future research.

I. Background

Before 1978, health insurance benefits for maternity were generally limited along two dimensions: either there was no coverage for pregnancy, or benefits were paid as a flat lump-sum cash amount, regardless of the ultimate costs of childbirth. This stood in contrast to coverage for common illnesses in this era, which was fairly complete.[2] During the 1975–1979 period, 23 states passed laws that outlawed treating pregnancy differently from comparable illnesses. This was also an important feature of the 1978 federal legislation, the PDA, which prohibited discrimination against pregnant women more broadly. The employer cost of the state (and later federal) mandates depends on two factors: the extent of differential coverage before these laws and the cost of its removal.

A. The Extent of Differential Coverage

There are two previous estimates of the extent of differential coverage for maternity benefits in this era. Dorothy R. Kittner (1978) used a 1976 Labor Department survey of health insurance plans to show that, while over 90 percent of plans included maternity benefits, nearly 60 percent of the plans provided less generous benefits for childbirth than for other disabilities. However, the Health Insurance Association of America (1978) used data from a survey of new group health insurance policies written in early 1978 to estimate that only 52 percent of employees had any coverage for maternity. Both of these estimates are problematic: Kittner's only includes firms with more than 26 employees and does not include information on dependent coverage; the Health Insurance Association of America looks only at new policies, which may have been supplementary to existing policies (and therefore less generous), and does not focus on women of childbearing age.

To obtain more accurate estimates, I use the 1977 National Medical Care Expendi-

ture Survey (NMCES), which collected data on demographics and health insurance coverage for a nationally representative sample of more than 40,000 individuals. While this survey was completed before the PDA was put in place, many states had passed their own maternity mandates by 1977, so that my calculations will represent underestimates of the extent of discrimination in the early 1970's.[3]

The NMCES contains data on approximately 2,900 females between ages 20 and 40 who were covered through employment-based group health insurance, either in their own name or through a family member. I use "hospital room and board" and "other inpatient services" as comparable illnesses in order to define differential coverage. I find that about 20 percent of women did not have coverage for maternity benefits when they had coverage for either of these comparable illnesses. There were an additional 30 percent of women who received less coverage of the physician's "usual, customary, and reasonable charges" for delivery than for other services, or received only a flat lump-sum provision (less than $250) for a delivery fee. Thus, at least 50 percent of women faced either differential coverage or benefits.[4]

B. The Cost of Expanding Maternity Benefits

Estimating the cost of the maternity mandates would require information on the increase in premiums for adding maternity

---

[2] This differential coverage may have been a natural response to problems of adverse selection in the timing of pregnancy. Arleen Leibowitz (1990) finds that fertility rates of women with first-dollar coverage were 29-percent higher than those with some coinsurance in the RAND Health Insurance Experiment.

[3] The data do not contain state identifiers, so I was unable to control for the effects of state laws. Regional controls were not sufficient, due to the widespread passage of state laws in 1976 and 1977. By January 1, 1977, 28 percent of the U.S. population lived in states that had passed mandates; if all firms in these states had completely eradicated differential benefits by the time of the survey, then the discrimination figures should be multiplied by a factor of 1.39.

[4] Another 33 percent of women did not receive any major-medical coverage of normal pregnancies in the presence of major-medical coverage of comparable illnesses. However, it is unclear whether these laws should be construed to require major-medical coverage of normal childbirth.

benefits to a group health package, as well as the cost of increasing the generosity of benefits to the level of comparable illnesses. This sort of data is difficult to gather because nondifferential maternity benefits are now mandated nationally. However, as with all Equal Employment Opportunity Commission legislation, this mandate does not apply to firms with fewer than 15 employees. I have thus been able to gather information on the cost of adding maternity benefits to a small-group plan by using a premium-calculation package from a national insurer. This program is typical of that used by a group-health-insurance salesperson for calculating premiums for a small firm: it inputs the details of the plan and the demographic composition of the workforce and returns the premium cost.[5] For each of several demographic classifications, I use this program to observe the increase in premium cost with the addition of maternity benefits to a typical health insurance plan.

Table 1 presents the cost of adding maternity benefits to a group package for six demographic classifications, in 1990 dollars, in 1978 dollars, and as a percentage of average earnings for each group in 1978. The 1990 cost was deflated to 1978 by using a weighted average of the detailed CPI for hospital services and physician services, where the weights correspond to the fraction of costs in a typical delivery attributable to each.[6] The cost for each group varies widely as a percentage of wages, from less than 1 percent to almost 5 percent. To the extent that there was coverage for childbirth in health insurance plans before the

mandates but differential benefits, the figures in Table 1 will be overestimates of the mandates' costs.[7]

A check on these costs is provided by comparing them to the expected cost of childbirth for an employee in these categories. In 1989, the average cost of a normal delivery was $4,334 (Health Insurance Association of America, 1989); for married women 20–30 years old, the average probability of having a child in a year was 17.7 percent (U.S. Department of Health and Human Services, 1987). The annual expected cost of childbirth for this group is thus $767. Compared to the additional cost of $984 for maternity benefits in family coverage for this age group, this implies an insurance loading factor of 28 percent, which appears reasonable.[8] The high cost of childbirth meant that this mandate was an expensive one for many insured persons.

C. *The Economics of Group-Specific Mandated Benefits*

The advantages and disadvantages of mandates as tools of social policy are discussed by Thomas G. McGuire and John T. Montgomery (1982), Summers (1989), and Gruber (1992b). Summers presents the efficiency argument for mandates (relative to public provision), noting that when a benefit is provided through the workplace only, individuals will increase their labor supply in order to take advantage of it. Thus, mandates are benefit taxes; if employees value the benefit they are receiving, the increase in labor supply will reduce the deadweight

---

[5]Since much of the insurance price differential across firm sizes arises from fixed administrative costs, the incremental cost of maternity benefits should not be very sensitive to firm size. The fact that maternity benefits are now mandated nationally for large firms makes this contention difficult to confirm, although, within the range of this program, there is no effect of size differences. My source for this program requested anonymity.

[6]These were two-thirds and one-third, respectively (Health Insurance Association of America, 1989). Unfortunately, the detailed CPI for obstetrics was discontinued in 1978.

[7]These mandates raised the cost of individual workers due to the widespread existence of experience rating in insurance policies in this era (see the appendix to Gruber [1992a]).

[8]Furthermore, the costs in Table 1 will account for the possibility of a nonnormal delivery; in 1989, cesarean sections cost 66-percent more than normal births on average (Health Insurance Association of America, 1989). On the other hand, the fertility rate for working women may be somewhat lower than the average rate overall. A 28-percent loading factor is approximately the average for a firm of 50 employees, according to Congressional Research Service (1988).

TABLE 1—THE COST OF ADDING MATERNITY BENEFITS
TO A HEALTH INSURANCE PACKAGE

Coverage	Demographic group	Annual cost (1990 dollars)	Annual cost (1978 dollars)	Cost as percentage of 1978 weekly earnings
Family	20–29-year-old females	$984	$360	4.6
Family	30–39-year-old females	$756	$277	3.5
Individual	20–29-year-old females	$324	$119	1.5
Individual	30–39-year-old females	$252	$92	0.9
Family	20–29-year-old males	$984	$360	2.9
Family	30–39-year-old males	$756	$277	1.7

Notes: The source of the data is a premium-calculation program from an anonymous insurance carrier. The cost was calculated for a two-person firm in Maryland. Maryland was a location which approximately at the midpoint of the locational cost distribution. The results arc not sensitive to variations in firm size. Costs are for 1990; they are deflated to 1978 using a weighted average of the detailed CPI for hospital services and physician services, where the weights are $\frac{2}{3}$ and $\frac{1}{3}$, respectively. Costs are normalized by 1978 weekly wages from the May 1978 CPS. For single coverage, wages of unmarried persons are used; for family coverage, wages of married persons are used.

loss of finance. If valuation is full, then there is no deadweight loss from the mandate.

As I showed in an earlier version of this paper (Gruber, 1992a), this analysis is readily extended to the case of a group-specific mandate.[9] However, there may be a number of barriers to full group-specific shifting which are less important when the benefit is extended to everyone in the workplace. Most obviously, there are antidiscrimination regulations which prohibit differential pay for the same job across groups, or which prevent differential promotion decisions by demographic characteristic.[10] Furthermore,

workplace norms that prohibit different pay across groups or union rules about equality of relative pay may have similar effects to antidiscrimination rules. Finally, if the group that benefits is disproportionately composed of workers earning at or near the minimum wage, there may not be scope for shifting to wages.

As Grubcr (1992a) shows, these rigidities can cause mandates to have efficiency consequences even in the presence of full valuation, with resulting group-specific disemployment. Furthermore, the distortion will be higher than that which would arise if the group-specific benefit were financed by a payroll tax assessed on all workers. This is because the smaller tax base for a group-specific mandate will lead to a higher tax rate for a given level of expenditures, and the deadweight loss from taxation rises with the square of the tax rate. As Summers (1989 p. 182) states, referring to the effects of these types of impediments, "It is thus possible that mandated benefit programs can work against the interests of those who most

[9]Of course, if there is full valuation, the fact that the benefit is not part of the existing compensation package implies that there must be a market failure in its provision. In fact, there is a strong a priori argument for market failures in many cases of group-specific mandates, such as maternity leave, maternity insurance, or coverage for AIDS, due to problems of adverse selection in insurance markets.

[10]See Ronald G. Ehrenberg and Robert S. Smith (1991) for a discussion of U.S. antidiscrimination legislation, which was in place well before the mid-1970's. In this discussion, I focus only on laws prohibiting discrimination in rates of pay or promotion. In fact, if there are *also* binding restrictions on relative hiring

practices, then employers may be forced to bear the cost of the mandate. If discrimination rules are *only* binding on the hiring side, then they will not impede group-specific shifting in the case of full valuation.

require the benefit being offered. Publicly provided benefits do not drive a wedge between the marginal costs of hiring different workers and so do not give rise to a distortion of this kind."

Since the efficiency case for mandates rests largely on employee valuation which is reflected in wage adjustments, the empirical work below will estimate the extent of group-specific shifting to wages of the cost of mandated health insurance for maternity. If there is *not* shifting to wages, then either the group that benefits does not value the mandate, or there are impediments to the adjustment of relative wages to reflect that valuation. As a result, there may be large efficiency costs associated with such a policy.

In considering these results, two caveats are in order. First, I am not studying whether mandated maternity benefits represent sensible social policy, but instead only whether there appear to be large efficiency costs from the financing of such policies. In the conclusion, I will consider more broadly the desirability of mandated maternity coverage. Second, I have focused purely on efficiency considerations and have ignored equity considerations about the source of finance of a group-specific mandate. If the goal of a mandate is not to correct a market failure, but rather to provide benefits to some deprived group in society, then full shifting to wages may not be viewed as a desirable outcome. Thus, in considering the results that follow, it is important to understand the goal of government mandate policy: is it to correct a market failure, or to redirect resources across groups?[11]

II. Data and Identification Strategy

The goal of the empirical work is to identify the effect of laws passed by certain states (experimental states) which affected particular groups of individuals (treatment group). Identifying this effect requires controlling for any systematic shocks to the labor-market outcomes of the treatment group in the experimental states that are correlated with, but not due to, the law. I do so in three ways in the estimation below. First, I include year effects, to capture any national trends in the earnings of the treatment group. Second, I include state effects, to control for secular earnings differences in the states that passed the laws and those that did not. Finally, I include state-by-year effects, to control for state-specific shocks over this period which are correlated with the passage of these laws. That is, I compare the treatment individuals in the experimental states to a set of control individuals in those same states and measure the change in the treatments' *relative* outcomes, relative to states that did not pass maternity mandates. The identifying assumption of this "differences-in-differences-in-differences" (DDD) estimator are fairly weak: it simply requires that there be no contemporaneous shock that affects the relative outcomes of the treatment group in the same state-years as the law.[12]

The treatment group here comprises those insured workers who are "at risk" for having a child, or whose health insurance covers someone who is at risk for having a child. The controls are other individuals who were directly unaffected by the law. However, the Current Population Survey (before May 1979) contained no information on health insurance coverage. I am thus unable to identify exactly the employees for whom this was a costly mandate.

I address this problem in two ways in the empirical work below. First, I use as the treatment group married women of ages 20–40. This group will contain the individuals for whom the mandate was most costly (according to Table 1), married women of

---

[11]For the set of laws under study, the answer appears to be the former, as they were part of a larger set of state insurance-market regulations which appeared in the 1970's. See Gruber (1992b) for more detail on these state mandates.

[12]This name derives from the "differences-in-differences" estimator used, for example, by David Card (1990). Such estimation, in my context, would include only state and year effects and would assume that there were no state-specific shocks.

childbearing age. My control group is all individuals over age 40 and single males of ages 20–40. I exclude single 20–40-year-old women, as well as 20–40-year-old married males, who may also be affected by the laws if their insurance covers their wives.[13] This "treatment-dummy" approach has the virtue that it is relatively nonparametric.

Second, I use data on insurance coverage from other data sets to model the likelihood that individuals were covered by insurance and the type of insurance coverage that they receive, and I assign each individual a cost of the mandate based on these predictions and the cost data in Table 1. This approach has the advantage that I use individual variation, rather than differences across broad demographic groups, to identify the impact of the law. However, it has the disadvantage that it imposes strong parametric assumptions. If the functional form for the expected cost of the mandate is incorrect, then the demographic-group dummy may be a more effective means of capturing the law's impact. Thus, in the empirical work that follows, I will rely on both the treatment-group dummy and the individually parameterized cost measure.

I examine two sets of law changes in order to identify the effect of the maternity mandates. First, I study several of the states that passed the mandates in the mid-1970's, comparing them to similar states that did not pass mandates. Second, I study the effect of the federal mandate on the states that had not yet passed maternity mandates, using the states that had passed mandates as controls.

I focus on three of the 23 states that passed maternity mandates before the federal PDA: Illinois, New Jersey, and New York (the "experimental" states). The choice of these three states was motivated by two considerations. First, all of these laws went into effect between July 1, 1976, and January 1, 1977, so that they can be studied simultaneously, and there is sufficient time to examine their impact before the federal law was put into place (October 1978). Second, the data that I use to study the labor-market impact of these laws, the May Current Population Survey, did not identify all states separately before May 1977, but rather grouped some states into regional classifications. Thus, I can only use those states that were identified separately in the survey before 1977.

My set of "nonexperimental" states was chosen using similar criteria: these states had to be separately identified in these CPS's, and they had to be able to capture any regional shocks to the experimental states. For Illinois, the control states used are Ohio and Indiana; for New Jersey and New York, the controls are Connecticut, Massachusetts, and North Carolina.[14]

The data consist of observations on all individuals in these sets of experimental and nonexperimental locations for two years before the legislation (1974 and 1975) and for two years after the legislation (1977 and (1978). Because I use the May CPS, the 1978 survey collects data from before the passage of the federal law. The means of the data are presented in the left-hand panel of Table 2, for the experimental states and the nonexperimentals (both for the "before" years and for the "after" years), for all wage-earners.[15]

---

[13]That is, there are three demographic subsets of costly individuals under the mandate, and the treatment-dummy approach focuses on just one (married women). Approximately 56 percent of working married women had insurance from their employers in 1979; as I will show below, the expected cost of the mandate is roughly comparable across these three groups, as a fraction of wages. I therefore focus on married women for expositional ease; the effects on the other groups, as well as the overall treatment effect, is presented below.

[14]Pennsylvania could not be used as a "mid-Atlantic" control because it implemented broad anti-sex-discrimination insurance regulations during 1977, which included a "maternity mandate." North Carolina is included as a control in order to avoid comparing New York and New Jersey solely to New England; the results are similar if North Carolina is excluded.

[15]Hourly wages are in 1978 dollars. I exclude any individuals who report earning less than $1/hour or more than $100/hour in 1978 dollars. I also exclude any persons less than 20 years old or older than 65, and I likewise exclude the self-employed. The means are unweighted.

VOL. 84 NO. 3   *GRUBER: INCIDENCE OF MANDATED MATERNITY BENEFITS*   629

TABLE 2—MEANS FOR ALL WAGE-EARNERS

	State laws				Federal PDA			
	Nonexperimental states		Experimental states		Nonexperimental states		Experimental states	
Variable	Before law	After law	Before law	After law	Before law	After law	Before law	After law
Percentage female	41.4 [49.3]	43.9 [49.6]	41.4 [49.3]	43.1 [49.5]	44.4 [49.7]	45.6 [49.8]	44.5 [49.7]	45.8 [49.8]
Average age	38.1 [12.6]	37.6 [12.5]	38.9 [12.6]	38.4 [12.6]	37.6 [12.7]	37.5 [12.4]	37.5 [12.7]	37.2 [12.4]
Percentage married	75.0 [43.3]	70.8 [45.5]	71.6 [45.1]	67.9 [46.7]	65.7 [47.5]	63.8 [48.1]	70.0 [45.8]	67.0 [47.0]
Percentage nonwhite	8.8 [28.3]	9.2 [28.9]	10.2 [30.3]	12.0 [32.5]	12.3 [32.8]	13.5 [34.2]	10.9 [31.2]	11.2 [31.4]
Average education	12.1 [2.87]	12.3 [2.81]	12.4 [2.94]	12.7 [2.88]	12.5 [3.04]	12.7 [2.99]	12.3 [2.97]	12.6 [2.88]
Average hourly wage	5.68 [3.31]	5.59 [3.16]	6.61 [3.98]	6.40 [3.62]	6.33 [4.02]	5.88 [3.74]	5.80 [3.81]	5.49 [3.63]
Percentage union	27.0 [44.4]	26.8 [44.3]	33.4 [47.2]	33.8 [47.3]				
Percentage manufacturing	36.5 [48.2]	35.3 [47.8]	28.5 [45.1]	26.6 [44.2]	25.1 [43.3]	23.9 [42.6]	23.6 [42.5]	22.6 [41.8]
Percentage services	29.7 [47.2]	31.5 [46.5]	35.3 [47.8]	37.3 [48.4]	41.4 [49.3]	42.6 [49.4]	39.9 [49.0]	40.9 [49.2]
Weekly cost of mandate	4.01 [1.68]	3.87 [1.65]	3.92 [1.66]	3.85 [1.63]	3.64 [1.59]	3.56 [1.58]	3.71 [1.60]	3.64 [1.59]
Cost/wages	0.020 [0.010]	0.020 [0.010]	0.018 [0.009]	0.018 [0.010]	0.019 [0.012]	0.021 [0.013]	0.021 [0.013]	0.022 [0.013]
N:	9,954	10,180	10,597	10,636	41,772	45,332	48,713	59,647

Notes: Numbers in square brackets are standard deviations. Observations with wages below $1/hour or above $100/hour are dropped, as are individuals younger than 20 or older than 65 and the self-employed. See text for definitions of experimental and nonexperimental states and for definitions of before and after years.

There are not many striking differences across the groups of states: the experimental states have higher wages, are more unionized, and are less manufacturing-oriented. Differences in unionization and industry distribution, as well as systematic wage differences across locations, are controlled for in the estimation. Overall, wages fell more in the experimental states than in the nonexperimental states; below, I will assess whether the maternity mandates played any role in this relative fall.

The federal legislation provides a distinct opportunity to study the impacts of increasing the costs of health insurance coverage for maternity. In this case, the states that had already passed maternity mandates are the nonexperimentals, and those that had not are the experimentals. The advantage of this "experiment" is that by this later date the CPS was identifying all states separately, so that I am able to use as control states all those states that had passed laws by January 1, 1977 (12 states), and as experimentals all states that did not pass laws before 1979 (28 states).[16] These states are more broadly representative of the country

[16]The controls are Arkansas, California, Colorado, Hawaii, Idaho, Illinois, Iowa, Maryland, New Jersey, New York, Tennessee, and Wisconsin. The experimen-

as a whole, which should help to overcome any problems induced by using three (somewhat similar) states as experimentals in the earlier estimation. The disadvantage is that the PDA was more expansive than the state mandates, covering the entire employment relationship, rather than just health benefits. Thus, there may have been some effect on the cost of employing women of child-bearing age in the nonexperimental states as well.[17] Nevertheless, health-insurance industry representatives estimated that the effects on health benefit plans would represent two-thirds of the cost of implementing the PDA (Commerce Clearing House, 1978). To the extent that the net cost difference across these two sets of states represents the health insurance requirements of the law only, the shifting estimates should be comparable to those from the first (state mandates) strategy.

I use the 1978 and 1979 (before), and 1981 and 1982 (after) March CPS to study the impact of the federal law. The March data differ from the May data used earlier in that the earnings and labor-market data are retrospective; that is, individuals are asked for their annual earnings, weeks worked, and usual hours per week in the previous year.[18] The means for the federal law change are presented in the right-hand panel of Table 2. Once again, the two sets

of states are fairly similar: in this case, the experimental states have slightly lower wages and are less manufacturing-oriented.

III. The Labor-Market Impact of the State Laws

A. *DDD Estimation*

Table 3 illustrates DDD estimation of the effect of the maternity mandates on wages. The top panel compares the change in wages for 20–40-year-old married women in the states that passed the laws to the change for 20–40-year-old married women in the nonexperimental states. Each cell contains the mean average real wage for the group labeled on the axes, along with the standard error and the number of observations. There was a 3.4-percent fall in the real wages of women in the experimental states over this period, compared to a 2.8-percent rise in the real wages of women in other states. Thus, there was a (significant) 6.2-percent relative fall in the wages of women of child-bearing age in states that passed these laws; this is the differences-in-differences estimate of the law's impact. This figure seems somewhat large given the magnitude of the costs identified in Table 1.

However, if there was a distinct labor-market shock to the experimental states over this period, this estimate does not identify the impact of the law. I examine this in the bottom panel of Table 3, where I perform the same exercise for the control group, all those older than 40 and single males ages 20–40. For that group, I do find a fall in wages in the experimental states, relative to the other states, of 0.8 percent. Although not significant, this suggests that it may be important to control for state-specific shocks in estimating the impact of the law.

Taking the difference between the two panels of Table 3, there is a 5.4-percent fall in the *relative* wages of 20–40-year-old married women in the states that passed the laws, compared to the change in relative wages in the nonexperimental states. This statistically significant DDD estimate provides some evidence that the cost of a group-specific mandate is borne by

---

tals are Alabama, Alaska, Delaware, the District of Columbia, Indiana, Kentucky, Louisiana, Maine, Massachusetts, Mississippi, Missouri, Montana, Nebraska, New Hampshire, New Mexico, North Carolina, North Dakota, Ohio, Oklahoma, Rhode Island, South Carolina, South Dakota, Texas, Utah, Vermont, Washington, West Virginia, and Wyoming. Connecticut was excluded in this part of the study because the state mandated benefit nondiscrimination rules for all groups in 1979.

[17] For example, another major cost of the PDA was the requirement that firms offering disability coverage extend that coverage to include pregnancy.

[18] Thus, the actual labor-market data come from 1977, 1978, 1980, and 1981. The use of the March CPS was dictated by the fact that, starting in 1979, the May CPS only asked earnings information of one-quarter of the sample. The March CPS also does not report data on union status.

members of that group. However, its interpretation is problematic, since there may be important variation in the effect of the law within the set of married 20–40-year-old women; for example, only some of these women will have insurance on the job. This source of variation will be exploited below, where I build individual-specific measures of the impact of the law. First, however, I discuss how the analysis of Table 3 can be expressed within a regression framework.

B. *Regression Framework for DDD Estimation*

The sampling variance of the DDD estimate in Table 3 can be reduced by moving to a regression framework, which allows me to control for other observables that affect the outcome variables of interest. The regression equation has the following form:

$$(1) \quad W_{ijt} = \alpha + \beta_1 X_{ijt} + \beta_2 \tau_t + \beta_3 \delta_j$$
$$+ \beta_4 \text{TREAT}_i + \beta_5(\delta_j \times \tau_t)$$
$$+ \beta_6(\tau_t \times \text{TREAT}_i)$$
$$+ \beta_7(\delta_j \times \text{TREAT}_i)$$
$$+ \beta_8(\delta_j \times \tau_t \times \text{TREAT}_i).$$

In this equation, i indexes individuals, j indexes states (1 if experimental state, 0 if nonexperimental), and t indexes years (1 if after the law, 0 if before). W is the log real hourly wage, X is a vector of observable characteristics, δ_j is a fixed state effect, τ_t is a fixed year effect, and TREAT is a dummy for treatment group (1 if treatment, 0 if control).

The analogy of this regression to Table 3 is straightforward. The fixed effects control for the time-series changes in wages (β_2), the time-invariant characteristics of the experimental states (β_3), and the time-invariant characteristics of the treatment group (β_4). The second-level interactions control for changes over time in the experimental states (β_5), changes over time for the treatment group nationwide (β_6), and time-invariant characteristics of the treatment group in the experimental states (β_7). The third-level interaction (β_8) captures all

variation in wages specific to the treatments (relative to controls) in the experimental states (relative to the nonexperimentals) in the years after the law (relative to before the law). This is the DDD estimate of the extent of shifting of the cost of the mandate to group-specific wages. The set of demographic covariates used includes education, experience and its square, sex, marital status, a marital-status × sex interaction, a dummy for nonwhite, a dummy for union status, dummies for 15 major industries, and separate year dummies for 1974 and 1978.

The first row of Table 4 presents the estimates of the third-level interaction from (1), β_8. The coefficient indicates that wages fell by 4.3 percent for the treatment group; it is marginally statistically significant. While this is slightly smaller than the estimate from Table 3, the standard error has been reduced as well, so that the significance is approximately the same. The fact that introducing the other covariates did not have a sizeable impact on this coefficient is comforting, given the experimental interpretation of the estimate.[19]

The next two columns of Table 4 examine the effects of this mandate on hours of work and probability of employment. If this benefit is fully valued, on average, by workers in the treatment group, there should be no change in their net labor input. However, even with full valuation on average, it is possible that the mandate could affect the *composition* of labor input. This mandate represents an increase in the fixed costs of employment and is thus more costly (as a

---

[19]The other coefficients in the regression are of their expected signs and magnitudes. There is a 1.2-percent fall in wages for the within-state control group. This suggests that the experimental states, on average, saw a negative shock over this period. Alternatively, the mandate itself could be causing this fall for the control group, if the groups are complements or if there is cross-subsidization across groups due to relative pay restrictions. However, given the findings of substantial shifting to group-specific wages, such spillover seems unlikely. The full set of coefficients are reported in Gruber (1992a).

TABLE 3—DDD ESTIMATES OF THE IMPACT OF STATE MANDATES
ON HOURLY WAGES

Location/year	Before law change	After law change	Time difference for location
A. *Treatment Individuals: Married Women, 20 – 40 Years Old:*			
Experimental states	1.547 (0.012) [1,400]	1.513 (0.012) [1,496]	−0.034 (0.017)
Nonexperimental states	1.369 (0.010) [1,480]	1.397 (0.010) [1,640]	0.028 (0.014)
Location difference at a point in time:	0.178 (0.016)	0.116 (0.015)	
Difference-in-difference:	−0.062 (0.022)		
B. *Control Group: Over 40 and Single Males 20 – 40:*			
Experimental states	1.759 (0.007) [5,624]	1.748 (0.007) [5,407]	−0.011 (0.010)
Nonexperimental states	1.630 (0.007) [4,959]	1.627 (0.007) [4,928]	−0.003 (0.010)
Location difference at a point in time:	0.129 (0.010)	0.121 (0.010)	
Difference-in-difference:	−0.008: (0.014)		
DDD:	**−0.054 (0.026)**		

Notes: Cells contain mean log hourly wage for the group identified. Standard errors are given in parentheses; sample sizes are given in square brackets. Years before/after law change, and experimental/nonexperimental states, are defined in the text. Difference-in-difference-in-difference (DDD) is the difference-in-difference from the upper panel minus that in the lower panel.

fraction of labor payments) for low-hours employees. If employers are able to lower each worker's wages by the lump-sum cost of the mandate, then neither hours nor employment should change. However, if employers are not able to implement a percentage reduction in pay that is inversely proportional to hours worked, then part-time workers will become more expensive. Employers may thus react by increasing hours and lowering employment, reducing

the cost per hour of the mandate while leaving total labor input unchanged.

Of course, if the wage offset is lower for low-hours workers, workers will demand the opposite outcome; there will be increasing demand for part-time work, with hours falling and employment increasing. Furthermore, since part-time workers may be more readily excluded from health insurance coverage, there may also be a countervailing effect on the employer side, as full-time

TABLE 4—TREATMENT-DUMMY RESULTS ACROSS DEMOGRAPHIC GROUPS

Group	Log hourly wage	Log hours/week	Employment (probit)	Percentage changes in labor input
Married women, ages 20–40	−0.043 (0.023)	0.049 (0.022)	−0.047 (0.048) [−0.016]	1.40
Single women, ages 20–40	−0.042 (0.026)	−0.014 (0.024)	−0.095 (0.064) [−0.030]	−5.95
Married men, ages 20–40	−0.009 (0.018)	0.030 (0.015)	−0.139 (0.072) [−0.038]	−1.08
All treatments	−0.023 (0.015)	0.027 (0.014)	−0.079 (0.039) [−0.024]	−0.88

Notes: Standard errors are given in parentheses. The coefficient is that on the third-level interaction in equation (1). The treatment group is the group indicated for each row. The control group is the same as that for Table 3 (all those older than 40 and single men younger than 40). The number in brackets in the employment column is the marginal probability (see text). The change in total labor input is the change in hours at the average-employment/population ratio plus the change in employment in terms of average hours per employed person. This is then divided by the ratio of employment to population to get per-worker figures and then divided by average hours per week for the treatment group to get a percentage change.

employees are replaced with their (uninsured) part-time counterparts. In this case as well, hours would fall, and employment would rise.[20] Thus, the effects on hours and employment are uncertain, even if the cost of the mandate can be shifted to wages on average.

Table 4 confirms the conclusion of full shifting, on average, but does show some compositional changes. In the second column, the dependent variable is the log of weekly hours of work; hours rise by a significant 4.9 percent for the treatment group. I measure employment by a dummy variable which equals 1 if the individual is employed, and 0 otherwise (unemployed or out of the labor force); the employment regressions are run as probits. Table 4 also shows an insignificant fall in employment; it implies that the treatments saw a 1.6-percent fall in employment over this period, relative to the

sets of controls.[21] There is a small net positive effect on total labor input of 0.48 hours per week per worker; this amounts to a rise in hours of about 1.4 percent of average hours per week for the treatment group.[22] This is consistent with the large wage offsets uncovered in the columns for log hourly wage and log hours/week.

As mentioned above, married women represent only one of three groups of workers that are potentially affected by these mandates. The costs of employing single women of childbearing age rose as well, as did costs

---

[20]Of course, another option for employers is to drop insurance coverage altogether. Gruber (1992b) finds that there was little effect of other expensive state-mandated benefits on the propensity of firms to offer health insurance.

[21]This is calculated by using the probit coefficients to predict the probability of employment as if all individuals in the experimental state/years were treatments, then predicting the probability as if none were treatments, and taking the average of the differences of these predictions across individuals.

[22]I calculate the change in total labor input as the change in hours at the average employment-to-population ratio plus the change in employment at average hours per employed person. This is then divided by the employment-to-population ratio to get per-worker figures.

of employing married males, who may cover their wives in their insurance policies. The effects on these other groups, as well as the effect on all of these groups together, are presented in the remaining rows of Table 4. There are some differences in the results across groups: shifting to wages is small and insignificant for married males, and there is evidence of a sizable fall in total labor input for single females, which is of the same magnitude as the fall in wages for that group. However, the overall results across all groups (i.e., from a regression in which the treatment dummy is 1 for members of all of these groups) is consistent with that for married women only: a decrease in wages, a rise in hours, and a fall in employment, with an overall labor input effect that is small relative to the wage effect.

The reasons for this differential effect across the demographic subgroups may be heterogeneity in the impact of this law across the groups, due to differential probabilities of insurance coverage and costs of extending maternity health-insurance benefits. In the next subsection, I address this heterogeneity by attempting to model the individual-specific cost of these mandates.[23]

C. *Individual Parameterization of the Cost of the Mandates*

In assessing the cost of these maternity mandates for each individual, one must consider (i) whether the individual is covered by insurance and whether that insurance provides differential maternity benefits; (ii)

whether this coverage is from the individual's own job or is through a family member; (iii) whether the coverage is for the entire family, or just the individual;[24] and (iv) the individual's (or spouse's) age-specific probability of childbearing. Unfortunately, the CPS does not contain information about insurance coverage during the 1974–1978 period. I have thus calculated *predicted* individual-specific costs, drawing on three sources of data: the estimates of age-specific costs from the premium program; data on the probability of insurance coverage in the 1979 May CPS Pension Supplement; and data on type of insurance coverage from the 1977 NMCES. These cost calculations are described in detail in the appendix to Gruber (1992a); I will briefly review them here.

For all individuals over age 40, and for single males ages 20–40, a cost of zero is assigned. I divide the remaining 20–40-year-olds into three treatment groups: single females, married females, and married males. I use the CPS Pension Supplement, which collects data on employer-provided insurance, to model the probability of insurance coverage as a function of individual demographics, hours of work, union status, and industry of employment. Separate predictor regressions are run for each of the three groups. I then create an extract from the NMCES of all persons in each of these three groups who are employed, who have insurance on the job, and who are the primary insured for their household. For each group I model the probability that a worker will have family coverage versus individual coverage as a function of demographics, industry, spouse's employment status, and spouse's industry.

---

[23]As I discuss in the next subsection, the expected costs of the mandates across the three groups are roughly equal. The reason for the much smaller wage effect for married males is therefore unclear; it may be that employers perceived the law as having a larger effect on the cost of employing women for other reasons. In any case, the coefficients across the different groups are not significantly different from each other, and the more appropriate test of the effect of the laws is to use the variation in the cost across individuals, which I do next. The overall conclusions from the individually parameterized results below are not sensitive to the exclusion of any one of these three groups from the analysis.

[24]The premium-pricing program described earlier assigns a much higher incremental cost of adding maternity benefits to family coverage than to individual coverage. Presumably, this proxies for differences in the probability of childbearing. Indeed, the relative cost difference between the two types of policies is almost exactly the same as the difference in the relative probabilities of childbearing between single and married women (U.S. Department of Health and Human Services, 1987).

Finally, I use Table 1 to assign age-specific costs: I take a weighted average of the costs of individual and family coverage (where the weights are the predicted probabilities of each type of coverage from the NMCES) and multiply by the predicted probability of having insurance coverage on the job. This yields a predicted weekly cost which varies by the six 10-year age groupings in Table 1.[25] The results of this exercise, for all treatment individuals, are presented at the bottom of Table 2. The cost averages $3.91 per week, which is 1.9 percent of wages on average; it has a maximum value of 28 percent of wages. The average cost is not appreciably different across the experimental/ nonexperimental locations, nor does it change much over time. The weekly cost is highest for married males, reflecting both the high cost for that group from Table 1 and the fact that they are more likely than married females to be the primary insured. However, once costs are normalized by wages, they are roughly equal for married men and women, and slightly lower for single women.

Since a fixed-cost-of-employment mandate is more costly for part-time workers, the predicted cost should also be normalized by hours worked per week, given that the probability of insurance coverage has been appropriately downweighted for that group in the predictor equation. However, for workers who report weekly wages in the CPS, the hourly wage is calculated as the weekly wage divided by hours worked. Thus, if there is measurement error in hours, this may induce a spurious correlation between

hourly wage and hourly mandate cost. I will present results below both with and without the normalization for hours worked, as the results are sensitive to the specification chosen.

The individually parameterized cost measure can be introduced in place of the treatment dummy in equation (4). Since the calculated cost of the mandate is expressed in dollars, it would be interpreted most straightforwardly in a levels wage equation, rather than the log wage specification used earlier. However, since wages are distributed lognormally, a levels wage equation is potentially misspecified. In a log wage equation, the linear cost measure estimates the percentage fall in wages for a one-dollar increase in cost, which varies along the wage distribution. Ideally, this problem could be solved by normalizing costs by individual wages, but this would induce a spurious negative correlation between the dependent and independent variables in the wage regression. Instead, I note that the wage equation can be specified as $W = (e^{\beta X} + \text{COSTNN})e^{\varepsilon}$, where COSTNN is the individual hourly mandate cost, and ε is a normally distributed error term. Taking logs of both sides of this equation, one obtains: $\log(W) = \log(e^{\beta X} + \text{COSTNN}) + \varepsilon$. This nonlinear model thus has both a normally distributed error and a directly interpretable coefficient on the individual mandate cost in dollars.[26]

To the extent that my estimate of the cost of the mandate is correct, a coefficient of -1 on the third-level interaction would in-

---

[25] In an earlier version of this paper, I also let the cost vary by single-year age-specific probabilities of childbearing. The results were similar; I rely on the 10-year averages because this seems to be the level at which the costs of insurance vary. For married males, I use own age rather than wife's age, since this appears to be the relevant variable for the premium calculation. Ideally, I would also control for the probability that the individual has differential benefit coverage; however, I am not confident enough in my estimates of the incidence of differential benefits to make this an integral part of the analysis. This implies that the result may underestimate the extent of shifting.

[26] The results are quite similar when the cost is included linearly in the log wage regression and normalized by average wages (see Gruber, 1992a). I have also tried entering hourly cost, not normalized by wages, into a linear wage equation: the estimated third-level interaction is -3.76, with a standard error of 0.99. Furthermore, the coefficient on cost (not normalized by wages) in a log wage regression should fall as the wage rises, since a dollar cost increase represents a smaller percentage of wages. This prediction is testable by cutting the sample by some measure of *permanent* income, such as education. In fact, the shifting coefficient for workers who did not graduate from high school is twice that of those who did, although estimates are not significantly different from each other.

TABLE 5—WAGES AND LABOR INPUT RESULTS—PARAMETRIZED COST OF THE MANDATE

	Specification				
	(i)	(ii)	(iii)	(iv)	(v)
		Log wage	Log wage	Log	Employment
Coefficient	Log wage	(no hours)	(full-time)	hours/week	(probit)
β_8	−2.140	−0.028	−0.037	0.0049	−0.027
	(0.759)	(0.019)	(0.019)	(0.0031)	(0.011)
					[−0.022]
Shifting (percentage):	214	109	156		
N:	41,367	41,367	35,868	41,367	84,305

Notes: All regressions are estimated by nonlinear least squares, as described in the text. Standard errors are given in parentheses. The mandate cost in columns (ii) and (iii) is not normalized by hours worked; shifting is calculated at average hours for the treatments. The sample in column (iii) is restricted to those who work at least 35 hours per week. Column (v) is a probit. Cost is assigned by demographic group average. The number in brackets shows the change in the probability of employment for a $1 increase in costs.

dicate full shifting to wages. Even if the *level* of the estimate is incorrect, however, so long as I capture the *relative costliness* across individuals appropriately, I will gain efficiency in estimation over the treatment-dummy case by using individual variation in relative costs.[27]

D. *Individual Parameterization: Results*

Table 5 presents the coefficient of interest from wage regressions with the individually parameterized costs. In column (i), the cost is normalized by hours worked. The regression indicates very sizable shifting to wages, on the order of 210 percent of the cost of the mandate. While this coefficient is significantly different from 0, it is not significantly different from 1, which would imply full shifting to wages.

In column (ii), I remove the normalization of the mandate cost for hours worked. At the mean hours worked for the treat-

[27] Using this estimated cost in place of a demographic dummy does introduce more imprecision into the estimation, since I have predicted the cost from earlier regression models. This imprecision will not be appropriately reflected in the standard errors in my outcome regressions, which will therefore be too small. However, this problem can be shown to disappear as the precision of the predictor equations increases; the predictor equations used fit fairly well, predicting between 73 percent and 85 percent of the cases correctly.

ment group, there is 109 percent shifting to wages, but the estimate is not significant. This reduction in the shifting coefficient implies that the fall in wages was greater for the low-hours workers, since they saw the greatest increase in predicted costs when predicted costs were normalized by hours worked. To the extent that these part-time workers were covered by health insurance, this is a sensible finding, since the hourly cost of the mandate was highest for them. However, only 20 percent of individuals who worked less than 35 hours per week in 1979 were covered by health insurance (based on tabulations from the May 1979 CPS). The predictor equation for the probability of insurance coverage controls for hours worked, a dummy for part-time work, and interactions of union status with hours of work and the part-time dummy; nevertheless, it would be disturbing if these results were driven solely by low-hours workers.

Thus, in column (iii) of Table 5, I focus only on full-time workers (35 hours per week or more); over 75 percent of this group is covered by insurance on the job. Cost is not normalized by hours worked for full-time workers, since the noise-to-signal ratio in hours is presumably quite high for this group.[28] The results reveal that the conclu-

[28] The shifting estimate is similar if cost is normalized.

sion of group-specific shifting was not driven by low-hours workers. The shifting estimate for full-time workers lies between the estimates of columns (i) and (ii).

If these estimates are correct, and there is full shifting of the cost of this mandate to the wages of the treatment group, then there should be no net effect on labor input. I test this in columns (iv) and (v) of Table 5. In column (iv), the dependent variable is the log of hours worked, and the cost is not normalized by average wages or hours.[29] The regression reveals a rise in hours worked by about 0.5 percent of their average level for a $1 increase in cost.

For the cost measure in the employment regression, I cannot predict individual probabilities of insurance coverage or type of coverage, since I cannot measure industry of employment or hours worked for the unemployed. I thus assign each individual the average probability of insurance coverage and the average probability of family/individual coverage for his or her demographic group (single females, married females, and married males). That is, I assume that if nonemployed individuals were employed, they would face the same probabilities of insurance coverage and buy the same type of insurance as their demographic counterparts who are employed. As before, the employment regression is run as a probit.

As column (v) of Table 5 shows, there is a significant fall in employment for the treatment group. The probit coefficient implies that a $1 increase in cost would lead to a 0.22-percent fall in probability of employment.[30] Taken together with the hours co-

efficient, this implies a rise in total labor input per worker of 0.63 percent of its average value for a 100-percent rise in cost. This can be contrasted to the estimate of a fall in wages of 4.7 percent of their average value. Thus, the estimated effect on net labor input is small, which confirms the conclusion of substantial shifting to wages.[31]

IV. The Federal Experiment

Tables 4 and 5 find extensive shifting of the cost of the maternity mandates to group-specific wages, both in a relatively unrestrictive treatment-group-dummy model and in a more parametric specification which tried to capture individual variation in the cost of the mandates. However, these results emerged from the analysis of only three experiments, using a select set of control states. This suggests the desirability of finding an example of a group-specific mandate that affected a broader range of states. The federal PDA of 1978 provides such an example.

The federal law can be studied within the same regression framework used above, with the exceptions that there are no data on union status and that the year dummies are now for 1978 and 1981. These results

---

[29] While normalizing by hours is once again theoretically appropriate, it would induce a spurious negative correlation between predicted cost and hours worked. Furthermore, the predictor equation for the probability of insurance coverage used here does not control for hours worked, since this would induce a spurious positive correlation.

[30] This is calculated similarly to the earlier case: predicted employment is calculated at average cost and at average cost plus one dollar for the treatment group in the experimental state/years; the average difference

in predicted probability of employment across treatment individuals gives the effects of a dollar increase in costs.

[31] I have also performed two specification checks to assess the robustness of this result. First, I assessed whether one of the law changes was driving the results, by running the regression separately by state, relative to the regional controls. While I found stronger results for New York and weaker results for New Jersey, the result was not driven by any one state's experience; the shifting estimate was significant at the 10-percent level even if New York was excluded. In all cases the net labor-input effect was very small relative to the wage effect, confirming the conclusion of full shifting. Second, in an attempt to include more detailed controls for industry-specific shocks which may be driving the results, I allowed the industry dummies to vary by state and year. This is a very general specification, which allows for state-specific, year-specific, and state×year-specific shocks by industry. Nevertheless, the shifting estimate is virtually identical to that in column (i) of Table 5. These results are reported in Gruber (1992a).

638   THE AMERICAN ECONOMIC REVIEW   JUNE 1994

TABLE 6—FURTHER RESULTS—FEDERAL EXPERIMENT

Demographic group/treatment	(i) Log wage	(ii) Log wage (no hours)	(iii) Log wage (full-time)	(iv) Log hours/week	(v) Employment (probit)	(vi) Change in total labor input
			Specification			
Married women, ages 20–40	−0.021 (0.012)			0.0012 (0.0098)	−0.018 (0.028) [−0.0055]	−0.0071
Single women, ages 20–40	−0.014 (0.014)			0.0157 (0.0101)	0.0184 (0.0374) [0.0050]	0.0219
Married men, ages 20–40	−0.008 (0.0012)			−0.0008 (0.0073)	0.0020 (0.0046) [0.0005]	−0.0003
All treatments	−0.0014 (0.0009)			0.0032 (0.0064)	0.0001 (0.0233) [0.00004]	0.0033
Individual parameterization	−0.587 (0.412)	−0.023 (0.010)	−0.017 (0.010)	−0.0002 (0.0015)	0.0007 (0.0068) [0.00005]	−0.0005
Shifting (percentage):	59	90	75			

Notes: The coefficient is β_8 in equation (1). Standard errors are given in parentheses. In column (v), the number in brackets interprets the probit coefficient for employment, by calculating the change in probability of employment for a \$1 increase in the cost of the mandate. Change in total labor input is the change in total hours per week per worker for a 100-percent rise in the cost of the mandate. It is calculated by adding the change in hours at average employment to the change in employment at average hours, for a \$1 rise in cost, for the relevant treatment group. This is then divided by average labor input (hours times employment/population ratio) for the treatment group (and multiplied by cost per week in the parameterized cost case) to get the percentage change in labor input for a 100-percent rise in the dollar cost.

are reported in Table 6. The first row repeats the estimation using the demographic dummy, which is once again equal to 1 for married women aged 20–40, and 0 for all others (excluding married 20–40-year-old males and single 20–40-year-old women). There is evidence of shifting to wages, although the magnitude is approximately half that of the earlier regressions and is only significant at the 10-percent level. There is also an increase in hours and a fall in employment, as before, although neither the hours nor the employment coefficient is as large as the respective standard errors. The net effect on labor input is approximately zero. Thus, once again one finds a fall in group-specific wages with no effect on net labor input.

The next three rows of Table 6 examine the other demographic groups. The wage results for both single women and married men are weaker than those for married women, although in no case are the estimates significantly different from each other. The overall treatment effect is about two-thirds the size of the effect for married women only. The labor-input results are once again mixed; overall, there is a small rise in hours and no effect on employment.

As above, moving to the individually parameterized cost yields further variation which can be used to pin down the extent of shifting to wages more precisely. The individually parameterized cost is calculated in the same way as for the state laws, and this is presented at the bottom of the right-hand side panel of Table 2.[32] The results are quite similar to those from the state laws,

[32] The only difference is that the predictor equations now no longer include controls for union status and its interaction with hours worked and part-time status.

with the cost averaging about 2 percent of wages.

The regression results using the individually parameterized costs are reported in Table 6; the same nonlinear specification described earlier is used. In column (i) the cost is normalized by hours worked, and in column (ii) it is not normalized. Here, the results are reversed from the previous case; the shifting estimate is higher and more significant when cost is *not* normalized. When cost is normalized by hours, the estimate indicates 60-percent shifting, but the estimate is insignificant. When it is not normalized, the shifting estimate rises to 90 percent, once again indicating approximately full shifting to wages, and it is statistically significant.

One reason for the worse results when cost is normalized by hours could be the fact that hours per week in the March CPS are for the previous year, while in the May survey they are the usual hours per week worked currently. The May measure may be a less noisy proxy for actual hours, which makes the estimate of cost per hour more precise and reduces the problems that arise from dividing both the dependent and independent variables by hours. To address this point, as well as to reduce the possible spurious influence of low-hours workers who are not covered by health insurance, I focus only on individuals who worked 35 hours per week or more in column (iii). The non-normalized estimate is similar for this restricted sample, and it indicates shifting of about 75 percent of the cost of the mandate; it is significant at the 10-percent level.

The fifth row of Table 6 reports labor-input results for the individually parameterized costs. Here, the results are the opposite of those uncovered earlier; there is now a *fall* in hours and a *rise* in employment. However, both the hours coefficient and the employment coefficient are completely insignificant, and there is no net effect on labor input. This confirms the conclusion that, on average, the cost of the mandate was fully shifted to wages.[33]

[33] I have also performed the two specification checks described above for the federal law change. First, I

V. Conclusions

Mandated employer provision of employee benefits is a topic of increasing interest in America today, and many of the proposed mandates are group-specific ones. When there is a market failure in the provision of a particular benefit, a mandate may be an efficient means of correcting the failure. By exploiting the fact that employees value the benefit that they are receiving, mandates act as a benefits tax, and can (in the limit) be as efficient as lump-sum financing of the benefit expansion. However, this argument rests crucially on the ability of wages to adjust freely to reflect employee valuation of the mandated benefit; in the case of group-specific mandates, there may be a number of impediments to such free adjustment of relative wages.

The evidence in this paper supports the contention that there will be group-specific shifting of the costs of mandates such as comprehensive health insurance coverage for maternity. This finding was robust to a variety of different specifications of the effect of these maternity mandates. The fact that the wages of women of childbearing age and their husbands were free to reflect the valuation of these benefits suggests that group-specific mandates do not change the relative cost of employing the targeted group of workers. This is an important precondition for arguing that mandates are an efficient tool of social policy.

It is important to highlight that this paper focused only on the efficiency case for mandates as a tool of public policy. In fact, there are at least two equity arguments

reran the regressions within each of four regions of the country: the Northeast, the Midwest, the South, and the West. Within each region, there was evidence of wage offsets, with the shifting estimates (from the regressions in which cost is not normalized by hours) ranging from 56 percent to 122 percent. However, none of the estimates was individually statistically significant, and none was significantly different from any of the others. Second, I controlled for industry-specific shocks by once again including industry-by-area-by-year controls. As with the earlier state laws, this had no effect on the coefficient of interest.

640   THE AMERICAN ECONOMIC REVIEW   JUNE 1994

against mandates. First, the goal of the mandate may be to redistribute resources toward a certain group in society. In this case, group-specific shifting of the costs of a mandate undoes this redistributive policy. Second, mandates may be relatively regressive policies for financing benefit expansions. As Rodrigo Vergara (1990) shows, a tax on all labor which finances a benefit expansion will be more progressive than a mandate if the distribution of income is sufficiently unequal.

Furthermore, the case of maternity health benefits may illustrate how correcting one market failure can serve to exacerbate another. Health economists have shown that full insurance may lead to large welfare losses through the overutilization of medical resources (Martin S. Feldstein, 1973). Indeed, it is interesting to note that the number of cesarean births per 1,000 population doubled from 1975 to 1981 and that cesarean sections are now the second most frequently performed surgical procedure in the country (Health Insurance Association of America, 1989; U.S. Department of Commerce, 1990). More research is needed on the effects of increased coverage for maternity after the mid-1970's on the *costs* of childbirth. Did full insurance coverage lead to more costly treatment of the complications of childbirth?

Finally, this analysis has focused solely on the financing of expansions of insurance coverage and has ignored the potential benefits of mandates. If expanded coverage of maternity did lead to a change in the style of treatment of childbirth, this may have had beneficial effects on birth outcomes. Similarly, if maternity-leave provisions increase the continuity of labor-force participation of women, there could be important gains in terms of reducing workplace inequality. There have also been almost 1,000 other mandated benefits at the state level which are similar to these maternity mandates; that is, they dictate the inclusion of minimum levels of certain benefits in existing health insurance plans. Some mandates, such as mental illness and alcoholism treatment, may have substantial "offset" effects in terms of reducing medical expenditures in other parts of the health-care system

(McGuire and Montgomery, 1982). If these benefits can be estimated, they could be weighed against the wage costs to employees in evaluating the efficacy of future workplace benefit expansions.

REFERENCES

Alan Guttmacher Institute. *Blessed events and the bottom line: Financing maternity care in the United States.* New York: Alan Guttmacher Institute, 1987.

Card, David. "The Effects of Minimum Wage Legislation: A Case Study of California, 1987–89." Industrial Relations Section Working Paper No. 278, Princeton University, 1990.

Commerce Clearing House. *New 1978 pregnancy benefit and discrimination rules, with explanation and state survey.* Chicago: Commerce Clearing House, 1978.

Congressional Research Service. *Costs and effects of extending health insurance coverage.* Washington, DC: U.S. Government Printing Office, 1988.

Ehrenberg, Ronald G. and Smith, Robert S. *Modern labor economics: Theory and public policy.* New York: Harper Collins, 1991.

Feldstein, Martin S. "The Welfare Loss of Excess Health Insurance." *Journal of Political Economy*, March/April 1973, *81*(2), pp. 251–80.

Gruber, Jonathan. "The Efficiency of a Group-Specific Mandated Benefit: Evidence from Health Insurance Benefits for Maternity." National Bureau of Economic Research (Cambridge, MA) Working Paper No. 4157, September 1992a.

_____. "State Mandated Benefits and Employer Provided Insurance," National Bureau of Economic Research Working Paper No. 4239, December 1992b.

Gruber, Jonathan and Krueger, Alan B. "The Incidence of Mandated Employer-Provided Insurance: Lessons from Workers' Compensation Insurance," in David Bradford, ed., *Tax policy and the economy.* Cambridge, MA: MIT Press, 1991, pp. 111–44.

Health Insurance Association of America. *New group health insurance.* Washington, DC: Health Insurance Association of America, 1978.

_____. *Source book of health insurance data*, Washington, DC: Health Insurance Association of America, 1981.

_____. *The cost of maternity care and childbirth in the United States, 1989*. Washington, DC: Health Insurance Association of America, 1989.

Kittner, Dorothy R. "Maternity Benefits Available to Most Health Plan Participants." *Monthly Labor Review*. May 1978, *101*(5), pp. 53–56.

Leibowitz, Arleen. "The Response of Births to Changes in Health Care Costs." *Journal of Human Resources*, Fall 1990, *25*(4), pp. 697–711.

Leshin, Geraldine. *EEO law: Impact on fringe benefits*. Los Angeles: UCLA Institute of Industrial Relations, 1981.

McGuire, Thomas G. and Montgomery, John T. "Mandated Mental Benefits in Private Health Insurance." *Journal of Health Politics, Policy, and Law*, Summer 1982, *7*(2), pp. 380–406.

Summers, Lawrence H. "Some Simple Economics of Mandated Benefits." *American Economic Review*, May 1989 (*Papers and Proceedings*), *79*(2), pp. 177–83.

U.S. Department of Commerce. *Statistical abstract of the United States*. Washington, DC: U.S. Department of Commerce, 1990.

U.S. Department of Health and Human Services. *Vital statistics of the United States*. Washington, DC: U.S. Department of Health and Human Services, 1987.

Vergara, Rodrigo. "The Economics of Mandatory Benefits Programs." Mimeo, Harvard University, 1990.

[14]

THE ECONOMIC CONSEQUENCES OF PARENTAL LEAVE MANDATES: LESSONS FROM EUROPE*

CHRISTOPHER J. RUHM

This study investigates the economic consequences of rights to paid parental leave in nine European countries over the 1969 through 1993 period. Since women use virtually all parental leave in most nations, men constitute a reasonable comparison group, and most of the analysis examines how changes in paid leave affect the gap between female and male labor market outcomes. The employment-to-populations ratios of women in their prime childbearing years are also compared with those of corresponding aged men and older females. Parental leave is associated with increases in women's employment, but with reductions in their relative wages at extended durations.

Over 100 countries have enacted some form of parental leave policies, with most assuring at least two to three months of paid job absences [Kamerman 1991]. Nevertheless, the effects of providing rights to time off work in the period surrounding childbirth remain poorly understood. Proponents believe that parental leave results in healthier children and improves the position of women in the workplace. Opponents counter that the mandates, by restricting voluntary exchange between workers and employers, reduce economic efficiency and may have a particularly adverse effect on women.

The results of previous research on parental leave are ambiguous. Some U. S. studies suggest that time off work is associated with increases in employment and wages [Dalto 1989; Spalter-Roth and Hartmann 1990; Waldfogel 1994, 1997]. However, since these analyses cover a period when most leaves were voluntarily provided by employers, rather than being required by law, the differences in labor market status may result from nonrandom selection into jobs providing the benefit, and the evidence is difficult to interpret. Other researchers have attempted to overcome the selection problem by examining legislated parental leave benefits. Klerman and Leibowitz [1997] uncover mixed

*I have benefited greatly from my discussions with Jackqueline Teague on the history of European parental leave policies. I would like to thank David Blau, Andrew Brod, Bruce Meyer, Stephen Machin, Kenneth Snowden, Jane Waldfogel, and workshop participants at the Center for European Economic Research, Northwestern University, Princeton University, University of North Carolina Chapel Hill, University of North Carolina Greensboro, University of Wisconsin, Society of Labor Economics Meetings, and American Economic Association Meetings for helpful comments on earlier versions of this manuscript.

employment effects of maternity leave mandates instituted by some states during the late 1980s. Waldfogel [1996] finds that recently enacted federal legislation in the United States had little effect on wages, while modestly increasing employment; but this last result is sensitive to the model estimated. The ambiguous results of these studies may reflect the limited scope of the federal and state mandates or inadequacies of the data. Finally, Ruhm and Teague [1997], using information for seventeen nations, show that short to moderate entitlements to parental leave are positively related to per capita incomes, employment-to-population ratios (EP ratios), and labor force participation rates. However, there is little indication of stronger effects for women than for men, raising concern that the direction of causation may be misidentified.

This study investigates the labor market consequences of rights to paid parental leave using data for nine European countries over the 1969 through 1993 period.[1] The dependent variables are EP ratios and hourly wages.[2] Since women use virtually all parental leave in most countries, men constitute a reasonable comparison group, and the "natural" experiment examines how changes in leave entitlements affect the gap between female and male outcomes.[3] Limited analysis is also undertaken using 25–34 year old women as the treatment group and corresponding men or females aged 45–54 as the comparison group. The younger women are in their prime childbearing years and so should be strongly affected by leave mandates. Time and country effects are controlled for throughout the analysis to provide "difference-in-difference-in-difference" (DDD) estimates. Country-specific time trends are frequently included to capture the effects of group-specific factors that vary over time within countries.

European data are particularly useful for investigating the effects of parental leave. All Western European countries cur-

---

1. A distinction is sometimes made between "maternity leave," which is granted to mothers for a limited period around the time of childbirth, and "parental leave," which permits additional time off work to care for infants or young children. Both are included in the definition of parental leave used below.
2. An earlier version of this paper also included weekly work hours as an outcome. There was little indication of a strong parental leave effect, and the results were sensitive to the specification chosen, probably partly because sex-specific data on work hours were unavailable for many countries.
3. Gruber [1994] and Waldfogel [1996] have similarly used men as a comparison group when examining the effects of mandated maternity benefits and parental leave legislation in the United States.

rently offer at least three months of paid maternity benefits, but many of the policies have been instituted or significantly revised during the last 30 years, resulting in substantial variation over time and across countries in the type and duration of the entitlements. Conversely, the United States did not require employers to provide parental leave until the 1993 passage of the Family and Medical Leave Act (FMLA).[4]

Better understanding the effects of parental leave mandates is important in both the European and United States contexts. Europe has been grappling with the question of whether extensive social protections inhibit economic flexibility and are a cause of low rates of recent employment growth [Blank 1994]. These concerns have recently led a number of countries to shorten the period of leave or reduce payments provided during it, at the same time that other nations have increased them [Organization for Economic Cooperation and Development 1995]. Conversely, advocates (e.g., the Carnegie Task Force on Meeting the Needs of Young Children [1994]) have argued for broadening the U. S. federal law to include small employers and provide payment during the time off work.

To preview the results, rights to paid leave are found to raise the percentage of women employed, with a substantial effect observed for even short durations of guaranteed work absence. In the preferred econometric specifications, leave legislation raises the female employment-to-population ratio by between 3 and 4 percent, with larger effects for women of childbearing age. Around one-quarter of this change probably results from increases in the number of women who are reclassified as "employed but absent from work" due to the availability of leave. Brief leave entitlements have little effect on women's earnings, but lengthier leave is associated with substantial (2 to 3 percent) reductions in relative wages.

---

4. The FMLA requires employers with more than 50 workers in a 75-mile area to allow twelve weeks of unpaid leave following the birth or adoption of a child or for personal illness or the health problem of a family member. Health insurance contributions must be continued during the period. Firms need not provide leave to the highest paid 10 percent of their workforce or persons employed less than 1250 hours during the previous year [Ruhm 1997]. Ten states and the District of Columbia legislated job-protected work absences prior to the FMLA, and eight others supplied limited rights to parental leave without guaranteeing the reinstatement of employment [Waldfogel 1994]. The state laws were enacted in the late 1980s or early 1990s and included numerous exemptions.

I. The Economics of Parental Leave Mandates

In a competitive spot labor market with perfect information and no externalities, mandated benefits such as parental leave reduce economic efficiency by limiting the ability of employers and workers to voluntarily select the optimal compensation package. Nevertheless, supporters argue that parental leave entitlements improve the health and well-being of children (e.g., Zigler, Frank, and Emmel [1988] and the Carnegie Task Force on Meeting the Needs of Younger Children [1994]). This might occur if the benefits represent externalities that are not adequately valued by agents negotiating labor contracts. For instance, the gains might not be fully taken into account if workers have inadequate information concerning the advantages of staying at home with infants, if they pay only a portion of the costs of their children's medical care (as with most types of health insurance), or if they have higher than socially optimal discount rates. Employers may also be less aware or supportive of the advantages of parental leave to dependents than of the corresponding benefits to the workers themselves.

It is also frequently asserted that leave mandates decrease female unemployment and increase firm-specific human capital by reducing the need for women to change jobs, if they wish to spend time at home with young children [Kamerman 1988; Bookman 1991; Bravo 1991; Trycinski 1991]. Lacking some source of market failure, this argument is unconvincing. Employers and workers can always voluntarily negotiate maternity leave, mitigating the joblessness and retaining the specific investments. Moreover, with competitive labor markets, the groups most likely to use parental leave will pay for it by receiving lower wages, implying that females of childbearing age will continue to obtain lower and possibly reduced compensation if the benefit is mandated.[5] Entitlements that allow substantial time off work may cause employers to limit women to jobs where absences are least costly, thereby increasing occupational segregation, as Stoiber [1990] suggests has occurred in Sweden.

Adverse selection under asymmetric information provides a potential source of market failure. A company voluntarily offering leave is likely to attract a disproportionate number of "high-risk" employees and be forced to pay lower wages. Persons with small

---

5. See Gruber [1994] for an excellent discussion of group-specific mandates and Summers [1989], Mitchell [1990], or Krueger [1994] for more general discussions of the economics of mandated benefits.

THE ECONOMICS OF PARENTAL LEAVE MANDATES   289

probabilities of using the benefit will avoid these firms and so do without even socially optimal leave.[6] A government mandate eliminates the incentive for this type of sorting behavior and has the potential to raise welfare.[7]

Companies in the United States rarely provided explicit paid maternity leave prior to the FMLA. Only 3 percent of full-time employees in private medium and large establishments (greater than 100 workers) were entitled to such leaves in 1993 and 1 percent of those working for small employers in 1992 [U. S. Department of Labor, Bureau of Labor Statistics 1994a, 1994b]. These low coverage rates could indicate that the costs of the entitlements exceed the benefits or that market imperfections limit their unregulated provision. Alternatively, most workers may have been able to take time off work through vacation, sick leave, or temporary disability policies, even without explicit maternity leave.[8]

Parental leave mandates are likely to shift the labor supply curve of the groups most probable to use it to the right (relative to those workers less likely to take leave).[9] The demand curve simultaneously moves to the left. However, since leave benefits are paid primarily by the government in most European countries, demand only shifts to the extent that nonwage costs (e.g., expenses associated with hiring and training temporary replace-

6. This is analogous to Rothschild and Stiglitz's [1976] argument for market failure in insurance markets. Aghion and Hermalin [1990] suggest that in some situations socially optimal parental leave might not be voluntarily provided to any workers. In their model, low-risk individuals signal this to employers by agreeing to contracts providing for little or no leave. High-risk workers sometimes do better by mimicking their counterparts, by taking positions without leave, than by revealing their propensity toward absenteeism.

7. The inefficiency of privately negotiated labor contracts under asymmetric information has been demonstrated across a variety of contexts. For example, McGuire and Ruhm [1993] indicate that employer-drug testing is likely to be excessive, and Levine [1991] and Kuhn [1992] argue that just-cause employment security regulations and advance notice of job terminations may be under-provided.

8. The Pregnancy Discrimination Act (PDA) of 1978 requires companies offering leave for temporary disabilities, which includes most medium and large establishments, to cover pregnancy and childbirth in the same way as other temporary disabilities. Several states have supplemented the PDA with stronger temporary disability laws or maternity leave mandates [Ruhm 1997]. During the 1986–1988 period, 73 percent of "employed" women in the United States with one-month old infants were on leave (and 41 percent on paid leave) rather than working, as were 41 percent (16 percent) of those with two-month old babies [Klerman and Leibowitz 1994].

9. In particular, some individuals will increase their labor supply prior to having children in order to meet the qualification conditions for parental leave. I return to this point below. Mortensen [1977] makes an analogous argument with regard to unemployment insurance.

ments) increase.[10] Thus, the shift in supply is likely to be large compared with that in demand, implying that the relative employment of women will rise and their relative wages will fall in the new equilibrium.[11]

Increased leave-taking could reduce work in the period immediately surrounding childbirth, even if leave entitlements raise overall employment. However, Klerman and Leibowitz [1997] illustrate that employment may increase even during this time span. The reason is that some persons who would otherwise have terminated their jobs to take more leave than previously permitted, may now find it worthwhile to return to work sooner in order to remain with their old employers. This occurs because the gap between desired leave duration and that offered by the firm decreases, while the benefits of maintaining the employment relationship (e.g., higher future compensation) are little changed.

There could be additional "dynamic" effects. For instance, labor productivity will rise if parental leave increases firm-specific human capital by allowing individuals to return to their old jobs. This will shift the demand curve to the right, further increasing employment and attenuating or reversing the decline in wages. Alternatively, if human capital depreciates during lengthy leave periods, the employment increases will be smaller, and the earnings reductions larger than in the static case.

II. Parental Leave Policies in Europe

Legislated maternity benefits have a long history in Europe. The German Imperial Industrial Code of 1891 set maximum work hours and *prohibited* the employment of women within four weeks of childbirth. Amendments to the code in 1903 and 1911 increased the leave period to six weeks and supplied women with paid time off work in the two weeks before delivery. By the turn of the century there was discussion of providing maternity insurance in many European countries.[12] Most early legislation emphasized concern for the health of the child and mother. Prenatal and postnatal leave was typically compulsory, and income support or

10. More precisely, this refers to the movement of the demand curve compared with groups not using leave. The demand for all types of labor may decline if the parental leave benefits are financed by payroll taxes levied on employers.
11. If the group-specific mandate is imposed in the presence of binding equal pay legislation or union rules that restrict wage reductions, female employment is likely to rise less (or may even fall), the decline in wages will be smaller, and the deadweight loss is likely to be larger [Gruber 1994].
12. See Frank and Lipner [1988] or Teague [1993] for discussions of early maternity leave policies.

THE ECONOMICS OF PARENTAL LEAVE MANDATES 291

job-protection was seldom provided. The 1919 and 1952 International Labour Organization *Maternity Protection Conventions* recommended that women not be permitted to work during the six-week period following confinement. Payment during leave and rights to return to the old job were also advocated, but many countries did not adopt these suggestions until much later.[13]

After the end of World War II, many nations that had recruited women into previously male-dominated occupations wished to return them to the home [Moeller 1993]. The motivation for policies related to family allowances, protective legislation, and family-law reform was often to restore women to their "proper" roles as mother and wife [Frank and Lipner 1988]. In the postwar period some countries mandated compulsory pregnancy leave but failed to prohibit dismissal from jobs.

By the late 1960s the concept of maternity leave began to evolve from a prohibition on employing women during the period surrounding childbirth to one of job-protected time off work to care for newborns and young children. Portugal, Spain, and Finland instituted employment reinstatement provisions during the 1969–1971 period; France and the Netherlands passed similar legislation in 1975 and 1976; as did Denmark, Ireland, and Greece between 1980 and 1984. Other nations, such as Switzerland and the United Kingdom, inaugurated regulations providing job-protected maternity leave. Nonetheless, vestiges of protective legislation still persist in some countries. Postnatal leave remains compulsory, rather than voluntary, in many nations, and some (such as Austria, France, and Italy) continue to require prenatal leave [Brocas et al. 1990].

Income support is now provided during at least a portion of the work absence throughout Europe. Wage replacement rates often exceed 80 percent and are typically financed by a combination of payroll taxes and general government revenues, although some nations require direct employer contributions. Although a few countries have recently reduced replacement rates or leave durations, the overall trend has been toward longer leave periods, with fathers increasingly gaining rights to time off work [Organization of Economic Cooperation and Development 1995]. The European Community Social Charter recently established a mini-

13. The 1919 convention advocated twelve weeks of paid leave and job-reinstatement upon return to employment. The 1952 conference recommended a cash benefit equal to at least two-thirds of previous earnings, compared a previously suggested unspecified amount "sufficient for the full and healthy maintenance of the working mother and her child" [International Labor Office 1984].

mum standard leave period of fourteen weeks, with pay no less than the individual would receive if absent from work because of sickness [Addison and Siebert 1993].

Even where parental leave extends to fathers, mothers take the vast majority of time off work.[14] There are a variety of reasons why men take leave so sparingly. In addition to cultural norms and differences in earnings capacity, the entitlements are generally restricted to mothers during the period immediately surrounding confinement, and fathers often can subsequently take time off work only if the mother qualifies for but waives her rights to it.

III. Data

This analysis uses aggregate data covering the 1969 through 1993 period for nine European countries (Denmark, Finland, France, Germany, Greece, Ireland, Italy, Norway, and Sweden). Labor market data for years prior to 1969 are frequently incomplete, and parental leave policies changed little during the early and middle 1960s. The nine nations chosen are all Western European countries with significant changes in their paid parental leave policies during the sample period.[15]

Paid parental leave is defined to include rights to time off work during the period surrounding childbirth where the size of the income support is directly related to previous employment. This is distinguished from payments that are available to all individuals, regardless of their work histories. Most of the analysis focuses on job-protected leave, where dismissal is prohibited during pregnancy and job-reinstatement is guaranteed at the end of the leave, since employment security is likely to be a key characteristic of leave policies that workers consider a "benefit." During the period analyzed, several nations added job security provisions to previously enacted compulsory "maternity protection" laws.

14. Even in Sweden, which provides the strongest encouragement for men to take some leave, males accounted for just 7 percent of total weeks of parental leave in 1988 [Organization of Economic Cooperation and Development 1995]. More typical is Germany, where fewer than 1 percent of those receiving parental leave in 1989 were men [Der Bundesminister fuer Jugend, Familie, Frauen und Gesundheit 1989]. (I thank Katharina Spiess for providing me with and translating this information.)

15. Eight other countries (Austria, Belgium, Canada, the Netherlands, Portugal, Spain, Switzerland, and the United Kingdom) were included in an earlier investigation of paid and unpaid leave by Ruhm and Teague [1997]. Canada was excluded from this analysis in order to restrict the sample to European nations. The other seven nations were deleted because they had little or no change in paid leave entitlements during the sample period.

A measure of "full-pay" weeks of leave is calculated by multiplying the number of weeks of paid leave by the average wage replacement rate during the period. The replacement rates are approximations because they do not account for minimum or maximum payments which sometimes exist. Also, some nations provide a "flat rate" payment or a fixed payment plus a percentage of earnings. In these cases, the replacement rate was estimated as a function of average female wages.

The leave durations apply to persons meeting all eligibility criteria. This overstates actual time off work, since some individuals do not fulfill the employment requirements and others use less than the allowed absence. Qualifying conditions either have not changed or have loosened over time in most countries, and increased labor force participation rates imply that more women are likely to meet given work requirements. Therefore, a greater share of females are expected to qualify for benefits at the end of the period than at the beginning, implying that the secular increase in parental leave entitlements is understated.

Unpaid leave has not been incorporated into this analysis for two reasons. First, many employers may be willing to grant unpaid time off work, even in the absence of legislation, making it difficult to distinguish between the effects of job absences voluntarily granted by employers and those required by law. Second, the actual use of legislated rights to unpaid leave may be quite limited, particularly for the extremely lengthy entitlements now provided in some countries. I also do not distinguish between leave available only to the mother and that which can be taken by either parent. Nor do I model differences in "take-up" rates.

These restrictions should be kept in mind when interpreting the results. If (within-country) growth in paid leave entitlements is positively correlated with changes in either the proportion of women with qualifying work histories or rights to additional unpaid leave, the econometric estimates will represent the combined effects of these factors, and so will overstate the impact of an increase in paid leave which occurs in isolation.

Data for Germany are only included through 1985. In 1986, Germany simultaneously lengthened the duration of job-protected leave and extended to nonworkers the income support payments previously restricted to persons meeting qualifying employment conditions [Ondrich, Spiess, and Yany 1996]. Using the criteria discussed above, this would be defined as a reduction in paid leave, since the payments are no longer tied to previous employment. Such a classification seems problematic, given that the duration of job-protected time off work was substantially increased in 1986 and again in 1988. The easiest way of dealing with the problem was to delete observations after 1985.[16]

Information on parental leave was obtained from the International Labour Office's *Legislative Series,* their 1984 global survey on "Protection of Working Mothers," and from *Social Security Programs Throughout the World,* which is published biennially by the United States Social Security Administration. A subset of the leave data was previously used by Teague [1993] and Ruhm and Teague [1997]. The time period has been extended in the present paper, and the data have been rechecked and modified as appropriate for greater accuracy.

The dependent variables are (natural logs of) employment-to-population ratios and hourly wage rates. Data on EP ratios are from various issues of the OECD publication *Labour Force Statistics;* those on wages are from several volumes of the ILO *Yearbook of Labour Statistics.*[17] Employment information is available for all nine countries but gender-specific wage data are more difficult to obtain. This analysis uses information on the wages of manufacturing workers for six nations (Finland, France, Greece, Ireland, Norway, and Sweden), for all nonagricultural workers in the case of Denmark and Germany, and with no wage data obtained for Italy. The frequent restriction to manufacturing implies that the results for wages should be interpreted cautiously. Nominal wages were deflated by purchasing power parities, using OECD *National Accounts* data, and by the Consumer Price Index. Age-specific information on the EP ratios of 25–34 and 45–54 year old women and 25–34 year old men was also used for all countries except Greece and Norway.[18] Finally, demographic data were obtained from *Labour Force Statistics* on population (of civilians aged 15–64), birth rates (per 1000 resident

16. As an alternative, I estimated a preliminary set of models with observations for Germany included through 1990 (the year before German Unification) and parental leave entitlements assumed to either remain constant (at 32 weeks) after 1985 or to increase in accordance with the extensions granted in 1986 and 1988. In the first case, the estimated parental leave effects were virtually identical to those obtained when the post-1985 data were excluded. In the second, the predicted increases (decreases) in female EP ratios (wages) were slightly larger (smaller).

17. The employment-to-population ratio is calculated as civilian adult employment divided by the population between the ages of 15 and 64, using standardized OECD definitions. Wages generally refer to hourly straight-time pay (either wages or salaries), excluding overtime premiums, bonuses, or gratuities, and averaged over both full- and part-time workers.

18. The data for Italy refer to 25–39 and 40–49 year olds.

population), total unemployment rates, and the proportion of the working age population employed in service or agricultural jobs (with manufacturing the excluded reference category).

The data are not always completely comparable between or within countries. For example, purchasing power parities provide the best method of adjusting nominal wages but are unlikely to supply exactly equivalent information across time and place. Similarly, nations sometimes alter their methods of collecting or aggregating data. The estimation strategy is designed to minimize biases resulting from such noncomparabilities. The inclusion of country fixed-effects controls for differences (between countries) in collection methods that remain constant over time. Most of the analysis focuses on gender differences in labor market outcomes. This automatically accounts for breaks in series (within-countries) which have the same effect on the male and female aggregates. Examination of the ratio of (the log of) female-to-male outcomes for periods immediately preceding and following each interruption in series revealed only one case, Norway in 1971, where the break led to a substantial change in the relative size of male and female EP ratios. Norwegian data for the years 1969 and 1970 were therefore deleted from the analysis.

IV. TIME-TRENDS

Parental leave entitlements increased sharply between 1969 and 1993. Weighting observations by the country's working age population, the mean duration of paid leave for the eight countries (excluding Germany for which no data were collected after 1985) rose from 10 to 33 weeks while average full-pay weeks grew from 7 to 22 weeks (see Fig Ia). The increases were most dramatic during the first ten years of the period, with a particularly large jump occurring at the end of the 1970s when six countries (Finland, France, Germany, Italy, Norway, and Sweden) almost simultaneously raised entitlements to job-protected leave. Since 1980, there has been little overall rise in leave durations, as increases in some countries have offset declines in others. Full-pay weeks grew more slowly than partially paid leave because some of the additional entitlements to time off work were provided at relatively low wage replacement rates.

Table I summarizes parental leave provisions in the last year of the data (1993 except for Germany). At that time, the countries offered a minimum of fourteen weeks of paid leave, and

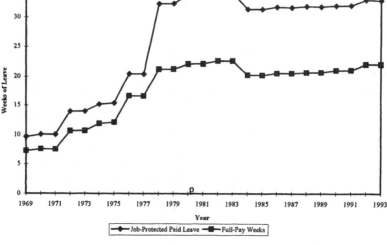

FIGURE Ia
Average Weeks of Parental Leave

six nations provided rights to more than six months off work. Full-pay weeks ranged from 9 weeks in Greece to 58 weeks in Sweden, with a positive correlation between replacement rates and leave durations. Income support during the work absence was typically financed through a combination of payroll taxes and general revenues. The conditions required to qualify for leave varied, but persons with more than a year of service were usually covered.

Table II displays paid leave durations and estimated replacement rates for each country at four-year intervals. The number of nations providing some job-protected paid entitlement rose from four in 1969 to eight in 1977, with all nine doing so after 1983. Countries supplying parental benefits in 1969 extended them during the sample period, with the result that the dispersion of leave durations tended to increase over time.[19] There were 30 observed changes in durations over the sample period and 5

19. The standard deviation of the (population-weighted) duration of paid leave (full-pay weeks) for the eight countries other than Germany was 10.8, 22.7, and 18.0 (8.6, 11.5, and 12.4) weeks in 1969, 1981, and 1993, respectively. The difference between minimum and maximum entitlement was 21, 57, and 50 (17, 37, and 49) weeks in these same years.

THE ECONOMICS OF PARENTAL LEAVE MANDATES 297

TABLE I
PAID PARENTAL LEAVE IN 1993

Country	Amount of leave	Rate of pay	Source of funds	Qualification conditions
Denmark	28 weeks	90% with maximum	Employers, Government	120 hours of employment during preceding 3 months.
Finland	44 weeks	80% with minimum; lower rate at high incomes	Payroll taxes, Government	Residence in country.
France	16 weeks	84% with minimum and maximum	Payroll and dedicated taxes	Insured 10 months before leave; minimum work hours or insurance contributions.
Germany	32 weeks	100% with minimum and maximum	Payroll taxes, Government	12 weeks of insurance or 6 months of employment.
Greece	15 weeks	60% with minimum	Payroll taxes, Government	200 days of contributions during last 2 years.
Ireland	14 weeks	70% with maximum	Payroll taxes, Government	39 weeks of contributions.
Italy	48 weeks	53% (80% first 5 months; 30% next 6 months)	Payroll taxes, Government	Employed and insured at start of pregnancy.
Norway	42 weeks	100% with maximum	Payroll taxes, Government	Employed and insured at least 6 of the last 10 months.
Sweden	64 weeks	90%	Payroll taxes, Government	Insured 240 days before confinement.

Information for Germany refers to 1985.

additional cases where nations modified replacement rates without altering the length of leave.

The relative wages and EP ratios of women also rose over time. This is shown in Fig Ib, which displays the (population-

TABLE II

ENTITLTEMENTS TO JOB-PROTECTED PAID PARENTAL LEAVE (IN WEEKS)
AND WAGE REPLACEMENT RATES IN SELECTED YEARS

	1969	1973	1977	1981	1985	1989	1993
Denmark	0	0	0	18	28	28	28
				[.90]	[.90]	[.90]	[.90]
Finland	0	12	29	43	43	44	44
		[.55]	[.55]	[.55]	[.80]	[.80]	[.80]
France	0	0	14	16	16	16	16
			[.90]	[.90]	[.90]	[.90]	[.84]
Germany	14	14	14	32	32		
	[1.00]	[1.00]	[1.00]	[1.00]	[1.00]		
Greece	0	0	0	0	12	12	15
					[.60]	[.60]	[.60]
Ireland	0	0	0	12	14	14	14
				[.55]	[.70]	[.70]	[.70]
Italy	21	21	31	57	48	48	48
	[.80]	[.80]	[.80]	[.57]	[.53]	[.53]	[.53]
Norway	12	12	12	18	18	24	42
	[.13]	[.32]	[.32]	[1.00]	[1.00]	[1.00]	[1.00]
Sweden	16	16	30	52	52	52	64
	[.55]	[.55]	[.90]	[.71]	[.71]	[.90]	[.90]

The unbracketed entry shows the number of weeks of job-protected paid parental leave employers are required to offer. The bracketed entry displays wage replacement rates. These are sometimes subject to minimum or maximum amounts. The average replacement rate is estimated in cases where the income support during early and later portions of the leave or includes a flat rate payment.

weighted) female-to-male ratios of these outcomes for the eight countries other than Germany.[20] Women were employed less than half as often as men (40 percent versus 82 percent) in 1969 but worked 70 percent as frequently (47 percent versus 67 percent) in 1993; the earnings gap fell from 25 percent to under 20 percent during the same period. Since many factors other than parental leave will have contributed to the declining gender differentials, it is important that the econometric methods control for these sources of spurious correlation.

One issue deserving mention is that European countries often count individuals on parental leave as "employed but absent from work" rather than "not employed." The extension of leave entitlements will therefore raise reported EP ratios if the work absences of "employed" persons increase. As discussed below, this is likely to

20. Specifically, the figure shows $(EP_f/EP_m) - 1$ and $(W_f/W_m) - 1$, for EP_i and W_i representing the EP ratios and wages of the ith group, with i equal to f for females and m for males.

THE ECONOMICS OF PARENTAL LEAVE MANDATES   299

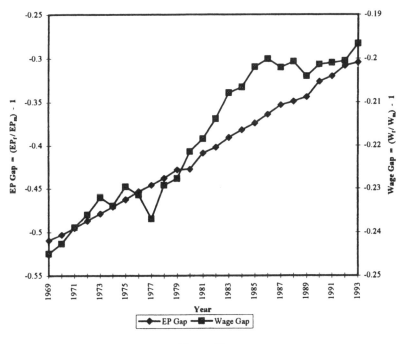

FIGURE Ib
Gender Gap in EP Ratios and Wages

account for one-quarter to one-half of the observed positive
relationship between parental leave durations and EP ratios.

V. ESTIMATION STRATEGY

Labor market outcome Y, measured in natural logs, for sex
group i (where f indicates females and m males) in country j at
year t, is assumed to be determined by

$$(1) \quad Y_{ijt} = a_1 S_i + a_2 C_j + a_3 T_t + b_1(S_i \times C_j)$$
$$+ \ b_2(S_i \times T_t) + b_3(C_j \times T_t) + d_i L_{jt} + e_{ijt}.$$

The key dependent variable L_{jt} is weeks of paid parental leave
entitlement. S_i is a group-specific intercept, C_j a country effect, T_t
a time effect, and e_{ijt} an i.i.d. error term. The second level
interactions allow for sex-specific country and time effects and for
a general time-varying country effect. Other observables are
excluded for ease of exposition.

The sex difference in outcomes can be expressed as

$$(2) \quad Y_{fjt} - Y_{mjt} = a_1(S_f - S_m) + b_1(S_f - S_m)C_j$$
$$+ b_2(S_f - S_m)T_t + (d_f - d_m)L_{jt} + (e_{fjt} - e_{mjt})$$

or equivalently

$$(3) \qquad \Delta Y_{jt} = \alpha + \beta_1 C_j + \beta_2 T_t + \delta L_{jt} + \epsilon_{jt}$$

Equation (3) is a DDD model. β_1 and β_2 indicate gender-specific country and time differences; δ shows the sex-difference in the impact of parental leave. Thus, these estimates measure how growth in the gender gap in labor market outcomes varies as a function of within-country changes in leave entitlements.

Since women use almost all parental leave, it may be reasonable to assume that $d_m = 0$. In this case δ supplies an unbiased estimate of d_f. By contrast, if d_m is nonzero and has the same (opposite) sign as d_f, the regression coefficient will be biased toward (away from) zero. One reason why d_m and d_f might have the same sign is that some men do use some parental leave. However, the resulting bias is likely to be small, since males take only a tiny fraction of total weeks of leave in most countries. Conversely, d_m and d_f will have the opposite sign if employers or households respond to lengthened entitlements by substituting employment away from females and toward males (or away from younger and toward older women) or vice versa. In this case, δ provides an upper bound estimate of d_f.

It is useful to contrast the DDD model to the corresponding equation without a comparison group:

$$(4) \qquad Y_{ijt} = \alpha + \beta_1 C_j + \beta_2 T_t + \delta L_{jt} + \epsilon_{ijt},$$

where $\alpha = a_1 S_i$, $\beta_1 = a_2 C_j + b_1(S_i \times C_j)$, $\beta_2 = a_3 T_t + b_2(S_i \times T_t)$, and $\epsilon_{ijt} = b_3(C_j \times T_t) + e_{ijt.}$. Equation (4) examines within-country growth in the dependent variable as a function of modifications in leave durations, but it does not contrast these changes to those of a comparison group expected to be unaffected by the leave entitlements (the third difference in the DDD model). Bias will therefore be introduced if time-varying country-specific effects $(C_j \times T_t)$ are correlated with changes in parental leave, as might occur if nations choose to increase entitlements when employment is rising.[21]

---

21. If $d_m = 0$, the parental leave coefficient in equation (4), estimated for male outcomes, provides a direct indication of this bias.

The DDD specification in equation (3) accounts for time-varying factors that affect both sexes equally. However, the estimates may still be inconsistent if within-country changes in parental leave are correlated with unobservables that have different effects on female and male labor market outcomes. This can be seen by adding a third level interaction $c_1(S_i \times C_j \times T_t)$ to equation (1). The error term in (3) becomes $\epsilon_{ijt} = c_1 (S_f - S_m)(C_j \times T_t) + (e_{fjt} - e_{mjt})$, which may be correlated with L_{jt}. Omitted explanatory variables represent a potentially important source of sex-specific time-varying factors.[22] A vector of country-specific time trends will therefore frequently be added to the models. These eliminate the bias, to the extent that sex differentials in omitted characteristics follow the specified trend.

To adjust for heteroskedasticity resulting from differences in population sizes, most of the models are estimated by weighted least squares (WLS). The weights are determined using the following procedure. First, the equations are estimated by OLS. Second, the squared residuals from these models are regressed against a constant term and the reciprocal of the working age population. Finally, the square root of the inverse of the predicted values from the second-stage regression are used as weights in the final set of estimates. Blackburn [1995] shows that this procedure is more efficient than weighting by (the square root of) population size or using OLS and reporting Huber-White standard errors, if there is a common group effect or group-time interaction across individuals in a country.[23]

VI. RESULTS

A first set of econometric estimates is displayed in Table III. Vectors of country and time dummy variables are included, observations are weighted to adjust for heteroskedasticity using the procedure described above, and the leave regressor is weeks of job-protected paid entitlement (irrespective of the replacement rate) divided by 100. The first two rows of each panel show results of equation (4), separately estimated for males and females. The dependent variable in the third row is the difference between

---

22. For instance, if the education of women is rising relative to men in countries extending leave, increased schooling could induce a spurious positive correlation between leave durations and female employment or earnings.

23. A large and significant constant term is obtained in virtually all of the second-stage regressions, which confirms that such group effects are important and justifies the use of this weighting procedure.

TABLE III

ECONOMETRIC ESTIMATES OF PARENTAL LEAVE EFFECTS USING
LINEAR SPECIFICATIONS

Group	(a)	(b)	(c)
Employment-to-population ratio (n = 203)			
Females (Y_{fjt})	.2550	.1372	.0564
	(.0650)	(.0528)	(.0485)
Males (Y_{mjt})	.1887	.0494	−.0028
	(.0449)	(.0299)	(.0386)
Difference ($Y_{fjt} - Y_{mjt}$)	.0583	.0859	.0597
	(.0467)	(.0426)	(.0320)
Hourly wages (n = 173)			
Females (Y_{fjt})	−.3923	−.1993	−.0757
	(.0977)	(.0885)	(.0791)
Males (Y_{mjt})	−.3197	−.2159	−.0119
	(.0823)	(.0813)	(.0749)
Difference ($Y_{fjt} - Y_{mjt}$)	.0152	.0426	−.0624
	(.0400)	(.0380)	(.0303)
Demographics	No	Yes	No
Time trends	No	No	Yes

The table displays coefficients on parental leave regressors. Data are for nine European countries over the 1969–1993 period. All specifications include vectors of year and country dummy variables. Parental leave refers to weeks of job-protected paid entitlement (irrespective of the wage replacement rate) divided by 100. Demographic variables include birthrates, unemployment rates, and the fraction of employment in service and agricultural jobs. Dependent variables are natural logs of female and male labor market outcomes in the first two rows of each panel and differences in the natural log of female and male outcomes in the third. Observations are weighted to correct for heteroskedasticity. Standard errors are in parentheses.

female and male outcomes; hence this is the DDD model specified by equation (3).

Demographic characteristics (birthrates, unemployment rates, and the employment shares in agriculture and services) are controlled for in column (b), as are country time trends in column (c). The demographic variables are likely to capture a portion of the impact of time-varying factors that influence the gender gap in EP ratios or wages. However, some of these regressors may be endogenous (e.g., countries may use parental leave policies as part of a strategy to raise birthrates). Moreover, since the set of characteristics controlled for is quite limited, the inclusion of country time trends may more adequately proxy the sex-specific time-varying effects.

The table demonstrates the importance of including a comparison group. The leave coefficients are of roughly similar magnitude for men and women in specification (a), with the result that the DDD coefficient in the third row is small and insignificant for both EP ratios and wages. Demographic variables capture the effects of some of the confounding factors, as evidenced by the reduction in the absolute value of the leave coefficients in the first two rows of each panel in column (b). However, the parameter estimates decrease substantially more in column (c), suggesting that the country-specific time trends do a better job of accounting for sex-specific time-varying effects. Indeed, the leave coefficients for the male outcomes are small and statistically insignificant in this specification, which is consistent with the hypothesis that parental leave has no effect on the male labor market. The DDD estimates in the third row are fairly insensitive to the choice of regressors for EP ratios but show more variation for wages.

A. Quadratic Specifications

Table IV summarizes the results of DDD models where the dependent variable is the difference between (the log of) female and male outcomes, LEAVE indicates weeks of job-protected paid leave divided by 100, and a quadratic term is included to allow for nonlinearities. The p-value refers to the null hypothesis that the parental leave coefficients (LEAVE and its square in these regressions) are jointly equal to zero. The lower panel shows the predicted impact of specified paid leave entitlements, compared with the case of no mandate.[24] Models (c) and (d) differ in that the latter is estimated by OLS, but with Huber-White robust standard errors reported, rather than using the WLS procedure.

Paid leave is positively related to the percentage of females employed, but there is some evidence that lengthy entitlements reduce their relative wages. The null hypothesis of no parental leave effect is not rejected in model (a), but the estimates are large and significant when time trends are controlled for (specification (c)); intermediate results are obtained when demographic variables are included (column (b)).[25] This further suggests that the basic model fails to capture the effects of gender-specific confounding factors. Once again, the demographic variables appear to account for some of these but less adequately than the country

24. These are calculated as $[\exp{(b_1 \text{LEAVE} + b_2 \text{LEAVESQ})}] - 1$, for b_1 and b_2 the regression coefficients on the parental leave variables.

25. Female EP ratios are negatively related to birth and unemployment rates and positively correlated with employment shares in agriculture and services. Relative wages decline with birthrates and the share of agricultural employment but are unrelated to unemployment rates or the size of the service sector.

TABLE IV
DDD ESTIMATES OF THE EFFECTS OF PAID PARENTAL LEAVE
USING QUADRATIC SPECIFICATIONS

Leave duration	Employment-to-population ratio				Hourly wages			
	(a)	(b)	(c)	(d)	(a)	(b)	(c)	(d)
Regression coefficients								
LEAVE	.0686	.1268	.2030	.2044	.0905	−.0922	−.1517	−.1350
	(.0806)	(.0710)	(.0593)	(.0867)	(.0672)	(.0611)	(.0532)	(.1100)
LEAVE								
SQUARED	−.0160	−.0647	−.2500	−.2521	−.1324	.2654	.2144	.1658
	(.0984)	(.0886)	(.0883)	(.1189)	(.0899)	(.0937)	(.1057)	(.1559)
p-value	.4616	.1071	.0034	.0628	.3281	.0096	.0167	.4704
Estimated differential versus no leave								
10 weeks	0.7%	1.2%	1.8%	1.8%	0.8%	−0.7%	−1.3%	−1.1%
20 weeks	1.3%	2.3%	3.1%	3.1%	1.3%	−0.8%	−2.2%	−2.0%
30 weeks	1.9%	3.3%	3.8%	3.9%	1.5%	−0.4%	−2.6%	−2.6%
40 weeks	2.5%	4.1%	4.2%	4.1%	1.5%	0.6%	−2.7%	−2.7%
Demographics	No	Yes	No	No	No	Yes	No	No
Time trends	No	No	Yes	Yes	No	No	Yes	Yes

See note to Table III. The dependent variables are differences in natural log of female and male labor market outcomes. LEAVE refers to the number of weeks of job-protected paid parental leave (irrespective of the wage replacement rate) divided by 100. The p-value refers to the null hypothesis that the coefficient on LEAVE and LEAVESQ are jointly equal to zero. All regressions include vectors of the country and year dummy variables. The lower panel of the table shows predicted differences in labor market outcomes, compared with no paid leave entitlement; these are calculated as $[\exp(b_1\text{LEAVE} + b_2\text{LEAVESQ})] - 1$, for b_1 and b_2 the regression coefficients on the parental leave variables. Specifications (a) through (c) are estimated using weighted least squares. OLS is used in specification (d), with Huber-White robust standard errors reported.

time trends. For this reason, the econometric models in the remainder of the paper include vectors of country-specific trends.[26] The results are insensitive to the method of accounting for heteroskedasticity, as evidenced by the virtually identical point estimates obtained in models (c) and (d). However, the Huber-

26. When demographic factors and country time trends are simultaneously controlled for, the results are close to those obtained with just time trends included (e.g., twenty weeks of paid leave increase predicted EP ratios by 3.8 percent and wages by 1.9 percent). The findings are also similar when time trends and unemployment rates (but no other demographic factors) are held constant. In this case, a twenty-week entitlement raises the expected EP ratio by 3.2 percent and lowers predicted hourly earnings by 2.1 percent. I also estimated models that included *lead* values of parental leave (at year $t + 1$), to provide a crude test of whether reverse causation is a problem. The leads of the leave variables did not jointly approach statistical significance (the p-value was .37 in the EP ratio equation and .85 for wages), and their inclusion had virtually no effect on the parameter estimates for contemporaneous leave in the wage models while modestly reducing the coefficients in the employment equations.

THE ECONOMICS OF PARENTAL LEAVE MANDATES   305

White standard errors are much larger than those obtained using the WLS procedure.

The estimates in Table IV suggest that parental leave mandates have large effects. For instance, rights to 40 weeks of job-protected paid leave are predicted to raise female EP ratios by 4.2 percent and lower hourly wages by 2.7 percent (in column (c)). As already mentioned, a portion of the positive relationship between leave durations and EP ratios may result because persons on parental leave are counted as "employed but absent from work," rather than "not employed." Some indication of the size of this effect at lengthier durations may be obtained by noting that 0.9 percent of the "employment" of 15–49 year old women in twelve EC countries was accounted for by maternity leave in 1983, as was 1.9 percent in 1992 [OECD 1995].[27] Since this rise in maternity leave usage occurred during a period when the average length of paid entitlements remained essentially constant, it may be reasonable to assume that around one percentage point of the increase in female EP ratios associated with extended paid entitlements is due to increased leave-taking, with two percentage points representing a likely upper bound.[28] Thus, this probably accounts for between one-quarter and one-half of the total estimated employment effect.

Table V provides information on the robustness of the results. Column (a) allows for lagged effects by including controls for job-protected leave (and its square) at year $t - 1$ as well as at time t. The table reports the sum of the coefficients, over the two years, along with the corresponding standard error; predicted effects in the bottom panel refer to changes in leave policies enacted at least one year previously. Column (b) controls for all types of paid leave, whether job-protected or not. The independent variable in column

27. The twelve countries include Belgium, Denmark, France, Germany, Greece, Ireland, Italy, Luxembourg, the Netherlands, Portugal, Spain, and the United Kingdom. An additional 0.6 percent of female employment in 1983 and 1.0 percent in 1992 was composed of work absences for personal or family reasons, a small portion of which may be due to parental leave. However, maternity leave will account for a smaller percentage of the employment of 15–64 year olds (the age group in this analysis) than of 15–49 year olds.

28. The population-weighted average duration of paid leave (full-pay weeks) declined from 34.1 (22.6) weeks in 1983 to 32.9 (22.0) weeks in 1992 for the eight countries (excluding Germany). There are three likely explanations for the increase in maternity leave over the period. First, some countries dramatically extended entitlements to unpaid leave, often with generous nonwork-related social insurance payments. Second, the persistence of high unemployment rates in many European nations may have made leave-taking relatively more attractive when compared with working. Third, increased labor force participation may have allowed women to meet the work history requirements needed to qualify for leave.

TABLE V
ADDITIONAL QUADRATIC SPECIFICATION ESTIMATES OF THE EFFECTS
OF PAID PARENTAL LEAVE

Leave duration	Employment-to-population ratio				Hourly wages		
	(a)	(b)	(c)	(d)	(a)	(b)	(c)
Regression coefficients							
LEAVE	.2182	.0975	.3426	.2571	−.1694	−.2198	−.1944
	(.0667)	(.0984)	(.0692)	(.0664)	(.0609)	(.0913)	(.0604)
LEAVE SQUARED	−.2515	−.1322	−.6869	−.3662	.2428	.3110	.2676
	(.0965)	(.1337)	(.1333)	(.1314)	(.1192)	(.1550)	(.1225)
p-value	.0299	.6033	.0000	.0006	.0687	.0573	.0046
Estimated differential versus no leave							
10 weeks	1.9%	0.8%	2.8%	2.2%	−1.4%	−1.8%	−1.7%
20 weeks	3.4%	1.4%	4.2%	3.7%	−2.4%	−3.0%	−2.8%
30 weeks	4.4%	1.7%	4.2%	4.5%	−2.9%	−3.6%	−3.4%
40 weeks	4.8%	1.8%		4.5%	−2.8%	−3.4%	
Specification	Lagged leave	All paid leave	Full-pay weeks of leave	Balances sample	Lagged leave	All paid leave	Full-pay weeks of leave

See notes to Table III and IV. All regressions include country and year dummy variables, as well as country-specific time trends. Specification (a) controls for contemporaneous job-protected paid leave and parental leave lagged one year. The sum of the coefficients at t and $t − 1$ are reported and the predicted effects refer to entitlements enacted at least one year previously. Specification (b) controls for all paid entitlements, whether or not job-protection is provided. In specification (c) the leave variable is full-pay weeks of leave, calculated as the weeks of job-protected paid leave multiplied by the estimated wage replacement rate. Specification (d) displays estimates for a sample restricted to observations where information on both employment-to-population ratios and hourly wages is available.

(c) is full-pay weeks of leave, defined as the average wage replacement rate multiplied by weeks of paid entitlement. In this case, the lower panel does not display an estimate for 40 weeks because fully paid entitlements of this duration are almost never observed in the sample. Finally, specification (d) displays results of an employment equation estimated for the eight countries (excluding Italy) for which wage data are available. These "balanced sample" estimates are directly comparable to those previously reported for wages.

Female EP ratios (wages) are positively (negatively) related to leave durations in all specifications. The estimated employment effects are larger for the "balanced sample" or when lags are included than the corresponding estimates in column (c) of Table IV, but the differences are modest, and the addition of lagged durations has virtually no effect on predicted wages. The coefficients on leave at $t - 1$ (not shown) suggest that changes in the entitlements have both an immediate impact and a considerably larger long-run effect, as anticipated if some laws are changed in the middle of the year or if adjustment to the new leave rights occurs over a period of time.[29]

Controlling for all types of paid leave, rather than just job-protected entitlements, results in smaller estimated employment effects and larger reductions in wages (see column (b)). For instance, 30 weeks of leave increases predicted female EP ratios by 1.7 percent and reduces expected wages by 3.6 percent, as compared with changes of 3.8 percent and −2.6 percent for rights to job-protected time off work. Countries instituting employment security provisions during the sample period initially moved from relatively short periods of nonprotected leave to similarly brief but protected entitlements. Therefore, the key issue determining whether the regressions should control for all leave or just job-protected absences is whether the addition of employment security provisions to existing leave rights (of short duration) has a substantial impact. As shown below, such changes are empirically important, particularly for EP ratios, implying that job-security provisions do need to be taken into account.

The wage replacement rate averages around 80 percent (85 percent for the first six months of leave and 72 percent thereafter), implying that a given duration of full-pay weeks would be expected to have roughly the same effect as a 25 percent longer entitlement to partially paid time off work. This is generally the case. For example, 30 full-pay weeks are predicted to increase female EP ratios by 4.2 percent and reduce wages by 3.4 percent (see column (c)), which is quite similar to the estimated effects previously obtained for 40 weeks of partially paid leave (4.2 percent and −2.7 percent).

B. "Step-Effects"

Continuous regressors may poorly capture the effects of the parental leave mandates, even when quadratic or higher order terms are included. For example, if women strongly wish to stay at home for a brief amount of time following childbirth, but with rapidly diminishing marginal utility of doing so thereafter, entitle-

---

29. The timing of the changes in parental leave policies is also frequently measured with an error of up to one year, which could induce the appearance of lagged effects and precludes a more sophisticated analysis of the dynamics of the adjustment process.

TABLE VI
Alternative DDD Specifications Examining the Effects of Job-Protected Paid Leave

	Employment-to-population ratio			Hourly wages		
	(a)	(b)	(c)	(a)	(b)	(c)
Regression estimates						
ANYLEAVE	.0261	.0327	.0164	.0157	−.0109	.0078
	(.0137)	(.0084)	(.0104)	(.0119)	(.0070)	(.0090)
LEAVE	.0583		.2552	−.2507		−.2367
	(.0960)		(.0885)	(.0913)		(.0774)
LEAVESQ	−.0659		−.5634	.3647		.3259
	(.1302)		(.1541)	(.1541)		(.1395)
p-value	.0019	.0001	.0000-	.0189	.1254	.0088
Estimated differential versus no leave						
10 weeks	3.2%		3.7%	−0.6%		−1.3%
20 weeks	3.6%		4.6%	−2.0%		−2.6%
30 weeks	3.8%		4.3%	−2.6%		−3.3%
40 weeks	4.0%			−2.6%		

See the notes to Tables III through V. All specifications include country and year dummy variables and country-specific time trends. ANYLEAVE is a dummy variable taking the value one if the country has established an entitlement to job-protected paid leave and zero otherwise. LEAVE and LEAVESQ refer to weeks of paid job-protected leave (divided by 100) in column (a) and full-pay equivalent weeks of leave (weeks of job-protected paid leave entitlement multiplied by the average wage replacement rate) in specification (c). The *p*-value refers to the null hypothesis that the coefficients on ANYLEAVE, LEAVE, and LEAVESQ are jointly equal to zero.

ments to short job absences could have a substantial impact, whereas longer leave periods have little additional effect. The previously estimated models would then be misspecified since they restrict the consequences of rights to brief leaves to be small, relative to those of more extended durations. To permit this type of "step-effect," a dummy variable ANYLEAVE, which equals one if the country has enacted a leave mandate and zero otherwise, is included in Table VI. ANYLEAVE therefore indicates the impact of paid leave guarantees of arbitrarily short duration, with LEAVE and its square capturing the effects of extending an existing mandate. Job-protected paid leave is controlled for in the first two columns of the table; full-pay weeks are held constant in the third.

The coefficient on ANYLEAVE is of substantial size and has a *t*-statistic exceeding one in most specifications. The point estimates indicate that legislation requiring employers to offer minimal amounts of paid leave raise the relative employment of

THE ECONOMICS OF PARENTAL LEAVE MANDATES 309

women by 1.7 to 2.6 percent and increase their hourly earnings by 0.8 to 1.6 percent (see specifications (a) and (c)). The predicted effect of further extending the leave period is summarized in the lower panel of the table.

These estimates confirm that paid leave is positively related to the EP ratios of women but suggest a more complicated story for wages. Whereas leave guarantees of substantial duration continue to be associated with sizable earning reductions, rights to brief periods away from the job now have less of an effect on expected wages. For instance, ten weeks of job-protected paid leave are predicted to reduce hourly earnings by 0.6 percent, as compared with a 1.3 percent reduction in the corresponding model that does not control for ANYLEAVE.

The results for all paid leave and full-pay weeks are also consistent. Since the average wage replacement rate is around 80 percent, we expect 10, 20, 30, and 40 weeks of job-protected paid leave to have approximately the same impact as 8, 16, 24, and 32 full-pay weeks. The estimated changes in EP ratios at these durations are 3.2, 3.6, 3.8, and 4.0 percent for (partially) paid leave versus 3.4, 4.3, 4.5, and 4.0 percent for full-pay weeks. The corresponding relative wage changes are −0.6, −2.0, −2.6, and −2.6 percent for job-protected entitlements, as compared with −0.9, −2.1, −3.0, and −3.4 percent for full-pay weeks.[30]

C. Women of Childbearing Age

I next compare the EP ratios of 25–34 year old women with those of same aged men or 45–54 year old females. (The lack of age-specific wage data precludes a similar analysis of earnings.) Since 25–34 year old females are in their prime childbearing years, they are expected to be strongly affected by parental leave mandates. Males of the same age constitute one possible comparison group; older women who have completed their fertility are

---

30. The robustness of the results was tested for by estimating specifications that included the ANYLEAVE dummy variable and a linear spline function. The results are similar to those reported. For example, when the break point is set at the median leave, conditional upon a positive entitlement (21 weeks for paid leave and 18 weeks for full-pay weeks), 10, 20, 30, and 40 weeks of job-protected paid leave raise predicted female EP ratios by 3.2, 3.6, 3.9, and 4.1 percent and decrease expected wages by 0.7, 2.2, 3.2, and 4.2 percent. Similarly, 10, 20, and 30 full-pay weeks raise employment by 3.0, 4.1, and 5.1 percent while cutting predicted wages by 0.9, 2.7, and 4.4 percent. Comparable results were obtained when setting the break points at 16 and 14 weeks, respectively (the twenty-fifth percentiles of nonzero entitlements).

310   *QUARTERLY JOURNAL OF ECONOMICS*

TABLE VII

DDD ESTIMATES OF THE EFFECTS OF JOB-PROTECTED PAID PARENTAL LEAVE
ON THE EP RATIOS OF WOMEN OF CHILDBEARING AGE

	Comparison group:			
	45–54 year old women		25–34 year old men	
	(a)	(b)	(a)	(b)
Regression estimates				
ANYLEAVE		.0465		.0285
		(.0259)		(.0238)
LEAVE	.0731	−.1559	.1291	−.0104
	(.1406)	(.1880)	(.1281)	(.1730)
LEAVESQ	.2313	.5076	.2366	.4052
	(.1748)	(.2309)	(.1594)	(.2124)
p-value	.0052	.0034	.0001	.0001
Estimated differential versus no leave				
10 weeks	1.0%	3.7%	1.5%	3.2%
20 weeks	2.4%	3.6%	3.6%	4.4%
30 weeks	4.4%	4.6%	6.2%	6.4%
40 weeks	6.8%	6.8%	9.4%	9.3%

See the notes to Tables III through VI. All specifications include country and year dummy variables and country-specific time trends. The dependent variable is the difference in the natural log of EP ratios between 25–34 year old women and either 45–54 year old women or 25–34 year old men. The sample contains 150 observations.

another.[31] Thus, the natural experiments in this section contrast changes in the percentage of the younger women employed to those of corresponding aged men or older females, as a function of variations in leave entitlements.

Table VII summarizes the econometric estimates. The dependent variable is the difference between (the log of) the EP ratios of 25–34 year old females and those of the comparison group. Time and country dummy variables are included, as are nation-specific time trends. Estimation is by weighted least squares. In addition to the quadratic in weeks of job-protected paid leave (divided by 100), specification (b) includes the ANYLEAVE dummy variable. Once again, the coefficient on ANYLEAVE is of substantial size

---

31. It is not obvious which comparison group is preferred. The use of younger men has the advantage of accounting for cohort differences that affect both sexes (such as the trend to extend education and delay entry into the labor force). However, changes in the employment of young females may have stronger effects on males of the same age, due to household labor supply decisions, than on older women.

THE ECONOMICS OF PARENTAL LEAVE MANDATES   311

and its inclusion improves the model fit, as measured by the adjusted R^2.

The table confirms that parental leave guarantees raise the employment of young women. The predicted changes in the EP ratios are larger than those for all females, as anticipated, since 25–34 year olds are in their prime childbearing years. For instance, entitlements to 40 weeks away from the job are predicted to increase the EP ratios of 25–34 year olds by 7 to 9 percent, compared with around 4 percent for all women.[32] However, these differences are less pronounced at short durations of leave.[33]

VII. Discussion

This analysis suggests that rights to short periods (three months) of paid parental leave increase the employment-to-population ratios of women by 3 to 4 percent while having little effect on wages. More extended entitlements (nine months) raise predicted female EP ratios by approximately 4 percent but decrease hourly earnings by around 3 percent. These effects are of similar magnitude to those obtained in some studies of other types of employment regulations and so need not be implausible.[34] Nevertheless, there are several reasons why they may overstate the true impact of parental leave guarantees. Most obviously, some countries may have provided additional rights to unpaid leave or implemented other "family-friendly" policies (such as subsidized child-care) at the same time they extended durations of paid time off work. In addition, if there are uncontrolled-for factors that simultaneously shift the female labor supply curve out and create political pressure to extend parental leave, lengthier leave would be correlated with higher EP ratios and reduced

---

32. The accounting bias resulting from counting persons on parental leave as "employed but absent from work" is likely to be larger for women of childbearing age than for all females. In 1983, 8.5 percent of "employed" women with children under five years of age, in twelve EC countries, were on maternity leave or were absent from work due to personal or family reasons; in 1992 the figure was 12.6 percent [OECD 1995]. Of course, many 25–34 year olds do not have children of this age.

33. Larger increases in employment are obtained in models that include the ANYLEAVE dummy variable and a linear spline. For instance, with a break point at 21 weeks, 30 weeks of parental leave are predicted to raise EP ratios of 25–34 year old women by 12 percent, compared with corresponding aged men, and by 14 percent compared with 45–54 year old females.

34. For example, Gruber [1994] estimates that mandated maternity benefits decrease the wages of some groups by up to 5 percent.

relative wages. Finally, it is possible that the entitlements encourage households to substitute female employment for male labor, violating the assumption that the legislated changes have no effect on the comparison group.

As mentioned, a positive relationship between leave durations and EP ratios may also occur because some individuals on parental leave are counted as "employed but absent from work" rather than "not employed." This cannot provide a full explanation for the findings, since a substantial rise in female EP ratios is predicted for rights to even short periods of paid leave, where the accounting bias should be relatively small. However, it may explain one-quarter to one-half of the increase in employment associated with longer entitlements.

Two primary factors are likely to account for the remaining 2 to 3 percent rise in women's employment. First, females who would not otherwise participate in the labor force may obtain jobs prior to childbirth in order to subsequently qualify for leave benefits. Some of the new entrants might also choose to remain employed after having children, but there is little evidence on the size of this effect, and it is not discussed further. Second, parental leave is likely to speed the return to work of new mothers.

The incentive for an individual to enter the labor force before having a child in order to qualify for parental leave is often strong. Persons working during the previous twelve months are generally eligible for leave benefits. Thus, a law establishing rights to three months of fully paid leave raises the effective wage for holding a job in the year prior to childbirth by 25 percent. Combined with substantial female labor force participation elasticities, this is likely to induce a substantial temporary increase in participation. Zabel [1996] estimates that the participation elasticities of women are between 0.5 and 1.0, implying that a 25 percent wage increase will raise female participation rates by 10 to 25 percent in the year before pregnancy.[35] With a baseline female EP ratio of 45 percent (the population-weighted sample average in these data), the enactment of three months of parental leave is therefore expected to induce a four to eleven percentage point increase in women's participation in the year before delivery which, if women average two children each, raises the average female EP ratio by between

35. Since the participation equation is nonlinear and the wage change is large, this should be viewed as a rough approximation.

THE ECONOMICS OF PARENTAL LEAVE MANDATES   313

0.4 and 1.0 percent.[36] Lengthier entitlements would presumably induce still larger entry into the labor force.

Previous research indicates that the availability of parental leave accelerates reentry into work. Klerman's [1993] analysis of the National Longitudinal Survey of Youth (NLSY) shows that the median time away from work for women receiving either paid or unpaid leave is around seven weeks. Conversely, the typical female who quits her job at or immediately before childbirth (presumably because she could not obtain sufficiently lengthy leave) does not return to work for more than one year. Waldfogel [1997] compares changes in work experience for NLSY women who do and do not return to the same employer after childbirth. The increase in experience, between the ages of 22 and 30, is 0.9 years greater for those who stay with the same employer than for those who do not (6.3 years versus 5.4 years).

Rönsen and Sundström [1996] study how parental leave affects the return to work in Norway and Sweden. Although both countries have relatively lengthy leave entitlements, those in Sweden are considerably more generous. It is presumably for this reason that Norwegian women are somewhat more likely to return to their jobs in the initial months following childbirth. However, Swedish reemployment rates ultimately considerably surpass those in Norway, with the result that young mothers in Sweden are almost twenty percentage points more likely to be employed three years after the first child is born.

These studies probably do not adequately control for all relevant sources of heterogeneity, so it remains uncertain to what extent leave mandates accelerate return to the labor force. Nevertheless, based on the available evidence, it may be reasonable to assume that entitlements of short-to-moderate length reduce the average time out of work by at least three months per child. If the typical woman has two children, this implies a six-month increase in job-holding which, with an average of around 23 years of lifetime employment, would raise the overall EP ratio by slightly over 2 percent. Longer leave periods may allow still more women to retain preexisting employment attachments but need not have a larger effect on female EP ratios, since

36. Female EP ratios average 45.3 percent, implying 1178 weeks of work between the ages of 15 and 64. Parental leave that induces a four percentage point increase in employment during the 52-week period preceding each of two births therefore raises the average EP ratio by 0.4 percent (4 percent × 104/1178). Similarly, a temporary eleven percentage point rise in employment elevates the EP ratio by 1.0 percent (11 percent × 104/1178).

314   *QUARTERLY JOURNAL OF ECONOMICS*

they are likely to delay the return to work of individuals who would have otherwise done so fairly quickly.

Next consider wages. Entitlements to short periods of paid leave are estimated to have little impact on hourly earnings, whereas rights to lengthier time away from the job significantly reduce them. This seems reasonable. Brief periods of leave probably impose few costs on employers, particularly when the benefits are paid by the government. The entry of some new workers into the labor force will lower wages (as discussed below) but this may be more than offset by the increased experience associated with faster return to work following childbirth.

There are several reasons why rights to extended parental leave might substantially reduce wages. First, increases in labor supply in the period immediately prior to childbirth are likely to significantly lower female earnings. A small portion of this decline will result from the reductions in average experience levels.[37] It will mostly occur, however, because the outward shift of the labor supply curve is combined with inelastic demand for labor. Hamermesh [1993] estimates that the long-run own-price elasticity of demand for homogeneous labor is around -0.3, implying that a 1 percent rise in labor supply will reduce wages by more than 3 percent. The decrease in women's relative wages will be less than this, to the extent that male and female labor is easily substitutable, but Hamermesh suggests that such substitutability is limited.

Second, extended work absences may impose substantial nonwage costs on firms. As the leave entitlement lengthens, it is likely to become much harder to schedule replacement workers, particularly in countries placing restrictions on the duration of employment on temporary fixed-term contracts. The costs may be sizable even when workers do not use all of the allowed leave, since employers face considerable uncertainty regarding the timing and ultimate likelihood of the individual's return to the job.

Third, extremely lengthy leave guarantees introduce the possibility that women having multiple children in a short period of time may be away from their jobs for several years consecutively, or with just brief spells of intervening employment, causing substantial depreciation of human capital. This becomes even

---

37. If the leave entitlements induce a 1 percent rise in the female EP ratios and inexperienced workers earn 20 percent less than the average women, the compositional change will decrease female wages by less than 0.2 percent.

THE ECONOMICS OF PARENTAL LEAVE MANDATES   315

more likely when paid leave is supplemented by rights to unpaid but job-protected time off work.

To summarize, this study indicates that parental leave guarantees raise the employment of women but, at longer durations, may be paid for through the receipt of lower relative wages. Several mechanisms have been identified as possible sources of the relatively large estimated effects. Nevertheless, beyond the caveats already mentioned, these findings should be viewed as tentative for a variety of reasons. The sample sizes are quite small, resulting in imprecise estimates in some models. The data on leave are incomplete—a more comprehensive investigation would explicitly consider eligibility and take-up rates. And the information on wages is often restricted to manufacturing workers. Ideally, this analysis would be supplemented by research using microdata from several countries. Finally, other benefits or costs may also be associated with the mandates. Most significantly, it is often argued that parental leave improves the health and well-being of children. This represents an important area for future research.

UNIVERSITY OF NORTH CAROLINA GREENSBORO AND
NATIONAL BUREAU OF ECONOMIC RESEARCH

REFERENCES

Addison, John T., and W. Stanley Siebert, *Current Controversies, No. 6: Social Engineering in the European Community: The Social Charter, Maastricht and Beyond* (London: The Institute of Economic Affairs, 1993).

Aghion, Philippe, and Benjamin Hermalin, "Legal Restrictions on Private Contracts Can Enhance Efficiency," *Journal of Law, Economics, and Organization*, VI (1990), 381–409.

Blackburn, McKinley L., "Misspecified Skedastic Functions for Grouped-Data Models," mimeo, University of South Carolina, 1995.

Blank, Rebecca M., "Introduction," in Rebecca M. Blank, ed., *Social Protection Vs. Economic Flexibility* (Chicago, IL: University of Chicago Press, 1994).

Bookman, Ann, "Parenting without Poverty: The Case for Funded Parental Leave," in Janet Shibley Hyde and Marilyn J. Essex, *Parental Leave and Child Care* (Philadelphia, PA: Temple University Press, 1991).

Bravo, Ellen, "Family Leave: The Need for a New Minimum Standard," in Janet Shibley Hyde and Marilyn J. Essex, eds. *Parental Leave and Child Care* (Philadelphia, PA: Temple University Press, 1991).

Brocas, Anne-Marie, Anne-Marie Cailloux, and Virginie Oget, *Women and Social Security: Progress Towards Equality of Treatment* (Geneva: International Labour Office, 1990).

Bundesminister fuer Jugend, Familie, Frauen und Gesundheit, *Erziehungsgeld, Erziehungsurlaub und Anrechung von Erziehungszeiten in der Rentenversicherung* (Berlin: Verlag W. Kohlhammer, 1989). [The Federal Ministry of Youth, Family and Health, *Child Rearing Benefit, Parental Leave and Credits for Rearing Children in the Social Security System* (Berlin: W. Kohlhammer, 1989)].

Carnegie Task Force on Meeting the Needs of Young Children, *Starting Points: Meeting the Needs of Young Children* (New York, NY: Carnegie Corporation of New York, 1994).

Dalto, Guy C., "A Structural Approach to Women's Hometime and Experience-Earnings Profiles: Maternity Leave and Public Policy," *Population Research and Policy Review*, VIII (1989), 247–266.

Frank, Meryl, and Robyn Lipner, "History of Maternity Leave in Europe and the United States," in Edward F. Zigler and Meryl Frank, eds. *The Parental Leave Crisis* (New Haven, CT: Yale University Press, 1988).

Gruber, Jonathan, "The Incidence of Mandated Maternity Benefits," *American Economic Review*, LXXXIV (1994), 622–641.

Hamermesh, Daniel S., *Labor Demand* (Princeton, NJ: Princeton University Press, 1993).

International Labour Office, *Yearbook of Labour Statistics* (Geneva: International Labour Office Publications, various years).

International Labour Office, *Legislative Series* (Geneva: International Labour Office Publications, various years).

International Labour Office, "Protection of Working Mothers: An ILO Global Survey (1964–84)," *Women at Work*, II (1984), 1–71.

Kamerman, Sheila B., "Maternity and Parenting Benefits: An International Overview," in Edward F. Zigler and Meryl Frank, eds., *The Parental Leave Crisis* (New Haven: Yale University Press, 1988).

——, "Child Care Policies and Programs: An International Overview," *Journal of Social Issues*, XCVII (1991), 179–196.

Klerman, Jacob A., "Characterizing Leave for Maternity: Modeling the NLSY Data," National Longitudinal Surveys Discussion Paper No. 95–21, Bureau of Labor Statistics, December 1993.

Klerman, Jacob A., and Arleen Leibowitz, "Labor Supply Effects of State Maternity Leave Legislation," in Francine Blau and Ronald Ehrenberg, eds., *Gender and Family Issues in the Workplace* (New York: Russell Sage Foundation Press, 1997).

Klerman, Jacob A., and Arleen Leibowitz, "The Work-Employment Distinction among New Mothers," *Journal of Human Resources*, XXIV (1994), 277–303.

Krueger, Alan B., "Observations on Employment-Based Government Mandates, with Particular Reference to Health Insurance," Working Paper No. 323, Industrial Relations Section, Princeton University, January 1994.

Kuhn, Peter, "Mandatory Notice," *Journal of Labor Economics*, X (1992), 117–137.

Levine, David I., "Just-Cause Employment Policies in the Presence of Worker Adverse Selection," *Journal of Labor Economics*, IX (1991), 294–305.

McGuire, Thomas G., and Christopher J. Ruhm, "Workplace Drug Abuse Policy," *Journal of Health Economics*, XII (1993), 19–38.

Mitchell, Olivia, "The Effect of Mandatory Benefit Packages," in L. Bassi, D. Crawford, and R. Ehrenberg, eds., *Research in Labor Economics, Vol. 11* (Greenwich, CT: JAI Press, 1990).

Moeller, Robert G., *Protecting Motherhood: Women and the Family in the Politics of Postwar West Germany* (Berkeley, CA: University of California Press, 1993).

Mortensen, Dale T., "Unemployment Insurance and Job Search Decisions," *Industrial and Labor Relations Review*, XXX (1977), 505–517.

Ondrich, Jan, C. Katharina Spiess, and Quing Yang, "Barefoot and in a German Kitchen: Federal Parental Leave and Benefit Policy and the Return to Work After Childbirth in Germany," *Journal of Population Economics*, IX (1996), 247–266.

Organization for Economic Cooperation and Development, "Long-Term Leave for Parents in OECD Countries," in *Employment Outlook: July 1995* (Paris: OECD, Department of Economics and Statistics, 1995).

Organization for Economic Cooperation and Development, *Labour Force Statistics: 1966–1986, 1968–1988, 1971–1991, 1973–1993* (Paris: OECD, Department of Economics and Statistics, various years).

Rönsen, Marit, and Marianne Sundström, "Maternal Employment in Scandinavia: A Comparison of After-Birth Employment Activity of Norwegian and Swedish Women," *Journal of Population Economics*, IX (1996), 267–285.

Rothschild, Michael, and Joseph Stiglitz, "Equilibrium in Competitive Insurance Markets: An Essay on the Economics of Imperfect Information," *Quarterly Journal of Economics,* XC (1976), 629–649.

Ruhm, Christopher J., "Policy Watch: The Family and Medical Leave Act," *Journal of Economic Perspectives,* XI (1997), 175–186.

Ruhm, Christopher J., and Jackqueline L. Teague, "Parental Leave Policies in Europe and North America," in Francine Blau and Ronald Ehrenberg, eds., *Gender and Family Issues in the Workplace* (New York, NY: Russell Sage Foundation Press, 1997).

Spalter-Roth, Roberta M., and Heidi I. Hartmann, *Unnecessary Losses: Costs to Americans of the Lack of Family and Medical Leave* (Washington, DC: Institute for Women's Policy Research, 1990).

Stoiber, Susanne A., "Family Leave Entitlements in Europe: Lessons for the United States," *Compensation and Benefits Management,* VI (1990), 111–116.

Summers, Lawrence, "Some Simple Economics of Mandated Benefits," *American Economic Review,* LXXIX (1989), 177–183.

Teague, Jackqueline L., "An International Analysis of the Effects of Family Leave Policies on Employment and Labor Force Participation," unpublished M.A. thesis, University of North Carolina at Greensboro, 1993.

Trzcinski, Eileen, "Employers' Parental Leave Policies: Does the Labor Market Provide Parental Leave?" in *Parental Leave and Child Care,* Janet Hyde and Marilyn Essex, eds. (Philadelphia, PA: Temply University Press, 1991).

U. S. Department of Labor, Bureau of Labor Statistics, *Employee Benefits in Medium and Large Private Establishments, 1993, Bulletin No. 2456* (Washington, DC: U. S. Government Printing Office, November 1994a).

U. S. Department of Labor, Bureau of Labor Statistics, *Employee Benefits in Small Private Establishments, 1992, Bulletin No. 2441* (Washington, D.C.: U. S. Government Printing Office, May 1994b).

U. S. Social Security Administration. *Social Security Programs throughout the World* (Washington, DC: U. S. Government Printing Office, various years).

Waldfogel, Jane, "The Family Gap for Young Women in the US and UK: Can Maternity Leave Make a Difference?" mimeo, Columbia University, 1994.

——, "The Impact of the Family and Medical Leave Act on Coverage, Leave-Taking, Employment and Earnings," mimeo, Columbia University, 1996.

——, "Working Mothers Then and Now: A Cross-Cohort Analysis of the Effects of Maternity Leave on Women's Pay," in Francine Blau and Ronald Ehrenberg, eds., *Gender and Family Issues in the Workplace* (New York: Russell Sage Foundation Press, 1997).

Zabel, Jeffrey, E., "Estimating Wage Elasticities for Lifecycle Models of Labor Supply Behavior," mimeo, Tufts University, 1996.

Zigler, Edward F., Meryl Frank, and Barbara Emmel, "Introduction," in Edward F. Zigler and Meryl Frank, eds., *The Parental Leave Crisis: Toward a National Policy* (New Haven, CT: Yale University Press, 1988).

Part IV
Unions

[15]

What Do Unions Do for Economic Performance?

BARRY T. HIRSCH

Trinity University, San Antonio, TX 78212 and IZA, Bonn

I. Introduction

The publication in 1984 of Richard Freeman and James Medoff's *What Do Unions Do?*, which summarized and synthesized results from their broad-based research program, was a landmark in labor economics and industrial relations. *What Do Unions Do?* quickly changed the subject matter and approach for scholars studying unions. The models (or descriptions) of unions employed by labor economists were extended to include a collective voice face of unions in addition to its microeconomic monopoly face. Empirical analyses of unions, which once focused almost exclusively on union wage effects, began to address the large variety of topics studied in *What Do Unions Do?* Industrial relations scholars, who had never abandoned a broad multi-disciplinary approach to what unions do, increasingly were expected to include data and econometric analysis in their research.

The appearance of *What Do Unions Do?* coincided with the beginnings of the long-term decline in private sector unionism in the United States. Although unionism was declining, the steady stream of research fueled by *What Do Unions Do?* provided us with a far richer understanding of the nature of unions and collective bargaining than we would otherwise have had. Twenty years later, the approach adopted and empirical regularities found by Freeman and Medoff hold up reasonably well. The continuing decline of private sector unionism, however, eventually eroded interest in and research on this topic. Freeman and other scholars increasingly have turned their attention toward issues such as public sector unions, alternative union and nonunion forms of worker representation, and workplace institutions outside the United States.

This essay focuses on perhaps the most contentious topic in *What Do Unions Do?* — union effects on productivity, growth, profits, and investment. Contentious first because the monopoly and voice approaches to unions provide different expectations about union effects on performance, and second, because the empirical evidence on which conclusions were based was extremely limited in 1984 (and remains limited today). Much of their story on unions and economic performance holds up well.[1] Freeman and Medoff rightly emphasize that union effects on productivity vary with respect to the labor relations environment and degree of competition, that unions generally decrease profitability, and that there exists slower growth in the union sector of the economy. Subsequent research suggesting that average union productivity effects are close to zero does not support Freeman and Medoff's conclusion that unions are generally good for productivity. Although they conclude that monopoly profits provide the principal source for union wage increases, subsequent research suggests that unions also tax the normal returns to long-lived tangible and intangible capital investments. And while it is true that much of the negative relationship between unions and growth is not causal, slower growth is partly attributable to the lower profits and investment resulting from union rent seeking.

I first summarize what Freeman and Medoff say about unions and performance in *What Do Unions Do?* A brief section on issues of measurement follows. I then provide an analysis of subsequent evidence on unions and performance, focusing on studies examining the U.S. private sector. This lengthy section is not intended to provide an exhaustive survey of each topic but, rather, to evaluate the themes, evidence, and conclusions presented in *What Do Unions Do?*[2] The next section is rather speculative, looking forward and asking what types of policy changes might better encourage workplace voice and participation in a world of declining unionism. A concluding section follows.

II. *What Do Freeman and Medoff Do?*

Freeman and Medoff examine the effects of unions on firm performance in two chapters of *What Do Unions Do?* Chapter 11 asks whether unionism is good or bad for productivity. Chapter 12 provides evidence on unions and profitability. They rightly emphasize that: "What unions do to productivity is one of the key factors in assessing the overall economic impact of unions" (p. 180). They conclude that in general unions tend to increase productivity, although the effect varies to no small extent with respect to time and place and the associated labor relations environment. In contrast, unionism almost always lowers profitability. Taken together, these pieces of evidence present a paradox. In Freeman and Medoff's words: "Beneficial to organized workers, almost always; beneficial to the economy, in many ways; but harmful to the bottom line of company balance sheets: this is the paradox of American trade unionism, which underlies some of the ambivalence of our national policies toward the institution" (p. 190).

Freeman and Medoff identify three routes through which unions affect productivity. One is via price-theoretic effects from standard microeconomic theory. Given union monopoly wage gains, firms may shift toward more capital and higher quality labor. As discussed later, a union wage gain need not produce such responses, but this point can be ignored for now. Although capital deepening or skill upgrading increase output per hour, this is not what is being tested (in principle) in the unions-productivity literature. Rather, the thesis is that unions increase "technical efficiency" — output for a given mix of inputs. Empirical literature in this area is clear on the issue, attempting to quantitatively control for capital investment and labor quality. If unions affect output per worker exclusively by moving up a labor demand schedule, such price-theoretic responses should not show up as union productivity gains in the empirical estimates.[3]

As outlined by Freeman and Medoff, what should show up in the empirical literature (which controls for the input mix) is the net effect of restrictive union work rules and voice/response interaction, the former depressing and latter raising productivity (1984, Figure 11–1, p. 163). These categories should be interpreted broadly. "Restrictive work rules" can include not only inefficient staffing requirements ("featherbedding"), but also any decrease in productivity resulting from limited incentives for worker effort or restrictions on management discretion (obviously, union formalization of the workplace governance structure can increase or decrease productivity).[4] As for voice/response, Freeman and Medoff highlight lower quits and improved personnel policies as key to increased productivity, emphasizing that positive outcomes require good labor relations. Productivity enhancing institutional response might also include a "shock effect" to management induced by higher union wages. Whether such a response should be considered a union voice/response effect or a monopoly effect is not clear, raising the more fundamental question as to whether the two faces of unions are truly distinct. I return briefly to this question. Given both positive and negative effects, the net effect of unions on productivity is an empirical question.

Empirical evidence on unions and productivity was rather sketchy in 1984; it remains less than clear-cut today. As Freeman and Medoff state: "This 'answer' to the debate over what unions do to productivity is probably the most controversial and least widely accepted result in this book" (1984, p. 180). Freeman and Medoff summarize evidence on manufacturing studies and sector-specific studies in construction, wooden furniture, cement, and coal (1984, Table 11–1, p. 166). The strongest evidence for a large positive effect of unions on productivity comes from Brown and Medoff's (1978) rightly influential study using manufacturing industry-by-state data. Depending on one's assumption regarding capital usage, one obtains estimates of union effects on total factor productivity of either 20–25 percent or 10–15 percent. Additional unpublished work with Jonathan Leonard using 1972 and 1977 Census of Manufacturers data produces positive estimates of union productivity effects.

In contrast to the Brown and Medoff study, Clark's (1984) analysis of manufacturing lines of business indicated a –2 percent average difference in the productivity of union and nonunion businesses. Freeman and Medoff cite but do not emphasize Clark's results, despite the fact that business-level analysis has numerous advantages over Brown and Medoff's highly aggregated data.

Sector-specific studies using value-added measures of output during the 1970s indicate extremely large union productivity effects in construction and moderate productivity effects in wooden household furniture. Studies using physical output measures confirm large union productivity effects in construction. Clark's studies of cement plants indicate a moderate union productivity advantage (6–8 percent) in his cross-sectional analysis and a roughly similar increase in productivity among the relatively few plants changing from nonunion to union status. Among the more interesting results in Freeman and Medoff's table are productivity results in underground bituminous coal for four years, 1965, 1970, 1975, and 1980, with union productivity effects swinging from highly positive in 1965 to highly negative in 1975 and 1980. Freeman and Medoff link these changes to deterioration in labor relations within the industry, emphasizing that union effects in the workplace vary depending on labor and management policies and their working relationship.

Despite the rather mixed empirical evidence on productivity, even in 1984, Freeman and Medoff interpret these findings as follows: "In sum, most studies of productivity find that unionized establishments are more productive than otherwise comparable nonunion establishments" (1984, p. 169).

Freeman and Medoff recognize the importance of union effects on productivity growth as well as levels. They analyze three alternative data sets, in each case finding industry union density associated with slower productivity growth. The magnitude of the estimates is nontrivial (relative to mean growth rates), but none is statistically significant, reflecting the large variation across industries in growth rates and their relationship to unionism. Freeman and Medoff conclude: "In sum, current empirical evidence offers little support for the assertion that unionization is associated with lower (or higher) productivity advance" (p. 170).

The final sections of Chapter 11 explore *why* or *how* unions affect productivity. There is no single metric to be estimated here; rather the authors assemble various observations or findings across otherwise disparate studies. Each of their explanations fits into their collective voice/institutional response framework, although in different ways. They first give prominence to the Brown and Medoff (1978) estimate that one-fifth of the union productivity effect found in their study can be attributed to lower quit rates. They also emphasize Clark's (1980a) findings that cement plants switching from nonunion to union changed their plant managers, replacing previously authoritarian or paternalistic managerial practices with more professional and structured supervision and governance. Freeman and Medoff next cite studies showing a link between productivity at unionized plants and the industrial relations climate in those plants, as reflected in number of grievances. Returning to the coal industry, where productivity swung from positive to negative, Freeman and Medoff state (italics in original): "The lesson is that *unionism per se is neither a plus nor a minus to productivity. What matters is how unions and management interact at the workplace*" (p. 179). They then note the importance of competition, suggesting that the coal industry's deterioration in labor relations and failure to maintain productivity gains along with wage gains stems in part from limited competition in that sector. In the concluding section of their productivity chapter, the authors declare: "Higher productivity appears to run hand in hand with good industrial relations and to be spurred by competition in the product market, while lower productivity under unionism appears to exist under the opposite circumstances" (p. 180).

Chapter 12, entitled "But Unionism Lowers Profits," summarizes what at the time was very limited evidence on unions and profitability. Freeman and Medoff (1984, Table 12–1, p. 183) rely on their own unpublished work using aggregate industry data from the Census of Manufacturers or from the Internal Revenue Service, as well as line-of-business data subsequently published in Clark's (1984) paper. Clark's study finds that union plants realize a price-cost margin 16 percent lower than nonunion plants, and "quasi-rents divided by capital" 19 percent lower. The aggregate data likewise indicated substantially lower profits associated with unionism, but with a wider range of estimates. The authors also cite Ruback and Zimmerman's (1984) subsequently published study showing that stock values fall as a result of successful union organizing drives. Despite the paucity of data on profitability, they conclude that unions lower profits. Subsequent work fully supports this conclusion.

Evidence is less clear as to *whose profits* are hardest hit. Freeman and Medoff emphasize work using aggregate industry data showing that unions reduce profits substantially in highly concentrated industries, but not in low-concentration industries. They also cite a subsequently published paper by Salinger (1984) arriving at the same conclusion using company data (although concentration is only weakly related to market value in Salinger's study). As discussed below, Salinger's conclusion is based on a restrictive specification that *forces* the union profit effect to interact with concentration and other variables (Hirsch and Connolly, 1987). Freeman and Medoff downplay Clark's (1984) finding that the largest impact of unions on profits is among lines of business with *low* market shares, noting in a footnote Clark's "contrary result . . . limited to a special group of businesses rather than to the entire economy" (1984, p. 278, fn. 7). Freeman and Medoff conclude that "the union profit effect appears to take the form of a reduction of monopoly profits" (1984, p. 186). Freeman and Medoff, however, are quick to point out that lower profits, whatever their source, can be associated with lower investment and growth. They explore the relationship between concentration and growth, find conflicting evidence, and safely conclude that the evidence relating unions, profitability, concentration, and growth is mixed. They rightly recognize "an important point about the impact of unions on profits: there is little normative content in the direction of the effect per se; rather, what matter are the market conditions and routes by which unionism alters profits" (p. 189).

In summary, Freeman and Medoff conclude that "the evidence on profitability shows that, on average, unionism is harmful to the financial well-being of organized enterprises or sectors" (p. 190). Beneficial to organized workers but harmful to the bottom line of companies — this paradox of American labor unions is one that Freeman and Medoff fully recognize. I return to this point subsequently.

III. *Two Faces Revisited: What Does Theory Do?*

By the time that *What Do Unions Do?* was published in 1984, Freeman and Medoff's "two faces of unions" dichotomy (Freeman and Medoff, 1979; Freeman, 1980) had become a standard framework or cataloging device to address the labor market effects of unions and remains so twenty years later. Although not a formal model in the sense that economists typically use the term, the two-faces approach has provided a broad umbrella under which labor economists and industrial relations scholars either have organized their thoughts about what unions do or, less frequently, based their explicit theoretical models of union behavior. The beauty of the framework is that the two faces — monopoly and voice — provide a sufficiently accurate description or shorthand for unions' principal activities, while at the same time being sufficiently broad to permit inclusion of a wide range of union effects in the workplace and economy.

The monopoly-voice distinction is not without limitations, however; the most serious is that these categories are neither distinct nor without ambiguity. Three examples should suffice. First, worker preferences and demand for wages, benefits, employment security, and working conditions depend in no small part on union bargaining power. Is this union's voice or monopoly face? Second, Freeman and Medoff stress that workplace outcomes depend crucially on management's response to its union. Is tighter management control in response to a union wage increases (a "shock effect") an example of labor union's voice/response or monopoly face? Or should one speak of a monopoly/response face? Finally, surveys indicate that workers have a desire for greater voice and cooperation in the workplace (Freeman and Rogers, 1999). Should this be considered an unsatisfied demand for union representation and the types of *collective* voice/response associated with unions? Or is it instead a desire for forms of individual voice and workplace interaction more typically found in nonunion than in union establishments (Kaufman, 2001)?

To address such questions, it is necessary to delineate a much clearer theory of what unions do. Fortunately, such an endeavor is not essential for this essay (but see the contribution to this symposium by Addison and Belfield on union voice). Herein, it is sufficient to identify those elements associated with unions that are likely to improve or detract from productivity, growth, profits, and investment. The monopoly/voice framework is a useful device to organize parts of the discussion. Once the focus turns to empirical evidence, one typically identifies (at best) the net effect of unions on various outcomes and rarely identifies the specific routes at work.

The monopoly face typically refers to what are mostly negative results emanating from union distortions relative to what might otherwise exist in a competitive labor market.[5] This face emphasizes the role of bargaining power, recognizing that the ability of unions to extract monopoly gains for its members is determined by the degree of competition and constraints on substitution facing both the employer and union. The standard microeconomic model has unions affecting labor (and product) market outcomes via wages above opportunity costs. The wage premium distorts relative factor prices and factor usage, thus producing a (presumably small) deadweight welfare loss. Independent of price distortions, unions may cause losses in output through strikes and decrease productivity in some workplaces through contractual work rules, reduced worker incentives, and limited managerial discretion.

Taken more broadly, the monopoly face can catalog any union effect that decreases efficiency or total value (the "size of the pie") to firm stakeholders (workers and owners) and consumers. Literature since *What Do Unions Do?* emphasizes unions' role in taxing returns on tangible and intangible capital and the resulting effects on profitability, investment, and growth.

The other face of unions is what Freeman and Medoff call "collective voice/institutional response." This face focuses on value-enhancing aspects of unions, emphasizing the potential role that collective bargaining has in improving the functioning of internal labor markets. For example, legally protected unions can effectively allow workers to express their preferences and exercise "collective voice" in the shaping of internal industrial relations policies. Collective bargaining may be more effective than individual bargaining or regulation in overcoming workplace public-goods problems and attendant free-rider problems. As the workers' agent, unions may facilitate the exercise of the workers' right to free speech, acquire information, monitor employer behavior, and formalize the workplace governance structure (Weil, 2003). Unions may better represent average or inframarginal workers, as opposed to workers who are most mobile and hired at the margin. In some settings, the exercise of collective voice should be associated with higher workplace productivity, an outcome that depends not only on effective voice, but also on a constructive "institutional response" and a cooperative labor relations environment. Freeman and Medoff emphasize that supportive management response to union voice is a necessary condition for positive union outcomes. Less clear is whether management actions that produce positive outcomes are responses to union voice (or voice bolstered by bargaining power) or responses to monopoly gains.

The monopoly and voice faces of unionism operate side-by-side, the importance of each being influenced by the economic environment. For a union firm in a reasonably competitive, largely nonunion industry, cost increases cannot be passed forward to consumers through higher prices. Thus, absent a productivity offset, unions should have little bargaining strength. Substantial union wage premiums in a competitive setting absent productivity improvements should lead establishments to contract over time. If a sizable proportion of an industry is unionized, industry-wide wage increases absent productivity offsets increase costs throughout the industry, costs increases are passed through to consumers, and no individual firm is at a severe disadvantage. But such a situation is difficult to sustain in the long run, if entry/expansion of nonunion companies is possible or products are tradable in world markets. On the one hand, the more competitive the market, the more limited is unions' bargaining power and ability to organize. On the other hand, the more competitive the market the greater the pressure on *union* companies to increase productivity. From a measurement standpoint, union companies that prosper or survive in a competitive environment are not a random draw from among all possible (and largely unobserved) union-firm experiences.

Unions have considerably greater ability to organize and to acquire and maintain wage gains in less competitive economic settings. Such settings include regulated industries in which entry and rate competition is legally restricted and oligopolistic industries in which entry is difficult because of economies of scale or limited international competition. Examples of the former include the previously regulated U.S. trucking and airline industries and the currently protected U.S. Postal Service, in each of which unionized workers have captured regulatory rents (Hirsch, 1988; Hirsch and Macpherson, 1998; Hirsch et al., 1999). Examples of the latter include the *deregulated* airline industry and the automobile industry. Following deregulation, unions' considerable strike power in the airline industry was maintained, allowing unions to capture a sizable share of potential profits during periods of strong demand but requiring concessions during downturns (Hirsch and Macpherson, 2000). In the automotive industry, labor relations have adapted in response to more limited market power and union power following the influx of European and Japanese imports, foreign-owned nonunion assembly plants in the United States, and labor-saving technological change and production innovations (Katz and MacDuffie, 1994).

Absent an offsetting productivity effect, a critical question concerns the source from which a union premium derives. Were it entirely a tax on *economic* profits (returns above opportunity costs), union rent seeking might be relatively benign. But for most firms in a competitive economy, above-normal returns are relatively small and short-lived. What appear to be abnormally high profits often represent the reward to firms for developing new and successful products, a reward for implementing cost-reducing production processes, or simply the quasi-rents that represent the normal returns to prior investment in long-lived physical and R&D capital. These profits serve an important economic role, providing incentive for investment and attracting resources into those economic activities most highly valued. To the extent that union gains vary directly with the quasi-rents emanating from long-lived capital, union wage increases can be viewed as a tax on *capital* that lowers the net rate of return on investment. In response, union firms reduce investment in physical and innovative capital, leading to slower growth in sales and employment and shrinkage of the union sector (Baldwin, 1983; Grout, 1984). It no longer follows that capital-labor substitution in union workplaces is optimal, a subject discussed more fully in the section on investment.[6]

Skill upgrading has been a conventional argument in the union literature (Freeman and Medoff, 1984; Lewis, 1986; Hirsch and Addison, 1986). The argument is simple — a union wage premium both allows and provides incentive for employers to upgrade the skill level of their work forces, offsetting part of the higher wage. Yet empirical evidence for skill upgrading is weak. Absence of clear-cut evidence is not surprising, however, once one realizes that such behavior need not follow from theory. Wessels (1994) provides a simple but persuasive challenge to the skill-upgrading hypothesis. If firms upgrade in response to a union wage increase, the union can then bargain in a future contract for an even higher wage in order to restore the premium. Employers, anticipating this, may respond by not upgrading. Firms that upgrade will face higher future wage demands and will have distorted their factor mix, using a higher skill labor mix than is optimal given its technology. Wessels provides an explicit model in which it is assumed that labor quality augments capital productivity and the decision to hire higher (lower) skill workers results if the elasticity of substitution between labor and capital is greater (less) than unity. Wessels concludes that available evidence is not consistent with skill upgrading.

Longitudinal evidence from wage equations also suggests that skill upgrading is not important. Freeman (1986) and Card (1996) conclude that wage-level and change estimates of the union-nonunion wage gap are similar, once one adjusts for bias from measurement error in union status (which is exacerbated in longitudinal estimates). This implies that, on average, *unmeasured* skills do not differ substantially for union and nonunion workers. Were skill upgrading important, we should observe high measured and unmeasured skills among union as compared to nonunion workers. The selection mechanism within union companies might better be characterized as a form of two-sided selection with positive selection among those with low measured skills and negative selection among those with high measured skills (Abowd and Farber, 1982; Card, 1996). Because of a queue of workers for union jobs, employers are able to avoid hiring workers in the lower tail of the skill distribution (skill here is defined broadly to include productivity-related attributes such as motivation and reliability). Yet few workers from the upper-tail of the skill distribution are either in or chosen from the union queue. Wage compression within union firms, both compression in skill differentials and contractually standardized wages, discourages applications by many of the most able workers. And following the logic of Wessels, firms may not have incentive to screen for and select the most able workers in the union queue if such action may lead to an increase in future wage demands. Card (1996) and Hirsch and Schumacher (1998) find clear evidence of two-sided selection.

The lack of strong longitudinal evidence for high unmeasured skills among union workers provides indirect evidence on unions and productivity. Were there a substantial positive union productivity effect (with measured worker skills and other inputs controlled for), then it seems likely that *some* of this higher productivity would be reflected in high unmeasured skills among union workers. We see no such thing. It seems implausible that union productivity effects would be embedded entirely in the workplace environment and not at all in workers, although such an outcome would be compatible with the collective voice view of how unions affect the workplace.

As the above discussion indicates, evidence is required to assess the relative importance of the monopoly and collective voice faces of unionism. Two additional points warrant emphasis. First, the effects of unions on productivity and other aspects of performance should differ substantially across industries, time, and countries. This is hardly surprising given that both the collective voice and monopoly activities of unions depend crucially on the labor relations and economic environment. Second, union effects are typically measured by differences in performance between union and nonunion firms or sectors. Such differences do not measure the effects of unions on aggregate or economy-wide economic performance as long as resources are free to move across sectors. For example, evidence presented below indicates that union companies in the United States have performed poorly relative to nonunion companies. To the extent that output and resources are mobile, poor union performance has led to a shift of production and employment away from unionized industries, firms, and plants and into the nonunion sector. Overall effects on economy-wide performance have been relatively minor.

IV. *Measurement: The Binding Limitations of Data and Inference*

What unions do is largely an empirical question. The evidence on this topic has greatly enhanced our knowledge and understanding of union effects on performance. But the availability and quality of data leave much to be desired. Even were better data available, identifying causal relationships is difficult. In this section, a few of the inherent problems associated with empirical studies are reviewed. My purpose is not to denigrate the value of this work — we would have far less understanding of what unions do absent such evidence. But given present limitations, caution must be used in drawing inferences. Were it possible to analyze these issues using better data and alternative methods, our assessment of how unions affect economic performance would require modification, certainly quantitatively if not qualitatively.

Most studies utilize cross-sectional data (at single or multiple points in time), measuring differences in outcomes (productivity, profitability, etc.) across establishments, firms, or industries with different levels of union coverage. Regression estimates from production functions, profit equations, and the like provide estimates of union-nonunion differences in performance, controlling for other *measurable* determinants. The key question is whether one can conclude that the estimated difference in performance associated with differences in unionization truly represents the causal effect of unions.[7]

There are several reasons why one must exhibit caution in drawing such a conclusion. First is potential bias from omitted variables. If one fails to control for an important productivity determinant and that factor is correlated with union density, then one obtains a biased estimate of the causal effect of unionism on performance. For example, older plants tend to have lower productivity, and union density is higher in older plants. If a study were to estimate the union impact on productivity among plants, the inability to measure and control for plant age (or its correlates, such as age of capital) would mean that part of the effect of plant age on productivity would be included in the (biased) estimate of the effect of unions upon productivity. Of course, omitted variables always exist in empirical work. One should have concern only where theory and supplemental evidence strongly suggest that there may exist substantial bias owing to some specified omission.

A second concern is bias resulting from union status being endogenous, rather than determined randomly (or independently of other correlates of the outcome measure). For example, unions likely will organize and survive in firms (or industries) with high potential profits; in this case, standard estimates of union effects on profitability (typically negative) would understate the impact of unions on profits. Alternative methods exist to deal with selection, but generally require identification (and measurement) of at least one variable that affects union status (say, state differences in labor law or sentiment toward unions), but not the outcome variable of interest (e.g., profitability).

A third reason for caution in making inferences is concern about "external validity." Even where one has obtained "internal validity" — unbiased estimates of union effects for the population being studied (e.g., a particular industry, time period, or country) — it is not clear whether these results have external validity that permit generalization. The most reliable estimates of union effects on productivity may well be based on specific industries (e.g., cement, sawmills) where output is homogeneous and can be measured in physical units rather than by value added. Yet it is not clear to what extent results in, say, the western sawmill industry (Mitchell and Stone, 1992) can be generalized to the economy as a whole, particularly given that we expect union effects to differ across time, establishment, industry, and country.

Several studies combine cross-sectional and longitudinal (i.e., time-series) analysis, typically examining *changes* in performance over time resulting from changes in union status (or, similarly, controlling for establishment fixed effects). For example, several studies examine changes in firm market value (measured by stock price changes), investment, or employment following the announcement of union representation elections and their outcomes. A limited number of studies examine changes in productivity or other performance measures following changes in unionization within plants. The advantage of longitudinal analysis is that each individual firm (or plant) forms its own control group — that is, a firm's performance once unionized is compared to its performance prior to unionization (as compared to changes among firms not changing union status). In this way, unmeasured, observation-specific, attributes fixed over time are controlled for in estimating the causal effect of unionization. Although such studies have strong advantages, inference can be difficult. Because unions may affect performance gradually over time, it is difficult to correctly correlate changes in unionization and changes in performance.[8] Moreover, firms or establishments changing union status are not randomly determined, making it unclear whether or not the measured effect among those receiving "treatment" (union status change) can be generalized to those not treated.

V. *What Have Unions Done? Revisiting the Evidence*[9]

As described in the previous section, union effects on performance must be estimated using imperfect data and statistical models and techniques that permit alternative interpretations of the evidence. Because of these limitations, one must carefully assess individual studies and the cumulative evidence before drawing strong inferences regarding unions' *causal* effect on performance. Even where the evidence is reasonably compelling, we often know little about the precise mechanisms through which these results are produced. In most of the studies reviewed below, unionization is treated as exogenous and we have little or no information on differences across unions in behavior or strategy. We can estimate the strength of the relationship between union status and productivity, profits, investment, or other performance outcomes. But we do not learn much else. The industrial relations and human resources literature has shed a bit of light inside the union-performance black box. But the literature provides few answers to the types of questions asked by unions regarding appropriate strategies, by management about personnel policies, or by policy makers about appropriate legislative and regulatory reforms.[10]

Discussion herein is largely restricted to the U.S. private sector, as in *What Do Unions Do?* There is growing international evidence on unions and performance (recent surveys include Aidt and Tzannatos, 2002; Metcalf, 2003; and, tangentially, Nickell and Layard, 1999). It is doubtful that results from other economies can be readily generalized to the United States, or vice-versa. As we have seen, the effects of unions are specific to the economic, legal, and structural environment. The institution of collective bargaining differs substantially across countries, making comparison difficult (the exception may be Canada and the United States). And changes in the economic, legal, and institutional structure surrounding collective bargaining have real effects on outcomes, as seen most notably by the changes in the United Kingdom since 1980 (Addison and Siebert, 2003; Pencavel, 2003). By the same token, variation across countries in the collective bargaining environment and in the legal structure, if clearly correlated with differences in union effects on performance, can offer clues as to the specific routes through which unions affect the workplace, something lacking in much of the U.S. literature. And non-U.S. studies frequently offer superior data. This is hardly surprising, given that in the U.S. data on firm or plant union density are not publicly available in any systematic fashion. Research may well provide more reliable answers to the question *"What Do Unions Do?"* for other countries than for the United States.

Productivity and Productivity Growth. Freeman and Medoff rightly emphasize the importance of what unions do to productivity. If collective bargaining in the workplace were systematically to increase productivity and not to retard growth, a strong argument could be made for policies that facilitate union organizing (this statement assumes that union-induced distortions in factor mix and economy-wide resource allocation are minor). A pathbreaking empirical study by Brown and Medoff (1978), followed by the body of evidence summarized in *What Do Unions Do?*, made for what appeared to many a persuasive case that collective bargaining in the United States is, on average, associated with substantial improvements in productivity.

The thesis that unions substantially increase productivity has not held up well. Subsequent studies are as likely to find negative as positive union effects on productivity. Critics have pointed out that a large union enhancement of productivity is inconsistent with the far less controversial evidence on profitability and employment (Addison and Hirsch, 1989; Wessels, 1985). And attention has focused on the dynamic effect of unions and their apparently negative effects on *growth* in productivity, sales, and employment. Surveys of the unions-productivity literature for the most part have concluded that union effects are highly variable but on average close to zero (see endnote 2). A "meta-analysis" of the unions-productivity literature concludes similarly that the average effect in the United States is very small but positive, while negative in the United Kingdom (Doucouliagos and Laroche, 2003). A survey of labor economists at leading universities asking for an assessment of the union effect on productivity produced a median response of zero and mean of 3.1 percent (Fuchs et al., 1998).[11]

A typical productivity study estimates Cobb-Douglas or (less restrictive) translog production functions in which measured outputs are related to inputs. To fix the discussion, a variant of the Cobb-Douglas production function developed by Brown and Medoff (1978) is:

$$Q = AK^{\alpha} (L_n + cL_u)^{1-\alpha}, \tag{1}$$

where Q is output; K is capital; L_u and L_n are union and nonunion labor; A is a constant of proportionality; and α and $(1-\alpha)$ are the output elasticities with respect to capital and labor. The parameter c reflects productivity differences between union and nonunion labor. If $c>1$, union labor is more productive, in line with the collective-voice model; if $c<1$, union labor is less productive, in line with conventional arguments concerning the deleterious impact of such things as union work rules and constraints on merit-based wage dispersion. Manipulation of equation (1) yields the estimating equation

$$\ln(Q/L) \cong \ln A + \alpha \ln(K/L) + (1-\alpha)(c-1)P, \qquad (2)$$

where P represents proportion unionized (L_u/L) in a firm or industry or the presence or absence of a union at the plant or firm level (a zero/one categorical variable). Equation (2) assumes constant returns to scale, an assumption relaxed by including a $\ln L$ variable as a measure of establishment size. The coefficient on P measures the logarithmic productivity differential of unionized establishments. If it is assumed that the union effect on productivity solely reflects the differential efficiency of labor inputs, the effect of union labor on productivity is calculated by dividing the coefficient on P by $(1-\alpha)$.

The conclusion that unions in general raise productivity substantially rests almost exclusively on the results of the influential Brown and Medoff (1978) study. Using aggregate two-digit manufacturing industry data cross-classified by state groups for 1972, Brown and Medoff's preferred coefficient estimates on union density are from .22 to .24, implying values (obtained by dividing the union coefficient by $1-\alpha$) for c-1 of from .30 to .31. Using alternative assumptions about capital usage (that increase union relative to nonunion capital), estimates of union productivity effects fall roughly in half. Absent this study, it would have been difficult to sustain the conclusion in *What Do Unions Do?* that in general unions raise productivity.

Limitations attach to the production function test and to the results in their paper, many of which were identified by Brown and Medoff. The use of value added as an output measure confounds price and quantity effects, since part of the measured union productivity differential may result from higher prices in the unionized sector. Not surprisingly, estimated effects of unions on productivity tend to be lower when price adjustments are made (Allen, 1986b; Mitchell and Stone, 1992). Union firms can more easily pass through higher costs when they operate in product markets sheltered from nonunion and foreign competition. Use of value added, therefore, is most likely to confound price and output effects in aggregate analyses relating industry value added to industry union density. It is less of a concern in firm- or business-level analyses that measure firms' union status *and* industry union density or other industry controls (Clark, 1984; Hirsch, 1991a). These studies tend to find small, generally negative, effects of unions on productivity.

It is difficult to reconcile the Brown-Medoff findings with other pieces of evidence. As argued by Addison and Hirsch (1989), parameter estimates from Brown and Medoff would most likely imply an *increase* in profitability associated with unionism, contrary to the rather unambiguous evidence of *lower* firm and industry profitability resulting from unionization. Wessels (1985) casts further doubt on these findings by showing that it is difficult to reconcile the productivity and wage evidence in Brown and Medoff with evidence on employment. Offsetting increases in productivity due to unionization and relative labor costs would imply substantial decreases in union employment (holding output constant) if firms shift toward labor-saving capital. Yet unions appear to have little effect on capital-labor ratios (Clark, 1984).

There are surprisingly few manufacturing-wide or economy-wide productivity studies and, except for Brown and Medoff, none reports consistent evidence of an overall positive effect of unions on productivity.[12] Clark (1984) provides one of the better broad-based studies. He uses data for 902 manufacturing lines-of-business from 1970 to 1980 to estimate, among other things, value-added (and sales) productivity equations. He obtains marginally significant coefficients on the union variable of from −.02 to −.03. The Clark study has the advantage of a large sample size over multiple years, business-specific information on union coverage, and a detailed set of control variables. In Clark's separate two-digit industry regressions, positive effects by unions on productivity are found only for textiles, furniture, and petroleum. A similar study is conducted by Hirsch (1991a), who examines over 600 publicly traded manufacturing firms during 1968–1980 (firm union data, collected by the author, is for 1977). Hirsch finds a strong negative relationship between union coverage and firm productivity when including only firm-level control variables, but the union effect drops sharply after including detailed industry controls. The results prove somewhat fragile when subjected to econometric probing. Hirsch interprets his results as providing no evidence for a positive economy-wide productivity effect and weak evidence for a negative effect. As in the Clark study, Hirsch finds considerable variability across industries.

A particularly rich data set has been developed recently by Black and Lynch (2002). They estimate production functions for a large sample of U.S. manufacturing plants over the period 1987–1993. Their study focuses on the effects of various workplace practices, information technology, and management procedures, but union status is also measured and analyzed. Absent interaction terms, Black and Lynch find slightly lower productivity in unionized plants following inclusion of detailed controls, a result equivalent to that in the Clark and Hirsch studies. The authors, however, find that this result is driven by low productivity among unionized plants using traditional management systems. Unionized plants that adopt human resource practices involving joint decision making (i.e., total quality management or TQM) and incentive-based compensation (i.e., profit sharing for nonmanagerial employees) are found to be more productive than their nonunion counterparts, which in turn had higher productivity than union plants using traditional labor-management relations (Black and Lynch, 2002). These results reinforce the conclusion that union effects are not a given, but depend highly on the specific economic and labor relations environment in which unions operate. Although one is reluctant to put too much emphasis on these specific results, they comport well with our priors. The suggestion is that union plants with high-performance systems, presumably adopted with union agreement, can realize enhanced productivity, whereas traditional top-down managed union plants realize no such enhancement.[13] Such research reinforces the need to get inside the union black box, helping us understand why there is high variation in performance across different unionized settings.[14]

Productivity studies based on firms within a single industry have advantages as compared to the manufacturing-wide studies. Output can sometimes be measured in physical units rather than value added, information on plant or firm-level union status is more readily available, and more flexible functional forms can be reliably estimated. From a methodological perspective, among the best analyses are Clark's studies of the cement industry (Clark 1980a, 1980b), Allen's analyses of the construction industry (Allen 1986a, 1986b), and Mitchell and Stone's (1992) work on western sawmills. Each of the studies provides a rather wide array of evidence. Clark finds positive, albeit small, effects of unions on productivity among cement plants. Allen (1986b) finds positive union effects in large office building construction and negative effects in school construction. Similarly, Allen (1986a) finds positive and negative union effects on productivity, respectively, in privately and publicly owned hospitals and nursing homes. Mitchell and Stone find negative effects of unions on output in sawmills, following appropriate adjustments for product quality and raw material usage. Although methodological advantages of the industry-specific studies are achieved at the price of a loss in generality, they do increase our understanding of how unions affect the workplace.[15]

Despite substantial diversity in the literature about union productivity, several systematic patterns are revealed (Addison and Hirsch, 1989). First, productivity effects tend to be largest in industries where the union wage premium is most pronounced. This pattern is what critics of the production function test predict — that union density coefficients reflects in part a wage rather than a productivity effect. These results also support a "shock effect" interpretation of unionization, i.e., management responds to an increase in labor costs by organizing more efficiently, reducing slack, and increasing measured productivity. Second, positive union productivity effects are typically largest where competitive pressure exists (consistent with the expectations of Freeman and Medoff, 1984, pp. 179–80), and these positive effects are largely restricted to the private, for-profit, sectors. Notably absent are positive productivity effects in public school construction, public libraries, government bureaus, schools, and law enforcement.[16]

This interpretation of the productivity studies has an interesting twist. The suggestion is that a relatively competitive, cost-conscious environment is a necessary condition for a positive effect of unions on productivity, and that managerial response should be stronger the larger the union wage premium. Yet it is precisely in such competitive environments that there should be little managerial slack and the least scope for union organizing and wage gains. This implies that steady-state union density in the U.S. private sector must remain small, absent a general union productivity advantage. By the same token, introduction of unions or the strengthening of other instruments for collective voice into highly competitive sectors of the U.S. economy is unlikely to have large downside risks for economy-wide performance. Although individual firms may fail to be competitive and perform poorly, market pressures should induce other firms and unions to develop labor relations systems providing the voice/response benefits envisaged by Freeman and Medoff. In short, as the U.S. economy has become more competitive over time (White, 2002), we might expect to see more favorable union-productivity outcomes among surviving and newly unionized establishments.

A concern expressed about the production function test is that there might be survivor bias, a form of selection that would bias upward estimates of union performance (Addison and Hirsch, 1989). In workplaces where unions have the most deleterious effects, businesses fail, contract, or grow slowly. Thus, the sample of union establishments sampled at any point in time includes a large proportion of establishments with positive performance outcomes, while those with poor outcomes are underrepresented.[17] Subsequent evidence indicates that survivor bias is not as serious as once believed. As discussed later, differences in failure rates among union and nonunion establishments and firms (following controls) appear small. If there is no union impact on business failure, survivor bias would arise only through use of weighted regressions, the use of current employment weights giving too large a weight to establishments with good performance (and growing employment) and too little to those with slow growth. Much of the literature uses unweighted regression estimates, however, which should avoid this particular form of bias.

Overall, the evidence produced since *What Do Unions Do?* suggests that the authors' characterization of union effects on productivity was overly optimistic. Freeman and Medoff were certainly correct that union productivity effects vary across workplaces, in particular with respect to the labor relations environment. They were correct to emphasize the role of management response, although one might just as readily emphasize the role of union response to management initiatives. And they were correct to note the role that a competitive market environment has on productivity outcomes. What appears incorrect is their conclusion that "productivity is generally higher in unionized establishments than in otherwise comparable establishments that are nonunion. . . "(p. 180). The empirical evidence does not allow one to infer a precise estimate of the average union productivity effect, but my assessment of existing evidence is that the average union effect is very close to zero, and as likely to be somewhat negative as somewhat positive.

Discussion now turns to the effects of unions on the *growth* in productivity. Productivity growth is typically measured by the change in value added after controlling for changes in factor inputs. Studies examining union effects on growth typically control (when possible) for union-nonunion differences in the accumulation of tangible and intangible capital and other measurable factors of production. Thus, what is being measured is a "direct" effect of unions on growth. Unions may also decrease productivity growth indirectly through their effects on investment and capital accumulation, a topic addressed shortly. Union effects on productivity levels and growth need not be the same. For example, unionization could initially be associated with higher levels of productivity, owing to a "shock effect" or "collective voice," but at the same time retard the rate of growth. In the long run, of course, low rates of productivity growth should produce lower productivity levels relative to comparison firms or industries.

As discussed earlier, Freeman and Medoff (1984) find lower (but not significant) union productivity growth using alternative industry-level data sets. They regard their results as inconclusive. A more comprehensive analysis using firm-level data (thus permitting control for industry effects) is provided by Hirsch (1991a), based on a sample of 531 firms and covering the period from 1968 to 1980. Following an accounting for company size and firm-level changes in labor, physical capital, and R&D, union firms have substantially lower productivity growth than nonunion firms. Accounting for *industry* sales growth, energy usage, and trade, however, cuts the estimate of the union effect by more than half. Addition of industry dummies cuts the estimate further, while the remaining effect proves fragile when subjected to econometric probes regarding the error structure. In short, union firms clearly display substantially lower productivity growth than do nonunion firms, but most (if not all) of this difference is associated with effects attributable to industry differences, union firms being located in industries or sectors with slow growth. There exists no strong evidence that unions have a *direct* effect on productivity growth.

Despite the contentiousness surrounding the effects of unions on productivity and growth, the most comprehensive studies find little effect that can be deemed causal. Results are simply too variable and not particularly robust to econometric probing. Five points surrounding this conclusion are worth emphasizing. First, union firms can be found to have lower productivity and productivity growth absent detailed controls. This is important in and of itself, although it tells us little about unions' causal effects. Second, a small or zero impact of unions on productivity is difficult to interpret. Does this mean that the positive and negative effects of unions are each close to zero, or that they simply cancel each other out with each having an important independent effect? Third, economy-wide studies measure the average effects of unions. There is considerable diversity in outcomes across firms and industries, consistent with the considerable emphasis given to the importance of the economic and labor relations environments. Fourth, studies of productivity and productivity growth control for differences in levels or changes in factor-input usage. But unionization is associated with lower rates of investment and accumulation of physical and innovative capital. This indirect route is primarily how we obtain slower growth in sales and employment in the union sectors of the economy. Finally, absence of a large positive union effect on productivity implies that union compensation gains are not offset, implying lower profitability and (typically) lower investment. The most important point to bring away from the productivity evidence may be the *absence* of a large positive effect due to unions.

Profitability. Absent sufficient productivity enhancements in the workplace or higher prices in product markets, union wage gains decrease profitability. The evidence on productivity does not suggest sufficiently higher productivity to offset higher compensation. Nor is it plausible that higher prices can offset wage increases, apart from regulated industries where prices are administered to approximate average costs. In more competitive settings, where union firms compete with nonunion domestic companies and traded goods, there is little possibility for passing forward higher costs. Lower profits will be seen in current earnings, in measured rates of return on capital, and in lower stock market values of a firm's assets. Ex-ante returns on equity (risk-adjusted) should not differ between union and nonunion companies, since stock prices adjust downward to reflect lower expected earnings (Hirsch and Morgan, 1994).

The responses of firms to differences in costs (union-related or otherwise) should in the long run mitigate differences in profitability. These are mitigated through the movement of resources out of union into nonunion sectors — investment in and by union operations decreasing until post-tax (post-union) rates of return are equivalent to nonunion rates of return. Stated alternatively, union coverage will be restricted to economic sectors realizing above-normal, pre-union rates of returns. Because the quasi-rents accruing to long-lived capital may provide a principal source for union gains and complete long-run adjustments occur slowly, however, we are likely to observe differences in profitability as these adjustments take place.

Consistent with Freeman and Medoff's conclusion in *What Do Unions Do?*, sub-sequent evidence points unambiguously to lower profitability among union companies, although studies differ in their conclusions regarding the source of union gains. Lower profits are found using alternative measures of profitability. Studies using aggregate industry data typically employ as their dependent variable the industry price-cost margin (PCM) defined by (Total Revenue –Variable Costs) / Total Revenue — and typically measured by (Value Added – Payroll – Advertising) / Shipments. Line-of-business studies and some firm-level studies use accounting profit-rate measures: the rate of return on sales, measured by earnings divided by sales, and the rate of return on capital, measured by earnings divided by the value of the capital stock. Firm-level analyses of publicly traded firms (Salinger, 1984; Hirsch, 1991a, 1991b) use market-value measures of profitability, a common measure being Tobin's q, defined as a firm's market value divided by the replacement cost of assets. Finally, "events" studies in which changes in market value attributable to votes for union representation or to unanticipated changes in collective bargaining agreements have been examined (Ruback and Zimmerman, 1984; Bronars and Deere, 1990; Abowd, 1989; Olson and Becker, 1990; Becker and Olson, 1992).

The finding of lower profitability from unionization is not only invariant to the profit measure used, but also holds regardless of the time period under study and holds for analyses using industries, firms, or lines-of-business as the observation unit. Although results vary, studies typically obtain estimates suggesting that union firms have profits 10 to 20 percent lower than nonunion firms. Firm-level studies that include large numbers of firm and industry controls tend to obtain the lower estimates. Economists are understandably skeptical that large profit differentials could survive in a competitive economy. Because rates of profit are not typically large, small absolute differences can produce large percentage differences. Whether one believes 10–20 percent differences in profitability can be sustained for "long" period of times depends on the definition of "long" and one's beliefs regarding the competitiveness of the U.S. economy.

Two potential sources of bias that can be identified cause the effects of union-ization to be *understated*. First, profit functions are estimated only for *surviving* firms, since those for which the effects of unionization are most deleterious may be less likely to remain in the sample. As stated previously, survival rates of firms do not appear to vary substantially with union status, so bias should be minor. Second, one expects unions to be more likely to organize where potential profits are higher; hence, the negative effect of unions on profits should be understated if union density is treated as exogenous. In fact, studies that attempt to account for the simultaneous determination of union status and profitability obtain larger estimates of union effects on profits (Voos and Mishel, 1986; Hirsch, 1991a), although such estimates are not precise. Because unionization in most firms was established long ago, however, the correlation between union status and current potential (i.e., nonunion) profits should be weak.

Although there is a consensus that unions decrease profitability, there is no agreement on the source of union wage gains. Influential early studies cited in *What Do Unions Do?* concluded that monopoly power provides the primary source for union gains, based on evidence that unions reduce profits primarily in highly concentrated industries (Freeman, 1983; Salinger, 1984; Karier, 1985). Subsequent research calls such a result into question. An early paper by Hirsch and Connolly (1987) criticizes this conclusion on several fronts. Market power arises not only from industry concentration, and rents from market power need not be the only source of union gains. Hirsch and Connolly provide firm-level evidence (but with an industry-level union measure) and find that unions gains derive from the returns associated with firm market share (with industry concentration constant), R&D capital, and weak foreign competition. With data similar to that used by Salinger, Hirsch and Connolly replicate the result from which he concluded that unions capture concentration-related profits. They show that the Salinger outcome is entirely the product of a restrictive specification that forces all union gains to vary with concentration. A more general specification rejects a positive interaction between union density and concentration.

Hirsch and Connolly also argue that if concentration were a major source of union gains, one should see union *wage* premiums larger for workers in more concentrated industries. Yet wage studies reject this outcome. In short, there is little evidence from either product or labor markets to support the hypothesis that profits associated with industry concentration provide a source for union rents. In a subsequent analysis using a data set with a firm union coverage measure, Hirsch (1990) more clearly rejects the hypothesis that concentration-related profit is a source of union rents.

The conflict in results with respect to concentration is not simply a result of the use of industry-level versus firm-level data. An industry study by Domowitz et al. (1986) finds no difference in union effects on profitability with respect to concentration. Likewise, using 1977 four-digit manufacturing-industry data, Chapell et al. (1991) find that unions have similar negative effects on price-cost margins among industries with low, medium, and high concentration. They also find that within concentration categories, unions have a larger effect on the profits of large than small firms.

Note that the studies summarized above do not reject the conclusion that union bargaining power and wage gains derive in part from firm market power. They reject the thesis that *concentration*-related profits provide a major source for union gains, in part because of the tenuous link between firm profitability and industry concentration

(Ravenscraft, 1983).[18] As discussed above, unions can and do capture rents stemming from sources of limited competition other than concentration, such as limited trade penetration or firm special advantages. Obvious examples of union gains stemming from market power (or specifically, restrictions on entry) include large wage premiums in the unionized U.S. Postal Service and among union workers in the trucking and airline industries under regulation.

Research appearing since *What Do Unions Do?* suggests that in addition to capturing rents stemming from market power, unions appropriate quasi-rents, in particular those that make up the normal returns to long-lived investments. This has important implications for investment and long-term growth (addressed below). For example, Hirsch (1991a) concludes that unions capture current earnings associated with limited foreign competition, both current and future earnings associated with disequilibrium or growing demand in the firm and industry (sales growth), future earnings emanating from R&D capital, and current and future quasi-rents emanating from long-lived physical capital (for related evidence, see Cavanaugh, 1998).

An interesting question is the extent to which the poor profit performance of unionized companies during the 1970s and early 1980s helps explain the decline in union membership during the 1980s and beyond. Blanchflower and Freeman (1992) note the unusually high union wage premiums in the United States as opposed to other countries (for recent evidence, see Blanchflower, 2003), arguing that this has consequences for employment and membership. Linneman et al. (1990) show that employment declines have been concentrated in the unionized sectors of the economy; nonunion employment has expanded even in highly unionized industries (for an update and extension, see Bratsberg and Ragan, 2003). That is, shifts in industry demand and employment are an insufficient explanation for the decline in private sector unionism. The complement of wage evidence linking large union premiums to declines in membership is the evidence summarized in this section on poor profit performance among union companies. A reasonable inference is that *profitability* differences between union and nonunion firms help explain declining unionization. Hirsch (1991a) finds a negative correlation between firm-level profitability in the late 1970s and subsequent changes in firm union density between 1977 and 1987. But the relationship between the wage premium, profits, and changes in union density is complex, and the verdict is out on how much of the decline in private sector density is related to lower profitability. Although smaller union wage premiums would lessen management response to unionization, they might also weaken the appeal that union representation has to workers.

Investment in Tangible and Intangible Capital. An area of theoretical and empirical research receiving attention since publication of *What Do Unions Do?* has been the union effect on investment, based on rent-seeking models in which unions appropriate (i.e., tax) the returns from investments in tangible and intangible capital. The theoretical origins for this literature reach back to Simons (1944); influential papers include Baldwin (1983) and Grout (1984). The earliest empirical paper in this literature appears to be Connolly et al. (1986). Rent-seeking models focus on the fact that unions capture some share of the quasi-rents that make up the normal return to investment in long-lived capital and R&D. "Rationally myopic" unions (Hirsch, 1991a; 1992b) find it optimal to tax capital when the time horizon of their members is short relative to owners' time horizon for long-lived, nontransferable capital (it need not follow from theory that the union always has the shorter time horizon; Addison and Chilton, 1998). In response, firms rationally reduce their investment in vulnerable tangible and intangible capital until returns on investment are equalized across the union and nonunion (i.e., taxed and nontaxed) sectors. Contraction of the union sector, it is argued, results from the long-run response by firms to such rent seeking.

As discussed earlier, the union tax or rent-seeking framework both complements and contrasts with the standard economic model of unions. In the standard model, a union wage increase causes a firm to move up and along its labor-demand schedule by decreasing employment, hiring higher quality workers, and increasing the ratio of capital to labor. Capital investment can increase or decrease owing to substitution and scale effects working in opposing directions. In the rent-seeking framework, union wage premiums are a tax on the returns to capital. Firms know that if they invest now in long-lived and nontransferable capital, union bargaining power will result in higher future wages. Stated alternatively, *wage* increases to unions are in part a tax on capital and need not lead firms to shift their factor mix away from labor and toward capital (Hirsch and Prasad, 1995; Addison and Chilton, 1996).[19]

Union rent seeking reduces investment not only in physical capital but also in R&D and other forms of innovative activity (Connolly et al., 1986). The stock of knowledge and improvements in processes and products emanating from R&D are likely to be relatively long-lived and firm specific. To the extent that returns from innovative activity are appropriable, firms will respond to union power by reducing these investments. Collective-bargaining coverage within a company is most likely to reduce investment in product innovations and relatively factor-neutral process innovations, while having ambiguous effects on labor-saving processes. Expenditures in R&D also tend to signal — or be statistically prior to — investments in physical capital. Therefore, firms reducing long-range plans for physical capital investment in response to unions' rent-seeking behavior are likely to reduce investment in R&D.

Patents applied for, or granted, are a measure of innovative *output* emanating from a company's R&D stock. Unionized companies may be more likely to patent, given their stock of innovation capital, to reduce union rent appropriation (Connolly et al., 1986). Although the patent application process is often costly and reveals trade secrets, patents offer firms opportunity to license product and process innovations and transform what might otherwise be firm-specific innovative capital into general capital, and lessen a union's ability to appropriate the quasi-rents from that capital.[20]

Hirsch (1991a) provides an empirical analysis of union effects on investment, both tangible and intangible capital. He distinguishes between "direct" and "indirect" investment effects of unions. The direct effect, discussed above, stems from the union tax on the returns to long-lived and relation-specific capital, leading firms to decrease investment to equate the marginal post-tax rate of return with the marginal financing cost. The indirect effect of unions on investment arises from the higher financing costs owing to reduced profits (and, thus, reduces internal funding of investment) for union firms. With data for 1968–1980 for approximately 500 publicly traded manufacturing firms and a model with detailed firm and industry controls, including profitability, Hirsch estimates the effect on investment for a typical unionized company compared to a nonunion company. Other things equal, the typical unionized firm has 6 percent lower capital investment than its observationally equivalent nonunion counterpart. Allowing for the profit effect increases the estimate to about 13 percent; that is, about half of the overall union effect is indirect. Hirsch repeats the exercise for intangible capital (annual investments in R&D), and his findings imply that the average unionized firm has 15 percent lower R&D, holding constant profitability and the other determinants. Allowing for the indirect effects induced by lower profitability only modestly raises the estimate. These deleterious union effects on capital investment have been confirmed in subsequent U.S. studies (e.g., Hirsch, 1992; Becker and Olson, 1992; Bronars and Deere, 1993; Bronars et al., 1994; Cavanaugh, 1998). Fallick and Hassett (1999) examine *changes* in firms' capital investment in response to a union win in a certification election. They find a substantial reduction, likening the effects of a vote for certification to the effects of a 30 percentage point increase in the corporate income tax.

Given reasonable similarities in the Canadian and U.S. collective bargaining systems and economic environment, two studies warrant mention. Consistent with U.S. evidence, Odgers and Betts (1997) conclude that unions significantly reduce investment in physical capital, while Betts et al. (2001) conclude likewise for R&D. Despite use of industry data (for multiple years), the authors make a convincing case that they have measured causal union effects.

A comparative study of the United States and Britain also warrants attention. Menezes-Filho et al. (1998) provide a detailed analysis of the effects of unions on R&D, concluding that although unionized establishments invest less in R&D, in the United Kingdom this is primarily an effect of the industry location and not of unions. They then subject firm-level data from the United States (provided by Hirsch) to the same battery of econometric tests to which they subject the British data. They conclude that, unlike the British evidence, the U.S. evidence of a deleterious effect of unionization on R&D investment is robust. Whereas the union tax model applies well to the United States, the authors speculate that British unions have fewer deleterious effects on R&D than do American unions owing to more explicit bargaining over employment levels and a preference for longer contracts. A recent survey by Menezes-Filho and Van Reenen (2003) reaffirms this conclusion — in the U.S. labor unions appear to substantially decrease R&D investment, but this same effect is not evident in Britain. The R&D evidence is consistent with labor market evidence finding far smaller union wage effects in Britain than in the United States (Blanchflower and Bryson, 2003).

Employment Growth and Survival. The effect of unions on employment growth and survival is not independent of its effects on productivity, profits, and investment.

It would be surprising were lower profits and investment not accompanied by slower growth, and this exactly what the evidence indicates. Linneman et al. (1990) show that much of what has been represented as a "de-industrialization" of America was in fact a *de-unionization*. Using Current Population Survey data for the 1980s, they show that within narrowly defined manufacturing industries, most displayed increases in nonunion employment while at the same time witnessing substantial decreases in union employment. The rate of decline in union employment is related to the magnitude of the union wage premium. In one of the few studies to examine firm-level employment growth, Leonard (1992) finds that unionized California companies grew at significantly slower rates than did nonunion companies. Dunne and Macpherson (1994) utilize longitudinal plant-level data (grouped by industry-by-size) to show that there are more employment contractions, fewer expansions, and fewer plant "births" in more highly unionized industries. They find that unions have no effect upon plant "deaths," even after controlling for plant size (larger plants are less likely to fail but more likely to be unionized). Freeman and Kleiner (1999) analyze two sets of data, one including insolvent and solvent firms, each with information on union status, and a second on individuals surveyed in the CPS Displaced Worker Surveys. Using the first data set, Freeman and Kleiner conclude that failed firms or lines of business (most lines of business remain in operation following bankruptcy) have similar union density as do solvent firms and lines of business. Using individual data, they find that being a union worker does not lead to a higher probability of permanent job loss from plant closure or business failure.

Two carefully executed studies examine the results of successful NLRB elections. In a study using longitudinal plant-level data, LaLonde et al. (1996) show that employment (and output) decrease following a vote in favor of union certification. DiNardo and Lee (2002) examine the causal effect of union elections on the subsequent survival of establishments. Previous literature is hobbled by a paucity of firm — and establishment-level unionization data and concerns about exogeneity. The authors address each of these issues. Combining NLRB election data for 1983–1999 with a matched listing of whether establishments named in the NLRB file continue to exist at that address in May 2001, they compare survival rates for establishments that have *just under* and *just over* a 50 percent vote in union elections. The authors make a convincing argument that the only important difference between these two sets of establishments is the union vote, so that subsequent differences in survival probabilities are likely to be causal. DiNardo and Lee conclude that the effects of successful union organizing drives on subsequent survival rates (from one to 18 years after an election) are negligible. The authors make a persuasive case that the results they find are causal and internally valid. It is less clear to what extent their results generalize to the larger population of existing (or previously existing) union establishments.

In short, the empirical literature finds that U.S. unions are associated with slower employment growth, but exhibit little or no difference in rates of business failure or survival.[21] These seemingly inconsistent results require explanation. The argument (Freeman and Kleiner, 1999) is that rent-seeking unions are willing to drive enterprises toward the cliff but not over it.[22] But in an uncertain world, it is implausible that unions will not sometimes miscalculate economic conditions or management actions, resulting in "accidental" business failures in the union sector. An alternative explanation is that because of wage premiums, union firms may have substantial wage flexibility via contract concessions as compared to nonunion firms with close to opportunity cost wages. Thus, nonunion companies are at a disadvantage when they try to cut costs during a prolonged downturn in business. Such wage flexibility may operate only for the minority of union firms at risk for bankruptcy, plant closures, or significant layoffs; the economy-wide evidence indicates that nonunion wages are procyclical but union wages largely acyclic (Grant, 2001).

VI. *What Should Unions Do? Assessing the Future of CV/IR and Public Policy*

Freeman and Medoff (1984) expressed considerable concern for the future of labor unions and the exercise of voice in the workplace. It is obvious, 20 years later, that such concern was warranted. By 2002, traditional collective bargaining serves few workers in the U.S. private sector; only one in twelve (8.6 percent) are union members and one in eleven (9.3 percent) are covered by a collective bargaining agreement (Hirsch and Macpherson, 2003). Given a competitive world, there is good reason to expect private sector unionism to continue its decline and little reason to predict any "spurt" in organizing success (Freeman, 1998). Such a conclusion is reinforced by the research discussed herein. Given lower profitability in union companies and widespread management resistance to unionization, organizing levels are likely to remain below replacement levels (i.e., normal union job loss) (Farber and Western, 2001).

What does the status quo imply? Continuation of current trends means that workers' desire for effective voice, cooperation with supervisors and management, and participation in decision making will remain unrealized for much of the nonunion (and perhaps union) work force. Absent a formal voice mechanism in the workplace, there is likely to be a continued reliance on governmental regulation and mandates, which by many accounts is insufficiently flexible and overly litigious (for analysis, see Addison and Hirsch, 1997). Labor law reforms could improve fairness, mitigate the contentiousness of the union organizing process, and facilitate organizing, thus slowing the decline in union density.[23] But union representation would remain very much the exception rather than the rule in the private sector. The case for labor law reforms that would *substantially* enhance organizing is weakened by what on balance appears to be a deleterious impact of unions, in their current form, on long-run economic performance. More fundamentally, labor unions as they now operate may not be the ideal organizational form to deliver the individual voice and cooperative work environment that workers want.[24]

Perhaps the fundamental problem with our current collective bargaining framework is the tension between a union's role as an agent of workplace democracy and voice and its role in redistributing income from owners (or consumers) to workers (Freeman and Lazear, 1995). A principal goal of labor law reform should be to encourage collective bargaining that enhances voice and cooperation while discouraging rent seeking. I salute any such efforts, but success is unlikely. Reforms that might work in this direction and that might muster sufficient political support are likely to have at most a modest effect on the steady-state level of union density. It is difficult to envision changes in labor law that will substantially change workplace governance for the more than 90 percent of private sector workers not covered by collective bargaining.

Continuation of the status quo appears likely, perhaps coupled with modest reforms in labor law and a growing role for government regulation in the workplace. Although not a preferred outcome, it is hardly a nightmare scenario. More of the same would permit continued economic growth and improvement in workers' standard of living. The economic pie would get larger and competition among employers would ensure that most (but not all) workers receive shares of the pie roughly commensurate with their economic contribution. Such a labor market, however, may produce less than the optimal level of worker participation and voice, with lower wealth and well-being than is at least theoretically possible (Levine and Tyson, 1990; Freeman and Lazear, 1995; Kaufman and Levine, 2000).

The remainder of this section is speculative, attempting to outline a general direction in which we might head in order to enhance worker voice and participation, an outcome that Freeman and Medoff once envisioned being possible through the positive face of traditional labor unions. As previous discussion has indicated, I am skeptical that labor unions can provide the principal road to enhanced voice in the workplace. If enhanced individual voice and participation are to occur, they must develop using a variety of approaches in multiple types of largely nonunion workplaces. Successful approaches to enhanced voice are unlikely to be mandated from above. Rather, they are likely to evolve through experimentation and cooperation among employers and their workers, with successful forms being imitated throughout the economy. Organized labor either will be reinvigorated and reinvented via competition — or will continue to whither.

I will not describe the specifics of what the future ought to look like. Rather, I first outline a set of criteria that workplace innovations should satisfy in order to evolve and flourish, followed by proposals that appear to satisfy these criteria. Whether beneficial changes (either those proposed here or elsewhere) can be identified and adopted via the political process is a different question, one about which I have little to say.

Criteria for Value-Enhancing Reforms in the Workplace.[25] A prerequisite for discussion of workplace reforms is to identify criteria that labor and employment law changes should satisfy. I offer the following. Reforms should: (1) be value enhancing for the parties and the economy;[26] (2) involve a greater role for individual and group voice within nonunion and union workplaces; (3) should encourage cooperation and participation across and among all levels of workers; (4) allow for variation in workplace governance type across heterogeneous workplaces; (5) allow flexibility within workplaces over time; (6) limit rather than facilitate rent seeking among worker organizations, including but not limited to labor unions; and (7) facilitate the evolution of workplace agents and institutions that best represent workers' interests and rights (Weil, 2003).

Absent major reforms and changes in current labor law, it is difficult to see how the current system can evolve toward adoption of employment governance structures embodying these characteristics. Meaningful change requires several things to occur. First, management must have incentives to initiate and encourage changes in workplace governance, changes that require removal of current legal barriers. Second, competitive pressures in product and labor markets are probably necessary. And third, pro-active changes in employment law and labor market regulations are likely necessary.

I discuss below two general approaches that have the potential to be value enhancing. The first approach is termed *conditional deregulation.* The second approach involves a change in the *labor law default* from no union to some alternative state. For each of these approaches, a move away from either the default regulatory structure or default governance structure within the firm requires approval of both management and workers (discussed below). The requirement for mutual agreement encourages management and workers to develop value-enhancing alternatives to the default structure.

• *Conditional Deregulation.* Here I describe a variant of a proposal suggested by Levine (1995), which he describes as conditional deregulation. Levine recognizes that there are a large number of governmental mandates and regulatory measures regarding workplace safety, hours and overtime requirements, pensions, discrimination, family leave, and the like. Under a system of conditional deregulation, the default for all (or nearly all) firms would be that they are covered by the full extent of these labor market regulations. These requirements would be divided into those that are non-waivable and those waivable. Non-waivable rights would include some minimum set of standards (say, with respect to discrimination or safety) that could not be waived by any employer. Conditional deregulation would permit employers to be exempt from the waivable set of regulatory standards and be subject only to the minimum standards if they voluntarily adopt alternative regulatory systems with employee oversight and approval.

In order to waive the regulations or "deregulate" workplace standards, firms must have in place independent worker committees to perform the approval and oversight functions. For union companies, the union would provide the employee voice with authority to waive government standards (the employer must also approve the waiver). For nonunion employers, worker committees or councils would be created with authority to approve the waiver on behalf of workers. A contentious issue would be the nature of these committees and the permissible employer role. Unlike Levine, I would argue for abolishment or major reform of 8(a)(2) of the NLRA, which restricts the creation of and role for worker associations other than traditional labor unions. (I would support abolishment of 8(a)(2) even absent other reforms.) I would permit a reasonably active role for the firm in setting up such worker councils, as long as the worker groups meet minimum requirements regarding independence, democratic choice of worker spokespersons, secret balloting on key issues, and antidiscrimination provisions protecting workers active in the worker associations.[27]

An important benefit of such an approach would be that it would spur the establishment of worker associations throughout the private sector and provide a vehicle to enhance worker voice and participation, and possibly cooperation between management and its workers. In those establishments where worker associations are formed, its major role will likely be to facilitate the exchange of information and provide workers a collective voice. Such worker groups, however, may also serve as a vehicle to transfer rents or quasi-rents from shareholders to workers, since their approval of waiving workplace regulations is likely to be conditional on the receipt of monetary or nonmonetary gains. Because the employer has the option of staying with the default regulatory standard, this makes it likely that any gains to workers through rent transfer will be less than the additional gains to shareholders from deregulation. In short, such a policy encourages value-enhancing choices by the firm and workers, while constraining the extent of rent seeking.

Adoption of conditional deregulation, as outlined above, would likely accelerate Congressional passage of waivable labor market mandates and employment regulations. Moreover, such regulations would likely set more stringent standards and contain fewer exemptions (based on company size and the like) than in the past. More stringent regulations could be costly absent the option to waive coverage. Given the availability of an opt-out, however, those establishments where regulations would prove costly are the ones most likely to agree on a mutually preferred set of alternative standards. The hope is that establishments will create workers' associations that gradually evolve into effective vehicles for voice, encouraging cooperation between management and its employees and facilitating value-enhancing changes in the workplace.

Conditional deregulation and the widespread creation of worker associations would have uncertain effects on unions. To the extent that nonunion worker associations substitute for traditional organizing, workers in some sectors may see even less reason to unionize. Just as likely an outcome is that conditional deregulation would provide the impetus for fundamental changes in and growth of labor unions in the private sector. With independent nonunion worker groups in place, workers in some firms will decide to turn to traditional collective bargaining and a more formalized union voice.

• *Changing the Labor Law Default.* A second proposed approach would shift the labor law default from its current setting of not unionized to some alternative invoking a governance structure providing independent worker voice. The default structure could be waived or replaced following the joint approval of workers and management. A point to emphasize is that the choice of the labor law and employment regulation defaults matter a lot, even where there exist procedures to modify those outcomes (Sunstein, 2001). For example, current labor law has a nonunion default, but allows majority worker choice of union representation. Imagine the opposite, with union representation the default, but workers free to reject representation by majority vote. In a frictionless system in which preferences are unaffected by the initial allocation, one might expect the two systems to produce the same outcomes.[28]

Obviously, eventual representation outcomes would differ enormously depending on a union versus a nonunion default. For one thing, the NLRA union certification and decertification processes are far from frictionless. Even absent such frictions, however, evidence from behavioral economics (Sunstein, 2001; Choi et al., 2003) indicates that workers would be more likely to stick to their initial endowment (collective bargaining) than would have chosen to adopt it through free elections. Were union coverage the workplace default, far more than 10 percent of private sector workers would remain unionized, even with frictionless decertification elections.

Why does the default affect outcomes? First, change is costly. Second, individuals exhibit behavioral inertia, often sticking with an existing rule or environment as long as it does not differ too much from the preferred choice. Third, and very important, is that the default signals a norm that the state (or employer, etc.) has deemed appropriate. That is, the choice of a norm affects individuals' evaluation of alternative arrangements. Whatever the relative importance of these reasons, a default governance structure must be chosen carefully since many workplaces will not change from it.[29] That being said, the default is not a mandate, but a starting point or endowment (or bargaining "threat point") from which the parties can move.

What might be an appropriate labor law default other than the current nonunion default? My preference is for a default that establishes some form of independent worker association, although not one with full collective bargaining rights. As part of any default, workers would retain their current right to form independent unions (without management approval). An important feature of a default mechanism is that it designates a standard procedure by which workers and management might discuss, negotiate, and approve mutually beneficial changes. It would be important that 8(a)(2) of the NLRA be crippled or abolished. This would permit and encourage management to be involved in the development of their firm's labor relations system, but with workers now starting from an enhanced endowment or bargaining position. Although one cannot predict precisely how any given system might evolve and operate, the widespread availability of the Internet makes it likely that both management and employee groups will use electronic communications to provide and exchange information (Diamond and Freeman, 2001; Freeman, 2002).

Note that the proposal for a change in the employment default can be combined with Levine's proposal for conditional deregulation. Assume that the selected default establishes a relatively independent worker association in the workplace. Management and workers could then make a joint decision to opt-out of waivable federal workplace standards.

Whatever default, it will not function well in all workplaces. The same is true for our current labor law default. In these workplaces, the employer and workers (either in the form of unions or worker associations) have incentive to move away from the default and develop proposals for participatory value-enhancing governance structures. Over time, operation of the system and the observed choices of workers and firms will produce legislated and administrative changes in the default. The inability to identify in advance all outcomes of a given reform should not necessarily be regarded as a serious criticism. The same can be said about any change — or the status quo. Laws and regulations do evolve over time.

The important point is that not only can workplaces opt out of the default, but the search for an alternative governance structure involves a productive exchange of information and the exercise of worker and management voice. Adoption of such a proposal should encourage management, workers, and workers' agents (be they traditional unions or worker associations) to communicate, negotiate, and arrive at alternatives that make all parties better off relative to the default. Clearly, the current labor law default provides little incentive for management or traditional unions to develop alternatives. An alternative default that permitted greater flexibility, be it through conditional deregulation or nonunion worker associations, would encourage value-enhancing innovations.

A major change in employment law and the default governance structure obviously requires thorough analysis and careful design.[30] The actual working of such a system, however, will be determined in no small part by the way it evolves in the workplace, courts, and regulatory agencies. Surprises will occur. Unanticipated outcomes may be good or bad. One simply hopes (perhaps naïvely) that policy evolves to minimize undesirable and encourage desirable results. An important concern is that a shift in the default away from the nonunion standard toward one emphasizing collective voice might shift too much power to incumbent workers (insiders), leading to employer cost levels inconsistent with full employment. It may prove difficult to limit the ability of worker associations or works councils to appropriate rents within a framework that promotes voice and the evolution of value-enhancing arrangements (Freeman and Lazear, 1995). But it strikes me that it's worth a try.

I sensibly end this rather speculative section on a sober note. The most likely prospect for the future, or at least the near future, is not adoption of any proposal discussed above, but continuation of the status quo. Changing the status quo in employment law does not appear feasible. Major changes cannot occur politically until there is strong dissatisfaction with our current system and a consensus that change is likely beneficial. While such a consensus may exist among legal and industrial relations scholars, it does not exist among workers or the general public. The emergence of a consensus for major workplace changes could result from some future economic and social upheaval. Whether such an upheaval will occur, its form if it does so, and the nature of a new majority consensus are far beyond the scope of this paper — and my imagination.

An alternative scenario is that major changes in workplace governance will occur, but that they will occur incrementally, absent a major upheaval or a spur via major public policy changes. A premise of my discussion has been that there are potential gains from greater employee voice and worker participation. What is needed is a governance form or workplace arrangements to make these gains possible. If 8(a)(2) were abolished, one can imagine such arrangements gradually evolving, working well in some workplaces, and then being adopted elsewhere in various forms. The Internet will likely play a major role in any such evolution (Diamond and Freeman, 2001; Freeman, 2002).

Labor unions, companies, and other workplace organizations already use the Internet heavily to communicate with their members or workers. There are isolated examples (Wal-Mart, IBM) where union-like worker voice groups, with little prospect for collective bargaining coverage, have emerged through the Internet, facilitating exchange of information and sometimes influencing company policies (Freeman, 2002). Employee voice is about communication and information, both of which are facilitated through electronic communication over networks. Whether effective nonunion employee voice and participation, coupled with an evolving and increasingly supportive legal and regulatory structure, will emerge, remains to be seen. Twenty years ago, Freeman and Medoff saw little need to address alternative nonunion forms for worker voice. Were *What Do Unions Do?* being written today, this is no doubt a subject the authors would consider.

VII. *Conclusion*

A common characterization of *What Do Unions Do?*, one heard largely although not exclusively from outside the research community, is that Freeman and Medoff argue that unions are unambiguously good — good for their members, good for economic performance, and good for society as a whole. Such a simplistic generalization about unions was inaccurate in 1984 and is still inaccurate today. But this is not what Freeman and Medoff say in *What Do Unions Do?* It is true that they tend to emphasize positive aspects of unionism. But this must be seen in context. A major and legitimate goal of *What Do Unions Do?* was to critique neoclassical economists for their then disproportionate focus on the "single face" monopoly aspects of labor unions. (Their challenge to industrial relations scholars has not been to broaden scope but to provide evidence.) They emphasize that there is a second and perhaps primary face of unions — the collective voice/institutional response face. *What Do Unions Do?* establishes that voice or nonmonopolistic aspects of unions should not be ignored and are worthy of serious analysis. Freeman and Medoff then provide a comprehensive empirical analysis of labor unions and interpret their findings in an intellectually honest manner. A broader "multi-face" view of unionism became widely accepted following the book's publication in 1984, and this perspective remains widely accepted today. And the analysis summarized in *What Do Unions Do?* has served as a reference point and stimulant for much of the subsequent literature on unions, much of which is examined in this and other papers in this symposium.

How have the empirical findings summarized in *What Do Unions Do?* held up over time? For the most part, the empirical regularities that they identify as union effects have been sustained in subsequent research. I have focused on the chapters on unions and economic performance — productivity, investment, growth, and profitability. The subsequent literature has proven less favorable for unions than the conclusions reached by Freeman and Medoff. That being said, little literature existed at the time *What Do Unions Do?* was written and, even now, the empirical evidence in this area is (understandably) limited and cannot establish (or reject) causal union effects or their magnitudes nearly so conclusively as one might like. Freeman and Medoff are clearly correct that variation in union productivity effects vary substantially across workplaces.

But their conclusion that union effects are generally positive, which I interpret to mean a nontrivial positive average effect, cannot be sustained, subsequent evidence suggesting an average union productivity effect near zero and at most modestly positive (say, 2–5 percent). Their speculation that productivity effects are larger in more competitive environments appears to hold up, but more evidence on this score would be desirable. Subsequent literature has continued to find unions associated with lower profits. Unlike Freeman and Medoff, several of the studies conclude that unions tax not just monopoly profits, but also the quasi-rents or long-run normal returns emanating from long-lived physical capital and R&D. Lower profits and the union tax on tangible and intangible capital has led to slower employment and productivity growth among union companies, reinforcing the downward trend in private sector unionism. Although union firms grow more slowly, Freeman and Medoff appear correct that unions do not lead to higher rates of business failure.

Even adopting a positive view of the evidence on unions and performance, union effects have not been sufficient to offset what are large (by international standards) union wage premiums in the United States. Because the voice face of unions depends so crucially on cooperative labor relations, management resistance to unionism and union organizing in the years since *What Do Unions Do?* has precluded any chance there might have been for this to be a period of expanding, cooperative, value-enhancing unionism. In short, the collective-voice face of unionism has been muted (or swamped) during the 20 years since publication of *What Do Unions Do?* One can argue as to how much of the management opposition is ideological, how much stems from the economic incentives of management to hold down costs in the face of union wage premiums and a highly competitive environment (Freeman and Kleiner, 1990), and how much is the result of labor law enforcement and generally low penalties (Kleiner, 2002). All three explanations clearly matter.

What Do Unions Do? has provided scholars and the public with a comprehensive and innovative documentation of the economic effects of unions. Yet whatever one's assessment of the evidence, old-style private sector unionism will continue to play a smaller and smaller role in the U.S. workplace. The publication date of *What Do Unions Do?* was doubly timely. It could not have appeared much sooner, given that the micro-level data sets on which much of the analysis is based had only recently become available. And although the empirical relationships uncovered by Freeman and Medoff look much the same today as twenty years ago, the focus of the book inevitably would have had to shift toward public sector unionism, alternatives to private sector unionism, or international comparisons (precisely the topics on which Freeman has subsequently focused). Labor economists and industrial relations scholars truly have been fortunate. Freeman and Medoff told us what private sector unions do while there remained unions doing it.

The research program ignited by *What Do Unions Do?* has continued apace as private sector unionism has declined. This program has been a rich one, extending beyond economists' earlier focus on monopoly unionism and union wage gaps and instead pursuing the ambitious agenda set by Freeman and Medoff. A principal con-

446   JOURNAL OF LABOR RESEARCH

cern among scholars has been the same concern made explicit in *What Do Unions Do?* How can we encourage value-enhancing workplace arrangements that facilitate voice among workers, while constraining unions' monopoly face? Freeman and Medoff focus their attention on traditional labor unionism. But with union density unlikely to rebound in the foreseeable future, the focus in recent literature is increasingly on the 90 percent of private sector workers without a formal mechanism for individual or collective voice and on new forms of workplace governance that might facilitate such voice.

I have provided some rather speculative ideas on the future of workplace voice. A likely path is that we will remain with something akin to the status quo, thus foregoing potential benefits from increased voice and participation. I have described new employment law defaults that might encourage the development of value-enhancing workplace governance structures — that is, those that make possible the benefits of voice with minimal rent seeking. "Radical" changes of this sort, however, appear politically impossible absent major social or political upheavals that economists have little ability to foresee (Freeman, 1998). A more likely avenue for change will be the gradual evolution of the workplace environment, employment law, and workplace governance in ways conducive to voice, participation, technological change (affecting what workers do), and the economic environments in which companies and households operate. There is of course no guarantee that the evolutionary changes produced in a competitive world will result in the type of arrangements described in the industrial relations literature. Nor can we envision what precise paths might be taken to effect such changes, although intensive Internet use for exchanging information, coordination of activities, and facilitating collective action appears likely. If future paths lead to workplace governance structures that take advantage of worker voice while restraining collective rent seeking, it will be in no small part a product of the productive discourse fueled by *What Do Unions Do?*

NOTES

*The paper benefited from the detailed comments of Bruce Kaufman and helpful discussion with John Addison.

[1]When I refer to Freeman and Medoff's "story" I refer to what the authors actually state in *What Do Unions Do?* and not to the simplistic (and incorrect) caricature of their work as saying that unions are everywhere good.

[2]There have been numerous surveys or appraisals of unions and performance in the United States and in other countries; see, for example, Becker and Olson (1987), Addison and Hirsch (1989), Booth (1995), Belman (1992), Freeman (1992), Kuhn (1998), Hirsch (1997), Doucouliagos and Laroche (2003), Aidt and Tzannatos (2002), Metcalf (2003), and Van Reenen and Menezes-Filho (2003).

[3]Addison and Hirsch (1989) make this point, largely rejecting the critique of Brown and Medoff (1978) made by Reynolds (1986).

[4]More broadly, what shows up using the production function approach is the effects of any factor (not elsewhere controlled for) affecting productivity and correlated with unionism. For example, the impact of union pay compression, which can positively or negatively affect productivity, would be included in estimated union productivity effects.

[5]Recent literature (Manning, 2003) argues that many firms face upward sloping supply curves (i.e., have a work force with limited mobility) and thus have leeway in their choice of wage policies. Unlike classical

monopsony theory, the "new monopsony" literature downplays the importance of market structure and provides few implications about employment and efficiency (just as price discrimination does not have clearcut implications for output and efficiency). A principal outcome of new monopsony is wage heterogeneity. It is not clear if this literature has a lot to say about union performance outcomes, apart from the obvious point that the nonunion counterfactual is more complex than a textbook competitive labor market. The empirical importance of the new monopsony literature remains to be seen.

[6]Using standard theory, a wage gain can decrease capital if scale effects exceed substitution effects, but the capital-labor ratio unambiguously rises. If unions tax capital (i.e., the returns on capital facilitate wage gains), there is no presumption that the factor mix is either more or less capital intensive in union firms (Hirsch and Prasad, 1995). No distortion in the factor mix also follows from bargaining models with "strong efficiency" outcomes (a vertical contract curve). Empirical tests of contract models are particularly difficult (Farber, 1986; Abowd, 1989; Pencavel, 1991).

[7]I provide no discussion of experimental methods, which have so far played little role in the literature on unions and performance. The experimental literature in personnel economics has added much to our knowledge about how workers perceive and respond to alternative compensation schemes and workplace policies. Such results have potential to inform discussion of how unions impact the workplace, getting inside the proverbial black box.

[8]This criticism does not apply to events studies measuring changes in equity value, since changes in stock price quickly reflect investors' expectations as to the present value of future changes due to unionism. A separate question is whether investors are good at predicting how unionization will affect firm performance.

[9]Portions of this section rely on my earlier survey of unions and performance (Hirsch, 1997).

[10]In a paper on "what unions do now" Turnbull (2003) makes this point forcefully, arguing for increased multidisciplinary research on unions and the need for greater relevance.

[11]The specific question asked was: "What is your best estimate of the percentage impact of unions on the productivity of unionized companies?" (Fuchs et al., 1998, pp. 1392, 1418).

[12]I exclude a study by Cooke (1994), who examines data on 841 Michigan manufacturing firms. Cooke's principal focus is on union-nonunion differences in the effect of employee participation programs and profit sharing on productivity. In his sample of firms, union companies have substantially higher output per worker, but Cooke has no measure of firm capital intensity, instead controlling for two-digit industry capital per employee, which assigns the same capital intensity to union and nonunion firms. Its coefficient is small and barely significant. Prior studies of manufacturing firms or businesses (Clark, 1984; Hirsch, 1991a) find that the capital-labor ratio is the single most important determinant of labor productivity, union firms are somewhat more capital-intensive (unions are more likely to organize successfully in capital-intensive plants), and resulting union-nonunion productivity differences are negative and close to zero. There is little way to know how much of the union-nonunion productivity difference in Cooke's study results from differences in capital intensity; it is unlikely to explain all the difference. The Michigan sample is likely to contain many firms in motor vehicles and transportation supply, an industry where Hirsch (1991) finds union firms to have a large productivity advantage.

[13]Nickell and Layard (1999) and Metcalf (2003) reach similar conclusions in their evaluation of international evidence. Human resource management (HRM) practices such as TQM do not automatically increase productivity. It appears that the circumstances under which they are adopted make a difference (Kleiner et al., 2002). HRM practices that increase productivity typically increase worker compensation; thus, costs need not decline (Cappelli and Neumark, 2001).

[14]Ichniowski et al. (1997) also examine the effect of HRM practices on productivity. They collect data on steel finishing lines with a common technology but different HRM practices. They conclude that innovative practices increase productivity when introduced jointly (rather than individually). The authors estimate union effects, but say little about these, no doubt due to the paucity of nonunion lines (8 percent of the 2,190 line months and what may be just 5 of their 60 steel lines). They obtain union coefficients that are generally small and vary across specifications.

[15]A general point in the literature is that union productivity effects depend on the state of labor relations. Recent studies provide evidence that productivity or quality suffers as a result of strikes and labor unrest. Kleiner et al. (2002) conclude that the productivity effects of strikes and slowdowns at a commercial airline manufacturer are temporary. Using auction data, Mas (2002) finds that construction equipment produced by Caterpillar at its U.S. plants during periods of labor unrest was more likely to be subsequently resold and sold at a deeper discount. Krueger and Mas (2004) find that tire defect rates were particularly high at a Bridgestone/Firestone plant during periods of labor unrest.

[16]See Addison and Hirsch (1989) and Booth (1995) for references (a study not cited is Byrne et al., 1996). There are exceptions to the conclusion regarding productivity effects in noncompetitive settings. An analysis of hospitals by Register (1988) finds higher productivity in union than in nonunion hospitals. A recent paper by Ash and Seago (2004) concludes that there are lower rates of heart attack mortality in California among hospitals with union rather than nonunion registered nurses. This conclusion is based in large part on declines in mortality among a relatively small number of hospitals that became unionized during the sample period.

[17]The logic here is identical to the survivor bias argument in measuring returns to mutual funds. If one measures past returns (over, say, ten years) of surviving funds (a balanced panel), average performance is relatively favorable. If one measures the average across all funds in each of the ten years (an unbalanced panel) average performance, which now includes funds that failed, is below the market as a whole (for evidence, see Malkiel, 2003). Even if no funds failed, an upward bias exists if one weights the funds based on current fund assets, since poorly performing funds would have decreased in relative size over time.

[18]Using business-level data, Ravenscraft (1983) finds that market share, but not industry concentration, is related to profitability. Following aggregation, he shows that the positive relationship between industry profit measures and concentration derive from the correlation of concentration with mean market share and not concentration per se.

[19]An additional challenge to the standard model comes from the literature on efficient contracts. There are settlements off the labor-demand curve, with lower wages and higher employment, preferred by both the union and management. Efficient contracts require simultaneous bargaining (explicit or implicit) over wages and employment rather than sequential determination (agreement on the wage followed by the firm's choice of employment). If settlements are not on the labor-demand curve, the effect of unions on factor mix cannot be predicted in straightforward fashion (for analysis of these models, see Farber, 1986; Pencavel, 1991).

[20]Using firm-level Compustat data and union data from Hirsch (1991a), Cavanaugh (1996) shows that the deleterious union effects on market value and investment are directly related to the ease with which quasi-rents can be appropriated.

[21]Canadian evidence on unions and employment growth appear consistent with that in the United States. Long (1993) utilizes survey data from a survey of 510 Canadian business establishments in the manufacturing and nonmanufacturing sectors. Union establishments (i.e., establishments with employees covered by collective bargaining agreements) had considerably slower employment growth between 1980 and 1985, although in manufacturing roughly half of the slower growth resulted not from unionism per se but from location in industries showing slower growth (industry effects were not important in the nonmanufacturing sector). After accounting for industry controls, firm size, and firm age, union establishments in the manufacturing (nonmanufacturing) sector had growth rates 3.7 (3.9) percent per year below those of nonunion establishments (union employment growth was negative over the period). For European evidence, see the recent paper by Addison et al. (2003) and the literature survey by Metcalf (2004).

[22]In their words: "Unions reduce profits but they do not 'destroy the goose that lays the golden egg'" (Freeman and Kleiner, 1999, p. 526). Using even more colorful language, Kuhn (1998, p. 1039) states: "Like successful viruses, unions are smart enough not to kill their hosts." Kremer and Olken (2001) apply a formal evolutionary biology model to unions, noting that parasites that kill their hosts do not spread, whereas those that do little harm spread and may evolve to become essential to their hosts. They conclude that unions maximizing the present value of members' wages are likely to be displaced by more moderate unions. Exoge-

nous firm turnover lowers equilibrium union density since unions must work harder (organize more) to stay in place.

[23]Discussion of labor law reforms is beyond the scope of the paper. Among the recommendations proposed by the Dunlop Commission during the mid-1990s were: narrowing the definition of supervisory and managerial workers who are exempt from the NLRA, shortening the time between the call for union elections and conduct of the elections, increased access of workers to union organizers, procedures such as mediation to facilitate newly certified unions to achieve first contracts, and fast injunctive relief against discriminatory action by employers. Estreicher (1996) discusses various labor law reforms intended to facilitate "value-added unionism" in the workplace. He starts from the premise that labor markets are overregulated and that greater freedom of contract would enhance development of preferred labor-management arrangements.

[24]For a description and data on what workers want, see Freeman and Rogers (1999). Kaufman (2001) provides a discussion and critique. Workers appear to desire individual voice and cooperation — not union voice per se.

[25]These proposals follow discussion previously presented in Hirsch and Schumacher (2002).

[26]For change to be enhancing for the parties, the "value of the enterprise" must increase. Abowd (1989) defines the value of the enterprise as the sum of firm market value and worker rents.

[27]The TEAM Act, passed by Congress but vetoed by President Clinton in July 1996, would have limited the scope of 8(a)(2) and allowed employer-organized and employer-funded worker participation groups in nonunion plants and offices. I support such legislation, whereas Levine would continue protections that prevent creation of "company unions." For evidence on how company unions worked prior to passage of the NLRA, see Kaufman (2000).

[28]In order to focus on the role of defaults, I assume that majority approval is synonymous with union coverage, ignoring the issue of obtaining a first contract following a union win.

[29]Choi et al. (2003) make the interesting point that where preferences are diverse and the firm (or state in our case) cannot readily identify a preferred default rule, it can make sense to assign a highly inefficient default, thus encouraging parties to select a preferred alternative. Where preferences are homogeneous and change is costly, it is important to choose a default close to the parties' preferred outcome. Choi et al. analyze pension contribution rules for workers within a firm. Our situation is more difficult, since a common governance structure is being assigned for workers within the firm who may have heterogeneous preferences.

[30]Relevant is the experience that other countries have had or will have with worker councils and alternative forms of organization, particularly in countries with relatively decentralized wage setting. The European Union Charter of Fundamental Rights of December 2000 provides for what appears to be broad-based guarantees for workers to have rights for information, consultation, and collective agreements (European Union, 2000, Articles 27, 28). How the Charter will be interpreted and implemented is unclear, but European experiences deriving from the Charter may well hold lessons for U.S. employment law reforms.

REFERENCES

Abowd, John M. "The Effect of Wage Bargains on the Stock Market Value of the Firm." *American Economic Review* 79 (September 1989): 774–800.

_____ and Henry S. Farber. "Job Queues and the Union Status of Workers." *Industrial and Labor Relations Review* 35 (April 1982): 354–67.

Addison, John T. and Clive R. Belfield. "Union Voice." In James T. Bennett and Bruce E. Kaufman, eds. *What Do Unions Do? The Evidence Twenty Years Later*, forthcoming.

Addison, John T. and John B. Chilton. "Self-Enforcing Union Contracts: Efficient Investment and Employment." *Journal of Business* 71 (July 1998): 349–69.

Addison, John T., John S. Heywood, and Xiangdong Wei. "New Evidence on Unions and Plant Closings: Britain in the 1990s." *Southern Economic Journal* 69 (April 2003): 822–41.

Addison, John T. and Barry T. Hirsch. "Union Effects on Productivity, Profits, and Growth: Has the Long Run Arrived?" *Journal of Labor Economics* 7 (January 1989): 72–105.

_____. "The Economic Effects of Employment Regulation: What Are the Limits?" In Bruce E. Kaufman, ed. *Government Regulation of the Employment Relationship*. Madison, Wisc.: *Industrial Relations Research Association*, 1997, pp. 125–78.

Addison, John T. and W. Stanley Siebert. "Recent Changes in the Industrial Relations Framework in the UK." In John T. Addison and Claus Schnabel, eds. *International Handbook of Trade Unions*. Northampton, Mass.: Edward Elgar, 2003, pp. 415–60.

Aidt, Toke and Zafiris Tzannatos. *Unions and Collective Bargaining: Economic Effects in a Global Environment*. Washington, D.C.: World Bank, 2002.

Allen, Steven G. "The Effect of Unionism on Productivity in Privately and Publicly Owned Hospitals and Nursing Homes." *Journal of Labor Research* 7 (Winter 1986a): 59–68.

_____. "Unionization and Productivity in Office Building and School Construction." *Industrial and Labor Relations Review* 39 (January 1986b): 187–201.

Ash, Michael and Jean Ann Seago. "The Effect of Registered Nurses on Heart-Attack Mortality." *Industrial and Labor Relations Review* 57 (April 2004): 422–42.

Baldwin, Carliss Y. "Productivity and Labor Unions: An Application of the Theory of Self-Enforcing Contracts." *Journal of Business* 56 (April 1983): 155–85.

Becker, Brian E. and Craig A. Olson. "Labor Relations and Firm Performance." In M. Kleiner, R. Block, M. Roomkin, and S. Salsburg, eds. *Human Resources and the Performance of the Firm*. Madison, Wisc.: Industrial Relations Research Association, 1987, pp. 43–86.

_____. "Unionization and Firm Profits." *Industrial Relations* 31 (Fall 1992): 395–415.

Belman, Dale. "Unions, The Quality of Labor Relations, and Firm Performance." In Lawrence Mishel and Paula B. Voos, eds. *Unions and Economic Competitiveness*. Armonk, N.Y.: M.E. Sharpe, 1992, pp. 41–107.

Betts, Julian R., Cameron W. Odgers, and Michael K. Wilson. "The Effects of Unions on Research and Development: An Empirical Analysis Using Multi-Year Data." *Canadian Journal of Economics* 34 (August 2001): 785–806.

Black, Sandra E. and Lisa M. Lynch. "How to Compete: The Impact of Workplace Practices and Information Technology on Productivity." *Review of Economics and Statistics* 83 (August 2001): 434–45.

Blanchflower, David G. and Alex Bryson. "Changes Over Time in Union Relative Wage Effects in the UK and the US Revisited." National Bureau of Economic Research Working Paper 9395, December 2002.

Blanchflower, David G. and Richard B. Freeman. "Unionism in the United States and Other Advanced OECD Countries." In M. Bognanno and M. Kleiner, eds. *Labor Market Institutions and the Future Role of Unions*. Cambridge, Mass.: Blackwell Publishers, 1992, pp. 56–79.

Booth, Alison L. *The Economics of the Trade Union*. Cambridge: Cambridge University Press, 1995.

Bratsberg, Bernt and James F. Ragan, Jr. "Changes in the Union Wage Premium by Industry." *Industrial and Labor Relations Review* 56 (October 2002): 65–83.

Bronars, Stephen G. and Donald R. Deere. "Union Representation Elections and Firm Profitability." *Industrial Relations* 29 (Winter 1990): 15–37.

_____. "Unionization, Incomplete Contracting, and Capital Investment." *Journal of Business* 66 (January 1993): 117–32.

_____ and Joseph S. Tracy. "The Effects of Unions on Firm Behavior: An Empirical Analysis Using Firm-Level Data." *Industrial Relations* 33 (October 1994): 426–51.

Brown, Charles and James Medoff. "Trade Unions in the Production Process." *Journal of Political Economy* 86 (June 1978): 355–78.

Byrne, Dennis, Hashem Dezhbakhsh, and Randall King. "Unions and Police Productivity: An Econometric Investigation." *Industrial Relations* 35 (October 1996): 566–84.

Cappelli, Peter and David Neumark. "Do 'High Performance' Work Practices Improve Establishment Level Outcomes?" *Industrial and Labor Relations Review* 54 (July 2001): 737–75.

Card, David. "The Effect of Unions on the Structure of Wages: A Longitudinal Analysis." *Econometrica* 64 (July 1996): 957–79.

Cavanaugh, Joseph K. "Asset Specific Investment and Unionized Labor." *Industrial Relations* 37 (January 1998): 35–50.

Chappell, William F., Walter J. Mayer, and William F. Shughart II. "Union Rents and Market Structure Revisited." *Journal of Labor Research* 12 (Winter 1991): 35–46.

Choi, James J., David Laibson, Brigitte C. Madrian, and Andrew Metrick. "Optimal Defaults." *American Economic Review* 93 (May 2003): 180–85.

Clark, Kim B. "The Impact of Unionization on Productivity: A Case Study." *Industrial and Labor Relations Review* 33 (July 1980a): 451–69.

_____. "Unionization and Productivity: Micro-Econometric Evidence." *Quarterly Journal of Economics* 95 (December 1980b): 613–39.

_____. "Unionization and Firm Performance: The Impact on Profits, Growth, and Productivity." *American Economic Review* 74 (December 1984): 893–919.

Connolly, Robert A., Barry T. Hirsch, and Mark Hirschey. "Union Rent Seeking, Intangible Capital, and Market Value of the Firm." *Review of Economics and Statistics* 68 (November 1986): 567–77.

Diamond, Wayne J. and Richard B. Freeman. "Will Unionism Prosper in Cyber-Space? The Promise of the Internet for Employee Organization." National Bureau of Economic Research Working Paper 8483, September 2001.

DiNardo, John and David S. Lee. "The Impact of Unionization on Establishment Closure: A Regression Discontinuity Analysis of Representation Elections." National Bureau of Economic Research Working Paper 8993, June 2002.

Domowitz, Ian R., Glenn Hubbard, and Bruce C. Peterson. "The Intertemporal Stability of the Concentration-Margins Relationship." *Journal of Industrial Economics* 35 (September 1986): 13–34.

Doucouliagos, Chris and Patrice Laroche. "What Do Unions Do to Productivity? A Meta-Analysis." *Industrial Relations* 42 (October 2003): 650–91.

Dunne, Timothy and David A. Macpherson. "Unionism and Gross Employment Flows." *Southern Economic Journal* 60 (January 1994): 727–38.

Estreicher, Samuel. "Freedom of Contract and Labor Law Reform: Opening Up the Possibilities for Value-Added Unionism." *New York University Law Review* 71 (June 1996): 827–49.

European Union. "Charter of Fundamental Rights of the European Union." *Official Journal of the European Communities* C 364 (December 2000): 1–22, at http://www.europarl.eu.int/charter/pdf/text_en.pdf.

Fallick, Bruce C. and Kevin A. Hassett. "Investment and Union Certification." *Journal of Labor Economics* 17 (July 1999): 570–82.

Farber, Henry S. "The Analysis of Union Behavior." In Orley C. Ashenfelter and Richard Layard, eds. *Handbook of Labor Economics, Vol. II*. Amsterdam: Elsevier, 1986, pp. 1039–89.

_____ and Bruce Western. "Accounting for the Decline of Unions in the Private Sector, 1973-1988." In James Bennett and Bruce Kaufman, eds. *The Future of Private Sector Unionism in the United States.* Armonk, N.Y.: M.E. Sharpe, 2002, pp. 28–58.

Freeman, Richard B. "The Exit-Voice Tradeoff in the Labor Market: Unionism, Job Tenure, Quits and Separations." *Quarterly Journal of Economics* 94 (June 1980): 643–74.

_____. "Longitudinal Analyses of the Effects of Trade Unions." *Journal of Labor Economics* 2 (January 1984): 1–26.

_____. "Is Declining Unionization of the U.S. Good, Bad, or Irrelevant?" In Lawrence Mishel and Paula B. Voos, eds. *Unions and Economic Competitiveness.* Armonk, N.Y.: M.E. Sharpe, 1991, pp. 143–69.

_____. "Spurts in Union Growth: Defining Moments and Social Processes." In Michael D.Bordo, Claudia Goldin and Eugene N. White, eds. *The Defining Moment: The Great Depression and the American Economy in the Twentieth Century.* Chicago: University of Chicago Press (NBER), 1998, pp. 265–96.

_____. "The Labor Market in the New Information Economy." National Bureau of Economic Research Working Paper 9254, October 2002.

_____ and Morris M. Kleiner. "Employer Behavior in the Face of Union Organizing Drives." *Industrial and Labor Relations Review* 43 (April 1990): 351–65.

_____. "Do Unions Make Enterprises Insolvent?" *Industrial and Labor Relations Review* 52 (July 1999): 510–27.

Freeman, Richard B. and Edward P. Lazear. "An Economic Analysis of Works Councils." In Joel Rogers and Wolfgang Streeck, eds. *Works Councils: Consultation, Representation, and Cooperation in Industrial Relations.* Chicago: University of Chicago Press (NBER), 1995, pp. 27–50.

Freeman, Richard B. and James L. Medoff. "The Two Faces of Unionism." *Public Interest* 57 (Fall 1979): 69–93.

_____. *What Do Unions Do?* New York: Basic Books, 1984.

Freeman, Richard B. and Joel Rogers. *What Workers Want.* Ithaca, N.Y.: Cornell University Press, 1999.

Fuchs, Victor R., Alan B. Krueger and James M. Poterba. "Economists' Views about Parameters, Values, and Policies: Survey Results in Labor and Public Economics." *Journal of Economic Literature* 36 (September 1998): 1387–425.

Grant, Darren. "A Comparison of the Cyclical Behavior of Union and Nonunion Wages in the United States." *Journal of Human Resources* 36 (Winter 2001): 31–57.

Grout, Paul A. "Investment and Wages in the Absence of Binding Contracts: A Nash Bargaining Approach." *Econometrica* 52 (March 1984): 449–60.

Hirsch, Barry T. "Trucking Regulation, Unionization, and Labor Earnings: 1973–1985." *Journal of Human Resources* 23 (Summer 1988): 296–319.

_____. "Market Structure, Union Rent Seeking, and Firm Profitability." *Economics Letters* 32 (January 1990): 75–79.

_____. *Labor Unions and the Economic Performance of U.S. Firms.* Kalamazoo, Mich.: Upjohn Institute for Employment Research, 1991a.

_____. "Union Coverage and Profitability among U.S. Firms." *Review of Economics and Statistics* 73 (February 1991b): 69–77.

_____. "Firm Investment Behavior and Collective Bargaining Strategy." In Mario F. Bognanno and Morris M. Kleiner, eds. *Labor Market Institutions and the Future Role of Unions.* Cambridge, Mass.: Blackwell Publishers, 1992, 95–121.

_____. "Unionization and Economic Performance: Evidence on Productivity, Profits, Investment, and Growth." In Fazil Mihlar, ed. *Unions and Right-to-Work Laws*. Vancouver, B.C.: Fraser Institute, 1997, pp. 35–70.

_____ and John T. Addison. *The Economic Analysis of Unions: New Approaches and Evidence*. Boston: Allen & Unwin, 1986.

Hirsch, Barry T. and Robert A. Connolly. "Do Unions Capture Monopoly Profits?" *Industrial and Labor Relations Review* 41 (October 1987): 118–36.

Hirsch, Barry T. and David A. Macpherson. "Earnings and Employment in Trucking: Deregulating a Naturally Competitive Industry." In James Peoples, ed. *Regulatory Reform and Labor Markets*. Norwell, Mass.: Kluwer Academic Publishing, 1998, pp. 61–112.

_____. "Earnings, Rents, and Competition in the Airline Labor Market." *Journal of Labor Economics* 18 (January 2000): 125–55.

_____. "Union Membership and Coverage Database from the Current Population Survey: Note." *Industrial and Labor Relations Review* 56 (January 2003): 349–54, and accompanying data site http://www.unionstats.com/.

Hirsch, Barry T. and Barbara A. Morgan. "Shareholder Risk and Returns in Union and Nonunion Firms." *Industrial and Labor Relations Review* 47 (January 1994): 302–18.

Hirsch, Barry T. and Kislaya Prasad. "Wage-Employment Determination and a Union Tax on Capital: Can Theory and Evidence Be Reconciled?" *Economics Letters* 48 (April 1995): 61–71.

Hirsch, Barry T. and Edward J. Schumacher. "Unions, Wages, and Skills." *Journal of Human Resources* 33 (Winter 1998): 201–19.

_____. "Private Sector Union Density and the Wage Premium: Past, Present, and Future." In James Bennett and Bruce Kaufman, eds. *The Future of Private Sector Unionism in the United States*. Armonk, N.Y.: M.E. Sharpe, 2002, pp. 92–128.

Hirsch, Barry T., Michael L. Wachter, and James W. Gillula. "Postal Service Compensation and the Comparability Standard." *Research in Labor Economics* 18 (1999): 243–79.

Ichniowski, Casey, Kathryn Shaw, and Giovanna Prennushi. "The Effects of Human Resource Management Practices on Productivity: A Study of Steel Finishing Lines." *American Economic Review* 87 (June 1997): 291–313.

Karier, Thomas. "Unions and Monopoly Profits." *Review of Economics and Statistics* 67 (February 1985): 34–42.

Katz, Harry C. and John Paul MacDuffie. "Collective Bargaining in the U.S. Auto Assembly Sector." In Paula B. Voos, ed. *Contemporary Collective Bargaining in the Private Sector*. Madison, Wisc.: Industrial Relations Research Association, 1994, pp. 181–224.

Kaufman, Bruce E. "Accomplishments and Shortcomings of Nonunion Employee Representation in the Pre-Wagner Act Years: A Reassessment." In Bruce E. Kaufman, and Daphne Taras, eds. *Nonunion Employee Representation: History, Contemporary Practice, and Policy*. Armonk, N.Y.: M.E. Sharpe, 2000, pp. 21–60.

_____. "The Employee Participation/Representation Gap: An Assessment and Proposed Solution." *University of Pennsylvania Journal of Labor and Employment Law* 3 (Spring 2001): 491–550.

_____ and David I. Levine. "An Economic Analysis of Employee Representation." In Bruce E. Kaufman and Daphne Taras, eds. *Nonunion Employee Representation: History, Contemporary Practice, and Policy*. Armonk, N.Y.: M.E. Sharpe, 2000, pp. 149–75.

Kleiner, Morris. "Intensity of Management Resistance: Understanding the Decline of Unionization in the Private Sector." In James Bennett and Bruce Kaufman, eds. *The Future of Private Sector Unionism in the United States.* Armonk, N.Y.: M.E. Sharpe, 2002, pp. 292–316.

_____, Jonathan Leonard, and Adam Pilarski. "How Industrial Relations Affect Plant Performance: The Case of Commercial Aircraft Manufacturing." *Industrial and Labor Relations Review* 55 (January 2002): 195–219.

Kremer, Michael and Benjamin A. Olken. "A Biological Model of Unions." National Bureau of Economic Research Working Paper 8257, April 2001.

Krueger, Alan B. and Alexandre Mas. "Strikes, Scabs and Tread Separations: Labor Strife and the Production of Defective Bridgestone/Firestone Tires."*Journal of Political Economy* 112 (April 2004): 253–89.

Kuhn, Peter. "Unions and the Economy: What We Know; What We Should Know." *Canadian Journal of Economics* 31 (November 1998): 1033–56.

LaLonde, Robert J., Gérard Marschke, and Kenneth Troske. "Using Longitudinal Data on Establishments to Analyze the Effects of Union Organizing Campaigns in the United States." *Annales d' Économie et de Statistique* 41/42 (1996): 155–85.

Leonard, Jonathan S. "Unions and Employment Growth." In Mario F. Bognanno and Morris M. Kleiner, eds. *Labor Market Institutions and the Future Role of Unions.* Cambridge, Mass.: Blackwell Publishers, 1992, pp. 80–94.

Levine, David I. *Reinventing the Workplace: How Business and Employees Can Both Win.* Washington, D.C.: Brookings Institution, 1995.

_____ and Laura D'Andrea Tyson. "Participation, Productivity, and the Firm's Environment." In Alan S. Blinder, ed. *Paying for Productivity: A Look at the Evidence.* Washington, D.C.: Brookings Institution, 1990, pp. 183–237.

Lewis, H. Gregg. *Union Relative Wage Effects: A Survey.* Chicago: University of Chicago Press, 1986.

Linneman, Peter D., Michael L. Wachter, and William H. Carter. "Evaluating the Evidence on Union Employment and Wages." *Industrial and Labor Relations Review* 44 (October 1990): 34–53.

Long, Richard J. "The Effect of Unionization on Employment Growth of Canadian Companies." *Industrial and Labor Relations Review* 46 (July 1993): 691–703.

Malkiel, Burton G. *A Random Walk Down Wall Street,* 8th ed. New York: Norton, 2003.

Manning, Alan. *Monopsony in Motion: Imperfect Competition in Labor Markets.* Princeton, N.J.: Princeton University Press, 2003.

Mas, Alexandre. "Labor Unrest, Fairness and the Quality of Production: Evidence from the Construction Equipment Resale Market." Princeton University, November 2002.

Menezes-Filho, Naercio, David Ulph, and John van Reenen. "R&D and Unionism: Comparative Evidence from British Companies and Establishments." *Industrial and Labor Relations Review* 52 (October 1998): 45–63.

Menezes-Filho, Naercio and John van Reenen. "Unions and Innovation: A Survey of the Theory and Empirical Evidence." Center for Economic Policy Research, Discussion Paper 3792, January 2003.

Metcalf, David. "Unions and Productivity, Financial Performance and Investment: International Evidence." In John Addison and Claus Schnabel, eds. *International Handbook of Trade Unions.* Northampton, Mass.: Edward Elgar, 2003, pp. 118–71.

Mitchell, Merwin W. and Joe A. Stone. "Union Effects on Productivity: Evidence from Western Sawmills." *Industrial and Labor Relations Review* 46 (October 1992): 135–45.

Nickell, Stephen and Richard Layard. "Labor Market Institutions and Economic Performance." In Orley C. Ashenfelter and David Card, eds. *Handbook of Labor Economics*, Vol. 3C. Amsterdam: Elsevier, 1999, pp. 3029–84.

Odgers, Cameron W. and Julian R. Betts. "Do Unions Reduce Investment? Evidence from Canada." *Industrial and Labor Relations Review* 51 (October 1997): 18–36.

Olson, Craig A. and Brian E. Becker. "The Effects of the NLRA on Stockholder Wealth in the 1930s." *Industrial and Labor Relations Review* 44 (October 1990): 116–29.

Pencavel, John H. *Labor Markets Under Trade Unionism: Employment, Wages, and Hours.* Cambridge, Mass.: Basil Blackwell, 1991.

_____. "The Surprising Retreat of Union Britain." National Bureau of Economic Research Working Paper 9564, March 2003.

Ravenscraft, David J. "Structure-Profit Relationships at the Line of Business and Industry Level." *Review of Economics and Statistics* 65 (February 1983): 22–31.

Register, Charles A. "Wages, Productivity, and Costs in Union and Nonunion Hospitals." *Journal of Labor Research* 9 (Fall 1988): 325–45.

Reynolds, Morgan O. "Trade Unions in the Production Process Reconsidered." *Journal of Political Economy* 94 (April 1986): 443–47.

Ruback, Richard S. and Martin B. Zimmerman. "Unionization and Profitability: Evidence from the Capital Market." *Journal of Political Economy* 92 (December 1984): 1134–57.

Salinger, Michael A. "Tobin's q, Unionization, and the Concentration-Profits Relationship." *Rand Journal of Economics* 15 (Summer 1984): 159–70.

Simons, Henry C. "Some Reflections on Syndicalism." *Journal of Political Economy* 52 (March 1944): 1–25.

Sunstein, Cass R. "Human Behavior and the Law of Work." *Virginia Law Review* 87 (April 2001): 205–76.

Turnbull, Peter. "What Do Unions Do Now?" *Journal of Labor Research* 24 (Summer 2003): 491–527.

Voos, Paula B. and Lawrence R. Mishel. "The Union Impact on Profits: Evidence from Industry Price-Cost Margin Data." *Journal of Labor Economics* 4 (January 1986): 105–33.

Weil, David. "Individual Rights and Collective Agents: The Role of Old and New Workplace Institutions in the Regulation of Labor Markets." National Bureau of Economic Research Working Paper 9565, March 2003.

Wessels, Walter J. "The Effects of Unions on Employment and Productivity: An Unresolved Contradiction." *Journal of Labor Economics* 3 (January 1985): 101–108.

_____. "Do Unionized Firms Hire Better Workers?" *Economic Inquiry* 32 (October 1994): 616–29.

White, Lawrence J. "Trends in Aggregate Concentration in the United States." *Journal of Economic Perspectives* 16 (Fall 2002): 137–60.

[16]

John T. Addison

University of South Carolina and Universität Potsdam

John B. Chilton

Columbia, South Carolina

Self-Enforcing Union Contracts: Efficient Investment and Employment*

I. Introduction

Carliss Baldwin's "Productivity and Labor Unions: An Application of the Theory of Self-Enforcing Contracts" (1983), provides a rich set of strategies firms might employ to counter union opportunism in the context of long-lived relation-specific capital. This work both anticipated and in an important (dynamic) sense outflanked the collective voice view of unionism (e.g., Freeman and Medoff 1984) and the ensuing slew of union productivity effects studies (e.g., Addison and Hirsch 1989). Our purpose here is to update Baldwin's influential work, renewing it to incorporate advances in game theory that have taken hold since 1983.

Baldwin's work has had staying power because it is a leading-edge application of the idea that long-term interests can form the foundation for credible self-enforcement of contracts. Her core conclusion is that the union's temptation for opportunistic conduct is strongest if the life of sunk capital is long in relation to the union's horizon. Because unions represent current membership and property rights in the union are not transferable, these tendencies are likely to prevail.

Baldwin (1983) asks whether a firm can credibly deter union opportunism that would lead to underinvestment. We show that the punishments Baldwin considers credible exclude tougher threats that only have the appearance of being self-destructive. If the firm's discount factor is sufficiently close to one, union opportunism can indeed be deterred. Moreover, we show that given the firm's discount factor, a shorter lifetime of capital does not necessarily promote efficiency. Although, as Baldwin emphasizes, it does enhance the firm's ability to punish union opportunism, it also creates adverse incentives for the firm to engage in opportunistic employment cuts.

* We thank, without implicating, an unusually generous referee for extensive comments on previous drafts of this article.

(*Journal of Business*, 1998, vol. 71, no. 3)

Baldwin provides a variety of ingenious remedies. These include the use of inefficient capacity to make substantial cuts in employment, a short-run profit-maximizing response to wage demands. Other proposed counterstrategies include a variety of measures designed to extend the union's horizon and thereby avoid the use of an inefficient defense by the firm.

The debate over the efficiency of union contracts has long been dominated by a separate literature that takes capital to be exogenous and focuses on the temptation of the firm to make an opportunistic cut in employment. Espinosa and Rhee (1989) bridge the underlying monopoly-union and efficient contracts models in this literature by showing that in a repeated game setting efficient self-enforcing contracts are guaranteed to exist, provided the firm is sufficiently patient. There is some irony here. Although Baldwin neglects opportunism by the firm, her application of repeated games to investment did predate their application to union employment.

Our update of Baldwin incorporates the potential for opportunistic behavior *from both sides* by extending the repeated game of Espinosa and Rhee (1989) to include sunk capital. We conclude that with sufficient patience on the part of the firm self-enforcing contracts will exist that are efficient with respect to employment and investment. This bottom-line result is of course sharply at odds with Baldwin in that it holds irrespective of the union's horizon or the productive life of capital.

One key to this result lies in the natural order of play. The firm observes the wage demand before selecting the concurrent level of employment, thereby permitting immediate punishment of union opportunism. In Espinosa and Rhee (1989) retaliating to wage breaches simply by choosing employment to maximize profit will deter union opportunism in any of the set of efficient-contract core of outcomes that are mutually acceptable relative to the monopoly union equilibrium. With exogenous capital this set is nonempty.

Even with endogenous capital, there are conditions under which an immediate one-period relocation to the labor demand curve is adequate to enforce an efficient contract acceptable to the firm. Echoing Baldwin, there are also conditions in which they will not because the firm finds it privately advantageous to cope with union opportunism up front by underinvesting. Further echoing Baldwin, the firm's ability to deter union malfeasance is strengthened if capital is finitely durable, provided the union places some weight on the future. Following an extortionate union wage demand, the firm can reduce investment and in so doing carry forward a deeper employment penalty into the future.

But capital flexibility is a two-edged sword: there is also the possibility that the finite durability of capital will itself cause inefficiency. Suppose that efficient employment and investment would obtain with perfect durability. With finite durability, the firm may lose the incentive to honor the contract if its discount factor is not sufficiently close to one. The cost to the firm of losing the union's trust is no longer so severe because the firm can counter by reducing investment.

Baldwin rightly requires that retaliation to union opportunism be credible. Relocating to the labor demand curve if the union cheats is a credible form of punishment by the firm. Baldwin sees tougher punishment as self-destructive and thus not credible. However, the logic of the cost of future consequences applies not only to breach of contract but also to the credibility of enforcement mechanisms. If its discount factor is sufficiently close to one, the firm will defend a reputation for toughness, a reputation for immediate cuts in employment severe enough to remove the union's temptation to cheat.

This insight implies that even unions with no concern for future consequences can be deterred from cheating. Baldwin's remedies for efficient deterrence of union opportunism all boil down to extending the union's concern for punishment into the future. On our analysis, these remedies are a substitute for a firm discount factor that is not sufficiently close to one.

The one-shot game that forms the foundation of our analysis is set out in Section II. The focus of Section III is to establish a common metric for the subsequent discussion of repeated play. Section IV then examines Espinosa and Rhee's (1989) result in the context of repeated play of the one-shot game, while sections VA and VB consider on-the-demand punishment with perfectly durable and finitely durable capital, respectively. Section VI introduces the innovation of more severe firm punishment of opportunistic behavior on the part of the union. Section VII concludes.

II. The One-Shot Game

A one-period multistage game forms the foundation for the repeated game analysis to follow.[1] This one-period game extends the monopoly-union model of wage and employment determination by including capital as an additional endogenous variable. There are two players, the firm and the union. The firm's objective is to maximize profit

$$\pi(w, N, K; r) = R(N, K) - wN - rK,$$

where N = labor, K = capital, $R(N, K)$ = revenue, w = wage, and r = rental price of capital. Exogenous to the model, r appears after a

---

1. Similar one-period models have been considered by Anderson and Devereux (1988) and Hirsch and Prasad (1995).

semicolon to distinguish it from the endogenous variables. It is assumed that the firm's revenue function $R(N, K)$ is strictly concave, that $R_N(N, K) > 0$ and $R_K(N, K) > 0$, and that $R_{NK}(N, K) > 0$.

The union's objective is to maximize utility $U(w, N)$. To simplify matters, its utility function is assumed to take the familiar union-rent form

$$U(w, N) = (w - w_0)N,$$

where w_0 is the competitive market wage. The workers can and will leave the firm if wage falls below the competitive wage. In the relevant region $w \geq w_0$, the union-rent utility function is quasiconcave.

The order of play in the one-shot multistage game is

firm chooses $K \to$ union chooses $w \to$ firm chooses N.

That is, the firm moves first, choosing K. Observing K and taking it as given, the union moves second and sets w. Finally, knowing K and w, the firm chooses N in the third stage. The last two moves follow the order of play in the monopoly-union model in which the union sets the wage unilaterally but the firm, retaining the right to manage, determines employment. Appending the firm's investment in K as the first move of the extended model captures the notion that capital is relatively inflexible, thereby possibly exposing the firm to subsequent holdup by the union.

A strategy for a player is a complete set of instructions specifying what the player would do in each possible contingency. In the one-period model, a strategy for the union expresses the wage as a function of capital. For the firm in this one-period model, a strategy designates a level of capital and specifies employment as a function of capital and the wage. Nash subgame-perfect equilibrium is adopted as the solution concept both for this one-period model and in the subsequent repeated-game analysis. Under the Nash requirement, each player's strategy must be a best response to the other's strategy. Subgame perfection rules out strategies that embody incredible threats. Specifically, a threat is credible only if the player would be prepared to carry it out if called on to do so. Credible mutual best responses can be thought of as forming a self-enforcing contract.

Before turning to the determination of the equilibrium, some preliminary results and notation regarding factor demand and efficiency will prove useful. First, contrary to the order of play given, suppose the firm chooses N and K taking the prices w and r as given. The firm's choices will satisfy the profit-maximizing first-order conditions of a competitive firm:

$$R_N(N, K) = w \qquad (1)$$

and

$$R_K(N, K) = r. \tag{2}$$

The long-run labor and capital demands, $LN(w; r)$ and $LK(w; r)$, solve the system (1) and (2). Each demand has the familiar property that the quantity of the factor demanded is decreasing in its own price. Solving equation (1) alone for employment yields the short-run labor demand function $N = SN(w; K)$, the semicolon signifying that K is given in the short run. It, too, has the property that employment and the wage are inversely related. Further, because $R_{NK}(N, K) > 0$, $SN(w; K)$ increases with an increase in K. In addition, it is well known that $SN[w; K(w'; r)] = LN(w; r)$ evaluated at $w = w'$ and that at this point of coincidence the short-run demand for labor is less elastic than the long-run demand.

The efficient (w, N) pairs for a *given* K lie on the contract curve of tangencies between the iso-profit and iso-utility curves. Specifically, the tangency condition under the rent maximand is

$$-[R_N(N, K) - w]/N = -(w - w_0)/N, \tag{3}$$

where the left-hand side is the short-run iso-profit slope and the right-hand side is the iso-utility slope. As is easily confirmed from (3), under the union-rent utility function, the contract curve is vertical at the competitive-equilibrium employment level $SN(w_0; K)$, the solution to (1) evaluated at $w = w_0$. Thus, the competitive employment level is the efficient level as well.

For a given level of capital, K_A, the relations among the short-run labor demand, the iso-profit contours, the iso-utility contours, and the contract curve are illustrated in figure 1. The function $SN(w; K_A)$ is the short-run labor demand curve. The quantity demanded at the competitive wage, $SN(w_0; K_A)$, then identifies the position of CC_A, the contract curve given K_A. Representative iso-profit and iso-utility contours have also been included.[2]

Since the union's payoff does not depend directly on capital, the efficient level of capital is simply the profit-maximizing choice as determined by equation (2). Thus, the efficient levels of labor and capital happen to be the competitive-equilibrium levels, the solution to (1) and (2) with w in (1) set equal to w_0. Denote these $N^* = LN(w_0; r)$ and $K^* = LK(w_0; r)$.

With these preliminaries completed, next consider the determination

---

2. As indicated by the arrow in fig. 1 pointing toward the northeast, union utility is increasing in w and N (in the relevant region, $w \geq w_0$). Given N, the firm's profit increases with a fall in w. Given w, profit increases as employment moves toward the demand curve. Thus, the downward pointing arrow in fig. 1 is a shorthand to indicate the firm's preference for moving toward inner–nested iso-profit contours. Further, each iso-profit curve has a slope of zero where it crosses the demand curve.

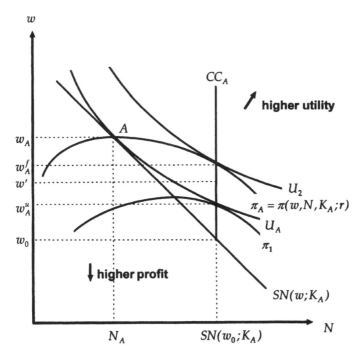

FIG. 1.—The monopoly-union equilibrium, A, and the contract curve showing efficient employment given K_A.

of a Nash subgame-perfect equilibrium of the one-period model. The credibility condition is implicit in the familiar solution given for the monopoly-union model of wage and employment determination. For a given $K = K_A$, and facing a price w, the firm's only credible choice of employment is dictated by the first-order profit-maximizing condition (1), the short-run labor demand $SN(w; K_A)$. As it is illustrated in figure 1, given K_A, the monopoly-union equilibrium (w_A, N_A) is characterized by the tangency at point A between the iso-utility curve U_A and the short-run labor demand curve $SN(w; K_A)$. Foreseeing that the firm will choose N to maximize profit, the union chooses w in order to maximize utility subject to the constraint $N = SN(w; K_A)$.[3]

3. Not all Nash equilibria are subgame perfect. Consider the strategies $w = w_0$ and N solves $R_N(N, K) = w_0$ if $w = w_0$, and $N = 0$ otherwise. These are Nash best replies for the monopoly-union game, given capital. They also produce the competitive wage and employment outcome, the most desirable outcome the firm can attain given that labor can always quit to earn at least the competitive wage. However, despite what the firm desires, if it was faced with a wage other than w_0, its only credible reply would be to set employment according to $N = SN(w; K)$, not $N = 0$.

In figure 1 the iso-profit contour $\pi_A = \pi(w, N, K_A; r)$ has a slope of zero at point A on the demand curve. So it must cross the iso-utility curve that is tangent to labor demand at point A, demonstrating that relative to any given K the monopoly-union equilibrium employment will be inefficiently low. Conditional on K_A, there exists a nonempty subset of efficient allocations that is mutually preferred to A. In figure 1, these mutually preferred efficient allocations, or core, lie on the contract curve CC_A at wages between w_A^f and w_A^u on the wage axis. Using A as the comparator, moving along the isoprofit contour $\pi_A = \pi(w, N, K_A; r)$ to its intersection with CC_A determines w_A^f, the highest wage the firm is willing to pay at the efficient level of employment. Likewise, again using A as the comparator, moving the iso-utility curve U_A to its intersection with CC_A determines w_A^u, the lowest wage the union would accept at the efficient level of employment. To anticipate later results, efficient employment at wages between these *reservation wages* w_A^f and w_A^u cannot be achieved under a monopoly-union equilibrium, but these allocations are certainly candidates for support in a repeated-game equilibrium.

As seen above, each choice of capital will yield a monopoly-union wage and employment pair. That is, each K will imply its own short-run labor demand, and each such labor demand will have an associated, tangent iso-utility curve. In figure 2, the locus of these equilibria is labeled *MUE*, for monopoly-union equilibria. Two such equilibria are illustrated: point A from figure 1, and another point T, the monopoly-union equilibrium associated with $K = K_T$. Note that because $SN(w; K_A)$ lies below $SN(w; K_T)$ in figure 2, it follows from assumptions that $K_A < K_T$.

Now the slope of *MUE* cannot be signed. It will be assumed its slope is positive, implying (as is plausible) that the greater is capital, the higher will be employment and wages.[4]

By its choice of K the firm determines which monopoly-union equilibrium along *MUE* will obtain. Anderson and Devereux (1988) provide a clever way of geometrically illustrating the equilibrium of the full one-shot game as a tangency between *MUE* and an appropriately constructed iso-profit contour. The trick is to recognize that first-order condition (1) for the profit-maximizing employment of labor is always true in equilibrium and then to use it to determine K, *not* N, as a function of N and w. (Whatever values of N and w emerge in equilibrium, (1) must hold and K can be inferred.) Label this function $K^1(w, N)$ to signify that K solves equation (1). Profit can then be determined from the

---

4. The slope of *MUE* is

$$\frac{-R_{LK}(R_{LL} + LR_{LLL}) + LR_{LL}R_{LLK}}{R_{LK} + LR_{LLK}}.$$

The ambiguity of its sign corresponds exactly to the ambiguous effect a shift in demand

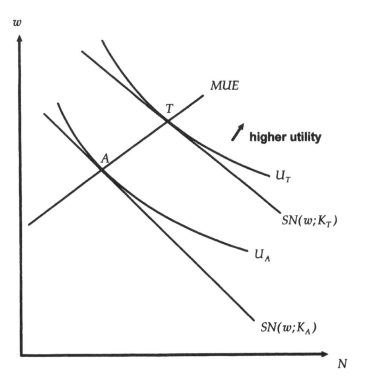

FIG. 2.—The locus of monopoly union equilibria, *MUE*, generated by varying capital.

composite function, $\pi[w, N, K^1(w, N); r]$, from which iso-profit contours in (w, N) space can be defined. These contours will of course differ from the short-run iso-profit curve family for which K is given.

The equilibrium of the one-shot game can thus be determined graphically in figure 3 in which the *MUE* locus is carried over from figure 2. Long-run labor demand $LN(w; r)$ and two key short-run labor demands are included. As mentioned earlier, at a point of intersection of a short-run demand curve with long-run demand, short-run demand is less elastic—and so the schedules cross only once. The curves π_E and π_F are representative iso-profit contours for the profit function $\pi[w, N, K^1(w, N); r]$. These iso-profit contours display the same features with respect to the long-run demand for labor as do capital-fixed iso-profit

_____

(in this case a change in capital shifts short-run labor demand) will have on the price (wage) set by a monopoly.

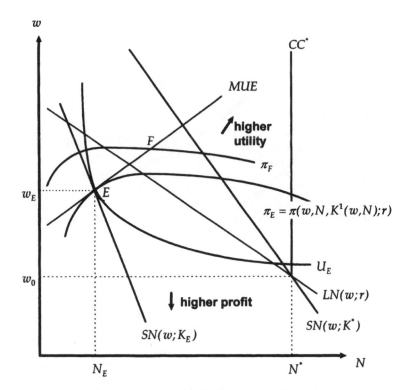

FIG. 3.—The inefficiency of the one-shot capital-first equilibrium E

contours with respect to the short-run demand.[5] In deciding how much to invest, the firm moves along MUE until it reaches tangency E between π_E and MUE, with the implication that equilibrium capital is $K_E = K^1(w_E, N_E)$. Higher levels of profit cannot be attained within the constraint of the model of union wage and employment determination.[6]

5. That is, they have positive (negative) slope to the left (right) of long-run demand, and zero slope where they cross that demand. As before, the firm's profit increases as it moves to lower iso-profit contours.

6. The interpretation due to Hirsch and Prasad (1995) is instructive, and for some readers perhaps more intuitive. Express the locus MUE in parametric form $[w(K), N(K)]$. The firm's problem reduces to the maximization of $\pi(w(K), N(K), K; r))$. The first-order condition for this problem is

$$[R_N - w(K)]dN/dK + [R_K - r - (dw/dK)N] = 0.$$

From (1) the first term is zero, leaving $R_K = r + (dw/dK)N$. With a positively sloped MUE, $dw/dK > 0$: the firm faces an effective price of *capital*, $r + (dw/dK)N$, greater than the market rate r. At this effective price, the long-run demand for *labor* passes through E and lies below the long-run demand at a price of capital of r. The monopoly union, in essence, not only drives up the price of labor but also that of capital.

Finally, now that the full equilibrium has been determined, what of the efficiency of capital? As was established earlier, the unique efficient combination of labor and capital (N^*, K^*) is determined by first-order conditions (1) and (2) with the wage set equal to the competitive level w_0. Along long-run demand $LN(w; r)$ in figure 3 the first-order conditions (1) and (2) hold simultaneously. Thus, at the competitive wage w_0 the long-run demand curve determines N^*. The contract curve CC^* is accordingly positioned vertically at N^* in figure 3, while the identity $SN[w; K(w; r)] = LN(w; r)$ is used to establish the position of $SN(w; K^*)$ relative to the long-run demand. Note also that, because short-run demand is less elastic than long-run demand, $SN(w; K_E)$ lies below $SN(w; K^*)$. Thus, because short-run demand follows the marginal revenue product of labor R_N, and $R_{NK} > 0$, the implication is $K_E < K^*$. By the standard of efficiency, both capital and labor are underutilized in the equilibrium of the one-shot game. The extent to which the efficient outcome (N^*, K^*) can be sustained in a repeated-game context is the subject of the balance of the article.

III. Repeated Play: Preliminaries

In subsequent sections, three alternative repeated games are considered. The first of these is repeated play of the monopoly-union model taking capital to be exogenous. This is the repeated game considered by Espinosa and Rhee (1989). The second variant extends the first by appending at the outset a once-and-for-all choice of capital by the firm. Here, the natural interpretation is that capital is perfectly durable and irreversible. Also an extension of the first, the third variant is, strictly speaking, the repeated game of the one-shot game of Section II. Capital lasts one period and is chosen by the firm at the outset of each period.

To maintain comparability among the one-shot game and the two variants of repeated play with endogenous capital, the price of capital is expressed in terms of its rental price r per period. As a consequence, the efficient mix of labor and capital remains (N^*, K^*), the same as in the one-shot game. In particular, by holding constant the rental price of capital r, the firm's discount factor δ will have no effect on the efficient level of capital. The roles that the discount factor of the firm and the lifetime capital play *strategically* in sustaining an efficient equilibrium can thereby be addressed without ambiguity. It is well known that, for a given price of capital of a given lifetime, a decrease in the discount factor decreases the present value of the stream of capital services, thereby reducing the level of capital preferred by the firm. The analysis here instead takes the rental price for the services of capital as given, and therefore the efficient level of capital is the same throughout the analysis. The price of capital is not independent but is inferred from the exogenously given rental price and discount factor.

The firm's objective at date t is to maximize the discounted sum of profits, $\sum_{s=t}^{T} \delta^s \pi(w_s, N_s, K_s; r)$, where $\delta < 1$ is the aforementioned discount factor of the firm and T is the firm's time horizon.[7]

For the union objective at date t, two alternative specifications are considered. One is to assume the union has its own discount factor $\delta_u < 1$ and a horizon T matching that of the firm. Then, its objective is $\sum_{s=t}^{T} \delta_u^s U(w_s, N_s)$. In the second specification, the union has a horizon of just one period so that the objective of the union is simply $U(w_t, N_t)$. Equivalently, the second specification is a specialization of the first in which the union's discount factor is zero.

As in the one-shot game, the equilibrium concept of subgame perfection will also be applied to the repeated games. Note that subgame perfection means that the firm and the union are constrained by their own future objectives even if their discount factors are not zero. This is the reason for specifying the objectives not just at the start of the game but at every date.

In what follows, the horizon T is replaced with infinity. For a finite horizon it is well known that if the equilibrium of the one-shot game is unique, as it is here, then the repeated game equilibrium outcome will in each period duplicate this one-shot equilibrium (e.g., Telser 1980). The reason is that the last period of play is identical to a one-shot game. Recognizing that the last period of play has a unique equilibrium that is not influenced by earlier moves, the penultimate period also is equivalent to the one-shot game. Continuing back in this way, every period is identical to a one-shot game. In the monopoly-union context this precludes the possibility of an efficient outcome. Our subsequent analysis will, therefore, focus exclusively on infinitely repeated play.

Finally, only stationary equilibria will be considered—that is, for all t, $(w_t, N_t, K_t) = (w, N, K)$. Note that the assumptions of the model imply efficient equilibria are stationary in employment and capital.

---

7. The discount factor corresponds in continuous time to $\delta = \exp(-\rho D)$, where D is the length of the period and ρ is the firm's rate of time preference. It is plausible to suppose that the rate of time preference of the firm equals the market rate of interest. References below to the feasibility of cooperative outcomes "for a discount factor sufficiently close to one" can be interpreted to mean "for rates of time preference or length of period sufficiently close to zero." Game theorists typically regard the length of the period and the rate of time preference as beyond the scope of their analysis. Nevertheless, as a referee has pointed out, the results derived below do suggest two intriguing possibilities. First, if the length of the period is interpreted as the wage-contract length, then there are mutual benefits to *negotiating* a *shorter* contract length. Second, if the market rate of interest determines the rate of time preference, then the larger the market rate, the less likely is an efficient outcome.

Journal of Business

IV. Exogenous Capital

In Espinosa and Rhee (1989), the one-shot monopoly-union game is infinitely repeated. Although capital is exogenous, their results provide a useful stepping stone to the analysis of endogenous capital.

Let capital take any arbitrary value K_A. Refer to figure 1. What Espinosa and Rhee show is that, for any efficient allocation on the contract curve CC_A between w_A^u and w_A^f, the efficient allocations mutually preferred to the one-shot equilibrium A can be supported in equilibrium provided the firm's discount factor is close enough to one.

To review their results, consider the following strategies:

$$N_t = SN(w_0; K_A) \quad \text{if } w_t = w' \text{ and the action } N_s = SN(w_0; K_A) \text{ has}$$

$$\text{been taken each time that } w_s = w' \text{ for } s < t,$$

$$N_t = SN(w_t; K_A) \quad \text{otherwise;}$$

and

$$w_t = w' \quad \text{if the firm has always adhered to its strategy,}$$

$$w_t = w_A \quad \text{otherwise.}$$

If these strategies are used, then $[w', SN(w_0; K_A)]$ will be the outcome in each period. Also, let w' belong to the necessarily nonempty interval (w_A^u, w_A^f) as indicated in figure 1 so that the firm achieves greater profit and the union achieves greater utility than at point A, the one-shot equilibrium.

Under these strategies, any deviation by the union triggers on-the-demand punishment by the firm; specifically, a move back onto the firm's labor demand curve for that period only. A deviation by the firm triggers a permanent move to the monopoly-union equilibrium.

As long as the firm's discount factor is sufficiently close to one, these strategies will constitute an equilibrium. The sequencing of moves within a period permits the firm to condition employment on the contemporaneous wage, thereby enabling immediate retribution. At the wage $w' \geq w_A^u$, the simple threat to leave the contract curve CC_A in figure 1 and go to the demand curve for one period is adequate to deter the union—if it fails to choose w' in a period, the best it can achieve is its utility at A, which is no better than if it had not deviated. Importantly, irrespective of the union's horizon or its discount factor, the union's strategy is a best reply to the firm's strategy. And the firm's threat is credible. As can be seen in figure 1, beginning on CC_A at a given wage of w, the firm's profit is increasing as its employment declines until the short-run demand $SN(w; K_A)$ is reached. The firm can never do better in the current period than move to its demand curve, and under the strategies specified above there are no future consequences if that move is triggered by a deviation by the union.[8]

And what of the firm's promise to choose $SN(w_0; K_A)$ if it faces the wage demand w'? Unlike punishment of the union, any punishment of the firm by the union (or unions) must rely on future, rather than immediate, consequences. Under the strategies specified, if the firm ever chooses an employment level other than $SN(w_0; K_A)$ after the union has chosen w', then the union will react by demanding w_A in each subsequent period. This reaction can be interpreted as a permanent loss of trust in the firm. The players all revert to playing their one-shot strategies, yielding outcome A in figure 1. These one-shot strategies are mutual best replies in the infinitely repeated game regardless of the history of play and are thus available to the players as a credible punishment. In short, the loss of trust in the firm is a self-fulfilling prophecy.

Having seen that the union will punish the firm, it is left to check that this punishment will deter the firm from cheating. If the firm does cheat, its highest immediate payoff will be

$$\pi[w', SN(w'; K_A), K_A; r] > \pi[w', SN(w_0; K_A), K_A; r]$$

$$> \pi[w_A, SN(w_A; K_A), K_A; r],$$

which is achieved by moving to the short-run demand curve. The effects of cheating can be traced using figure 1; the firm receives an immediate one-period gain by moving from CC_A to $SN(w'; K_A)$, albeit at the cost of a permanent reduction in the future stream of profit when the union duly reacts by raising the wage to w_A. For any $w' < w_A^f$, there exists a discount factor δ sufficiently close to one such that the punishment will exceed the gain. Specifically, δ must satisfy

$$\frac{\pi[w', SN(w_0; K_A), K_A; r]}{1 - \delta} \geq \pi(w', SN(w'; K_A), K_A; r)$$

$$+ \delta \left\{ \frac{\pi[w_A, SN(w_A; K_A), K_A; r]}{1 - \delta} \right\} \quad (4)$$

or, rearranging,

$$\delta \geq \frac{\pi[w', SN(w'; K_A), K_A; r] - \pi[w', SN(w_0; K_A), K_A; r]}{\pi[w', SN(w'; K_A), K_A; r] - \pi[w_A, SN(w_A; K_A), K_A; r]}. \quad (5)$$

For any w' satisfying $w_A^u \leq w' \leq w_A^f$, therefore, there exists a δ such that an efficient outcome can be achieved as a self-enforcing equilibrium.

8. For more on efficient play between long-run and short-run players, a useful starting point is Kreps (1990).

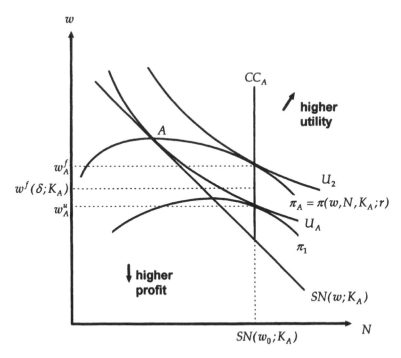

FIG. 4.—The sustainable set of efficient equilibria given K_A and δ

Alternatively, for a given δ, is there a *sustaining wage set*, a set of wages that will sustain efficient outcomes? Now, for $\delta = 0$, the sustaining wage set is empty. Under $\delta = 0$, condition (5) implies that the firm pays $w' = w_0$, which is in turn less than w_A^u, the lowest wage the union would accept at the efficient level of employment. It follows that a discount factor of zero is incompatible with efficiency. Rather, there exists a critical value δ_c, such that for all δ in the interval $\delta_c \leq \delta < 1$ there is a nonempty sustaining wage set, a proper subset of the interval $w_A^u \leq w' \leq w_A^f$. Replacing the inequality in (5) with an equality and solving for w' defines a function $w^f(\delta; K_A)$.[9] Values w_A^u and $w^f(\delta; K_A)$ are then the lower and upper bounds of the sustaining wage set. Figure 4 illustrates for the case $\delta \geq \delta_c$. The sustaining wage set is that portion of CC_A covering wages between w_A^u and $w^f(\delta; K_A)$. Note that if $\delta < \delta_c$, then the sustaining set is empty.[10]

9. Here it is assumed the right-hand side of (5) is monotonically increasing in w'.
10. Espinosa and Rhee (1989, p. 571) go on to show that a positive discount factor allows mutually beneficial improvements on the one-shot outcome, even if the discount

V. Endogenous Capital

A. Perfect Durability

The key insight in Espinosa and Rhee (1989) is that, because of the natural order of play, efficient outcomes can be achieved in equilibrium, even if only the firm has a long-run horizon. To what extent does this insight carry over once capital is endogenized?

Take Espinosa and Rhee's game tree and graft on to it an opening once-and-for-all choice of capital by the firm. The natural interpretation is that capital is perfectly durable and irreversible. The firm commits to a perpetual lease at a per period rental price of r for each unit of capital. As discussed in Section III, expressing the cost of capital in terms of its rental price achieves comparability of the perfect durability case with the earlier one-shot model and with the later case of finitely durable capital.

For each value of capital, there follows a subgame that is the repeated game of the exogenous capital model just considered. Subgame perfection implies that play from that point must itself be a Nash subgame-perfect equilibrium.

If an equilibrium is to be efficient, play subsequent to the installation of K must be efficient if the efficient level of capital K^* is chosen. Once K^* has been sunk, the preceding analysis of exogenous capital can be applied. Given a w', there is a minimal δ required to achieve efficient employment. Or, alternatively, δ must exceed a critical value in order for the sustainable set of efficient equilibria to be nonempty.

However, the firm must also find it attractive to choose K^* over any other K. Suppose that if K^* is not chosen the players go permanently to the one-shot monopoly-union equilibrium associated with the chosen K. (Again, this is always one equilibrium of such a subgame.) The best outcome for the firm amongst these alternatives ($K \neq K^*$) is the one-shot endogenous capital outcome, namely, point E in figure 5, which carries over from figure 3.

As can be seen from figure 5, the firm can guarantee itself more profit at E than it can achieve at point T, the one-shot equilibrium associated with K^*. As a result, some of the efficient outcomes that can be supported in the repeated game *given* K^* might not be achievable when capital is endogenous. To induce the firm to select K^* adds a further limitation: the firm must earn at least $\pi_E = \pi(w_E, N_E, K^1(w_E, N_E); r)$, not just $\pi_T = \pi(w_T, N_T, K^*; r)$.

---

factor is not sufficiently large to support an efficient outcome. As pointed out earlier, the discount factor depends on the rate of time preference and the length of a period (which can be interpreted as the contract length). If the rate of time preference equals the market rate of interest, then the discount factor can be computed from observable variables. But in order to quantify the effect these variables have on the sustainable set, the entire model would have to be parameterized.

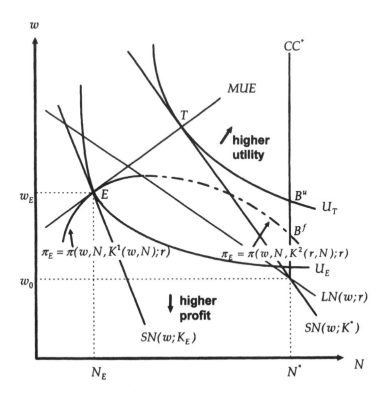

FIG. 5.—Efficiency, durability, and the repeated game

Figure 5 illustrates. The iso-profit contour π_E is a hybrid. Below $LN(w; r)$, it is drawn for K satisfying equation (1). Recall that this is done in order to find the one-shot endogenous capital equilibrium point E. But above the long-run demand, the continuation of π_E is drawn for K satisfying equation (2). (Along $LN(w; r)$, both (1) and (2) hold, so the contour π_E is continuous where it intersects long-run demand.) Let $K^2(r, N)$ be the function that solves equation (2) for K. At point B^f, the intersection of π_E with the contract curve CC^*, $N = N^*$ and, because $K^* = K^2(r, N^*)$, $K = K^*$. The wage coordinate of B^f establishes the highest wage the firm would be willing to pay to enter into an efficient contract.

The wage coordinate of B^u establishes the lowest wage the union would accept once K^* is installed, assuming for now that the firm's strategy is to deploy Espinosa and Rhee's (1989) on-the-demand punishment if the union cheats on the wage. In figure 5, B^u lies above B^f on the wage scale, although the reverse can also occur. In the case illustrated, no efficient contract that utilizes on-the-demand punishment is self-enforcing—irrespective of the firm's discount factor. The reason such a case can arise is that, unlike the exogenous capital model, the parties do not compare the proposed efficient outcome with the same monopoly-union equilibrium (point A in figure 1). Rather, the firm compares the proposed efficient outcome with point E in figure 5, while the union compares the proposed efficient outcome with point T in figure 5. Clearly, the comparators are different.

If, instead, B^u lies below B^f on the wage scale, then for each wage in that interval an efficient outcome is self-enforcing for δ sufficiently close to one. Alternatively, given δ there is a set of sustainable efficient equilibria *given* K^*, which defines one upper bound on the wage. Endogenizing capital adds an additional constraint on the set of sustainable efficient equilibria, a constraint that is binding if the upper bound on wages given K^* lies above B^f on the wage scale.

B. Finite Durability

Assume that rather than being perfectly durable, capital can be cost-lessly adjusted at the start of each period. From the standpoint of achieving an efficient outcome, the advantage is that a harsher punishment can be imposed on the union that cheats. This is an effect along the lines suggested by Baldwin. But there is also a downside risk. Flexible capital weakens the union's punishment of the firm that cheats.

To simplify the explanation of the latter effect, suppose that the union discounts the future entirely ($\delta_u = 0$). Further suppose that with perfectly durable capital an efficient outcome is possible. For any such equilibrium there is a minimum firm discount factor necessary to achieve that result. Now consider flexible capital. If the firm cheats on employment, then its per period payoff in the punishment phase is its one-shot equilibrium payoff, not the smaller *MUE* payoff at the efficient level of capital. This in turn raises the minimum firm discount factor necessary to achieve the same efficient result. As a consequence, efficient outcomes that could be achieved if capital were rigid become less likely with flexible capital.

The more familiar effect, working to expand the possible efficient outcomes, requires that the union's horizon extend beyond the present period. In comparison with perfect durability, the ability to choose capital each period enables the firm to respond to union misbehavior by reducing the union's future payoffs. Provided the discount factors of both the firm and the union are sufficiently close to one, there will exist efficient allocations that can be achieved in equilibrium that did not exist under rigid capital.[11] The reason is that the union can now be made to effect a comparison with the same alternative outcome as the

___

11. Similarly, there will exist values of δ for which flexibility is necessary to achieve an efficient equilibrium.

firm. To understand this, consider the one-shot monopoly-union equilibrium outcome (w_E, N_E, K_E), corresponding to point E in figure 5. Choose an efficient allocation (w', N^*, K^*) from the core of allocations that is mutually preferred by both the firm and the union to (w_E, N_E, K_E). For discount factors sufficiently close to one, such an allocation can be achieved in equilibrium by an appropriate mutually reinforcing credible deterrent. Specifically, if the outcome in a round ever differs for any reason from (w', N^*, K^*), play in subsequent rounds switches to the strategies used in the one-shot capital-first equilibrium.

VI. Reputation for Toughness

The foregoing discussion of endogenous capital limited the firm to using on-the-demand punishment for union malfeasance. However, harsher short-term cuts in employment can also be credible. The idea is to obtain more leverage from the firm's regard for the future. The firm has an interest in maintaining not only a reputation for honesty but also a reputation for toughness.[12]

Regarding the union horizon, let us focus on the most challenging case for achieving efficiency, namely, a union with a one-period horizon. Thus, attention will be duly restricted to one-period punishment in response to a union holdup.

Consider the following strategies:

1. For the firm, at each round t,
   a) if it has always adhered to its strategy,
      i) install $K_t = K^*$.
      ii) If $w_t = w'$, choose $N_t = N^*$. Otherwise, maximize profit subject to the constraint $U(w_t, N_t) \le U(w', N^*)$.
   b) If it has ever failed to adhere to its strategy prior to round t, then henceforth play according to its one-shot capital-first equilibrium strategy.
   c) If $K_t \ne K^*$, choose N_t according to its monopoly-union equilibrium strategy given K_t.[13]
2. For the union, at each round t,
   a) if the firm has never deviated from its strategy (including capital choice in round t), choose $w_t = w'$.
   b) Otherwise, choose w_t to maximize $U(w_t, N_t)$ subject to $N_t = SN(w_t, K_t)$.

---

12. This notion could also be applied to expand the set of efficient equilibria in Espinosa and Rhee's setting with exogenous capital.
13. Note that the firm's strategy here applies to the setting where capital has a one-period life. With small modifications it can be adapted to the infinitely durable case, and the equilibrium analysis will go through with little change.

Finally, (w', N^*, K^*) is an allocation located on the contract curve CC^* which gives the union at least $U(w_0, N^*)$ and gives the firm at least as much as the one-shot-capital-first equilibrium. It will be shown that these strategies constitute a Nash subgame-perfect equilibrium.

Note that the firm in 1*a* ii utilizes the least-cost "punishment schedule" for employment, namely, the employment schedule that maximizes profit in the current period subject to the condition that the union not gain from demanding a wage different from the contract wage w'. The intersection of $SN(w, K^*)$ and the locus given by $U(w, N) = U(w', N^*)$ defines a critical wage. Below that critical wage this schedule follows $SN(w, K^*)$, that is, on-the-demand punishment. Above that critical wage, the punishment schedule instead follows the locus $U(w, N) = U(w', N^*)$, namely, off-the-demand punishment.

If strategies 1 and 2 are deployed, the outcome is (w', N^*, K^*), which is a member of the set of efficient outcomes. Are 1 and 2 equilibrium strategies? Consider the union. It is enough to sort subgames according to whether the firm has deviated. First, consider the case where the firm has never deviated. The union cannot gain from departing from 2*a*, thereby initiating a deviation. If the union did deviate, the firm's response would be to implement the punishment in 1*a*ii, which, by construction, does not allow the union to gain from cheating. Second, consider histories where the firm has cheated. Because the firm's strategy says that once it cheats it will henceforth play as if engaged in a one-shot game, the union can do no better than choose a wage as if it were playing a one-shot game. The union will adhere to 2*b*.

And what of 1, the firm's strategy? To start, suppose the firm at some time fails to utilize strategy 1. The union's reaction according to 2*b* would be to play as if engaged in a one-shot game. The union in essence forms an unshakeable belief about the firm that deviates from its strategy. If the firm cheats on employment, the union concludes the firm is untrustworthy—just as in Espinosa and Rhee's (1989) analysis, the firm would lose its reputation for honesty. The firm's reputation for toughness is at stake in a subgame where the union has cheated. If the firm fails to carry out its off-the-demand punishment, the union concludes the firm is weak and will never carry out off-the-demand punishment. Once the union has been triggered to behave according to its one-shot strategy—that is, once it has formed an unshakeable belief the firm is untrustworthy or weak—the firm can do no better than to confirm those beliefs and play as specified in 1*b* and 1*c*.

So will the firm ever deviate? First, it will not cheat on capital. Given the union's immediate response, the firm can do no better from cheating than the one-shot capital-first equilibrium. But it prefers (w', N^*, K^*). Second, failure to be tough with a union that cheats yields a saving in the current period but at the price of permanently lower profitability. It follows that the firm will choose to carry out its threats, thereby maintaining its reputation for toughness, as long as its discount factor is sufficiently close to one. Finally, what of the firm's temptation to cheat on the employment agreement? The analysis is familiar. Compared with the constant stream of profit $\pi(w', N^*, K^*; r)$ along the equilibrium path of play, it obtains a one-time gain at the expense of a permanently lower stream of profit in the future. For a discount factor sufficiently close to one, cheating on the labor agreement does not pay.

VII. Conclusion

This article has sought to modify Baldwin's (1983) influential study of the efficiency of investment under self-enforcing union contracts in two major respects. First, it recasts her treatment by locating it in the context of the monopoly-union and efficient-contract models. Second, it adheres throughout to a formal game-theoretic approach. If the focus is narrowly on on-the-demand punishment, our game-theoretic results reaffirm Baldwin's prescription for deterring union malfeasance, namely, lengthen the union's time horizon or shorten the replacement cycle of capital. That said, much of our analysis has suggested that union malfeasance does not necessarily underpin suboptimal investment.

Moreover, the effect on efficiency of a shorter economic life of capital is itself not unambiguous. In particular, we identified the potential for malfeasance on the part of the firm and not just the union. This approach allowed us to obtain the more exotic result that, where capital has a short lifetime, the ability of the union to punish the firm for opportunistic behavior is reduced—a result that clearly turns one Baldwin prescription on its head.

It was also argued that the firm can credibly impose punishment that is harsher than the conventional on-the-demand form, buttressing the broad conclusion of the article that the union's horizon and the durability of capital are not necessarily crucial to efficiency. Specifically, sufficient patience by the firm will suffice to make credible retribution that has the superficial appearance of a self-destructive threat. Stated another way, underinvestment may stem from an insufficient firm discount factor.

In the world of efficient equilibria as constructed here, no punishment is ever meted out for the obvious reason that no one breaks the agreement. But the real world admits of such things as lockouts, walkouts, and slowdowns. Repeated-game models of oligopolistic collusion have dealt with a similar discrepancy by showing that incomplete information regarding market demand can produce alternating phases of collusion and price wars brought on by the suspicion of cheating. This suggests a promising development of the model would be to incorporate the effects of incomplete information on the efficiency of union contracts. Prior to that, however, a more important task is to further parameterize the model so as to gauge the likelihood of observing inefficient contracts and the relative contribution of their proximate causes.

Finally, we have not up to this point addressed the small but growing empirical literature dealing with union effect on investments in physical and intangible capital. That literature points unequivocally to lower investment in the presence of unions (see, e.g., Hirsch 1991; Bronars and Deere 1993; Bronars, Deere, and Tracy 1994; Cavanaugh 1996; Fallick and Hassett 1996). Whether this association is merely an artifact of selection or is underinvestment stemming from unionization has not been resolved empirically. Even if there is underinvestment, one should be more than usually careful in attributing blame. Without a union there can of course be no conflict over the division of the surplus. However, this conflict in and of itself does not lead to suboptimal investment. Other factors must be present as well. It has been shown here that these must encompass not just union myopia but also the firm's patience and the durability of its capital. The task for the empirical literature— abstracting from selection issues—is now to determine the contribution of each of these factors to the lower levels of investment observed in union settings.

References

Addison, J. T., and Hirsch, B. T. 1989. Union effects of productivity, profits, and growth: Has the long run arrived? *Journal of Labor Economics* 7 (January): 72–105.

Anderson, S. P., and Devereux, M. 1988. Trade unions and the choice of capital stock. *Scandinavian Journal of Economics* 90(1):27–44.

Baldwin, C. Y. 1983. Productivity and labor unions: An application of the theory of self-enforcing contracts. *Journal of Business* 56 (April): 155–85.

Bronars, S. G., and Deere, D. R. 1993. Unionization, incomplete contracting, and capital investment. *Journal of Business* 66 (January): 117–32.

Bronars, S. G.; Deere, D. R.; and Tracy, J. S. 1994. The effects of unions on firm behavior: An empirical analysis using firm-level data. *Industrial Relations* 29 (October): 426–51.

Cavanaugh, J. K. 1996. Asset specific investment and unionized labor. Unpublished manuscript. Dayton, Ohio: Wright State University.

Espinosa, M. P., and Rhee, C. 1989. Efficient wage bargaining as a repeated game. *Quarterly Journal of Economics* 104 (August): 565–88.

Fallick, B. C., and Hassett, K. A. 1996. Investment and union certification. Federal Reserve Board, Finance and Economics Discussion Series No. 1996–43. Washington, D.C.: Board of Governors of the Federal Reserve System, November.

Freeman, R. P., and Medoff, J. L. 1984. *What Do Unions Do?* New York: Basic Books.

Hirsch, B. T. 1991. *Labor Unions and the Economic Performance of Firms.* Kalamazoo, Mich.: W. E. Upjohn Institute for Employment Research.

Hirsch, B. T., and Prasad, K. 1995. Wage-employment determination and a union tax on capital: Can theory and evidence be reconciled? *Economics Letters* 48 (April): 61–71.

Kreps, D. 1990. Corporate culture and economic theory. In J. E. Alt and K. A. Shepsle (eds.), *Perspectives on Positive Political Economy.* New York: Cambridge University Press.

Telser, L. G. 1980. A theory of self-enforcing agreements. *Journal of Business* 54 (January): 27–44.

[17]

Southern Economic Journal 2003, 69(4), 822–841

New Evidence on Unions and Plant Closings: Britain in the 1990s

John T. Addison,* John S. Heywood,† and Xiangdong Wei‡

In this paper, we exploit the longitudinal element of the 1990 and 1998 Workplace Employee Relations Surveys for Britain to investigate the effect of unionism on establishment closings. Contrary to both recent U.S. research and long-standing British work, we find a strong positive association between two measures of unionism—union recognition for collective bargaining purposes and union coverage—and plant closings. This association is robust to the inclusion of highly detailed industry controls but is driven by plants that are parts of multiestablishment entities. No such relationship obtains in the case of single-plant enterprises. In explaining our findings, we address their consistency with the widely perceived reduction in the "disadvantages of (British) unionism" in recent years.

1. Introduction

The effect of unions on establishment closings is an important but poorly developed theme in empirical labor economics. This is unfortunate because the association may assist our understanding of union impact on economic performance while serving as a potential explanation for the ongoing decline in union membership. Both topics remain controversial in part because of the dearth of evidence of union impact on establishment closings.

In the present paper, we use British workplace data for the 1990s to investigate the issue. We obtain very different results from those reported in earlier U.S. and British studies. Specifically, we find a positive and well-determined association between unionization and establishment closings in the private sector that is driven by plants that are part of multiestablishment enterprises. In single independent establishments, a more conventional statistically insignificant association is reported. We argue that the empirical distinction between types of establishment reflects not only theoretical considerations but also former Prime Minister Margaret Thatcher's sustained legal challenge to the union movement during the decade of the 1980s (see Addison and Siebert, in press).

The plan of the paper is as follows. In the next section, we review the sparse empirical literature on unions and plant closings, which we preface with material on other performance indicators. After

* Department of Economics, Moore School of Business, University of South Carolina, Columbia, SC 29208, USA; E-mail ecceaddi@moore.sc.edu; corresponding author.

† Department of Economics, P.O. Box 413, University of Wisconsin, Milwaukee, Milwaukee, WI 53201, USA; E-mail heywood@uwm.edu.

‡ Department of Economics, Lingnan University, 8 Castle Peak Road, Tuen Mun, Honk Kong; E-mail xdwei@ln.edu.hk.

We thank, without implicating, Barry Hirsch and Paulino Teixeira for helpful comments on an earlier draft of this paper. We have also benefited from the comments and suggestions of an anonymous reviewer of this *Journal*. We acknowledge the Department of Trade and Industry; the Economic and Social Research Council; the Advisory, Conciliation and Arbitration Service; and the Policy Studies Institute as the originators of the 1998 Workplace Employee Relations Survey data and the Data Archive at the University of Essex as the distributor of the data. None of these organizations bears any responsibility for the authors' analysis and interpretations of the data.

Received February 2002; accepted September 2002.

that, we offer some applied theoretical conjectures on the expected association(s) between a union presence and closures. A brief review of the data set is then followed by presentation of our detailed findings. An interpretative section concludes.

2. The Empirical Literature

In both the United States and Britain, there is a large literature documenting union effects on firm and establishment performance. This literature offers a somewhat pessimistic view of union impact that, when taken in the round, might lead one to anticipate a positive association between union presence and plant closings.

In their review of U.S. productivity studies, Addison and Hirsch (1989) conclude that no compelling case emerges for a statistically or economically significant positive or negative union productivity effect. For its part, the British evidence points consistently to negative union productivity effects, subject to the important caveat that these have been much attenuated in recent years (see, e.g., Metcalf 1994, 2003). As far as productivity growth is concerned, the U.S. evidence points to a negative although not always robust association between unionism and changes in productivity (e.g., Hirsch 1991). The British evidence points to lower productivity growth in union regimes in the 1970s, although in later decades this result is sensitive to type of union (e.g., Gregg, Machin, and Metcalf 1993; Addison and Belfield 2001).

The evidence on profitability is both stronger and weaker than that for productivity: stronger in the sense that almost without exception the union effect is negative and well determined in both countries, albeit again subject to some erosion through time in the British case,[1] and weaker to the extent that there is lingering controversy as to the source of the profit effect. For the United Kingdom, although not it seems the United States, there are at least some indications that the union wage premium may accrue from product market power (e.g., Machin and Stewart 1996).

The U.S. evidence on investments in physical capital generally matches the productivity and profitability results for that country in indicating consistently lower investment in union regimes (e.g., Hirsch 1991, 1992; Fallick and Hassett 1999). Time-series studies for Britain also indicate some negative union effects (e.g., Denny and Nickell 1992), even if there is again evidence of a weakening in such effects in the 1980s compared with previous decades (see Metcalf 1994, p. 151). Research in the United States has also found rather strong evidence that unionization adversely affects investment in research and development (R&D) (Hirsch 1991). But this indication of union rent seeking acting as a tax on intangible capital is not replicated for the United Kingdom. In particular, Menezes-Filho, Ulph, and Van Reenen (1998a) report that the negative correlation between union density/recognition and R&D intensity that is observed in cross-section and panel data for plants and companies, respectively, disappears when one accounts for age effects and the availability of innovative activity in the relevant industry.

Finally, when one turns to the evidence on employment change, U.S. findings generally suggest that employment growth is lower (and employment contraction is greater) in the union sector (e.g., Linnemann, Wachter, and Carter 1990; Leonard 1992; Dunne and Macpherson 1994). British studies consistently point to the same result regardless of the time period examined (e.g., Blanchflower, Millward, and Oswald 1991; Fernie and Metcalf 1995; Booth and McCulloch 1999).

---

[1] For the United States, see the studies by Addison and Hirsch (1989), Hirsch (1991), Becker and Olson (1992), and Bronars, Deere, and Tracy (1994); for the United Kingdom, see Metcalf (1993, 1994), and Addison and Belfield (2002).

In sum, although the evidence is not always easy to interpret statistically (some theoretical ambiguities are aired in the next section), there are few grounds for optimism in the data concerning union impact on firm performance. The bright spot is the seeming improvement in the U.K. situation in recent years. Observed changes in the impact of British unions through time have been attributed to the Thatcher union reforms, which are widely seen as having reduced the "disadvantages of unionism" (Oulton 1990). Nevertheless, the union effects on profits, R&D, and productivity growth are causes for concern. Lower profitability may be expected to lower investment in vulnerable forms of capital both directly because of the union "tax" (most clearly evident for the United States) and indirectly because profits are a pool of resources from which investments are frequently financed. And even if many firms do not depend on formal R&D for their survival (but rather on organizational innovation), all will rely on their productivity growth if they are to prosper in the long run. Thus, it appears reasonable in these circumstances to anticipate higher rates of business failure in union regimes in both countries, even if in the case of the United Kingdom such effects might be more obvious in the pre-Thatcher era.

In any event, there is little concrete evidence of this in the few published studies of plant closings for the two countries. Beginning with the U.S. evidence, although there are case studies pointing to high union labor costs as a major reason for plant closings during the 1980s (see Gerhart 1987), the two best-known econometric studies fail to detect higher rates of attrition in unionized regimes. Thus, in a sectoral analysis based on establishment data from the 1977 and 1982 Census of Manufactures microdata files, Dunne and Macpherson (1994) report that sectors with high union membership did not experience significantly greater employment loss due to plant closings than their less unionized counterparts, controlling for the price-cost margin and establishment size. As noted earlier, however, the authors' separate analysis of sectoral contraction and expansion rates suggests that more heavily unionized sectors do downsize more and have (marginally) lower growth, other things being equal.

The more comprehensive U.S. analysis by Freeman and Kleiner (1999) uses three data sets: a sample of firms/business lines from the COMPUSTAT I and II files, 1983–1990, supplemented with union density information from Hirsch (1991); information on displaced workers from the Current Population Survey (CPS) Displaced Worker Supplements for 1994 and 1996, linked to control samples from the CPS outgoing rotation group, 1991–1995; and information on the rate of plant closure in union and nonunion regimes from the files of the Federal Mediation and Conciliation Service (FMCS).

Of most interest is Freeman and Kleiner's analysis of the union impact on insolvencies using the COMPUSTAT data files. Their final sample comprises 633 business units (319 firms and 314 business lines), of which 126 became insolvent (67 firms and 59 terminated business lines) between 1983 and 1990. For a probit specification that includes just a union dummy and union density, plus dummies for whether the observation was a firm or a line of business, it is found that union presence is negatively associated with the likelihood of failure but that as the union density increases the firm/business line is more likely to fail. Adding in controls for firm age, sales, and a vector of industry characteristics (namely, concentration ratios, growth rate of sales, import penetration rates, and bankruptcy rates) reduces the effect of union presence but not that of union density, each remaining statistically significant. Finally, replacing the union variable(s) with the categorical measures of low, medium, and high density indicates that only the last category is associated with greater rates of insolvency, compared with no union presence. Regardless of specification, however, insolvencies are higher than in nonunion regimes only where union density is at or above 60%, a level that is twice the average unionization rate of the sample.

Since even their sample of insolvent firms had been in business for some time, Freeman and Kleiner use the FMCS data to informally address the issue of whether newly unionized firms close more frequently than other companies. For the interval 1986–1993, it is found that just 341 out of 10,783 certification elections (and 3009 out of 168,945 dispute cases) resulted in plant closures. Expressed as rates of closure, these values compare favorably with estimates of business failures from the Annual Surveys of Manufactures, averaging 3.4% per year between 1974 and 1978. Equating the latter with average rates of plant closure in the absence of new unionism, Freeman and Kleiner (1999, p. 525) conclude that there is "virtually no union effect on closure of new plants."

Finally, Freeman and Kleiner use the CPS data to estimate the individual's probability of being displaced. It is found that the proportion of union workers among the displaced population is almost exactly predicted by their characteristics and that the probability that a worker will be displaced by plant closure—or indeed for any other reason—is not materially affected by his or her union status.

This use of multiple data sets is a response to a standard problem that arises in assessing union impact on failure rates: the absence of unambiguous identifying restrictions. The problem is whether union workplaces differ in unmeasured but systematic ways from their nonunion counterparts so as to bias estimates of the union effect. Unions may tend to be concentrated in less profitable, slower-growing industries with lower rates of new investment and productivity growth and higher failure rates. Alternatively, unions may alight on firms with larger economic rents that plausibly may be less likely to fail. Adverse union effects on closures from comparisons between union and nonunion establishments would, in these circumstances, alternately overstate or understate the true union impact.

The final U.S. study considered here offers a novel, quasi-experimental solution to (minimizing) this problem of selection/omitted variables bias. DiNardo and Lee (2002) exploit data on union representation elections, arguing that where union elections are close—namely, circumstances in which unions barely won or barely lost—the establishments in question are likely to be virtually identical *ex ante* so that examination of their subsequent survival rates should determine the causal impact of unionism, if any. The authors' sample is obtained from the universe of 27,000 establishments that experienced National Labor Relations Board representation elections between 1983 and 1999. Their regression discontinuity analysis reveals little or no effect of unions on establishment survival rates. Specifically, where the union vote share is between 45% and 55%, the difference in survival probabilities as between union wins and union losses is a statistically insignificant 0.7% (the confidence interval is from -3.7% to 2.3%). The raw data admit of negative selection, with unions tending to succeed in elections in smaller and potentially less robust plants.[2]

The sole published study for Britain is by Machin (1995), who exploits the longitudinal element from the 1984 and 1990 Workplace Industrial Relations Surveys (WIRS) to identify establishments that were in the 1984 survey but subsequently closed down. Machin's full sample comprises 704 trading sector establishments, of which 87 closed down between the two surveys. Machin presents several probit estimates of plant closure and in each case computes the marginal union effects. In the most parsimonious specification, the plant closure dummy is regressed on the presence or otherwise of a trade union recognized for collective bargaining purposes. The union coefficient estimate is negative and marginally significant. Establishments with union recognition emerge as some 4.8% less likely to have failed over the six-year sample period. A second specification adds controls for establishment employment size, the share of manual employees in the workforce, single independent establishment

---

[2] These findings should be viewed as only suggestive because of the small number of baseline characteristics of establishments and the virtual absence of information on what happens between the time of the election and the single point (2002) at which survival or death is recorded.

(the reference category being establishments that are part of a multiplant firm), and manufacturing industry. The effect is to reduce in absolute size the magnitude of the union coefficient estimate, which is now no longer statistically significant from zero. The effects of the other covariates are all well determined other than for the share of manual workers. In particular, larger establishments and single independent establishments are associated with a smaller likelihood of closure and conversely for manufacturing industry establishments. A third specification adds two inverse measures of establishment performance, namely, below-average financial performance and a low degree of capacity utilization. (Although both are positively signed, only the latter variable is statistically significant.) Their inclusion serves to increase the absolute value of the union coefficient estimate, although it remains statistically insignificant from zero.

Since British research has suggested that union premia have been highest in closed shop situations, Machin also tests whether such regimes were associated with higher risk of closure over the sample period. They are found not to be. Similarly, the basic result that unions have no discernible impact on closings is shown to be robust to the exclusion of some less-than-clear-cut instances of plant closings and the inclusion of one-digit industry controls and age-of-establishment dummies.

Machin thus rejects the null hypothesis that closure rates are higher in unionized establishments. He further asserts that there is no evidence to suggest that unions imperil firm survival in the long run or that plant failures have played a part in the waning fortunes of British unionism from 1984 to 1990, when the proportion of workers covered by a collective agreement fell from 71% to 54% and density declined from 54% to 38%.

3. Theoretical Conjectures

While the standard monopoly union or on-the-demand-curve model leads us to expect a positive union effect on establishment dissolution (see also Lazear 1983), in circumstances where the union bargains over wages and employment the contracts that result may be efficient. Indeed, in the strongly efficient (i.e., vertical contract curve) case, the union will have no real effects: Output and input usage, as well as product prices, will be the same as under perfect competition. The two sides will maximize the total surplus (i.e., the total value of the enterprise) and then bargain over its distribution. In this framework, there are few grounds for expecting unions to have any effect on plant closings. Yet this model is static: Capital is assumed fixed. In the long run, as is well known, union appropriation of the quasi rents from long-lived specific capital may reduce such investments and threaten the survival of the enterprise (see, e.g., Grout 1984). In other words, efficient bargains are not sufficient to ensure that investment will be unaffected and survival unimpaired.

That being said, one must be cautious in attributing a finding of lower physical investment in unionized firms to unions. While it is true that without a union there can be no conflict over the division of the surplus, this conflict does not lead in and of itself to suboptimal investment. There must be other factors at work as well. As Addison and Chilton (1998) have shown, these factors include not just union myopia but also the firm's patience and the durability of its capital. The contribution of these factors to lower levels of investment typically observed in union settings has not been modeled. It is also true that the incorporation of other theoretical insights, and in particular the strategic aspects of R&D rivalry under oligopolistic competition (see Menezes-Filho, Ulph, and Van Reenen 1998b), may mean that unions can increase the firm's incentive to innovate.

Since the theory is ambiguous on the dynamic implications of union rent seeking for plant closings—even if there is undoubtedly an investment problem in union regimes—the informality of applied exercises is scarcely surprising. Thus, Freeman and Kleiner (1999, p. 512) simply argue that unions care about the employment prospects of their membership and will make concessions to keep the firm afloat. Rational unions, we are told, should not push firms to the edge of bankruptcy and will grant wage concessions to sustain them (see also Kuhn 1986). Freeman and Kleiner do acknowledge that bargaining failures (induced by suboptimal information disclosure) and maintenance of the standard rate may on occasion be sufficient to generate differential failure rates between unionized and nonunion plants. Yet they argue that, in general, unions are not so foolish as to force organized firms out of business—their rationality being reflected in their organization of firms to begin with that have sufficient economic rent to deflect the probability of long-run business failure. Therefore, one should not expect to observe a positive association between union presence and bankruptcy, other things being equal.[3]

In light of the previous discussion, we combine Freeman and Kleiner's concessions argument with Machin's (1995) finding that single independent establishments have lower rates of closing. In particular, the concessions argument might be modified to reflect the status of firms as either multiplant or single-plant entities. The availability of more generous severance packages and transfer rights (by seniority) in multiestablishment entities might make workers, and insiders in particular, less prone to make concessions than their counterparts in single-plant firms.[4] More generally, one might formulate a calculus of plant closing that emphasizes the benefits and costs: Plants are more likely to close as the closing benefits rise and as the closing costs fall. Single-establishment operations can be viewed as having greater closing costs, as they involve the exit of the firm. Plants with greater flexibility and lower production costs—as proxied by, say, the share of female employees and the proportion of workers on fixed-term contracts—should have lower closing benefits and be less likely to close.

Returning to the union, the closure of a single independent establishment means that union workers will with certainty lose their jobs, so that the union may be prepared to grant concessions. The range of concessions may considerably exceed those available in nonunion establishments if we posit that a collective response by workers is likely to be more successful in circumstances where there is more room to cut rents. Although the latter considerations also obtain in union regimes that are part of multiestablishment operations, there are countervailing influences: Not only are union members likely to have transfer rights to other units of the enterprise, but also the ongoing firm is more likely to fulfill its contractual and legal requirements covering severance pay, pensions, and other fringes to which members might be entitled. In short, the costs of establishment closure to the union might be lower in the case of multiestablishment undertakings and as a result the concessions it offers much attenuated compared with those made in single-establishment firms. Perhaps counterintuitively, the end-game phenomenon (see Lawrence and Lawrence 1985) may also support the notion that it is more costly to close single-establishment undertakings. This is because the end game acts as an exit cost making closure less likely and/or delaying closure. If management expects a concessionary response, it may announce the possibility of closure and thereby capture the

---

[3] However, we note that Curme and Kahn (1990) find that U.S. workers discount the value of pensions and deferred compensation in the face of increasing risk of firm insolvency. They report that a greater risk of firm bankruptcy leads to a heightened emphasis on current earnings and a consequent reduction in pension coverage. Moreover, for workers who do have pensions, a rise in probability of closure steepens the tenure-earnings profile rewarding insiders. Such evidence highlights the potential role that insiders might play in the face of an uncertain future to actually raise the current costs of firms in distress.

[4] Thus, the *Los Angeles Times* (1987, p. 29) reported that "spirits remain high" as General Motors closed a plant in Massachusetts in the late 1980s. The article emphasized that workers with high tenure received 30 weeks of unemployment benefits and 95% of take-home pay for two years.

concessions that reduce the likelihood of closure. If management instead expects an end game, as other evidence might suggest they should (see footnote 3), the announcement of potential closure is likely to be delayed as long as possible to minimize the exit cost. Where the union has access to plant performance data, management may well take actions to prolong the life of the plant to avoid the exit. This again could serve to lower the likelihood of closure.

Finally, since we are looking at the United Kingdom, there is the overlay of antiunion legislation. In a general sense, the implied attenuation of union bargaining power—widely suggested by the British literature—might be expected to have reduced any effects of unions on plant closings. In short, we would expect a replay of Machin's (1995) results for 1984–1990, only more so. On the other hand, the weakened status of unions may have made plant closing easier, as unions had fewer political and economics resources with which to oppose them. Manning (1993) has argued that one element of the union reforms in Britain—specifically the 1984 requirement for prestrike ballots—may have led to a union loss of influence over employment (if not necessarily over wages on the grounds that wages, unlike closings, affect all workers equally) and to more plant closings. The argument is straightforward: In multiplant enterprises, unions were once able to keep open unprofitable plants by threatening to strike profitable ones. The need to ballot members destroyed the credibility of this mechanism because workers whose jobs are not in jeopardy would not vote for a strike. On this reasoning, there were too few plant closings in the 1970s and 1980s.

4. Data

The main data used in this study are taken from the British 1990 Workplace Employee Relations Survey (WERS) and from a trawl survey that served as a first step in the construction of the separate panel component of the 1998 WERS (see Millward, Bryson, and Forth 2000). The WERS is a long-standing government-funded establishment survey geared to mapping out the changes in industrial relations practice in Britain. The 1990 WERS was the third such inquiry in a series of surveys initiated in 1980. It covers a total of 2061 establishments (plants) with 25 or more employees in England, Scotland, and Wales. Establishment size–related weights are also provided for the data, so that the sample can be made nationally representative after weighting.

The trawl of the 1990 WERS establishments was conducted for the purpose of selecting a sample for a panel survey alongside the current 1998 WERS. It identifies the ongoing status of the 1990 establishments. The trawl confirms that of the 2061 establishments, 222 had closed by 1997–1998, while 1803 remained in operation[5] and 36 were no longer traceable. Accordingly, our initial usable sample comprises 2025 establishments including the 222 failures. For the purposes of the present inquiry, we necessarily focus on for-profit organizations. This private sector restriction reduces the sample to some 1,326 establishment observations, of which 179 had closed by 1998.

Our dependent variable is a dummy variable that takes the value of one if the establishment closed between the two survey dates. The covariates in our probit regressions are constructed from the 1990 WERS. Chief among these are our two union variables: union recognition and union coverage. The former measure is a dummy variable indicating whether the establishment had a written agreement recognizing unions (either manual or nonmanual) for purposes of negotiating pay and conditions of employment. The latter measure is a continuous variable indicating the percentage of

---

[5] Our definition of survivors includes those establishments whose size had fallen below 25, who had been subject to change in ownership, and whose address had been changed.

employees covered by the collective bargaining agreement. We prefer these constructs to the conventional union density measure—namely, the share of the workforce belonging to unions, also available in the WERS—as we believe that they more closely reflect union influence within an establishment. (As a practical matter, however, the results reported here were closely consistent across all three union measures. Results for the union density measure are available from the authors on request.)

We also assembled a number of other independent variables to control for establishment heterogeneity. These include—in addition to establishment type (a single independent establishment versus one that is part of a multiestablishment firm), size, age, and workforce composition—a wide variety of other variables designed to capture industrial relations factors (such as representative participation, financial participation and disclosure, employee involvement schemes, and the climate of industrial relations more generally), workplace flexibility, technology, ownership, and competitive position. Further, given the standard problem of union endogeneity, we include a much more detailed set of industry dummies than are usually deployed in studies of this nature. (We will also report the results of Durbin-Wu-Hausman tests for the influence of endogeneity.) Because detailed industry dummies are not provided as a matter of course with the WERS, we had to contact the data archive for the four-digit industry affiliation for each establishment. At the most detailed level, we employ a total of 93 industry dummies. Definitions of all the variables used and their means/standard deviations are provided in Table 1.

Finally, two limitations of the WERS should be noted. First, in respect of the outcome indicator, we do not know the date of the closure event. We know only that the establishment ceased trading sometime between the 1990 and 1998 surveys, so that in the limit we may be relating closures to arguments measured up to eight years earlier. Second, although we can distinguish between single independent establishments (i.e., firms) and establishments that are part of multiplant firms, among the latter group we cannot identify establishments belonging to the same entity. Not being able to link up establishments in the same firm limits the force of the distinction we seek to draw between the two types of establishment.

5. Estimation

Our estimation strategy builds up an increasingly complete set of controls to examine whether a robust association between unions and plant closure can be identified. Columns 1 and 2 of Table 2 provide results for a parsimonious specification in which the probability of plant closure depends on unionism and a narrow set of firm characteristics. Consistent with Machin (1995, table A1), single independent establishments and larger establishments are less likely to close than their multiestablishment and smaller counterparts. But the workforce composition variables are of opposing sign. The main result, however, is that union recognition and greater union coverage are each associated with a higher probability of closure. Note that the estimations do hold constant the broad industry affiliation of each plant.

Given the parsimonious set of controls deployed thus far, the union variables may of course be capturing other aspects of the establishments that correlate with the closure probability. To examine this possibility, columns 3 and 4 of Table 2 augment the previous specification with a very wide range of additional potential determinants while retaining the broad industry dummies. Perhaps surprisingly, the additional arguments generally do not take statistically significant coefficients, although it now appears that plants with larger shares of manual workers are more likely to close, while the previous results pertaining to establishment size and female composition are much attenuated. Despite the

Table 1. Descriptive Statistics of the Main Variables ($n = 1326$ for Variables without Missing Values)

Variable	Mean	Standard Deviation	Definition
Closed	0.154	0.361	Dummy = 1 if the establishment closed by 1997–1998
Union recognition	0.312	0.463	Dummy = 1 if union recognized for collective bargaining purposes
Union coverage	27.700	39.858	Percentage of employees covered by a collective agreement
Establishment size	4.132	0.753	Log establishment size
Establishment age	15.598	9.129	Number of years operating at current address
Single independent establishment	0.272	0.445	Dummy = 1 if single establishment firm
Percentage female	37.138	28.808	Percentage of female workers
Percentage manual	54.139	33.694	Percentage of manual workers
Percentage professional-technical	13.458	20.626	Percentage of professional/technical workers
Percentage part time	16.638	23.373	Percentage of part-time workers
Shift work	0.344	0.475	Dummy = 1 if shift work practiced
Percentage short term	0.086	0.280	Percentage of short-term contract workers
JCC	0.206	0.405	Dummy = 1 if joint consultative committee present
New EI schemes	0.425	0.494	Dummy = 1 if new employee involvement schemes introduced during the past three years
Financial disclosure	0.569	0.495	Dummy = 1 if financial information disclosed to workers
Climate	0.927	0.260	Dummy = 1 if industrial relations climate good/very good
ESOP	10.507	23.777	Percentage of workers covered by share-ownership schemes
Layoffs	0.141	0.348	Dummy = 1 if compulsory redundancies invoked in preceding year
Computer technology	0.061	0.239	Dummy = 1 if automated handling, storage, and centralized machine control
Technological change	0.438	0.496	Dummy = 1 if new plant/technology affecting jobs introduced during preceding three years
Takeover	0.144	0.351	Dummy = 1 if ownership change due to takeover during the past three years
Flexibility	0.360	0.480	Dummy = 1 if management implemented changes to reduce job demarcation or increase the flexibility of work

Table 1. Continued

Variable	Mean	Standard Deviation	Definition
Market power	0.267	0.443	Dummy = 1 if firm dominates product market or has few competitors
Foreign	0.074	0.262	Dummy = 1 if foreign ownership
Export	0.079	0.270	Dummy = 1 if establishment produces primarily for the export product
Unemployment	6.665	1.804	Regional unemployment rate (13 regions)
Manufacturing	0.292	0.455	Dummy = 1 for manufacturing sector
Financial performance	1.505	0.604	Index of financial performance relative to establishments in the same industry, where 0 = below average, 1 = about average, and 2 = above average
Capacity utilization	0.068	0.252	Dummy = 1 if capacity utilization is "considerably below average"

addition of the many—and possibly collinear—new controls, the results for the union variables remain largely unchanged. If anything, the finding for union recognition is now slightly stronger than before, increasing in both magnitude and level of statistical significance. In short, the prior finding that union establishments were more likely to close in the 1990s in Britain persists.

We next further augment our estimations to include as detailed a set of industry dummies as makes sense given the size of our sample. In most cases this is the relevant four-digit disaggregate dummy, but for the smallest sample sizes it is the slightly more aggregate three-digit dummy. The outcome is an estimation that includes 93 industry dummies as well as the two dozen controls. This is our first-pass procedure for dealing with problems stemming from the nonrepresentative distribution of union coverage and recognition across sectors and the possibility that unionized/more highly organized sectors are contracting for reasons independent of union influence. The estimations including the detailed industry dummies are contained in Table 3. It can be seen that larger plants and those with larger percentages of female employees continue to be less likely to fail. Establishments subject to a takeover appear more likely to close. Those with higher percentages of short-term contracts are also more likely to close, perhaps because such contracts indicate hard times at the plant. The addition of more detailed industry dummies adds to the explanatory power of the estimates as measured by the pseudo-R^2-statistic. The positive association between unions and plant closures is now stronger than before.

Despite the long list of controls and the very detailed industry dummies in Table 3, union endogeneity may still be a cause for concern. If unionization is endogenous, perhaps because plants more likely to close are more likely to become organized, the estimates of its influence are inconsistent. The resulting bias in the standard errors could erroneously indict unionization as a statistically significant determinant of closings. To test this possibility, we performed Durbin-Wu-Hausman tests for the influence of endogeniety (Davidson and MacKinnon 1993, pp. 237–42). These are augmented regression tests designed to determine whether a critical variable of interest (unionization in our case) should be replaced by an instrumented variable.

As an initial step, we identified a series of variables available to us in the WERS that are

832   *Addison, Heywood, and Wei*

Table 2. Probit Regressions with One-Digit Industry Dummies (Dependent Variable: Dummy = 1 if Establishment Closed by 1997–1998)

Variable	Specification			
	1	2	3	4
Constant	0.128	0.151	−0.269	−0.237
	(0.356)	(0.421)	(0.535)	(0.469)
Union recognition	0.187*		0.234**	
	(1.771)		(2.056)	
Union coverage		0.003**		0.003**
		(2.336)		(2.555)
Establishment size	−0.179**	−0.185**	−0.109	−0.113
	(2.730)	(2.813)	(1.424)	(1.475)
Establishment age	0.5E − 03	−0.001	0.001	0.4E − 04
	(0.011)	(0.162)	(0.125)	(0.008)
Single independent establishment	−0.341**	−0.333**	−0.232*	−0.230*
	(3.023)	(2.970)	(1.933)	(1.922)
Percentage female	−0.004**	−0.004**	−0.003	−0.002
	(2.305)	(2.170)	(1.214)	(1.080)
Percentage manual	0.002	0.002	0.005*	0.005*
	(1.709)	(0.963)	(1.910)	(1.829)
Percentage professional-technical			0.005	0.005
			(1.433)	(1.408)
Percentage part time			−0.005	−0.004
			(1.601)	(1.546)
Shift work			−0.130	−0.149
			(1.190)	(1.354)
Percentage short term			0.175	0.171
			(1.132)	(1.101)
JCC			−0.012	0.2E − 04
			(0.097)	(0.002)
New EI schemes			−0.061	−0.067
			(0.605)	(0.669)
Financial disclosure			0.021	0.013
			(0.198)	(0.848)
Climate			−0.112	−0.108
			(0.666)	(0.642)
ESOP			0.001	0.001
			(0.604)	(0.597)
Layoffs			0.084	0.107
			(0.667)	(0.848)
Computer technology			−0.128	−0.111
			(0.632)	(0.547)
Technological change			−0.049	−0.034
			(0.460)	(0.322)
Takeover			0.202	0.203
			(1.622)	(1.622)
Flexibility			0.028	0.010
			(0.280)	(0.101)
Market power			−0.023	−0.012
			(0.222)	(0.111)

Table 2. Continued

Variable	Specification			
	1	2	3	4
Foreign			−0.073	−0.048
			(0.402)	(0.264)
Export			−0.219	−0.197
			(1.184)	(1.062)
Unemployment			−0.017	−0.020
			(0.649)	(0.799)
Nine one-digit industry dummies	Included	Included	Included	Included
n	1289	1285	1274	1270
Pseudo-R^2	0.061	0.064	0.073	0.076
Log likelihood	−522.1	−518.8	−505.2	−501.9

t-statistics in parentheses.
** and * denote statistical significance at the .05 and .10 levels, respectively.

correlated with unionization but not with establishment closure. We relied on two theoretical conjectures. The first is that unionization is associated with greater industrial jurisprudence, such as formal procedures and due process. The four dummy variables in the WERS illustrative of this tendency identified whether the establishment had formal procedures for determining pay and conditions, discipline and dismissals, individual grievances, and health and safety issues. The second conjecture is that unions are a response to regimented work and that unions, in response to such regimentation, limit the ability of mangers to organize work (Duncan and Stafford 1980). Three variables captured these dimensions: whether work was organized around shifts, whether management was able to organize work as it wished, and whether the establishment used any "freelancers, home workers, or outworkers." None of these seven variables was individually significant when entered as additional arguments in the specifications contained in the first two columns of Table 3. Moreover, they were jointly insignificant as well: $\chi^2(7) = 7.17$ and $\chi^2(7) = 6.85$.

Next, the two union variables were separately regressed on the exogenous variables from the original specification plus the previously mentioned seven variables. Five of the seven variables in the first estimation and four of seven variables in the second estimation were statistically significant, and all seven were jointly significant in both estimations. The predicted values of unionization from these equations form the potential instrument to be added to an augmented equation.[6] The augmented equations are exactly those in the first two columns of Table 3 with the addition of the predicted values, and the test for the consistency of the original estimates of the influence of unionization is a test of significance on the predicted values. In each case, the coefficients on the predicted values fell very far from statistical significance, with *t*-statistics well below 1.0. This result allows us to reject the hypothesis that endogeneity is generating inconsistent estimates and validates our continued use of the two actual measures of unionization.[7]

Returning therefore to the point estimates of the union effect in Table 3, we can argue that the magnitudes in question are of economic as well as statistical significance. For example, using the result for union recognition alone (i.e., from the first column of the table), the projected probabilities of closure by establishment size are as follows:

---

[6] Note that an identical alternative is to add the residuals from the union equation to the augmented equation (see Davidson and MacKinnon 1993, p. 239).
[7] In the augmented regressions, actual coverage remained statistically significant, while collinearity with the potential instrument led actual union recognition to drop just below significance.

834   *Addison, Heywood, and Wei*

Table 3. Probit Regressions with Three-Digit Industry Dummies (Dependent Variable: Dummy = 1 if Establishment Closed by 1997–1998)

Variable	Specification	
	1	2
Constant	0.377	0.151
	(0.350)	(0.421)
Union recognition	0.304**	
	(2.044)	
Union coverage		0.005**
		(2.701)
Establishment size	−0.153*	−0.162*
	(1.649)	(1.729)
Establishment age	0.002	−0.001
	(0.371)	(0.177)
Single independent establishment	−0.203	−0.184
	(1.399)	(1.268)
Percentage female	−0.009**	−0.009**
	(3.115)	(2.940)
Percentage manual	$-0.6E-04$	$-0.4E-03$
	(0.017)	(0.141)
Percentage professional-technical	0.001	0.001
	(0.287)	(0.241)
Percentage part time	0.006	0.006
	(1.335)	(1.378)
Shift work	−0.047	−0.081
	(0.325)	(0.560)
Percentage short term	0.396**	0.387*
	(2.007)	(1.951)
JCC	0.073	0.073
	(0.480)	(0.476)
New EI schemes	0.025	0.024
	(0.198)	(0.192)
Financial disclosure	−0.021	−0.034
	(0.163)	(0.260)
Climate	−0.232	−0.236
	(1.198)	(1.217)
ESOP	0.003	0.003
	(1.179)	(1.234)
Layoffs	0.086	0.113
	(0.549)	(0.720)
Computer technology	0.029	0.040
	(0.119)	(0.163)
Technological change	−0.039	−0.026
	(0.305)	(0.208)
Takeover	0.258*	0.271*
	(1.660)	(1.733)
Flexibility	0.068	0.047
	(0.543)	(0.368)
Market power	−0.116	−0.083
	(0.898)	(0.641)
Foreign	−0.367	−0.328
	(1.499)	(1.357)

Table 3. Continued

Variable	Specification	
	1	2
Export	−0.240	−0.234
	(1.083)	(1.051)
Unemployment	−0.051	−0.059*
	(1.628)	(1.866)
93 three (four)-digit industry dummies	Included	Included
n	1211	1207
Pseudo-R^2	0.227	0.232
Log likelihood	−418.148	−414.298

t-statistics in parentheses.
** and * denote significance at the .05 and .10 levels, respectively.

	union recognition	no union recognition
small plants	.230	.159
large plants	.174	.107

In these calculations, small (large) plant size is defined as a value of one standard deviation below (above) the mean size, and all explanatory variables other than establishment size and union recognition are set at their sample means. As shown, in the case of small plants the increase in the probability of closure associated with union recognition for collective bargaining purposes is .071, almost a 50% increase. For large plants, the increase is smaller (.067), but this translates into a 65% rise in the probability of closure because of the reduced exposure of larger establishments to failure.

Picking up on our earlier evidence and that of Machin (1995) that single independent establishments may be less likely to close than establishments that are part of multiestablishment firms, Table 4 presents results for the two types of plant.[8] The results in the second column of the table, pertaining to multiestablishments, yield the familiar result that larger establishments are less likely to fail. Other findings for this sample are that plants with larger shares of part-time workers (perhaps proxying greater flexibility) are also less likely to close, while the incidence of short-time work and being involved in a takeover presage a higher likelihood of closure. Again note that despite the reduced degrees of freedom associated with use of a subsample, the union recognition coefficient estimate is larger than before and remains highly statistically significant.

This evidence contrasts with that provided for the (admittedly much smaller) sample of single independent establishments (i.e., firms) in the first column of Table 4. Here, for example, the presence of a joint consultative committee and compulsory redundancies are associated with an increased probability of closing and conversely for exposure to foreign trade. Interestingly, the by now familiar effects of unions and of plant size both vanish.

We also estimated a fully stacked model in which each control was interacted with a dummy variable identifying establishment type (see the final column of Table 4). This procedure allows us to reject the hypothesis that the estimates in the first two columns of Table 4 are identical (LR χ^2 [31] = 44.74). Moreover, it confirms that the effects of each of the variables identified in our brief discussion of the first two columns of the table are indeed significantly different as between the two types of establishment. The most important finding here is of course the large and well-determined difference in the effect of union recognition in the two samples. Note that this result is independent of the union

[8] The division of the sample into two categories makes it impossible to retain the full set of disaggregated industry dummies.

Table 4. Probit Regressions for Single Independent versus "Multiestablishments" (Dependent Variable: Dummy = 1 if Establishment Closed by 1997–1998)

Variable	Single Independent Establishment	Multiple Establishment	Difference
Constant	−2.626	−.0732	
	(1.394)	(0.138)	
Union recognition	−.7000	.3633**	−1.063**
	(1.241)	(3.040)	(2.429)
Establishment size	.2788	−.1686**	.4474**
	(0.988)	(2.079)	(1.988)
Establishment age	.0064	−.0020	.0084
	(0.365)	(0.346)	(0.582)
Percentage female	−.0008	−.0016	−.0024
	(0.534)	(0.677)	(0.444)
Percentage manual	−.0009	.0062**	−.0071
	(0.087)	(2.348)	(0.910)
Percentage professional-technical	.0067	.0058*	.0009
	(0.365)	(1.736)	(0.059)
Percentage part time	.0002	−.0073**	.0075
	(0.019)	(2.292)	(0.876)
Shift work	.3169	−.1914	.5084*
	(0.836)	(1.605)	(1.664)
Percentage short term	−.4049	.4034**	−.8083*
	(0.713)	(2.426)	(1.764)
JCC	.8812*	−.1676	1.048**
	(1.946)	(1.214)	(2.853)
New EI schemes	.2084	−.1563	.4366
	(0.817)	(1.419)	(1.553)
Financial disclosure	−.4105	.0985	−.5090*
	(1.164)	(0.866)	(1.762)
Climate	.1228	−.1126	.2353
	(0.152)	(0.690)	(0.376)
ESOP	−.0434	.0021	−.0454
	(0.361)	(1.012)	(0.510)
Layoffs	.8605**	−.0614	.9218**
	(2.308)	(0.426)	(2.904)
Computer technology	−2.313	.0941	−2.404
	(0.849)	(0.467)	(1.184)
Technological change	−.0650	−.0999	−.0349
	(0.186)	(0.873)	(0.122)
Takeover	−1.335	.2301*	−1.565*
	(1.215)	(1.874)	(1.895)
Flexibility	−.0194	.0898	−.1092
	(0.052)	(0.842)	(0.363)
Market power	.0597	.0324	.0273
	(0.172)	(0.279)	(0.095)
Foreign	−.1002	−.1834	.0632
	(0.113)	(1.002)	(0.123)
Export	−1.004*	−.0902	−.9103*
	(1.638)	(0.433)	(1.779)
Unemployment	.0036	−.0243	.0279
	(0.043)	(0.884)	(0.402)

Table 4. Continued

Variable	Single Independent Establishment	Multiple Establishment	Difference
Nine one-digit industry dummies	Included	Included	
n	189	1074	
Pseudo-R^2	.1604	.1022	
Log likelihood	−60.5	−431.2	

t-statistics in parentheses.
** and * denote significance at the .05 and .10 levels, respectively.

variable we employ. In otherwise identical estimates that substitute union coverage for union recognition, we obtain a union coefficient of −.0034 (0.669) for single independent establishments and of .0052 (3.493) for establishments that are part of multiestablishment firms.

As a final exercise, we replicated the basic specification used by Machin (1995) in examining data from the earlier workplace surveys with a view to establishing whether the specific variables he used in some way account for the profound differences in the British results through time. We note that his specification results in a drastic reduction in sample size due to missing data on two variables, namely, below-average financial performance and operating well below full capacity. Moreover, because of changes in the workplace survey, we can obtain a measure of the latter variable only for plants that are part of multiestablishment entities, leading to a further reduction in sample size.[9]

The first column of Table 5 presents results for a parsimonious specification that mimics that deployed by Machin (1995, table A1, col. 3) in containing the two new variables and replacing the broad industry controls with a single manufacturing-sector dummy variable. Two principal results emerge. First, establishments reporting superior financial performance emerge as less likely to close. Second, establishments recording considerable excess capacity are more likely to close. (Both results are also reported by Machin, although only the latter is statistically significant.) Third, and again most important, those establishments with union recognition remain significantly more likely to close with an estimated coefficient that is even larger than those already presented. Augmenting the explanatory variables and adding in the aggregate industry dummies (see the second and third columns of the table) does not materially alter any of these conclusions. The only new result that emerges within this reduced sample of multiestablishment plants is that rising levels of employee share ownership are now associated with a reduced likelihood of plant closure.

6. Interpretation

We have reported that British unions were associated with an increased probability of plant closings over the 1990s. This finding is sharply at odds with prior research results for the United Kingdom and, less directly, for the United States. Moreover, the association is of considerable economic magnitude and is independent of which measure of unionism we employ and which treatment of industry effects we follow.

This central result is, however, driven by plants that are part of multiestablishment entities. Within single independent establishments, no such effect is discernible. We earlier argued that a union

---

[9] The only difference in the two specifications is that our measure of financial performance is an index rather than the more parsimonious category of below-average financial performance used by Machin. When we replaced the index with the latter measure, the coefficient estimate for financial performance was statistically insignificant (as for Machin), but the union results were largely unaffected.

Table 5. Probit Regressions for "Multiestablishments" (Dependent Variable: Dummy = 1 if Establishment Closed by 1997–1998)

Variable	Specification		
	Parsimonious	Augmented	Full
Constant	−.2131	.3547	.5375
	(0.432)	(0.443)	(0.531)
Union recognition	.4776**	.3565*	.4707**
	(3.053)	(1.925)	(2.312)
Establishment size	−.1128	−.0815	−.1364
	(1.006)	(0.584)	(0.934)
Establishment age	−.0038	−.0087	−.0083
	(0.468)	(0.923)	(0.878)
Percentage female		−.0014	−.0007
		(0.371)	(0.163)
Percentage manual	−.0024	.0081*	.0073
	(1.041)	(1.895)	(1.529)
Percentage professional-technical		.0037	.0038
		(0.618)	(0.616)
Percentage part time		−.0173**	−.0173**
		(3.227)	(3.037)
Shift work		−.1655	.1536
		(0.844)	(0.769)
Percentage short term		.0794	−.0669
		(0.263)	(0.215)
JCC		−.2980	−.2331
		(1.325)	(1.006)
New EI schemes		−.0936	.0991
		(0.529)	(0.534)
Financial disclosure		−.0114	−.0654
		(0.062)	(0.339)
Climate		−.0425	.0493
		(0.149)	(0.162)
ESOP		−.0093**	−.0100**
		(2.546)	(2.615)
Layoffs		−.3484	−.3110
		(1.384)	(1.221)
Computer technology		−.0115	.3652
		(1.011)	(1.123)
Technological change		−.1292	−.1544
		(0.691)	(0.785)
Takeover		.0241*	−.0418
		(0.130)	(0.210)
Flexibility		0.1138	.1490
		(0.643)	(0.816)
Market power		−.1096	−.1579
		(0.628)	(0.860)
Foreign		−.1001	−.0881
		(0.388)	(0.331)
Export		.1142	−.0861
		(0.400)	(0.289)
Unemployment		−.0279	−.0464
		(0.678)	(1.060)

Table 5. Continued

	Specification		
Variable	Parsimonious	Augmented	Full
Manufacturing	−.0413	−.2496	−.2003
	(0.081)	(1.145)	(1.038)
Financial performance	−.4013**	−.5192**	−.5987**
	(3.402)	(3.990)	(4.274)
Capacity utilization	.7215**	.7293**	.7630**
	(2.964)	(2.729)	(2.788)
Nine one-digit industry dummies	Not included	Not included	Included
n	458	451	451
Pseudo-R^2	.0854	.1685	.1913
Log likelihood	−200.6	−181.5	−178.1

t-statistics in parentheses.
** and * denote significance at the .05 and .10 levels, respectively.

effect differentiated by type of establishment is *prima facie* consistent with several strands of the theory, reflecting game-theoretic considerations, insider-outsider distinctions, and incomplete information. But in line with piecemeal theoretical developments within this area, our arguments were ultimately informal and speculative. Nevertheless, the unions-cause-plant-closings hypothesis minimally requires some reformulation in the light of our results for single independent establishments, especially if they are sustained in future empirical work.

There is of course the possibility that our results are very sensitive to the particular circumstances of time and place. We have noted that our sample period was preceded by a major legislative attack on union bargaining power. As is well known, between 1980 and 1990, five major pieces of union reform legislation were enacted by successive Conservative administrations. At one level, the attack on union immunities might have been expected to curb union rent-seeking activity and mute any deleterious union effects on plant closings. Accordingly, we would expect Machin's results to carry over to the decade of the 1990s, which they clearly fail to do. But at another level, certain other aspects of the legislation may have operated in opposite fashion. First, the requirement for strike ballots may have led to a loss in union influence over employment in multiestablishment firms for the reasons identified by Manning (1993) and discussed earlier. Second, the weakening in union bargaining power implied by the legislation might have emboldened employers to close unionized establishments and either open new plants that unions have largely failed to organize or to expand their nonunion operations in double-breasted situations. Unfortunately, the WERS does not allow us to link establishments in the same firm, thereby precluding direct examination of these issues. Nonetheless, we think it entirely possible that the difference in results for Britain between Machin and ourselves has something to do with the sea change in the legislative framework confronting unionism in the past decade. The passage of New Labour's Employment Relations Act in 1998 (see Addison and Siebert, in press) marks another policy shift—this time in favor of unions—and provides a tantalizing opportunity to revisit the issue with further iterations of the WERS even if more fundamental progress perforce awaits better data sets and better theory.

References

Addison, John T., and Clive R. Belfield. 2001. Updating the determinants of firm performance: Estimation using the 1998 Workplace Employee Relations Survey. *British Journal of Industrial Relations* 39:341–66.
Addison, John T., and Clive R. Belfield. 2002. Unions and establishment performance: Evidence from the British Workplace/ Employee Relations Surveys. IZA Discussion Paper No. 455.

840   *Addison, Heywood, and Wei*

Addison, John T., and John B. Chilton. 1998. Self-enforcing union contracts: Efficient investment and employment. *Journal of Business* 71:349–69.

Addison, John T., and Barry T. Hirsch. 1989. Union effects on productivity, profits, and growth: Has the long run arrived? *Journal of Labor Economics* 7:72–105.

Addison, John T., and W. Stanley Siebert. 2003. Recent changes in the industrial relations framework in the U.K. In *International handbook of trade unions,* edited by John T. Addison and Claus Schnabel. Cheltenham, UK: Edward Elgar. In press.

Becker, Brian E., and Craig A. Olson. 1992. Unionization and firm profits. *Industrial Relations* 31:395–415.

Blanchflower, David G., Neil Millward, and Andrew J. Oswald. 1991. Unionism and employment behaviour. *Economic Journal* 101:815–34.

Booth, Alison L., and Andrew McCulloch. 1999. Redundancy pay, unions and employment. *Manchester School* 67:346–66.

Bronars, Stephen G., Donald R. Deere, and Joseph S. Tracy. 1994. The effects of unions on firm behavior: An empirical analysis using firm-level data. *Industrial Relations* 33:426–51.

Curme, Michael, and Lawrence M. Kahn. 1990. The impact of the threat of bankruptcy on the structure of compensation. *Journal of Labor Economics* 8:419–47.

Davidson, Russell, and James G. MacKinnon. 1993. *Estimation and inference in econometrics.* New York: Oxford University Press.

Denny, Kevin, and Stephen J. Nickell. 1992. Unions and investment in British industry. *Economic Journal* 102:874–87.

DiNardo, John, and David S. Lee. 2002. The impact of unionization on establishment closure: A regression discontinuity analysis of representation elections. NBER Working Paper No. 8993.

Duncan, Greg, and Frank Stafford. 1980. Do union members receive compensating wage differentials? *American Economic Review* 70:355–71.

Dunne, Timothy, and David A. Macpherson. 1994. Unionism and gross employment flows. *Southern Economic Journal* 60: 727–38.

Fallick, Bruce C., and Kevin Hasset. 1999. Investment and union certification. *Journal of Labor Economics* 17:570–82.

Fernie, Sue, and David Metcalf. 1995. Participation, contingent pay, representation and workplace performance: Evidence from Great Britain. *British Journal of Industrial Relations* 33:379–415.

Freeman, Richard B., and Morris M. Kleiner. 1999. Do unions make enterprises insolvent? *Industrial and Labor Relations Review* 52:510–27.

Gerhart, Paul. 1987. *Saving plants and jobs: Union-management negotiations in the context of threatened plant closing.* Kalamazoo, MI: W. E. Upjohn Institute for Employment Research.

Gregg, Paul, Stephen Machin, and David Metcalf. 1993. Signals and cycles? Productivity growth and changes in union status in British companies, 1984–9. *Economic Journal* 103:894–907.

Grout, Paul A. 1984. Investment and wages in the absence of binding contracts: A Nash bargaining approach. *Econometrica* 52:449–60.

Hirsch, Barry T. 1991. *Labor unions and the economic performance of firms.* Kalamazoo, MI: W. E. Upjohn Institute for Employment Research.

Hirsch, Barry T. 1992. Firm investment behavior and collective bargaining strategy. *Industrial Relations* 31:95–121.

Kuhn, Peter. 1986. Wages, effort, and incentive compatibility in life-cycle employment contracts. *Journal of Labor Economics* 4:28–49.

Lazear, Edward P. 1983. A competitive theory of monopoly unionism. *American Economic Review* 71:606–20.

Lawrence, Colin, and Robert Z. Lawrence. 1985. Manufacturing wage dispersion: An end game interpretation. *Brookings Papers on Economic Activity* 1:47–106.

Leonard, Jonathan S. 1992. Unions and employment growth. *Industrial Relations* 31:80–94.

Linneman, Peter D., Michael L. Wachter, and William H. Carter. 1990. Evaluating the evidence on union wages and employment. *Industrial and Labor Relations Review* 44:34–53.

Los Angeles Times. 1987. Workers' spirits remain high as GM prepares to close Massachusetts plant. December 1, p. 29.

Machin, Stephen. 1995. Plant closures and unionization in British establishments. *British Journal of Industrial Relations* 33: 55–68.

Machin, Stephen, and Mark Stewart. 1996. Trade unions and financial performance. *Oxford Economic Papers* 48:213–41.

Manning, Alan. 1993. Pre-strike ballots and wage-employment bargaining. *Oxford Economic Papers* 45:422–9.

Menezes-Filho, Naercio, David Ulph, and John Van Reenen. 1998a. R&D and unionism: Comparative evidence from British companies and establishments. *Industrial and Labor Relations Review* 52:45–63.

Menezes-Filho, Naercio, David Ulph, and John Van Reenen. 1998b. The determination of R&D: Empirical evidence on the role of unions. *European Economic Review* 42:919–30.

Metcalf, David. 1993. Industrial relations and economic performance. *British Journal of Industrial Relations* 31:255–83.

Metcalf, David. 1994. Transformation of British industrial relations? Institutions, conduct, and outcomes. In *The U.K. labour market: Comparative aspects and institutional developments,* edited by Ray Barrell. Cambridge, UK: Cambridge University Press, pp. 126–57.

Metcalf, David. 2003. Unions and productivity, financial performance and investment: International evidence. In *International handbook of trade unions,* edited by John T. Addison and Claus Schnable. Cheltenham, UK: Edward Elgar. In press.

Millward, N., A. Bryson, and J. Forth. 2000. *All change at work? British employment relations 1980–98, as portrayed by the Workplace Industrial Relations Survey series.* London: Routledge.

Oulton, Nicholas. 1990. Labour productivity in U.K. manufacturing in the 1970s and 1980s. *National Institute Economic Review* 132:71–91.

[18]

WHEN UNIONS "MATTERED": THE IMPACT OF STRIKES ON FINANCIAL MARKETS, 1925–1937

JOHN DINARDO and KEVIN F. HALLOCK*

This examination of the Stock Market's responsiveness to strikes looks specifically at strike actions that labor historians generally view as the major ones occurring in the United States in the years 1925–37. The authors find that strikes had large, negative effects on industry stock value. Longer strikes, violent strikes, strikes in which unions "won," industry-wide strikes, strikes that led to union recognition, and strikes that led to large wage increases were associated with larger negative share price reactions than were other strikes. Much of the "news" generated by the typical strike seems to have been registered by the Stock Market very early in the strike. However, there were also some fairly large stock price reactions to news that could be fully revealed only at the end of a strike.

This paper is an examination of the impact of important strikes on industry stock returns at a time when unions were rapidly evolving. We focus on the economic consequences of strikes during the interwar period as reflected in the behavior of the stock market. Our point of departure is the identification of strikes that, in contrast with most present-day strikes, were primarily an attempt by workers to change the "terms of trade" between workers and their employers. Using standard event-study methods, we evaluate the effect of various important strike characteristics on broad industry-level measures of equity prices. While several studies (for example, Becker and Olson 1986; Neumann 1980; Kramer and Vasconcellos 1996; Persons 1995) have investigated the link between strikes and stock prices, they have focused on a much more recent period—one for which data are publicly available—and the strikes they have examined arguably had a much smaller impact on the structure of industrial relations than did the strikes in our sample.

*John Dinardo is Professor of Economics and Public Policy, University of Michigan, and Kevin F. Hallock is Associate Professor of Economics and of Labor and Industrial Relations, University of Illinois at Urbana-Champaign. The authors thank Orley Ashenfelter, Sherrilyn Billger, Dale Belman, Richard Block, Kevin Denny, Benjamin Gordon, Wallace Hendricks, Margaret Chaplan, Mark Moore, Larry Neal, Martin Wagner, and participants at the Ninth Bargaining Group Conference at Michigan State University for discussions and suggestions. Matthew Artz and Xiang Yi provided excellent research assistance. For financial support, the authors thank the Institute of Labor and Industrial Relations at the University of Illinois. They are also extremely grateful to Margaret Chaplan and Katie Dorsey from the Industrial Relations Library at the University of Illinois for their help in identifying and locating data.

Industrial and Labor Relations Review, Vol. 55, No. 2 (January 2002). © by Cornell University.
0019-7939/00/5502 $01.00

Given our focus on strikes, our paper is directly related to two literatures. In one (see Neumann and Reder 1984), the effect of strikes on industry-wide output is measured using industry-wide measures such as inventories and shipments. In another, the lost value associated with strikes is measured using data on market valuation (see, for example, Ruback and Zimmerman 1984). This literature is closely related to the "event study" literature in finance and has focused exclusively on using stock market returns from individual firms. At its most basic level, our approach is a combination of these two approaches. Like the firm-level studies, our study uses information from the capital markets; unlike that literature, but in common with the literature on the "industry-wide" effect of strikes, our study focuses on broadly defined industrial aggregates.

Our study, therefore, begins with the premise that the extent of union effects is potentially easier to detect when changes in unionization are large and important than when they are modest. Toward that end, we focus on the period between the two World Wars, an important time for the U.S. labor movement. After witnessing a prodigious and rapid increase in membership at the end of the nineteenth century, American unionism experienced a decline of almost equal magnitude in the period leading up to the first World War. The ferocity of business and government hostility to the attempt to organize American workers left little doubt about the importance of the struggle. As we will argue below, this period and the period leading up to World War II provide a unique time to investigate the impact of strikes on firms.

Analytical Framework

At first glance, it might be surprising to find any effect of strike activity on *industry-wide* stock prices. The first puzzle involves why strikes should have any effect on the returns of individual firms. In the context of an infinitely long-lived firm, and when strikes have no effect on the terms of trade, the change in the value of discounted earn-

ings streams would be quite small. Given the considerable evidence that the measured change in market values of firms resulting from strikes is not negligible (for example, Becker and Olson 1986; Neumann 1980; Ruback and Zimmerman 1984), however, we follow the earlier literature and assume that it is meaningful to investigate the presence of such an effect.

Once we turn our attention away from the single firm and consider the entire industry, we must consider the effect of union bargains on non—unionized firms or those not immediately party to the contract negotiations.[1] One's *a priori* view of the sign and magnitude of these indirect effects depends on the mechanism by which unions (in this historical context) raise wages. If a "successful" strike is one resulting in a one-time "permanent" change in the share of the surplus going to workers, the strike's effect on the value of the firm will be proportional to the change in profits going to the firm. The effect on industrial activity at large will be small to the extent that the strike's effects are limited exclusively to the struck firm and the firm's share of output is small.

To prepare the way for our empirical analysis, consider the extreme case in which wage bargains reached by unions accrue to all workers in an industry.[2] Again for simplicity, we assume a constant real rate of interest r. Before the strike, the industry faces a probability π of a one-time permanent change in firm value due to the union calling a strike and winning.[3] If we denote earnings in a given time period by D and the percentage change in the share going to the firm by $-\delta$, the value of the firm prior to the strike decision is

---

[1]See Lazear (1983) for some of the subtleties involved.

[2]The presentation could be made more realistic by considering a finite time horizon or the possibility of future union wins or losses, but this would merely complicate the expressions without contributing additional insight.

[3]$1 - \pi$, then, is the probability that the union does not call a strike or calls one and loses.

IMPACT OF STRIKES ON FINANCIAL MARKETS, 1925–1937   221

(1) $E[V_0] = \pi \int_0^{\infty} e^{-rt}D(1-\delta)\,dt +$
        $(1-\pi)\int_0^{\infty} e^{-rt}Ddt$

If the union strikes and wins, the value of the firm is merely

(2) $V_{\text{union strikes and wins}} = \int_0^{\infty} e^{-rt}D(1-\delta)\,dt$

The percentage change in the value of the firm (or log difference) when the union wins is then given by

(3)   Percent change in
            the value of the firm =

$\log(E[V_0]) - \log(V_{\text{union strikes and wins}})$

$= \log\left(\dfrac{1-\delta\pi}{1-\delta}\right)$

$\approx (1-\pi)\delta$

This expression has a simple interpretation. The percentage change in the value of the firm when the union strikes and wins an important fight is equal to the product of the probability that the union loses or does not strike at all $(1-\pi)$ and the fraction of earnings that flow away from shareholders toward workers (δ). If firms completely anticipated a union strike and victory ($\pi = 1$) and this information were already incorporated into the value of the firm, a strike would have no effect on excess returns.

The analysis is completely symmetric for the case in which the union does not strike or strikes and loses. In this case, the magnitude of the measured effect of union losses on stock prices will be largest when the probability firms attach to a union loss is small. The measured effect of a union loss on stock returns will be small whenever a union defeat is likely. Put differently, the revision to stock prices depends not only on the direct effect of the union loss (or other event) on the firm's "bottom line" (δ) but also on how surprising the event is (π).

We focus on the relationship between strikes and industry stock prices during the period between the World Wars because this is a time viewed as very important in labor history by labor historians and other informed observers. Nevertheless, it is in-

teresting to compare our results with those of studies using data from a much more recent time period. Several such studies are noteworthy. Becker and Olson (1986), in a comprehensive study of the impact of strikes on individual firm stock prices from 1962 to 1982, found that the average large strike was associated with a 4.1% decline in stock prices.[4] Persons (1995) found that the share price reaction to struck automobile producers and steel suppliers was around 1.6% on the days around the strike. Neumann (1980) found a share price reaction of about 0.5% on the day of an announced strike for a sample of firms struck in the late 1960s and mid-1970s.[5] Using Canadian data, Nelson et al. (1994) studied 124 strikes between January 1983 and July 1989 and found a loss in stock price of about 1% for the 5-day window around the strike.[6] Although each of these studies used a different time period, sample of strikes, and event window, they all suggest a negative share price reaction of between 1% and 4% around the start of the strike.

A goal of our work is to assess the impact of strikes on industry stock prices during the interwar period. As a practical matter, the most straightforward way to do so would be merely to examine industry stock returns before and after the strike and then attribute the entire stock price change to the effects of the strike. The problem with such a comparison is that it implicitly assumes that *had the strike not occurred*, industry returns after the strike ended would have been exactly equal to industry returns just before the strike—an assumption that is justifiable only in the improbable case that general economy-wide conditions were

---

[4]The Center for Research in Security Prices (CRSP) at the University of Chicago only published daily stock prices after 1962. All of the previous studies concentrated on years after this date.

[5]Neumann (1980) went on to suggest that the stock market seems to have predicted the occurrence of strikes quite well during this period.

[6]Also see Kramer and Vasconcellos (1996), Davidson et al. (1988), and Ruback and Zimmerman (1984) for related studies.

unchanging during the strike period. A more realistic analysis generates an assessment of the movement of stock prices that *would have occurred in the absence of the strike.* This *counterfactual* can then be compared to the actual behavior of stock prices to generate an estimate of the strike's effect.

One approach to making such a comparison, and the one we use in this paper, is often referred to as "the event study method." It has been widely used in industrial relations research, including, for example, Becker and Olson (1986) and Abowd, Milkovich, and Hannon (1990). As the technical aspects of the method we employ are carefully described in Brown and Warner (1985), Campbell, Lo, and MacKinlay (1997), Fama et al. (1969), and MacKinlay (1997), we will describe the basic ideas only briefly.

We begin by concentrating on the effect of a strike around the strike's start. Cumulative average excess returns are calculated using the simple method outlined below. Let t index time in trading months, let s indicate the "event month" (the month of the start of the strike), and let i indicate industries. First the industry monthly stock return, R_{it}, is regressed on R_{mt}, the average market return for month t, which we also collected from the Cowles (1938) data. This regression,

$$(5) \qquad R_{it} = \alpha_i + \beta_i R_{mt} + \eta_{it},$$

is estimated for a period[7] from month $s-24$ to month $s-12$. The coefficients from this regression, as well as the values of R_{mt} during the strike period, allow us to generate an estimate—$\hat{R}_{it}$—of what would have happened had the strike not occurred, where

$$(6) \qquad \hat{R}_{it} = \hat{\alpha}_i + \hat{\beta}_i R_{mt},$$

and where $\hat{\alpha}_i$ and $\hat{\beta}_i$ are OLS estimates of the parameters in equation (5) and $\hat{R}_{it}$ is merely the predicted return. Our reason for estimating this regression using data for

a period preceding the strike is to avoid potential contamination of our counterfactual by expectations of a strike.

With our estimates of the counterfactual in hand, the next step is to compute the following for each month around the event date:

$$(7) \qquad ER_{it} = R_{it} - \hat{R}_{it},$$

where ER_{it} (usually called the "excess return") for each industry i for each month t is merely the difference between the actual return R_{it} and the predicted return $\hat{R}_{it}$. In the absence of a strike, the average of ER_{it} should clearly equal zero.

The excess returns calculated for each month around the start of a strike are used to form the average excess returns for each strike. These are easily computed by averaging the monthly excess returns for each strike. We also compute "cumulative" excess returns by adding monthly excess returns for various intervals (called event "windows") around the date of the strike. Cumulative average excess returns are merely the average of these cumulative excess returns across all strikes.

The precise statistic used to assess whether average excess returns or cumulative excess returns are "statistically significant" are discussed in Campbell, Lo, and MacKinlay (1997). These tests proceed by observing, as noted previously, that average excess returns and cumulative average excess returns should be zero in the absence of "news" that permanently alters the value of the firm. The extent to which these returns differ from zero is evidence in support of the hypothesis that the events we have identified provided important news.

Another issue is the definition and timing of the event. In the typical event study, where excess returns over a period of a few *days* are being evaluated, defining the timing of the event is critically important and often very difficult. Researchers must be able to carefully identify when participants in capital markets first became aware of news. We are not as concerned with this issue, since our periods are measured in months. Other implications of the timing are discussed below.

---

[7]We tried other prediction periods with no meaningful effect on the results.

Historical Context

As mentioned in the introduction, the interwar period is a particularly interesting one for an investigation of this kind. The state policy vis-a-vis unionism was either nonexistent or hostile during most of the sample period. Moreover, it is clear that most participants firmly believed that the outcome of the battle between capital and labor was of great significance and the immediate stakes were enormous. For example, in the decades leading up to our sample period the Industrial Workers of the World began as "the last important national organization to challenge the philosophy of business unionism ... [but by the end of World War I had become] a tiny organization whose status as a labor union was questionable" (Rees 1977). Moreover, it is quite clear (particularly for years before 1934) that "unions existed in a predominantly non-institutionalized setting. Union recognition, collective bargaining and labor-management contractual agreements were not yet legal and, in fact, much of the conflict between labor and capital was over the right to organize" (Rubin 1986). At the same time, the government's attempts to avert strikes that might damage wartime production and other concerns led to the passage of the Clayton Act. The Clayton Act abolished the legal framework that had most limited union organizing—the principle that unions violated the Sherman Anti-Trust Act by acting as a "restraint on trade."[8] As a consequence, the interwar period was arguably the crucible that set the terms of trade under which unions would be tolerated by business and the government after World War II. As such, it is an ideal context in which to study the impact of strikes on stock prices.

In addition, unlike in the post–World War II period, the role of the state in providing income support (sometimes viewed as an "alternative" to unionism) was rather small. Moreover, the institutional features that were to mark postwar industrial relations, such as "pattern bargaining," were forged in part during this critical period. The formation of industrial relations schools reflected a perception that collective bargaining was a relatively permanent phenomenon. In contrast, during the interwar period the view of collective bargaining as "normal" or "inevitable" was not widespread. The absence of such a view was reflected in the nature of the strikes, which generally were driven by debates over fundamental aspects of workplace relations.

Data

The two main data sources for this paper are the information on the specific strikes and industry financial data. The first set of data come from Filippelli (1990), a history of significant strikes from the relevant time period. The stock price data are from a Yale University report (Cowles 1938). In each case, collecting the data required going through the sources by hand (or using scanning technology along with Optical Character Recognition [OCR] software).

We investigated a broad set of possible sources of data on strikes from this particularly important period in labor history, including, for example, Peterson (1938). However, only one that we were able to locate, Filippelli (1990), offered us the exact relevant dates associated with each strike, which are crucial to the event study method we employ. In *Labor Conflict in the United States: An Encyclopedia*, a host of contributors provide detailed accounts of various important strikes during the time period in question. Obviously, we only focus attention on a certain select set of strikes. Filippelli, the editor of the collection, examined a total of 254 strikes that occurred over a very long time period—the strikes "that appear in all standard labor histories," he claimed, and that represent, he hoped, "all of the conflicts that labor histo-

---

[8]In practice, of course, the Clayton Act was not a panacea for American trade unionism. Indeed, in the first 24 years after its passage, more cases of antitrust violations were brought against labor than in the 24 preceding years. See Fisher (1940).

rians have agreed are pivotal in American history" (p. xii). In part due to limitations of our financial market data, we examine only 36 strikes occurring over the time period we consider.

Importantly, this same source also provides us with a wealth of other valuable information about each strike that allows us to create another set of variables, including the duration of each strike, the industry involved in the strike, whether the union was recognized by the struck firm as a result of the strike, whether the union was new or established,[9] the number of strikers involved, whether there was violence during the strike, whether wages increased, decreased, or stayed the same after the strike, and who was the eventual "winner" of the strike (union or management).

Simple statistics for each of the strikes are contained in Table 1. Obviously, some of the data in this table, such as the strike's start date and the number of strikers involved, are based on purely "objective" criteria and are therefore easily culled from the strike narratives. Other data, such as whether the union or firm "won," are more subjective. We discuss these subjective measures below.

The first strike in our sample started in January 1925 and the last one started in May 1937.[10] The strikes occurred in 17 different industries. The average strike duration was 5.5 months. Violence was mentioned in the narratives in just over half of the strikes. Wages decreased in only a handful of cases, stayed the same in about half, and increased in just over a third of strikes. Following Card and Olson (1995),

we also attempted to identify the "winner" of each strike.[11]

To situate our sample in the universe of all strikes that occurred during this period, we present some information from Griffin (1939), who included a much larger set of strikes in his analysis of strikes from 1880 to 1937. Figure 1 (which was generated using data from the Griffin study) reveals that for the period 1925–37 (the period we analyze), the median annual percentage of strikes that were "successes" (from the perspective of the unions) was 35%; of "failures," 33.4%; and of compromises, 30.7%. Given the consistency with our estimates, we conclude that the strikes in our sample, apart from their greater "importance," are not radically different from the broader sample of strikes.

Our stock price data come from Cowles's *Common-Stock Indexes: 1871–1937* (1938). This book contains several series for common stocks by industry by month over a relatively long time period. One distinguishing characteristic of the book is the tremendous amount of effort and meticulous attention to detail that went into its description of the data and industries. Included are indexes on dividend payments, price-earnings ratios, earnings, stock prices, and stock prices including cash dividends. For each industry, we scanned in the stock prices, including cash dividends, for each month from 1906 to 1937 (although this paper examines strikes that occurred during the period 1925–37). Because of a four-month gap in the information during World War I, we are left with 380 months of data for each industry. Since we collected information on 69 industries, this gives us

---

[9]We define an "established" or "old" union by first identifying the name of the union from accounts in Filippelli (1990) and a variety of other sources (Gifford 1999; Reynolds and Killingsworth 1944; Fink 1977) to identify the date the union was established. Unions older than three years were defined as established. Our results are robust with respect to different definitions of "established."

[10]Later strikes are covered in the Filippelli (1990) volume, but our stock price data (described below) end at the conclusion of 1937.

[11]We identified the union as the winner in 53% of the strikes. Obviously it is not always easy to identify the "winner" of a strike. We determined the winner based on our subjective evaluation of the Filippelli narratives. In 10% of the cases, the winner of the strike is not clear (see Table 1). Our results are insensitive to our treatment of the ambiguous cases. Below, we further investigate the strikes that led to union recognition, often one of the key goals of the strikers.

IMPACT OF STRIKES ON FINANCIAL MARKETS, 1925–1937   225

Table 1. Sample Statistics for the Strikes.

Industry	Start Date of Strike	Strike Duration (months)	Number of Strikers	Violence during Strike?	Recognition Strike?	Wages Incr., Decr., or Same	Winner
Coal	Nov. 1925	5	500	No	No	Decreased	Unclear
	Apr. 1927	15	200,000	Yes	No	Same	Mgt.
	Apr. 1931	1	200	Yes	No	Same	Mgt.
	Jul. 1932	11	—	Yes	No	Decreased	Mgt.
	Aug. 1933	3	2,000	No	No	Same	Mgt.
Misc. Services	May 1934	3	3000	Yes	No	Increased	Union
	May 1935	3	20,000	Yes	No	Increased	Union
Shipping	May 1934	2	1,000	Yes	No	Increased	Union
	Jan. 1936	12	30,000	No	No	Increased	Unclear
Mining	May 1935	1	—	Yes	No	Same	Mgt.
Steel & Iron	May 1937	2	40,000	Yes	No	Same	Mgt.
Electrical Equipment	Feb. 1934	4	3,600	Yes	Yes	Increased	Union
Household Products	—	—	1,000	No	Yes	Decreased	Mgt.
Auto Tires, Rubber	June 1934	1	1,100	No	Yes	Increased	Union
	Jan. 1936	2	14,000	No	Yes	Same	Union
Food Products	Jan. 1930	0	5,000	Yes	No	Same	Mgt.
	Nov. 1932	2	400	Yes	No	Decreased	Mgt.
	May 1932	50	1,500	No	No	Same	Mgt.
	Jan. 1933	0	5,000	Yes	No	Same	Mgt.
	Sep. 1935	1	—	Yes	No	Increased	Union
	May 1936	—	35,000	Yes	No	Same	Mgt.
	May 1937	0	2,000	Yes	Yes	Same	Mgt.
Paper	Nov. 1934	4	36	No	No	Same	Union
	—	—	600	No	No	Same	Union
	Feb. 1936	9	36	No	No	Increased	Union
Textiles	Jan. 1925	23	16,000	Yes	Yes	Same	Union
	Apr. 1928	6	27,000	Yes	Yes	Decreased	Union
	Apr. 1929	5	1,000	Yes	No	Same	Mgt.
	July 1934	2	—	Yes	No	Same	Unclear
	Oct. 1936	5	3,700	No	No	Same	Mgt.
Tobacco	Nov. 1931	1	10,000	No	No	Same	Union
General Motors	Sep. 1933	2	5,000	No	No	Increased	Unclear
	Nov. 1936	—	—	No	No	—	—
	Dec. 1936	2	47,000	Yes	Yes	Same	Union
	—	—	7,600	No	Yes	Increased	Union
Autos, non-GM	Jan. 1933	1	12,000	No	No	Increased	Union
	—	—	24,000	No	No	Same	Union
	—	—	2,000	Yes	Yes	Same	Union
Meat Packing	Sep. 1933	—	—	Yes	Yes	Increased	Union
Radio, Phonograph	May 1936	2	6,000	Yes	Yes	Increased	Union
Air Transport	Feb. 1932	3	36	No	No	Increased	Union

Source: This information was gathered from narratives in Filippelli (1990).

26,220 industry/months of data.[12] It is also worth noting that we do not have complete

---

[12]The scanning technology, along with Optical Character Recognition (OCR) software, worked remarkably well. We hand-checked *each* observation and found that only about 4% were in error.

information on security prices for all industries for the entire time period. One example is absence of stock prices for automobiles and trucks, which, as of the late 19th century, had not yet been invented. Figure 2 displays the average stock price over time using these data. The dramatic

Figure 1. Fraction of Strikes in Which the Union Succeeded, Failed, or Accepted a Compromise, 1880–1937.

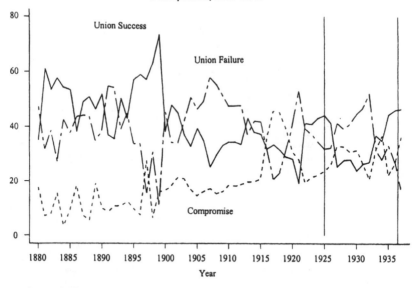

Source: Griffin (1939), Table XI.7.

increase up to the great crash of 1929 is clear from the figure, as is the subsequent increase.

Empirical Results

In many traditional financial event studies, it is transparent how one dates an "event." The same is not true for all strikes in our sample. In principle, the appropriate date is the date at which most of the "information" in the strike is incorporated. If the financial markets are forward-looking, and most of the information is revealed at the beginning of the strike, then the date of the strike announcement is most relevant. Table 2 presents our estimates of cumulative average excess industry stock returns for various windows relative to the strike announcement date. In Table 3, we concentrate on estimates of the cumulative average excess industry stock returns relative to the strike ending date.

We suspect that certain types of news provoke one reaction from financial mar-

kets at the start of the strike and a different one at the end.[13] Two examples may help explain this. The number of strikers is known at the start of the strike, so we expect this variable to affect prices at the start of the strike. Since this information is already known at the strike's beginning, no doubt it is already incorporated into stock prices by the end, and therefore has less of an effect at that juncture. On the other hand, we have also recorded information on whether wages went up, went down, or stayed the same. However, this is clearly only known for sure at the end of the strike (although markets may have an educated guess at the strike's onset as to what will happen to wages by strike's end) and, therefore, we expect a larger share price reaction to wage changes at the end of the strike. We will discuss share price changes around the start of the strike (Table 2),

---

[13]We are grateful to an anonymous referee for this suggestion.

around the end of the strike (Table 3), and including information from both the start and the end (Table 4).

Each column of Table 2 reports results based on a different event window: month 0 (simply the excess return during the strike start month, averaged over all strikes), month 0 to month +1 (the sum of the excess returns over the two-month period from the month of the strike announcement through the month after the announcement, averaged over all strikes), month −1 to month 0, month −1 to month +1, month −2 to month +2, and month −3 to month +3. In principle, results from all windows should be roughly the same. If the frequency of our stock price information were daily, we could date strike announcements perfectly, and if the transmission of "news" and the markets' reaction to it are both quick, we would expect the shortest window to be the most appropriate window. However, given the frequency of the stock data and our *a priori* expectations concerning the speed of transmission of economic news from strikes during the interwar period, our preferred results are those that use the windows from $t = -1$ to 1 month. For completeness, we also report results for other wider windows.

The first row of the table summarizes the information for all strikes. For example, the number −0.030 in the fourth column represents the cumulative average excess returns over the three months (−1, 0, and 1 relative to the strike start date) averaged over all strikes in the sample. This means that industry stock prices dropped by about 3% around the time of the start of the strike. The second pair of rows in the table compares union wins to union losses. That is, it repeats the same analysis but simply computes cumulative average excess returns separately for the sample of strikes that are defined as "won" or "lost" by the union (see below). Subsequent sets of rows report results contrasting "violent" strikes and nonviolent ones; strikes in which wages went up with strikes in which they went down or remained the same; strikes involving many strikers (more than the median of 3,700) with those involving few strikers; short strikes (lasting less than the median

Figure 2. Stock Prices over Time, 1925–1936.

Source: Industry averaged stock prices including cash dividends from Cowles (1938).

of 2 months) with longer ones; strikes that resulted in recognition of the union by the firm with those that did not; industry-wide strikes with strikes of less scope; and strikes by an established union (defined above) with other strikes.

The evidence from the table is generally consistent with the view that the financial markets viewed these strikes as important. If they had not, then excess share prices obviously would not have changed around the time of news about the strikes. In general, the results are economically significant and different from zero at conventional levels of statistical significance. For example, the point estimates in the row labeled "union win" indicate losses to the firm of about 7% for our preferred specification (month −1 to month +1) and are statistically different from zero. In contrast, union losses led to generally quite small stock price changes (−1%) that were not distinguishable from zero at conventional levels of significance. Note that given our earlier discussion, it is interesting that the share price reaction to a union win (which is not fully known until the strike is over) is reasonably large at the start of the strike. Perhaps financial markets could, to some degree, predict the outcome even at the start of the strike.[14]

_____

[14]We discuss what happens around the end of the strike below.

Table 2. Cumulative Average Abnormal Industry Stock Returns
for Strikes in the 1920s and 1930s, Where Event Is Defined as Start of Strike.
(T-Statistics in Parentheses)

	Months Relative to Strike Announcement Date					
	t = 0	*t = 0 to 1*	*t = -1 to 0*	*t = -1 to 1*	*t = -2 to 2*	*t = -3 to 3*
All Strikes	-0.011	-0.024	-0.017	-0.030	-0.013	-0.015
	(1.070)	(1.580)	(1.172)	(1.635)	(0.539)	(0.559)
Union Win	-0.020	-0.050	-0.038	-0.068	-0.038	-0.020
	(1.034)	(1.845)	(1.418)	(2.067)	(0.891)	(0.390)
Union Loss	-0.004	-0.004	-0.007	-0.008	0.007	-0.016
	(0.312)	(0.218)	(0.475)	(0.373)	(0.255)	(0.536)
Yes Violence	-0.019	-0.025	-0.033	-0.040	-0.049	-0.049
	(1.616)	(1.455)	(2.037)	(1.909)	(1.855)	(1.588)
No Violence	0.001	-0.021	0.008	-0.014	0.044	0.038
	(0.059)	(0.775)	(0.307)	(0.415)	(1.031)	(0.736)
Wages Down	0.037	0.092	0.032	0.087	0.128	0.095
	(1.916)	(2.096)	(1.159)	(1.814)	(2.264)	(1.478)
Wages Same	-0.014	-0.038	-0.027	-0.050	-0.052	-0.061
	(1.094)	(2.066)	(1.430)	(2.222)	(1.763)	(1.750)
Wages Up	-0.016	-0.031	-0.014	-0.029	0.016	0.040
	(0.804)	(1.085)	(0.473)	(0.807)	(0.344)	(0.732)
Many Strikers[a]	-0.013	-0.016	-0.005	-0.008	-0.015	-0.022
	(1.068)	(0.949)	(0.324)	(0.417)	(0.575)	(0.716)
Few Strikers	-0.012	-0.041	-0.026	-0.056	-0.005	0.008
	(0.674)	(1.636)	(1.037)	(1.792)	(0.123)	(0.160)
Short Strike[b]	-0.000	-0.004	-0.006	-0.010	0.047	0.045
	(0.001)	(0.172)	(0.268)	(0.352)	(1.242)	(1.009)
Long Strike	-0.019	-0.036	-0.024	-0.041	-0.048	-0.052
	(1.435)	(1.920)	(1.285)	(1.786)	(1.661)	(1.494)
Recognition	-0.037	-0.061	-0.041	-0.065	-0.088	-0.091
	(1.642)	(1.933)	(1.292)	(1.683)	(1.764)	(1.535)
Not Recognition	-0.001	-0.010	-0.008	-0.016	0.017	0.014
	(0.088)	(0.546)	(0.484)	(0.787)	(0.643)	(0.448)
Industry-Wide	-0.021	-0.040	-0.051	-0.070	-0.109	-0.125
	(0.650)	(0.871)	(1.125)	(1.254)	(1.515)	(1.461)
Not Industry-Wide	-0.010	-0.022	-0.014	-0.026	-0.004	-0.005
	(0.931)	(1.403)	(0.908)	(1.358)	(0.151)	(0.188)
New Union[c]	-0.002	-0.015	-0.008	-0.021	0.059	0.057
	(0.080)	(0.487)	(0.247)	(0.553)	(1.179)	(0.963)
Old Union	-0.011	-0.016	-0.019	-0.024	-0.049	-0.059
	(0.909)	(0.829)	(1.157)	(1.088)	(1.747)	(1.817)

Note: For description of the strikes, see Table 1.
[a]Above the median of 3,700 strikers.
[b]Below the median of 2 months.
[c]Less than 3 years old.

More arresting, perhaps, is that when wages fell in response to the strike, the estimated positive impact on the value of the industry was roughly 9% using our preferred window width, and statistically different from zero. In contrast, when wages remained the same or increased (a tiny fraction of our total observations), our point estimates indicate that the value of the industry fell between 3% and 5%, although our estimates for the cases of "wages up" are imprecise. The same issue of timing holds here as well. We discuss the reaction at the end of the strike below.

It is also interesting to note that strikes leading to the recognition of the union by the firm appear to have had a much larger negative share price reaction than strikes that did not lead to the recognition of a union. (Compare, for example, –0.065 to –0.016, in the month –1 to month +1 window in Table 2.) Also, as expected, strikes that involved an entire industry had a much larger negative effect (albeit an imprecisely estimated one) on industry stock prices than strikes involving a single firm (or a small number of firms).

Strikes that involved new versus established unions are the subject of the last two rows of Table 2. It appears that, on average, strikes by established unions led to larger negative industry share price reactions. Although these estimates are not precise, they are consistent with the view that more established unions have more power against management than do new unions.

The only apparently anomalous results for the start of the strike are those for the number of strikers: our point estimates for the effect on stock prices are larger in magnitude for small strikes (–5.6%) than for large strikes (–0.8%). This is less anomalous than meets the eye, however, since it is explicable by our mechanism for choosing strikes. If size is only one aspect of "importance," then strikes with fewer strikers that made it to the list had to be more important in other dimensions. The results for other window widths are generally insignificantly different from the results for our preferred window widths, and are generally less precise.

Table 3 repeats the analysis summarized in Table 2, except that windows are calculated around the end date of the strike. In general, the results are uniformly less precise and insignificantly different from zero at conventional levels of significance. One possible reason for this is that the end of the strike may be difficult to identify correctly, especially in those cases where management is defined as the winner. This is consistent with the view that most of the "news" in strikes occurs at the beginning of the strike, and also agrees with other research. However, as we noted above, it is

reasonable to expect that some of the information about the strike, such as who "won" and whether wages increased, would not be fully revealed until the end of the strike.

It turns out that the wage changes are perfectly in line with this idea.[15] From the "wages up," "wages down," and "wages same" section of Table 3, it is clear that this information had a larger effect around the strike ending date (where it was more likely to be fully revealed). In fact, the share price reaction to "wages down" was approximately +13%. The other piece of information that we expected to have a larger impact at the end of the strike than at the beginning is who "won" the strike. For some reason, our empirical findings do not support this idea. In addition, it is interesting to note what happened to overall stock prices around strike start times and strike end times. The initial news of a strike tended to send stock prices down (row 1 of Table 2), as clearly this was a signal of some disruption of business. On the other hand, the overall stock price reaction to strike ends was positive (row 1 of Table 3), which suggests that investors were happy that the strike was over and that firms could get back to business.

In Table 4, we combine both windows— around the start of the strike and around the end of the strike. This is an appropriate summary if both the strike announcement and its conclusion contain significant economic news. Our estimates become somewhat more precise and the magnitude of the effects becomes much larger. For our preferred window widths, union wins lead to a decrease of roughly 3% in the value of the firm. For wage changes, our point estimates are quite large. Strikes that resulted in lower wages led to increases of 22% in the value of the firm, and strikes with no wage increases led to losses on the order of 7%. Likewise, short strikes led to an increase of roughly 7%, and our longer

---

[15]Again, we thank an anonymous referee for this suggestion.

Table 3. Cumulative Average Abnormal Industry Stock Returns
for Strikes in the 1920s and 1930s, Where Event Is Defined as End of Strike.
(T-Statistics in Parentheses)

	Months Relative to Strike Ending Date					
	t = 0	*t = 0 to 1*	*t = -1 to 0*	*t = -1 to 1*	*t = -2 to 2*	*t = -3 to 3*
All Strikes	-0.001	0.009	0.011	0.020	0.013	-0.007
	(0.061)	(0.589)	(0.725)	(1.107)	(0.565)	(0.238)
Union Win	-0.006	0.009	0.021	0.036	0.012	-0.051
	(0.310)	(0.353)	(0.781)	(1.104)	(0.285)	(0.991)
Union Loss	0.001	-0.000	-0.001	-0.001	0.006	0.016
	(0.055)	(0.012)	(0.036)	(0.070)	(0.225)	(0.501)
Yes Violence	-0.003	-0.011	-0.008	-0.016	-0.030	-0.057
	(0.276)	(0.700)	(0.462)	(0.786)	(1.129)	(1.813)
No Violence	0.003	0.040	0.039	0.076	0.080	0.070
	(0.169)	(1.432)	(1.413)	(2.223)	(1.817)	(1.303)
Wages Down	0.081	0.092	0.119	0.130	0.156	0.153
	(3.629)	(3.034)	(3.421)	(3.221)	(3.216)	(2.760)
Wages Same	-0.013	-0.014	-0.018	-0.020	-0.022	-0.016
	(0.962)	(0.778)	(0.994)	(0.892)	(0.749)	(0.464)
Wages Up	-0.011	0.013	0.016	0.040	0.016	-0.046
	(0.531)	(0.459)	(0.543)	(1.121)	(0.348)	(0.809)
Many Strikers[a]	-0.001	0.002	-0.008	-0.005	0.000	0.002
	(0.089)	(0.091)	(0.455)	(0.250)	(0.013)	(0.062)
Few Strikers	-0.014	0.003	0.009	0.025	0.009	-0.032
	(0.760)	(0.098)	(0.329)	(0.785)	(0.215)	(0.632)
Short Strike[b]	0.018	0.041	0.055	0.079	0.077	0.029
	(1.147)	(1.924)	(2.470)	(2.927)	(2.231)	(0.682)
Long Strike	-0.018	-0.022	-0.030	-0.035	-0.046	-0.040
	(1.243)	(1.099)	(1.510)	(1.413)	(1.433)	(1.037)
Recognition	-0.022	-0.023	-0.031	-0.033	-0.035	-0.085
	(1.084)	(0.814)	(1.101)	(0.939)	(0.782)	(1.591)
Not Recognition	0.007	0.021	0.027	0.040	0.032	0.023
	(0.597)	(1.197)	(1.517)	(1.873)	(1.144)	(0.679)
Industry-Wide	-0.046	-0.086	-0.071	-0.111	-0.153	-0.217
	(1.034)	(1.379)	(1.132)	(1.454)	(1.546)	(1.854)
Not Industry-Wide	0.004	0.018	0.019	0.033	0.030	0.014
	(0.364)	(1.214)	(1.250)	(1.800)	(1.251)	(0.492)
New Union[c]	0.024	0.085	0.084	0.144	0.131	0.069
	(0.986)	(2.453)	(2.396)	(3.387)	(2.360)	(1.011)
Old Union	-0.007	-0.016	-0.023	-0.032	-0.040	-0.063
	(0.528)	(0.866)	(1.178)	(1.365)	(1.309)	(1.739)

Note: For description of the strikes, see Table 1.
[a]Above the median of 3,700 strikers.
[b]Below the median of 2 months.
[c]Less than 3 years old.

strikes led to losses of about 8%. In addition, using our preferred window width (month –1 to month +1), recognition strikes appear to have led to losses of about 10% (non-recognition strikes led to small gains), industry-wide strikes resulted in losses on the order of 18%, and strikes by established unions had much larger negative share price reactions than strikes involving new unions.

As we discuss above, several papers (for example, Becker and Olson 1986; Neumann 1980; Persons 1995; and Nelson et al. 1994) have found a negative share price reaction

IMPACT OF STRIKES ON FINANCIAL MARKETS, 1925–1937   231

Table 4. Cumulative Average Abnormal Industry Stock Returns
for Strikes in the 1920s and 1930s: Addition of Returns around Start of Strike and End of Strike.
(T-Statistics in Parentheses)

	Months Relative to Strike Starting and Ending Date					
	$t = 0$	$t = 0$ to 1	$t = -1$ to 0	$t = -1$ to 1	$t = -2$ to 2	$t = -3$ to 3
All Strikes	−0.012	−0.015	−0.006	−0.010	0.000	−0.022
	(1.072)	(1.686)	(1.378)	(1.975)	(0.781)	(0.608)
Union Win	−0.026	−0.041	−0.017	−0.032	−0.026	−0.071
	(1.079)	(1.878)	(1.619)	(2.343)	(0.935)	(1.065)
Union Loss	−0.003	−0.004	−0.008	−0.009	0.013·	0.000
	(0.317)	(0.218)	(0.476)	(0.380)	(0.340)	(0.734)
Yes Violence	−0.021	−0.036	−0.041	−0.056	−0.079	−0.106
	(1.639)	(1.615)	(2.089)	(2.064)	(2.172)	(2.410)
No Violence	0.004	0.019	0.047	0.062	0.124	0.108
	(0.179)	(1.629)	(1.446)	(2.261)	(2.089)	(1.496)
Wages Down	0.118	0.184	0.151	0.217	0.284	0.248
	(4.105)	(3.688)	(3.612)	(3.697)	(3.933)	(3.131)
Wages Same	−0.027	−0.052	−0.045	−0.070	−0.074	−0.077
	(1.457)	(2.208)	(1.742)	(2.394)	(1.916)	(1.810)
Wages Up	−0.027	−0.018	0.002	0.011	0.032	−0.006
	(0.964)	(1.178)	(0.720)	(1.381)	(2.262)	(0.085)
Many Strikers[a]	−0.014	−0.014	−0.013	−0.013	−0.015	−0.020
	(1.934)	(1.043)	(0.898)	(0.543)	(0.993)	(0.722)
Few Strikers	−0.026	−0.038	−0.017	−0.031	0.004	−0.024
	(0.680)	(1.639)	(1.132)	(1.809)	(0.124)	(0.172)
Short Strike[b]	0.018	0.037	0.049	0.069	0.124	0.074
	(0.760)	(0.198)	(0.424)	(0.860)	(1.260)	(1.191)
Long Strike	−0.037	−0.058	−0.054	−0.076	−0.094	−0.092
	(1.837)	(2.718)	(2.784)	(3.429)	(2.781)	(1.642)
Recognition	−0.059	−0.084	−0.072	−0.098	−0.123	−0.176
	(1.968)	(2.097)	(1.697)	(1.927)	(1.930)	(2.211)
Not Recognition	0.006	0.011	0.019	0.024	0.049	0.037
	(0.603)	(1.316)	(1.592)	(2.032)	(1.312)	(0.813)
Industry-Wide	−0.067	−0.126	−0.122	−0.181	−0.262	−0.342
	(1.221)	(1.631)	(1.596)	(1.920)	(2.165)	(2.360)
Not Industry-Wide	−0.006	−0.004	0.005	0.007	0.026	0.009
	(1.000)	(1.855)	(1.545)	(2.255)	(1.260)	(0.527)
New Union[c]	0.022	0.070	0.076	0.123	0.190	0.126
	(0.989)	(2.501)	(2.409)	(3.432)	(2.638)	(1.396)
Old Union	−0.018	−0.032	−0.042	−0.056	−0.089	−0.122
	(1.051)	(1.199)	(1.651)	(1.746)	(2.183)	(2.515)

Note: For description of the strikes, see Table 1.
[a]Above the median of 3,700 strikers.
[b]Below the median of 2 months.
[c]Less than 3 years old.

to strikes on the order of 1–4%. Our baseline reaction to stock prices (in row 1 of Table 2) is a loss of 3% of stock price for the three-month event-window (month −1 through month +1, our preferred specification). Despite this similarity, we should again point out some important differences between our study and the aforementioned studies.

First, our study concentrates on *monthly* returns; the others concentrate on *daily* returns. We argue that the decision to study monthly returns is more reasonable for our time period. This assumption would most obviously present problems for more recent time periods; no doubt, markets react more quickly today than in the past.[16] Second, our focus is on *industries* and previous research has focused on share price reactions in *individual firms*. Finally, we use data from a period in which labor historians believe strikes were "pivotal in American history." In any event, our results suggest a relatively large share price reaction to strikes for entire industries, and these effects are larger than those found in the aforementioned studies except for Becker and Olson (1986), although, like the others, their focus was on the reactions of individual firms.

Given our concentration on industry returns, the magnitude of our estimates might be surprising, since we expect industry-wide reactions to strikes to be smaller than the effect on specific firms (as business moves from struck to nonstruck firms, for example). Moreover, our evidence is roughly consistent with that reported by Kramer and Vasconcellos (1996), who found effects on nonstruck firms that were statistically indistinguishable from those on struck firms from 1982 to 1990. On the other hand, given our focus on the seminal industrial relations strikes of the interwar period, our results are consistent with the views of historians and others who have singled out this period as one of unusual importance in the development of postwar industrial relations.

Concluding Comments

The primary aim of this work has been to investigate the effect of strikes on industry stock prices at a time when unions were rapidly evolving. In contrast to recent work on the subject that has used data from the recent past, we have examined a period of time when changes in the level of unionization were more important. One advantage of this focus is that it is easier to measure the effect of "large changes" than it is to detect small changes in the current era of declining unionization. The time between the World Wars was particularly important in the history of unionization. Unlike most recent strikes, during that earlier period many strikes were an attempt by workers to change the "terms of trade" between workers and employers.

Our empirical approach melds two previous literatures: in one, the effects of strikes on industry-wide measures of output, such as inventories, are studied, and in the second, a standard "event study" approach is used to examine the relationship between strikes and *individual* firm stock valuations. We develop a data set with an unusually rich set of characteristics for each of the strikes for the time period 1925–37 and combine this information with stock return data. We use a very parsimonious model that helps provide one consistent interpretation of our results.

On a descriptive level, we find that strikes had large negative effects on industry stock valuation. In addition, longer strikes, violent strikes, strikes won by the union, strikes leading to union recognition, industry-wide strikes, and strikes that led to wage increases affected industry stock prices more negatively than strikes with other characteristics. We also examine industry stock price movements around the start and the end of the strike. It seems that "news" about the strike was revealed early and, in fact, there is some evidence that investors were able to predict strike outcomes. However, we do find larger reactions to some news that could only be completely revealed at the end of the strike (for example, worker wage changes).

The generally asymmetric response of stock prices to wins and losses is consistent with our expectations. Our analysis suggests that financial markets viewed union victories in the interwar period as very important determinants of the share of firm profits going to stockholders.

---

[16]Farber and Hallock (2000) discussed the changing stock price reaction to job loss announcements over time using data from 1970–97 and briefly discussed whether changes in technology have somehow made news less timely and therefore less "newsworthy." They found very little support for this hypothesis.

IMPACT OF STRIKES ON FINANCIAL MARKETS, 1925–1937   233

REFERENCES

Abowd, John M., George T. Milkovich, and John M. Hannon. 1990. "The Effects of Human Resource Management Decisions on Shareholder Value." *Industrial and Labor Relations Review*, Vol. 43, No. 3S (February), pp. 203S–236S.

Becker, Brian E., and Craig A. Olson. 1986. "The Impact of Strikes on Shareholder Equity." *Industrial and Labor Relations Review*, Vol. 39, No. 3 (April), pp. 425–38.

Brown, Steven J., and Jerold B. Warner. 1985. "Measuring Security Price Returns." *Journal of Financial Economics*, Vol. 14, No. 1 (March), pp. 3–31.

Campbell, John Y., Andrew W. Lo, and A. Craig MacKinlay. 1997. *The Econometrics of Financial Markets*. Princeton: Princeton University Press.

Card, David, and Craig Olson. 1995. "Bargaining Power, Strike Durations, and Wage Outcomes: An Analysis of Strikes in the 1880s." *Journal of Labor Economics*, Vol. 13, No. 1 (January), pp. 32–61.

Cowles, Alfred, and Associates. 1938. *Common-Stock Indexes*. Cowles Commission for Research in Economics Monograph No. 3, 2nd ed. Bloomington, Indiana: Principia.

Davidson, Wallace N. III, Dan L. Worrell, and Sharon H. Garrison. 1988. "Effect of Strike Activity on Firm Value." *Academy of Management Journal*, Vol. 31, No. 2, pp. 387–94.

Fama, Eugene, Lawrence Fisher, Michael Jensen, and Richard Roll. 1969. "The Adjustment of Stock Prices to New Information." *International Economic Review*, Vol. 10, No. 1 (February), pp. 1–21.

Farber, Henry S., and Kevin F. Hallock. 2000. "Have Employment Reductions Become Good News for Shareholders? The Effect of Job Loss Announcements on Stock Prices, 1970-97." Working Paper, Princeton University and University of Illinois, March.

Filippelli, Ronald L. 1990. *Labor Conflict in the United States: An Encyclopedia*. Garland Reference Library of Social Science. New York: Garland.

Fink, Gary M. 1977. *Labor Unions*. The Greenwood Encyclopedia of American Institutions. Westport, Conn.: Greenwood.

Fisher, Thomas R. 1940. *Industrial Disputes and Federal Legislation*. New York: Columbia University Press.

Gifford, Court. 1999. *Directory of U.S. Labor Organizations*. Washington, D.C.: Bureau of National Affairs.

Griffin, John Ignatius. 1939. *Strikes: A Study in Quantitative Economics*. New York: Columbia University Press.

Kramer, Jonathan K., and Geraldo M. Vasconcellos. 1996. "The Economic Effect of Strikes on the Shareholders of Nonstruck Competitors." *Industrial and Labor Relations Review*, Vol. 49, No. 2 (January), pp. 213–22.

Lazear, Edward. 1983. "A Competitive Theory of Monopoly Unionism." *American Economic Review*, Vol. 73, No. 4 (September), pp. 631–43.

MacKinlay, A. Craig. 1997. "Event Studies in Economics and Finance." *Journal of Economic Literature*, Vol. 35, No. 1 (March), pp. 13–39.

Nelson, Morton, Ben Amoako-Adu, and Brian Smith. 1994. "Impact of Labor Strikes: Canadian Evidence." *Journal of Economics and Business*, Vol. 46, No. 3 (August), pp. 153–65.

Neumann, George R. 1980. "The Predictability of Strikes: Evidence from the Stock Market." *Industrial and Labor Relations Review*, Vol. 33, No. 4 (July), pp. 525–35.

Neumann, George R., and Melvin W. Reder. 1984. "Output and Strike Activity in U.S. Manufacturing: How Large Are the Losses?" *Industrial and Labor Relations Review*, Vol. 37, No. 2 (January), pp. 197–211.

Persons, Obeua S. 1995. "The Effects of Automobile Strikes on the Stock Value of Steel Suppliers." *Industrial and Labor Relations Review*, Vol. 49, No. 1 (October), pp. 78–87.

Peterson, Florence. 1938. *Strikes in the United States, 1880–1936*. In *Bulletin of the United States Bureau of Labor Statistics*. Washington, D.C.: GPO.

Rees, A. 1977. *The Economics of Trade Unions*. Chicago: University of Chicago Press.

Reynolds, Lloyd G., and Charles C. Killingsworth. 1944. *Trade Union Publications: The Official Journals, Convention Proceedings, and Constitutions of International Unions and Federations, 1850-1941*, Vol. 1. Baltimore: Johns Hopkins Press.

Ruback, Richard, and Martin Zimmerman. 1984. "Unionization and Profitability: Evidence from the Capital Market." *Journal of Political Economy*, Vol. 92, pp. 1134–57.

Rubin, Beth A. 1986. "Class Struggle American Style: Unions, Strikes, and Wages." *American Sociological Review*, Vol. 51 (October), pp. 618–31.

[19]

Reconsidering Union Wage Effects:
Surveying New Evidence on an Old Topic

BARRY T. HIRSCH

Trinity University, San Antonio, TX 78212 and IZA Bonn

I examine evidence on private sector union wage gaps in the United States. The consensus opinion among labor economists of an average union premium of roughly 15 percent is called into question. Two forms of measurement error bias downward standard wage gap estimates. Match bias results from Census earnings imputation procedures that do not include union status as a match criterion. Downward bias is roughly equal to the proportion of workers with imputed earnings, currently about 30 percent. Misclassification of union status causes additional attenuation in union gap measures. This bias has worsened as private sector density has declined, since an increasing proportion of workers designated as union are instead nonunion workers. Corrections for misclassification and match bias lead to estimated union gaps substantially higher than standard estimates, but with less of a downward trend since the mid 1980s. Private sector union gaps corrected for these biases are estimated from the CPS for 1973–2001. The uncorrected estimate for 2001 is .13 log points. Correction for match bias increases the gap to .18 log points; further correction for misclassification bias, based on an assumed 2 percent error rate, increases the gap to .24. Reexamination of the skill-upgrading hypothesis leads to the conclusion that higher union gap estimates are plausible. The conventional wisdom of a 15 percent union wage premium warrants reexamination.

I. *Introduction*

The effect of labor unions on wages is one of the more heavily studied topics in empirical labor economics. There exists a reasonably strong consensus among economists that the average union-nonunion wage gap is about 15 percent, a consensus based in no small part on the influence of work by H. Gregg Lewis (1963, 1986). A survey of labor economists at leading universities by Fuchs, Krueger, and Poterba (1998) asked the question: "What is your best estimate of the percentage impact of unions on the earnings of their average member?" The median response was 15 percent and mean response 13.1 percent; dispersion was low. A meta-analysis by Jarrell and Stanley (1990), reexamining the studies surveyed by Lewis (1986), places the range of average union wage gaps at 9–12 percent, a bit lower than Lewis's summary of these same studies, with union gaps rising with unemployment. Likewise, labor economics textbooks place the union wage gap in the range of 10–20 percent.

I interpret recent evidence on the union impact on wages and make no attempt to provide a comprehensive survey of union wage gap studies. Rather, my analysis focuses in depth on recent strands in the literature, with particular attention given to my own work. The evidence on union wage effects is found to be far less clear-cut than might be expected given the consensus among labor economists. In the end, one concludes that the "Lewis consensus" centering on 15 percent (or less) is too low. Current private sector union wage gaps from the CPS appear well in excess of 20 percent, even following a gradual decline since the mid 1990s. How one arrives at this conclusion makes for an interesting story, one involving arguments and evidence not so well known among labor economists.

Although standard estimates of the union gap in the United States are in the neighborhood of 15 percent, these estimates fail to account for two measurement problems in CPS data (as well as other data sets), each of which causes a downward bias to wage gap estimates. The first problem, misclassification error in the reporting of union status, is well understood by labor economists and a central focus of studies using *longitudinal* analysis. Misclassification (measurement error) bias has not been considered a serious concern for standard wage level studies. This assumption is no longer tenable. As true union density in the U.S. private sector has fallen to below 9 percent, the noise-signal ratio in union status has risen and downward bias from misclassification has become a serious problem. I provide corrected estimates of union wage gaps based on alternative assumptions about rates of misclassification (1, 2, and 3 percent).

The second source of downward bias (currently about 5 percentage points) is the result of imputation "match bias" (Hirsch and Schumacher, 2004). Workers who do not report earnings have them assigned (imputed) based on the earnings of a matched donor with a set of characteristics identical to the nonrespondent. CPS match criteria do not include union status, however, so most union workers who fail to report earnings are assigned the earnings of nonunion workers, while a few nonunion workers are assigned the earnings of union workers. Hirsch and Schumacher show that the proportional attrition in the union coefficient is roughly equal to the proportion of workers with imputed earnings, currently about 30 percent.

The combined effect of match bias and misclassification error is substantial — a downward bias in union wage gap estimates on the order of .10 log points, from roughly .25 to .15 in recent years. Match bias and misclassification error have roughly equal effects, although the magnitude of the latter bias depends critically on the assumed rate of misclassification, something about which we know far too little. Each of these sources of bias has become more severe over time, with rising imputation rates leading to increased match bias and falling private sector density leading to greater misclassification bias. Standard estimates of union wage gaps, therefore, substantially understate the level of the union wage gap, but overstate decline in the union wage gap since the mid-1980s. Independent of the biases addressed herein, the magnitude of the decline in the union wage gap is uncertain due to conflicting evidence from alternative data surveys (Hirsch et al., 2004).

My principal focus centers on the level and changes over time in the union-nonunion wage gap in the U.S. private sector, following accounting for measurement biases. The analysis is based on OLS wage level estimates, which raises the question of whether such methods are appropriate, given the possibility of unmeasured skills correlated with union status and skill upgrading by union employers who pay high wages. I discuss alternative estimation approaches, in particular selection models and longitudinal analyses accounting for worker fixed effects. Longitudinal evidence shows that selection is two-sided, with positive selection among workers with low measured skills and negative selection among workers with high measured skills (Card, 1996; Hirsch and Schumacher, 1998). As emphasized by Card, this form of two-sided selection is inconsistent with single-index selection models, calling into question gap estimates from such studies (Lee, 1978; Robinson, 1989).

The theoretical basis for the skill-upgrading hypothesis also warrants examination. Theory and evidence suggest that unions may have little effect on *average* worker skills (Wessels, 1994). Union wage effects *following sorting* by employers and employees may differ little across worker skill groups, contrary to standard evidence. The average wage gap obtained across a broad sample of workers may be a better measure of the causal impact of unions on wages than are wage level estimates disaggregated by worker group, based on schooling, occupation, race, gender, etc. Absent good instruments for union status (i.e., predictors of union status that do not affect earnings), wage level analysis producing an average union wage effect may provide a reasonable approach for many (but not all) applications.

I first present an overview of union wage gap theory and estimation. This is followed by an analysis of two important measurement issues — match bias in wage gap estimates due to earnings imputation and bias from misclassification of union status. Estimates of union wage gaps that account for these biases are presented for the U.S. private sector for 1973–2001. That is followed by an appraisal of the skill-upgrading hypothesis and longitudinal union gap estimates. A final section examines briefly such topics as unions and earnings inequality, union wage effects in the public sector, differences in wage effects for union members and covered nonmembers, union effects on compensation (wages plus benefits), and the relationship between union status and working conditions.

II. *Union Wage Gaps: Estimation Methods and Measurement Issues*

What Wage Effects Are Being Measured? Union Gaps and Gains. Unions affect wages in a number of ways. Most important, union bargaining power leads to higher wages among covered workers. Collective bargaining leads to a more formalized governance structure and wage determination process, reducing management discretion. A result of this process is lower wage dispersion, evident through both a flattening of skill differentials and the standardizing of wages within job-seniority classifications (Freeman, 1980, 1982). As argued subsequently, the decrease in skill differentials is far less than suggested by standard wage regressions.

Unions also affect nonunion wages, albeit to a far lesser extent than union wages. On the one hand, "threat effects" lead nonunion employers to increase wages to deter union organizing. Threat effects are most apparent in sectors with highly unionized labor markets, defined by industry (e.g., airlines) or location. "Spillover" effects, on the other hand, produce downward pressure on nonunion wages. Such effects follow from a two-sector model in which the decrease in employment in the union sector increases labor supply in the nonunion sector. A number of studies find evidence consistent with threat effects, based on a positive relationship between nonunion wages and industry union density. The weight of the evidence suggests that union wages grow with respect to industry density at a rate equivalent to or greater than nonunion wages, implying a constant or increasing union wage gap with respect to density. Evidence is less clear-cut with respect to metropolitan area density.[1]

Spillover effects are difficult to detect since they are widely dispersed. Were the negative effects on nonunion wages from spillovers sufficiently large to offset both the wage gains among union members and positive threat effects on nonunion wages, the total wage bill or labor's share of income should be unaffected by unionization. But isolating how union density affects labor's share is not easy. Aggregate time series data require that one distinguish the effect of changes in (highly trended) union density from that of other time-series variables that may influence labor's share. Considerable cross-sectional variation occurs in union density across industry, but this reflects differences among industries heavily affected by threat effects and those most affected by spillover effects, rather than their net effect economy-wide.[2]

Lewis makes a useful distinction between wage "gaps" and "gains." Gaps are wage differentials between union and nonunion workers. Gains are the effect of unionism on union wages, relative to what wages would be absent unionism. Were the net effect of unionism on nonunion wages zero, union gaps and gains would be equivalent. If union threat effects are dominant (thus raising nonunion wages), estimates of union gaps understate union gains. If spillover effects are dominant, gaps exceed gains. The focus in the literature (and in this paper) has been on estimates of the average union wage gap. Union gains are difficult to estimate given that we do not observe what wages would be in absence of unionization or the institutional structure (e.g., labor law) that enables unions. One can estimate union and nonunion wages including a control for union density (say at the industry level), thus providing estimates of union gaps and gains for each level of union density (e.g., Freeman and Medoff, 1981). Lewis (1986) is skeptical about the reliability of this approach. He is concerned that union density coefficients capture more than the effects of unionization (for example, employer size), as seen by their sensitivity with respect to choice of control variables.

Finally, it is worth clarifying terminology. A term used frequently in the literature is union wage *premium*. The terms premium and gap are largely interchangeable, typically referring to the excess of union wages over wages for similar nonunion workers and jobs. As a matter of taste, I prefer the term gap; the term premium is used sparingly.

Specification. My focus is on union gaps estimated with cross-sectional wage level regressions. A subsequent section discusses longitudinal gap estimates and variation in wage effects across worker groups. The obvious starting point is the standard semilogarithmic wage equation. This earnings function can be interpreted, rather heroically, as a structural human capital model (Mincer, 1974; Willis, 1986) or, more generally, as a reduced form price equation in which supply and demand determinants, including union status, are explanatory variables. The semilog form of the earnings function is justified by theory (both human capital and probabilistic descriptions of the earnings generations process) and statistical evidence on functional form (Heckman and Polachek, 1974). Given a semilog wage equation, a natural metric for measuring union gaps is the log wage differential, which is simply the difference in mean union log wages and mean nonunion log wages, conditional on worker and (ideally) job characteristics. Although log wage gaps can be readily converted to (approximate) percentage differentials, I present gaps in log point form.[3]

A logical starting point is a general model of both wage and union status determination.

$$U = Z\psi + \gamma(W_u - W_n) + \mu_1. \tag{1}$$

$$W_u = X_u\beta_u + \mu_2. \tag{2}$$

$$W_n = X_n\beta_n + \mu_3. \tag{3}$$

Here U is union status; subscripts u and n designate union and nonunion; W is the individual log wage; X is a vector of wage determinants; β is the corresponding coefficient vector; and μ is the error term. Interpreted as a structural union choice equation, individual workers select a U job conditional on a vector Z of individual characteristics and their relative wage opportunities in union and nonunion jobs. As emphasized by Abowd and Farber (1982), workers must select the union job queue *and* be selected from the queue by union employers. Thus, the union status equation might better be interpreted as a reduced form equation in which vector Z includes job characteristics (employer size, working conditions, etc.) that influence the benefits and costs of union organizing and provision of union services (Hirsch and Berger, 1984).

Although reliable estimation of the general model is not typically possible, it is useful to think about what such a model involves, if for no other reason than to help understand the limitations inherent in models estimated in the literature. In the Heckman-Lee selection approach (Lee, 1978; Duncan and Leigh, 1980; Hirsch and Berger, 1984; Robinson, 1989), a reduced form union status probit equation is first estimated (i.e., with $W_u - W_n$, the log wage gap, excluded), from which selectivity variables for the union and nonunion wage equations are constructed (so-called lambda's). In principle, these are intended to yield unbiased estimates of wage equation parameters and thus each worker's wage in the union and nonunion sectors. Once such information is available, one can calculate both "unbiased" union-nonunion wage gaps and "structural" estimates of the union status equation (i.e., with inclusion of $W_u - W_n$). Such models can be identified and estimated in a statistical sense, based on (sometimes arbitrary) exclusion of a union status determinant from the wage equations or due to nonlinearity in the probit equation error term.

The reliability of results obtained from selection models has been questioned by prominent labor economists (Lewis, 1986; Freeman and Medoff, 1984). Skepticism initially stemmed from the enormous variance of estimates produced by such methods and because the high gap estimates sometimes obtained in such studies violated most economists' priors that skill upgrading should result in selectivity-adjusted estimates that are lower than standard estimates. Robinson (1989) provides a careful defense of such methods, but also obtains gap estimates exceeding those obtained from standard (nonselection) models.[4]

Selection model estimates of the union gap are unreliable for two principal reasons. First, economically meaningful identification of the selection model requires that there be at least one variable that determines union status but not the wage. Unfortunately, there are few obvious candidates among available measures. A less recognized but no less important shortcoming is that the selection model (as typically employed in the literature) is incompatible with the two-sided selection process that characterizes union status determination. Longitudinal evidence (Section V) implies that there is positive selection into unions (i.e., positive unmeasured attributes) among workers with low levels of measured skill and negative selection among workers with high levels of measured skill. As discussed by Card (1996), however, selection models used in the literature produce identical selectivity terms for those with equivalent probabilities of being a union member. Those in the bottom and top of the skill distribution have roughly equal union density rates (Card, 1996), implying that these workers are assigned similar selectivity adjustment terms, wholly inconsistent with there being two-sided selection. It is not surprising that selection models produce unreliable estimates of union wage effects.[5]

Absent the ability to estimate the full model shown above, a natural approach would be to "instrument" union status in order to avoid bias in the wage equations due to unmeasured wage determinants correlated with union status. But such an approach does not avoid the inherent problem of identifying appropriate instruments (i.e., good predictors of union status not correlated with unmeasured skills or other wage determinants). Apart from the issue of unmeasured skills, a union wage effect identified through IV methods would strictly apply only to the exogenous variation in union status associated with that particular variable(s) (Angrist and Krueger, 2001). It is uncertain whether such an estimate would be close to the average gap obtained (theoretically) with respect to all exogenous variation in union status. Despite these concerns, "discovery" of appropriate instruments, or other sources of exogenous variation in union status, would provide an important step toward estimation of unbiased union gaps.

In practice, union wage gaps are typically estimated with union status treated as exogenous. Union wage gaps can be and sometimes are estimated based on separate union and nonunion wage equations (Bloch and Kuskin, 1978). Decomposition of the union-nonunion wage differential into portions *explained* by differences in the X's and a portion that is a union wage premium (i.e., due to different coefficients or payoffs in the union sector), begins with the following (nonunique) identity:

$$w_u - w_n = (x_u - x_n)\beta_n + (\beta_u - \beta_n)x_u, \tag{4}$$

where lowercase w and x now represent *mean* values. Here the total union wage differential $w_u - w_n$ is shown as the sum of the portion explained by differences in the X's, evaluated using nonunion betas, and the union wage premium or gap, measured by union mean characteristics (X's) times the difference in coefficients (note that this portion includes the difference in intercepts). Coefficients (apart from the intercept) tend to be smaller or "flatter" in the union than in the nonunion sector due to greater wage standardization in the union sector and because of greater homogeneity in the union work force for a given set of measured characteristics. In calculating the union gap (the right-hand-side term in (4)), "flatter" union betas are more than offset by a larger union intercept.[6]

The simplest and most common method for obtaining union wage gap estimates is the single equation approach:

$$W = X\beta + \Gamma U + \mu. \tag{5}$$

This is simply a restricted form of the general model, making the assumptions that union status is exogenous and slope coefficients equal, with the union gap Γ measured by the difference in the union and nonunion intercepts. For estimates from the private sector, this simple method produces an estimate not too different from that obtained from the right-hand-side term in equation (4). Estimates of the private sector wage gaps shown in subsequent sections will be based on a single equation (by year), as seen in equation (5).

Choice of Control Variables. Estimates of the union gap can differ depending on the choice of control variables. That being said, most wage equations contain a fairly standard set of controls and, with a few exceptions noted below, estimates do not vary too greatly because of differences in controls (for an analysis, see Lewis, 1986; Blanchflower and Bryson, 2002). One of the more important choices is the use of occupation and industry controls (dummies). In general, control for occupation (even at a very broad level) is associated with higher union wage gap estimates, since union workers are concentrated in lower skill broad occupational categories. Detailed controls for industry, by contrast, tend to lower union gap estimates, since industry controls capture the effects of unions on industry-wide wages and may control for compensating differentials associated with adverse working conditions.

Blanchflower and Bryson (2002), for example, omit occupation dummies and include relatively detailed industry (and state) dummies. Using otherwise similar data and estimation methods, they obtain lower CPS union wage gap estimates than do Hirsch and Schumacher (2004), who include broad occupation and industry dummies. My own preference is that broad occupation be included and interpreted as a crude control for unmeasured skills, since the schooling and potential experience variables available in the CPS are incomplete measures of human capital. Supporting this proposition is Hirsch and Schumacher's (1998) evidence that inclusion of occupation dummies sharply increases estimated union gaps in wage level equations but have little effect in wage change equations where unmeasured worker-specific skills (fixed effects) have been netted out.

Including industry dummies are appropriate to the extent that they measure differences in working conditions or skills not captured by occupation or other controls.[7] They also may be appropriate as controls if substantial industry rents exist independent of union coverage. The concern with inclusion of *detailed* industry dummies is that they entangle industry differentials and union wage effects. For example, union bargaining power within industries included in the Census transportation category (e.g., airlines, railroads, the U.S. Postal Service) increases wages for union and nonunion workers. With detailed industry controls, one roughly makes a comparison of wages between union members and nonmembers within each detailed industry (since all get "credit" for the industry dummy), whereas absent industry dummies one makes a comparison between union and nonunion workers with similar characteristics within broad industries.[8]

Two controls typically excluded from regression estimates of union wage gaps are employer size (company and establishment size) and years of tenure with a worker's current employer. Neither of these wage correlates is available in the monthly CPS earnings files. Each of these exclusions leads to higher union gap estimates since employer size and tenure are positively correlated with earnings and union status. Whether it is better or worse to include these variables is not clear. The union wage gap is largest among small employers and relatively small among large employers. That is, unions do not increase wages by very much over and beyond what is obtained by nonunion employees in large firms and establishments. The wage advantage associated with employer size appears to be some combination of human capital (measured and unmeasured) matched with physical capital and economic rents (Brown and Medoff, 1989; Oi and Idson, 1999). If the size advantage were entirely due to skill, the question would then arise whether the matching on skill seen among nonunion employers applies equally to union employers. (Section V discusses unions and unmeasured skills.) If not, inclusion of employer size would bias downward union gap estimates. If matching on skill by large employers were the sole source of the size-wage advantage and occurred in both union and nonunion firms, control for employer size would be appropriate. My reading of the literature is that skill differences are insufficient to account for size-wage advantage in general and that selection on skill is less likely in union than in nonunion establishments. If my assessment is correct, exclusion of employer size may produce a less biased estimate of the union gap than would inclusion, albeit in opposite directions.

Control for tenure when estimating a union wage gap is problematic. The argument for inclusion is based on the presumption that tenure measures accumulated skills beyond those captured by an experience (or potential experience) variable. But length of tenure with an employer is simply an inverse function of quits (Farber, 1999). Quits are lower in union firms because of higher wages, benefits (e.g., defined-benefit pension plans that penalize mid-career quits), and union voice (Freeman, 1980). Thus, causality runs not only from tenure to wages but also from wages to tenure (Abowd and Kang, 2001; Farber, 1999). Inclusion of tenure necessarily biases the union gap downward since the tenure coefficient reflects in part how wages affect quits. To the extent that tenure measures skills not reflected in general experience and other control variables, its exclusion biases the union gap upward.

III. *Measurement Issues: Match Bias and Misclassification of Union Status*

Data quality is an important concern in most empirical endeavors. Estimation of union wage gaps is no exception. This section provides discussion of two measurement issues. The first issue, "match bias," refers to the downward bias in union gap estimates due to earnings imputation procedures that do not include union status as a match criterion. This problem is not well known, but has a major impact on union gap estimates. The second issue — misclassification in union status — is a well-known problem. Misclassification is generally thought to cause a substantial bias in longitudinal estimates of the union wage gap, but to have little effect on wage level estimates. Discussion here suggests that misclassification has a sizable effect on wage level estimates when true union density is low, as in the U.S. private sector. Taken together, match bias associated with earnings imputation and measurement error from misclassification of union status cause a large downward bias in estimates of union wage effects.

Match Bias from Earnings Imputation. A substantial proportion of workers surveyed in the CPS and in other household surveys do not report earnings, and these individuals have their earnings imputed by the Census. As analyzed by Hirsch and Schumacher (2004), earnings imputation in the CPS causes a substantial downward bias in union wage gap estimates, currently about 5 percentage points. Because of increases in nonresponse over time, match bias affects the trend as well as level of union gap estimates. CPS estimates that fail to account for match bias greatly understate the magnitude of the union gap and overstate a downward trend in the gap evident since the mid 1980s.

The monthly CPS-ORG (outgoing rotation group) files are a principal source of union gap estimates. Individuals who either refuse or are unable to report weekly earnings have earnings imputed using a "cell hot deck" method that matches each nonrespondent to an earnings "donor" with an identical set of match characteristics. There are 14,976 "cells" or combinations of match variables. Match criteria include categorical variables for schooling, age, occupation, hours worked, gender, and receipt of tips, commissions, or overtime. They do not include sectoral variables such as union status or industry.

Even if the Census matching provides an unbiased measure of average earnings, wage differential estimates are systematically understated when the attribute being studied is not a criterion used by the Census to match donors to nonrespondents. These include, among others, union-nonunion, industry, and public-private wage gap estimates. Hirsch and Schumacher (2004) derive a general expression for match bias.[9] Bias in the union wage gap, absent covariates, is shown to equal

$$B = [(1-\rho_u)\Omega_u + \rho_n\Omega_n]\Gamma, \qquad (6)$$

where Γ is the unbiased log wage gap and the term in brackets is the attenuation in the gap estimate. The terms Ω_u and Ω_n measure the rate of imputation or nonresponse for union and nonunion workers, whereas ρ_u and ρ_n measure the proportion of union donors matched to union and nonunion workers. The attenuation term in brackets is equal to the sum of match error rates, the proportion of false negatives (nonunion donors matched to union nonrespondents) and false positives (union donors matched to nonunion nonrespondents).[10]

Note that if the nonresponse rate for union and nonunion workers is similar ($\Omega_u = \Omega_n$) and the rate at which each is matched to a union donor is equivalent ($\rho_u = \rho_n$), equation (6) reduces to:

$$B = \Omega\Gamma. \qquad (7)$$

In this case, match bias can be approximated by $\Omega\Gamma$, where Ω is the proportion of workers with imputed earnings, and Γ is a log wage gap estimate free of match bias. Standard wage gap estimates from CPS samples including allocated earners must be multiplied by $1/(1-\Omega)$ to approximate a wage gap free of match bias. For example, if 30 percent of the estimation sample has earnings imputed, the gap estimate is attenuated by about 30 percent. Intuitively, the 30 percent of the sample for whom earnings is imputed displays little or no union gap, since both union and nonunion nonrespondents are matched to similar proportions of union and nonunion donors.

Introduction of covariates *increases* the downward bias in gap estimates due to earnings imputation. Hirsch and Schumacher explain how this can be likened to right-hand-side measurement error bias and employ a bias expression developed by Card (1996).[11] Correlation between union status and other match criteria reduces bias via improvements in imputation match quality. For a given match quality, however, correlation between union status and right-hand-side covariates exacerbates bias in the union coefficient, since bias increases with the ratio of error variance to total variance *conditional on covariates*.

Hirsch and Schumacher compare the difference in union gap estimates in samples including and excluding nonrespondents with the theoretical match bias (from Card) based on union and nonunion imputation and donor match rates and the correlation between union status and all other control variables. They conclude that excluding imputed earners from the estimation sample is a reasonable approach, the degree of *observed* attenuation being highly similar to the nonresponse or imputation rate. They show, however, that true bias exceeds the observed attenuation, with the nonrespondent population having a set of characteristics associated with a relatively high union gap. In short, the simplest approach for researchers is to exclude imputed earners from their estimation samples. This avoids the severe match bias that accompanies wage gap estimates associated with non-match criteria. In the case of union wage gaps, however, even this approach leaves gap estimates slightly biased downward.

Census imputation rates and the ability to identify imputed earners have varied over time, making it difficult to obtain time-consistent union gap estimates. For example, the 1973–1978 May CPS files do not provide imputed earnings for nonrespondents (earnings are recorded as missing). The apparent sharp decline in CPS union wage gap estimates after 1978, viewed as a puzzle in the literature (Freeman, 1984; Lewis, 1986), is in large part a result of the inclusion of imputed earners in CPS estimation samples beginning in 1979 following their exclusion in 1973–1978. During the period 1989–1993, only about a fifth of those with imputed earnings are identified as such by the Census allocation flag. For those years, Hirsch and Schumacher identify imputed earnings based on whether or not the "unedited" earnings field value is missing or contains an earnings value. Revisions in the earnings questions beginning in 1994 increased complexity and rates of imputation. There were no valid allocated earnings flags included with the CPS-ORG during 1994 and most of 1995. Hirsch and Schumacher address these issues and construct time-consistent union gap estimates for 1973–2001 that are purged of match bias.

Misclassification Bias. A second measurement issue concerns bias from the misclassification of union status. Random measurement error on a right-hand-side variable, such as union status, biases the coefficient toward zero, with attenuation increasing with the ratio of noise to signal.[12] The principal source of information on CPS reporting error in union status comes from a January 1977 CPS validation study that compared employer reports of union status with worker-reported union status in the CPS (Mellow and Sider, 1983). Freeman (1984) and Card (1996) have used information from the validation study to adjust longitudinal union wage gaps for misclassification bias. Card concludes that both workers and employers misreport union status and that misreporting is roughly symmetrical, the probability of a nonunion worker misreporting union status is equal to the probability of a union worker misreporting. Card's best estimate is that the misclassification rate for union status is between 2.5 and 3 percent. Based on Card's analysis, Farber and Western (2002), for example, assume a symmetric misclassification rate of 2.7 percent in order to calculate a "corrected" union density series for the United States.

I am not aware of any other data source with which to compare the 1977 CPS validation results. But there are reasons to be cautious in placing too much weight on estimates from this single survey. First, the sample size is small: Card's calculations from the validation survey were based on 1,718 men age 24–66. Second, as pointed out by Card, the union status question asked of employers and employees in the CPS validation survey is not identical to the union question(s) asked of employees in the CPS.[13] Misclassification rates could differ across the two sets of questions, although it is not obvious which set of questions should produce a higher error rate. Finally, the validation survey is now a quarter century old. Because of the small sample sizes, differences in the union question, and age of the survey, it is easy to imagine that the true union misclassification rate is below or above, say, 2.7 percent. In the discussion below, I use a "conservative" estimate of a 2 percent misclassification rate. Subsequent analysis presents union gap estimates adjusted for 1, 2, and 3 percent misclassification rates.

Misclassification bias is a first-order concern for longitudinal studies, which identify the union wage effect by the partial correlation of wage change with respect to changes in union status. Because true changes in union status over short time periods is a low-frequency event, much of the measured union status change reflects reporting error (Mincer, 1983; Freeman, 1984; Card, 1996).[14] Freeman and Card conclude that following adjustment for misclassification bias, longitudinal union wage gap estimates are similar to those obtained from OLS wage level regressions.

In contrast to the longitudinal studies, misclassification bias has not been regarded as serious for the estimation of union gaps from wage level regressions.[15] This assumption should be reconsidered. As Farber and Western (2002) show in their analysis of union density, were true union density 50 percent, symmetric misclassification would not bias density estimates, but bias becomes more serious as union density moves toward zero or one hundred percent. For example, if true union density were zero and there were a 2 percent misclassification rate, all 2 percent of the measured union density would be due to misclassification.

Letting u^* be the true but unobserved union status and u be observed union status, Farber and Western (2002) derive the following relationship between true union density $\hat{u}^*$ and observed union density $\hat{u}$ (likewise, see Card, 1996):

$$\hat{u}^* = (\hat{u}-\lambda)/(1-2\lambda), \tag{8}$$

where λ is the union misclassification rate, assumed in (8) to be the same for union and nonunion workers. For example, given an observed union density in the private sector of 9 percent in 2001and assuming that the misclassification rate is 2 percent, true union density is 7.3 percent (that is, $(.09-.02)/(1-.04) = .0729$).

I am concerned with bias in the estimation of union wage gaps, and not the measurement of union density. Given high *nonunion* density, a 2 percent misreporting rate distorts by very little observed nonunion wages. However, observed private sector union density is below 10 percent, implying that the proportion misclassified in the union sample is high and that union wages are understated accordingly. Thus, a substantial downward bias exists for standard union wage gap estimates, at least those for the private sector.

To estimate the bias in union gap estimates resulting from misclassification error, I rely on Card's attenuation coefficients. An attenuation coefficient, γ, is bounded [0, 1], with $\gamma = 1.0$ implying no attenuation or bias, and $\gamma = 0$ implying complete attenuation or a coefficient that goes to zero. Absent covariants, Card (1996, p. 959) derives the attenuation coefficient γ^0 equal to:

$$\gamma^0 = \hat{u}^*/\hat{u} \, [(q_1-\hat{u}) \, / \, (1-\hat{u})]. \tag{9}$$

Here $q_1 = \text{Prob}(u = 1 \mid \hat{u}^* = 1)$, the probability of a true union member being classified as union. This is simply equal to $(1-\lambda)$ or .98, if we assume a misclassification rate λ equal to .02. As previously stated, $\hat{u}^*$ and $\hat{u}$ are the true and observed union densities, respectively, with $\hat{u}^* = (\hat{u}-\lambda)/(1-2\lambda)$.

Based on equation (9) above and assuming a misclassification rate λ equal to .02 and an observed private sector union density $\hat{u} = .09$, the implied attenuation is $\gamma^0 = .792$. Thus, private sector union wage gaps (unadjusted for covariates) are biased downward by a fifth (.208) given a misclassification rate of 2 percent, and by considerably more if misclassification exceeds 2 percent.

Attenuation is more severe given positive correlation between union status and other regression covariates. Letting R^2 be the coefficient of determination from a regression of observed union status on other covariates, Card (1996, p. 960) derives an attenuation coefficient that for our application is equal to:

$$\gamma^1 = [\gamma^0 - (R^2/(1-2\lambda))]/(1-R^2).$$ (10)

If R^2 were equal to zero, $\gamma^1 = \gamma^0$. Assuming that $R^2 = .11$, its average value across recent years (Hirsch and Schumacher, 2004), the attenuation coefficient is $\gamma^1 = .761$, which implies that private sector union gap estimates are biased downward by almost a quarter (.239). Stated alternatively, private sector union wage gap estimates (for recent years) must be multiplied by $1/\gamma^1 = 1.31$ to eliminate misclassification bias.

Downward bias in the union coefficient is highly sensitive to the rate of misclassification, which I have assumed to be 2 percent (1 person in 50). A misclassification rate of $\lambda = .03$ or 3 percent implies $\gamma^0 = .686$ and $\gamma^1 = .642$. In short, downward bias in standard union gap estimates may be far more severe than previous figures suggest. Unfortunately, we simply know far too little about actual union misclassification rates. Given the importance of attenuation bias for low-frequency outcomes (e.g., union status in the private sector), future CPS validation surveys by the Census and BLS would have high value added.

The misclassification bias discussed in this section adds to what is already a substantial downward bias from imputation mismatch on union status. Obviously, attenuation from measurement error is less severe if misclassification rates are low or union density is high.[16] The clear implication of this section is that measurement error bias should be carefully considered not only in longitudinal analyses of union wage gaps, but also in wage level analyses. Moreover, the severity of this bias has increased over time as union density has fallen in the private sector, at the same time that match bias from imputation has worsened as CPS nonresponse rates have increased. Both misclassification and match bias result in standard analyses understating the level of the union wage gap and overstating its decline. We turn to this evidence below.

IV. *Private Sector Union Wage Effects Over Time*

In this section, changes over time in the U.S. private sector union wage gap are examined, based on regression results from the CPS. Following the analysis in the previous section, results are presented based on standard CPS samples with imputed earners included, with imputed earners excluded, and with alternative assumptions about the rate of union misclassification (1, 2, and 3 percent). Union wage gap estimates increase substantially once imputed earners are excluded, consistent with a downward match bias from imputation described in Hirsch and Schumacher (2004). As described in the previous section, union gap estimates also increase substantially with the assumed rate of misclassification. The downward trend in the private sector union gap seen in standard estimates from the CPS is shown to result in part from attenuation due to match bias and misclassification bias.

Union Wage Gaps with Match Bias and Misclassification Rate Adjustments. Figure 1 shows estimates of private nonagricultural sector union wage gaps from the CPS for 1973–2001, taken from recent work by Hirsch and Schumacher (2004).[17] The base series in Figure 1 (shown in diamonds) provides estimates from the sample including workers with imputed as well as reported earnings; hence, these estimates suffer from the downward match bias described in the previous section.[18] The next series (in squares) provides correction for match bias by omitting workers whose earnings are allocated (for details, see Hirsch and Schumacher, 2004). As evident from the two series, inclusion of imputed earners biases union estimates gap downward roughly 3–4 percentage points prior to 1994 and by roughly 5 percentage points in years since 1999. Standard estimates including workers with imputed earnings tend to understate the magnitude of the union wage gap, but exaggerate its decline.

Relying on estimates from the series corrected for match bias, the average private sector union gap rose during the 1970s, hit a high of .23 in 1984, and has slowly declined since that time, the exception being the early 1990s economic slowdown. By 2001, the private sector union gap is estimated to be .18 log points, not too far above the 15 percent "conventional wisdom" based on a much earlier period. The CPS sample including imputed earners, which makes up 30 percent of the CPS sample, produces a union wage gap estimate of .13 in 2001. The differences between series 1 and 2 illustrate clearly that union wage gap estimates from the CPS must account for what is a severe downward bias, either through removal of imputed earners or the use of alternative imputation methods (Hirsch and Schumacher, 2004).

Apart from the issue of match bias due to Census earnings imputation, are the estimates in Figure 1 consistent with what other researchers would obtain? A recent paper by Blanchflower and Bryson (2002) helps answer this question. Blanchflower and Bryson also use the CPS for 1973–2001 and provide adjustments for imputation bias based on the methods described in Hirsch and Schumacher. However, they choose a specification that excludes broad occupation dummies but includes rather detailed industry dummies and state fixed effects. For reasons described in an earlier section, each of these adjustments drive down the union premium. Moreover, correlation between union status and the other covariates in the Blanchflower-Bryson specification will be higher than in Hirsch-Schumacher, since union status differs substantially by detailed industry and state. As seen in the previous section, such correlation exacerbates downward bias in the union gap estimate owing to misclassification error in union status. Whereas our log wage gap estimate for 2001, corrected for match bias, is .18, the corresponding Blanchflower-Bryson estimate is .14. Changes in the union wage gap over time

Figure 1

Private Sector Union Wage Gaps, with and without Match Bias and Misclassification Bias Corrections, 1973–2001

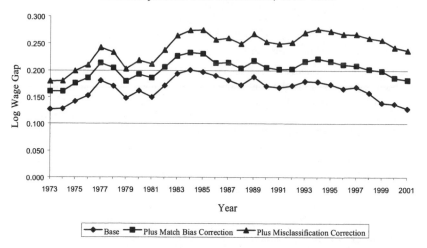

Source for the "Base" and "Base Plus Match Bias Correction" is Hirsch and Schumacher (2004). The series shown with "triangles" corrects for misclassification bias based on a 2 percent misclassification rate (see text). Data for 1973–1981 are from the May CPS Earnings Supplements and for 1983–2001 from the monthly CPS-ORG earnings files. There was no union status variable in 1982. The sample includes employed private sector nonagricultural wage and salary workers ages 16 and over with positive weekly earnings. The union gap for each year is the coefficient on a membership dummy variable in a regression where the log of hourly earnings is the dependent variable. Control variables included are years of schooling, experience and its square (allowed to vary by gender), and dummy variables for gender, race and ethnicity (3), marital status (2), part-time status, region (8), large metropolitan area, industry (8), and occupation (12). The series labeled "Base" include the full sample (workers with and without earnings imputed) for the years 1979–2001 and estimates of the full sample for 1973–1978. The "Corrected" series include only workers reporting earnings. Researchers who use all valid earnings records in CPS files would obtain gap estimates similar to the "squares" for 1973–1978 when CPS files do not include imputed earnings, and the "diamonds" beginning in 1979 when CPS files include imputed earnings values. See Hirsch and Schumacher (2004) and the text for details.

are similar in the two studies. Blanchflower and Bryson provide further checks on specification sensitivity.

Shown next in Figure 1 is the estimated union wage gap series (in triangles) including not only the match bias adjustment, but also a correction for misclassification bias using the Card (1996) correction formula (equation 10). The diamond series is based on an assumed misclassification rate of 2 percent, which earlier discussion characterized as "conservative." Adjustment for misclassification has a substantial effect on union gap estimates. The attenuation coefficient γ^1 is about .89 in 1973 and declines throughout the nearly thirty-year period, to a value of .77 in 2001 (downward bias of 11 and 23 percent, respectively). Comparing wage gap estimates from series 2 and 3, those adjusted for misclassification bias are about 2 percentage points higher during the mid 1970s, a bit over 4 percentage points in the mid 1980s, and currently in excess of 5 percentage points higher.

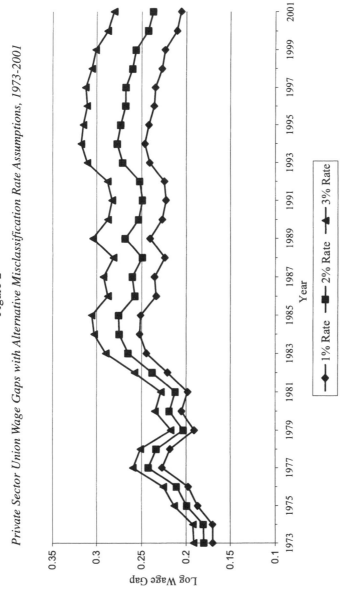

Figure 2

Private Sector Union Wage Gaps with Alternative Misclassification Rate Assumptions, 1973-2001

See the note to Figure 1. Each set of wage gap estimates starts with the series corrected for match bias, followed by corrections for misclassification bias based on assumed rates of 1 percent (diamonds), 2 percent (squares), and 3 percent (triangles). See the text for details.

The bias from misclassification is sensitive to the assumed rate of misreporting. Figure 2 shows alternative union wage gap series, with corrections to the Hirsch-Schumacher series based on the assumption of misclassification rates of 1, 2, and 3 percent (the 2 percent series was shown previously in Figure 1). A misclassification rate of 1 percent has little effect on estimates, at least in early years when private sector density was well above current levels. In 2001, a 1 percent misclassification rate implies an attenuation coefficient γ^1 of about .88 (downward bias of 12 percent) or about .02 log points off the union gap (.182 versus .206). A rate of 3 percent misclassification implies a large bias, with an attenuation coefficient γ^1 of .65 (downward bias of 35 percent) or nearly .10 log points off the union gap (.182 versus .281).

These results show clearly that as private sector union density has fallen to low levels, attenuation in wage gap estimates due to misclassification of union status has increased. The bias is now serious, causing a substantial understatement of union wage gaps. Unfortunately, the exact degree of attenuation is highly sensitive to the rate of misclassification, a number about which we know little, apart from the error rate of 2.5–3 percent found in the 1977 CPS validation survey (Card, 1996).[19]

Although the precise degree of misclassification bias is uncertain, enough is known to cause us to reconsider the conventional wisdom of a 15 percent union wage gap (Fuchs et al., 1998). A misclassification rate of 3 percent (1 in 33 workers), in line with evidence from the 1977 CPS validation survey, yields estimates of union wage gaps since the mid 1980s of about .30 log points (this includes both the match bias and misclassification bias corrections). An error rate of 2 percent (1 in 50 workers) implies union wage gaps of roughly .25 since the mid 1980s. Union wage gaps at these levels are well beyond conventional beliefs. Based on the discussion in this section, I would argue that the profession should adjust upward its belief about the magnitude of union wage effects in the U.S. private sector. Just how large that upward adjustment ought to be, however, requires further study.

Union and Nonunion Wage Trends in the CPS, ECI, and ECEC: Troubling Puzzles. Adjustment for match bias and misclassification affect inferences regarding changes in the union wage gap over time. The evidence from standard estimates not accounting for these biases can be readily summarized. As recognized in the literature, union wage gaps tended to increase during the 1970s, a period of both a strong and weak recession and high unanticipated inflation.[20] Sample sizes were very small during 1979–1981 (there was no 1982 union question in the CPS), but it appears that union wage gaps peaked around 1984, consistent with evidence from the Employment Cost Index (ECI). Union wage gaps appeared to ease downward after around 1984, and then declined steadily after 1996, with a particularly sharp drop beginning in 1999. Inferences about the size of the decline must be moderated once one adjusts for imputation match bias and then again following a correction for misclassification bias.

Nothing in the analysis causes us to question the conventional wisdom that the union wage gap is countercyclical, noted long ago by Lewis (1963, 1986). Stated alternatively, one observes a lesser degree of wage cyclicality among union than among

Figure 3

Union and Nonunion Differences in ECI Annual Wage Change

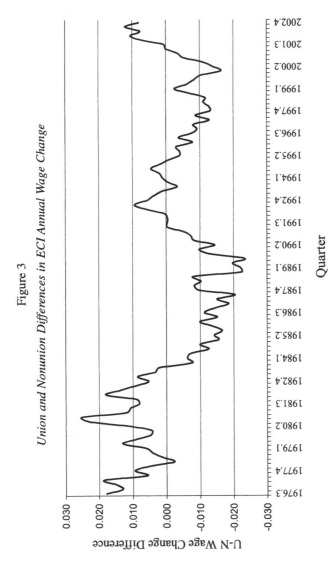

ECI Wage index values for 1975:3 through 2002:4 are from U.S. Bureau of Labor Statistics, Office of Compensation Levels and Trends, Employment Cost Index: Historical Listing, January 30, 2003, Table 7. U-N Wage Change Differences represent the 4-quarter change in log values for the union ECI index minus the nonunion change. A positive (negative) value represents an increase (decrease) in the union-nonunion wage gap.

nonunion workers. An article by Grant (2001) surveys the literature and provides new evidence, concluding that nonunion wages tend to be somewhat procyclical and union wages largely acyclical.

As seen in Figures 1 and 2, all union gap series indicate a decline in the gap since 1984, but the extent of the decline is affected by adjustments for imputation and misclassification bias. Each of these adjustments lessens the decline in the union gap. In our preferred series with the 2 percent misclassification rate, much of the decline that occurs takes place in the years after 1997, a period when the labor market was relatively strong. This evidence supports the conclusion reached by Blanchflower and Bryson (2002) that there has been little underlying change in the union wage premium, the 1990s decline being the result of an unusually strong economy and likely to be temporary.

Does evidence on union and nonunion wages from other data surveys match the CPS? The most commonly used measure of wage growth is the Employer Cost Index (ECI), derived from the National Compensation Survey, published by BLS (USDOL, 2003). Its observational unit is occupation-by-establishment job cells observed in consecutive quarters. The ECI measures quarterly wage and compensation growth and has separate indices for private sector union and nonunion jobs beginning in 1975:3. Shown in Figure 3 is an updated version of a figure from Hirsch, Macpherson, and Schumacher (2003) (hereinafter HMS). It provides ECI union-nonunion differences, by quarter, in rates of wage growth during the previous four quarters (thus beginning with 1976:3). A positive value indicates faster union than nonunion wage growth (a rising union gap) and a negative value indicates slower growth (a falling gap).

The ECI evidence is qualitatively the same as that seen in the CPS. As evident in Figure 3, union wage growth exceeded nonunion growth during the late 1970s and early 1980s, briefly during the early 1990s recession, and once again in late 2001 and 2002 during the most recent recession, consistent with a countercyclical wage gap (BLS, 2003). Despite the recent pattern, for most of the years since the early to mid-1980s, union wages have risen more slowly than have nonunion wages. Figures on total compensation indicate less of a decline in the union compensation gap than in the wage gap, with greater growth in union than in nonunion benefits (Hirsch et al., 2004).

Despite the broad similarity in the ECI and CPS evidence on relative union-nonunion wage growth, HMS identify several troubling puzzles. The ECI indicates far more rapid decline in relative union wages than seen in CPS regression analysis of union wage gaps. Decline in the ECI is similar to that seen in the *unadjusted* (i.e., non-regression) CPS figures. HMS show that about half of the CPS decline in the unadjusted union gap is accounted for by changes in the relative composition of union to nonunion wage attributes, with the remaining half representing decline in the adjusted gap. The puzzle is that the ECI is intended to represent a fixed-weight index, much akin to what is effected through regression controls. The ECI unit of observation holds the occupation, occupation skill level, industry, and establishment constant, as well as changes in employment (through the use of fixed weights). It cannot take into account (i.e., hold constant) worker characteristics such as schooling, age, or gender.

Even more puzzling is that the Employer Costs for Employee Compensation (ECEC), also drawn from the NCS, shows a different pattern than the ECI. The ECEC uses current rather than fixed weights and allows job cells to move into and out of the sample. In principle, the ECEC should yield results more similar to the *unadjusted* CPS, rather than regression estimates. Surprisingly, the ECEC indicates highly similar union and nonunion wage growth, at odds with both the ECI and the CPS (unadjusted or adjusted for worker characteristics and sector). HMS are unable to resolve these puzzles in a satisfactory manner.

A reasonable conclusion seems to be that the weight of the evidence shows a decline in relative union to nonunion wages. The magnitude of the decline is in doubt, as is the question of whether the decline since the mid-1990s will be short-lived or permanent. Closing over time between union and nonunion *compensation* has been less than the closing in wages. Blanchflower and Bryson (2002) conclude that the 1990s decline in the union gap is likely to be temporary, primarily the result of the unusually strong economy. Focusing on the CPS evidence in Figure 1, it is clear that the series corrected for match bias and misclassification bias (the triangles) is more consistent with the "no trend thesis" than are uncorrected estimates (the diamonds). Given the increased competitiveness of the U.S. economy and the continuing decline in private sector union density, a rebound in the union gap to its peak level would be surprising. Evidence will tell (or may tell), but not for some time.

V. *Employer/Employee Selection, the Skill-Upgrading Hypothesis, and Longitudinal Wage Gaps*

Preceding sections have argued that union wage gaps are higher than standard estimates and conventional wisdom suggest. Whether union gap estimates well above 15 percent are plausible depends to no small degree on one's priors regarding the relationship between union status and worker skills. This section addresses the issue, focusing on the skill-upgrading hypothesis.

Interpretation of union wage gap estimates depends in part on the correlation between union status and worker skills that are unmeasured in typical wage equations.[21] If unmeasured skills are positively correlated with union status, union gap estimates are likely to be biased upward, and vice-versa. A conventional argument, sometimes referred to as the "skill-upgrading" hypothesis, is that a union wage premium both allows and provides incentive for employers to upgrade the skill level of their work forces, offsetting part of the higher wage. Despite a substantial empirical effort to account for unmeasured skills and facilitate estimation of unbiased union gap estimates, the literature does not point clearly toward the existence of substantial skill upgrading in union workplaces.

Absence of clear-cut evidence in favor of skill upgrading by union employers is not so surprising once one realizes that such behavior need not follow from theory. Wessels (1994) has provided a simple but persuasive challenge to the skill-upgrading hypothesis. If firms upgrade in response to a union wage increase, the union can then bargain in a future contract for an even higher wage in order to restore the premium.[22] Employers, anticipating this, may respond by not upgrading. Firms that upgrade will face higher future wage demands and will have distorted their factor mix, using a higher skill labor mix than is optimal given its technology. Wessels provides an explicit model in which it is assumed that labor quality augments capital productivity and the decision to hire higher (lower) skill workers results if the elasticity of substitution between labor and capital is greater (less) than unity. Wessels concludes that available evidence is not consistent with skill upgrading. In short, once one takes into account that unions acquire wage gains through bargaining power, it no longer follows that firms can offset, or will attempt to offset, cost increases through skill upgrading.

The selection mechanism within union companies may best be characterized as a form of two-sided selection (Abowd and Farber, 1982; Card, 1996). A queue of workers exists for union jobs. Hence, employers are able to avoid hiring workers in the lower tail of the ability distribution (ability is used broadly to include productivity-related attributes such as motivation and reliability). Yet few workers from the upper-tail of the ability distribution are either in or chosen from the union queue. Wage compression within union firms, both compression in skill differentials and contractually standardized wages, discourages applications by many of the most able workers. And, following the logic of Wessels, firms may not have incentive to screen for and select the most able workers in the union queue if such action may lead to an increase in future wage demands. In short, realistic models of worker and firm selection lead to the prediction that unionized work forces need not be systematically more or less skilled than a nonunion labor force, but the skill distribution is more likely to be compressed. Not only are unions associated with compression in wages, but also compression in worker ability (Hirsch and Schumacher, 1998).

The estimation issue arising from the nonrandom determination (i.e., endogeneity) of union status is how to account for the possible bias in union gap estimates owing to correlation between unmeasured skill and union status. The literature has attempted to account for skill bias in two principal ways: (a) selection models that explicitly account for the process through which union status is determined, and (b) longitudinal models relating wage changes for individual workers to changes in union status, thus netting out unmeasured worker-specific skills fixed over time, i.e., transferable across jobs.[23]

Selection models were discussed in a previous section, where I argued that selection results on union wage gaps are unreliable for two reasons. First, these models typically employ a single index selection measure that is equivalent for workers with the same probability of union status. This is inconsistent with the two-sided selection results in Card (1996) in which workers with low and high measured skills have similar union probability rates, but opposite selectivity (e.g., positive selection for workers with low measured skills, and negative selection for those with high measured skills). Second, even were the single index selection model appropriate, meaningful identification requires use of one or more variables that are good predictors of union status but not earnings.

Longitudinal models identify a union wage effect from the wage changes of workers who switch union status (Mellow, 1981; Freeman, 1984; Card, 1996, Hirsch and Schumacher, 1998), thus controlling for unmeasured skills transferable across jobs. That is, if union workers possess high unmeasured skills, their wages would be higher than predicted in nonunion jobs and we should observe relatively small wage gains in moving from nonunion to union jobs, as well as small wage losses in moving from union to nonunion jobs.[24]

Absent an accounting for misclassification error in union status, longitudinal analysis typically obtains far lower union gap estimates than those obtained from wage level equations. Some authors conclude that the lower estimates support the proposition that union workers have high unmeasured skills. As emphasized by Freeman (1984) and others, longitudinal estimates are seriously biased toward zero owing to measurement error. Although misclassification rates for union status may be relatively low, so is the incidence of true union switching over short time periods (one year in studies using the CPS). Thus a large proportion of those recorded as union switchers have not changed union status and display no correlation between wage change and recorded union status change. Freeman and Card correct their estimates based on union status information from the 1977 matched CPS-employer survey. Although using different methods and assumptions to correct bias, each concludes that corrected longitudinal estimates are similar to those from wage level equations. Hirsch and Schumacher (1998) make no explicit correction for misclassification, but instead rely on union gap estimates among workers who change detailed industry and occupation as well as union status, since such workers are most likely to be true job and union status changers. Their longitudinal estimates are lower than their wage level estimates. Taken together, longitudinal studies suggest that omitted ability bias has at most a modest effect on average union wage gap estimates.[25]

Although longitudinal studies do not greatly alter our assessment of *average* union wage effects, they very much affect assessment of union wage differences across worker skill groups. The conventional wisdom is that union wage premiums are largest for workers with low skills and smallest for workers with high skills. For example, standard union gap estimates are substantially larger for high school than for college graduates and for blue-collar than for white-collar workers. Such findings reinforce the thesis that unions decrease skill-based wage differentials.

As emphasized by Card (1996) and Hirsch and Schumacher (1998), longitudinal union gap estimates, which control for worker-specific skills, are far more similar across skill groups than are standard estimates. Among union workers with low measured skills (e.g., high school dropouts), there exists positive selection, union employers hiring and retaining those with high unmeasured skills (motivation, dependability, etc.). By contrast, among union workers with high measured credentials (e.g., college graduates), negative selection is more typical, with the most motivated and skilled workers not sorting into the union sector or being so highly valued as by nonunion employers. Union wage compression and rate standardization help produce this pattern of two-sided selection. But, following sorting and a more complete accounting for worker skills, union wage gap differences across skill groups are far less than commonly believed.

A vivid example is provided in Hirsch and Schumacher (1998). When they segment their sample by educational group, they obtain the following log point union gap estimates — dropouts: 0.24; high school grads: 0.20; some college: 0.17; and college graduates: 0.08. This is the standard pattern found in the literature, gap estimates falling sharply with measured skill (if occupational dummies are excluded, a far steeper gradient with respect to schooling is found). In sharp contrast, longitudinal union gap estimates for the same four groups of workers were as follows: 0.11, 0.12, 0.12, and 0.11 (longitudinal estimates, which control for worker-specific skills, are unaffected by occupational controls). That is, no discernable difference is found in union gap estimates across schooling groups, following sorting in the labor market. A similar result is seen using a multidimensional index of measured skills (i.e., predicted earnings from a sparse earnings function). Card obtains a similar qualitative pattern, but concludes that union wage effects do decline with skill level, although not by nearly so much as evident in standard estimates.[26]

In short, union-nonunion wage gaps for workers of equivalent ability do not vary nearly so much across worker groups as commonly believed. This result follows selection by individuals into the union queue and the selection of workers by firms from the queue. Union workplaces not only tend to have a compressed wage distribution, but also a compressed distribution of worker skills. The compressed skill distribution results in part from union success in compressing compensation. Moreover, work settings that best lend themselves to relative homogeneity in skills and wages are also the most likely to be successfully organized and maintain political support for union representation.

Besides aiding our understanding of what unions do, the conclusion that union wage effects vary relatively little across worker groups, following matching by workers and employers, has implications for empirical studies. Because union gap estimates from wage level equations differ so markedly by worker group, the response by some is to move away from a single union wage gap estimate and instead estimate a family of union wage effects. Some applied researchers recommend the use of quantile regression methods or other semi-parametric (or nonparametric) methods that permit gap estimates to better fit the data. Discussion in this section suggests that flexible estimation methods that fail to account for two-sided selection need not produce reliable measures of union wage gaps. Union wage gaps estimated across a broad cross-section of private sector wage and salary employees may well produce more appropriate estimates. Attention should be aimed at controlling for positive selection at the low end of the measured skill distribution and negative selection at the high end of the measured skill distribution. Studies that model and estimate this process in a principled manner would be a welcome contribution to the literature.

VI. *Further Topics: Inequality, Public Sector Unions, Membership vs. Coverage, Compensation, and Working Conditions*

I have focused on a narrow but important range of issues concerning unions and wages. In this section, brief mention is made of several additional issues. Some of these topics have been studied extensively in the literature (e.g., inequality), while others have not (e.g., working conditions).[27]

Unions and Earnings Inequality. Unionization is strongly associated with lower earnings dispersion or inequality. As carefully documented by Richard Freeman (1980, 1982), unions appear to lower dispersion in two major ways. First, union workplaces have compressed skill differentials — that is, smaller wage differences between workers in low- and high-skill positions. Second, wages are contractually determined or standardized, with pay often depending solely on a worker's job position and seniority. Management has less discretion and is limited in its ability to vary pay across workers in similar positions. The decline in private sector unionization is frequently identified as one of several important explanations for rising earnings inequality. In particular the sharp decline in union density during the 1980s corresponds to the period when earnings inequality rose most rapidly. A paper by Card et al. (2003) provides recent evidence and a careful documentation of the union-inequality relationship. Moreover, the strong empirical relationship between unions and inequality is consistent with the political economy of democratic unions that have incentive to foster support among average workers (the median voter) more than mobile marginal workers catered to by employers in a competitive labor market (Farber, 1986).

Despite the strong inverse correlation between unions and inequality, an important caveat is in order. It is difficult to know how much of this relationship is causal. As discussed in the previous section, longitudinal union gaps across measured skill groups vary little following sorting in the labor market (i.e., positive sorting on low-measured skill and vice-versa). Union wage policies affect sorting in the labor market between the union and nonunion sectors. Thus, differences in observed wage inequality between the union and nonunion sectors exaggerates unions' causal effects on economy-wide dispersion. Were unions to disappear, inequality among previously unionized *workers* would not rise to the level seen in nonunion sectors since there exists greater homogeneity or compression of worker skills and tastes within the union sector. Moreover, greater homogeneity is not only the result of sorting in response to union policies. Unions are more likely to organize successfully in sectors where worker preferences and skills are homogeneous (Hirsch, 1982). That is, causality runs from low dispersion to unionization as well as in the other direction.

Public Sector Unionization. Much of my discussion has concerned union wage effects in the private sector. Separate analyses of unionism in the private and public sectors are appropriate. First, the legal structure differs, the private sector being covered by the National Labor Relations Act (or the Railway Labor Act for workers in a few industries), while public sector workers are covered by a diverse mix of federal and state collective bargaining laws. Second, some public sector workers counted as members belong to employee associations that do not have collective bargaining rights or, more generally, the bargaining rights of public workers vary considerably across jurisdictions. Third, the impact of public sector workers may take place as much through the political process as through collective bargaining and show up not only in higher wages, but also in public appropriations and employment (Freeman and Medoff, 1984). Fourth, there is likely to be more misclassification error in union status in the public sector since what constitutes union membership and coverage may not be clear to some workers.[28]

As discussed previously, downward bias in union wage estimates from misclassification is a more serious problem than generally believed. Bias is a function of the ratio of noise to signal in the union measure. Misclassification in the public sector is probably more severe than in the private sector. Yet true density is far higher in the public than private sector. We simply do not have enough information to know whether misclassification bias is more or less severe in the public than in the private sector.

For the above reasons, estimation of private and public sector union gaps are best kept separate. My focus on private sector gaps should not be taken to imply that study of the public sector is not important. It is important and increasingly so. Whereas 26 percent of all union members and 28 percent of covered workers were government employees in 1977 (the year the CPS adopted its current set of union status questions), corresponding figures were 44 and 45 percent in 2001 (Hirsch and Macpherson, 2003).

Membership versus Coverage. Most of the literature on union wage gaps uses as its measure of union status a binary variable either for membership or coverage, comparing the selected union group to everyone else. Few studies distinguish between the three groups — union members, covered nonmembers, and non-covered nonmembers. Were there identical union wage effects from being a member and being a nonmember covered by a collective bargaining agreement, one would get a lower union gap estimate using membership, since covered nonmembers would be included in the control group (Jones, 1982). Just the opposite is found. As seen in Lewis (1986), the choice of union status variable typically has a small effect on union gap estimates, but membership gaps typically are a little larger than are coverage gaps.

In the work shown in this study, a union membership variable is used, since the coverage variable was not available until 1977. The number of private sector covered nonmembers is sufficiently small so that their inclusion in the nonunion control group produces union wage effect estimates nearly equivalent to what would be obtained were covered nonmembers included as a distinct group (or removed from the analysis).

In U.S. studies that distinguish among the three groups, union members display a substantial wage advantage relative to covered nonmembers (Jones, 1982; Schumacher, 1999; Budd and Na, 2000). For example, focusing exclusively on right-to-work states, where union gaps tend to be higher than across all states, Schumacher (1999) finds a –.14 lower union gap for covered nonmembers than for members (and a –.10 log wage difference when the estimation sample is limited to covered workers, members and nonmembers). An interesting question then arises. Why is there a wage advantage to membership versus coverage? Schumacher investigates a number of sources. He finds little evidence to support the following explanations for the gap: (a) higher unmeasured skills among members than covered nonmembers; (b) lower job tenure among covered nonmembers than among members; (c) higher misclassification rates for covered nonmembers; or (d) industry and occupational wage effects.

Schumacher (1999) and Budd and Na (2000) conclude that union wage gaps are lowest in industry-occupation sectors in which there are large numbers of "free riders" (the ratio of nonmembers to total covered). What is not clear is the direction of causation. One possibility is that less free riding provides unions with greater bargaining power. Alternatively, covered workers may be less likely to free ride in jobs where they realize a substantial wage advantage. Both explanations are plausible and likely to matter. It will be up to future studies to sort out the relative importance of these two explanations.[29]

Compensation. Discussion to this point has been in terms of union *wage* effects. Ideally we would like to focus on compensation (wages plus benefits). The difficulty is that micro data sets providing worker characteristics (e.g., the CPS) at most provide indicator variables on the receipt of benefits (e.g., pension payments and health insurance) but not the dollar value of benefits. Published data on employer costs for benefits, for example, from the BLS's Employer Costs for Employee Compensation surveys, do not permit the matching of dollar benefits to individual workers and their characteristics.

Although evidence is limited, that which exists indicates clearly that higher benefits are received by union than by nonunion workers. Work by Freeman (1981) finds that the union benefit gaps greatly exceed wage gaps, leading to a union compensation gap that exceeds the wage gap by about 2 percentage points. Freeman finds the union benefit advantage particularly large for insurance and pensions.

Recent wage and benefit data from the *Employer Costs for Employee Compensation* indicates the large gap in benefits between union and nonunion workers. In 2001, the ECEC data (USDOL, 2002) show hourly compensation for nonunion workers of $19.98, $14.81 in wages and $5.18 in benefits (included those government mandated). Compensation for union workers is $27.80, $18.36 in wages and $9.45 in benefits. Current data confirm that union wage gaps understate union compensation gaps, perhaps substantially so.[30]

Working Conditions. A shortcoming of most union wage gap estimates, including those herein, is that they fail to control (at least directly) for working conditions. To the extent that union jobs have more adverse working conditions than do nonunion jobs (Duncan and Stafford, 1980), union gap estimates are biased upward. The extent of this bias is not known. Even if appropriate data were available, estimation of compensating differentials associated with working conditions is notoriously difficult (Rosen, 1986; Hwang et al., 1992). To some extent, working conditions are controlled for through the inclusion of occupation and industry dummies. As discussed previously, control for occupation drives union gap estimates upward while control for industry drives gap estimates downward. Use of detailed industry controls, while helping control for working conditions, also captures some of what we consider a union effect and exacerbates downward bias from misclassification error in union status.

The literature on compensating differentials finds that union workers are compensated more highly for risks than are nonunion workers (Viscusi and Aldy, 2003). One explanation is that this reflects a lack of information or some form of market failure in nonunion companies, one that is mitigated by union voice. Alternatively, if compensating differentials in the nonunion sector reflect competitive returns, higher differentials in union jobs is simply one way in which unions produce a premium for their members. It is difficult to distinguish between these explanations (for an informal effort to do so with respect to workers' compensation claims, see Hirsch et al., 1997).

VII. *Summary*

Conventional wisdom among labor economists holds that the average union wage premium is approximately 15 percent. Accompanying this loose consensus have been various arguments that can lead one to argue that union gaps are either higher or lower than 15 percent. Whatever one's view, arguments presented herein show that there exists a substantial downward bias in standard union gap estimates. The bias emanates from two sources of measurement error. The first source, not well known among economists, is the "match bias" associated with Census earnings imputation procedures. The second is a well-know source of bias, but one thought to be unimportant for wage level estimates of union gaps — measurement error resulting from the misclassification of union status.

Based on a 2001 CPS sample of private sector nonagricultural workers, a .13 log wage gap is obtained using the full sample of workers with and without imputed earnings. The union gap rises to .18 when nonrespondents are excluded from the sample. Correcting for misclassification bias (with an assumed 2 percent rate) raises the private sector union wage gap from .18 to .24 log points in 2001. Based on misclassification rates of 1 or 3 percent, the union gap increases from .18 to .21 or .28, respectively.

The combined effect of misclassification and match bias is not only sizable, but has become larger over time as nonresponse rates have risen and private sector density has declined. I have presented time-consistent private sector union wage gaps for 1973–2001, with correction for match bias and misclassification bias. Absent these corrections, standard estimates substantially understate the true union wage gap and overstate decline in the union gap since the mid-1980s. The precise magnitude of the private sector gap and its decline depends very much on assumed rates of misclassification. Unfortunately, when one turns to data sources other than the CPS to clarify trends in union and nonunion wage growth, further puzzles arise.

How plausible is a union wage gap substantially greater than 15 percent? The answer depends in part on one's beliefs about employers' ability and incentives to off-set union wage increases with skill upgrading of their work forces. It is argued herein that in a repeated bargaining framework, skill upgrading need not follow. Nor does empirical evidence reveal substantial skill upgrading among union employers. Longi-tudinal studies indicate that two-sided selection produces a skill distribution among union workers that is more compressed than among a nonunion work force with the same distribution of measured earnings attributes. Although wage level evidence pro-duces union wage gap estimates that decline sharply with respect to measured skill attributes (e.g., schooling), true union gaps may differ little across skill groups fol-lowing labor market sorting and an accounting for two-sided selection.

Union wage gaps in the United States, long thought to be about 15 percent, have been considered high as compared to union gaps in other countries (Blanchflower and Freeman, 1992; Blanchflower and Bryson, 2002). I argue that the average union wage gap in the U.S. private sector is substantially higher than previously believed. An even higher U.S. union wage gap makes the international comparison all the more notable.[31] One cannot avoid the conclusion that a relatively high wage premium in the United States explains *part* of the fierce management opposition to union organizing and the inability of unions to maintain private sector union density at past or current rates.

The study of union wage gaps has a long history in labor economics, although interest in this topic may be waning as density declines. Recent research suggests that there remains much to be learned. There never has been a consensus on the most appro-priate methods by which union gaps should be estimated. The literature continues to await modeling and estimation approaches that can reliably identify the causal effects of unions on wages. Independent of the approach, the measurement issues addressed herein require one to revise one's assessment of both the level and trend in the aver-age union wage gap. The conventional wisdom of a 15 percent union gap requires reconsideration. Whether a new consensus will emerge is uncertain.

NOTES

[1]One of the first micro-level wage equation papers to include measures of union density at the industry level was Freeman and Medoff (1981). Curme and Macpherson (1991) include union density in union and nonunion wage equations at the industry and metropolitan-area levels.

[2]Macpherson (1990) examines union effects on labor's share based on cross-sectional variation in union density within manufacturing for the years 1973–1975 and 1983–1985. He obtains a positive relationship in each of the periods and concludes that unionization increases labor's share.

[3]A simple approximation of the percentage gap is $[\exp(\beta-1)]100$, where β is the log wage gap. Giles (1982) provides a comparison between this simple measure and more precise approximations.

[4]Robinson (1989) offers the explanation that skills are heterogenous, with union workers having an absolute advantage in skills in union jobs and nonunion workers an absolute advantage in nonunion jobs.

[5]Closely related critiques of the selection model, as applied to union wage gap estimates, are provided in Farber (1983) and Lemieux (1998). It is not surprising that estimation of a structural model is difficult, given

the complexity of the process by which union status is determined. There exists both worker demand for union services and a supply curve of union services based on the costs of organizing and satisfying the preferences of rank and file (Pencavel, 1971; Lazear, 1983; Hirsch and Addison, 1986, Ch. 2). Union employment requires both that workers be in the union queue and be selected by employers, with a wage premium creating excess demand for union jobs (Abowd and Farber, 1982). There is no presumption that there exists a price (dues) based equilibrium as in standard markets.

[6]The decomposition shown by (4) is not unique; for example, one can decompose the wage differential by:

$$w_u - w_n = (x_u - x_n)\beta_u + (\beta_u - \beta_n)x_n.$$

This provides a less intuitive decomposition, since the explained portion is based on the wage structure in the union sector and the union premium is measured by the additional wage that workers with nonunion characteristics would earn if paid according to the union wage structure. One could also take a weighted average of these two measures, letting the explained portion be the employment (or sample) weighted average of β_u and β_n times $(x_u - x_n)$ and the remainder of the differential a measure of the gap. Owing to a large nonunion share, the weighted average approach would produce a premium estimate for the U.S. private sector close to the estimate obtained in (4).

[7]As seen subsequently, misclassification bias is worsened by inclusion of industry dummies, since these are correlated with observed union status. Bratsberg and Ragan (2002) examine differences across industries in union wage gaps. They find that industry differences in union gaps have narrowed over time.

[8]A similar issue arises if one wants to measure an industry wage effect in a highly unionized sector. For example, in measuring wage comparability between unionized U.S. Postal Service workers and similar levels of work in the private sector (as required by statute) control for union status would effectively compare union postal workers to unionized private workers (i.e., postal workers would be credited with a union "endowment" variable in the same way they are credited with schooling or experience). Exclusion of a union control would effectively compare postal workers to a weighted average of union and nonunion workers throughout the private sector (Hirsch et al., 1999).

[9]Note that match bias is distinct from response bias. It would exist even if nonresponse were randomly determined.

[10]A similar but more complex match bias exists for longitudinal estimates of wage gaps, depending on whether a worker has earnings imputed in one or multiple years and whether the worker is a union joiner or leaver. Hirsch and Schumacher (2004) describe this bias. Unlike wage level studies, longitudinal studies often omit workers with allocated earnings in any year.

[11]When earnings are imputed, one is correctly measuring a *donor's* earnings and explanatory variables used in the match. The donor's union status and other nonmatch criteria are measured with error.

[12]See Aigner (1973) and Card (1996), among others. Absent covariates, misclassification bias looks very much like the match bias formula presented earlier, with attenuation (proportionate bias) equal to the sum of match error rates. As shown by Card, bias is exacerbated if there are covariates, since the relevant "signal" from union status is that net of its correlation with other explanatory variables.

[13]The validation survey asked employers and employees whether their wage was determined by collective bargaining. The CPS question asks workers if they are members of a labor union or employee association like a union. Nonmembers are asked if they are covered by a collective bargaining agreement on their principal job.

[14]Here two wrongs make a right, with consistent misreporters not being classified as changing union status.

[15]A notable exception is Bollinger (2001), who emphasizes the wide bounds that both cross-section and fixed-effects union gap estimates can take over the full range of union misclassification rates. Bollinger does not provide "preferred" estimates of union wage gaps based on "best guess" misclassification rates. He calculates that the misclassification rate must be below 0.8 percent for the true coefficient in his fixed effects model to be bounded below the true coefficient in a wage level model. The 1977 CPS validation study suggests a far higher misclassification rate.

[16]An interesting question is how misclassification rates differ between the private and public sectors (see Section VI). Because the meaning of union membership and coverage is not well understood by workers in some public sector jobs, my expectation is that misclassification is less severe in the private sector. On the other hand, union density levels are lower in the private sector, making attenuation bias more severe for a given misclassification rate.

[17]Details regarding estimation and a listing of wage gap estimates by year are in Hirsch and Schumacher (2004).

[18]The May 1973–1981 CPS does not include imputed earnings for nonrespondents. The "diamond" wage gap estimates for 1973–1978 are approximations of what gaps would be for the full sample were earnings imputed for nonrespondents (Hirsch and Schumacher, 2004).

[19]Note that adjusting for misclassification error requires knowledge of the error rate (assumed here), union density in each year, and the R^2 obtained from a regression of union status on the other covariates. The annual R^2, calculated in Hirsch and Schumacher (2004), declines over time from a high of about .25 in 1973 to .10 in 2001. Declining union density over time increases bias, while the declining correlation of union status with other covariates mitigates bias.

[20]The CPS did not include imputed earnings in May 1973–1978. So standard estimates in the literature are similar to the "squares" in Figure 1 for 1973–1978 and then show a large drop to the "diamonds" beginning in 1979, a puzzle addressed without satisfaction by Freeman (1984) and Lewis (1986).

[21]The same point holds true for omitted working conditions correlated with union status. This issue is discussed briefly in a final section.

[22]This process is aptly described by Kalachek and Raines (1980, p. 68), who nonetheless stress the importance of skill upgrading by union employers. "Hence the stage is set for a neverending chase between the employer and the union. The faster the employer liquidates rents, the greater the pressure on the union to recreate them."

[23]A distinct but related literature uses a production function approach to see if unionized firms or industries have higher technical efficiency, or measured output for given combinations of inputs (for surveys, see Addison and Hirsch, 1989; Booth, 1995). Studies attempt to measure whether union establishments are more productive owing to unionization, holding constant the capital-labor ratio and labor quality. If union status is a close proxy for unmeasured worker skills, it is likely that those same skills, unmeasured in a production function study, would show up as a positive union productivity effect. The most reliable economy-wide evidence, however, based on data at the line-of-business or firm level (Clark, 1984; Hirsch, 1991) does not indicate positive union productivity effects, on average. A survey measuring the views of labor economists at top universities asked the question: "What is your best estimate of the percentage impact of unions on the productivity of unionized companies." The median response was zero and mean response 3.1 percent (Fuchs et al., 1998, pp. 1392, 1418).

[24]Ignored is the important issue of whether union status change is exogenous.

[25]This same conclusion need not apply to specific worker groups. For example, Hirsch (1993) concludes that low longitudinal estimates among truck drivers support the proposition that union drivers have high unmeasured skill (e.g., driving experience, reliability).

[26]Hirsch and Schumacher (1998) also provide a direct measure of two-sided selection, reporting AFQT percentile scores for union and nonunion workers with low and high measured attributes. Among workers with high measured attributes, union workers have AFQT scores 14–15 percentile points less than nonunion workers.

[27]Space prevents discussion of additional topics. Two that warrant exploration are an evaluation of matching techniques and the use of sample weights. Matching estimators would calculate a union gap as the mean difference in log wages between each union worker and a matched nonunion worker, where each match is based on a random selection from among all nonunion workers with the exact combination of attributes (i.e., hot-deck matching) or among nonunion workers with similar propensity scores (i.e., the probability

of being a union member based on logit or probit estimates). In contrast to regression analysis, matching estimators provide an explicit weighting function based on union worker ("treatment group") characteristics (Angrist and Krueger, 1999). A second issue concerns use of sample weights. The CPS and other household surveys are not fully representative, although they do contain weights intended to provide population estimates. A weighted estimator should produce an average union gap estimate similar to what would be obtained based on a fully representative sample.

[28]In the CPS, nonmembers are asked if they are covered by a collective bargaining agreement at their workplace. Misclassification of the coverage variable is believed to be particularly severe among federal workers, with workers in the same work units providing different answers.

[29]Booth and Bryan (2001) use matched employer-employee data from Britain and instrumental variable estimation to account for membership endogeneity. Despite some variation across worker groups, the authors conclude that there is little systematic difference in wages between covered members and nonmembers.

[30]Before attaching too much weight to ECEC wage figures, note that nonunion (but not union) wage growth in the ECEC is substantially lower than that seen in the ECI or CPS (Hirsch et al., 2004).

[31]I do not know in which countries or data sources there exist match bias from earnings imputation. To the extent that union density is higher in other countries, measurement error bias will be less severe for given rates of misclassification. In countries where union status is less clearly defined than in the U.S., rates of misclassification may be high.

REFERENCES

Abowd, John M. and Changhui Kang. "Simultaneous Determination of Wage Rates and Tenure." Cornell University, March 2001.

Abowd, John M. and Henry S. Farber. "Job Queues and the Union Status of Workers." *Industrial and Labor Relations Review* 35 (April 1982): 354–67.

Addison, John T. and Barry T. Hirsch. "Union Effects on Productivity, Profits, and Growth: Has the Long Run Arrived?" *Journal of Labor Economics* 7 (January 1989): 72–105.

Angrist, Joshua D. and Alan B. Krueger. "Empirical Strategies in Labor Economics." In O. Ashenfelter and D. Card, eds. *Handbook of Labor Economics*, Vol. 3A. Amsterdam: North-Holland, 1999, pp. 1277–366.

_____. "Instrumental Variables and the Search for Identification: From Supply and Demand to Natural Experiments." *Journal of Economic Perspectives* 15 (Fall 2001): 69–85.

Blanchflower, David G. "Changes Over Time in Union Relative Wage Effects in Great Britain and the United States." In S. Daniel, P. Arestis and J. Grahl, eds. *The History and Practice of Economics. Essays in Honor of Bernard Corry and Maurice Peston, Vol. 2.* Northampton, Mass.: Edward Elgar, 1999, pp. 3–32.

_____ and Alex Bryson. "Changes Over Time in Union Relative Wage Effects in the UK and the US Revisited." NBER Working Paper #9395, December 2002.

Blanchflower, David G. and Richard B. Freeman. "Unionism in the United States and Other Advanced OECD Countries." In M. Bognanno and M. Kleiner, eds. *Labor Market Institutions and the Future Role of Unions.* Cambridge, Mass.: Blackwell Publishers, 1992, pp. 56–79.

Bloch, Farrell E. and Mark S. Kuskin. "Wage Determination in the Union and Nonunion Sectors." *Industrial and Labor Relations Review* 31 (January 1978): 183–92.

Bollinger, Christopher R. "Response Error and the Union Wage Differential." *Southern Economic Journal* 68 (July 2001): 60–76.

Booth, Alison L. *The Economics of the Trade Union.* Cambridge: Cambridge University Press, 1995.

_____ and Mark L. Bryan. "The Union Membership Wage-Premium Puzzle: Is There a Free-Rider Problem?" Center for Economic Policy Research, Discussion Paper No. 2879, July 2001.

Bratsberg, Bernt and James F. Ragan, Jr. "Changes in the Union Wage Premium by Industry." *Industrial and
Labor Relations Review* 56 (October 2002): 65–83.

Brown, Charles and James Medoff. "The Employer Size-Wage Effect." *Journal of Political Economy* 97
(October 1989): 1027–59.

Budd, John W. and In-Gang Na. "The Union Membership Wage Premium for Employees Covered by Collective Bargaining Agreements." *Journal of Labor Economics* 18 (October 2000): 783–807.

Card, David. "The Effect of Unions on the Structure of Wages: A Longitudinal Analysis." *Econometrica* 64
(July 1996): 957–79.

_____, Thomas Lemieux, and W. Craig Riddell. "Unionization and Wage Inequality: A Comparative Study
of the U.S., the U.K., and Canada." NBER Working Paper #9473, January 2003.

Clark, Kim B. "Unionization and Firm Performance: The Impact on Profits, Growth, and Productivity."
American Economic Review 74 (December 1984): 893–919.

Curme, Michael and David A. Macpherson. "Union Wage Differentials and the Effects of Industry and Local
Union Density: Evidence from the 1980s." *Journal of Labor Research* 12 (Fall 1991): 419–27.

Duncan, Greg J. and Frank P. Stafford. "Do Union Members Receive Compensating Wage Differentials?"
American Economic Review 70 (June 1980): 355–71.

Duncan, Gregory M. and Duane E. Leigh. "Wage Determination in the Union and Nonunion Sectors: A Sample Selectivity Approach." *Industrial and Labor Relations Review* 34 (October 1980): 24–34.

Farber, Henry S. "The Determination of the Union Status of Workers." *Econometrica* 51 (September 1983):
1417–38.

_____. "The Analysis of Union Behavior." In O. Ashenfelter and R. Layard, eds. *Handbook of Labor Eco-
nomics, Vol. II.* Amsterdam: North-Holland, 1986, pp. 1039–89.

_____. "Mobility and Stability: The Dynamics of Job Change in Labor Markets." In O. Ashenfelter and
D. Card, eds. *Handbook of Labor Economics, Vol. 3B.* Amsterdam: North–Holland, 1999, pp. 2439–83.

_____ and Bruce Western. "Accounting for the Decline of Unions in the Private Sector, 1973–1988." In
James T. Bennett and Bruce E. Kaufman, eds. *The Future of Private Sector Unionism in the United
States.* Armonk, N.Y.: M.E. Sharpe, 2002, pp. 28–58.

Freeman, Richard B. "The Exit-Voice Tradeoff in the Labor Market: Unionism, Job Tenure, Quits and Separations." *Quarterly Journal of Economics* 94 (June 1980): 643–74.

_____. "Unionism and the Dispersion of Wages." *Industrial and Labor Relations Review* 34 (October
1980): 3–23.

_____. "The Effect of Unionism on Fringe Benefits." *Industrial and Labor Relations Review* 34 (July
1981): 489–509.

_____. "Union Wage Practices and Wage Dispersion within Establishments." *Industrial and Labor Rela-
tions Review* 36 (October 1982): 3–21.

_____. "Longitudinal Analyses of the Effects of Trade Unions." *Journal of Labor Economics* 2 (January
1984): 1–26.

_____. "In Search of Union Wage Concessions in Standard Data Sets." *Industrial Relations* 25 (Spring
1986): 131–45.

_____ and James L. Medoff. "The Impact of the Percent Organized on Union and Nonunion Wages."
Review of Economics and Statistics 63 (November 1981): 561–72.

_____. *What Do Unions Do?* New York: Basic Books, 1984.

Fuchs, Victor R., Alan B. Krueger, and James M. Poterba. "Economists' Views about Parameters, Values, and Policies: Survey Results in Labor and Public Economics." *Journal of Economic Literature* 36 (September 1998): 1387–425.

Giles, D.E.A. "The Interpretation of Dummy Variables in Semilogarithmic Equations: Unbiased Estimation." *Economics Letters* 10 (1982): 77–79.

Grant, Darren. "A Comparison of the Cyclical Behavior of Union and Nonunion Wages in the United States." *Journal of Human Resources* 36 (Winter 2001): 31–57.

Heckman, James J. and Solomon W. Polachek. "Empirical Evidence on the Functional Form of the Earnings-Schooling Relationship." *Journal of the American Statistical Association* 69 (June 1974): 350–54.

Hirsch, Barry T. "The Interindustry Structure of Unionism, Earnings, and Earnings Dispersion." *Industrial and Labor Relations Review* 36 (October 1982): 22–39.

_____. *Labor Unions and the Economic Performance of U.S. Firms.* Kalamazoo, Mich.: Upjohn Institute for Employment Research, 1991.

_____ and John T. Addison. *The Economic Analysis of Unions: New Approaches and Evidence.* Boston: Allen & Unwin, 1986.

Hirsch, Barry T. and Mark C. Berger. "Union Membership Determination and Industry Characteristics." *Southern Economic Journal* 50 (January 1984): 665–79.

Hirsch, Barry T. and David A. Macpherson. "Union Membership and Coverage Database from the Current Population Survey: Note." *Industrial and Labor Relations Review* 56 (January 2003): 349–54, and accompanying data site http://www.unionstats.com/.

Hirsch, Barry T., David A. Macpherson, and J. Michael DuMond. "Workers' Compensation Recipiency in Union and Nonunion Workplaces." *Industrial and Labor Relations Review* 50 (January 1997): 213–36.

Hirsch, Barry T., David A. Macpherson, and Edward J. Schumacher. "Measuring Union and Nonunion Wage Growth: Puzzles in Search of Solutions." In P. Wunnava, ed. *The Changing Role of Unions: New Forms of Representation.* Armonk, N.Y.: M.E. Sharpe, 2004.

Hirsch, Barry T. and Edward J. Schumacher. "Match Bias in Wage Gap Estimates Due to Earnings Imputation." *Journal of Labor Economics* 22 (July 2004).

_____. "Unions, Wages, and Skills." *Journal of Human Resources* 33 (Winter 1998): 201–19.

Hirsch, Barry T., Michael L. Wachter, and James W. Gillula. "Postal Service Compensation and the Comparability Standard." *Research in Labor Economics* 18 (1999): 243–79.

Hwang, Hae-shin, W. Robert Reed, and Carlton Hubbard. "Compensating Wage Differentials and Unobserved Productivity." *Journal of Political Economy* 100 (August 1992): 835–58.

Jarrell, Stephen B. and T.D. Stanley. "A Meta-Analysis of the Union-Nonunion Wage Gap." *Industrial and Labor Relations Review* 44 (October 1990): 54–67.

Jones, Ethel B. "Union/Nonunion Wage Differentials: Membership or Coverage?" *Journal of Human Resources* 17 (Spring 1982): 276–85.

Kalachek, Edward and Frederic Raines. "Trade Unions and Hiring Standards." *Journal of Labor Research* 1 (Spring 1980): 63–75.

Lazear, Edward P. "A Competitive Theory of Monopoly Unionism." *American Economic Review* 73 (September 1983): 631–43.

Lee, Lung-Fei. "Unionism and Wage Rates: A Simultaneous Equations Model with Qualitative and Limited Dependent Variables." *International Economic Review* 19 (June 1978): 415–34.

Lemieux, Thomas. "Estimating the Effects of Unions on Wage Inequality in a Panel Data Model with Comparative Advantage and Non-Random Selection." *Journal of Labor Economics* 16 (June 1978): 261–91.

Lettau, Michael K., Mark A. Loewenstein, and Aaron T. Cushner. "Explaining the Differential Growth Rates of the ECI and the ECEC." *Compensation and Working Conditions* 2 (Summer 1997): 15–23.

Lewis, H. Gregg. *Unionism and Relative Wages in the United States: An Empirical Inquiry.* Chicago: University of Chicago Press, 1963.

_____. *Union Relative Wage Effects: A Survey.* Chicago: University of Chicago Press, 1986.

Macpherson, David A. "Trade Unions and Labor's Share in U.S. Manufacturing Industries." *International Journal of Industrial Organization* 8 (March 1990): 143–51.

Mellow, Wesley. "Unionism and Wages: A Longitudinal Analysis." *Review of Economics and Statistics* 63 (February 1981): 43–52.

_____ and Hal Sider. "Accuracy of Response in Labor Market Surveys: Evidence and Implications." *Journal of Labor Economics* 1 (October 1983): 331–44.

Mincer, Jacob. *Schooling, Experience, and Earnings.* New York: Columbia University Press, 1974.

_____. "Union Effects: Wages, Turnover, and Job Training." In J.D. Reid, Jr., ed. *New Approaches to Labor Unions.* Greenwich, Conn.: JAI Press, 1983, pp. 217–52.

Oi, Walter Y. and Todd L. Idson. "Firm Size and Wages." In O. Ashenfelter and D. Card, eds. *Handbook of Labor Economics, Vol. 3B.* Amsterdam: North-Holland, 1999, pp. 2165–214.

Pencavel, John H. "The Demand for Union Services: An Exercise." *Industrial and Labor Relations Review* 24 (January 1971): 180–90.

Robinson, Chris. "The Joint Determination of Union Status and Union Wage Effects: Some Tests of Alternative Models." *Journal of Political Economy* 97 (June 1989): 639–67.

Rosen, Sherwin. "The Theory of Equalizing Differentials." In O. C. Ashenfelter and R. Layard, eds. *Handbook of Labor Economics, Vol. 1.* Amsterdam: North-Holland, 1986, pp. 641–92.

Schumacher, Edward J. "What Explains Wage Differences between Union Members and Covered Non-members?" *Southern Economic Journal* 65 (January 1999): 493–512.

Viscusi, W. Kip and Joseph E. Aldy. "The Value of a Statistical Life: A Critical Review of Market Estimates Throughout the World." NBER Working Paper #9487, February 2003.

Wessels, Walter. "Do Unionized Firms Hire Better Workers?" *Economic Inquiry* 32 (October 1994): 616–29.

Willis, Robert J. "Wage Determinants: A Survey and Reinterpretation of Human Capital Earnings Functions." In O.C. Ashenfelter and R. Layard, eds. *Handbook of Labor Economics, Vol. 1.* Amsterdam: North-Holland, 1986, pp. 525–602.

U.S. Department of Labor, Bureau of Labor Statistics. *Employment Cost Index, Historical Listing.* January 30, 2003. Available at http://www.bls.gov/ncs/ect/.

U.S. Department of Labor, Bureau of Labor Statistics. *Employer Costs for Employee Compensation, Historical Listing (Annual) 1986–2001.* June 19, 2002. Available at http://www.bls.gov/ncs/ect/.

[20]

THE IMPACT OF DEUNIONISATION ON EARNINGS DISPERSION REVISITED

John T. Addison, Ralph W. Bailey and
W. Stanley Siebert

ABSTRACT

This paper examines the effects of union change in Britain on changes in earnings dispersion 1983–1995. We investigate not only the decline in union density but also the greater wage compression among unionised workers, as well as changes in union density across skill groups. For the private sector, we find that deunionisation accounts for little of the increase in earnings dispersion. What unions have lost on the swings (lower density), they have gained on the roundabouts (greater wage compression). But for the public sector we find strong effects, because unions are increasingly organising the more skilled. This change in the character of public sector unions means that they no longer reduce earnings variation nearly as much as they once did.

1. INTRODUCTION

The British earnings distribution has widened considerably since Mrs Thatcher's sustained attack on the unions. The possibility of there being a

Aspects of Worker Well-Being
Research in Labor Economics
ISSN: 0147-9121/doi:10.1016/S0147-9121(06)26009-6

JOHN T. ADDISON ET AL.

connection between the two developments has been the subject of a fairly large literature. In this paper, we revisit the subject, using the general variance decomposition technique first put forward by Freeman (1980) and Metcalf (1982). We follow Card's (2001) modification of this approach to allow for changes in the "structure" of unionisation across the workforce; specifically, the greater decline in union density among the lower paid than the higher paid. Using this method, and allowing for changes in union wage and variance gaps, as well as union density, we show that the effect of deunionisation on earnings dispersion has on the whole been more modest than generally believed. We concentrate on the period up to 1995, because most of the changes in unionisation and earnings dispersion had occurred by this point (see Fig. 1 below).

Certainly, casual inspection shows a striking association between movements in union density over time and changes in the earnings dispersion (see Leslie & Pu, 1996, Fig. 4d). Emphasising this link, Schmitt (1995, p. 201) has calculated that the decline in union density could account for 21 per cent of the rise in the pay premium for a university degree and for 13 per cent of the increase in the non-manual differential, 1978–1988. Machin (1997, p. 653) obtains more dramatic results: comparing 1983 with 1991, he calculates that the male earnings variance would have been 40 per cent less had the 1983 levels of union coverage prevailed in 1991. Bell and Pitt (1998, pp. 520–523)

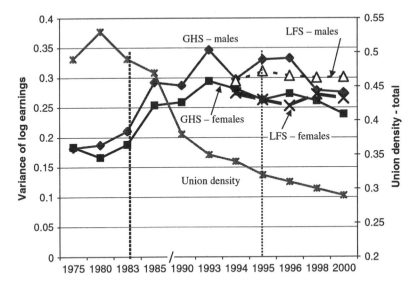

Fig. 1. Earnings Variance in the GHS and LFS Compared.

also conclude that deunionisation between the early 1980s and 1990s widened the male earnings distribution – in this case by about 20 per cent.

That said, not all research points the same way. Notably, in their thorough analysis of the wage distribution of U.K. males, Gosling, Machin, and Meghir (2000, p. 661) emphasise education rather than deunionisation: the way recent cohorts have improved their acquisition of education, as well as changes over time in the returns to education. Moreover, Card (2001) has pointed out that the equalising effects of unionism can be exaggerated if we do not allow for the fact that unionisation effects vary across the wage distribution. He shows that if the *structure* of unionisation changes, so that union density falls less over time for the higher paid – as has happened both in the U.S. and the U.K. (see below) – then estimates of the equalising tendency of unionisation can be reduced.

The plan of the paper is as follows. In the next two sections, we first describe the datasets used before reviewing the variance decomposition approach; here, we also derive some descriptive results on changes in unionisation over time. In the fourth section, we give the results of the variance decomposition analysis. (Because variance decomposition is central to our approach, our measure of wage dispersion is naturally the variance, rather than other commonly used measures such as the Gini coefficient or the ratio of the top to the bottom deciles.) Then, in the fifth section, given the diverging trends of unionisation in the public and private sectors, we present some results for the two sectors separately. The final section provides a summary and conclusion.

2. THE DATA

We require data on earnings, unionisation, and individual characteristics over the last two decades. Just about the earliest dataset available with good union and earnings information is the 1983 General Household Survey (GHS) (OPCS, 1986). 1983 is the only year in which the GHS included a union membership question, but this year is early enough to represent the "golden age" of unionism. The Family Expenditure Survey (Bell & Pitt, 1998), or British Social Attitudes Survey (Blanchflower & Bryson, 2003) also offer possibilities. The Family Expenditure Survey asks a question on whether union dues are paid, from which it would be possible to infer union membership beginning in 1982. However, as Bell and Pitt (1998, p. 515), acknowledge this method is likely to omit union members who do not pay dues regularly. For its part, the British Social Attitudes Survey has union

JOHN T. ADDISON ET AL.

membership and earnings data available from 1984 (SCPR, 1985). However, the earnings data provided are in categories rather than continuous in form, and there is a small sample (867 employees in 1984), which would raise problems for our study of earnings dispersion. The GHS, by contrast, has the advantage of a large sample of employees (over 8,000), which is important since we aim to split the sample into private and public sectors, and analyse males and females separately. Accordingly, we use the 1983 GHS for our early period, as have Machin (1997), Gosling and Lemieux (2001), and Bell and Pitt (1998).

For the later period, we use the Labour Force Survey (LFS), which provides detailed earnings data from 1993 onward. The LFS also provides a large sample of over 8,000 employees. We choose the 1995 LFS (OPCS, 2000), because 1995 represents the nadir of the union movement's fortunes, and well precedes Labour's 1997 election victory. Most of the changes in unionisation and earnings dispersion had occurred by 1995, as shown in Fig. 1 (see also Card, Lemieux, & Riddell, 2003), and we therefore concentrate on this period.

Fig. 1 further indicates that the two datasets are comparable. It can be seen that earnings inequality in the GHS steadily increased from the late 1970s to the early 1990s, with the two surveys yielding similar measures of inequality in 1995. While the measures are more divergent in 2000, both sources agree that the rise in inequality plateaued in the 1990s. Moreover, union status is measured by the same question in both surveys: 'Are you a member of a trade union or staff association?' As regards union coverage, however, which would arguably better address the issue of union impact on wages, the survey questions differ. In the GHS the question is: 'Is there a trade union or staff association where you work, which people in your type of job can join if they want to?' In the LFS the question is simply: 'At your place of work, are there unions, staff associations, or groups of unions?' Hence, as with most of the literature, we restrict the analysis to union membership alone.

As regards the wage variable, we take several steps to ensure comparability. For both datasets, we restrict the sample to individuals aged 16–66 years, and not self-employed. For both, we use the same hourly wage variable computed by dividing weekly earnings by usual hours. In addition, we convert the 1983 wage data to 1995 values using the retail price index. Finally, for both years we trim off observations with implausibly low or high wage rates, excluding hourly wages outside the £1–£45 range. These adjustments have a minor effect. Our 1995 figure for aggregate union density (the percentage of employees who are union members) is 33.1 per cent,

The Impact of Deunionisation on Earnings Dispersion Revisited

Table 1. Hourly Wage Distributions, Union and Non-Union Workers, 1983 and 1995.

	Men		Women	
	Non-Union	Union	Non-Union	Union
1983				
Union density (%)	56.7		42.1	
Overall variance log wages	0.223		0.192	
Variance log wage	0.289	0.151	0.197	0.147
Mean log wage	1.639	1.854	1.280	1.534
Adjusted union wage gap (*t*-value)	0.149 (12.9)		0.195 (15.5)	
1995				
Union density (%)	37.4		30.7	
Overall variance log wages	0.309		0.262	
Variance log wage	0.358	0.205	0.241	0.226
Mean log wage	1.876	2.066	1.55	1.89
Adjusted union wage gap (*t*-value)	0.091 (6.41)		0.195 (13.7)	

Notes: Samples are taken from the 1983 General Household Survey and the 1995 third quarter Labour Force Survey (LFS) with Northern Ireland excluded. Samples comprise respondents aged 16–66 years who were not self-employed and whose hourly wage was between £1 and £45 in 1995 pounds (1983 wages valued in 1995 pounds according to the retail price index). For the LFS, the income weights supplied with the data are used. The adjusted union wage gap is the union coefficient from a regression controlling for years of education, years of experience (plus experience squared and cubed), and dummies for non-white, marital status, and 5 regions.

comparable with Brook's (2002), (Table 1) figure of 32.3 per cent for employees in Great Britain.

3. ACCOUNTING FOR THE IMPACT OF DEUNIONISATION

There are different ways to account for the impact of deunionisation on earnings dispersion. First, various counterfactuals are possible. It is natural to compute the impact of deunionisation by asking what earnings dispersion would be if union density had not declined. However, there are two other important dimensions of unionism: the union wage gap, and the variance gap (the difference in the variance of wages for union and non-union workers). It is worth considering counterfactual changes in these dimensions as well. Second, as noted above, we can allow for differences in union density across skill groups. Let us look at these points in turn.

JOHN T. ADDISON ET AL.

Beginning with the basic two-sector formulation, average wages $\bar{w}$ are

$$\bar{w} = U\bar{w}^u + U'\bar{w}^n \tag{1}$$

where U is union density, $U' = 1 - U$ and the superscripts u and n refer to union and non-union, respectively. This equation can be rewritten in terms of union "power", namely, union density multiplied by the union/non-union wage gap

$$\bar{w} - \bar{w}^n = U\Delta_w \tag{2}$$

where $\Delta_w = \bar{w}^u = \bar{w}^n$ is the wage gap. This equation shows that the term $U\Delta_w$ determines the extent to which average wages are pushed above non-union wages; hence, the conventional use of the term "union power." It is important to consider how union power differs across the skill groups, which we do below.

The impact of unionism on the variance of average wages is what we wish to assess. Eq. (1) provides a framework for estimating this effect. According to this equation, the variance of wages can be expressed in terms of union density, and the union–non-union wage and variance gaps. Using Freeman's formula (1980, p. 19) the variance (V) is

$$V = V^n + U\Delta_v + UU'\Delta_w{}^2$$

or,

$$D = V - V^n = U\Delta_v + UU'\Delta_w{}^2 \tag{3}$$

where $\Delta_v = V^u - V^n$ is the union–non-union variance gap, V^u and V^n being the variance of wages in the union and non-union sectors, respectively. The impact of unionism on the overall wage variance is then D, namely, the overall wage variance minus the (larger) wage variance that would prevail without unionism. As can be seen, the impact can be decomposed into a term involving the union variance gap, $U\Delta_V$, the so-called *within-sector* effect, which is generally negative since Δ_v is generally negative. The impact will also depend on the term $UU'\Delta_w$, the *between-sector* effect, which is positive since unions widen wage dispersion due to the union wage gap. Note that the impact of unionism depends not only upon U but also upon the wage and variance gaps, Δ_w and Δ_v.

In assessing the impact of unionism on changes in wage variance over time – our focus here – we need to hypothesise what would have happened if unionism had taken a different path, that is, develop a counterfactual.

The Impact of Deunionisation on Earnings Dispersion Revisited

Various approaches are possible. First, let us write an equation for the change in union impact, ΔD, between time periods 0 and 1

$$\Delta D = \Delta V - \Delta V^n = U_1 \Delta_{1v} - U_0 \Delta_{0v} + U_1 U_1' \Delta_{1w}^2 - U_0 U_0' \Delta_{0w}^2 \quad (4)$$

where $\Delta D = D_1 - D_0$, $\Delta V = V_1 - V_0$, and $\Delta V^n = V_1^n - V_0^n$. The counterfactual here is then the change in the non-union wage variance, ΔV^n For example, if deunionisation is causing a decline in union impact on the wage variance, the (negative) impact of unionisation will be smaller absolutely in period 1 than period 0; that is, $\Delta D > 0$. This condition requires the change in the overall wage variance to be greater than the change in the non-union wage variance, or $\Delta V > \Delta V^n$. Thus, changes in the non-union wage variance are meant to control for changes in the "other factors" which determine the overall wage variance.

We can also develop a counterfactual by writing

$$\Delta D = \Delta_{1v} \Delta U + \Delta_{1w}^2 \Delta(UU') + U_0 \Delta \Delta_v + U_0 U_0' \Delta \Delta_w^2 \quad (5)$$

or,

$$\Delta D = \Delta D' + \Delta D'' \quad (5')$$

where $\Delta D' = \Delta_{1v} \Delta U + \Delta_{1w}^2 \Delta(UU')$; $\Delta D'' = U_0 \Delta \Delta_v + U_0 U_0' \Delta \Delta_w^2$; $\Delta U = U_1 - U_0$; $\Delta(UU') = U_1(1-U_1) - U_0(1-U_0)$; $\Delta \Delta_v = \Delta_{1v} - \Delta_{0v}$; and $\Delta \Delta_w^2 = \Delta_{1w}^2 - \Delta_{0w}^2$.

In other words, the change in union impact can be decomposed into two parts: $\Delta D'$, the change in impact due to movements in U alone, weighted by period 1's wage and variance gaps, and $\Delta D''$, the change in impact due to movements in wage and variance gaps, weighted by period 0's U level. $\Delta D'$ is sometimes reported (e.g., Machin, 1997, p. 653), since it builds a natural counterfactual based on changes in union density *alone*. However, variance gaps are also important as a measure of union power. These gaps have in fact increased over time in Britain, as we will see. Therefore, while we will report $\Delta D'$ values for comparative purposes, we will generally rely on the ΔD measure.

Let us now turn to the point that unionisation varies across skill groups. A way of showing this variation, following Card (2001), is to define skill groups using predicted earnings percentiles based on the non-union wage structure. We can then compare union densities across these skill groups.[1] We can also consider how union "power" (viz. density multiplied by the

JOHN T. ADDISON ET AL.

wage gap, noted earlier) varies across skill groups. The picture for males
(females) is given in Figs. 2a and 2b (Figs. 3a and 3b).

Fig. 2a shows that, for males in 1983, union density was lowest among the
least skilled (lowest decile), highest at the third decile and then somewhat
lower for the more skilled. Corresponding data for 1995 show density falling
most among the least skilled, leaving the highest density at the top decile.
The male union density measure thus suggests that unions help a labour

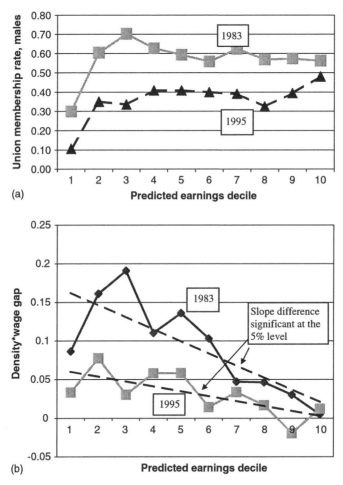

Fig. 2. (a) Union Density by Skill, (b) Union Power by Skill, Males in 1983 and
1995.

The Impact of Deunionisation on Earnings Dispersion Revisited

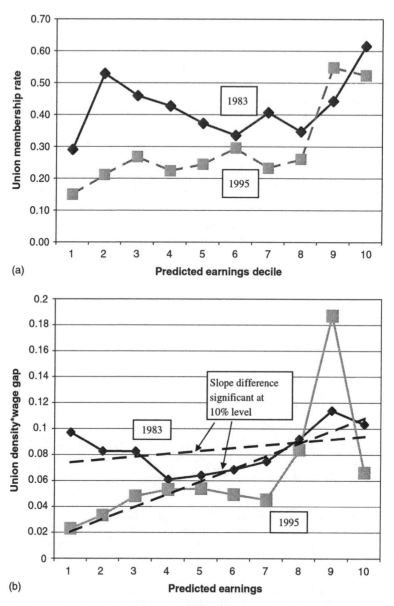

Fig. 3.   (a) Union Density by Skill, (b) Union Power by Skill, Females, in 1983 and 1995.

JOHN T. ADDISON ET AL.

"elite". However, the picture is different for union power. Fig. 2b shows that union power was definitely greater both in 1983 and in 1995 for the least skilled. Nevertheless, it is evident that there has been a significant fall in union power among this group by 1995. For females, the union density and union power graphs are more similar. Over time, both density and power have fallen among low-skill groups, but have remained quite steady in the top three deciles. Thus, Fig. 3b shows that, particularly in 1995, there is a positive covariance between union power and skill for women, so that unionisation appears to benefit an elite.[2]

Allowing for different union effects by skill category requires modification of Eq. (3). Card (2001, p. 298) shows that the formula becomes

$$V = V^{n*} + \overline{U\Delta_V} + \overline{U(1-U)\Delta_w{}^2} + \text{Var}[U(c)\Delta_w(c)]$$
$$+ 2\text{Cov}[w^n(c), \ U(c)\Delta_w(c)] \tag{6}$$

V^{n*} is the non-union wage variance, namely, the variance that would result if all workers were paid according to the non-union wage structure.[3] $U(c)$ is union density in the c groups, $\Delta_v(c)$ are the variance gaps, $\Delta_w(c)$ are the wage gaps, and $w^n(c)$ are the non-union wage rates. The over-bar terms indicate averages over the c skill categories, and are analogous to the terms in Eq. (3). But the terms for variance and covariance between categories are new, and in practise we will find the covariance to be the most important. This covariance is precisely that between skill, w^n, and union power, $U\Delta_w$, which we have been discussing above in connection with Figs. 2b and 3b. A negative covariance term will indicate that unions are more helpful to the least skilled, and this will pull the overall wage variance, $V(c)$, below the variance prevailing without unions, V^{n*}. A positive covariance term indicates the opposite.

Over time, as Figs. 2b and 3b have made clear, union power in the cases of both men and women has been shifting towards more skilled workers (the covariance term in Eq. (6) is becoming less negative). This factor will have offset the equalising tendency of unions brought about, in particular, by the variance gap. We now consider the size of these effects.

4. FINDINGS

4.1. The Economy as a Whole

Table 1 contains panels for 1983 and 1995 that show how the overall variance in log wages has increased over the period. For men the increase has

The Impact of Deunionisation on Earnings Dispersion Revisited

been 86 log points (from 0.223 to 0.309), and for women it has been 70 log points (from 0.192 to 0.262). These large increases are what we are concerned to explain. Notice that the increase in wage variance for non-union workers has been smaller: 69 points for men (0.289 to 0.358), and 44 points for women (0.197 to 0.241). Thus, forces operating on the non-union sector alone cannot explain the increase in overall wage variance, suggesting a role for deunionisation. The table also shows that the union wage variance is lower than the non-union variance, thereby pointing to the equalising effect of greater unionisation.[4] Interestingly, it can also be seen that while both the union and non-union wage variances have risen over time, the union variance for men remains much smaller than the corresponding non-union variance: the variance gap has even increased. In other words, even though they are less extensive than heretofore, male unions can still strongly "standardise" their members' wages.

Table 1 also contains information on the wage gap, both unadjusted and adjusted for a set of conventional human capital variables.[5] The unadjusted wage gaps are always larger than the adjusted gaps because union workers have higher skills than their non-union counterparts. However, the difference between adjusted and unadjusted wage gaps grows between 1983 and 1995, reflecting the increased unionisation of high skill groups in 1995. For men, the adjusted wage gap falls over time as well, reflecting reduced union power on this dimension (but we must remember that male unions can still standardise members' wages). By contrast, female unions seem to have increased their power to bring about a wide wage gap (0.205 in 1995, compared to 0.197 in 1983), but not so strongly to standardise their members' wages.

We now estimate basic union effects on wage dispersion, using Eq. (3). The results are given in Table 2. Taking males in 1983, for example, the within-sector effect is $U\Delta_V = -0.078$, which is negative because the variance gap is negative. The between-sector effect is $U(1-U)\Delta_W^2 = 0.006$ which is positive, following the wage gap, but bound to be small since the wage-gap term is squared. The total effect is -0.072. This figure represents a sizeable contribution – about one-third – to reducing male wage variance in 1983 (0.223 from Table 1). In 1995, the impact is smaller, -0.055, or about one-sixth of the male wage variance (0.309 from Table 1). Taking changes over time, as in Eq. (4), male deunionisation contributes to a rise in wage variance of 0.017, which is 19.8 per cent of the overall increase. Turning to women, we see that in 1983 unionism is weakly egalitarian, reducing wage variance by -0.012. By 1995, however, women's unionism actually *widens* the wage variance by 0.004. Over time, then, the impact of deunionisation for women is similar – namely, 22.9 per cent – but is achieved by a different route.

JOHN T. ADDISON ET AL.

Table 2. Basic Estimates of the Contribution of Declining Unionisation to Wage Inequality, 1983–1995.

	Men	Women	Remarks
1983			
Union density, U	0.567	0.421	From Table 1
Union wage gap, Δ_W	0.151	0.197	Adjusted difference between union and non-union wages (Table 1)
Union variance gap, Δ_V	−0.138	−0.050	Difference in union and non-union wage variances (Table 1)
Union effect, *between* sectors, $U(1-U)\Delta_W^2$	0.006	0.009	Small effect of unions in raising wage inequality by widening mean pay as between union and non-union sectors
Union effect, *within* sectors, $U\Delta_V$	−0.078	−0.021	Larger effect of unions is to reduce wage dispersion within union sectors
Total union effect	−0.072	−0.012	Estimated total effect of unions is to reduce wage variance; for example, for men the reduction is −0.072
1995			
Union density, U	0.374	0.307	⎫ From Table 1
Union wage gap, Δ_W	0.086	0.205	⎬
Union variance gap, Δ_V	−0.153	−0.015	
Union effect, *between* sectors, $U(1-U)\Delta_W^2$	0.002	0.009	⎫ See explanations for 1983 above ⎬
Union effect, *within* sectors, $U\Delta_V$	−0.057	−0.005	⎭
Total union effect	−0.055	0.004	Variance-reducing effect of unions is smaller for men in 1995 than 1983, and unions even increase dispersion for women in 1995
Changes: 1983–1995			
Change in variance of wages	0.086	0.070	See Table 1; for example, for men 0.086 = 0.309–0.223
Change in effect of unions	0.017	0.016	Change in total union effect derived above; for example, for men 0.017 = −0.055−(−0.072)
Contribution of unions (%)	19.8	22.9	For example, for men 0.198 = 0.017/0.086

The Impact of Deunionisation on Earnings Dispersion Revisited

Table 2. (*Continued*)

	Men	Women	Remarks
Memo item			
Amount 1995 V would be lowered given 1983 U (%)[a]	0.030 (34.3)	0.002 (2.4)	This figure depends mainly on $(U_1-U_0)\,\Delta_{v1}$, the change in U weighted by the 1995 variance gap. This gap is small for women; hence the 2.4% figure

[a]This number gives $\Delta D'$, the deunionisation effect assuming changes in union density alone; see Eq. (5′).

The last row of Table 2 shows the different estimates for deunionisation that are obtained when we use the counterfactual, $\Delta D'$, from Eq. (5′). It will be recalled that here we are estimating what the 1995 wage variance would have been had the 1983 level of union density prevailed, taking as given the 1995 union wage and variance gaps. Using this method, deunionisation contributes 34.3 per cent to the widening in the male wage variance, but only 2.4 per cent in the case of females. However, as we have also noted, this method ignores changes in wage and variance gaps.[6]

The next step is to allow for differences in union structure (i.e. in coverage and in wage and variance gaps) across skill groups, where the latter are defined using Card's (2001) predicted earnings deciles. We have already seen (from Fig. 2b) how union power, for men, although tending to be pro-poor, has become less so with the passage of time. And the trend is the same for women (Fig. 3b). Table 3 now quantifies the impact of these trends.

The estimates in Table 3 indicate a reduced impact of deunionisation on wage dispersion for men, although not for women. Looking first at men, unions reduce overall wage variance in both years: by -0.041 in 1983 and by -0.042 in 1995. However, as can be seen, the reduction is as great in 1995, which implies that deunionisation cannot be a factor in the widening male wage variance. To put this finding another way: the counterfactual variance of wages if all were paid according to the non-union wage structure, V^{n*}, has increased by 0.087, which is as much as the increase in the overall wage variance, 0.086. Since the male non-union wage variance has increased so much, there is little room for a deunionisation effect.

The main factor behind the strong variance-reducing effect of unions for men in 1995 is the larger variance gap term: $\overline{U\Delta_V} = -0.033$ in 1995 compared with -0.024 in 1983 (see the lower panel of the table). In other words, unions standardise their members' pay more in 1995 than 1983. This factor

JOHN T. ADDISON ET AL.

Table 3. Adjusted Estimates of the Contribution of Declining Unionisation to Wage Inequality, Allowing for Different Union Effects across Pay Deciles.

	Men	Women	Remarks
1983			
Variance of wages, V	0.223	0.192	From Table 1
Adjusted variance of non-union wages, V^{n*}	0.264	0.207	Allowing for different union impacts across pay deciles (see Notes below)
Adjusted union effect	−0.041	−0.015	Example for men −0.041 = $V - Vn*$; (see text Eq. (6))
1995			
Variance in wages	0.309	0.262	From Table 1
Adjusted variance in non-union wages, V^{n*}	0.351	0.261	Allowing for different union impacts across pay deciles (see Notes below)
Adjusted union effect	−0.042	0.001	E.g. for men −0.041 = $V - Vn*$; (see text Eq. (6))
Changes: 1995 − 1983			
Variance of wages ΔV	0.086	0.070	For men, unionism reduces
Adjusted variance of non-union wages ΔV^{n*}	0.087	0.054	wage dispersion about as much in 1995 as 1983. So decline of unions cannot
Adjusted union effect	−0.001	0.016	have increased dispersion.
Union effect is % of ΔV	0	23	But for women, unionism has a role

	Men		Women	
	1983	1995	1983	1995
$\overline{U \Delta_V}$	−.024	−0.033	−0.030	−0.022
$\overline{U(1-U)\Delta_w{}^2}$	0.009	0.003	0.011	0.009
$Var[U(c)\Delta_w(c)]$	0.003	0.001	0.001	0.002
$2Cov[w^n(c), U(c)\Delta_w(c)]$	−0.028	−0.013	0.004	0.013
Total	−0.041	−0.042	−0.016	0.001
Memo: Average variance gap $\overline{\Delta_V}$	−0.04	−0.09	−0.06	−0.06

Notes: The adjusted formula, allowing for different union effects on wage variance by skill category, is given in Eq. (6) in the text. Values for the terms in the equation (taken from the $c = 10$ decile groups in Appendix B) are given above.

The Impact of Deunionisation on Earnings Dispersion Revisited

counteracts the tendency for union power to become less pro-poor, as shown by the diminution of the covariance term (see also the significant flattening of the union power line in Fig. 2b). On the other hand, the adjusted and simple estimates are similar for women. The variance-reducing effect of unions is estimated to be much larger in 1983 (at -0.015) than in 1995 (0.001). For women, union power has tended over time to become less egalitarian (see also Fig. 3b).[7] Consequently, the change in the *character* of women's unionisation appears to play a considerable role in the widening of women's wage variance.

These results differ from the received wisdom. In particular, it seems that the increase in wage dispersion for men can hardly be attributed to deunionisation. What unions have lost on the swings (less power among the unskilled) they have gained on the roundabouts (more wage compression for their members). It is true that deunionisation still seems to have a role to play in explaining increased wage dispersion among women. Nevertheless, we conclude that the equalising effects of unions are less than might be thought. Let us now consider whether distinguishing between the public and private sectors upsets this conclusion.

4.2. Public-Private Sector Comparisons of Unionism

It is interesting to assess the impact of deunionisation on wage inequality in the public and private sectors separately, since union trends have been so different. As can be seen from Table 4, public sector union density in 1995 is 78–86 per cent of its 1983 value. Indeed, some public sector groups such as women with further or higher education, have even maintained or increased their union density reflecting the rise in unionism among teachers and nurses. However, private sector density has declined considerably. In particular, the 1995 value for women (men) is now only 57 (69) per cent of the 1983 value.

At the same time, the private and public sectors are similar in that the more educated categories have maintained their union density better than less educated groups. The picture is best appreciated with the aid of Figs. A1 through A4 in Appendix A, which graph the union power variable – union density multiplied by the wage gap – against predicted earnings (the covariance term in Eq. (6)). Men and women are shown separately by sector. As can be seen, the 1995 relationship is significantly less negatively sloped than that for 1983 in all cases (though marginally for private sector males),

JOHN T. ADDISON ET AL.

Table 4. Trade Union Membership Rates, 1983 and 1995.

	Men			Women		
	1983	1995	Ratio 1995/1983	1983	1995	Ratio 1995/1983
(a) Private sector						
Overall	41.4	27.5	68.8	26.0	14.9	57.3
By education						
Degree or equivalent	13.4	18.4	94.8	30.2	14.2	47.0
Further education	40.6	24.3	59.9	27.3	21.8	79.8
'A' level or equivalent	39.3	32.2	81.9	20.2	17.7	87.6
'O' level or equivalent	30.0	17.2	57.3	21.4	14.4	67.3
Other	47.8	38.3	80.1	21.4	11.8	55.1
None	49.8	25.5	51.2	30.9	13.4	43.4
Observations	2,851	3,199		2,149	2,875	
(b) Public sector						
Overall	85.1	66.3	77.9	68.9	59.4	86.2
By education						
Degree or equivalent	81.2	71.9	88.5	76.1	73.3	96.3
Further education	85.2	78.1	91.7	73.9	79.0	1.07
'A' level or equivalent	83.6	56.2	67.2	68.2	45.2	66.3
'O' level or equivalent	79.5	60.8	76.5	64.3	46.8	72.8
Other	85.5	55.4	64.8	65.0	49.0	75.4
None	88.9	75.8	85.3	67.9	46.5	68.5
Observations	1,535	979		1,334	1,582	

Note: Public sector employment is defined to include nationalised industries, public corporations, or central or local government.

indicating that the more educated have maintained their union power better than the less educated.

We now calculate the basic union effects on wage dispersion. The necessary data on union density, and the wage and variance gaps are assembled in Table 5. It is interesting to note how, in the public sector, even though union density has been maintained, there have been considerable changes in wage gaps and variance gaps. For males, the wage gap – both the raw and the adjusted gap – has fallen almost to zero. However, the *variance gap* has been maintained, indicating that public sector unions have retained the power to compress male wages. However, for females in the public sector, there have been opposite tendencies, with the wage gap in particular rising.

Basic estimates of the impact of deunionisation, following Eq. (3), are given in Table 6. This table is analogous to Table 2 for the whole economy. For example, for private-sector men in 1983, −0.062 is an estimate of the amount by which unionisation reduces the wage variance. As can be seen,

The Impact of Deunionisation on Earnings Dispersion Revisited

Table 5.   Hourly Wage Distributions, 1983 and 1995.

	Men		Women	
	Non-Union	Union	Non-Union	Union
(a) Private sector				
1983				
Union density (%)	41.4		26.0	
Overall variance log wages	0.231		0.168	
Variance log wage by group	0.291	0.131	0.179	0.112
Mean log hourly wage	1.62	1.78	1.22	1.41
Adjusted union wage gap (*t*-value)	0.128 (8.60)		0.202 (10.9)	
1995				
Union density (%)	28.5		15.1	
Overall variance log wages	0.314		0.239	
Variance log wage by group	0.359	0.187	0.242	0.198
Mean log hourly wage	1.85	1.97	1.52	1.68
Adjusted union wage gap (*t*-value)	0.113 (6.3)		0.133 (5.96)	
(b) Public sector				
1983				
Union density (%)	85.1		68.9	
Overall variance log wages	0.178		0.172	
Variance log wage by group	0.250	0.162	0.201	0.154
Mean log hourly wage	1.77	1.89	1.49	1.61
Adjusted union wage gap (*t*-value)	0.112 (4.46)		0.095 (4.99)	
1995				
Union density (%)	66.5		59.5	
Overall variance log wages	0.238		0.235	
Variance log wage, by group	0.294	0.206	0.216	0.206
Mean log hourly wage	2.09	2.18	1.67	2.00
Adjusted union wage gap	0.016 (0.57)		0.191 (9.49)	

Note: See Table 2.

the impact of unions has fallen over time in both public and private sectors, just as for the economy as a whole. However, the fall has been particularly marked for women in the public sector, implying a greater role for de-unionisation (in terms of Eq. (4), the inequality $\Delta V > \Delta V^n$ holds strongly for this group). This is a surprising result given the fact that their union density has fallen least. The penultimate row gives the basic estimates for the contribution of deunionisation to the increased wage variance: 18.1 per cent for private-sector men, 5.6 per cent for private-sector women, 23.3 per cent for public-sector men, and 54.0 per cent for public-sector women. The final row shows, as a matter of interest, the very different estimate we would obtain using the counterfactual $\Delta D'$ of Eq. (5').

JOHN T. ADDISON ET AL.

Table 6. Basic Estimates of the Contribution of Declining Unionisation to Wage Inequality in the Private and Public Sectors, 1983–1995.

	Private Sector		Public Sector	
	Men	Women	Men	Women
1983				
Union effect, *between* sectors, $U(1-U)\,\Delta_W^2$	0.004	0.008	0.002	0.002
Union effect, *within* sectors, $U\Delta_V$	−0.066	−0.017	−0.075	−0.032
Total effect	−0.062	−0.009	−0.073	−0.030
1995				
Union effect, *between* sectors, $U(1-U)\,\Delta_W^2$	0.002	0.002	0.000	0.010
Union effect, *within* sectors, $U\Delta_V$	−0.049	−0.007	−0.059	−0.006
Total effect	−0.047	−0.005	−0.059	0.004
Changes: 1983–1995				
Change in variance of wages	0.083	0.071	0.060	0.063
Change in effect of unions	0.015	0.004	0.014	0.034
Contribution of unions (%)	18.1	5.6	23.3	54.0
Memo item				
Amount 1995 V would be lowered given 1983 U (%)	0.022	0.005	0.016	0.001
	(26.7)	(6.8)	(27.3)	(1.5)

Note: See Table 2.

We now turn to estimates that allow for different union effects by skill category. The results are given in Table 7, which is analogous to Table 3 for the whole economy. For men in the private sector, as for the economy as a whole, the adjusted estimate is smaller than the basic estimate. This outcome is primarily because the variance gaps within skill categories are smaller than the variance gap for the sector. An indication of this fact is provided in the memo item in the last row of the table, which gives the average variance gap across skill categories, $\overline{\Delta_V}$. For private sector men in 1983 this gap averages −0.05, whereas for the private sector as a whole it is −0.160 (= 0.131 − 0.291, Table 5).[8] At the same time, notice how the variance gap for men in this group has increased over time, from −0.05 to −0.07, as the memo item in the bottom panel indicates. On this measure, then, unions have increased their power over male wages in the private sector, even as union density has declined.

Pushing against this equalising effect of unions for private sector men has been the shift in union membership towards the labour elite. The shift is given by the decline (in absolute value) in the covariance term given in the lower panel of Table 7. The shift is also illustrated by the flatter union power graphs for 1995 (see Fig. A1 in Appendix A). For private-sector men, the net

The Impact of Deunionisation on Earnings Dispersion Revisited

Table 7. Adjusted Estimates of the Contribution of Declining Unionisation to Wage Inequality, Allowing for Different Union Effects across Pay Deciles.

	Private Sector		Public Sector	
	Men	Women	Men	Women
1983				
Variance in wages	0.231	0.169	0.178	0.172
Adjusted variance of non-union wages, V^{n*}	0.263	0.177	247	0.215
Adjusted union effect	−0.032	−0.008	−0.069	−0.044
1995				
Variance in log wages	0.314	0.239	0.238	0.235
Adjusted variance of non-union wages, V^{n*}	0.343	0.242	287	0.251
Adjusted union effect	−0.029	−0.003	−0.049	−0.016
Changes: 1983–1995				
Variance of wages, ΔV	0.083	0.070	0.060	0.063
Adjusted variance of non-union wages, ΔV^{n*}	0.080	0.065	040	0.036
Adjusted union effect	0.003	0.005	020	0.028
Union effect as % of ΔV	3.6%	7.1	33	44

	Private Sector				Public Sector			
	Men		Women		Men		Women	
	1983	1995	1983	1995	1983	1995	1983	1995
$\overline{U\Delta_V}$	−0.020	−0.021	−0.012	−0.007	010	−0.021	−0.018	−0.041
$\overline{U(1-U)\Delta_w^2}$	0.007	004	0.009	0.003	0.007	0.002	0.004	008
$\mathrm{Var}[U(c)\Delta_w(c)]$	0.003	001	000	000	023	004	006	0.002
$2\mathrm{Cov}[w^n(c),\ U(c)\Delta_w(c)]$	−0.021	−0.013	−0.006	0.001	−0.109	−0.034	−0.035	0.016
Total	−0.032	−0.029	−0.008	−0.003	−0.069	−0.049	−0.044	−0.016
Memo: average variance gap $\overline{\Delta_V}$	−0.05	−0.07	−0.05	−0.04	01	−0.03	−0.03	−0.06

Notes: See Table 4. The adjusted formula (allowing for different union effects by skill category) for the effect of unions on the variance of wages is given in Eq. (6) in the text. Values for the terms in the equation are given above.

result is that unions reduce earnings variance by about the same amount (around −0.03) in both 1983 and 1995. Therefore, deunionisation has apparently not contributed to the rise in male private sector wage variance.

For the other groups, the adjusted estimates are similar to the basic estimates, though the new method reveals interesting consequences of the change in the nature of unionism, particularly in the public sector. As can be seen, for public-sector men and women, the deunionisation effect remains large, 0.020 and 0.028 respectively (33–44 per cent of the increase in

JOHN T. ADDISON ET AL.

variance). The large effect in the public sector does not result from a fall in union density, as might be thought, but rather from the shift towards elite workers in union organising. This effect is shown by the decline in the covariance term in the lower panel of Table 7, which we have already noted for private sector men, and is also shown in Appendix A's Figs. A3 and A4. In fact, for public-sector women in 1995, the usual negative, pro-poor covariance between skill and union power turned positive, 0.016, as Table 7 shows. This change in the covariance term overwhelms the dispersion-reducing effect of a tendency towards larger variance gaps (for example, for public sector women, the last row of Table 7 shows the average variance gap to have increased in absolute value from −0.03 to −0.06). In short, there has been a change in the character of public-sector women's unionism, which the union density figures alone do not capture.

5. CONCLUSIONS

In this paper, we have analysed the impact of deunionisation on earnings dispersion over the period 1983–1995, taking men and women separately and also distinguishing between the private and public sectors. We have seen that unionism is a many-dimensioned entity. Union density is by no means the most important dimension. The variance and wage gaps attributable to unions are also important. So, too, is the "pro-poor" – or otherwise – distribution of union density. In fact, we show (following Card, 2001) that the distribution of union density has become less pro-poor over time, shifting for example from the less educated to the better educated. Accordingly, the "sword of justice" effect of unions (see Metcalf, 2005, p. 102) has become weaker.

Our headline finding is that the large decline in union density accounts for little of the increase in earnings variation in the private sector, either for men or women. This finding can be explained by allowing for unionism's other dimensions. We show that the variance gap has widened sufficiently over time to offset both the decline in density and the adverse shift in density towards the more skilled. In the private sector, therefore, unions appear to have maintained their power – at least as regards standardising their members' wages – notwithstanding all Mrs Thatcher's reforms.

In the public sector there has been less of a decline in union density. Yet, paradoxically, it is here that unionism has had more of a role to play. In the public sector, as in the private sector, variance gaps – and thus the power to standardise – have been maintained. The difference lies in the shift towards

The Impact of Deunionisation on Earnings Dispersion Revisited

organising the more skilled in the public sector, particularly amongst women. This means that unions no longer reduce earnings variation as much as they once did. Changes in the character of public sector unionism – not so much deunionisation as "re-unionisation" – can thus account for a large percentage (30–40 per cent) of the increased earnings dispersion in the public sector. But, to repeat, of the private sector no such statement can be made.

NOTES

1. The prediction equation is based on Card's (2001, p. 303) specification, and includes years of education, dummies for race, marital status and (5) regions, linear, quadratic and cubed experience, and interactions of five levels of education with linear and quadratic experience. It is fitted to non-union workers only, and then used to assign union and non-union workers into 10 equally sized groups.

2. It is likely that union power is overstated for low-skilled workers, and understated for the high skilled. Card (2001, p. 300) finds that low-skilled union workers have higher unobserved skills than their non-union counterparts, and the opposite for high-skilled union workers. Hence, the true wage (in efficiency units) for the low-skilled union worker will be lower than the observed wage, leading to an overstatement of union power here, with precisely the opposite result for the high skilled. We do not make an adjustment for this factor, but it should be kept in mind when assessing the extent to which union power is "pro-poor".

3. V^{n*} will differ from V^n in Eq. (3). $V^{n*} = \overline{V_i^n} + \mathrm{var}(\overline{X_i^n})$, where $\overline{V_i^n}$ is the weighted average of wage variances of the c groups, and $\mathrm{var}(\overline{X_i^n})$ is the variance of wage averages of the c groups.

4. Union wage variance remains much lower than the non-union variance when we standardise the differences in the characteristics of union and non-union workers. The variance of residuals from a wage regression for union workers is also lower than that for non-union workers.

5. The adjusted union wage gap is the union coefficient from a regression controlling for years of education, years of experience (plus experience squared and cubed), and dummies for non-white, marital status, and 5 regions. As will be seen, this two-sector wage gap does not play a major role in later calculations, and so we do not refine it.

6. The position here would be assessed by computing $\Delta D''$. For men, Δ_v has increased, indicating that 1995 is *superior* for this dimension of union power. Hence, male V in 1995 would be reduced given 1983 Δ_v.

7. We have the counterintuitive result for women that their average variance gap within skill groups, $\overline{\Delta_V}$, is larger than the variance gap for the labour force as a whole, Δ_v. In 1995, for example, $\overline{\Delta_V} = -0.06$ (bottom panel, Table 3), yet $\Delta_v = -0.015$ (Table 2). The reason is that Δ_v depends upon the distribution of union density across skill groups, as well as variance gaps within groups. The fact that most female union members are in the high skill groups, coupled with the fact that variance gaps are small for some of these groups, drives Δ_v down to -0.015.

JOHN T. ADDISON ET AL.

8. For public sector males in 1983 we have the extreme result that the average within skill group gap $\overline{\Delta_V} = 0$ (Table 7, bottom panel), while the overall gap $\Delta_v = -0.088$ ($= 0.162–0.250$, Table 5b). This result arises because males in public sector unions in 1983 tended to be found in skill groups with high variance gaps, although variance gaps were zero averaged across skill groups (going the "wrong" way for several groups, with higher variance for union than non-union workers).

ACKNOWLEDGMENTS

The authors acknowledge the Office of Population Censuses and Surveys, Social Survey Division (OPCS), as the originator of the 1983 General Household Survey; the OPCS, the Central Statistical Office, the Departments of Finance and Personnel and of Economic Development (Northern Ireland) and the Commission of the European Communities as originators and sponsors of the 1995 Quarterly Labour Force Survey; and the Data Archive at the University of Essex as the distributor of the data. None of these organisations bears any responsibility for the authors' analysis and interpretation of the data. The authors also thank participants at the July 2004 IZA *Workshop on Wage Inequality* and an anonymous reviewer for their comments.

REFERENCES

Bell, B., & Pitt, M. (1998). Trade union decline and distribution of wages in the UK: Evidence from kernel density estimation. *Oxford Bulletin of Economics and Statistics, 60*(4), 509–528.

Blanchflower, D., & Bryson, A. (2003). Changes over time in union relative wage effects in the UK and the US revisited. In: J. T. Addison & C. Schnabel (Eds), *International handbook of trade unions* (pp. 197–245). Cheltenham: Edward Elgar.

Brook, K. (2002). Trade union membership: An analysis of data from the autumn 2001 LFS. *Labour Market Trends, 110*(7), 343–354.

Card, D. (2001). The effect of unions on wage inequality in the U.S. labor market. *Industrial and Labor Relations Review, 54*(2), 296–315.

Card, D., Lemieux, T., & Riddell, W. C. (2003). Unions and the wage structure. In: J. T. Addison & C. Schnabel (Eds), *International handbook of trade unions* (pp. 246–292). Cheltenham: Edward Elgar.

Freeman, R. (1980). Unionism and the dispersion of wages. *Industrial and Labor Relations Review, 34*(1), 3–23.

Gosling, A., Machin, S., & Meghir, C. (2000). The changing distribution of male wages in the U.K. *Review of Economic Studies, 67*(4), 635–666.

Gosling, A., & Lemieux, T. (2001). *Labor market reforms and changes in wage inequality in the United Kingdom and the United States.* NBER Working Paper No. 8413, Cambridge, MA: National Bureau of Economic Research.

The Impact of Deunionisation on Earnings Dispersion Revisited

Leslie, D., & Pu, Y. (1996). What caused rising earnings inequality in Britain? Evidence from time series, 1970–1993. *British Journal of Industrial Relations, 34*(1), 111–130.

Machin, S. (1997). The decline of labour market institutions and the rise in wage inequality in Britain. *European Economic Review, 41*(3-5), 647–657.

Metcalf, D. (1982). Unions and the distribution of earnings. *British Journal of Industrial Relations, 20*(2), 163–169.

Metcalf, D. (2005). Trade unions: Resurgence or perdition? In: S. Fernie & D. Metcalf (Eds), *Trade unions: Resurgence or demise?* London: Routledge.

OPCS. (1986). General Household Survey, 1983 [computer file]. London: Office of Population Censuses and Surveys Social Survey Division; Colchester, U.K.: The Data Archive [distributor], SN: 2099.

OPCS. (2000). Quarterly Labour Force Survey, June–August, 1995 [computer file]. 3rd ed., Office of Population Censuses and Surveys Social Survey Division, Department of Finance and Personnel (Northern Ireland) Central Survey Unit, Colchester, Essex: UK Data Archive [distributor], SN: 3490.

Schmitt, J. (1995). The changing structure of male earnings in Britain, 1974–1988'. In: R. B. Freeman & L. F. Katz (Eds), *Differences and changes in wage structures* (pp. 177–204). Chicago, Il.: University of Chicago Press.

SCPR. (1985). Social and Community Planning Research, British Social Attitudes Survey, 1984 [computer file]. Colchester, Essex: UK Data Archive [distributor], 1985. SN: 2035.

JOHN T. ADDISON ET AL.

APPENDIX A

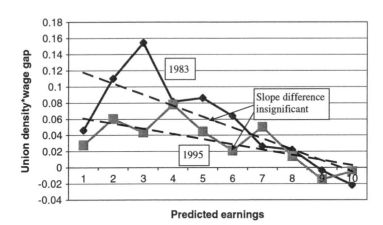

Fig. A1. Union Power by Skill, Private-Sector Males 1983 and 1995.

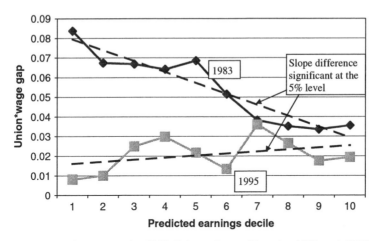

Fig. A2. Union Power by Skill, Private-Sector Females 1983 and 1995.

The Impact of Deunionisation on Earnings Dispersion Revisited

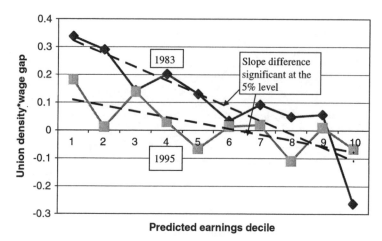

Fig. A3.   Union Power by Skill, Public-Sector Males 1983 and 1995.

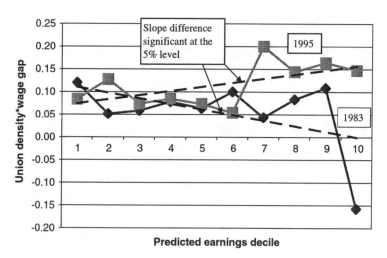

Fig. A4.   Union Power by Skill, Public-Sector Females 1983 and 1995.

JOHN T. ADDISON ET AL.

APPENDIX B

Table B1. Union Membership Rates and Union Wage Effects by Pay Decile.

Predicted Earnings Decile	Men				Women			
	Proportion Union	Log W_N	Wage Gap	Variance Gap	Proportion Union	Log W_N	Wage Gap	Variance Gap
1983								
1	0.22	0.99	0.38	−0.03	0.30	0.93	0.32	−0.11
2	0.52	1.35	0.31	−0.01	0.49	1.12	0.17	−0.05
3	0.68	1.45	0.28	−0.04	0.42	1.13	0.20	−0.04
4	0.66	1.57	0.17	−0.02	0.46	1.19	0.13	−0.03
5	0.64	1.54	0.21	−0.02	0.37	1.24	0.17	−0.05
6	0.55	1.61	0.19	0.06	0.36	1.27	0.19	−0.07
7	0.60	1.71	0.08	−0.02	0.37	1.31	0.20	−0.11
8	0.57	1.83	0.07	−0.05	0.39	1.39	0.24	−0.07
9	0.57	2.00	0.05	−0.05	0.38	1.46	0.30	0.01
10	0.57	2.28	0.01	−0.12	0.59	1.79	0.18	−0.17
1995								
1	0.12	1.24	0.28	−0.06	0.16	1.22	0.15	−0.03
2	0.36	1.53	0.21	−0.06	0.23	1.31	0.14	−0.06
3	0.34	1.72	0.09	−0.09	0.28	1.37	0.18	−0.04
4	0.42	1.73	0.14	−0.10	0.23	1.46	0.24	−0.02
5	0.44	1.83	0.13	−0.02	0.28	1.54	0.17	−0.05

The Impact of Deunionisation on Earnings Dispersion Revisited

Table B1. (*Continued*)

Predicted Earnings Decile	Men				Women			
	Proportion Union	Log W_N	Wage Gap	Variance Gap	Proportion Union	Log W_N	Wage Gap	Variance Gap
6	0.43	1.98	0.03	-0.12	0.27	1.57	0.18	-0.04
7	0.41	2.02	0.08	-0.02	0.26	1.66	0.18	-0.07
8	0.36	2.14	0.05	-0.12	0.28	1.73	0.30	-0.04
9	0.39	2.42	-0.05	-0.05	0.57	1.85	0.33	-0.11
10	0.48	2.54	0.03	-0.18	0.51	2.21	0.13	-0.14

Notes: Predicted earnings decile is based on a prediction equation for the non-union sector, using an equation with years of education, experience, experience squared and cubed, dummies for marital status, non-white and 5 regions, and interaction of five levels of education with education and linear and quadratic experience. The wage gap is the difference between the log of hourly earnings between union and non-union workers for the given decile. The variance gap is the difference in the variance of log earnings between union and non-union workers for the given decile.

[21]

THE EFFECT OF UNIONS ON
WAGE INEQUALITY IN THE U.S. LABOR MARKET

DAVID CARD*

This study uses Current Population Survey micro data for 1973–74 and 1993 to evaluate the effect of changing union membership on trends in male and female wage inequality. Unionization rates of men fell between the two sample periods, with bigger declines among lower skill groups. These trends account for 15–20% of the rise in male wage inequality. Union membership rates of low-wage women also declined, while unionization increased among higher-wage women. On balance, shifting unionization accounts for very little of the rise in female wage inequality. Economy-wide trends in unionization mask a sharp divergence between the private sector, where unionism was declining, and the public sector, where it was rising. Comparisons across sectors suggest that unionization substantially slowed the growth in wage inequality in the public sector.

The fraction of trade union members in the U.S. labor market has fallen dramatically in recent decades (see, for example, Farber 1990; Riddell 1992), while the level of wage inequality has risen (for example, Katz and Autor 1999; Blackburn, Bloom, and Freeman 1990; Bound and Johnson 1992). Since unions historically exerted an equalizing effect on the distribution of wages (Freeman 1980; Freeman and Medoff 1984), many analysts believe that the fall in unionization has contributed to the rise in wage inequality. Indeed, a number of recent studies—including Freeman (1993) and DiNardo, Fortin, and Lemieux (1996)—estimate that the fall in union membership can account for up to one-quarter of the rise in male wage dispersion over the 1980s.[1]

This paper presents new estimates of the effect of changing unionization on wage inequality for male and female workers over

A data appendix with additional results, and copies of the computer programs used to generate the results presented in the paper, are available from the author at the Department of Economics, University of California–Berkeley, 549 Evans Hall #3880, Berkeley, CA 94720-3880.

[1]The effect of unions on female wage inequality is relatively under-studied. DiNardo, Fortin, and Lemieux (1996) estimated that changing patterns of unionization explain relatively little of the recent rise in female wage dispersion. DiNardo and Lemieux (1997) studied the relative effect of unions on male wage inequality in the United States and Canada.

*The author is Professor of Economics, University of California–Berkeley. He thanks Thomas Lemieux, John DiNardo, and Henry Farber for helpful comments.

Industrial and Labor Relations Review, Vol. 54, No. 2 (January 2001). © by Cornell University.
0019-7939/00/5402 $01.00

the period from 1973 to 1993. The methodology extends the traditional two-sector framework developed by Freeman (1980) for measuring the equalizing effect of trade unionism in two ways. First, explicit attention is paid to the fact that unionization rates vary across the wage distribution, and that union membership has fallen disproportionately for lower-wage workers. This trend has reduced the equalizing effect of unionism in the economy. Second, the method accounts for differences in the relative wage effect of unions on different skill groups. A long-standing hypothesis in the literature is that unions raise wages more for lower-skilled workers (Lewis 1986). Indeed, conventional (ordinary least squares) estimates of the union wage gap for low-skilled workers are large and positive, while estimates for highly skilled men are small or even negative. Taken at face value, this pattern implies a substantial equalizing effect of unions. Evidence presented in Card (1996), however, suggests that unionized workers with low observed skill characteristics tend to have higher unobserved skills than their nonunion counterparts, contributing to their apparent wage advantage. Conversely, union members with higher observed skills tend to have below-average unobserved characteristics, explaining the negative union wage gap for highly educated and experienced workers. Estimates of the equalizing effect of unions that ignore these differential selectivity biases (for example, the re-weighting method used by DiNardo, Fortin, and Lemieux) may therefore overstate the role of unions in compressing wage differences across the skill distribution.

Although private sector union membership rates have declined sharply over the past 30 years, union densities have actually risen in the public sector (Freeman 1988). In light of this divergence, it is interesting to examine the effect of changing unionization on the growth of wage dispersion *within* the public and private sectors. An evaluation of the effect of unions on inequality in the public sector is particularly compelling because many observers believe that rises in public sector unionism have

occurred for exogenous reasons, associated with changes in legal barriers to unionization, rather than for potentially endogenous reasons, such as shifts in demand that may have also contributed to rising wage inequality (Freeman 1986). Moreover, an analysis of union wage effects in the public and private sectors presents an opportunity to ask whether unions act differently in the two sectors—in particular, whether unions exert a greater equalizing effect across skill groups in a noncompetitive versus a competitive environment.

Methods

To illustrate the potential effect of unions on wage inequality, it is useful to begin by assuming that workers can be classified into homogeneous skill groups—for example, categories based on detailed levels of education and age.[2] Let $w_i^n(c)$ represent the log wage that individual i in skill category c would earn in the nonunion sector, and let $w_i^u(c)$ represent the log wage for the same individual if he or she worked in a unionized job. Assume that

$$w_i^n(c) = w^n(c) + \varepsilon_i^n,$$
$$w_i^u(c) = w^u(c) + \varepsilon_i^u,$$

where $w^n(c)$ and $w^u(c)$ are the mean nonunion and union wages for individuals in skill group c, respectively, and that the residual components ε_i^n and ε_i^u satisfy the conditions

$$E[\varepsilon_i^n] = E[\varepsilon_i^u] = E[\varepsilon_i^n|\text{nonunion}] = E[\varepsilon_i^u|\text{union}] = 0.$$

One interpretation of these assumptions is that all workers in the same skill group are viewed as exchangeable (that is, equally productive) by potential employers. The observed union-nonunion gap in mean wages for workers in skill group c is

$$\Delta_w(c) = w^u(c) - w^n(c).$$

---

[2] The following presentation borrows from Lemieux (1992); see Card (1992) for a parallel development.

Under the assumption that the conditional expectations of ε_i^n and ε_i^u are both zero, this is also the expected wage gain that a nonunion worker in skill group c would receive if she could find a unionized job, or alternatively the expected wage loss that a union worker would suffer if he moved to the nonunion sector.

In addition to affecting the mean level of wages, unions can potentially influence the distribution of wages within skill categories. Let

$$\text{Var}[\varepsilon_i^n | c] = v^n(c)$$

and

$$\text{Var}[\varepsilon_i^u | c] = v^u(c)$$

denote the variances of log wage outcomes for individuals in skill group c in the nonunion and union sectors, respectively. The union-nonunion variance gap for skill group c will be denoted by

$$\Delta_v(c) = v^u(c) - v^n(c).$$

Finally, let $u(c)$ denote the fraction of workers in group c whose wages are set by union contracts. In principle, $u(c)$ may be different from the fraction of trade union members. However, given the limitations of the available data (discussed below), such differences will be ignored.

Under the preceding assumptions, the mean log wage of all workers in group c is

$$(1) \qquad w(c) = w^n(c) + u(c)\Delta_w(c).$$

The second term on the right-hand side of this expression is the average wage *gain* for workers in skill group c associated with the presence of unionism (Lewis 1986), and is simply the product of the union coverage rate and the union wage gap. The variance of log wage outcomes for workers in skill group c is[3]

$$(2) \qquad v(c) = v^n(c) + u(c)\Delta_v(c) \\ + u(c)(1 - u(c))\Delta_w(c)^2.$$

This equation shows that unions exert a "within-sector" effect associated with any change in the dispersion of wage outcomes relative to those in the nonunion sector (the second term in equation 2), and a "between-sector" effect associated with the potential widening of mean wage outcomes between the union and nonunion sectors (the third term in equation 2).

Using equation (2), the variance of wage outcomes across all skill groups can be written as

$$(3) \qquad v = \text{Var}[w(c)] + \text{E}[v(c)] \\ = \text{Var}[w^n(c) + u(c)\Delta_w(c)] + \text{E}[v^n(c) \\ + u(c)\Delta_v(c) + u(c)(1 - u(c))\Delta_w(c)^2] \\ = \text{Var}[w^n(c)] + \text{Var}[u(c)\Delta_w(c)] \\ + 2\text{Cov}[w^n(c), u(c)\Delta_w(c)] + \text{E}[v^n(c)] \\ + \text{E}[u(c)\Delta_v(c)] + \text{E}[u(c)(1 - u(c))\Delta_w(c)^2],$$

where expectations (denoted by $\text{E}[\,]$), variances (denoted by $\text{Var}[\,]$), and covariances (denoted by $\text{Cov}[\,]$) are taken over the skill categories. In contrast, if all workers were paid according to the existing wage structure in the nonunion sector, the variance of wage outcomes would be

$$(4) \qquad v^n = \text{Var}[w^n(c)] + \text{E}[v^n(c)].$$

Thus, the effect of unions on the variance of wage outcomes, relative to the situation that would be observed if all workers were paid according to the existing wage structure in the nonunion sector,[4] is

$$(5) \qquad v - v^n = \text{Var}[u(c)\Delta_w(c)] \\ + 2\text{Cov}[w^n(c), u(c)\Delta_w(c)] \\ + \text{E}[u(c)\Delta_v(c)] + \text{E}[u(c)(1 - u(c))\Delta_w(c)^2].$$

A helpful aid to understanding this equation is to compare it to the simplified basis case in which union coverage rates, wage gaps, and variance gaps are all constant across skill groups (that is, $u(c) = u$; $\Delta_w(c) = \Delta_w$; $\Delta_v(c) = \Delta_v$). In this case the first two

---

[3]This equation follows from the standard decomposition of a variance into within-sector and between-sector components.

[4]Of course, in the absence of unions, the wage structure in the nonunion sector might change, as Lewis (1986) and others have often pointed out.

terms in equation (5) are zero and the effect of unions on the variance of wages reduces to the simple two-sector formula

$$(5') \qquad v - v^n = u\Delta_v + u(1 - u)\Delta_w^2.$$

Relative to this benchmark case, variation in either the union coverage rate $u(c)$ or the union wage effect $\Delta_w(c)$ across skill groups introduces two additional factors into the overall wage dispersion effect. The first is a positive variance component that arises if the union wage gain $u(c)\Delta_w(c)$ varies across groups. The second is a covariance term that may be positive or negative, depending on whether the union wage gain is larger or smaller for higher- or lower-wage workers. If the unionization rate is higher for less-skilled workers, or if the union wage gap is higher for such workers, then the covariance will be negative, enhancing the equalizing effect of unions on wage dispersion.[5]

Unobserved Heterogeneity

The preceding formulas have to be modified slightly if the union and nonunion workers in a given skill category have different productivity levels and would earn different wages even in the absence of unions. Such a phenomenon will arise if workers have productivity characteristics that are known to employers but not fully captured in the observed skill categories, and if the mean level of these unobserved skills is different between union and nonunion workers in a given skill group. As before, assume that workers are classified into skill categories on the basis of *observed* characteristics, and suppose that

$$(6a) \qquad w_i^n(c) = w^n(c) + a_i + \varepsilon_i^n,$$

$$(6b) \qquad w_i^u(c) = w^u(c) + a_i + \varepsilon_i^u,$$

where a_i represents an unobserved skill component, and $E[\varepsilon_i^n|\text{nonunion}] = E[\varepsilon_i^u|\text{union}] = 0$. Note that a_i is assumed to shift wages by the same amount in the union and nonunion sectors. Let

$$\theta(c) = E[a_i|\text{union}, c] - E[a_i|\text{nonunion}, c]$$

represent the difference in the mean of the unobserved skill component between union and nonunion workers in group c. The mean wage gap between union and nonunion workers in skill group c then includes the true union wage premium and the difference attributable to unobserved heterogeneity:

$$E[w_i^u(c)|\text{union}] - E[w_i^n(c)|\text{nonunion}]$$
$$= \Delta_w(c) + \theta(c).$$

Taking account of unobserved productivity differences between union and nonunion workers, the difference in the variance of wages in the presence of unions and in the counterfactual situation in which all workers are paid according to the nonunion wage structure is

$$(7) \qquad v - v^n = \text{Var}[u(c)\Delta_w(c)]$$
$$+ 2\text{Cov}[w^n(c), u(c)\Delta_w(c)] + E[u(c)\Delta_v(c)]$$
$$+ E[u(c)(1-u(c))\{(\theta(c)+\Delta_w(c))^2 - \theta(c)^2\}].$$

Only the last term of this equation, which reflects the gap in mean wages between union and nonunion workers with the same observed skills in the presence and absence of unions, differs from equation (5).[6]

The possibility that there are unobserved skill differences between union and nonunion workers with the same observable characteristics introduces a difficult empirical problem: how do we distinguish the

---

[5]If the unionization rate varies across skill groups but the union wage gap and union variance gap are constant (that is, $\Delta_w(c)=\Delta_w$ and $\Delta_v(c)=\Delta_v$), then $v-v^n$ $= u\Delta_v + u(1 - u)\Delta_w^2 + 2\Delta_w\text{Cov}[w^n(c), u(c)]$, where u is the average rate of unionization.

---

[6]The relatively simple form of equation (7) depends crucially on the assumption that unobserved skills are equally valuable in the union and nonunion sectors. If, for example,

$$w_i^u(c) = w^u(c) + k_c a_i + \varepsilon_i^u,$$

where $k_c < 1$, then the formula has to be modified to account for the fact that unionization affects the rewards to unobserved skills. Lemieux (1998) presented a model with this property.

true union wage effect $\Delta_w(c)$ for workers in a given skill group from the heterogeneity component $\theta(c)$? In the absence of unobserved heterogeneity, $\Delta_w(c)$ can be estimated by the mean wage difference between union and nonunion workers in skill group c. More generally, however, the observed difference in mean wages between union and nonunion workers reflects the sum of the true union wage effect and the mean difference in unobserved skills.[7]

A natural solution to this problem is to use longitudinal data on union status changers to evaluate the wage gains of union joiners and the wage losses of union leavers. Assuming that unobserved skills are rewarded equally in the union and nonunion sectors, the change in wages "differences out" the unobserved heterogeneity component, leaving only the change in the true union wage premium. In Card (1996) I considered wage changes for a longitudinal sample stratified into five observable skill groups on the basis of predicted wages in the nonunion sector. Lemieux (1992) considered wage changes in a Canadian data set for three similarly defined skill groups. The empirical results in these papers point to two important conclusions. First, in both the United States and Canada the "true" (that is, longitudinally based) union wage effect is higher for less-skilled workers. For example, the results in Card (1996) suggest that the union wage effect ranges from about 30% for men in the bottom quintile of the observed skill distribution to about 10% for men in the top quintile.[8] Second, in both countries union

[7]A similar problem arises in the estimation of $\Delta_s(c)$, if Var[a_i|union] ≠ Var[a_i|nonunion]. In particular, if the distribution of unobserved heterogeneity is not the same in the union and nonunion sectors, conditional on skill group, then there is a distinction between the observed gap in wage dispersion between union and nonunion workers and the gap attributable to the effect of unions. A full consideration of this possibility is beyond the scope of this paper.
[8]Lemieux's results for Canadian men and women are comparable, although the variation in the union wage effect across skill groups for women is smaller than for Canadian (or U.S.) men.

workers with lower observed skills tend to have higher *unobserved* skills than their nonunion counterparts,\ whereas union workers with higher observed skills tend to have lower unobserved skills than their nonunion counterparts. In terms of the notation introduced above, $\theta(c) > 0$ for lower skill groups and $\theta(c) < 0$ for higher skill groups.

This pattern suggests that the selection process controlling workers' union status differs between more- and less-skilled workers. In Card (1996) I hypothesized that the differences arise because workers must pass two "hurdles" to be observed in a union job. First, they have to find a unionized employer who will hire them. Second, they must prefer a union job to any nonunion alternatives. (See Abowd and Farber [1982] and Farber [1983] for similar models.) For workers with lower observed skills, the first of these hurdles is more likely to bind, because unionized employers typically have a queue of applicants and will reject workers with low education or limited experience unless they possess other skills that are not observable in a typical micro data set. For workers with higher observed skills the second hurdle is more likely to bind if unionized employers offer a "flatter" pay structure that is less attractive to older and better-educated workers. In this case, a union job will be more attractive to workers whose unobserved skills are below average. Thus, union workers with lower observed skills will be positively selected while those with higher observed skills will be negatively selected. In the analysis below I use results from Card (1996) to make a rough adjustment to the observed union wage gaps for workers in different deciles of the predicted wage distribution to account for these different selection biases.

Data

This paper uses Current Population Survey (CPS) data on wages from the May 1973 and 1974 surveys, and from the 12 monthly surveys in 1993. The May 1973 sample is the first CPS that contains both union status information and wage data for individuals' current jobs. This sample is therefore

UNIONS AND WAGE INEQUALITY IN THE U.S.   301

Table 1. Union Membership Rates for Men and Women: 1973–74 versus 1993.

	Men			Women		
Group	1973–74	1993	Ratio 1993/1973–74	1973–74	1993	Ratio 1993/1973
1. All	30.8	18.7	0.61	14.1	13.3	0.94
2. By Education:						
< High School	35.1	14.3	0.41	17.4	9.8	0.56
High School	39.3	24.5	0.62	13.5	11.8	0.87
Some College	22.7	19.5	0.86	9.0	10.5	1.17
College or More	10.7	12.4	1.16	14.8	20.4	1.38
3. By Age:						
16–30	24.9	10.4	0.42	11.5	7.3	0.63
31–45	32.6	20.7	0.63	15.5	15.0	0.97
46–65	37.3	26.5	0.71	16.7	18.0	1.08
4. By Race:						
White	30.2	18.3	0.61	13.5	12.4	0.92
Black	37.5	23.4	0.62	18.6	19.2	1.03
Other	28.3	14.8	0.52	18.8	14.6	0.78
5. By Region:						
Northeast	36.8	25.4	0.69	21.2	19.1	0.90
Midwest	38.2	23.9	0.63	17.2	14.9	0.87
South	19.5	10.9	0.56	6.8	7.4	1.09
West	31.3	18.7	0.60	13.8	15.4	1.12
6. By Sector:						
Private	31.1	14.9	0.48	13.0	7.1	0.55
Public	28.9	39.3	1.36	18.0	37.3	2.07
7. No. Obs.	43,189	86,270	—	30,500	82,624	—

Notes: Based on samples derived from the May 1973/74 CPS and 1993 merged outgoing rotation group files. Samples include individuals age 16–65 who are not self-employed, and whose reported or constructed hourly wage is between $2.01 and $90.00 per hour in 1989 dollars. Samples are weighted by CPS sample weights.

the earliest benchmark to compare against later levels of unionization and wage inequality. In view of the relatively small sample size of the monthly CPS, I elected to pool the May 1973 and May 1974 data.[9] The 1993 CPS is the last survey prior to the introduction of a new computer-assisted survey instrument that substantially changed the nature of the earnings questions. I therefore use this sample to measure recent patterns of unionism and wage inequality.

Table 1 presents a descriptive overview of the changes in union membership between the early 1970s and the early 1990s.

The samples underlying this table (and all subsequent tables in this paper) include employed individuals between the ages of 16 and 65 who reported an hourly or weekly wage for their main job.[10] Union status is measured by the individual's response to the question, "On this job (the main job) is the respondent a member of a labor union or an employee association similar to a union?" Recent CPS surveys have also collected union coverage information for non-

---

[9]The wage data from the two surveys are deflated to a common basis using the CPI.

[10]Self-employed workers are excluded. About 20% of individuals refuse to provide information on their earnings to the CPS. The 1993 sample includes allocated wages for these individuals, while non-respondents are dropped from the 1973 and 1974 samples.

302   INDUSTRIAL AND LABOR RELATIONS REVIEW

Table 2. Characteristics of Union and Nonunion Workers in 1973–74 and 1993.

	Men		Women	
Variable	Nonunion	Union	Nonunion	Union
1973–74				
1. Education (years)	12.3	11.2	12.1	11.7
2. Experience (years)	16.9	21.5	17.6	20.8
3. Nonwhite (percent)	9.1	11.7	11.8	16.4
4. Married (percent)	71.1	81.4	59.5	63.1
5. Public Sector (percent)	16.9	15.5	21.4	28.6
6. Mean Log Wage	1.323	1.519	0.947	1.177
7. Unadjusted Union Wage Gap	—	0.196	—	0.230
8. Adjusted Union Wage Gap	—	0.178	—	0.220
9. Std. Dev. Log Wages	0.553	0.354	0.442	0.383
10. Residual Std. Dev. Log Wage	0.416	0.324	0.372	0.328
1993				
1. Education (years)	13.1	12.8	13.1	13.9
2. Experience (years)	16.8	22.1	17.5	21.2
3. Nonwhite (percent)	13.6	15.8	14.9	21.5
4. Married (percent)	58.6	70.8	53.8	60.1
5. Public Sector (percent)	11.4	32.2	14.7	57.3
6. Mean Log Wage	2.359	2.613	2.153	2.466
7. Unadjusted Union Wage Gap	—	0.254	—	0.313
8. Adjusted Union Wage Gap	—	0.168	—	0.166
9. Std. Dev. Log Wages	0.590	0.415	0.515	0.456
10. Residual Std. Dev. Log Wage	0.446	0.363	0.423	0.379

Notes: See note to Table 1 for sample description. Education categories in 1993 CPS are re-coded to earlier basis. The adjusted union wage gap is the union coefficient from a regression model that also includes education, a cubic in potential experience, and indicators for nonwhite race, Hispanic ethnicity, marital status, and three regions. The residual standard deviation of log wages is the residual standard error from a similar regression fit separately to the union and nonunion samples.

members of unions; however, this information was not collected in the 1973 or 1974 surveys. For comparability over time I therefore use union membership status in both 1973–74 and 1993.[11]

The first row of Table 1 shows the well-known decline in union membership among male workers between 1973 and 1993, along with the fairly stable rate of union membership among women. Comparisons of membership patterns for different subgroups reveal that within the male and female labor forces some groups lost union membership while others gained.

Younger and less-educated men and women experienced the largest drops in union membership, whereas union rates among college-educated men and women rose significantly. Men in different race groups and regions had fairly similar relative declines in union membership, whereas the patterns by race and region for women were more variable.

Row 6 of Table 1 illustrates what is probably the most important fact about union membership in the U.S. labor market over recent decades: the dramatic decline in unionism in the private sector (for both men and women) and the fairly rapid rise in public sector unionization. These figures indicate that the relative stability in union membership of women actually masked a shift in unionization from the private sector to the public sector. In 1973–

[11]In 1993, 2.1% of male nonunion members and 2.5% of female nonunion members reported that their wages were set by union contracts.

74, 29% of female union members worked in the public sector. By 1993 this ratio had risen to 57%. For men there was a similar shift—from 16% to 32%.

Table 2 presents comparisons of the characteristics of union and nonunion workers in the two sample periods. Unionized men were typically older, less educated, and more likely to be married than their nonunion counterparts. Interestingly, the mean gap in education narrowed over the two decades (from 0.9 years in 1973–74 to 0.3 years in 1993). This is consistent with the data in Table 1 showing that union densities fell most rapidly for less-educated workers. In 1973–74 unionized women were also older and less educated than nonunion women, but by 1993 the education differential had reversed, again consistent with the rapid rise in union membership of more-educated women.

The sixth through eighth rows of the upper and lower panels in Table 2 report mean log wages of union and nonunion workers in the two sample periods (row 6), the unadjusted differences in mean log wages between the sectors (row 7), and the adjusted wage gaps between union and nonunion workers (row 8), estimated from ordinary least squares (OLS) regression models for log hourly wages that include a union membership dummy and a standard set of control variables.[12] In 1973–74, the unadjusted gaps in mean log wages between union and nonunion men and women were very similar to the adjusted wage gaps (compare rows 7 and 8). In 1993, however, the unadjusted wage gaps were higher than the corresponding adjusted gaps (especially for women), implying that union workers had higher average skill characteristics than nonunion workers.

The ninth and tenth rows of Table 2 present measures of the dispersion in wages

within the union and nonunion sectors. The entry in row 9 is just the standard deviation of log wages within each sector, while the entry in row 10 is the residual standard deviation after adjusting for the effects of a standard set of covariates (allowing separate coefficients in the union and nonunion sectors). Note that the union-nonunion difference in the residual standard deviation of earnings is smaller than the difference in the standard deviation in wages, particularly for men. This is mainly attributable to the compressed distribution of observable skill characteristics in the union sector. Comparisons of either measure of wage dispersion between sectors and over time illustrate three important facts. First, wages were less dispersed in the union sector, even after adjusting for differences in observable skills. Second, wages of women (in either union or nonunion jobs) had lower dispersion than wages of men, and the union-nonunion difference in dispersion was smaller for women than men. Third, wage inequality of male and female workers in both the union and nonunion sectors rose substantially between 1973–74 and 1993.

Effects of Unions on Wage Inequality

Naive Estimates

As a starting point for evaluating the contribution of changing unionism to the rise in inequality of wages, it is useful to begin with the simple two-sector framework developed by Freeman (1980).[13] Recall that if the union density $u(c)$ and the union relative wage effect $\Delta_w(c)$ are constant across skill groups, then the effect of unions on the variance of wages (relative to what would be observed if all workers were

---

[12]These are years of education, a cubic in potential experience, indicators for nonwhite race, hispanic ethnicity (available in 1993 only), and marital status, and a set of three indicators for region of residence.

[13]Freeman (1980) did not apply this framework to the overall labor force, but rather used it to study wage inequality within the manufacturing sector, assuming that unions raise the relative wages of blue-collar workers and lower their dispersion but have no effect on white-collar wages.

Table 3. Naive Estimates of
the Contribution of Unions to
Rising Wage Inequality, 1973–74 to 1993.

Description	Men	Women
1973–74		
1. Variance of Log Wages	0.258	0.195
2. Union Rate (*U*)	0.308	0.141
3. Union Wage Gap (Δw)	0.196	0.230
4. Union Variance Gap (Δv)	−0.180	−0.049
5. Between-Sector Effect	0.008	0.006
6. Within-Sector Effect	−0.056	−0.007
7. Total Effect	−0.047	0.000
1993		
1. Variance of Log Wages	0.325	0.269
2. Union Rate (*U*)	0.187	0.133
3. Union Wage Gap (Δw)	0.254	0.313
4. Union Variance Gap (Δv)	−0.176	−0.057
5. Between-Sector Effect	0.010	0.011
6. Within-Sector Effect	−0.033	−0.008
7. Total Effect	−0.023	0.004
Changes from 1973–74 to 1993		
Change in Variance of Wages	0.067	0.074
Change in Total Effect of Unions	0.024	0.004
Share Attributable to Unions	0.365	0.056

Note: See text for formulas and Tables 1 and 2 for underlying data.

paid according to the existing nonunion wage structure) is

$$(5')\qquad v - v^n = u\Delta_v + u(1 - u)\Delta_w^2.$$

A comparison of the size of this differential over time provides a first-pass estimate of the changing effect of unionism on wage inequality. Table 3 illustrates the application of this formula to data for men and women in 1973–74 and 1993, using the summary statistics from Table 2. Note that if the union density is constant across skill groups, and the union wage and variance effects are constant across skill groups, then it is appropriate to use the *unadjusted* union wage gap and unadjusted union variance gap in equation (5').[14] In fact, under these

assumptions the adjusted union wage gap should equal the unadjusted gap, since the union membership rate is orthogonal to individual characteristics. As noted, this was roughly true in 1973–74, but not in 1993.

The results in Table 3 show that ignoring differences in union coverage rates and union effects across groups, the decline in unionism between 1973–74 and 1993 would have been expected to cause the variance of male wages to rise by 0.024 and the variance of female wages to rise by 0.004. Virtually all of the difference for men is attributable to the change in average union density (−0.121 = 0.308 − 0.187) multiplied by the union variance gap ($\Delta v \approx -0.18$). For women, the union variance gap is smaller than for men, and the decline in union density is negligible, so the net contribution of unionism to widening inequality is trivial. As shown at the bottom of Table 3, between 1973–74 and 1993 the variance of wages rose by 0.067 for men and 0.074 for women. Thus, a naive calculation suggests that falling unionism can explain about 36% of the rise in male wage inequality, but none of the rise in female inequality.

Allowing for Differences across Skill Groups

As pointed out in the first section ("Methods"), there are several reasons to suspect that the naive calculations in Table 3 overstate the role of unions in the growth of wage inequality. Using the framework of equation (5) or (7), it is possible to refine these estimates to allow for differences in union coverage rates and union wage effects by skill group. A necessary first step, however, is to define skill groups. In this study I divided workers into observable groups based on their predicted wages in

---

[14]To see this, assume that the expected union wage in skill category *c* is $w^u(c) = w^n(c) + \Delta_w$, and the variance of union wages in group *c* is $v^u(c) = v^n(c) + \Delta_v$. Assuming that the union rate is constant across all skill

groups, the mean union wage is $E[w^u(c)] = E[w^n(c)] + \Delta_w$, and the variance of union wages is $E[v^u(c)] = E[v^n(c)] + \Delta_v$.

UNIONS AND WAGE INEQUALITY IN THE U.S.   305

Table 4. Distribution of Union Membership and Union Effects across Skill Deciles.

	1973–74				1993			
Decile	Percent Union	Decile Share of Union (%)	Raw Union Gaps: Wage	Raw Union Gaps: Variance	Percent Union	Decile Share of Union (%)	Raw Union Gaps: Wage	Raw Union Gaps: Variance
A. Men								
1	12.1	3.9	0.42	0.02	5.3	2.9	0.29	0.05
2	26.2	8.5	0.35	−0.01	11.0	5.9	0.29	0.02
3	35.2	11.4	0.31	−0.03	16.3	8.7	0.29	−0.02
4	39.5	12.8	0.25	−0.08	21.1	11.3	0.29	−0.05
5	40.9	13.3	0.23	−0.06	24.8	13.3	0.26	−0.07
6	39.9	13.0	0.18	−0.07	26.7	14.3	0.20	−0.11
7	36.3	11.8	0.11	−0.10	27.6	14.8	0.17	−0.11
8	38.1	12.4	0.08	−0.09	22.2	11.9	0.10	−0.11
9	27.8	9.1	0.00	−0.09	15.9	8.5	−0.01	−0.11
10	11.6	3.8	−0.10	−0.10	15.5	8.3	−0.05	−0.09
B. Women								
1	9.9	7.0	0.38	−0.01	5.0	3.7	0.26	0.03
2	15.1	10.7	0.27	−0.02	7.6	5.7	0.25	0.00
3	15.9	11.2	0.23	−0.03	10.5	7.9	0.25	−0.01
4	14.6	10.4	0.23	0.01	10.8	8.2	0.23	−0.05
5	13.9	9.8	0.21	−0.04	13.2	9.9	0.19	−0.04
6	14.1	10.0	0.21	−0.06	14.7	11.1	0.18	−0.04
7	14.4	10.2	0.19	−0.03	11.6	8.7	0.18	−0.05
8	15.7	11.1	0.13	−0.05	13.5	10.2	0.14	−0.07
9	13.2	9.4	0.17	−0.03	17.9	13.5	0.12	−0.07
10	14.4	10.2	0.23	−0.06	27.8	20.9	0.11	−0.10

Notes: Skill deciles are based on the predicted wage in the nonunion sector. The decile share of union represents the percentage of all union workers in the skill decile. The wage gap is difference in mean log wages between union and non-union workers in the skill decile. The variance gap is the difference in variance of log wages between union and nonunion workers in the skill decile. See Table 1 for the sample definition; see text for a description of wage prediction models.

the nonunion sector (conditional on education, age, and race). In particular, I fit a set of wage prediction models to data for nonunion workers by gender and sample period, and then used the resulting coefficient estimates to assign all workers in a gender/year group to 10 equal-sized predicted wage deciles.[15]

---

[15]The prediction equation includes education, indicators for nonwhites and Hispanics (in 1993 only), a third-order polynomial in experience, interactions of indicators for three main levels of education with linear and quadratic experience, and interactions of the ethnicity dummies with education and linear and quadratic experience.

Table 4 shows unionization rates, unadjusted union wage gaps, and unadjusted union variance gaps across skill deciles for men and women in 1973–74 and 1993. A key feature of the table is the pattern of union membership rates across skill groups. In 1973–74, union membership rates of men followed an "inverted-U" pattern, with the highest membership rates for workers in the middle of the skill distribution. The pattern of 1993 membership rates was similar, but with lower membership levels for all but the top skill decile. Among women, union rates were fairly constant across skill groups in 1973–74, but were rising across skill groups in 1993, with the highest membership rate in the top group.

Table 5. Estimates of the Contribution of Unions to Rising Wage Inequality, 1973–74 to 1993.

Description	1973–74	1993	Change
A. Male Workers			
Variance in Log Wages	0.258	0.325	0.067
Effect of Unions Using Naive Calculation (Equation 5')	−0.047	−0.023	0.024
Effect of Unions Using Raw Union Wage Differentials (Equation 5)	−0.027	−0.015	0.012
Effect of Unions Using Adjusted Differentials (Equation 7)	−0.019	−0.011	0.008
B. Female Workers			
Variance in Log Wages	0.195	0.269	0.074
Effect of Unions Using Naive Calculation (Equation 5')	0.000	0.004	0.004
Effect of Unions Using Raw Union Wage Differentials (Equation 5)	0.000	−0.002	−0.002
Effect of Unions Using Adjusted Differentials (Equation 7)	−0.002	−0.004	−0.002

Notes: See text for methods. Raw union wage differentials are actual differences in mean log wages between union and nonunion workers in each skill decile. Adjusted union wage differentials assume that the true union wage effect declines linearly from 0.30 for the lowest skill decile to 0.075 for the highest skill decile.

A second interesting feature is the pattern of the union wage gaps across skill groups. For men in 1973–74, these ranged from 40% for the lowest skill group to –10% for the highest skill group. Taken at face value, these estimates suggest that unions exerted a substantial "flattening" effect on the male wage structure in the early 1970s. This effect seems to have moderated slightly over the next two decades. In particular, the union wage gap for the bottom skill group was lower in 1993 than in 1973–74 (29% versus 42%). For women, the union wage gaps at the bottom of the skill distribution are comparable to those for men, but the decline in the unadjusted wage gaps across the skill distribution is less pronounced. Thus, it appears that unions may exert a more modest flattening effect on the female wage structure than on the male wage structure.

An important caveat to the interpretation of the wage gaps in Table 4 is the potential role of unobserved heterogeneity. Recall that the unadjusted union wage gap for any skill group is actually a combination of the true union wage effect and a selection effect equal to the difference in the unobserved skills of union versus nonunion workers in the group. If unionized workers in lower skill groups are positively selected and those in higher skill groups are negatively selected, then the flattening effect of unions is overstated by the unadjusted union wage gaps in Table 4. In Card (1996), I used longitudinal CPS data from 1986 and 1987 to estimate unadjusted and adjusted union wage gaps for five skill groups, based on predicted wages in the nonunion sector. As in Table 4, the unadjusted wage gaps decline sharply across the skill groups, from a high of 36% in the bottom skill quintile to a low of –13% in the top skill decile. The *adjusted* union wage gaps (based on wage changes for those who change union status) also decline across the skill distribution, but are lower for the least skilled group (28%) and higher for the most skilled group (11%).[16] Thus, the unadjusted union wage gap for low-skilled men overstates the true union wage effect for these workers, while the unadjusted gap for high-skilled workers actually understates the true union wage effect.

Table 5 presents a series of calculations that use the data in Table 4, together with

---

[16]A similar pattern arises in Lemieux's (1992) study of the Canadian labor market, based on wage changes for men in three skill groups.

the formulas given by equations (5) or (7), to re-estimate the contribution of changing unionism to rising wage inequality. (For reference, the table also reproduces the naive calculations from Table 3.) The estimates based on equation (5) ignore any unobserved skill differences between union and nonunion workers in the same skill decile, and use the unadjusted union wage gaps in Table 4 as estimates of the true union wage effects. The estimates based on equation (7) use adjusted wage gaps for each skill group derived from my 1986 paper. In the absence of longitudinal estimates for different time periods, or for women, I use a single set of estimates of the "true" union wage effects for each skill group that range from 30% for the lowest skill decile to 8% for the highest skill group.[17]

For women, the estimates of the effect of unionization are qualitatively and quantitatively similar, regardless of the method. In all cases, unions are estimated to have a negligible effect on cross-sectional wage inequality, or on changes in inequality. For men, the results from equation (5) or (7) are qualitatively similar to the results of the naive calculation (based on equation 5′), but the magnitude of the union effect is reduced. The main source of the difference between the estimate based on (5) versus the estimate from the naive two-sector model is that the average "within sector" effect of unions on the variance of wages (that is, the average of the $\Delta_v(c)$ terms across skill groups) is substantially smaller than the gross difference in the variance of wages between the union and nonunion sectors.[18] This difference arises because male union members tend to be drawn from the middle of the skill distribu-

tion—consequently, the union-nonunion gap in the overall variance of wages overstates the gap within any skill group. The main source of the difference between calculations based on the selection-adjusted wage gaps versus the unadjusted wage gaps is that the covariance term $(\text{Cov}[w^n(c),$ $u(c)\Delta_w(c)])$ in equation (7) is smaller in magnitude (less negative) when the wage gaps are adjusted for selection biases. The unadjusted gaps overstate both the positive effect of unions on low-wage workers and the negative effect on high-wage workers.

In principle, it is also possible to implement equation (7) using longitudinally based estimates of the union variance effect (Δ_v) rather than the simple differences in the variances of wages between the union and nonunion sectors shown in Table 4. This would be appropriate if unobserved skills are rewarded equally in the union and nonunion sectors (as is assumed in equations 6a and 6b), but the variance of unobserved skill is different in the two sectors. Card (1992) and Lemieux (1992) both presented estimates of the effect of unions on the variance of wages based on the wage outcomes of union status changers. The longitudinal variance gap estimates presented in Card (1992) are relatively noisy, and on average only slightly smaller in absolute value than the corresponding cross-sectional estimates. Lemieux's estimates are also noisy but tend to be smaller (in absolute value) than the cross-sectional estimates. If the cross-sectional variance gaps in Table 4 are viewed as bounding the likely effect of unions on wage dispersion, then the estimates in Table 5 should be interpreted as *upper bound* estimates of the contribution of changing unionization to rising wage inequality. Taken as whole, then, it appears that the effect of unions on widening wage inequality may be relatively modest.

Unionization and Inequality in the Public and Private Sectors

In light of the diverging rates of union membership in the public and private sectors, it is interesting to ask how much chang-

---

[17]These estimates were obtained by fitting a linear model to the adjusted union wage gaps for the five skill groups used in Card (1996), and then interpolating to a set of 10 skill groups. The adjusted union gap for skill decile *j* is $0.30 - 0.0244 \times (j - 1)$.

[18]From Table 4, the average value of $\Delta_v(c)$ is about −0.06, while from row 4 of Table 3, $\Delta_v = -0.18$.

Table 6. Union Membership Rates in the
Public Sector for Men and Women, 1973–74 versus 1993.

	Men			Women		
Group	1973–74	1993	Ratio 1993/1973–74	1973–74	1993	Ratio 1993/1973
1. All	28.9	39.3	1.36	18.0	37.3	2.07
2. By Education:						
< High School	30.2	29.0	0.96	17.6	24.1	1.37
High School	40.5	46.0	1.14	17.0	32.9	1.94
Some College	25.8	42.7	1.66	14.2	29.6	2.08
College or More	19.5	34.2	1.75	20.6	46.1	2.24
3. By Age:						
16–30	24.9	28.8	1.16	16.4	27.0	1.65
31–45	29.7	42.9	1.44	18.6	38.5	2.07
56–65	31.7	40.8	1.29	19.2	41.5	2.16
4. By Race:						
White	27.8	39.7	1.43	16.9	37.5	2.22
Black	37.0	39.8	1.08	23.9	36.9	1.54
Other	35.2	29.5	0.84	24.2	35.1	1.45
5. By Region:						
Northeast	48.2	65.3	1.35	35.1	61.5	1.75
Midwest	31.9	44.1	1.38	20.9	41.7	2.00
South	14.7	21.0	1.43	6.0	19.9	3.32
West	28.0	41.2	1.47	17.5	42.7	2.44
6. By Industry:						
Education	24.1	40.2	1.67	17.9	44.9	2.51
Health/Hospital	23.8	31.2	1.31	20.1	28.6	1.42
Public Admin.	32.8	36.7	1.12	17.2	28.1	1.63
Other	28.9	43.1	1.49	17.6	31.7	1.80
7. By Level of Government:						
Federal	—	14.9	—	—	26.4	—
State	—	39.3	—	—	30.6	—
Local	—	39.3	—	—	42.8	—
8. No. Obs.	7,081	13,583	—	6,814	17,117	—

Notes: Based on samples derived from the May 1973/74 CPS and 1993 merged outgoing rotation group files.
Samples include individuals age 16–65 who are not self-employed, and whose reported or constructed hourly
wage is between $2.01 and $90.00 per hour in 1989 dollars.

ing unionism affected the inequality of wages within and between the two sectors. Tables 6 and 7 present some simple comparisons of unionization rates across different subgroups of the two sectors, while Figures 1 and 2 show unionization rates in the two sectors by predicted skill group in 1973–74 and 1993.[19]

An examination of the data for the public sector in Table 6 and Figure 1 suggests that public sector union rates rose for almost all groups after the early 1970s, with relatively larger gains for workers in the top two predicted skill deciles. Much of this rise is attributable to the rise in unionization among teachers: as shown in Table 6,

---

[19]The predicted skill groups for the two sectors are based on sector-specific wage equations, fit to the nonunion workers in each sector. The estimated coefficients from the two wage models were used to

assign a predicted nonunion wage for all workers in each sector, and the samples of public and private sector workers were then divided into 10 equal-sized groups.

the union membership rate of men in the education sector rose by 67% between the early 1970s and the early-1990s, while the rate for women rose by 150%. Since teachers and related workers make up such a large share of public sector employment (30% of men and around 50% of women), the rise of teacher unions has been a key determinant of the growth of public sector unionism, accounting for 40% of the rise in union membership among public sector men between 1973 and 1993, and 70% of the rise for public sector women.

The institutional factors controlling the process of unionization in the public sector vary by state: some states prohibit collective bargaining for certain groups of state or local employees, while others have adopted more or less "pro-union" legislation (see, for example, Freeman [1986], and the papers in the volume edited by Freeman and Ichniowski [1988]). This variation is reflected in Table 6 by the widely different levels of public sector unionization across regions. Nevertheless, the rates of growth between 1973 and 1993 are fairly similar across regions, especially for men. It is also interesting to compare unionization rates between the federal, state, and local levels. Unfortunately, information on the level of government was not collected in the 1973 or 1974 CPS surveys, so this comparison is not possible for the base period, but the data for 1993 show generally higher union rates at the local level, and fairly comparable densities across regions at the federal and state levels.

In contrast to the pattern of increasing union membership in the public sector, the data in Table 7 and Figure 2 show uniformly decreasing private sector union rates. On average, union rates fell by about 50%, with larger declines for younger and less-educated workers, but with fairly similar declines across regions and major industries.[20] The similarity of the trends in

Figure 1. Union Membership Rates in the Public Sector by Skill Group.

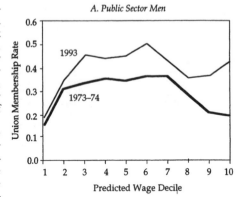

A. Public Sector Men

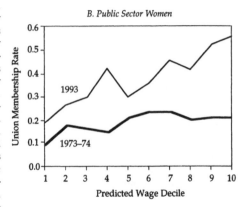

B. Public Sector Women

union membership for men in construction, manufacturing, transportation, communications, and retail trade is notable because these industries experienced very different employment trends over the sample periods. As noted by Farber (1990), the fact that unionization rates declined at comparable rates across industries that experienced very different sectoral growth rates makes it difficult to find support for a theory of union decline linked to sector-specific demand conditions. On the other hand, explanations linked to the institutional or legal environment might be bet-

---

[20]The union membership trend for women in construction is very imprecisely estimated because of the small number of women in this industry.

Table 7. Union Membership Rates in the
Private Sector for Men and Women, 1973–74 versus 1993.

	Men			Women		
Group	1973–74	1993	Ratio 1993/1973–74	1973–74	1993	Ratio 1993/1973
1. All	31.1	14.9	0.48	13.0	7.1	0.55
2. By Education:						
< High School	35.7	13.3	0.37	17.4	8.4	0.48
High School	39.1	21.7	0.55	12.8	8.2	0.64
Some College	22.0	15.0	0.68	7.5	6.3	0.84
College or More	5.9	5.2	0.88	5.2	5.5	1.06
3. By Age:						
16–30	24.9	8.5	0.34	10.3	4.6	0.45
31–45	33.2	16.4	0.49	14.4	8.0	0.56
56–65	38.7	22.6	0.58	15.9	9.4	0.59
4. By Race:						
White	30.6	14.6	0.48	12.5	6.3	0.50
Black	37.6	19.0	0.51	16.4	12.5	0.76
Other	26.7	11.8	0.44	17.0	9.4	0.55
5. By Region:						
Northeast	34.7	18.3	0.53	17.8	9.8	0.55
Midwest	39.2	20.8	0.53	16.2	8.7	0.54
South	20.5	9.0	0.44	7.0	3.8	0.54
West	32.1	14.3	0.45	12.6	7.8	0.62
6. By Industry:						
Construction	40.9	21.6	0.53	2.0	3.3	1.65
Durable Mfg.	45.3	22.9	0.51	28.6	14.9	0.52
Nondurable Mfg.	37.7	21.2	0.56	27.4	11.6	0.42
Transportation	59.8	31.7	0.53	20.7	21.2	1.02
Communication	54.3	30.6	0.56	53.9	36.2	0.67
Public Utilities	45.8	36.6	0.80	19.7	20.8	1.06
Retail Trade	13.3	7.2	0.54	9.5	5.5	0.58
7. No. Obs.	36,108	72,687	—	23,686	65,507	—

Notes: See notes to Table 6.

ter able to explain the uniformity of trends across private sector industries.

How do unions affect the structure of wages in the public versus private sectors? Figures 3 and 4 plot unadjusted union wage gaps by skill decile for men and women in the two sectors. A comparison of the wage gaps by skill level in the public and private sectors suggests that unions exerted a surprisingly similar effect on the wage structures in the two sectors. In particular, the union wage gaps are large and positive for the least skilled men in both sectors, and decline rather quickly across skill groups, with *negative* wage gaps for the most highly skilled men in both sectors. Nevertheless, the average union wage gap is smaller for

men in the public sector than in the private sector (Lewis 1988), primarily because the wage gaps for workers in the middle of the skill distribution are lower in the public sector.[21] The unadjusted union wage gaps

---

[21]Conventional union wage gaps by sector (estimated from simple models fit by sector and gender) are presented in Appendix Table A1, and show wage gaps of about 10% for public sector men in both 1973–74 and 1993, versus 19% for private sector men in both years. One caveat to comparison of union-nonunion wage gaps in the public and private sectors is the possibility that "spillovers" from the unionized sector to the nonunionized sector may be more important in the public sector—see Belman, Heywood, and Lund (1997), for example. If this is the case, then the presence of public sector unionism may have a

UNIONS AND WAGE INEQUALITY IN THE U.S.   311

for women in the public and private sectors are even more similar, and indeed the averages of the unadjusted wage gaps across all 10 skill deciles are comparable in the two sectors.[22]

Another interesting feature of the wage gaps in Figures 3 and 4 is the similarity of the patterns in 1973–74 and 1993. Despite the rapid growth of public sector unionism, the effects of unions on wages in the public sector seem to have changed relatively little over the 1970s and 1980s. By the same token, despite dramatic declines in private sector unionization, union wage effects for different skill groups remained fairly constant, with only a modest decline in the union wage advantage for the least skilled men in the private sector. In the absence of longitudinally based estimates of the "true" union wage effects for the two years, these changes must be interpreted cautiously, however, since the processes of selection into the union sector may have also changed, leading to shifts in the magnitude of selection biases in the observed wage gaps.

Table 8 uses data by predicted skill decile for men and women in the public and private sectors to estimate the effects of unions on wage inequality in the two sectors in 1973–74 and 1993. As in Table 5, I have computed the effects of unions using two alternative sets of union wage gaps: the observed gaps (shown in Figures 3 and 4) and adjusted gaps based on the estimates in my 1996 paper.[23]

The results for private sector men and women in Table 8 are fairly close to the

Figure 2. Union Membership Rates in the Private Sector by Skill Group.

A. Private Sector Men

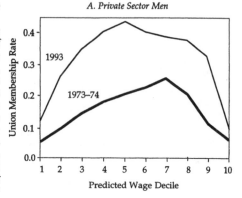

B. Private Sector Women

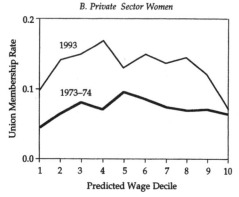

---

relatively bigger effect than is estimated using the counter-factual of the current nonunion wage structure.

[22]As shown in Appendix Table A1, conventional union wage gaps for women based on models fit to the public and private sectors are only slightly smaller in the public sector than in the private sector.

[23]In principle, one might prefer to modify the adjusted gaps for the public and private sectors. I experimented with several alternatives and found that they gave results similar to the ones presented in Table 8.

results for all workers in Table 5: changes in unionism can account for 15–20% of the rise in wage inequality among private sector men, and virtually none of the rise in inequality for private sector women. The results for public sector workers suggest a more important role for unions. Changes in public sector unionism apparently "held back" rising wage inequality to a significant degree. For men, the estimates suggest that the variance of wages would have risen an additional 30–40% in the absence of unions, while for women the variance of

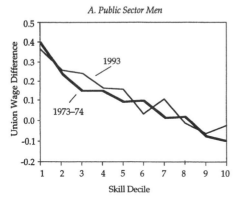

Figure 3. Union Wage Gaps in the Public Sector by Skill Group.

A. Public Sector Men

B. Public Sector Women

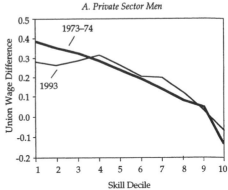

Figure 4. Union Wage Gaps in the Private Sector by Skill Group.

A. Private Sector Men

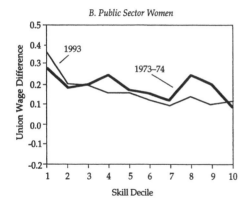

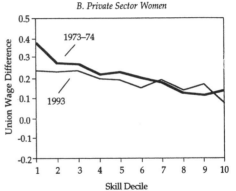

B. Private Sector Women

wages would have risen an additional 40%. Comparing the changes in wage inequality in the public and private sectors, differential trends in union membership can potentially account for 50–80% of the slower rise in wage inequality for men in the public sector, and 20–30% of the slower rise in wage inequality for women in the public sector.

Another important aspect of the differential trends in unionization in the public and private sectors is the potential effect on public-private wage gaps. For men, union membership rose 10.4 percentage points in

the public sector and fell 16.2% in the private sector, implying a 26.6 percentage point divergence. Assuming a mean union wage gap of about 15%, this divergence would have caused mean public sector wages to rise by about 4 percentage points relative to private sector wages. A similar calculation for women shows a 25.2 percentage point divergence in union coverage, also implying a roughly 4 percentage point widening of the mean public-private wage gap. On average, the public-private wage gap for men rose slightly (about 3 percentage points) between 1973 and 1993, whereas it

Recent Developments in Labor Economics III

UNIONS AND WAGE INEQUALITY IN THE U.S.   313

Table 8. Estimates of the Contribution of Unions
to Rising Wage Inequality: Public and Private Sectors, 1973–74 to 1993.

Description	1973–74	1993	Change
A. *Public Sector Male Workers*			
Variance in Log Wages	0.233	0.266	0.033
Effect of Unions Using Raw Union Wage Differentials (Equation 5)	−0.029	−0.043	−0.014
Effect of Unions Using Adjusted Differentials (Equation 7)	−0.024	−0.033	−0.009
B. *Public Sector Female Workers*			
Variance in Log Wages	0.204	0.237	0.033
Effect of Unions Using Raw Union Wage Differentials (Equation 5)	0.001	−0.013	−0.014
Effect of Unions Using Adjusted Differentials (Equation 7)	−0.003	−0.016	−0.013
C. *Private Sector Male Workers*			
Variance in Log Wages	0.260	0.328	0.068
Effect of Unions Using Raw Union Wage Differentials (Equation 5)	−0.024	−0.009	0.015
Effect of Unions Using Adjusted Differentials (Equation 7)	−0.018	−0.008	0.010
D. *Private Sector Female Workers*			
Variance in Log Wages	0.173	0.264	0.091
Effect of Unions Using Raw Union Wage Differentials (Equation 5)	−0.002	0.000	0.002
Effect of Unions Using Adjusted Differentials (Equation 7)	−0.002	−0.001	0.001

Notes: See notes to Table 5.

fell about 8% for women.[24] Thus, differential shifts in unionization can potentially explain most of the movement of the mean public-private wage gap for men over the two decades, but none of the shift for women. Indeed, in the absence of changing relative union patterns, the public sector wage gap for women would have fallen even faster.

Conclusions

The primary objective of this paper has been to reassess the connection between declining unionization and widening wage inequality using data for men and women from the early 1970s and early 1990s. The

evidence points to three main findings on this issue. First, since the fraction of women belonging to unions was relatively stable over the two decades under examination, shifts in unionization explain almost none of the rise in overall wage inequality among female workers. Second, the decline in union membership among men explains a modest share—15–20%—of the rise in overall male wage inequality. Third, within the public sector, rising unionism was a significant force in forestalling rising wage inequality for both male and female workers. For men, the differences in trends in union membership between the public and private sectors can explain 50–80% of the slower growth of wage inequality in the public sector than in the private sector. For women a similar calculation shows that differences in unionism can explain 20–30% of the difference in the growth of wage inequality between the sectors.

A secondary goal of the paper has been to develop a deeper understanding of union membership patterns and union wage effects in the labor market as a whole and in the public and private sectors. As late as

---

[24]In 1973/74, public sector men earned about 1% lower wages than private sector men, controlling for education, experience, and race, whereas public sector women earned about 14% more than private sector women, controlling for the same factors. In 1993, comparable public-private wage gaps were 2% for men and 6% for women.

314   INDUSTRIAL AND LABOR RELATIONS REVIEW

1974, union membership in the U.S. economy was concentrated among men with average or slightly below-average education working in the private sector. In 1993, the highest union membership rates occurred for highly educated women in the public sector. Despite this dramatic shift, an important characteristic of unions— their tendency to raise wages more for workers with lower measured skills—persisted. Indeed, there was remarkable stability in the structure of union-nonunion wage gaps across different skill groups over the sample periods. A comparison of union relative wage structures in the public and private sectors over time suggests that unions exerted about the same effect on different skill and gender groups in the two sectors, and that despite the dramatic shifts in union membership, the structure of union relative wage effects was about the same in the mid-1990s as in the mid-1970s. How and why unions were able to maintain such a stable effect on the structure of wages among their membership is an interesting question for further research.

Appendix Table A1
Conventional Union Wage Gaps by Sector

Year	Men			Women		
	All	Public	Private	All	Public	Private
1973–74	0.178	0.095	0.194	0.220	0.182	0.213
	(0.004)	(0.011)	(0.005)	(0.006)	(0.020)	(0.007)
1993	0.168	0.096	0.194	0.166	0.142	0.183
	(0.004)	(0.008)	(0.005)	(0.004)	(0.007)	(0.007)

Notes: Standard errors in parentheses. Entries are estimated union coefficients from weighted OLS regression models that include years of education, a cubic in experience, dummies for marital status, nonwhite race, Hispanic ethnicity (in 1993 only), and three region dummies. The estimation uses CPS sampling weights.

REFERENCES

Abowd, John M., and Henry S. Farber. 1982. "Job Queues and the Union Status of Workers." *Industrial and Labor Relations Review,* Vol. 35, No. 3 (April), pp. 354–67.

Belman, Dale, John S. Heywood, and John Lund. 1997. "Public Sector Earnings and the Extent of Unionization." *Industrial and Labor Relations Review,* Vol. 50, No. 4 (July), pp. 610–28.

Blackburn, McKinley, David Bloom, and Richard B. Freeman. 1990. "The Declining Position of Less-Skilled American Males." In Gary Burtless, ed., *A Future of Lousy Jobs?* Washington, D.C.: Brookings Institution.

Bound, John, and George Johnson. 1992. "Changes in the Structure of Wages in the 1980s: An Evaluation of Alternative Explanations." *American Economic Review,* Vol. 82, No. 3 (June), pp. 371–92.

Card, David. 1992. "The Effect of Unions on the Distribution of Wages: Redistribution or Relabelling?" National Bureau of Economic Research Working Paper 4195. Cambridge, Mass., October.

_____. 1996. "The Effect of Unions on the Structure of Wages: A Longitudinal Analysis." *Econometrica,* Vol. 64, No. 4 (July), pp. 957–79.

Card, David, and Thomas Lemieu. 1996. "Wage Dispersion, Returns to Skill, and Black-White Wage Differentials." *Journal of Econometrics,* Vol. 74, No. 2 (October), pp. 319–61.

DiNardo, John, Nicole Fortin, and Thomas Lemieu. 1996. "Labor Market Institutions and the Distribution of Wages, 1973–1992: A Semi-Parametric Approach." *Econometrica,* Vol. 64 (September), pp. 1001–44.

DiNardo, John, and Thomas Lemieu. 1997. "Diverging Male Wage Inequality in the United States and Canada, 1981–1988: Do Institutions Explain the Difference?" *Industrial and Labor Relations Review,* Vol. 50 (July), pp. 629–51.

Farber, Henry S. 1983. "The Determination of the Union Status of Workers." *Econometrica,* Vol. 51, No. 5 (September), pp. 1417–37.

_____. 1990. "The Decline of Unionization in the

United States: What Can Be Learned from Recent Experience?" *Journal of Labor Economics,* Vol. 8 (January, Part 2), pp. S75–S105.

Freeman, Richard B. 1980. "Unionism and the Dispersion of Wages." *Industrial and Labor Relations Review,* Vol. 34, No. 1 (October), pp. 3–23.

____. 1986. "Unionism Comes to the Public Sector." *Journal of Economic Literature,* Vol. 24, No. 1 (March), pp. 41–86.

____. 1988. "Contraction and Expansion: The Divergence of Private Sector and Public Sector Unionism in the United States." *Journal of Economic Perspectives,* Vol. 2, No. 2 (Spring), pp. 63–88.

____. 1993. "How Much Has De-Unionization Contributed to the Rise in Male Earnings Inequality?" In S. Danziger and P. Gottschalk, eds., *Uneven Tides: Rising Inequality in America.* New York: Russell Sage Foundation.

Freeman, Richard B., and James L. Medoff. 1984. *What Do Unions Do?* New York: Basic Books.

Katz, Lawrence F., and David H. Autor. 1999. "Inequality in the Labor Market." In Orley Ashenfelter and David Card, eds., *Handbook of Labour Economics.*

Amsterdam and New York: North Holland.

Lemieux, Thomas. 1992. "Unions and Wage Inequality in Canada and the United States." In David Card and Richard B. Freeman, eds., *Small Differences That Matter: Labor Markets and Income Maintenance in Canada and the United States.* Chicago: University of Chicago Press.

____. 1998. "Estimating the Effects of Unions on Wage Inequality in a Panel Data Model with Comparative Advantage and Non-Random Selection." *Journal of Labor Economics,* Vol. 16 (April), pp. 261–91.

Lewis, H. Gregg. 1986. *Union Relative Wage Effects: A Survey.* Chicago: University of Chicago Press.

____. 1988. "Union Nonunion Wage Gaps in the Public Sector." In Richard B. Freeman and Casey Ichniowski, eds., *When Public Sector Workers Unionize.* Chicago: University of Chicago Press.

Riddell, W. Craig. 1992. "Unionization in Canada and the United States: A Tale of Two Countries." In David Card and Richard B. Freeman, eds., *Small Differences That Matter: Labor Markets and Income Maintenance in Canada and the United States.* Chicago: University of Chicago Press.

Part V
Personnel Economics

[22]

Personnel Economics: Past Lessons and Future Directions

Presidential Address to the Society of Labor Economists, San Francisco, May 1, 1998

Edward P. Lazear, *Hoover Institution and Graduate School of Business, Stanford University*

In 1987, the *Journal of Labor Economics* published an issue on the economics of personnel. Since then, personnel economics, defined as the application of labor economics principles to business issues, has become a major part of labor economics, now accounting for a substantial proportion of papers in this and other journals. Much of the work in personnel economics has been theoretical, in large part because the data needed to test these theories have not been available. In recent years, a number of firm-based data sets have surfaced that allow personnel economics to be tested. Using two such data sets, I give support to the implications of theories that relate to life-cycle incentives, tournaments, piecework incentives, pay compression, and peer pressure. I conclude that personnel economics is real. It is far more than a set of clever theories. It has relevance to the real world. Additionally, firm-based data make asking and answering new kinds of questions feasible. The value of research in this area is high because so little is known compared with other fields in labor economics. Questions about the importance of a worker's relative position in a

This research was supported in part by the National Science Foundation. Comments from Joseph Guzman and participants of the Institute for International Economic Studies seminar at Stockholm University are gratefully acknowledged.

[*Journal of Labor Economics*, 1999, vol. 17, no. 2]

firm, about intrafirm mobility, about the effect of the firm's business environment on worker welfare, and about the significance of first impressions can be answered using the new data. Finally, I argue that the importance of personnel economics in undergraduate as well as business school curricula will continue to grow.

Personnel economics, defined as the use of economics to understand the internal workings of the firm, has grown in importance over the last decade. Questions that relate to internal labor markets, incentives, compensation, promotion, evaluation, recruitment, turnover, and other resource practices have been investigated at some length in the labor literature. Indeed, in the first three meetings of the Society of Labor Economists, submissions of papers on personnel economics have played a prominent role, accounting for about 25% the total.

My own interest in personnel economics was an outgrowth of my move from the University of Chicago's economics department to its business school. When I was confronted with students whose focus was primarily business, it became clear to me that traditional labor economics was less central to their interests than were the topics covered in the organizational behavior curriculum. But economics provides a rigorous and in many cases better way to think about these human resources questions than do the more sociological and psychological approaches. Certain questions, especially those dealing with compensation, turnover, and incentives, are inherently economic. Others, like those associated with nonmonetary aspects of the job—norms, teamwork and peer relationships—while seemingly noneconomic, are capable of being informed by economic reasoning.

Most of the early work in personnel economics was theoretical. Primarily because of data shortcomings, research focused on dreaming up theories that might explain the empirical regularities of human resources practices. Few papers made serious attempts to test the theories, although other researchers have provided some evidence on the ideas advanced in the earlier papers.[1]

It is now time to take stock. Have the ideas in personnel economics been useful, and are they an accurate description of the real world? What kind of evidence can be used to support or refute the claims? Where is the field going? In this essay, I examine three themes:

First, is personnel economics real or merely a series of clever models proposed by abstract thinkers who have little contact with reality? To answer this question, two firm-based data sets are used that can provide

---

[1] See e.g., Hutchens (1987, 1989); Bull, Schotter, and Weigelt (1987); Knoeber (1989); Ehrenberg and Bognanno (1990); Knoeber and Thurman (1994); Drago and Garvey (1998); and Erikkson (in press).

direct evidence on a large number of theoretical predictions. The evidence shows that personnel economics has much going for it. Not only does it make sense at an intuitive level, but it finds support in the data. Economics works well in explaining the world, and not the least so in the area of human resources. Although it is always prudent to be critical of one's own work, we have much reason to be proud of the success of economic analysis in helping us understand labor markets, both external and internal.

Second, because new firm-level databases are becoming available, labor economists can answer different kinds of questions than the did in the past. Many of these questions are not only interesting, but as a result of their novelty, the answers remain largely unknown. Thus, this is a field that is wide open to discovery. It is much easier to make a mark here than it is in the historically more active, traditionally important fields like labor supply, labor demand, and human capital. In the second part of this article, I attempt to make the argument by posing some questions and providing some preliminary answers.

Third, because most students who take labor courses, both at the undergraduate and masters levels, are more likely to end up in business than in academic economics or policy analysis, personnel economics is a natural part of their labor economics training. Those less-than-objective economists who work in the field of personnel economics might argue that personnel economics is at least as relevant to the typical economics program as to the traditional economics curriculum. Thus, the essay concludes by suggesting that personnel economics should become an important part of our teaching programs because of the field's relevance and because of its demonstrated validity.

I. Personnel Economics Is Real

There are a number of theories that have been proposed over the past 2 decades that purport to explain a variety of human resources phenomena observed in firms.[2] Since an author cannot expect anyone else to take his theories seriously if he does not, the first part of this essay is devoted to providing evidence that theoretical ideas presented in a number of my previous papers are supported by empirical evidence. The evidence presented comes from two firm-based data sets. One is from an autoglass installation chain named Safelite. The other is from a large financial services company. The approach used is to outline the predictions of the

[2] Actually, the work in personnel economics goes back much further. The earliest mention in relatively modern literature is found in Slichter (1928). Reder (1955) is an excellent example of pioneering work in this area. More recent is the well-known book by Doeringer and Piore (1971).

theory, to discuss how the theory could be refuted, to compare the predictions to those of other competing theories, and then to present the results.

A. Deferred Compensation as a Motivator

My initial foray into personnel economics took the form of a paper entitled, "Why Is There Mandatory Retirement?" (Lazear 1979), written in the late 1970s when mandatory retirement was still legal in the United States, as it currently is elsewhere. Although the purpose of the paper was to explain this particular, somewhat puzzling institution, my main contribution was probably in proposing a theory of deferred compensation as a motivator. I argued that senior workers receive high wages not so much because they are worth what they are paid during their senior years but because high wages served to motivate them during the early stages of their careers. Since the young want to grow old in the firm and reap the benefits of high-wage, perhaps cushy jobs, they put forth higher levels of effort than they would for flat wages.[3] A brief description of the theory follows.

A worker can choose to work at a high level of effort, or he may shirk, putting forth a low level of effort. A worker who works at a high level produces output given by the V profile in figure 1. If he shirks, his output is V'. The $\tilde{W}$ curve in is the value of the worker's alternative use of time, in this context most easily thought of as the value of his leisure. Time T is the date of voluntary and efficient retirement. If workers receive compensation V, they would choose to retire voluntarily at time T because that is the point at which the alternative use of time just equals the worker's marginal product or payment.

Consider two schemes, W and V, where W is constructed such that the present value of the W path from zero to T equals the present value

---

[3] This theory (see Lazear [1981] for more detail) predated the literature on efficiency wages but had an efficiency-wage mechanism embedded in it. High wages are paid to motivate workers, and an oversupply of labor would result were it not for mandatory retirement or some other hours constraint. The subsequent efficiency-wage literature deviated from the approach used in Lazear (1979, 1981) by obtaining an equilibrium with unemployment. In my work, unemployment does not result. The market clears because workers buy their jobs by taking wages that fall short of the marginal products during the early years on the job. As long as the profile is set up appropriately, and in competition this would be the expected result, the labor market operates efficiently. It is not the incentive component that causes unemployment in efficiency wage models. The incentive component is present in Lazear (1979, 1981), where the labor market clears. Unemployment results in the subsequent efficiency wage models (see Shapiro and Stiglitz 1984) because sufficiently rich compensation structures are ruled out. It is the wage-rigidity part that creates unemployment, just as it does in the traditional Keynesian story.

Wage, Output

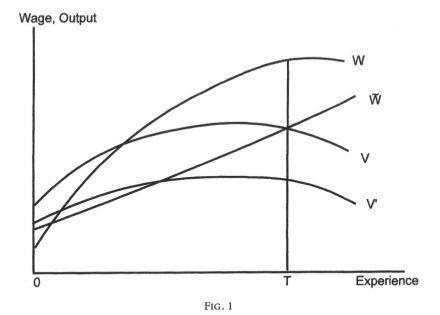

FIG. 1

of the *V* path over the same period. With perfect capital markets, workers would be indifferent between paths *W* and *V* if all else were equal, but all else is not equal. Consider a worker who is being paid according to *V* and is nearing time *T.* At that point, the incentives to shirk become overwhelming. On the day before *T,* the worker may either work at the high level of effort, or he may shirk. If he shirks, the worst thing that can possibly happen is that he gets fired. If he gets fired, he does not receive wage *V* during the next period, but he does get to enjoy the value of his leisure, which is equal to his wage at time *T.* Thus, nothing is lost by shirking. If instead the worker were paid *W,* things would be different. Under such circumstances, shirking allows him to enjoy the value of his leisure *W̃* next period, but he forgoes wage *W.* Since *W* is set such that it is well above *V* at time *T,* a worker would forfeit quasi rents by shirking. Thus, the a sufficiently steep *W* profile induces workers to perform at a higher level of effort than they would were they paid their marginal product at each point in their careers.[4]

The key prediction of this model is that wages rise more rapidly than marginal product. There was some early corroboration of this idea. Med-

---

[4] Actually, a discrete payment after retirement is necessary to prevent shirking in the last moment on the job. See Akerlof and Katz (1989) for a good discussion of this point.

off and Abraham (1980) used subjective performance data and found that wages rose more rapidly than performance. Their work has been criticized as being less than definitive because the subjective ratings might reflect overall ability, relative position within the job, or some other factor that was not well correlated with productivity levels. The theory begged for quantitative productivity measures to prove the case.

Spitz (1991) had more objective data. She was able to examine the productivity of supermarket retail clerks and found that their productivity did not rise as rapidly with experience as their wages.

The Safelite data set allows a detailed examination of the relation between experience-earnings and experience-productivity profiles. Safelite is the nation's largest autoglass installer, headquartered in Columbus, Ohio. Safelite has a very sophisticated information system and keeps detailed machine-readable records of weekly output for each installer in the company. The data used cover the period from January 1994 to July 1995. During the period, Safelite switched from paying installers hourly wages to paying piece rates. Piece-rate compensation is an alternative to career motivation schemes, so most of the discussion in this section will focus on the period during which workers were paid time rates. More will be said about the time-rate/piece-rate distinction below.

The data on output per week and compensation per week were used to estimate the relation of both productivity and pay to tenure. The results are unambiguous. Irrespective of the specification, the tenure coefficient in the pay regression is always higher than the tenure coefficient in the output regression.

Two equations are estimated. The first is the standard log of earnings (pay per day) on tenure and tenure squared. The second has the same right-hand variables but uses actual daily output as the dependent variable.[5] Both regressions allow full interaction with the pay regime by including a dummy equal to one if pay during the person-month is piece rate and zero if pay is hourly wage, and also PTENUR and PTENUR2, which are tenure and tenure squared multiplied by PPPFLAG, the piece-rate dummy.

The key result is that tenure has a greater effect in the wage regression than it does in the output regression.[6] The model reported table 1 includes individual-specific effects and a quadratic tenure specification. Using the coefficients from the hourly wage regime, figure 2 shows the slopes of

[5] The period is a month so that the figures are the average daily figures in a given month.

[6] Although this is true for the raw numbers, it is necessary to normalize these coefficients because output is in windshield units and pay is in dollars. To normalize, I assumed that the present value of the pay equaled the present value of output over a 10-year period. The results are insensitive to assumptions about the length of the work life.

Table 1

ln(Pay per Day)	Coefficient		SE
Pay regression:			
Piece rate dummy	.1060902		.0052568
Tenure	.1723315		.0051049
Piece rate dummy × tenure	−.0080443		.0013366
Tenure squared	−.0027871		.0004152
Piece rate dummy × tenure squared	.0002437		.000063
Constant	3.998284		.0129329
N		29,586	
R^2		.7451	
Root mean square error		.15432	
Output regression:			
Piece rate dummy	.2337737		.0135927
Tenure	.0809399		.013193
Piece rate dummy × tenure	−.0395036		.0034563
Tenure squared	−.0046519		.0010741
Piece rate dummy × tenure squared	.0014897		.0001629
Constant	.6658699		.0334352
N		29,412	
R^2		.7562	
Root mean square error		.39814	

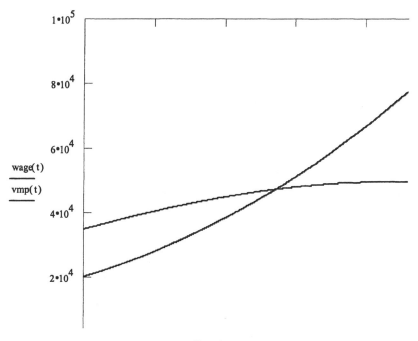

FIG. 2

the two estimated profiles. The estimated diagram (figure 2) resembles the predicted diagram (figure 1) in that the slope of tenure in the earnings regression is steeper than that of the productivity regression.

The model is estimated in a number of different ways. Fixed effects are omitted, time dummies are included, and a different definition of tenure is used.[7] The results are unchanged: tenure has a greater effect on pay than on output.

How do these results compare against those that might be expected from traditional human capital theory?[8] It is necessary to distinguish on-the-job training (OJT) that takes the form of general human capital from OJT that is firm-specific. When investment in OJT is general, the worker bears the full cost of the training. As a result, he is paid exactly his productivity at each moment in time. Thus, if OJT were general, then the slope of the experience-productivity profile should be the same as that of the experience-earnings profile. The fact that the slope of the earnings profile is steeper than that of the productivity profile is inconsistent with investment in general OJT being the complete explanation of the experience-earnings relation.

The situation is even more compelling when the alternative considered is that of investing in firm-specific OJT. Because workers and the firm share the costs and benefits of investment, experience-earnings are flatter than experience-productivity profiles. But the Safelite results clearly indicate that experience-earnings rise more steeply than experience-productivity. Thus, firm-specific OJT cannot be the full story either.

The idea that earnings rise more rapidly than productivity is not a rejection of the idea that investment in human capital is important. The large tenure coefficients in the experience-productivity relation suggest that learning on the job is very important at Safelite. The question is about the link between productivity growth and earnings growth, not about productivity growth per se. The conclusion from this section is that innovations in personnel economics, which take the form of worklife incentive theory, are necessary to reconcile earnings growth with productivity growth, at least at this one company.

B. Tournament Theory

Somewhat related to worklife incentive schemes is tournament theory,[9] which maintains that firms use promotions to motivate workers. There are

---

[7] Within-period tenure rather than total tenure was used. The results were qualitatively the same.

[8] The empirical implications were first spelled out by Becker (1962) and Mincer (1962).

[9] See Lazear and Rosen (1981).

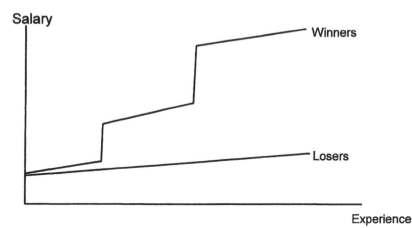

FIG. 3

two major differences between tournament theory and worklife incentive theory. First, tournament theory emphasizes relative comparisons between individuals; worklife incentive theory does not rely on interpersonal comparisons of any kind.[10] Second, tournament theory focuses on pay changes that are associated with promotions, which correspond in the real world to job title changes. The emphasis in the worklife incentive scheme is on wage growth that occurs within a job rather than the growth between them. Both schemes can be at work within the same firm. The salary hierarchy that corresponds to a particular job structure can be modeled by tournament theory. The within-job wage growth that is associated with work experience is modeled by worklife incentive theory, particularly for those who are past the stages where a great deal of human capital investment is occurring. At the normative level, promotions are used to motivate young managers. Middle-level managers who know that future promotions are highly unlikely can be motivated through worklife incentive schemes.[11]

The important component of tournament theory is that job changes carry with them significant wage increases and that the paths of winners and losers diverge. This is shown in figure 3. Not only do winners have steeper experience-earnings profiles than losers, but winners' profiles are

[10] Actually, direct relative comparisons are unnecessary. Each worker is assumed to be competing against the equilibrium level of effort, which could also be represented by an effort output standard.

[11] This distinction is somewhat overstated because promotions need never cease. There is no reason that changes in job titles must be associated with changes in tasks. "Promotions" could merely signify wage increases.

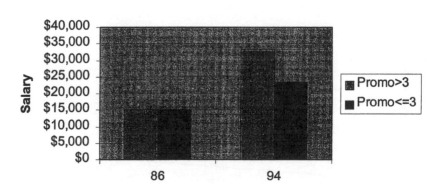

FIG. 4.—Wage growth for high- and low-promotion workers

characterized by discontinuous jumps at promotion points. Neither worklife incentive theory nor human capital theory imply any discrete salary changes. Unless learning were extremely discontinuous, human capital theory, taken literally, would imply smooth wage growth. Similarly, there is no reason for discontinuity (except at the retirement date) in the worklife incentive story. In order to generate discrete jumps, it is necessary to resort to tournament theory or some other explanation.[12]

It is possible to get some sense of whether promotions are associated with discrete wage growth above that implied by changes in the levels of experience. McCue (1996) examined this using the Panel Study of Income Dynamics and found that promotions were important in explaining job growth. McCue's study is enlightening but draws inferences from examining workers at many different firms. To complement her approach, it is useful to examine the entire salary structure of a given firm. To do this, firm based data are needed. The data used here come from a large financial services firm with approximately 42,000 employees at the end of the sample period in 1994. Data were obtained on all employees of this firm (including the CEO) for the period 1986 through 1994. Some workers who were present in 1986 were not present in 1994. Many working in 1994 were not present in 1986. The data set consists of a series of snapshops of the payroll file on the same date each year. Thus, the exact career path of each employee can be described and compared to others in the same firm.

To see that promotion matters for wage growth, examine figure 4. The sample is the group of individuals who were with the firm continuously

---

[12] Rosen (1986) shows how skew in within-firm earnings results in a multistage tournament context.

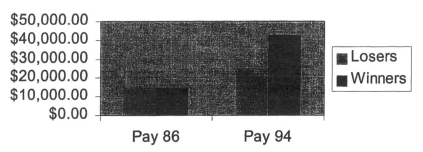

FIG. 5.—Pay changes: losers and winners

from 1986 through 1994. Those with more than three promotions over the period experienced an increase in log of pay of .80. Those with three or fewer promotions experienced a wage increase in log of pay of .45. Two individuals who both started with the mean wage for young workers of just under $15,000 would diverge significantly by 1994.[13] Those with more than three promotions would have on average a salary in 1994 of about $33,400, whereas those with three or few promotions would have a salary in 1994 of about $25,500.

Figure 5 presents similar information, but for a slightly different cut. Here, workers who stay during the entire period and are young at the beginning of the period are split into two groups. "Winners" are defined as those with five or more promotions over the period. "Losers" are defined as those with no promotions over the 8-year period. The losers are not really losers, however, because they have managed to remain with the firm for at least 8 years. Still, the difference in wages at the end of the period between the two groups is large, as is shown in figure 5.

Table 2 reports regression result that examine the effect of promotions on wage growth. This is done in two ways.[14] First, each person-year is treated as a separate observation, and the effect of promotion on annual wage growth is estimated. Second, wage growth is estimated over the entire 8-year period for the sample of individuals who were with the firm continuously from 1986 through 1994. These are reported in table 2.

The first regression reports a coefficient on TOTPROMO of .13. This variable measures the total number of promotions between 1986 and 1994. Thus, an individual with one promotion during the 8-year period would have wage growth that is about 13% higher than one who did not

---

[13] "Young" is defined as having been with the firm for 3 or fewer years in 1986.

[14] Summary statistics on the variables in table 2 are reported in appendix table A1.

Table 2
The Effect of Promotions on Wage Growth

	DPAY	
	Coefficient	SE
Regression (1). Dependent variable = change in log wages between 1986 and 1994:		
TENURE	−.0216384	.0011618
TOTPROMO	.1345333	.0072543
_CONS	.6218923	.0236682
N	4,891	
R²	.17	

	DLNPAY	
	Coefficient	SE
Regression (2). Dependent variable = annual change in log wages (unit of analysis = person-year):		
TENURE	−.0176034	.0002819
PROMO	.1400868	.0050373
_CONS	.2186578	.0030998
N	123,233	
R²	.04	
Regression (3). Dependent variable = annual change in log wages (unit of analysis = person-year):		
TENURE	.0009663	.0002725
PROMO	.1078641	.0052318
PROMOLAG	.0778803	.0049764
PROMOLAG2	.0165095	.0047457
_CONS	−.0704595	.0039956
N	57,005	
R²	.0115	
Regression (4). Dependent variable = annual change in log wages (unit of analysis = person-year):		
TENURE	−.0031468	.0001521
PROMO	.0540001	.0028358
_CONS	.0849271	.0018738
N	57,390	
R²	.0160	
Regression (5). Dependent variable = annual change in log wages (unit of analysis = person-year):		
TENURE	−.0025411	.000155
PROMO	.0565873	.0028276
PROMOLAG	.0596881	.0026912
PROMOLE	.005603	.0029692
_CONS	.0653392	.0021526
N	57,390	
R²	.0244	

have any promotions during the period. The second regression examines
1-year wage growth and reports a coefficient of .14 on PROMO, which
is a dummy equal to one if a promotion occurred in a given year.

There are two points. First, promotions do create kinks in the earnings

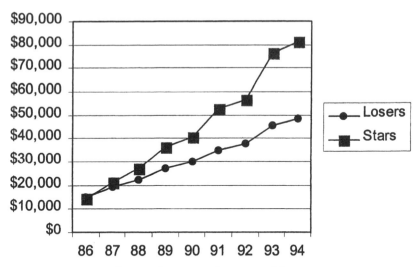

FIG. 6.—Pay progression: stars and losers

function. From the second regression, it is clear that earnings grow about 14% faster in a year during which a promotion occurred than in a year without a promotion.

The importance of promotions is demonstrated in figure 6, which shows two profiles. The profile labeled "Stars" corresponds to an individual who started with wages of just under $15,000 (the mean for young workers in 1986) but enjoyed five promotions during the 8-year interval. These were assumed to occur in 1987, 1988, 1989, 1991, and 1993. The stars' profile has kinks that correspond to promotion years. There are no jumps like the ones shown in figure 3 because we cannot determine the exact point at which the promotion and raise associated with it was given. Thus, the picture assumes that growth occurred smoothly throughout the year.[15]

Second, stars end up with earnings that are 4.4 times their initial earnings, whereas losers end up with wages that are 2.3 times their initial earnings. This corresponds to annual earnings growth rates of 23.5% and 16.2%, respectively. So promotion clearly matters at this firm in a way consistent with tournament theory. Because promotion implies a kink in the profile, neither human capital theory nor worklife incentive theory provides an explanation of the pattern of wage growth that is both observed and a reflection of within-firm tournaments.

---

[15] The same is true for all raises. These come in discontinuous fashion, but they are assumed to raise wages continuously throughout the year.

The effect of a promotion on wage growth may be misstated by the contemporaneous coefficient on PROMO. The coefficient may overstate the effect of promotion on wage growth if the firm takes in a subsequent year what it gives up this year in promotion. It may understate the effect on wage growth if promotion opens up opportunity for future wage growth. It is possible to examine this directly. One can look at the effect of past promotion on this year's wage growth. This is done in regression (3) of table 2.

This regression contains variables that reflect promotion lagged 1 year (PROMOLAG) and 2 years (PROMOLAG2). These reduce the coefficient on contemporaneous promotion somewhat, but the total effect of a given promotion is now estimated to be .20 on change in log wages, or about .06 greater than that of contemporaneous promotion alone. Evidently, promotion implies additional within-job wage growth. Some of this may reflect ability differences that were observed at the time of hire. Such differences could show up in the promotion decision. Some of the wage growth associated with promotion may reflect reward or ability learned after the time of hire. It is possible to examine the two effects separately. Ability known at the time of hire is as likely to be reflected in future promotions as it is in past promotions, but the effect of the rewards or new knowledge of ability is reflected only in lagged coefficients. Regression (5) in table 2 reports these results. Leads on promotion are shown as PROMOLE. Note that the effect of the PROMOLE variable on this period's wage growth is very small compared with that of last period's promotion. Learning about ability after hire or reward as reflected in promotion seem to be an important source of wage growth. Information on ability that shows up generically in promotion does not appear to determine wage growth.[16]

C. Salaries and Piece Rates

The most direct application of personnel economics is to the provision of incentives, and one of the cleanest incentive schemes is piecework. When individuals are paid on the basis of their output, their incentives are aligned with those of the firm. Of course, output may be difficult to measure, and these practical difficulties may induce firms to offer salaries, defined as payment on input, rather than piece rates, defined as payment on output.

---

[16] Note that the coefficients in this regression on promotion are smaller than in the previous regressions. The sample size is different because individuals had to have been in the sample for the next year as well to be in these regressions. The basic regression on this sample is reported in regression (4). The same pattern is observed when two-period lags and leads are included.

The groundwork for the analysis of compensation methods was laid in a number of papers,[17] but the specific application to worker compensation is found in Lazear (1986*b*). Two issues arise in the discussion. First, how do firms select a compensation scheme? More specifically, what are the factors that affect the choice between payment on input and payment on output? Second, do workers respond to incentives in the predicted fashion?

Knowing the answer to the second question is a prerequisite to answering the first. The analysis of a firm's choice of compensation scheme proceeds in two steps. The worker's behavioral response to various schemes is modeled. Then the firm chooses the parameters that maximize profits, given the labor supply response behavior derived in the first stage. It is therefore important to establish that workers do indeed respond to incentives as predicted by basic theory.

Incentive responses are difficult to test. In order to do so, it is necessary to observe workers in two different situations and compare the outcomes. But this presents two problems. First, since in most circumstances only one scheme is likely to be optimal, only one scheme is observed for each worker if optimality obtains. Second, in the context of salaries and piece rates, the major reason for choosing input-based pay is that some or all components of output are not perfectly observable.[18] This is problematic because it is difficult to test a theory in which the predictions are about components that cannot be observed.

Sometimes it is possible to test behavioral predictions by examining related factors that are observable. In rare cases, however, the researcher is presented with data that are well suited to the purpose and allow direct testing of the theory. Recently, a number of cases of this sort have arisen.[19]

I have personally been the fortunate recipient of what is, for the purpose of testing whether workers respond to incentives, perhaps the best of the available data sets. A change in management induced Safelite, the autoglass firm mentioned above, to switch from paying hourly wages to paying piece rates. The available data set provides detailed information on each worker's output of autoglass installed, both before and after the change to piece rates. This allows testing of the theory set out in Lazear (1986*b*).

This case is instructive not only because it reveals the importance of compensation policy in affecting productivity but because it demonstrates the power of economics in explaining the real world. The predictions that come from the theory are quite precise and are borne out by the evidence.

---

[17] These include Johnson (1950); Cheung (1969); Stiglitz (1975); Ross (1973); and Hölmstrom (1979).

[18] See Baker (1992).

[19] See Paarsch and Shearer (1996); Fernie and Metcalf (1997); and Prendergast (in press).

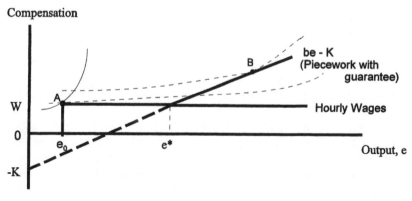

Compensation

FIG. 7

The theory emphasizes two effects of compensation scheme choice: incentives and sorting.[20] A simple diagram, taken from Lazear (1996), illustrates both mechanisms and the predictions.

Safelite gradually switched its workforce from an hourly wage payment structure to piecework over about a 1-year period between 1994 and 1995. Autoglass installers were previously paid hourly wages. They were moved to a system of payment by number of units of glass with a minimum hourly wage guarantee. If the piece rate pay fell short of what the worker would have earned under the old system, he was paid according to the old hourly wage formula.

Implicit in every wage guarantee is a required minimum standard of effort or, when it can be observed, output. Safelite's plan guaranteed W to anyone who would have earned less than W under the piece rate and paid the piece rate to all of those whose compensation by the piece rate formula would have exceeded W. The scheme used is

$$\text{Compensation} = \max[W, be - K].$$

Here, W is the guaranteed wage, b is the piece rate based on number of units of output, e, and K is a constant term to satisfy the individual rationality constraint. The situation is shown in figure 7.

Indifference curves shown in the diagram represent individuals with different tastes or abilities. Low-ability workers have steep indifference curves because additional effort must be compensated by large increases

---

[20] The sorting approach was suggested earlier in another context by Salop and Salop (1976).

in income. Solid indifference curves are those for relatively low-ability workers, and dotted indifference curves are those for higher-ability workers.

The hourly wage schedule is shown by the function that starts at zero, becomes vertical at e_0 and then horizontal at point A. The piece rate schedule with guarantee is the same, except that compensation rises with output above e^*, as shown by the upward-sloping segment.

If workers are offered the hourly wage schedule, then everyone chooses point A since there is no value to working at higher levels of effort. But high-ability workers choose to move from A to B when offered the piece rate schedule with a guarantee. The least able remain at point A. There are three implications.[21]

First, average effort does not decrease and generally increases when the firm switches from hourly wages to piece rates. As long as some workers put forth enough effort to be in the piece rate range, then average output rises. This is the incentive effect associated with moving from hourly wages to piece rates.

Second, average ability of the workforce increases because the ability of the lowest-quality worker does not change as a result of the switch in compensation scheme, but the ability of the highest-quality worker rises. Now, some workers who were previously unwilling to work at Safelite because hourly wages were too low, given their ability and alternatives, now find that the piece rate allows them to work harder and receive more from the job. The least able worker is indifferent between the two schemes. Switching to piece rates has the effect of improving retention and recruitment of high-quality workers. This is the sorting effect.

Third, variance of worker ability and output rises after the switch to piece rates. Even if underlying ability levels did not change, variance in productivity would rise because some workers remain at A, whereas others work in the piece-rate range, with output levels exceeding e^*. This, coupled with the fact that the maximum ability level increases under a piece rate, implies that the increase in output variance becomes even greater.

The evidence on these points is presented in table 3, which comes from Lazear (1996). It can be summarized as follows:

1. Overall productivity increased about 44% (an increase in the log equal equal to .368) as a result of the switch from the hourly wage contract to piecework.

2. The increase can be split into two components. Because individual workers can be followed and their output can be measured before and after the switch, the incentive effect can be taken out. It is defined as the

---

[21] The formal derivation of this material is contained in Lazear (1996).

Table 3
Regression Results
Dependent Variable: ln(Units Installed per Worker, per Day)

	PPPFLAG	R^2	Description
Regression (1)	.368 (.013)	.04	Dummies for month and year included
Regression (2)	.197 (.009)	.73	Dummies for month and year; worker-specific dummies included (2,755 individual workers)

SOURCE.—Lazear (1996).
NOTE.—$N = 29,837$. Standard errors are in parentheses.

increase in output for a given worker after the switch to piece rates occurred, averaged across all workers. This amounts to a log increase of .197, or a 22% increase in productivity for the average worker, as shown by the coefficient in the second row of table 3.

3. The sorting effect can be seen as the difference between the incentive effect and the total effect.[22] Sorting can also be examined more directly. Since high-ability workers are made most happy by the new plan, their turnover rates should fall. Table 4 presents some evidence.

Separation rates went down for high-output individuals after the switch to piecework, from 3.5% to 2.9% per month, but went up from 4.6% to 5.3% per month for normal-output individuals after the switch. As a result of these very high turnover rates and new hiring, the company had a very different workforce composition in July 1995 after the firm was completely switched to the new plan than it did in January 1994 before any switch had occurred.

4. Finally, variance in output rose. Under hourly wages, the variance in average output was 2.02. Under piecework, the variance rose to 2.53.

All predictions of the model are borne out. The effects are large and statistically precise. The Safelite data support the predictions from personnel economics.

Table 4
Separation Rates by Regime and Worker Type

	Hourly Wage Observations	Piecework Observations
Normal output (lower 90%)	.046	.053
High output (upper 10%)	.035	.029
Total	.045	.050

[22] There are some other possibilities for this component, however, which result from the way in which the plan was implemented. See Lazear (1996) for the details.

D. Pay Compression

The argument in Lazear (1989) is that it is rational for firms hiring in a competitive labor market to compress the wage structure. Whenever any part of compensation is relative, a large spread between the wages of "winners" and "losers" results in a competitive, rather than cooperative, work environment. For this reason, firms and workers may choose to adopt a more compressed wage structure.

Compression must be defined relative to something, and the appropriate metric is productivity. Again, the Safelite data permit an examination of productivity directly. Since there is also detailed information on compensation, it is possible to examine the relation between compensation and productivity to assess the amount of compression.

The Safelite data are not ideal for this purpose because the pay compression argument has its greatest force when individuals work together in teams. To the extent that installers are working individually, there is much less motivation for using a compressed pay structure. Still, it is instructive to examine the Safelite data.

The data are split into two regimes. Data are examined from the period when workers were paid hourly wages and from the piece-rate period. The hourly wage period would appear to be more relevant because the piece-rate structure, almost by construction, implies that compensation and productivity are matched. Once a firm chooses to base pay on the piece, it has moved away from pay compression, so the only question would be, "Why does the firm choose to pay on the basis of output?" But this is not quite true. Because the firm has choice over the piece rate formula, wages can be compressed even under piece rates. For example, if compensation is given by

$$\text{Pay} = be - K,$$

where e measures output, setting $b = 0$ and K equal to some negative number would result in completely compressed pay. As b goes to one, the correlation between pay and productivity increases.

Table 5 presents some data on wage and productivity variation. First note that the amount of variation in wages is always less than the amount of variation in productivity. This is true both in absolute terms and relative to the means. At some level, this result is almost guaranteed during the hourly wage period. Since the hourly wage does not change from day to day, even as daily output in units varies, it is necessarily the case that productivity variation will exceed wage variation at least on a daily basis.

The kind of variation that is of more interest is variation across workers, rather than variation for a given worker over time. To get at this, fixed

Table 5
Variations in Wages and Productivity at Safelite

Pay Status and Variables	Mean	SD	N
All:			
log (units per worker, per day)	.895	.762	31,059
log (pay per worker, per day)	4.62	.291	31,059
Fixed effect—units	−.082	.773	2,610
Fixed effect—pay	−.009	.228	2,610
Hourly wages:			
log (units per worker, per day)	.792	.838	15,478
log (per worker, per day)	4.59	.312	15,478
Fixed effect—units	−.062	.721	2,111
Fixed effect—pay	−.020	.236	2,111
Piece rates:			
log (units per worker, per day)	.998	.663	15,581
log (pay per worker, per day)	4.65	.265	15,581
Fixed effect—units	−.169	.991	499
Fixed effect—pay	.037	.184	499

effects on output were computed from the fully specified regression used in Lazear (1996), which relates log of output to month and year dummies, tenure variables, a piece rate dummy, and interaction effects. Fixed effects on wages were computed from an analogous regression with log of pay per day as the dependent variable.

Again, the result is the same. The amount of variation in output fixed effects exceeds that in wage fixed effects.[23] Interpersonal variations in output are larger than interpersonal variations in compensation. As before, this is true for the whole sample period and also for each regime taken independently. Figure 8 shows a histogram of the fixed effects for output (FIXEDU) and for pay (FIXEDP).

The results of table 5 are clear evidence of pay compression relative to productivity. They may or may not support the view that firms compress wages so as to bring about more harmony at the workplace. There is a fundamental difficulty in testing the latter proposition. In order to provide evidence on this point, it is necessary to be able to observe individual output so that output can be compared to productivity. But when individual output is observable, it is less likely that team production and cooperation are important. As a result, the evidence presented should be viewed

[23] The mean of the fixed effects differ (slightly) from zero for two reasons. First, only individuals who have values of fixed effects on both output and wages are included in the table, whereas each regression includes all individuals who have values only for the variables in that regression. Second, the weighting is different because table 5 computes the mean of each individual's fixed effect and does not weight by the number of observations used in computing each fixed effect.

Presidential Address 219

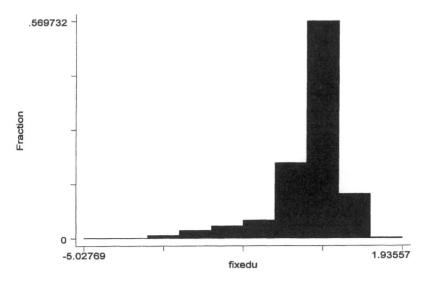

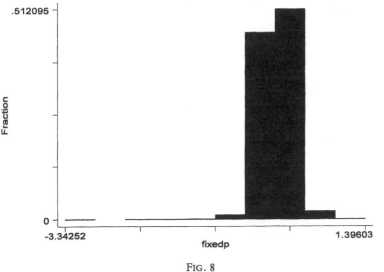

FIG. 8

as consistent with, but not conclusive, proof that firms compress wages to foster cooperation.

E. Norms

Kandel and Lazear (1992) analyze the effects of peer pressure on output. To the extent that norms are important at the workplace, they are most likely to be in force at the small stores that Safelite operates throughout its company.[24] It is possible to evaluate the effect of peer pressure by comparing the change in output of individuals who never produced enough to be in the piece-rate range to the change in output to those who do make it into the piece-rate range.

The effects of peer pressure could have operated in a number of ways at Safelite. First, the announcement that the firm was going to move from hourly wages to piece rates could have a direct effect on worker behavior. This effect is picked up in the time dummies, though, and cannot be disentangled from other variations in output that are caused by seasonality and idiosyncratic weather events.

Second, when a given store moves to the piece-rate system, there may be effects on all workers. As low-output workers see other workers putting forth higher levels of effort, they may become less secure in their positions. This might be true even if the low-output workers are never even close to being in the piece rate range.

Recall that hourly wages are always coupled with some (implicit or explicit) minimum standard on input or, if observable, output. This was labeled e^* on figure 7. A worker may not know e^* but may try to infer it by looking at the output of his peers. As average output rises, a worker who feels that he is close to the minimum cutoff level may be induced to increase his output. This can be tested using the Safelite data.

Let us define two groups of workers. A dummy variable, L, for low output, is set equal to one if a worker never averaged more than four units per day for any month during which he was employed. The piece-rate range does not start until a worker has produced at least 4.5 units, so these workers probably assumed that they would be earning the guaranteed hourly wage. In terms of figure 7, they are the workers who should have chosen to be at point A.

The fixed-effects regression reported in table 3 was rerun on two groups separately, namely those having $L = 1$ and those having $L = 0$. To determine whether there is implicit pressure on those who are not affected directly by the piece rate structure, it is only necessary to compare the effect of switching from hourly wages to piece rates across groups. Because the group with $L = 1$ is never in or very close to the piece rate range, there should be no direct effect of the switch on those workers. The results are reported in table 6.

Workers who are or have potential to be in the piece-rate range experienced an average increase in output of .55 units. Those who never reached (or close to reaching) the piece-rate range experienced an increase in output of .32 units. The model, as illustrated by figure 7, taken literally,

---

[24] Encinosa, Gaynor, and Rebitzer (1998) examine peer pressure and profit sharing in medical practices.

Table 6
The Effect of a Switch to Piece Rates by Group

Group	Increase in Output Associated with Switch to the Piece-Rate System	N
All workers	.44	29,837
Low output workers		
(piece rates never paid)	.32	16,995
All other workers	.55	12,842

implies that there should be no change in output for those who are going to be out of the piece-rate range. Workers should choose either to be on the upward-sloping segment of the compensation schedule or to locate at point A.[25]

Workers who are out of the piece rate range probably increased their effort level because they sensed that e^*, the minimum acceptable output, depended on what other workers were producing. Since the output of others went up substantially, the low-output workers may have felt compelled to increase their output. This is best interpreted as the effect of peer pressure. Because the increase in output is associated directly with the actual switch to the new compensation scheme and not merely with the announcement that a switch is going to occur, it seems reasonable that the increase among the low-output workers results when they see others' outputs rise. The rise in peer output makes more credible the implicit increase in e^*.

F. The Evidence Supports the View
That Personnel Economics Is Real

The evidence presented in this section supports the view that personnel economics is real and that the theories have the power to explain patterns that are observed in the real world. Of course, the data used to demonstrate this proposition come from only two firms. As such, this is little more than a case study.[26] But more data of this type are becoming available, so additional evidence is likely to be presented in the near future.

---

[25] Note that the coefficients in table 6 are the effect only of the switch to piece rates. Thus, output of low-output workers increased by .32 units net of all other effects when the store in which the individual worked switched to piece rates. Since this is net of any time dummies, the .32 is not the effect of improvement in general conditions at Safelite in general.

[26] The results that pertain to worker reaction to Safelite's change should not be interpreted as coming from one case study. It is best interpreted as a shock that hits about 3,000 workers. It is the behavior of the 3,000 workers, not the one firm, that is reported.

In order to demonstrate that personnel economics is real, I believed it most appropriate to examine the validity of my own theories first. A number of the propositions that I have put forth over the past 20 years were checked. The evidence supports the following views:

1. Age-earnings profiles are steeper than age-productivity profiles, consistent with the view that the earnings profile serves an incentive and perhaps a retention role, in addition to compensating workers for the enhanced skills that they acquire on the job.

2. Consistent with tournament theory, promotion is an important source of wage growth for "winners." Further, the difference between the earnings of those who are promoted and those who are not are substantial. The prize associated with winning the race up the corporate ladder is large enough to matter to most workers. Finally, some of the gains from being promoted are received as additional wage growth within the position after the promotion is granted.

3. The theory of incentives, specifically as applied to the difference between hourly or time-based compensation and piece-rate compensation, finds strong support in the data. Worker behavior, both in terms of sorting and response to incentives, matches the predictions of incentive theory very well.

4. Pay compression seems to be an important force in the firm studied. Personnel economics predicts that compression will be used to facilitate cooperation among workers. The evidence is consistent with this view, but the firm examined is not one in which cooperation effects are likely to be strongest. As such, additional corroboration is needed.

5. Peer pressure, perhaps through demonstration effects, seems to be a force in motivating workers. Even workers who were not able to take advantage of the piece-rate schedule directly increased their output when the compensation scheme was switched. This probably reflected the message that standards had risen, which was made credible by the fact that overall output rose.

II. New Directions for Research in Personnel Economics

As a result of firm-based data becoming available, there is a whole range of new questions that can be answered. Most of these are quite new, at least to economics. As such, the potential for for significant breakthroughs is great. Indeed, I believe that the rate of return to research on these new questions in personnel economics is likely to be much greater than that on research in more traditional labor economics areas. It is not that the older questions are less important than they were in the past. Rather, it is much more difficult to make substantial advancements on our knowledge in areas that have been investigated for 30 or 40 years than it is in a new area. As such, the issues discussed below may yield greater payoffs, at least in the near future.

I first proposed that we turn our attention to empirical issues that used job-based or firm-based data in Lazear (1992) and used a panel data set constructed from one firm's complete personnel records over about a 10-year period. This work was followed by Baker, Gibbs, and Hölmstrom (1994) who made similar uses of company-based data. The basic pitch in Lazear (1992) was that taking the job as the relevant unit of analysis leads us to consider different questions and to use different kinds of data sets. In what follows, the questions outlined there are expanded, and new ones are discussed.

To investigate the issues, the financial services company data will be used. Recall that this is a 9-year panel on everyone who worked at the firm between 1986 and 1994. In addition to information on pay and position, scores on annual evaluations done by supervisors are reported. Although admittedly subjective, the evaluation data allow for some interesting areas of investigation that are less standard in the economics literature. Some questions and preliminary answers, which are based on the financial services data, follow.

A. Relative vs. Absolute Performance

The essence of tournament theory is that relative performance matters. The most direct test of this basic premise of tournament theory involves an examination of whether promotions are based on relative performance. The theory predicts that workers should be judged and rewarded on the basis of their performance relative to others in their comparison group. It is only possible to assess a worker's relative position by having data on the group against which he is compared, in this case, the other workers at his firm in his same job. One of the firm-based data sets discussed above makes this comparison possible.

In the financial services data set, individuals are rated by their supervisors annually. Those scores, numerical values between 0 and 5, can be used to rank individuals relative to one another. This is done on a job-year basis. That is, for each year and job, the average score on the performance evaluation is computed. Then a variable that measures the difference between an individual's performance level and the mean for his or her job can be computed.

Before analyzing relative performance, it is important to define the group of which the individuals is part for the purposes of comparison. The tournament model predicts that those with high relative performance in their job are the ones most likely to be promoted. The job is relevant because all individuals competing at the same round of the tournament, should, ex ante, have the same estimated ability. At the empirical level, the job-year has been used as the group. All individuals in the same job title in a given year are assumed to be in the comparison group for the

Recent Developments in Labor Economics III

Table 7
Logit Estimates
Dependent Variable = Promotion Dummy

	Coefficient	SE	z
Performance score	.0312077	.0219066	1.4
Difference in performance	.3825541	.0267416	14.3
Constant	−1.989317	.0767519	−25.9
N		142,038	
log likelihood		−55,629.363	

purposes of this analysis. Deviations from the mean of that group in a given year define relative performance.

The results of the estimation are reported in table 7, where the probability of promotion is posited to depend on absolute and relative performance scores.

As is clear from table 7, "difference in performance," defined as the difference between the absolute level on the performance rating and the job-year mean, is more important than the absolute level of performance in determining promotion probability. (The standard deviation of the level of performance is .61, whereas that of the difference is .50. The means are 3.48 and zero, respectively.) Two individuals, A and B, who each receive, say, 4s on their evaluations are only equally likely to be promoted if the mean for their comparison groups are the same. If individual A is in a job where the average score is 3 and B is in a job where the average score is 2, then B is more likely to be promoted than A. These findings are supportive of the tournament view of promotion and could only be obtained by using firm-based data, which allow the relative comparisons to be made.[27]

B. The Dynamics of Intrafirm Status

Are relative positions in the firm stable over time? Is the person who is situated at the firm's 95th percentile of income in 1986 also likely to be at the same position in 1994, or do relative positions shift around? Is there a "once a star, always a star—once a loser, always a loser" effect, or is there a great deal of intrafirm mobility? Simple human capital theory suggests that there must be some upward mobility in relative positions as individuals start at the bottom, acquire skills, and move up in the income distribution. What is the typical pattern?

---

[27] The same qualitative results are obtained for wage growth instead of promotion as the dependent variable. Furthermore, using rank on the performance evaluation, rather than the deviation from the mean, has the same type of effect on determining promotion in a linear probability model with job-specific fixed effects.

Table 8
Transition Matrix

QUINT90	QUINT94					Total
	15,775.76	20,884.08	27,033.33	39,549.12	415,000	
10,839.38	899	457	232	143	64	1,795
	10.02	5.09	2.59	1.59	.71	20.00
15,393.04	558	802	297	109	28	1,794
	6.22	8.94	3.31	1.21	.31	19.99
20,029.28	191	466	861	231	47	1,796
	2.13	5.19	5.59	2.57	.52	20.01
29,725.08	101	57	364	1,073	199	1,794
	1.13	.64	4.06	11.96	2.22	19.99
275,001	46	27	26	239	1,457	1,795
	.51	.30	.29	2.66	16.24	20.00
Total	1,795	1,809	1,780	1,795	1,795	8,974
	20.00	20.16	19.84	20.00	20.00	100.00

The transition matrix shown in table 8 enables us to answer these questions. Columns reflect quintiles in earnings in 1994. Rows reflect quintiles in earnings in 1990. Thus, the entry of 457 with 5.09 under it in row 1, column 2, is interpreted as 457 individuals, or 5.09% of the total sample consisted of individuals who were in the lowest quintile in earnings of 1990 and in the second lowest quintile of earnings in 1994.

It is obvious that the lowest level individuals tend to move up in the firm. This is simple arithmetic. They cannot move down, so they either all remain in the same quintile or some move up. In fact, conditional on remaining with the firm for the period, half of the individuals who were in the lowest quintile in 1990 have moved up by 1994.

Within-firm mobility can be measured in another way. The cells above the diagonal all reflect upward mobility. Those on the diagonal reflect no movement out of the quintile. Those below the diagonal reflect downward mobility. It is useful, therefore, to look at the proportion in each category.

The results are that 57% stayed in the same quintile but 43% moved out of their quintile during the 4-year period. Twenty percent of the initial sample moved up at least one quintile, and 23% moved down at least one quintile. There is a great deal of upward and downward mobility in this firm. This is not surprising, given the rapid growth during the period. But the same pattern is observed when the transition matrix for 1986–90 is examined. In this earlier period, not shown on the table, 61.6% remained in the same quintile; 17% moved up, and 21.4% moved down.

The fact that more move down than up suggests that new hires come in at higher wages or levels than incumbents and their position erodes over time. This is examined in another way below.[28]

---

[28] See Section IIE below, "What Have You Done for Me Lately?"

Perhaps a more important point is that the chances for moving up and down in this firm are substantial. Since most personnel economics models postulate the necessity for internal reward or punishment, it is encouraging to see that mobility is common. Were all workers locked into a particular position, most of the theories that discuss schemes for addressing moral hazard would be suspect.

C. Turnover—Who Stays and Who Goes?

Although there is a large literature on worker mobility, it is based on individual-based data sets that do not permit an examination of the worker's situation in his current firm. Do firms keep their best workers, or do they lose them to the competition? Firm-based data allow us to determine how workers do in relation to their peers and broaden the set of theoretical propositions that can be tested.

Again, using the financial services data, it is possible to look at turnover probabilities and their determinants. This is done in two ways. First, each person-year is treated as a distinct observation, and a logit is run that has as its dependent variable a dummy (SEPAR) that is equal to one in the year during which the individual left the firm. Second, a proportionate hazard model for censored data is estimated. The results are contained in table 9.

In panel A, observe that the higher is total compensation, the lower is the likelihood of a separation. This could reflect one of two factors. One possibility is that within grade, those who are better performers are likely to be better rewarded, which results in fewer quits. Alternatively, it could be that those who are better compensated are at higher levels in the firms hierarchy and that higher level jobs exhibit more stable employment. The second explanation is contradicted by the positive coefficient on "comparable salary." This variable is the salary on jobs comparable to the one held and is an indicator of level in the hierarchy but is a measure different from the individual's own salary. At this firm, it is the higher-level workers, not the lower-level ones, who separate most often. Within grade, however, the more highly paid and presumably better-suited workers are the ones who remain on the job.

There seems to be a "play me or trade me" mentality in this firm. Workers who have experienced a recent promotion are less likely to separate than those who have not been promoted. This may seem to be an obvious finding, but it is not. Promotion also signals to the outside that a worker is valuable (see Waldman 1984) as well. If all human capital were general, one would expect no relation between promotion and separation because the worker's value inside and outside would be identical. The current firm should be willing to match outside offers. However, as long as some human capital is firm-specific, then a promotion may signal that the worker is better suited to the current firm than to other firms.

Table 9
Separation Results

A. Logit Estimates: Dependent Variable is SEPAR

SEPAR	Coefficient	SE	z
Year	−.1601774	.0044923	−35.656
Date hired	−.0137769	.0020442	−6.740
Total compensation	−.00018	1.67E−06	−107.887
Comparable salary	.0001243	1.71E−06	72.485
Age	−.0021733	.0011614	−1.871
Promoted	−.6322732	.0350984	−18.014
Performance	−.4020703	.0190723	−21.081
_CONS	15.14701	.3854178	39.300
N		134,632	
log likelihood		−31,588	

B. Hazard Ratio Estimation for Job Length*

	Coefficient	SE	z
Date hired	−1.99E−06	4.94E−07	−4.036
Age	−.0272142	.0035962	−7.567
Average compensation	−.0000142	2.99E−06	−4.758
Comparable salary	.00002	3.79E−06	5.274
Average performance	.0941915	.0552432	1.705
N		26,072	
log likelihood		−13,964.678	

* This was estimated correcting for censored data since only some individuals have completed their employment.

Under these circumstances, promotion would be negatively associated with turnover.[29]

The coefficient on performance is similar. It, too, suggests that better performers are less likely to separate. Better performance may reflect general skills, which would have no implications for turnover, or specific skills, which would reduce turnover. The fact that separation is negatively associated with performance suggest that at least some of what is measured by the internal performance evaluation is firm-specific.

There is an additional complication in interpretation. The logit holds wages constant. For these explanations to hold, it is necessary that performance and promotion measure rents to at least one side. Thus, at a given wage, those with higher levels of performance must have lower alternatives and/or must be worth more to the firm. Either would result in lower turnover, holding wage constant.

Panel B of table 9 estimates a proportional hazard model. The variables

[29] This is the mechanism that is discussed in Jovanovic (1979) and more directly applicable to the context here, in Lazear (1986a).

Table 10
Promotions and Performance Evaluation Scores

	Not Promoted during the Year	Promoted during the Year
PDIFF (change in the performance score)	.052	.003
	(.003)	(.006)

NOTE.—Standard errors are in parentheses.

mimic those in the panel A except that they reflect the averages over the period during which the individual is employed by the firm.[30] All coefficients, except the one on age, have the same sign as those in the annual separation logit. The coefficient on age is positive, but not significantly different from zero, in the hazard model.

One somewhat surprising result is that the date of hire is negatively related to separation probability. Those who are hired most recently are less likely to leave in this firm. Of course, this is after age, wage, and other performance factors are held constant so the interpretation is different from that in the usual separation models. Additionally, this firm experienced major growth throughout the period, and those workers hired in the past may not have been well suited to the new environment.

D. Promotions and Performance

Are those who are promoted likely to perform less well in their new job than they did in their previous job? There are two reasons to expect this to be so. First, there may be learning that takes place on the job. Individuals who were recently promoted are necessarily new to the job and are likely to be acquiring new skills. Those who were not recently promoted do not have as steep a learning curve. Second, a recently promoted individual has moved into a higher-ability pool, and the comparison with his peers is likely to be less favorable than that with his prior jobmates. An extreme version of this is the Peter Principle,[31] which states that workers are promoted to their level of incompetence. That is, workers stop being promoted only after they are found to be lacking in their new job.

Table 10 provides some evidence on these issues. Here, the observation is a person-year. All person-year observations are divided into two categories: those in which promotions occurred and those in which they did not. For each person-year, a performance evaluation score is reported. Those workers who remained with the firm for the next 2 years also have

---

[30] Promotion is deleted because including number of promotions over the period is a proxy for job length since there can be no more than one promotion per year.
[31] See Peter (1968).

Table 11
Halo Effects
Dependent Variable = Change in log of Total Annual Pay over 1-Year Period

DLNPAY	Coefficient	SE	t
Tenure	.0007322	.0002941	2.4
Age	−.0015321	.0002077	−7.3
Performance	.0708476	.0037186	19.0
Last year's performance	.0074964	.0042266	1.7
Performance 2 years ago	−.001714	.0037154	−.4
Constant	−.2455407	.0146196	−16.7
Simple correlations:			
Performance with lagged performance			
($N = 100{,}310$)		.63	
Change in log wage with lagged			
change ($N = 84{,}369$)		.70	
N		69,296	
R^2		.0109	

performance evaluation scores in each of those 2 years. Thus, PDIFF is the difference in the performance score that was received by a given individual 2 years after the date of the observation and the performance score for that same individual during the year of the observation.

The main finding is that performance evaluation scores tend to rise for workers who are not promoted. They get better in their current jobs or, at least are perceived to improve over time. This is consistent with acquiring job-specific human capital. Those who are promoted do not experience the same performance evaluation growth over the 2-year period. Relative to the average employee, their performance falls with time. To the extent that performance evaluations measure objective productivity, those who are promoted are less likely to be as productive in their new jobs. This finding is consistent with the view that the firm sorts workers by ability and promotes those with higher levels of ability to higher level jobs. Because job evaluations have a relative component, the tougher the competition, the less improvement in an individual's performance score as he acquires additional experience.

E. What Have You Done For Me Lately?

It is possible to ask whether there are halo effects within the firm. Are employees who are identified as good performers during prior years more likely to be treated well, given their performance this year? Table 11 reports the results of a regression where the change in the log of annual pay is the dependent variable. The right-hand variables include age, tenure, and performance measures for this year, last year, and 2 years ago. The results suggest that there are no halo effects. Neither last year's

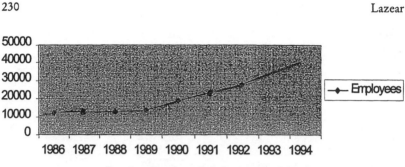

Fig. 9.—Number of employees over time

nor the previous year's performance, as measured by the evaluation, affects wage growth this year. But there is a very strong effect of this year's performance on wage growth. Apparently, this firm continually asks, "What have you done for me lately?"[32]

F. The Effect of the Business Environment on Worker Welfare

What is the effect of macroeconomic variables on worker welfare, as reflected by wage growth and or promotion? Specifically, how does firm growth affect wages and promotions? The firm in question experienced two different growth paths during the sample period. These are shown in figure 9. The period from 1986 through 1989 was one of slow growth, whereas the period from 1990 through 1994 was one of rapid growth. It is possible to examine how employees did in the two different time periods.

The evidence in table 12 makes it quite clear that firm growth, wage growth, and promotion all move together in this firm. Wages grew about 50% faster during the high-growth period (after 1989) than during the

Table 12
Wage Growth and Promotion in Low- and High-Growth Environments

Period	Average Growth Rate in Number of Workers	Average Growth Rate in Wages	Promotion Rate
Low growth, 1986–89	.039	.083	.114
		(.0007)	(.0014)
High growth, 1990–94	.223	.123	.135
		(.0007)	(.0009)

NOTE.—Standard errors are in parentheses. Partial year observations were dropped from the wage growth calculations.

---

[32] It is also possible that the current evaluation score is "rigged" to justify the wage increase that a supervisor wants to give his subordinate.

Presidential Address   231

Table 13
Regression of log of Total Pay on Year, Job Effects Removed

lnpay	Coefficient	SE	t
Year	−.0811626	.0029928	−27.119
Constant	16.26978	.2712165	59.988
N		63,430	
R^2		.4765	
Root mean square error		.95392	

NOTE.—Absorbs (job) $F_{(8248,55180)}$ = 5.744 (8,249 categories).

low growth period (1986–89). Additionally, promotions were almost
20% more likely during the high-growth period than during the low-
growth period. New hiring and/or acquisition of other firms is clearly
good for the workers at this particular firm.

The relation of worker welfare to firm growth is not well understood. Again, it belongs in the realm of personnel economics to a large
extent because of the required unit of analysis. Firm-based data are
almost essential. This is not the kind of question that can be answered
using standard national panel data (like the National Longitude Study
or the Panel Study of Income Dynamics) because those data sets do not
contain the relevant information about the firm in which the individual works.

G. Within-Firm Cohort Effects

Market conditions seem to affect the wage at which an individual is
hired into a job. It is commonly alleged that brand new assistant professors earn more than the second-year group, who arrived a year earlier.
Are cohort effects a reflection of different firms doing the hiring in different years, or does a given firm pay attention to a worker's entering cohort?

Why should one even care about the firm-specific cohort effect? If
wages are market driven, then the national data sets that use the individual
as the unit of analysis incorporate all market effects. Although firms may
not be able to affect the wage function, the can choose where on the
pay-quality spectrum to locate. This, by itself, may be interesting to
researchers.

The financial services data allow us to examine within-firm cohort
effects, at least at this one firm. In table 13, a regression that removes the
average job effect is reported. The year effects are large and significant
and amount to more than the average rate of inflation. A worker who is
hired 1 year later earns about 8% more than a worker hired into the same
job during the previous year. This is another manifestation of the effects
of firm growth on worker wages since the latter period was also one
during which the firm was growing.

H. Many Questions, Some Answers

A number of somewhat unconventional questions were addressed in this section. These questions can be answered only with the use of firm-based data. It is the increased availability of this kind of data that makes answering these question feasible today. In this analysis, only one firm's data were used, so the results are hardly conclusive. Still, they suggest that further research along these lines may be useful. Specifically,

1. Relative performance as measured by annual evaluations matter. It is the within-job rather than within-firm comparisons that determine promotions, consistent with tournament theory.

2. Internal mobility is substantial. Theories that require internal reward and punishment of workers are bolstered by these findings.

3. Turnover is less likely among the high-wage, high-performing workers. Also, those who have been recently promoted are more likely to stay with the firm.

4. Individuals who are recently promoted do not experience as much growth in their performance scores as those who are not promoted. This is consistent with job-specific learning and with ability differences that sort by levels in the firm's hierarchy.

5. Rapid growth in the size of the firm produced both more rapid wage growth and higher promotion rates.

6. Cohort effects are important and large, even within a given firm.

III. The Role of Personnel Economics in the University Curriculum

Although personnel economics is becoming a standard part of the business school curriculum, particularly at the graduate level, the material has not become a major part of the education programs of economics departments. This is beginning to change and will accelerate over the next few years.

There are a few reasons. First, most economics students at the undergraduate level do not go to graduate school in economics. The majority enter business. Personnel economics, with its direct focus on business issues, is at least as relevant to these students as the standard material taught in an undergraduate labor economics course.

Second, there is precedent set by other business school fields, most notably finance. Fifty years ago, finance was a field with little solid theoretical or empirical literature. As a result of breakthroughs in the theory of finance, an enormous empirical literature was generated. Subsequently, finance started being taught in business schools and used by practitioners and consultants in business. Now, finance has become a part of the subject matter taught by economics departments, especially among the best departments in the country.

We may expect similar developments for personnel economics. Thirty years ago, personnel economics did not exist. The literature in personnel was descriptive, loose, and ad hoc. But personnel economics is now an intellectually respectable field. It is rigorous, analytic, and rich in empirical predictions that are starting to be tested. It was the lack of substance, not the lack of interest that kept the subject out of the economics curriculum in the past. That reason no longer exists.

Third, many more people are working in this area than was the case even 10 years ago. These researchers are well equipped to bring personnel economics into the classroom and have an interest in doing so. At the time of this writing, I am the only economist to have written a book or textbook in the field,[33] but despite my willingness to monopolize the market, others are sure to follow.

Fourth, personnel economics is not just a fad. The field has been around now for at least 20 years. The growing availability of firm-based data and other data that are appropriate for testing the theories will only strengthen the interest and activity in personnel economics. It is a field that is here to stay.

IV. Conclusion

I began by arguing that personnel economics is real. There are a large number of theories that relate to the use of labor economics in business that now form the crux of personnel economics. The theories are not just ideas; when evidence can be brought to bear on them, the evidence supports the theories.

Furthermore, the theories and new data sets lead to additional issues and researchable questions. Some of those have been discussed here, and some preliminary evidence has been presented. The evidence illustrates that it is possible with data now available to answer questions that could not be addressed in the past.

Finally, because of the relevance and newly found rigor of personnel analysis, personnel economics should and will become a more important part of the educational curriculum. The field is growing and is one that has a large potential audience, of both students and practitioners.

---

[33] Lazear (1995) is a short book that describes the field at a mildly technical level. Lazear (1998) is a genuine textbook intended to bring the material to the MBA and undergraduate classroom.

Appendix

Table A1
Summary Statistics on the Variables in Table 2

Variable	N	Mean	SD	Minimum	Maximum
DLNPAY	123,233	.124132	.7226912	−7.592198	7.047651
DPAY	33,659	.3180266	1.246648	−7.683821	8.80177
PROMO	131,110	.2006102	.4004584	0	1
PROMOLAG	86,590	.2157524	.4113457	0	1
PROMOLE	131,110	.2006102	.4004584	0	1
TOTPROMO	4,966	1.288361	1.037569	0	6

References

Akerlof, George A., and Katz, Lawrence F. "Workers' Trust Funds and the Logic of Wage Profiles." *Quarterly Journal of Economics* 104 (August 1989): 525–36.

Baker, George. "Incentive Contracts and Performance Measurement." *Journal of Political Economy* 100 (June 1992): 598–614.

Baker, George; Gibbs, Michael; and Hölmstrom, Bengt. "The Internal Economics of the Firm: Evidence from Personnel Data." *Quarterly Journal of Economics* 109 (November 1994): 598–614.

Becker, Gary S. "Investment in Human Capital: A Theoretical Analysis." *Journal of Political Economy* 70 (October 1962): 9–49.

Bull, Clive; Schotter, Andrew; and Weigelt, Keith. "Tournaments and Piece Rates: An Experimental Study." *Journal of Political Economy* 95 (February 1987): 1–33.

Cheung, Steven N. S. *The Theory of Share Tenancy: With Special Application to Asian Agriculture and the First Phase of Taiwan Land Reform.* Chicago: University of Chicago Press, 1969.

Doeringer, P., and Piore, M. *Internal Labor Markets and Manpower Analysis.* Lexington, MA: D. C. Health, 1971.

Drago, Robert, and Garvey, Gerald T. "Incentives for Helping on the Job: Theory and Evidence." *Journal of Labor Economics* 16 (January 1998): 1–25.

Ehrenberg, Ronald G., and Bognanno, Michael L. "Do Tournaments Have Incentive Effects?" *Journal of Political Economy* 98 (December 1990): 1307–24.

Encinosa, William E., III; Gaynor, Martin; and Rebitzer, James B. "Sociology of Groups and the Economics of Incentives: Theory and Evidence on Compensation Systems." Working paper. Cleveland, OH: Case Western Reserve University, May 1998.

Eriksson, Tor. "Executive Compensation and Tournament Theory: Empirical Tests on Danish Data." In this issue.

Fernie, Sue, and Metcalf, David. "It's Not What You Pay, It's the Way That You Pay It and That's What Gets Results." Jockeys' Pay and

Performance. Centre for Economic Performance Discussion Paper no. 295. London: London School of Economics, 1997.

Hölmstrom, Bengt. "Moral Hazard and Observability." *Bell Journal of Economics* 10 (Spring 1979): 74–91.

Hutchens, Robert M. "A Test of Lazear's Theory of Delayed Payment Contracts." *Journal of Labor Economics* 5 (October 1987): S153–S170.

———. "Seniority, Wages and Productivity: A Turbulent Decade." *Journal of Economic Perspecitives* 3 (Fall 1989): 49–64.

Johnson, D. Gale. "Resource Allocation under Share Contracts." *Journal of Political Economy* 58 (1950): 111–23.

Journal of Labor Economics. "Supplement: The New Economics of Personnel," edited by Arthur Blakemore. Vol. 5, no. 4, pt. 2 (October 1987).

Jovanovic, Boyan. "Firm-Specific Capital and Turnover." *Journal of Political Economy* 87 (December 1979): 1246–60.

Kandel, Eugene, and Lazear, Edward P. "Peer Pressure and Partnerships." *Journal of Political Economy* 100, no. 4 (August 1992): 801–17.

Knoeber, Charles R. "A Real Game of Chicken: Contracts, Tournaments, and the Production of Broilers." *Journal of Law, Economics and Organization* 5 (Fall 1989): 271–92.

Knoeber, Charles R., and Thurman, Walter N. "Testing the Theory of Tournaments: An Empirical Analysis of Broiler Production." *Journal of Labor Economics* 12 (April 1994): 155–79.

Lazear, Edward P. "Why Is There Mandatory Retirement?" *Journal of Political Economy* 87 (December 1979): 1261–84.

———. "Agency, Earnings Profiles, Productivity, and Hours Restrictions." *American Economic Review* 71 (September 1981): 606–20.

———. "Raids and Offer-Matching." In *Research in Labor Economics,* edited by Ronald Ehrenberg, 8, pt. A: 141–65. Greenwich, CT: JAI Press, 1986. (*a*)

———. "Salaries and Piece Rates." *Journal of Business* 59 (July 1986): 405–31. (*b*)

———. "Pay Equality and Industrial Politics." *Journal of Political Economy* 97 (June 1989): 561–80.

———. "The Job as a Concept." In *Performance Measurement and Incentive Compensation,* ed. William J. Bruns, Jr. Cambridge, MA: Harvard Business School Press, 1992.

———. *Personnel Economics.* Cambridge, MA: MIT Press, 1995.

———. "Performance Pay and Productivity." Working Paper no. 5672. Cambridge, MA: National Bureau of Economic Research, August 1996.

———. *Personnel Economics for Managers.* New York: Wiley, 1998.

Lazear, Edward P., and Rosen, Sherwin. "Rank-Order Tournaments as Optimum Labor Contracts." *Journal of Political Economy* 89 (October 1981): 841–64.

McCue, Kristin. "Promotions and Wage Growth." *Journal of Labor Economics* 14 (April 1996): 175–209.

Medoff, James, and Abraham, Katharine. "Experience, Performance, and

Earnings." *Quarterly Journal of Economics* 95 (December 1980): 703–36.

Mincer, Jacob. "On-the-Job Training: Costs, Returns, and Some Implications." *Journal of Political Economy* 70 (October 1962): S50–S79.

Paarsch, Harry J., and Shearer, Bruce S. "Fixed Wages, Piece Rates, and Intertemporal Productivity: A Study of Tree Planters in British Columbia." Unpublished manuscript. Iowa City: University of Iowa, 1996.

Peter, Lawrence. *The Peter Principle.* New York: Morrow, 1968.

Prendergast, Canice. "The Provision of Incentives in Firms." *Journal of Economic Literature* (in press).

Reder, Melvin W. "Theory of Occupational Wage Differentials." *American Economic Review* 45 (December 1955): 833–52.

Rosen, Sherwin. "Prizes and Incentives in Elimination Tournaments." *American Economic Review* 76 (September 1986): 701–15.

Ross, Stephen A. "The Economic Theory of Agency: The Principal's Problem." *American Economic Review* 63 (May 1973): 134–39.

Salop, Joanne, and Salop, Steven. "Self-Selection and Turnover in the Labor Market." *Quarterly Journal of Economics* 90 (November 1976): 619–27.

Shapiro, Carl, and Stiglitz, Joseph E. "Equilibrium Unemployment as a Worker Discipline Device." *American Economic Review* 74 (1984): 433–44.

Slichter, Sumner. *Modern Economic Society* New York: Henry Holt, 1928.

Spitz, Janet. "Productivity and Wage Relations in Economic Theory and Labor Markets." Ph.D. dissertation, Stanford University Graduate School of Business, 1991.

Stiglitz, Joseph E. "Incentives, Risk, and Information: Notes toward a Theory of Hierarchy." *Bell Journal of Economics and Management Science* 6 (August 1975): 552–79.

Waldman, Michael. "Job Assignments, Signalling, and Efficiency." *Rand Journal of Economics* 15 (Summer 1984): 255–67.

[23]

HOW TO COMPETE: THE IMPACT OF WORKPLACE PRACTICES AND INFORMATION TECHNOLOGY ON PRODUCTIVITY

Sandra E. Black and Lisa M. Lynch*

Abstract—Using data from a unique nationally representative sample of businesses, we examine the impact of workplace practices, information technology, and human capital investments on productivity. We estimate an augmented Cobb-Douglas production function with both cross section and panel data covering the period of 1987–1993, using both within and GMM estimators. We find that it is not whether an employer adopts a particular work practice but rather how that work practice is actually implemented within the establishment that is associated with higher productivity. Unionized establishments that have adopted human resource practices that promote joint decision making coupled with incentive-based compensation have higher productivity than other similar nonunion plants, whereas unionized businesses that maintain more traditional labor management relations have lower productivity. Finally, plant productivity is higher in businesses with more-educated workers or greater computer usage by nonmanagerial employees.

I. Introduction

HOW do managerial decisions such as whether or not to adopt a Total Quality Management (TQM) system or expand an employee involvement program affect labor productivity? Does the implementation of "high-performance" workplace practices ensure better firm performance? Does the presence of a union hinder or enhance the probability of success associated with implementing these practices? Do computers really help workers be more productive? These questions and others have been raised in recent years as many firms have reorganized or reengineered their work sites from the old Fordist model of work organization to new high-performance work systems that decentralize decision making within a firm. Using data from a unique nationally representative sample of businesses (the Educational Quality of the Workforce National Employers Survey (EQW-NES)), we begin to examine these and other important questions about the determinants of productivity.

Although there have been many studies on the impact of capital investments and R&D on firm or establishment productivity, until recently there has been very little direct

Received for publication November 5, 1997. Revision accepted for publication August 2, 2000.

* Federal Reserve Bank of New York, and Tufts University and NBER, respectively.

Part of the work reported herein was supported under the Education Research and Development Center program, agreement number R117Q00011-91, CFDA 84.117Q, as administered by the Office of Educational Research and Improvement, U.S. Department of Education. This funding was administered through the National Center on the Educational Quality of the Workforce (EQW), University of Pennsylvania. The authors have benefitted from comments by Martin Bailey, Richard Freeman, Dale Jorgenson, John Halitwanger, and participants in seminars at the NBER, Census Bureau, London School of Economics, Institute for Fiscal Studies, MIT, and the Universities of Bristol, Essex, Mannheim, Maryland, Oxford, and Warwick. We would especially like to thank Fabio Schiantarelli for his extensive comments on this paper and Steve Bond, Joyce Cooper, Wayne Gray, Arnie Reznek, and Steve Rudolph who provided much assistance on the data used in this project. The findings and opinions expressed in this report do not necessarily reflect the position or policies of OERI, the U.S. Department of Education, the Bureau of the Census, Federal Reserve Bank of New York, or the Federal Reserve System.

analysis of the impact of workplace practices on productivity. Some of these studies have been hindered by problems such as low survey response rates, firm-level rather than establishment-level productivity data, limited workplace practice data, and subjective measures of productivity. Moreover, although there is ample micro-based evidence on the impact of human capital accumulation on individuals' wages, much less is known about the direct effect of human capital on the productivity of businesses. Finally, although there has been some research using firm data on the impact of computers on productivity, these studies have not been able to simultaneously control for workplace practices and human capital investments.

Our work builds upon this research by using a large, nationally representative sample of manufacturing businesses. Because of the survey design, we have detailed information on workplace practices (beyond just their incidence), human capital investments, and a measure of the diffusion of computer usage, that can be matched with standard cross-sectional and longitudinal measures of inputs and outputs of the production process. More specifically, the EQW-NES provides information on workplace practices such as TQM systems, benchmarking, the diffusion of computer usage among nonmanagerial employees, recruitment strategies, the use of profit sharing, and the extent of employee participation in decision making. We also have information on the average educational level of the establishment and the numbers of employees trained, along with other characteristics of the business such as whether or not it is unionized, employee turnover, the age of the capital stock, and the demographic composition of the workforce. Finally, one unique design feature of the EQW-NES is that we are able to match it with the Bureau of the Census' Longitudinal Research Database (LRD) so that we can utilize the panel data dimension of the LRD.

We first estimate a standard Cobb-Douglas production function with cross-sectional data that is augmented by our measures of workplace practices, information technology, and human capital investments. We then estimate a standard production function on the LRD panel covering the period from 1987 to 1993 using both within and generalized method of moments (GMM) estimators to address omitted variable and endogeneity bias. The average establishment residual over this period is then used as a measure of the establishment fixed effect and is regressed on our measures of workplace practices, human capital investments, diffusion of computer usage, and other employee and employer characteristics to determine their association with productivity. In this way, we try to see how the information on workplace practices we obtained in our survey is related to

The Review of Economics and Statistics, August 2001, 83(3): 434–445

which businesses did better or worse on average over the period 1988–1993.

We find that workplace practices do matter, no matter how the production function is estimated. However, it is not so much whether or not an employer adopts a particular work practice but rather how that work practice is actually implemented within the establishment that is associated with higher productivity. For example, simply adopting a TQM system has an insignificant or even negative impact on productivity, whereas increasing the proportion of workers meeting regularly to discuss workplace issues or extending profit sharing to production workers has a significant and positive impact on productivity.

We also see important differences across plants on the basis of the type of labor-management relations within the plant. Unionized plants that have adopted new workplace practices such as incentive-based compensation or greater employee participation in decision making have substantially higher productivity than similar nonunion plants or establishments with more traditional labor-management relations. In addition, those plants with more-educated workers also have significantly higher productivity, everything else constant. Finally, the greater the proportion of nonmanagerial workers who use computers, the higher is plant productivity.

II. Background Discussion

Our paper is not the first to examine the impact of workplace practices on the productivity of businesses, but much of the previous work on this topic has been limited in several ways. Some of the most detailed research on the adoption and nature of new workplace practices has been done on a case study basis. This includes work by Krafcik (1988), Womack, Jones, and Roos (1991), Ichniowski (1992), Berg et al. (1996), and Batt (1995). These studies have provided us with a wealth of information on the chain of events that resulted in the adaptation of new workplace practices, but it is difficult to generalize these results to a broader spectrum of the economy.

One solution to this problem is to conduct a detailed intra-industry study of the adoption of workplace practices to see their impact on a range of industry-specific performance measures. Examples of intra-industry studies include work by Ichniowski, Shaw, and Prennushi (1997), Arthur (1994), Kelley (1994, 1996), Bailey (1993), and Dunlop and Weil (1996). By examining human resource practices associated with one specific production process, it is possible to greatly reduce problems of the underlying heterogeneity of production processes. Most of the intra-industry studies conclude that the adoption of a coherent system of new human resource management practices such as flexible job definitions, cross-training, and work teams, along with extensive reliance on incentive pay, results in substantially higher levels of productivity than more traditional human resource management practices. Although these results represent an important contribution to the literature on workplace practices and productivity, again it is not easy to generalize these findings for a broader segment of the economy.

Another research strategy is to examine a more representative cross-sectional sample of firms to see the impact of workplace practices on broader measures of performance such as productivity or profitability. Examples of this strategy include Bartel (1989), Ichniowski (1990), Huselid (1995), Huselid and Becker (1996), and Delaney and Huselid (1996). These studies have found that there is a correlation between human resource management systems and business performance as measured by labor productivity, Tobin's q, or present value gain in cash flow and firm market value. Unfortunately, much of this work has been limited by low survey response rate, high levels of aggregation of human resource management practices and performance measures, and the use of an index of human resource practices. Examining human resource management practices at the firm or business line level may miss the degree of heterogeneity in practices within multiple establishment firms. Therefore, we believe that the preferable level of analysis for the issues we wish to examine is the establishment level. In addition, using an index of workplace practices can lead to ambiguities in the interpretation of the results. Although it probably makes sense to combine subjective responses that are centered on a particular theme into an index, it is not clear why it is necessary to group these responses when there are more detailed data available on factors such as the proportion of workers involved in decision making.

Nevertheless, there is a burgeoning theoretical and empirical debate on the existence of synergies in bundles of human resource management practices. The theoretical work of Milgrom and Roberts (1995) and Kandel and Lazear (1992), along with the empirical studies mentioned above, are important contributions in this area. Milgrom and Roberts argue that the impact of a system of human resource practices will be greater than the sum of its parts because of the synergistic effects of bundling practices together. Kandel and Lazear argue that introducing a profit-sharing plan for all workers in a firm may have little or no impact on productivity unless it is linked with other practices that address the inherent free rider problem associated with corporate-wide profit sharing plans. The empirical evidence on synergies is mixed, with Huselid and Ichniowski arguing that bundles matter more than individual practices and Delaney and Huselid finding no evidence of bundles. Empirically, we have opted to interact a wide range of practices with each other to see if there are interaction effects beyond the own effect of specific HR practices. We believe that this is a less restrictive strategy than arbitrarily grouping our businesses into three or four types of HR practice bundles or using factor analysis to generate an index of HR practices. As Osterman (1994) has shown, in spite of widespread diffusion in the 1980s of new workplace practices, U.S. companies use a range of combinations of workplace practices and as a result are not neatly classified into discrete types.

As part of our analysis of the role of synergies in human resource management practices, we also look at the impact of unions on productivity and how the results are affected by the interaction between the presence of unions and other workplace practices. Theoretically, the presence of unions can have a positive impact on labor productivity, because they lower the costs of introducing new workplace practices; workers are more willing to participate in employee involvement programs because they feel the union will protect their employment security. As discussed by Malcomson (1983), agreements made between managers and workers may not be legally enforceable, so the presence of unions can address incentive compatibility problems that may arise at the workplace. In addition, negotiations that management undertakes with workers about the introduction of new workplace practices are less expensive if the company has to deal only with union specialists rather than each individual worker.

On the other hand, unions can lower productivity if they constrain the choice set of management and pursue restrictive practices such as over manning rules. Empirically, the evidence on the impact of unions on productivity is mixed. The range of estimates on the impact of unions on labor productivity runs from minus 3% in Clark (1984), to plus 22% in Brown and Medoff (1978), to no effect in Freeman and Medoff (1984). We try to reconcile these disparate findings by interacting the union status of an establishment with other workplace practices. In this way, we try to distinguish between different types of labor-management relations—traditional and new—and their impact on labor productivity.[1]

We are also able to look at the effect of education on productivity. To date, most of the micro work on education's impact on individual firm productivity has been indirect or focused on industry-level trends.[2] Researchers have examined the impact of education on wages and from this inferred the impact of education on productivity. Empirical analysis on the returns to schooling suggests that an additional year of post high-school education can raise wages of a worker from 5% to 12%. Therefore, researchers have assumed that productivity increases for a more highly educated workforce are of similar magnitude. Again, one of the features of the EQW-NES is that we are able to construct a

measure of the average educational level of an establishment and directly examine its effect on productivity.

Finally, we also examine the relationship between computer use and productivity. The impact of computers on productivity and wages has been analyzed by several researchers, but it nevertheless remains a controversial issue. Research in the 1980s (such as Bailey and Gordon (1988)) found little impact of computers on trends in aggregate productivity growth, although more recent work by Oliner and Sichel (1994) argues that this is to be expected given that they represent such a small percentage of the capital stock. Researchers who have used more micro-based data (such as Brynjolfsson and Hitt (1993)) have found a positive relationship between computers and productivity. In addition, Alan Krueger (1993) found that workers who worked with computers were paid approximately 15% more than similar workers who did not work with computers. However, none of these papers have the detailed information that we have in the EQW-NES to control for a wider range of factors when examining the impact of computer usage on productivity.

In sum, this paper seeks to address many of the limitations in previous work on the impact of workplace practices, human capital, and information technology on productivity. We examine a more objective measure of labor productivity using a data set that is more representative, has a higher response rate than most previous studies on the manufacturing sector, and contains very detailed information on specific employer practices. We allow for a less restrictive bundling of human resource management practices, match plant-level practices with plant-level outcomes, and use both cross-sectional and longitudinal data to estimate production functions.

III. The Data

To understand the nature and importance of our contribution, it is useful to start with a description of the data set on which we base our empirical analysis. The EQW National Employers Survey was administered by the U.S. Bureau of the Census as a telephone survey in August and September of 1994 to a nationally representative sample of more than 3,000 private establishments with more than twenty employees. The survey represents a unique source of information on how employers recruit workers, organize work, invest in physical capital, and utilize education and training investments. The survey oversampled establishments in the manufacturing sector and establishments with more than 100 employees. Public sector employees, not-for-profit institutions, and corporate headquarters were excluded from the sample. The target respondent in the manufacturing sector was the plant manager and in the nonmanufacturing sector was the local business site manager. However, the survey was designed to allow for multiple respondents so that information could be obtained from establishments that kept financial information such as the

---

[1] The only other paper that has tried to do something similar to this is by Cooke (1994), where he examines the interaction of union status, profit sharing, and employee involvement on productivity in a sample of manufacturing establishments in Michigan in 1989.

[2] See Jorgenson and Griliches (1967) and Jorgenson, Gallop, and Fraumeni (1987) for a discussion of education, labor quality, and productivity using industry-level data, and the Bureau of Labor Statistics, U.S. Department of Labor (1993) for a discussion of how educational attainment and workforce composition explain patterns of productivity growth from 1948 to 1990.

book value of capital or the cost of goods and materials used in production at a separate finance office (typically at corporate headquarters for multi-establishment enterprises). Computer-assisted telephone interviewing (CATI) was used to administer each survey, which took approximately 28 minutes to complete.[3]

The sampling frame for the survey was the Bureau of the Census SSEL file, one of the most comprehensive and up-to-date listings of establishments in the United States. Although the survey included establishments in both the manufacturing and nonmanufacturing sectors, this paper examines responses from manufacturing respondents only. This is because we link this survey with the Census Longitudinal Research Database (LRD) that includes longitudinal information for manufacturing establishments only. In other work (Lynch and Black (1998) and Black and Lynch (1996)), we analyze the cross-sectional data from the EQW-NES for both manufacturing and nonmanufacturing establishments.

The response rate for manufacturing establishments in the EQW National Employers Survey was 75%, which is substantially higher than most other voluntary establishment surveys. Probit analysis (available from the authors upon request) of the characteristics of nonrespondents indicates that there was no significant pattern at the two-digit industry level in the likelihood of participating in the survey. The only businesses more likely not to participate were manufacturing establishments with more than 1,000 employees. Of the 1,831 manufacturing establishments that participated in the survey, not all respondents completed all parts of the survey by the interview cutoff date of October 1, 1994. Therefore, the final number of manufacturing establishments in the sample for which all parts of the survey was completed were 1,621 establishments. This represents a 66% overall completed survey response rate.

As mentioned above, we are able to match many of the establishments in our survey to the Longitudinal Research Database (LRD). The LRD, housed at the Center for Economic Studies at the Bureau of the Census, was created by longitudinally linking the establishment-level data from the Bureau of the Census's Annual Survey of Manufacturers (ASM). The LRD data include information on shipments, materials, inventories, employment, expenditures on equipment and structures, book values of equipment and structures, and energy use. (For more information on the LRD, see Davis and Haltiwanger (1991).) Because we are able to match the LRD with the EQW-NES, we have annual establishment-level data on inputs and outputs of production for the manufacturing employers in our survey.

Although we could, in theory, use data from the LRD from as far back as 1972, we restrict our analysis to just

those establishments in the LRD from 1987 through 1993.[4] We believe that this choice is a reasonable compromise between having a sufficiently large number of years of data to obtain an estimate of the establishment fixed effect, yet few enough to allow us to assume that some of the workplace characteristics are more or less constant over this period. Because of this balanced panel restriction, along with problems of missing data, our final estimation sample is reduced to 638 establishments. It is important to note that the LRD is basically the universe of all manufacturing establishments with more than 250 employees but is only a subsample of establishments with fewer than 250 employees. Therefore, by restricting our analysis to employers in the EQW-NES that were in the LRD from 1987 onwards, we are more likely to omit smaller establishments and establishments that were "born" after 1987. However, this does not mean that our sample does not include smaller establishments. In fact, almost 20% of our observations in this restricted sample are establishments with fewer than 100 employees. In addition, we are able to compare some of the results in this paper with those obtained using a larger sample that does not impose these restrictions (Black & Lynch, 1996).

IV. The Model

We base our empirical analysis of the determinants of establishment productivity on an augmented Cobb-Douglas production function containing real sales (Y), labor (L), capital (K), materials (M), and our workplace practices, human capital, and information technology variables. We test the restriction implied by constant returns to scale and find that for our data this restriction is always accepted. Therefor, our reported results use the following specification which imposes constant returns to scale:[5]

$$\ln(Y/L)_i = \alpha \ln(K/L)_i + \beta \ln(M/L)_i + \delta'Z_i + \epsilon_i \quad (1)$$

and

$$\ln(Y/P)_i = \alpha \ln(K/P)_i + \beta \ln(M/P)_i + \gamma \ln(N/P)_i \\ + \delta'Z_i + \epsilon_i, \quad (2)$$

and where ϵ_i is an error term and δ' is a vector of coefficients on Z_i which are establishment-specific workplace practices and characteristics of employees such as education and turnover. In equation (1) we treat all workers identically, and in equation (2) we differentiate between production workers (P) and nonproduction workers (N).

Before discussing in more detail the nature of our empirical estimation, it is necessary to describe the construction of the input variables derived from the LRD. Because we do

---

[3] For more detail on the data set and the particular questions asked, see Lynch and Black (1998).

[4] Note that if an establishment changed ownership it would still be included in the sample.
[5] A complete set of all the estimated equations is available upon request from the authors.

not have a measure of the capital stock every year in the LRD, we need to construct a measure. We use the standard perpetual inventory method to construct an estimate of the value of the capital stock in each year starting from the book value in a base year and using the information on new investment together with an estimate of the portion of the capital stock that depreciates each year.[6] We chose the total book value of the capital stock in 1987 as our starting point. We also tried using 1982 as the base year; however, we lose many observations when we do this. Nevertheless, when we do use 1982 as the base year, the major empirical findings change little.[7] In addition, we check the sensitivity of our estimates to the inclusion of end-of-period or beginning-of-period values of the capital stock. Again, our empirical results are not very sensitive to this distinction. Generally, we prefer results using the value of the beginning of period capital stock on the assumption that it takes time before new capital becomes productive.

Finally, we do not account for the value of assets sold, retired, scrapped, or destroyed, because these data are not available in the ASM after 1988. Total sales, capital, and material numbers were all adjusted using deflators from the NBER Productivity Database assembled by Eric Bartelsman and Wayne Gray (1995). These deflators were constructed from five-digit product deflators from BEA. These are largely created from the Bureau of Labor Statistics' (BLS) industry-based producer prices, which are extrapolated backwards using the old BLS product prices. (See the appendix for more information on the deflators used.)

We augment the standard Cobb-Douglas production function by also allowing productivity to depend upon workplace practices, plant-specific human capital measures, the diffusion of information technology, employee turnover rates, age of the establishment, R&D policy in the firm, age distribution of the capital stock, and other characteristics of the establishments using data from the EQW-NES. In spite of the fact that we are able to control for many more managerial practices than most previous studies on productivity, our cross section estimates may still be subject to omitted-variable bias (Griliches & Mairesse, 1995) due to unobserved establishment characteristics. Although we believe that the detailed information contained in our establishment survey allows us to extract much of the previously unobserved establishment-specific effect, one can remove any remaining biases due to omitted but time-invariant

establishment-specific effects using panel data. (See Schmidt (1985) for a discussion on using panel data to estimate firm-level efficiency.) Consider the following equation:

$$Y_{it} = \alpha' X_{it} + \delta' Z_i + v_i + \epsilon_{it}, \tag{3}$$

where Y is sales per production worker;

α' is a vector of coefficients on capital per production worker, materials per production worker, and the number of nonproduction workers per production worker;
δ' is our vector of coefficients on workplace practices from the EQW-NES survey;
v_i is an unobserved, time-invariant, establishment fixed effect; and
ϵ_{it} is the idiosyncratic component of the error term.

If we take deviations from a firm's mean or take first differences of equation (3), all firm observed and unobserved time-invariant fixed effects drop out, and we can remove the bias in estimating the coefficients in vector α' that occurs because of the omission of the establishment fixed effect. However, this means that we are unable to observe the impact of the observed but time-invariant employer fixed effects such as workplace practices and educational quality of the workforce on labor productivity. Therefore, we adopt the following two-step procedure. In the first step, we use the within estimator to obtain estimates of the coefficients (α') on capital, labor, and materials (X_{it}) from the 1988–1993 LRD panel. Year-industry specific constants are also included in the estimated equation to allow for differential technological progress by industry and to control for industry-year specific business cycle effects that lead to differential intensity of use of the factors of production.

The use of the within estimator deals with the correlation between the choice of inputs and the firm-specific, time-invariant component of the error term. However, if capital, employment, materials, and output are chosen simultaneously, or if there are measurement errors in the explanatory variables (particularly the measure of capital), the within estimator will be inconsistent. (See discussion by Griliches and Hausman (1986).) For this reason we have also estimated equation (3) using generalized method of moments (GMM), combining the equation in differences and levels. This approach involves using lagged value of both the levels and the changes over time of capital, materials, labor, and output as instruments for current values of capital, labor, and materials. These lagged values are assumed to be correlated with current values but independent of the error term. The technique is an extension of Arellano and Bond (1991) along the lines suggested by Arellano and Bover (1995) and is implemented in the revised version of

[6] In other words: $K_t = (1 - \delta_t)K_{t-1} + NI_t$ — where K_t is the real end-of-period capital stock, δ_t is the depreciation rate, and NI_t is real capital expenditures. The depreciation used is 0.1331 for machinery and 0.0343 for buildings. These numbers come from Hulten and Wykoff (1981).

[7] We also tried using the reported book value of the capital stock in each year as our measure of the capital stock. The problem with this measure is that it does not take into account depreciation or price inflation. In addition, in 1989, 1990, 1991, and 1993, the ASM did not include questions about the book value of the capital stock, only new investment. We did try various imputations of these data, but the results do not seem very sensitive to the definition of the capital stock.

the DPD program first developed by Arellano and Bond (1988).[8]

We generate predicted values of $Y_{it} - \alpha'X_{it} = \delta'Z_t + v_i + \epsilon_{it}$ using the within estimator or the GMM estimator of α'. We then average that value over the period 1988–1993 for each business to get an estimate of the firm-specific, time-invariant component of the residual.[9] In the second step, we regress our average residual on the various human resource management practices, human capital measures, a variable to capture diffusion of information technology, industry dummies, and other worker and employer characteristics we find in the EQW-NES in order to obtain estimates of δ'.

One advantage of this two-step procedure relative to the estimation of the cross section production functions (which include workplace practices and establishment characteristics) is that we can address the issue of biases in the estimates of the coefficients of capital, labor, and materials due to correlations with the firm-specific, time-invariant components of the error term, v_i. The GMM estimator can also address the issue of biases due to correlation with ϵ_{it}. These advantages complement the fact that the panel allows us to bring more information to bear in estimating capital, labor, and materials coefficients. However, biases can still arise in estimating the δ's in the second step. These biases will be discussed further below.

V. The Results

In this section, we discuss the econometric results concerning the effect of workplace practices, establishment, and worker characteristics on productivity.

A. Cross Section Estimation

Table 1 presents our cross section estimation of an augmented Cobb-Douglas production function with constant returns to scale. In equation (1), we use the total number of workers as our measure of labor, and then, in equation (2), we separate employees into production and nonproduction workers. Therefore, the dependent variable in the first regression is the log of annual sales per worker for 1993, and the dependent variable in equation (2) and (3) is the log of annual sales per production worker for 1993. Equation (3)

---

[8] If the error term is white noise, one can use levels of capital, labor, materials, and sales lagged at least twice as instruments for the equations in differences. For the equation in levels, differences of these variables lagged at least one period are legitimate instruments under the additional assumption that the correlation between the level of the variables and the firm-specific, time-invariant component of the error term is constant. (See Arellano and Bover (1995).) The orthogonality condition associated with the equations in differences and levels are estimated jointly.

[9] Note that ϵ_{it} are assumed to be zero mean disturbances so that averaging over time should eliminate (or at least very substantially reduce) its contribution to the residual. We estimate the first step using a larger sample than in the second step because we are not constrained to have information on all of the workplace practices to do this estimation. By including a larger number of observations, we hope to improve the precision of our estimates for capital, labor, and materials.

allows for interactions between various workplace practices.[10]

The estimated coefficients on capital, labor, and materials are consistent with previous estimates using the LRD through 1987, except that the coefficient on capital is rather small. This may be due in large part to measurement error, and we return to this issue in table 2. In terms of the variables we use from our survey, we find that investments in new technology are associated with significantly higher establishment productivity. Although the age of the capital stock appears to have insignificant effects on productivity, the existence of a R&D center within the firm is associated with significantly higher productivity. In addition, the more nonmanagerial workers who use computers, the higher the establishment's productivity. Interestingly, in results not reported here, the proportion of managers who use computers is never significant in any specification we tested.

In table 1, average education of nonproduction workers has a significant impact on establishment productivity. The coefficient on average educational level of nonproduction workers suggests that raising their average educational level 10% (approximately one more year of school) would increase productivity by approximately 4%. None of the training variables we included in our regressions were ever statistically significant. Unfortunately, in the EQW-NES, we do not have a measure of the accumulated stock of training for all workers, only training done at a point of time. This means that our estimates of the impact of training are most likely underestimates of the true returns to training. But, given our finding that the proportion of nonmanagerial workers using computers has a significant and positive relationship to establishment productivity, we conclude that human capital investments can have an important impact on labor productivity.

Workplace practices have very interesting effects on labor productivity. In particular, we find that simply introducing high-performance workplace practices is not enough to increase establishment productivity. As shown in equation two in table 1, the increased employee voice that is associated with these practices seems to be a necessary condition to making the practices effective. For example, although 70% of the establishments used in our analysis have some form of a TQM system in place, TQM is not itself associated with higher productivity. Instead, the percentage of workers involved in regular decision-making meetings is positively related to labor productivity. On average, approximately 53% of employees in our sample are involved in some sort of regular meeting to discuss workplace issues. Benchmarking[11] and profit sharing for production workers,

---

[10] All of our regressions include two-digit industry dummies. We also tested the sensitivity of our results by including three-digit industry dummies, and none of our major findings were changed.

[11] Benchmarking involves setting targets based on other firms' successes and attempting to meet these goals. For example, a manufacturer might use a competitor's or even another industry's scrap rate to establish standards for their own scrap rate.

TABLE 1.—DETERMINANTS OF LABOR PRODUCTIVITY: CROSS SECTION RESULTS

Variable	Mean (s.d.)	Eq. (1) Coefficient (t-statistic)	Eq. (2) Coefficient (t-statistic)	Eq. (3) Coefficient (t-statistic)
Log (capital/workers)		0.024* (1.77)	0.034** (2.32)	0.035** (2.41)
Log (materials/workers)		0.54** (29.81)	0.57** (29.04)	0.56** (28.59)
Log (Nonproduction/production)		—	0.18** (10.86)	0.18** (10.98)
Technology				
Share of equip < 1 yr.	0.069 (0.076)	0.09 (0.443)	0.06 (0.32)	0.05 (0.24)
Share of equip 1–4 yr. old	0.198 (0.191)	0.11 (1.42)	0.13 (1.58)	0.12 (1.43)
R&D center	0.77 (0.42)	0.07* (1.98)	0.08** (2.17)	0.08** (2.14)
Proportion nonmanagers using computers	0.36 (0.31)	0.13** (2.59)	0.12** (2.31)	0.11** (2.10)
Worker Characteristics				
Log (avg ed)	2.54 (0.06)	0.38 (1.45)	—	—
Log (avg ed nonproduction workers)	2.68 (0.083)	—	0.45** (2.02)	0.45** (1.97)
Log (avg ed production workers)	2.51 (0.055)	—	0.05 (0.16)	0.10 (0.30)
Turnover (proportion employees less than one year)	0.10 (0.12)	−0.29** (−2.18)	−0.18 (−1.34)	−0.21 (−1.51)
Proportion employees women	0.34 (0.20)	−0.07 (−0.84)	0.03 (0.30)	0.03 (0.30)
Proportion employees minority	0.24 (0.22)	−0.10 (−1.52)	−0.10 (−1.43)	−0.11 (−1.52)
Use of High-Performance Work Systems				
TQM	0.71 (0.45)	−0.005 (−0.15)	−0.022 (−0.66)	−0.08 (−1.32)
Benchmarking	0.49 (0.50)	0.072** (2.46)	0.07** (2.24)	0.06** (1.97)
Number of managerial levels	2.9 (2.0)	0.001 (0.20)	0.003 (0.43)	0.003 (0.30)
# employees per supervisor	24.4 (21.7)	0.0003 (0.40)	0.0004 (0.55)	0.0004 (0.62)
Proportion workers in self-managed teams	0.145 (0.264)	0.05 (0.90)	0.04 (0.72)	0.05 (0.85)
log number of employees in training	4.69 (2.45)	−0.004 (−0.66)	−0.003 (−0.47)	−0.002 (−0.31)
Employee Voice				
Unionized	0.50 (0.50)	0.04 (1.18)	0.03 (0.75)	−0.10 (−1.48)
Proportion workers meeting regularly in groups	0.528 (0.407)	0.09** (2.39)	0.08** (2.17)	0.05 (0.58)
Profit Sharing				
Managers and supervisors	0.78 (0.42)	−0.027 (−0.60)	−0.04 (−0.78)	−0.04 (−0.76)
Production/clerical/technical	0.64 (0.48)	0.064* (1.67)	0.067* (1.64)	0.013 (0.02)
Recruitment Strategies				
Grades a top priority in recruitment	0.20 (0.40)	−0.006 (−0.17)	−0.008 (−0.21)	−0.011 (−0.29)
Communication a top priority in recruitment	0.73 (0.45)	0.033 (1.03)	0.03 (0.96)	0.027 (0.80)
Interaction Terms				
union*profit sharing for nonmanagerial workers	0.29 (0.46)	—	—	0.11* (1.72)
union*TQM	0.36 (0.48)	—	—	0.08 (1.21)
% meet*profit sharing for nonmanagerial workers	0.36 (0.42)	—	—	0.014 (0.19)
% meet*TQM	0.42 (0.43)	—	—	0.04 (0.51)
N =	638	638	638	638
Adjusted R^2 =		0.78	0.82	0.82

t-statistics in parenthesis.
** denotes significant at the 5% level and * denotes significant at the 10% level.
Estimated equations also include a constant term, two-digit SIC industry controls, age of the establishment, a dummy variable if the establishment is part of a multiple-establishment firm, and a dummy variable if the primary product is exported.

both considered high-performance workplace practices, are also associated with higher establishment productivity.

Given the impact that certain workplace practices seem to have on establishment productivity, we turn to an examination of the synergistic effects of bundling certain practices. We tried a wide range of interaction effects and found that most were not even remotely significant. However, equation (3) in table 1 presents results when we interact unionization

and TQM, unionization and profit sharing for nonmanagers, the percentage meeting in groups and profit sharing for nonmanagers, and the percentage meeting in groups and TQM. When these interactions are included, the own effect of unionization becomes negative although not statistically significant, whereas the interaction of unionization and profit sharing for nonmanagers is significant and positive. This indicates that more traditional labor management relations, where employees have little voice in decision making and pay is not linked to performance, is associated with lower establishment productivity. At the same time, more cooperative unionized labor management relations (where employees have a greater role in decision making but also have part of their compensation linked to firm performance) are associated with higher labor productivity.[12]

Our regression coefficients in equation (3) of table 1 imply that a unionized plant with no benchmarking, no TQM, no profit sharing for nonmanagerial workers, and no employee involvement programs will have 10% lower productivity than an otherwise similar plant that is nonunion. A nonunion plant that uses benchmarking, TQM, has 50% of its workers meeting on a regular basis, and profit sharing for nonmanagerial workers will have 4.5% higher productivity than an otherwise similar nonunion plant that has not adopted any of these "high-performance workplace" practices. However, a unionized plant with benchmarking, TQM, 50% of its workers meeting on a regular basis, and profit sharing for nonmanagerial workers will have 13.5% higher productivity than an otherwise similar nonunion plant with none of these high-performance workplace practices.

Finally, it is interesting to note the lack of significance of the percentage of employees who are women or minorities. Other results of interest that are not reported in table 1 include the fact that newer establishments have significantly higher productivity, all else constant, than older establishments. We also tried interacting capital, materials, and labor with industry to see how robust our estimates of the effect of workplace practices on labor productivity were when a more flexible specification for the impact of capital, materials, and labor was allowed for. Our estimates on workplace practices were unchanged with the exception of TQM, which became significantly negative.

B. Panel Data Two-Step Estimation Based on Within Estimator

In this section, we discuss how the results in table 1 alter when we incorporate panel data on establishment inputs and outputs into the estimation in order to begin to address the problem of unobserved time-invariant characteristics of the establishment. Our first step is the estimation of a simple Cobb-Douglas production function with establishment fixed effects using the panel data from the LRD that includes controls for capital, labor, materials, and industry by time dummies. We run this on the full set of establishments in our survey that are matched to the LRD and contain data from 1987 through 1993 (984 establishments). We again test and accept the restriction of constant returns to scale; our dependent variable is sales per production worker. The estimates from the first-stage estimation using the within esti-

mator are reported in column 1 of table 2. As in table 1, capital is small although still significant and positive.[13] Because we had to construct a measure of the capital stock, there is likely to be significant measurement error in our proxy for the capital stock. The estimated coefficient on materials is larger than in table 1, while that on nonproduction workers is smaller.

Using these first-step estimates, we then calculated the average residual for each establishment in the sample.[14] The second column in table 2 contains the second-step results obtained from regressing the average residual on various workplace practices and employee characteristics.[15] Almost all of the estimated effects are similar to those in equation (3) of table 1. Again we see that the proportion of nonmanagerial workers using computers has a significant and positive effect on having higher-than-average productivity over the period 1988–1993. The average educational level of nonproduction workers and benchmarking are also positively related to those businesses that did better on average over this six-year period. Our finding on the importance of worker education for labor productivity is consistent with evidence presented by Hellerstein, Neumark, and Troske (1996). Unionization itself has no significant effect on which businesses did better or worse on average, but the interaction of unionization and profit sharing for nonmanagers is associated with better than average performance. One result that does change is that we now find that those employers who cite communication skills as a priority in recruitment also did better than average over the period 1988–1993. In addition, we find that those establishments with a larger share of new capital (one to four years old) in their capital stock have higher productivity. All of these findings are consistent with the idea that increased employee voice is positively related to establishment productivity and that new forms of labor-management relations are significantly related to better-performing businesses.

C. Panel Data Two-Step Estimation Based on GMM Estimator

Although the fixed-effects estimator corrects for the omitted-variable bias associated with unobserved time-invariant factors in the cross section estimation, the fact that

---

[12] We tested the joint null that all four interaction terms are equal to zero and rejected it at the 5% level.

[13] The coefficients on capital, materials, and nonproduction workers cannot be exactly compared with those in table 1 because the sample is different (and larger) in the first step in table 2 than in table 1.

[14] The first stage is estimated on the larger sample of 984 establishments in order to obtain more-precise estimates of the first-stage coefficients, because we will use these estimates to calculate the average residual over the period for each plant. The second stage contains fewer observations (638) due to missing workplace practices data. We have also redone the first-stage estimation just using the sample of 638 plants that we examine for the second stage. This does not significantly affect any of our second-stage results, only the standard errors in the first stage.

[15] It is important to note the distinction between the results presented in this table and those in table 1. In table 1, the dependent variable was labor productivity at a point in time (1993), whereas, in table 2, the dependent variable in the second step is the average residual (that is, the firm fixed effect) over the period 1988–1993.

TABLE 2.—DETERMINANTS OF LABOR PRODUCTIVITY 1988–1993 TWO-STEP ESTIMATES USING WITHIN AND GMM ESTIMATORS IN THE FIRST STEP

	Within Estimator		GMM Estimator	
	First Step	Second Step	First Step	Second Step
Dependent Variable:	sales/production employees	avg. residual 1988–1993	sales/production employees	avg. residual 1988–1993
Independent variables:				
Log (capital/production workers)	0.03** (3.16)		0.18** (4.24)	
Log (materials/production workers)	0.61** (58.54)		0.42** (9.38)	
Log (nonproduction/production)	0.07** (7.47)		0.15** (4.36)	
			Sargan test = 44.8 [$p = 0.25$]	
Technology				
Share of equip < 1 yr.		−0.04 (−0.19)		0.01 (0.03)
Share of equip 1–4 yr. old		0.16** (2.13)		0.14* (1.67)
R&D center		0.05 (1.53)		0.05 (1.36)
Proportion nonmanagers using computers		0.15** (3.17)		0.05 (1.02)
Worker Characteristics				
Log (avg ed nonproduction workers)		0.57** (2.78)		0.31 (1.43)
Log (avg ed production workers)		0.24 (0.76)		0.22 (0.64)
Turnover (proportion employees less than 1 year)		−0.32** (−2.51)		−0.16 (−1.17)
Proportion employees women		−0.02 (−0.25)		−0.01 (−0.07)
Proportion employees minority		−0.11* (−1.74)		−0.13* (−1.89)
Use of High-Performance Work Systems				
TQM		−0.03 (−0.47)		−0.11* (−1.87)
Benchmarking		0.07** (2.34)		0.07* (2.19)
Number of managerial levels		−0.001 (−0.08)		−0.008 (−1.04)
# employees per supervisor		−0.001 (−1.12)		−0.0002 (−0.23)
Proportion workers in self-managed teams		−0.02 (−0.40)		0.01 (0.20)
Log number of employees trained		0.001 (0.19)		0.004 (0.63)
Employee Voice				
Unionized		−0.012 (−0.21)		−0.12* (−1.81)
Proportion workers meeting regularly in groups		0.17** (2.31)		0.09 (1.15)
Profit Sharing				
Managers and supervisors		−0.03 (−0.76)		−0.08* (−1.67)
Production/clerical/technical		0.014 (0.22)		0.034 (0.50)
Recruitment Strategies				
Grades a top priority in recruitment		−0.005 (−0.37)		−0.01 (−0.80)
Communication a top priority in recruitment		0.03** (2.08)		0.03 (1.49)
Interaction Terms				
union*profit sharing for nonmanagerial employees		0.09* (1.62)		0.15** (2.34)
union*TQM		0.02 (0.32)		0.10 (1.52)
% meet*profit sharing for non-managerial workers		−0.05 (−0.69)		−0.02 (−0.34)
% meet*TQM		−0.05 (−0.68)		0.02 (0.30)
N for the first stage = 984		*N* for the second stage = 638		
Adjusted R^2 =		0.22		0.07

T-statistics in parenthesis.
** Significant at the 5% level and * at the 10% level. First-stage estimation also includes a constant term, year dummies, and two-digit SIC industry controls interacted with the year dummies. Second-stage equations also include a constant term, two-digit SIC industry controls, age of the establishment, a dummy variable if the establishment is part of a multiple-establishment firm, and a dummy variable if the primary product is exported. Appropriately lagged values of capital, labor, materials, and sales are used as instruments for the GMM estimator. The Sargan test is distributed as χ^2 with degrees of freedom equal to the number of instruments minus the number of estimated coefficients.

current values of capital, labor, and materials are simultaneously determined with output leads to an upward bias of the estimates. However, measurement error in the capital and materials variables may be biasing our first-step estimates of the vector of coefficients α' on capital, labor, and materials in the opposite direction. To attempt to correct for these potential biases, we use GMM techniques to instrument for capital, labor, and materials in the first stage.

If the coefficients in the equation using the within estimator are relatively more tainted due to measurement error, we would expect to see larger and more significant coefficients in the GMM first-differences estimation. This is, in fact, what we see for capital in the third column of table 2. If one calculates what our reported GMM estimates in table 2 imply about the share of capital and share of labor (production and nonproduction workers) in value added (output minus materials costs), we find that labor accounts for two-thirds of value added and capital one-third. This is consistent with what we see in national income and product accounts. Note that the Hansen-Sargan test of overidentifying restrictions does not suggest misspecification of the model.

When we look at the second-step estimates based on the GMM estimation (the fourth column of table 2), we see a similar pattern of results compared to the within estimator or even the cross section estimates presented in equation (3) of table 1. One major change, however, is that the percentage of nonmanagers using computers becomes insignificant. This may reflect in part the improved precision in the estimate on capital. In addition, TQM now enters with a large negative and statistically significant coefficient.

While our two-step procedure in table 2 addresses the biases that may arise in estimating the vector of coefficients α′ on capital, labor, and materials, it does not address biases that may arise in the second step when we estimate the vector of coefficients δ′ associated with observed workplace practices and characteristics. These biases may be due to correlations between the second-stage regressors and unobserved, time-invariant, plant-level characteristics or with the average of the idiosyncratic shocks (because the time period over which we average is relatively short). Although we believe that our vector δ′ extracts a substantial part of the previously unobserved fixed effect and that most of the endogeneity issues are related to labor, capital, and materials, these potential biases may be affecting our estimates of the impact of workplace practices on labor productivity. For example, a firm's decision to adopt particular workplace practices may be related to business performance, although it is unlikely that it will be performance in just one year. If an employer decides to adopt a new workplace practice in times of trouble because it becomes less expensive to switch systems (as suggested theoretically by Caballero and Hammour (1994) and shown empirically for a sample of British employers by Nickell, Nicolitsas, and Patterson (1996)), then our coefficients on workplace practices will likely be biased downwards. This would mean that it would be more difficult to find a positive effect of a workplace practice on labor productivity. If, instead, employers are more likely to adopt new workplace practices when times are very good, then our coefficients will be biased upwards.

Therefore, as a further check we adopted a strategy detailed by Doms, Dunne, and Troske (1997) to see if the plants that have implemented our various measures of

high-performance workplace practices in 1993 were also the more productive plants in 1982 (a period well before the introduction of many of these practices in U.S. manufacturing). If they were also more productive in the earlier period, one might worry that it is really some omitted firm fixed effect that is driving our results. To do so, we estimated equation (3) from table 1 but used the 1982 LRD data for labor productivity, capital, and materials instead of our 1993 data. We find no evidence that firms with high-performance workplace practices were more productive; in fact, none of our workplace practices variables were significant except average education of nonproduction workers. This suggests that it is not just the most productive firms that implement these workplace practices.

Nevertheless, an omitted variable that may be correlated with our workplace practices and consequently generate biases is managerial quality. It could be argued that the presence of good managers is more likely to be observed in firms with high-performance workplace practices. Therefore, what looks like an effect of workplace practices on productivity is just good management. But if good managers are those who adopt incentive-based compensation, get a higher proportion of their workers involved in decision making, and train a higher proportion of workers to use computers, then the fact that we are able to include these variables explicitly as regressors in our analysis means that it is unlikely that there is much unobserved managerial quality left.

One might think that having a follow-up survey on workplace practices would at least help us address any bias associated with unobserved but time-invariant employer fixed effects. Unfortunately, short panels on workplace practices are not going to be a magic elixir. First, workplace practices change very slowly, so if the period of time between surveys is not long enough there may be very few employers who change practices. Second, measurement error affecting workplace practices may bias our coefficients. Huselid and Becker (1996) present estimates on the impact of measurement error on the coefficients on workplace practices on various firm outcome measures for a two-period panel of 218 employers. They find large measurement error (some variables containing a 30% to 40% error variance), and, when they try to adjust for this, they find that their corrected coefficients on workplace practices are similar to those found in cross section estimation. In other words, the upward bias associated with omitted employer fixed effects is almost exactly offset in their sample with the downward bias associated with measurement error. Nevertheless, in recent work (Black & Lynch, 2000), we find that many of the results presented in this paper on the impact of workplace practices on productivity persist when we examine a panel of manufacturing establishments over the period 1993–1996. Clearly, a long panel on establishments that included repeated information on workplace practices would be preferable so that we could use a GMM estimation procedure to adjust for endogeneity and omitted fixed-effects biases on these variables. Even though these types of data are unlikely to be produced in the near future, we believe our results shed some light on the impact of workplace practices and information technology on productivity.

VI. Conclusion

New technologies and changing workplace practices have altered the nature and organization of work. There have been many stories in the popular press about the successes associated with the introduction of high-performance workplace systems and the revolution computers have caused on the job. At the same time, the gains to completing a college degree relative to a high school diploma have doubled over the past fifteen years in response to what many have argued are the skill demands associated with new technologies and changing work organization. We have tried in this paper to get a better understanding of how workplace practices, human capital investments, and information technology are related to establishment productivity. By using a large representative sample of businesses, we have been able to examine these factors on a broader cross section of employers, unlike previous studies that have focused on one particular industry, product, or even firm.

By relying on detailed measures of human resource practices included on their own and interacted with each other, rather than just using summary indices, we have been able to see that what appears to matter most for productivity is how HR systems are implemented. Adopting a TQM system per se does not raise productivity. Rather, allowing greater employee voice in decision making is what seems to matter most for productivity. Instituting a profit-sharing system has a positive effect on productivity, but only when it is extended to nonmanagerial employees. Finally, those unionized establishments that have adopted what have been called new or "transformed" industrial relations practices that promote joint decision making coupled with incentive-based compensation have higher productivity than other similar nonunion plants, and those businesses that are unionized but maintain more traditional labor-management relations have lower productivity.

Although the two-step procedure used in this paper addresses some of the biases that may arise in estimating the impact of workplace practices and characteristics on productivity, it does not address all potential biases. Longitudinal data that enabled us to follow businesses over time to examine changes in performance resulting from implementation of high-performance workplace practices would help provide further evidence on the role of the new workplace in productivity. A long panel on establishments that included repeated information on workplace practices would allow us to use a GMM estimation procedure like we did on capital, materials, and labor to adjust for endogeneity and omitted fixed-effects biases on our estimates of the impact of work-

place practices on productivity. Nevertheless, by using this two-step method, this paper has highlighted the importance of measuring the intensity of workplace practices in an establishment and not just the incidence. In addition, it suggests an important role for considering synergies among workplace practices. Understanding what constitutes a productive workplace environment is not limited to whether or not an establishment has TQM, but also how it is implemented including the mechanisms and institutions in place to address incentive compatibility problems that may arise as employers seek greater employee involvement in labor productivity improvements. Other studies have been limited in their ability to identify these important relationships or by the fact that it was not easy to generalize their findings to a broader segment of the economy.

REFERENCES

Arellano, M., and S. Bond, "Dynamic Panel Data Estimation Using DPD—A Guide for Users," Institute for Fiscal Studies working paper no. 88/15 (1988).
———, "Some Tests of Specification for Panel Data: Monte Carlo Evidence and a Application to Employment Equations," *Review of Economic Studies* 58(2) (1991), 277–297.
Arellano, M., and O. Bover, "Another Look at the Instrumental Variable Estimation of Error-Components Models," *Journal of Econometrics* 68(1) (1995), 29–51.
Arthur, Jeffrey, "Effects of Human Resource Systems on Manufacturing Performance and Turnover," *Academy of Management Journal* 37(3) (1994), 670–87.
Bailey, Martin, and Robert Gordon, "The Productivity Slowdown, Measurement Issues and the Explosion of Computer Power," *Brookings Papers on Economic Activity* 19(2) (1988), 347–420.
Bailey, Thomas, "Organizational Innovation in the Apparel Industry," *Industrial Relations* 32(1) (1993), 30–48.
Bartel, Ann, "Formal Employee Training Programs and Their Impact on Labor Productivity: Evidence from a Human Resource Survey," NBER working paper no. 3026 (1989).
Bartelsman, Eric J., and Wayne Gray, "The NBER Manufacturing Productivity Database," unpublished manuscript. Board of Governors of the Federal Reserve System (January 1995).
Batt, Rosemary, "Performance and Welfare Effects of Work Restructuring: Evidence from Telecommunications Services," unpublished doctoral dissertation, MIT Sloan School of Management (1995).
Berg, Peter, Eileen Appelbaum, Thomas Bailey, and Arne Kalleberg, "The Performance Effects of Modular Production in the Apparel Industry," *Industrial Relations* 35(3) (1996), 356–373
Black, Sandra E., and Lisa M. Lynch, "Human Capital Investments and Productivity," *American Economic Review* (May 1996).
———, "What's Driving the New Economy: The Benefits of Workplace Innovation," NBER working paper no. 7479 (January 2000).
Brown, Charles, and James Medoff, "Trade Unions in the Production Process," *Journal of Political Economy* 86(3) (1978), 355–378.
Brynjolfsson, Eric, and Loren Hitt, "New Evidence on the Returns to Information Systems," working paper, MIT Sloan School of Management (1993).
Bureau of Labor Statistics, U.S. Department of Labor, *Labor Composition and U.S. Productivity Growth, 1948–90*, Bulletin 2426, (Washington, DC: U.S. Government Printing Office, December 1993).
Caballero, R., and M. L. Hammour, "The Cleansing Effects of Recessions," *American Economic Review* 84(5) (1994), 1350–1368.
Clark, Kim B., "Unionization and Firm Performance: The Impact on Profits, Growth, and Productivity," *American Economic Review* 74 (December 1984), 893–919.
Cooke, William, "Employee Participation Programs, Group-Based Incentives, and Company Performance: A Union-Nonunion Comparison," *Industrial and Labor Relations Review* 47(4) (1994), 594–609.

Davis, Steve, and John Haltiwanger, "Wage Dispersion Between and Within U.S. Manufacturing Plants: 1963–1986." *Brookings Papers on Economic Activity: Microeconomics (1991)*, 115–180.

Delaney, John, and Mark Huselid, "The Impact of Human Resource Management Practices on Perceptions of Performance in For-Profit and Nonprofit Organizations," *Academy of Management Journal.*

Doms, Mark, Timothy Dunne, and Kenneth Troske, "Workers, Wages and Technology," *Quarterly Journal of Economics* 112 (February 1997), 235–290.

Dunlop, John, and David Weil, "Diffusion and Performance of Modular Production in the U.S. Apparel Industry," *Industrial Relations* 35 (July 1996), 334–354.

Freeman, Richard, and James Medoff, *What Do Unions Do?* (New York: Basic Books, 1984).

Griliches, Z., and J. A. Hausman, "Errors in Variables in Panel Data," *Journal of Econometrics* 31(1) (1986), 93–118.

Griliches, Z., and J. Mairesse, "Production Functions: The Search for Identification," NBER working paper no. 5067 (1995).

Hellerstein, Judith, David Neumark, and Kenneth Troske, "Wages, Productivity and Worker Characteristics: Evidence from Plant-Level Production Functions and Wage Equations," NBER working paper no. 5626 (June 1996).

Hulten, Charles, and Frank Wykoff, "Measurement of Economic Depreciation" (pp. 81–125) in C. R. Hulten (Ed.), *Depreciation, Information, and the Taxation of Income from Capital.* (Washington, DC: Urban Institute, 1981).

Huselid, Mark A., "The Impact of Human Resource Management Practices on Turnover, Productivity, and Corporate Financial Performance." *Academy of Management Journal* 38(3) (1995), 635–672.

Huselid, Mark A., and Brian E. Becker, "High Performance Work Systems and Firm Performance: Cross-Sectional Versus Panel Results." *Industrial Relations* 35(3) (1996), 400–422.

Ichniowski, Casey, "Human Resource Management Systems and the Performance of U.S. Manufacturing Businesses," NBER working paper no. 3449 (1990).

———, "Human Resource Practices and Productive Labor-Management Relations" (pp. 239–271), in D. Lewin, O. Mitchell, and P. Sherer (Eds.), *Research Frontiers in Industrial Relations and Human Resources.* (Ithaca, NY: ILR Press, Cornell University Press, 1992).

Ichniowski, Casey, Kathryn Shaw, and Gabrielle Prennushi, "The Effects of Human Resource Management Practices on Productivity," *American Economic Review,* 87(3) (1997), 291–313.

Jorgenson, Dale, and Zvi Griliches, "The Explanation of Productivity Change," *Review of Economic Studies* 34(3) (1967), 249–283.

Jorgenson, Dale, Frank Gallop, and Barbara Fraumeni, *Productivity and U.S. Economic Growth.* (Cambridge: Harvard University Press, 1987).

Kandel, E., and Edward Lazear, "Peer Pressure and Partnerships," *Journal of Political Economy* 100(4) (1992), 801–817.

Kelley, Maryellen, "Information Technology and Productivity: The Elusive Connection," *Management Science* 40(3) (1994), 1406–1425.

———, "Participative Bureaucracy and Productivity in the Machined Products Sector," *Industrial Relations* 35 (1996), 374–399.

Krafcik, John, "Triumph of the Lean Production System," *Sloan Management Review* 30(1) (1988), 41–52.

Krueger, Alan, "How Computers Have Changed the Wage Structure: Evidence from Micro Data, 1984–1989." *Quarterly Journal of Economics* (February 1993), 33–60.

Lynch, Lisa M., and Sandra E. Black, "Determinants of Employer Provided Training," *Industrial and Labor Relations Review* 52(1) (October 1998), 69–79.

Malcomson, James, "Trade Unions and Economic Efficiency," *Economic Journal* 93 (1983), 50–65.

Milgrom, P., and Roberts, J., "Complementarities and Fit: Strategy, Structure and Organizational Change in Manufacturing," *Journal of Accounting and Economics* 19 (1995), 179–208.

Nickell, S. J., Daphne Nicolitsas, and Malcolm Patterson, "Does Doing Badly Encourage Management Innovation?" Oxford Institute for Economics and Statistics working paper (August 1996).

Oliner, Stephen, and Daniel Sichel, "Computers and Output Growth Revisited: How Big is the Puzzle?" *Brookings Papers on Economic Activity* 2 (1994), 273–317.

Osterman, Paul, "How Common is Workplace Transformation and Who Adopts It?" *Industrial and Labor Relations Review* 47(2) (January 1994), 173–187.

Schmidt, Peter, "Frontier Production Functions: A Review," *Econometric Reviews* 4 (1985), 353–355.

Womack, James, Daniel Jones, and Daniel Roos, *The Machine That Changed the World* (New York: Rawson/Macmillan, 1991).

APPENDIX

The capital deflator was created by first generating a three-digit industry real net capital stock value. The three-digit data is converted to the four-digit level by assuming that the industry-asset type flows are the same for all four-digit industries within a three-digit industry. With this information, four-digit investment deflators were created for equipment and structures separately. The materials deflator was created by averaging together price deflators for 529 inputs (369 manufacturing industries and 160 nonmanufacturing industries), using as weights the relative size of each industry's purchases of that input in the Input-Output Tables. The inflation in materials prices was calculated as a Tornquist index (weighting each product's inflation rate by the average of the previous and current-year's shares in total materials used).

The energy price deflator is based on each industry's expenditures on six types of energy (electricity, residual fuel oil, distillates, coal, coke, and natural gas). These six types of energy represent 94.6% of all energy expenditures by the manufacturing sector in 1976. They were a majority of the energy costs for all but one industry, and more than 90% of energy costs for 300 of the industries.

Finally, because the deflator data were unavailable for 1993, we regressed current price levels (using two- or three-digit level SIC data, depending upon availability) on the previous year's price level and the current year's producer price index for stage of processing groupings from the BLS. We then generated an imputed value for 1993 deflators using the predicted values from this regression.

[24]

HUMAN RESOURCE MANAGEMENT AS A SUBSTITUTE FOR TRADE UNIONS IN BRITISH WORKPLACES

STEPHEN MACHIN and STEPHEN WOOD*

The authors use British workplace data for 1980–98 to examine whether increased human resource management (HRM) practices coincided with union decline, consistent with the hypothesis that such practices act as a substitute for unionization. Two initial analyses show no important differences between union and non-union sectors or between newer workplaces (which are likelier to be non-union) and older ones in the pattern of HRM practices over time; and the study's longitudinal analysis picks up no evidence of faster union decline in workplaces or industries that adopted HRM practices than in those that did not. Not only is the hypothesized substitution effect thus not supported, but the authors even uncover some evidence of a complementarity between unions and HRM practices. The authors conclude that increased use of HRM practices is probably not an important factor underpinning union decline in Britain.

T he decline of trade unionism has been a feature of many countries in recent years (Verma et al. 2002) and the subject of a large body of research. Union decline has been especially strong in Britain over the past 25 years. In the late 1970s over 13 million people—or around 58% of workers—were trade union members, and wages for over 70% of workers were set by collective bargaining. Since reaching its peak in 1979, unionization (however measured) has fallen year after year, so that by 2004 less than 30% of workers were members of a trade union.

Coinciding with the decline in trade unionism has been an increase in the use of human relations practices and new forms of work organization. These are often subsumed under labels such as high-involvement, high-commitment, and high-performance management, or simply human resource management. For convenience we shall follow Fiorito (2001), a major U.S. writer on union substitution, and use the term human resource management (HRM).

*Stephen Machin is Professor of Economics, University College London, and Research Director of the Centre for Economic Performance, London School of Economics; Stephen Wood is Professor of Work Psychology, Deputy Director of the Institute of Work Psychology, and Co-Director of the ESRC Centre for Organisation and Innovation, University of Sheffield, and Associate of the Centre for Economic Performance, London School of Economics. This research is part of a joint project between the Leverhulme Foundation–funded research on the Future of Trade Unionism in Modern Britain and the ESRC Centre for Innovation and Organisation (Grant Number RA013461). The empirical research is based on data from the Workplace Industrial/Employee Relations series, which is deposited at the Data Archive at the University of Essex, U.K. (http://www.esrc.ac.uk). The authors thank Alex Bryson, Peter Cappelli, and participants at the Labor seminar at Wharton Business School for comments, and Alison Geldart for editorial assistance.

Industrial and Labor Relations Review, Vol. 58, No. 2 (January 2005). © by Cornell University.
0019-7939/00/5802 $01.00

The increased adoption of HRM practices has been presented, particularly in the prescriptive management literature, as providing the basis for a new win-win relationship between workers and managers. It is argued that they offer management the prospect of improved performance while improving workers' job satisfaction, security, and perhaps pay and benefits.

The increasing adoption of the term high-performance methods, even in the industrial relations literature, implies an acceptance of the validity of this chain of argument. If it is indeed the case that these modern HRM methods enhance workers' satisfaction, they might be expected to reduce the demand for trade unions. This possibility forms the basis of what has become known as the HRM-substitution explanation of union decline. The argument is that unions may become redundant in the eyes of workers (and employers) because of "the effects that positive employer practices ... have in reducing the *causes* of unionism, i.e., worker dissatisfaction" (Fiorito 2001:335; italics in original).

This paper explores empirically whether HRM/union substitution has been a major factor in the decline of trade unionism in Britain. It asks whether there is indeed a link between the rise of HRM and declining trade unionism in British workplaces. To investigate this question, we use rich data on workplaces over time from the British Workplace Industrial/Employee Relations Surveys for 1980, 1984, 1990, and 1998.

HRM Substitution in Britain

The initial tendency to associate HRM practices with non-unionism was perhaps never as strong in the United Kingdom as it was in the United States, except when the practices were associated with U.S. multinationals. A lot of the discussion of HRM as an alternative to trade unions never appeared in published sources, but remained as a point of debate and speculation in conferences and seminars. HRM was often assumed to be antithetical to trade unionism, and hence much of the subtext of the debate concerned the future of industrial

relations as a field (Godard and Delaney 2000). Keith Sisson, editor of a textbook on personnel management, summed up the published sources well in his introduction to the book's second edition: "Although there are formulations which give an important place to trade unions ..., most are silent on the issues or assume a non-union environment" (Sisson 1994:12). From this, he wrote, we can infer that these writers regard unions as "at best unnecessary and at worst to be avoided."

At least one British commentator, however, did explicitly associate HRM with non-unionism: "An organisation pursuing HRM," he wrote, "will almost always prefer a non-union path, emphasising individual rather than collective arrangements" (Guest 1989:48) Yet while HRM might be associated with non-unionism, non-unionism "unfortunately" could not be equated with HRM, Guest noticeably added, as "a company may pursue non-union policies or remain fortuitously non-union without practising HRM."

The implication is that HRM is viewed as a major, if not the only effective, means of remaining non-union. Consistent with that, HRM is inherent to the definition of union substitution in some of the U.S. literature, certainly when distinctions are made between union substitution and union suppression. When Kochan (1980:183) first made the distinction—on the basis that direct union suppression involved "hard line opposition" through, for example, the use of blacklists, while union substitution was comparatively indirect—he certainly associated substitution with the growth of personnel management. More recently, Fiorito (2001:335) similarly made the distinction on the basis that "union *suppression* refers to direct attacks on *symptoms* of 'unionism' (pro-union attitudes, intentions or actions) among workers" (italics in original). Since union substitution refers to employer practices designed to offer good pay and conditions or certain kinds of employee involvement, it is often conceived as being aimed at reducing worker dissatisfaction. Given that for Fiorito the adoption of such practices does not have to be consciously motivated by anti-unionism, any increase in their use that acts to enhance job satisfaction and discourage unionism could be taken to be union substitution.

Nonetheless, this prejudges too much ahead of empirical research on the purported link between HRM and non-unionism. Fiorito has in fact implicitly recognized the empirical nature of the question by designing and conducting studies to test whether HRM practices do indeed act as substitutes for unions (Fiorito 2001; Fiorito et al. 1987).

Union Decline and the Increased Incidence of HRM Practices

The sharp union decline in Britain that dates from 1979 is by now well known. Aggregate union density showed a remarkable stability in the postwar period (at around 40–45% membership), followed by a sharp rise in the 1970s, but then an even sharper fall from the late 1970s onward. Since 1979 aggregate union density has trended downward so that, by the end of the 1990s, less than 30% of workers were members of trade unions.[1]

Alongside the evidence on the decline of unionization in the United Kingdom is research demonstrating that managers' increasing interest in HRM has translated into increased adoption of HRM practices. Wood and Albanese (1995:232–34) showed that the use of an extensive set of 15 HRM practices typically associated with high-involvement, high-commitment, or high-performance management—including team briefing, team working, formal assessment, merit pay, flexible job descriptions, and quality circles—all increased in their sample of 132 U.K. manufacturing plants between 1986 and 1990. Team briefing and flexible

job descriptions had the highest rate of increase.

For a similar period in the subsequent decade, a study of manufacturing showed increases in both the adoption and extent of use by companies of three key high-involvement practices—team working, empowerment, and learning culture (Wood et al. 2005). Analyses of the British Workplace Employee Relations Survey of 1998 have also documented the rise of direct communication methods and certain kinds of pay systems (Forth and Millward 2002; Millward et al. 2000; Sisson 1993). Several more qualitative studies (for example, for the United Kingdom, Clark 1995; Scott 1994; Starkey and McKinlay 1993:40–81; and Wickens 1987) have concentrated on the development of HRM practices in the past two decades, Storey's (1992) being the first to document the freshness of these in key U.K. organizations (as Kochan et al. [1986] and Appelbaum and Batt [1994] did for the United States).

Existing Empirical Work from Britain

To date, empirical research on the link between HRM practices and unionism has almost exclusively been based on point-in-time cross-sectional analysis. Wood (1996), examining the full range of HRM practices in U.K. manufacturing, found that unionized workplaces did not differ from non-unionized workplaces in the extent of either major HRM practices or, more generally, "high commitment management" (as judged by a composite measure) in either 1986 or 1990. Appraisal and merit pay were, however, more likely to be used in non-unionized plants, and the rate of change in high-commitment management between 1986 and 1990 was greater in non-union plants.

Various analyses of aspects of the Workplace Industrial/Employee Relations Survey Series (of 1980, 1984, 1990, and 1998) have explored the link between human resource management practices and unionism. Most of these studies have concentrated on merit pay and non-union voice mechanisms and have concluded that they

---

[1]For selected years, aggregate union density was as follows: 1946—43%; 1950—41%; 1960—41%; 1970—46%; 1975—51%; 1980—52%; 1985—46%; 1990—38%; 1995—32%; 2003—29%. Sources for these numbers are Price and Bain (1983), Waddington (1992), Cully and Woodland (1998), and Hicks and Palmer (2004).

are not associated with non-unionism, being either neutral with respect to union recognition or positively associated with it (Sisson 1993; Cully et al. 2000; Gospel and Willman 2003).

Wood and de Menezes (1998) developed a composite measure of high-commitment management based on a mixture of data from WIRS for 1990 and a sister survey from 1990–91 (the Employers' Manpower and Skills Practices Survey) and found that this variable had no association with unionism. Analysis of a fuller range of HRM practices that were included for the first time in the WIRS/WERS series in 1998 found that the number of these practices used was associated with unionism (Cully et al. 2000:110–11), but that this was mostly because they were especially widespread in large private sector workplaces and throughout the public sector.

A more in-depth analysis of the practices that were included in Cully et al.'s aggregate index of high commitment by Wood, de Menezes, and Lasaosa (2003) revealed that the relationship was more complex. The family-friendly practices, for example, and internal labor market employment practices included in Cully et al.'s index were not among the core high-involvement practices associated with changes in work organization. The validity of indices based on simply aggregating practices is questionable. Using their superior measures, Wood et al. (2003) found no strong relationship between union recognition or density and high-involvement management (nor, indeed, family-friendly management).

Forth and Millward (2002) conducted a more direct assessment of the union substitution hypothesis, but again only using cross-sectional data (the 1998 Workplace Employee Relations Survey). They tested to see if direct communication channels were more prevalent where managers reported that they were generally not in favor of union membership than where managers were either neutral or positive toward unions. Forth and Millward first examined the subsample of workplaces with union recognition and then the non-union subsample, and found that direct communication was unrelated to management's orientation toward unionism in the unionized sample. In the non-unionized sample the existence of some direct communication channels was related to negative attitudes toward unions on the part of management, but the extent of their use was greater where these attitudes were positive. The authors concluded that managers in non-union workplaces attempting union substitution provide the minimum direct communication necessary and "do not provide further channels of communication that might be superfluous to the aim of union avoidance" (p. 23). This conclusion seems inconsistent with the union substitution thesis, and chimes more with Millward et al.'s (1992:350–65) earlier argument that the previously union-based British system of industrial relations has not been replaced by an alternative union-free model of employee representation.

Interpretation

Regardless of whether the relationship between HRM and unionism can be gleaned from cross-sectional analysis, any association that does exist could reflect a variety of processes. First, those who associate HRM with non-unionism may see the relationship simply as a transitional state or aberration. For example, Guest by 1995 admitted the co-existence of unionism and HRM, but implied that this could reflect that one or other was in a weak form: either the trade unionism was not robust or the HRM was fragmented or limited (Guest 1995:121). Moreover, statistical results could, to some extent, be mirroring the rise of industrial relations situations in which neither HRM nor unionism existed; this is what Guest (1995:125–27) called the black hole cases, or Sissons (1993:207) referred to as the bleak houses. According to Guest, HRM could not exist at high levels of unionization. Consistent with this view, he certainly saw a mutually supportive relationship between unions and HRM as less likely than "black holes" or "bleak houses"—much as Millward et al. (1992) had, a few years before. Any meaningful juxtaposition of unions and HRM along the mutual gains lines is by implication dependent on a change of union attitudes so that they embrace the HRM model. This implies that union members accept a role in enhancing economic performance, which in turn means that they accept the validity of the purported HRM-performance link. The implication is that the mutual gains for employees arise regardless of the presence of a union. Subsequently, Guest and Conway (1999) reported research that bore this out, as they observed that a high rate of adoption of HRM was associated with higher job satisfaction and commitment and reduced intentions to leave regardless of the union status of the individual. Further, those employees in unionized workplaces with little or no HRM had more negative attitudes than their equivalents in the non-union sector (that is, those in Guest's black hole).

Second, and linked to this, there is the possibility that the cross-sectional analysis masks multiple processes. There may be cases in which HRM and unionism are mutually supportive, as they seemingly were in the original Saturn experiment in the United States (Rubinstein and Kochan 2001); cases in which managers are using HRM to undermine an existing union or at least reduce its influence; and cases in which it is being used to keep unions at bay, alongside the black hole cases. There may also be a separation of the major HRM practices from unionism, with the former focused on changing task systems, the latter on governance. This is consistent with the more general point that the relationship between HRM practices and unionism may vary across practices, as Fiorito et al. (1987) indeed observed in their study of the effects of human resource practices on voting behavior in union organizing campaigns (see also Fiorito 2001).

In the most prominent HRM literature, that which has sought to test HRM's performance effects, quite diverse practices are taken to fall under the umbrella of HRM. They can be classified as practices concerned with job and work design (particularly with local empowerment), communications and representation, skill acquisition and training, appraisal, recruitment and selection, compensation, and internal mobility (Appelbaum et al. 2000; Wood and Wall 2002). Several of the practices that fall under these headings are ones that unions have campaigned for or that are at least consistent with their demands, the most obvious being representation, training, job security, fair selection processes, and priority given to internal recruitment. Yet this is not to deny that if management were to offer these practices independently of employee pressure, dissatisfactions that spur unionism might disappear, reducing workers' willingness to join unions. Nonetheless, some practices—especially functional flexibility in a situation of negotiated work rules and job demarcations—may constitute substitutes for union-inspired rules and practices. As such, these may bring their own problems for workers, such as an increase in workloads, in supervisors' power, and in the scope for arbitrary management, as well as erosion of the union's power base.

The practices that most directly constitute alternatives to unions are those that can replace bargaining and voice roles. More specifically, there are two core substitutes for unions: forms of individualized pay determination such as individual bargaining or imposed merit- and performance-related pay awards, and methods of communication that purport to give workers a direct voice and avoid any third party such as a union or at least union representatives. Neither of these is likely to offer full alternatives to unions. First, under individualized pay determination, individuals negotiate without the strength of their fellow workers, and awards may be subject to the arbitrariness of managers, one of the very forces that unions were historically established to counter. Second, direct or non–union representative communication methods may offer lower levels of involvement and information-sharing, providing consultation rather than bargaining, and may not have the formal independence from management that the union has. Nonetheless, such practices remain the ones that are most important for testing the link between HRM and unionization.

Given the above considerations, the key test of union substitution is whether the increased adoption of HRM practices over time led to declines in unionism that are detectable after the analysis controls for the influence of other factors, thus allowing us to conclude that HRM systems acted to replace collective bargaining and union voice. Therefore the issue of substitutability is best explored with data on direct substitutes for unions over time. This is consistent with Fiorito's (2001:351) conclusion, based on his finding of only modest support for union substitution in a study of the effects of human resource practices on union voting intentions, that we require measures of "the use of HR practices over time" to really assess "the extent to which they have contributed to the decline of unions over recent decades." It is this cross-time approach emphasizing dynamics that we adopt in our empirical investigation.

The Study

Data Description

The data used in this paper are drawn from the British Workplace Industrial/Employee Relations Surveys of 1980, 1984, 1990, and 1998. These are workplace-level surveys[2] containing rich data on the industrial relations environment of workplaces that have been widely used by researchers to study a range of issues (see the bibliography of Millward et al. 2002, for details of these studies). Of most relevance for our analysis is the fact that the surveys were carried out over time, as this permits us to address the question of whether HRM adoption paralleled union decline. The survey data contain a number of measures of union presence and of HRM practices. The cross-time angle offered by the four cross-sec-

tions is important, as we wish to see whether the rapid union decline over the period corresponded in some way with changes in the incidence of HRM practices.

Measures of Union Presence and HRM

The union data in the WIRS/WERS series have been used by many researchers, both to look at union decline (Disney, Gosling, and Machin 1994, 1995; Machin 2000, 2003) and to study the economic effects of trade unions (Millward et al. 2002). The usual measure on which researchers focus is trade union recognition—whether management recognizes trade unions for collective bargaining purposes—but there are also data on workplace-level union density (the proportion of workers who are union members) and union coverage (the proportion of workers covered by collective bargaining).

The coverage of data on HRM variables became broader over the series, so that the 1998 survey covered most areas associated with HRM. Fortunately for our present concerns, the variables that have been included throughout the series (or in at least three surveys) relate to pay methods or employee voice, which are most apposite for testing the HRM/substitution hypothesis. For our empirical analysis we have therefore identified the following variables that we can observe over time (with those years that are available on a consistently defined basis in square brackets):

— the incidence of flexible pay (profit-sharing or share ownership) [1984, 1990, 1998, trading sector workplaces only];

— the presence of a Joint Consultative Committee [1980, 1984, 1990, 1998];

— the presence of problem-solving groups [1990, 1998];

— whether team briefings occur [1984, 1990, 1998];

— whether there are regular meetings in which management communicates or consults with the entire work force present [1984, 1990, 1998];

— whether management makes systematic use of a management chain for communication

---

[2]The first three surveys were representative samples of establishments with at least 25 employees, while the 1998 survey lowered this size threshold to 10 employees. To maintain consistency over time, we restrict our analysis to workplaces with at least 25 employees.

[1984, 1990, 1998];

— whether a suggestions scheme is in operation [1984, 1990, 1998]; and

— whether the workplace has a personnel specialist in place [1980, 1984, 1990, 1998].

Analysis Strategy

We start by examining whether, in the era of union decline, HRM practices more rapidly permeated non-union workplaces than unionized workplaces. If they did, this would suggest that HRM practices do increasingly provide a voice for workers in non-union environments, and may well make trade unions anachronisms in the workplace. In other words, the implication would be that in this world of HRM, workers do not need union representation in their workplace to ensure that grievance procedures, health and safety arrangements, and other forms of involvement are there for them if required. The first approach we adopt thus considers differences over time in the use of HRM practices in the union and non-union sectors. This enables us to look at whether one can identify differential trends through time in HRM incidence between union and non-union workplaces. If HRM substitution is present, we ought to see faster increases in HRM in the non-union sector.

An observed correlation between non-unionism and HRM could, however, merely reflect a higher presence of HRM practices in newer workplaces, where unionization is especially low. That is, because HRM practices are themselves relatively new, it is plausible that they could be taken up more by new workplaces than by established ones; and it is well established that unions have organized much less consistently in newer British workplaces than in older ones (Machin 2000, 2003). To ensure that we are not conflating workplace age and union status effects, our second approach therefore considers whether the incidence of HRM is higher in newer workplaces than in older ones, and thus is a stronger test than the first approach.

Finally, we consider longitudinal data on workplaces and industries and explore whether the rise of HRM has, in fact, gone hand-in-hand with union decline. While the data are for only a limited number of HRM practices, we are able to look at the dynamics of change to see whether within-workplace or within-industry changes in unionization display any correlation with changes in HRM incidence. We do this in two ways: first, by asking whether unionized workplaces that introduced HRM practices between 1990 and 1998 saw falls in union presence relative to those that did not introduce practices; and second, by modeling changes in HRM and unionism in industries between 1980 and 1998.

Union/Non-Union Differences in HRM Incidence over Time

Descriptive Statistics

Sharp union decline is revealed in the WIRS/WERS data since 1980. Panel A of Table 1 shows that the percentage of establishments recognizing trade unions for collective bargaining fell from 64% to 42% between 1980 and 1998. Union density and coverage also fell sharply (to 36% and 41%, respectively) over the same time period.[3]

Panel B of Table 1 gives means of the HRM variables over the relevant cross-sections. For most HRM practices—particularly flexible pay, team briefing, and having a personnel specialist—the table shows increased incidence. But this is not true of all measures. The presence of the more traditional Joint Consultative Committee actually falls, and the frequencies of some of the other practices (regular meetings with senior management, presence of a management chain) remain fairly constant over time.

Changes over Time by Union Status

Table 2 shows changes over time in the incidence of HRM practices separately for union and non-union workplaces, and also

---

[3]Note that the 1980 number for density is based only on full-time workers (see Millward, Bryson, and Forth 2000).

Table 1. Changes in Union Presence and the
Incidence of HRM Practices over Time (Proportions).

			Year		
Variable		1980	1984	1990	1998
A. Union Variables					
Union Recognition		.64	.66	.53	.42
Union Density[a]		.62	.58	.48	.36
Union Coverage		—	.71	.54	.41
B. HRM Variables					
Flexible Pay		—	.30	.54	.50
Joint Consultative Committee		.34	.34	.29	.29
Problem Solving Groups		—	—	.35	.42
Team Briefing		—	.36	.48	.53
Regular Meetings with Senior Management		—	.34	.41	.37
Management Chain		—	.62	.60	.60
Suggestion Schemes		—	.25	.28	.33
Personnel Specialist		.19	.20	.27	.27

Notes:
Aggregate weighted proportions (that is, proportions across all establishments with 25 or more workers) in Panel A are taken from the sourcebooks for the 1980, 1984, and 1990 Workplace Industrial Relations Surveys and the 1998 Workplace Employee Relations Surveys (1980: Daniel and Millward 1983; 1984: Millward and Stevens 1986; 1990: Millward et al. 1992; 1998: Cully at al. 1998, 1999). For 1998 recognition data, recognition is recoded to zero for fifteen workplaces that recognized teacher unions but that in fact had pay set by the Pay Review Bodies (this follows the same procedure as in Chapter 10 of Cully at al. 1999). John Forth and Neil Millward kindly provided the serial codes for these fifteen workplaces.
   Panel B weighted proportions are the authors' own calculations from the WIRS/WERS data.
   [a]Union density is for full-timers in 1980 and all workers in other years.

displays comparisons between the two sectors. The table shows the percentage of workplaces with each of the practices for a start year and end year, and the change in the percentage between those years. The penultimate column shows the gap between sectors in those changes in percentages. For example, between 1984 and 1998, the percentage of workplaces that had flexible pay increased by 17 percentage points in the union sector and by 25 percentage points in the non-union sector, making for a gap of 8 percentage points between the changes in the two sectors. The final column displays the level of statistical significance of those inter-sectoral differences.

The numbers in Table 2 reveal several patterns. First, at a given point in time, the incidence of the HRM factors tends to be higher in the union sector than in the non-union sector. At face value, this would suggest a complementarity between unions

and HRM practice. However, of most interest to us is whether there were any changes in HRM practices over the period of union decline. Table 2 shows an increased adoption of most practices in both sectors, but the results concerning increased substitution into the non-union sector are uneven (see the last two columns). Indeed, the only practice that seems to show a strong, statistically significant, faster differential increase in incidence in non-union workplaces than in union workplaces is flexible pay. As noted above, there was an eight percentage point faster increase in flexible pay incidence in the non-union sector—a statistically significant difference between sectors, as shown by the p-value of the significance test given in the final column. However, this really is the only evidence of substitution. The next nearest is a four percentage point increase in Joint Consultative Committees, with an associated p-

Table 2. Union/Non-Union Differences in
Changes in the Incidence of HRM Practices over Time.

HRM Practice	Start and End Years	Union Sector			Non-Union Sector			Difference in Change between Non-Union/ Union Sectors	Test of Signif. of Difference in Change (p-value)
		Percent in Start Year	Percent in End Year	Change	Percent in Start Year	Percent in End Year	Change		
Flexible Pay	1984, 1998	38	55	17	23	48	25	8	.04
Joint Consultative Committee	1980, 1998	41	38	-3	21	22	1	4	.11
Problem Solving Groups	1990, 1998	39	49	10	30	37	7	-3	.26
Team Briefing	1984, 1998	39	58	19	31	49	18	-1	.69
Regular Meetings with Senior Management	1984, 1998	36	41	5	30	35	5	0	.83
Management Chain	1984, 1998	68	70	2	51	52	1	-1	.75
Suggestion Schemes	1984, 1998	31	42	11	15	26	11	0	.82
Personnel Specialist	1980, 1998	23	32	9	12	23	11	2	.51

value of .11. For the other HRM practices, we find very similar patterns of change between the non-union and union sectors, all statistically insignificant (in the +2 to −3% range of differences).

To the practice-specific results shown in Table 2, it is worth adding a brief mention of the pattern of results obtained when we look at the practices jointly. Notably, there is no statistically significant differential increase in the use of multiple practices across sectors. In 1984, union sector workplaces had, on average, 2.67 of the seven HRM practices for which we have data over the 1984–98 period, and this figure rose to 3.30 by 1998; in the non-union sector the number rose from 1.85 to 2.53 over the same period. The scale of change is similar across the two sectors (a rise of .53 in the union sector and .68 in the non-union sector), and in statistical terms one cannot reject the null hypothesis of the same change across sectors (p-value of significance test = .68).

HRM Substitution and Workplace Age

Links with Workplace Age

The evidence so far has not revealed much in support of the HRM substitution thesis. In this section we consider the question another way, looking instead at the extent to which newer workplaces differentially introduced HRM practices. We adopt this approach in the light of the evidence that union decline in Britain has been driven, at least partially, by unions' failure to secure recognition and build up membership in newer workplaces (Machin 2003). Consider the upper panel of Table 3. Among workplaces set up before 1980, 63% recognized unions for collective bargaining, and union membership density was 58%. In stark contrast, union recognition and density were 36% and 31%, respectively, in workplaces set up in the 1980s, and only 27% and 22%, respectively, in those set up in the 1990s. Hence one sees very sharp falls in unionization rates by age of workplace. Columns (6) and (7) of Table 3 show the scale of the declines, which was very strong in statistical terms (the numbers in parentheses are standard errors).

This pattern offers promise as a means to try and identify HRM substitution. In new workplaces the absence of unions may well mean that managers used HRM to pre-

Table 3. Changes in Union Status and in the Incidence
of HRM Practices over Time Related to Age of Workplace.

(1) Years of Data	(2) Measure	(3) Set up before 1980	(4) Set up in 1980s	(5) Set up in 1990s	(6) Gap 1980s – before 1980 (4) – (3)	(7) Gap 1990s – before 1980 (5) – (3)	(8) Number of Workplaces
A. Differences in Union Status by Age of Workplace							
1980, 1984, 1990, 1998	Union Recognition	.63	.36	.27	–.27 (.02)	–.36 (.02)	8,022
1980, 1984, 1990, 1998	Union Density	.58	.31	.22	–.27 (.01)	–.36 (.02)	7,028
B. Differences in HRM Incidence by Age of Workplace							
1980, 1984, 1990, 1998	JCC	.33	.24	.26	–.09 (.01)	–.07 (.02)	8,004
1984, 1990, 1998 Trading Sector	Flexible Pay	.42	.50	.52	.08 (.02)	.10 (.02)	4,194
1990, 1998	Problem-Solving Groups	.39	.38	.37	–.01 (.02)	–.02 (.02)	3,955
1984, 1990, 1998	Team Briefing	.45	.46	.50	.01 (.02)	.05 (.02)	5,961
1984, 1990, 1998	Regular Meetings with Senior Management	.36	.40	.42	.05 (.02)	.07 (.02)	5,978
1984, 1990, 1998	Management Chain	.61	.63	.53	.02 (.02)	–.07 (.02)	5,978
1984, 1990, 1998	Suggestion Schemes	.28	.29	.32	.01 (.01)	.04 (.02)	5,977
1980, 1984, 1990, 1998	Personnel Specialist	.32	.42	.48	.10 (.02)	.16 (.02)	4,194

Notes: Standard errors in parentheses.

empt unionism, or that workers, either as a consequence or independently, preferred an alternative form of voice. If so, we should see more rapid inflows of HRM practices into newer workplaces than into older, more unionized workplaces. This is what we first look at in the lower panel (B) of Table 3, which presents indicators for HRM practices using the same structure as Panel A.

The numbers in Table 3 show something of a mixed pattern, but they are in part conducive to the idea that HRM practices were more likely to be present in newer workplaces. The strongest evidence in favor of this distribution is for flexible pay and for the presence of a personnel specialist. The prevalence of flexible pay was 8 percentage points higher in workplaces set up in the 1980s, and 10 percentage points higher in those set up in the 1990s, than in older workplaces; and corresponding numbers for the presence of a personnel specialist were 10 and 16 percentage points higher, respectively. Age of workplace gaps are less marked for some of the other measures, but most are positive, the main exception being the more traditional practice, the Joint Consultative Committee.

However, over the time period being studied there were also some important compositional changes, such as the increased incidence of smaller workplaces, and a move away from manufacturing to services. So we next present some empirical estimates of the relationship with age of workplace derived from statistical models that control for such shifts in composition. This is important because some of these HRM practices may be much more likely to be prevalent in certain workplaces. For example, larger workplaces are more likely to have a personnel specialist than are their smaller counterparts.

Statistical Estimates

Table 4 reports estimates derived from probit equations in which either union status measures (upper panel) or various measures of HRM incidence (lower panel) were the dependent variables. The table reports the marginal effects of workplace age derived from the estimated probit equations. In Table 4 (as in Table 3) workplace age is defined as either "set up in the 1980s" or "set up in the 1990s." A number of control variables were in-

HRM AS A SUBSTITUTE FOR TRADE UNIONS 211

Table 4. Statistical Estimates of the Relationship between Changes in
Union Status and the Incidence of HRM Practices over Time and Age of Workplace.

Years of Data	Measure	Set up in 1980s	Set up in 1990s	Sample Size
	A. Union Equations			
1980, 1984, 1990, 1998	Union Recognition	−.120 (.019)	−.100 (.026)	7,483
1980, 1984, 1990, 1998	Union Density	−.102 (.011)	−.106 (.016)	6,623
	B. HRM Equations			
1984, 1990, 1998 Trade Sector	Flexible Pay	.003 (.024)	−.024 (.033)	3,915
1980, 1984, 1990, 1998	JCC	−.052 (.021)	−.019 (.028)	7,466
1990, 1998	Problem-Solving Groups	.000 (.021)	−.010 (.027)	3,640
1984, 1990, 1998	Team Briefing	−.003 (.020)	.011 (.027)	5,480
1984, 1990, 1998	Regular Meetings with Senior Management	−.003 (.019)	.046 (.027)	5,497
1984, 1990, 1998	Management Chain	.001 (.018)	−.013 (.025)	5,497
1984, 1990, 1998	Suggestion Schemes	−.020 (.019)	−.008 (.027)	5,496
1980, 1984, 1990, 1998	Personnel Specialist	−.010 (.022)	.004 (.030)	7,483

Notes: Probit marginal effects; standard errors in parentheses. All specifications include controls for establishment size (dummies for 50–99, 100–199, 200–499, 500–999, 1000+ workers relative to 25–49), female proportion, part-time proportion, part of a larger organization, private sector, industry (one-digit industry dummies), and survey year.

cluded in the probit equations, which were chosen to capture the most important compositional changes in the economy over the time period under study. The variables included are establishment size (five dummy variables compared to a base of 25–49 workers), whether the establishment was part of a larger organization, the proportions of part-time and female workers, whether the workplace was in the private sector, and a set of one-digit industry dummies.

The upper panel of Table 4 reconfirms what is known from earlier work, revealing union recognition to be around 10 to 12 percentage points lower in workplaces set up in the 1980s or 1990s conditional on the factors measuring compositional change.

This is a sizeable effect, and the same is true for union density, as given in the second specification of the upper panel, where 1980s and 1990s effects are very similar indeed.

The lower panel (B) of Table 4 considers the HRM practices. It is immediately striking that the inclusion of the controls is much more important for the HRM regressions than for the union ones. In statistical terms, all of the correlations with workplace age are wiped out in the statistical models. Unlike for union decline, the changing composition of workplaces seems to fully explain the link between the incidence of HRM practices and workplace age. This, like the evidence reported in the previous section, seems inconsistent with

Table 5. Differences in Age of Workplace Effects by
Union Status from Models of the Incidence of HRM Practices.

(1)	(2)	Union Workplace		Non-Union Workplace		Non-Union/ Union Difference		
		(3)	(4)	(5)	(6)	(7)	(8)	
	Set up in	*Set up in*	*Set up in*	*Set up in*	*Set up in*	*Set up in 1980s*	*Set up in 1990s*	*Sample*
Years of Data	*Measure*	*1980s*	*1990s*	*1980s*	*1990s*	*(5) – (3)*	*(6) – (4)*	*Size*
1984, 1990, 1998 Trading Sector	Flexible Pay	−.009 (.037)	.057 (.052)	.020 (.031)	−.053 (.040)	.029 (.047)	−.110 (.061)	3,915
1980, 1984, 1990, 1998	JCC	−.018 (.027)	−.000 (.037)	−.074 (.030)	−.025 (.039)	−.056 (.039)	−.025 (.050)	7,466
1990, 1998	Problem-Solving Groups	.028 (.029)	.036 (.037)	−.022 (.031)	−.050 (.037)	−.049 (.042)	−.084 (.048)	3,640
1984, 1990, 1998	Team Briefing	−.008 (.027)	.041 (.037)	.022 (.029)	.004 (.037)	.030 (.038)	−.036 (.049)	5,480
1984, 1990, 1998	Regular Meetings with Senior Management	−.017 (.026)	.011 (.036)	.022 (.028)	.089 (.037)	.039 (.038)	.077 (.048)	5,497
1984, 1990, 1998	Management Chain	−.015 (.025)	.032 (.033)	.034 (.023)	−.029 (.033)	.048 (.031)	−.061 (.048)	5,497
1984, 1990, 1998	Suggestion Schemes	−.019 (.025)	−.014 (.034)	.019 (.030)	.032 (.037)	.039 (.039)	.046 (.049)	5,496
1980, 1984, 1990, 1998	Personnel Specialist	.010 (.029)	.040 (.039)	−.013 (.031)	−.018 (.040)	−.022 (.041)	−.057 (.051)	7,483

Notes: Probit marginal effects; standard errors in parentheses. All specifications include controls for establishment size (dummies for 50–99, 100–199, 200–499, 500–999, 1000+ workers relative to 25–49), female proportion, part-time proportion, part of a larger organization, private sector, industry (one-digit industry dummies), and survey year.

HRM substitution taking place during the period of union decline in Britain.

Non-Union/Union Differences

Before accepting that conclusion, however, we need to examine whether or not predominantly new non-union workplaces were increasingly introducing HRM practices. We do so in Table 5, which reports the marginal effects of workplace age on the incidence of various HRM incidence measures derived from probit equations estimated separately for union and non-union workplaces. HRM substitution related to workplace age predicts that one should see more of a positive new workplace effect in non-union workplaces. The table therefore presents coefficient estimates associated with indicators of whether workplaces were set up in the 1980s and 1990s for the union sector (columns 3 and 4), analogous effects for the non-union

sector (in columns 5 and 6), and then non-union/union gaps (columns 7 and 8).

Table 5 shows that the positive non-union/union gaps that HRM substitution would predict are rarely seen. In fact, none of the non-union/union differences in columns (7) and (8) are positive and statistically significant, and many are actually negative. This result reflects the fact that a number of the non-union effects are negative and they rarely are more positive than the union effects. None of this supports the HRM/union substitution thesis.

Longitudinal Changes in the Union-HRM Relation

Our analysis so far rejects the idea that HRM substitution, in its orthodox sense of substituting between union and non-union sectors, has occurred. But one more possibility remains: that where the use of HRM has risen within the union sector, it weak-

Table 6. Changes in Union Density (%) Associated with Changes
in the Presence of HRM Practices in Unionized Workplaces, 1990–97.

	Introduced Practice	*Removed Practice*	*No Change*
Flexible Pay	−8.9	−9.6	−5.8
Number of Workplaces	87	42	319
JCC	−8.6	−8.8	−5.8
Number of Workplaces	80	64	307

Notes: Authors' own calculations from 1990–97 WIRS panel. The sample covers workplaces that recognized trade unions for collective bargaining purposes in 1990 and 1997.

ened unions. This would represent a form of HRM substitution occurring within the union sector.

We investigate this hypothesis by drawing on the longitudinal sample of workplaces that the WIRS/WERS series covered between 1990 and 1997. Due to limitations of the available data on HRM practices, however, we can only look here at the JCC and Flexible Pay measures. Table 6 shows the within-establishment change in union density broken down by the change, or lack thereof, in the status of each HRM practice (practice newly introduced; practice removed; or no change). The hypothesis that HRM substitution weakened unions within the union sector implies larger falls in union density in workplaces that introduced an HRM practice than in those that did not.

The results in Table 6 are not in line with that prediction. For example, although workplaces that introduced a JCC between 1990 and 1997 saw union density fall by 9 percentage points, density also fell by 9 percentage points in workplaces that removed a JCC and by 6 percentage points in workplaces where JCC status remained unaltered. The same pattern is true of Flexible Pay. While density fell by 9 percentage points in workplaces that introduced Flexible Pay, it also fell by 10 percentage points in those that abandoned the practice and by 6 percentage points in workplaces with no change in their use of flexible pay.

The results remain robust in regressions with the change in union density as the dependent variable and control variables including the 1990 to 1997 change in employment, the proportion of manual workers, and a set of one-digit industry dummies, as shown in Table 7. Overall, there seems to be little evidence of faster union decline in workplaces that introduced HRM practices in the 1990s.

Another way of using the WIRS/WERS data to study longitudinal changes is to aggregate the workplace data in the four surveys of 1980, 1984, 1990, and 1998 to industry level so as to study industry-level changes in the relationship between unionization and HRM incidence over time. To perform that exercise, we aggregated the data to 44 industries that we track over time. Table 8 reports the coefficients on various HRM practices from a regression in which the proportion of workplaces in the industry with recognized unions was the dependent variable and industry fixed effects were included in some of the equations. Where industry fixed effects were controlled for, one can infer the relationship between within-industry changes in unionization and within-industry changes in HRM practices. We can use the fixed effect equations to assess the following question about HRM substitution: in industries where HRM incidence went up by more, did unionization fall by more? Evidence confirming this would be a negative coefficient on the HRM measures in the industry fixed effects specifications reported in Table 8.

Table 8 is structured to show results that enter the HRM incidence measures separately (in columns 1–7, where no controls are included, and in columns 9–15, where controls are included) and all together (in column 8, without controls, and in column

Table 7. Changes in Union Density Associated with Changes
in the Presence of HRM Practices in Unionized Workplaces, 1990–97.
(Dependent Variable: Changes in Proportion Union Members, 1990–97)

	Introduced Practice	*Removed Practice*	*Sample Size*
Flexible Pay	−.008 (.025)	−.017 (.034)	444
JCC	−.026 (.027)	−.042 (.025)	451

Notes: All specifications include controls for change in log(employment), change in proportion manual, and a set of one-digit industry dummies; standard errors in parentheses.

16, with controls). The pattern of results shows that while there are a few negative coefficients, these are the exception to the rule, and only one of them is statistically significant (for Regular Meetings with Senior Management when no control variables are entered in column 4). In the specifications with control variables in the lower panel of Table 8 there is no evidence of union decline being faster where HRM incidence increased. As such, neither set of longitudinal data considered in this section supports the hypothesis of HRM substitution.

Concluding Remarks

In this paper we have considered one of the key hypotheses of modern industrial relations, namely that unionism has been replaced by alternative non-union forms of voice and communication through the adoption of HRM practices. Were such HRM substitution taking place, one would expect to see a swifter introduction of HRM practices in non-union workplaces than in unionized workplaces; certainly one would expect to find the presence of these practices and the absence of a recognized trade union, in the new kinds of workplaces being set up in recent years. A finding of a more rapid diffusion of HRM into non-union workplaces would also cast doubt on the argument, expressed by those encouraging unions to embrace HRM, that HRM practices and unions can be complementary. Moreover, were such a pattern a long-term trend, it would seemingly contradict the "mutual gains" argument (Kochan and Osterman 1994) that HRM's performance

effects will be enhanced when unions are present.

Our empirical investigation, using workplace data from the Workplace Industrial/Employee Relations series of surveys in Britain between 1980 and 1998, uncovers no evidence to support the hypothesis of HRM/union substitution, at least operating in the commonly accepted and frequently stated way, with HRM replacing unions. This finding emerges from several empirical strategies. First we compared changes over time in the incidence of HRM practices across union and non-union sectors, and found little difference between sectors. Second, we asked whether newer workplaces (because these have been shown to be more likely to be non-union) have experienced differentially faster HRM incidence. We were unable to find much evidence of such a pattern, and certainly we found no evidence of statistically significant union/non-union differences. Third, an analysis of longitudinal changes also failed to yield any evidence of faster union decline in workplaces or industries with faster adoption of HRM practices. Overall, one can only conclude that HRM substitution does not seem to be a very important factor in explaining trade union decline in Britain.[4]

However, we do not know how generalizable these findings are to other countries. It is sometimes argued that in Britain managers have not fully embraced human re-

_____

[4]See Pencavel (2004) for a general and wide-ranging account of other factors underpinning union decline in the United Kingdom.

Table 8. Industry Panel (44 Industries) Relating Changes
in Union Recognition to Changes in HRM Practices, 1980–98.

	(1)	(2)	(3)	(4)	(5)	(6)	(7)	(8)
Flexible Pay	.105							.042
	(.070)							(.069)
JCC		.077						−.007
		(.092)						(.095)
Team Briefing			.219					.061
			(.081)					(.090)
Regular Meetings with Senior Management				−.166				−.151
				(.088)				(.078)
Management Chain					.160			.048
					(.096)			(.095)
Suggestion Schemes						.166		.003
						(.106)		(.094)
Personnel Specialist							.355	.291
							(.061)	(.081)
Controls	No	No	No	No	No	No	No	No
R-Squared	.87	.90	.91	.91	.91	.91	.89	.93
Sample Size	176	130	132	132	132	132	176	130

	(9)	(10)	(11)	(12)	(13)	(14)	(15)	(16)
Flexible Pay	.097							.103
	(.082)							(.072)
JCC		−.057						−.160
		(.091)						(.122)
Team Briefing			.193					.102
			(.089)					(.085)
Regular Meetings with Senior Management				−.068				−.057
				(.092)				(.085)
Management Chain					.057			−.028
					(.103)			(.112)
Suggestion Schemes						.146		.022
						(.099)		(.105)
Personnel Specialist							.264	.261
							(.056)	(.094)
Controls	Yes	Yes	Yes	Yes	Yes	Yes	Yes	Yes
R-Squared	.91	.92	.93	.93	.93	.93	.91	.94
Sample Size	176	130	132	132	132	132	176	130

Notes: Based on an estimation that aggregates the 1980, 1984, 1990, and 1998 WIRS/WERS establishment data to the industry level; weighted by industry cell sizes; standard errors in parentheses.

source management practices, adopting them in a largely piecemeal way. This may involve cherry-picking the latest fashion or introducing the practices that are most easily implemented. Fragmented adoption may also be common in the United States (Appelbaum and Batt 1994:124), and it may be linked to the more general argument about the way in which Anglo-Saxon financial systems and corporate governance are said to encourage "short-termism." However, there is evidence to suggest a pattern to the use of human resource practices that is not consistent with the ad hoc adoption of such practices. Studies in the United Kingdom by Wood, in particular, using a variety of data sets, suggest some integrated use of practices (Wood and Albanese 1995; Wood and de Menezes 1998; de Menezes and Wood 2005; Wood et al. 2004), and Storey's (1992:113) report of the adoption of HRM practices in the 1980s described a growing systematic use of those practices during the period of his study. Moreover, similar work by Wood (1999) using Osterman's U.S. data set pointed to integrated use. Our analysis of changes in the aggregate use of HRM found no statistically significantly greater adoption of HRM practices in non-union workplaces than in unionized ones. If the results of our research are uniquely British in some way, there seems little cause to believe that the ad hoc adoption of practices accounts for that uniqueness.

It may also be that stronger substitution effects would be evident where management's attitudes toward unions are more markedly negative than in the United Kingdom. Some observers cite the United States as a decidedly union-unfriendly environment, and claim that HRM is being used more overtly there than in the United Kingdom as a form of union suppression. However, there have certainly been enough genuflections to the co-existence of unions and HRM practices in other countries (for example, Kochan et al. 1986; Weitbrecht 2003) to suggest that were this study replicated outside Britain, similar results might be found. Moreover, we have little evidence to indicate that strong anti-union employers, particularly in low-wage sectors of the economy, are any more likely to use any employee involvement, performance-related pay, or sophisticated personnel methods than are their counterparts in the United Kingdom.

Its generalizability aside, this study has implications for the wider debate about industrial relations as a field of study, which has been largely fueled by events in Anglo-Saxon economies. If new management practices of the sort we have considered are actually no less likely (and possibly are more likely) to be introduced in the union sector than in the non-union sector, then an important premise undergirding some of the discussion of the future of industrial relations—that HRM and unionism are alternatives—comes under challenge. In fact, it may be the case that HRM is as complementary to the organization of work in unionized workplaces as it is elsewhere. Critical to this is a subject that we have not considered here: the nature of the collective use of HRM practices and the impact of their introduction on workplace performance, a question that is far from resolved in favor of the positive link (Wood 1999; Wood and Wall 2002) that is often assumed. A related question we have not investigated here is whether there are different reasons for introducing HRM practices in union and non-union environments. Such matters remain firmly on the agenda for future research.

REFERENCES

Appelbaum, Eileen, Thomas Bailey, Peter Berg, and Arne L. Kalleberg. 2000. *Manufacturing Advantage: Why High-Performance Work Systems Pay Off.* Ithaca, N.Y.: ILR Press (an imprint of Cornell University Press).

Appelbaum, Eileen, and Rosemary Batt. 1994. *The New American Workplace.* Ithaca, N.Y.: ILR Press (an imprint of Cornell University Press).

Barker, James. 1993. "Tightening the Iron Cage: Concertive Control in Self-Managing Teams." *Administrative Science Quarterly,* Vol. 38, No. 3 (September), pp. 408–37.

Clark, Jon. 1995. *Managing Innovation and Change: People, Technology, and Strategy.* Thousand Oaks and London: Sage.

Cully, Mark, Stephen Woodland, Andrew O'Reilly, and Gill Dix. 1999. *Britain at Work: As Depicted by the 1998 Workplace Employee Relations Survey.* London: Routledge.

Daniel, William, and Neil Millward. 1983. *Workplace Industrial Relations in Britain.* London: Heinemann.

Disney, Richard, Amanda Gosling, and Stephen Machin. 1994. "British Unions in Decline: An Examination of the 1980s Fall in Trade Union Recognition." *Industrial and Labor Relations Review,* Vol. 48, No. 3 (April), pp. 403–19.

____. 1995. "What Has Happened to Union Recognition in Britain?" *Economica,* Vol. 63, No. 249, pp. 1–18.

Edwards, Paul K. 1995. "Human Resource Management, Union Voice, and the Use of Discipline: An Analysis of WIRS3." *Industrial Relations Journal,* Vol. 26, No. 3 (Autumn), 204–20.

Fiorito, Jack. 2001. "Human Resource Management Practices and Worker Desires for Union Representation." *Journal of Labor Research,* Vol. 22, No. 2 (Spring), pp. 335–54.

Fiorito, Jack, Christopher Lowman, and Forrest D. Nelson. 1997. "The Impact of Human Resource Policies on Union Organizing." *Industrial Relations,* Vol. 26, No. 1 (Winter), pp. 113–26.

Forth, John, and Neil Millward. 2002. *The Growth of Direct Communication.* London: Chartered Institute of Personnel and Development.

Godard, John, and John Delaney. 2000. "Reflections on the High-Performance Paradigm's Implications for Industrial Relations as a Field." *Industrial and Labor Relations Review,* Vol. 53, No. 3 (April), pp. 482–502.

Gospel, Howard, and Paul Willman. 2003. "Dilemmas in Worker Representation: Information, Consultation and Negotiation." In Howard Gospel and Stephen Wood, eds., *Representing Workers: Trade Union Recognition and Membership in Modern Britain.* London: Routledge, Chapter 8, pp. 144–65.

Guest, David E. 1989. "Human Resource Management: Its Implications for Industrial Relations and Trade Unions." In John Storey, ed., *New Perspectives on Human Resource Management.* London: Routledge, pp. 41–55.

____. 1995. "Human Resource Management, Trade Unions, and Industrial Relations." In John Storey, ed., *Human Resource Management.* London: Routledge, pp. 110–41.

Guest, David, and Neil Conway. 1999. "Peering into the Black Hole: The Downside of the New Employment Relations in the U.K." *British Journal of Industrial Relations,* Vol. 37, No. 3 (September), pp. 367–90.

Hicks, Stephen, and Tom Palmer. 2004. "Trade Union Membership: Estimates from the Autumn 2003 Labour Force Survey." *Labour Market Trends,* Vol. 112, pp. 99–101.

Kochan, Thomas A. 1980. *Collective Bargaining and Industrial Relations.* Homewood, Ill.: Richard D. Irwin.

Kochan, Thomas A., Harry C. Katz, and Robert B. McKersie. 1986. *The Transformation of American Industrial Relations.* New York: Basic Books.

Kochan, Thomas A., and Paul Osterman. 1994. *The Mutual Gains Enterprise.* Boston: Harvard Business School Press.

Koys, Daniel J. 1991. "Fairness, Legal Compliance, and Organizational Commitment." *Employee Responsibilities and Rights Journal,* Vol. 4, pp. 283–91.

Machin, Stephen. 2000. "Union Decline in Britain." *British Journal of Industrial Relations,* Vol. 38, No. 4 (December), pp. 631–45.

____. 2003. "New Workplaces, New Workers: Trade Union Decline and the New Economy." In Howard Gospel and Stephen Wood, eds., *Representing Workers: Trade Union Recognition and Membership in Modern Britain.* London: Routledge, Chapter 2, pp. 15–28.

de Menezes, Lilian, and Stephen Wood. 2005. "Identifying HRM in Britain Using the Workplace Industrial Relations Survey." *International Journal of Human Resource Management,* forthcoming.

Metcalf, David. 2001. "British Unions: Dissolution or Resurgence Revisited?" In Richard Dickens, Jonathan Wadsworth, and Paul Gregg, eds., *The State of Working Britain.* London: Centre for Economic Performance, Chapter 4, pp. 25–33.

Millward, Neil, Alex Bryson, and John Forth. 2000. *All Change at Work? British Employment Relations, 1980–1998, as Portrayed by the Workplace Industrial Relations Survey Series.* London: Routledge.

Millward, Neil, and Mark Stevens. 1986. *British Workplace Industrial Relations, 1980–84.* Aldershot: Gower.

Millward, Neil, Mark Stevens, David Smart, and W. R. Hawes. 1992. *Workplace Industrial Relations in Transition.* Aldershot: Dartmouth Publishing.

Millward, Neil, Stephen Woodland, Alex Bryson, John Forth, and Simon Kirby. 2002. "A Bibliography of Research Based on the British Workplace Industrial Relations Survey Series." September 2002 version available at http://www.niesr.ac.uk/niesr/wers98/BIBLIOGR.HTM.

Ng, Ignace, and Dennis Maki. 1994. "Trade Union Influence on Human Resource Management Practices. Industrial Relations." *Industrial Relations,* Vol. 33, No. 1 (January), 121–35.

Pencavel, John. 2004. "The Surprising Retreat of Union Britain." In Richard Blundell, David Card, and Richard Freeman, eds., *Seeking a Premier League Economy*. New York: National Bureau of Economic Research, pp. 181–232.

Price, Robert, and George Sayers Bain. 1983. "Union Growth in Britain: Retrospect and Prospect." *British Journal of Industrial Relations*, Vol. 21, No. 1 (March), pp. 46–68.

Rubinstein, Saul A., and Thomas A. Kochan. *Learning from Saturn*. Ithaca, N.Y.: ILR Press (an imprint of Cornell University Press).

Scott, Andrew. 1994. *Willing Slaves?* Cambridge: Cambridge University Press.

Sisson, Keith. 1993. "In Search of HRM." *British Journal of Industrial Relations*, Vol. 31, No. 2 (June), pp. 201–11.

Starkey, Ken, and Alan McKinlay. 1993. *Strategy and the Human Resource*. Oxford: Blackwell.

Storey, John. 1992. *Developments in the Management of Human Resources*. Oxford: Blackwell.

Verma, Anil, Thomas A. Kochan, and Stephen J. Wood. 2002. "Union Decline and Prospects for Revival: Editors' Introduction." *British Journal of Industrial Relations*, Vol. 40, No. 3 (September), pp. 373–84.

Waddington, Jeremy. 1992. "Trade Union Membership in Britain, 1980–87: Unemployment and Restructuring." *British Journal of Industrial Relations*, Vol. 30, No. 2 (June), pp. 287–324.

Weitbrecht, Hansjörg. 2003. "Human Resource Management and Co-Determination." In Walter Muller-Jentsch and Hansjörg Weitbrecht, *The Changing Contours of German Industrial Relations*. Muchen

and Mering: Rainer Hampp Verlag, pp. 57–79.

Wickens, Peter. 1987. *The Road to Nissan*. Houndsmill: MacMillan.

Wood, Stephen. 1996. "High Commitment Management and Unionization in the U.K." *International Journal of Human Resource Management*, Vol. 7, No. 1 (March), pp. 41–58.

____. 1999. "Getting the Measure of the Transformed Organization." *British Journal of Industrial Relations*, Vol. 37, No. 3 (September), pp. 391–419.

Wood, Stephen, and Maria Teresa Albanese. 1995. "Can We Speak of High Commitment Management on the Shop Floor?" *Journal of Management Studies*, Vol. 32, No. 2 (March), pp. 215–47.

Wood, Stephen, and Lilian De Menezes. 1998. "High Commitment Management in the U.K.: Evidence from the Workplace Industrial Relations Survey, and Employers' Manpower and Skills Practices Survey." *Human Relations*, Vol. 51, No. 4 (April), pp. 485–515.

Wood, Stephen, Lilian de Menezes, and Ana Lasaosa. 2003. "Family Friendly Management in Great Britain: Testing Various Perspectives." *Industrial Relations*, Vol. 42, No. 2 (Spring), pp. 221–50.

Wood, Stephen, C. B. Stride, Toby D. Wall, and Chris W. Clegg. 2004. "Revisiting the Use and Effectiveness of Modern Management Practices." *Human Factors and Ergonomics in Manufacturing*, Vol. 14, No. 4, pp. 415–32.

Wood, Stephen, and Toby Wall. 2002. "Human Resource Management and Business Performance." In Peter Warr, ed., *The Psychology of Work*. Harmondsworth: Penguin, Chapter 14, pp. 351–74.

Name Index

Oswald, A.J. 193, 197, 410
Oulton, N. 411

Paarsch, H.J. 541
Pakes, A. 6
Palmer, T. 579
Pattanaik, P.K. 281
Patterson, M. 574
Peltzman, S. 267
Pencavel, J.H. 358, 379, 380, 472, 590
Persons, O.S. 431, 440
Peter, L. 556
Peterson, F. 433
Phelps, E.S. 201, 210
Piore, M. 529
Pischke, J.-S. 172
Pissarides, C.A. 219, 225, 250
Pitt, M. 479, 480
Polachek, S.W. 448
Portugal, P. 184, 225
Posner, R. 153
Poterba, J.M. 444
Prasad, K. 367, 379, 390, 396
Prendergast, C. 541
Price, R. 579
Prunnushi, G. 566

Ragan, J., Jr. 366, 472
Raines, F. 473
Ramey, V. 83, 90
Ravenscraft, D.J. 366, 380
Rebitzer, J.B. 548
Reder, M.W. 430, 529
Rees, A. 433
Reibel, M. 123, 133
Reinhardt, U. 265
Reynolds, L.G. 434
Rhee, C. 389–90, 397, 399, 401–3, 406
Riddell, W.C. 481, 505
Rissman, E. 157
Robbins, D.J. 35, 58
Roberts, J. 566
Robinson, C. 446, 448, 448, 449, 471
Rogers, J. 352, 381
Rogerson, R. 170, 244, 274
Ronson, M. 339
Roos, D. 566
Rosen, H. 162
Rosen, S. 469, 534, 536
Rosenblum, L.S. 34
Ross, S.A. 541
Rothschild, M. 267, 273, 315
Ruback, R.S. 351, 364, 430, 431
Rubenstein, S.A. 581

Rubin, B.A. 433
Ruhm, C.J. 273, 312, 313, 315, 320
Ryan, A. 43

Sachs, J. 77, 78, 81, 87, 99, 210, 211, 224
Salinger, M.A. 351, 364, 365
Salomaki, A. 220
Salop, J. 542
Salop, S. 542
Sargent, T. 225
Scarpetta, S. 170, 175, 176
Schmidt, P. 569
Schmitt, J. 99
Schoeni, R.F. 109, 113, 143
Schotter, A. 528
Schumacher, E.J. 355, 381, 445, 450, 452–4, 457, 462, 464–6, 468, 469, 472, 473
Scott, A. 579
Seago, J.A. 380
Shapiro, C. 267, 530
Shatz, H. 77, 78, 81, 87, 99
Shaw, K. 566
Shearer, B.S. 541
Shepard, I. 157, 159
Sichel, D. 567
Sider, H. 454
Siebert, W.S. 175, 184, 318, 358, 409, 426
Siegel, D. 34
Simons, H.C. 366
Sisson, K. 578, 579, 580
Slaughter, M. 11, 34, 61, 81, 87, 91, 99
Slichter, S. 529
Smith, R.S. 295
Somers, A. 162
Somers, H. 162
Spalter-Roth, R.M. 311
Spiess, C.K. 319
Spitz, J. 532
St. Antoine, T. 157
St. Paul, G. 170
Stafford, F.P. 41, 114, 420, 469
Staiger, R. 61, 77
Stanley, T.D. 444
Starkey, K. 579
Stern, J. 200
Stewart, J. 273
Stewart, M. 410
Stieber, J. 162
Stiglitz, J.E. 267, 273, 315, 530, 541
Stone, J.A. 356, 359, 361
Storey, J. 579, 592
Stuart, C. 268
Summers, L.H. 224, 273, 274, 280, 289, 294–5, 314

The International Library of Critical Writings in Economics